SWITZERLAND
43RD EDITION

Where to Stay and Eat
for All Budgets

Must-See Sights
and Local Secrets

Ratings You Can Trust

Fodor's Travel Publications   New York, Toronto, London, Sydney, Auckland
www.fodors.com

FODOR'S SWITZERLAND
Editors: Andrea Lehman, Mark Sullivan, Matthew Lombardi

Editorial Production: David Downing
Editorial Contributors: Sue Birrer, Nancy Coons, Katrin Gygax, Tania Inowlocki, Jennifer McDermott, Marton Radkai, Lito Tejada-Flores, Sharon-Anne Wilcox, Kay Winzenried
Maps: David Lindroth *cartographer;* Bob Blake and Rebecca Baer, *map editors*
Design: Fabrizio La Rocca, *creative director;* Guido Caroti, *art director;* Moon Sun Kim, *cover designer;* Melanie Marin, *senior picture editor*
Cover Photo (View above Zermatt over lake to Matterhorn, Valais Alps): D.C. Lowe/Stone/Getty Images
Production/Manufacturing: Colleen Ziemba

Forty-Third Edition

ISBN 1–4000–1432–8

ISSN 0071–6553

SPECIAL SALES
This book is available for special discounts for bulk purchases for sales promotions or premiums. Special editions, including personalized covers, excerpts of existing books, and corporate imprints, can be created in large quantities for special needs. For more information, write to Special Markets/Premium Sales, 1745 Broadway, MD 6-2, New York, New York 10019, or e-mail specialmarkets@randomhouse.com.

AN IMPORTANT TIP & AN INVITATION
Although all prices, opening times, and other details in this book are based on information supplied to us at press time, changes occur all the time in the travel world, and Fodor's cannot accept responsibility for facts that become outdated or for inadvertent errors or omissions. So **always confirm information when it matters,** especially if you're making a detour to visit a specific place. Your experiences—positive and negative—matter to us. If we have missed or misstated something, **please write to us.** We follow up on all suggestions. Contact the Switzerland editor at editors@fodors.com or c/o Fodor's at 1745 Broadway, New York, New York 10019.

PRINTED IN THE UNITED STATES OF AMERICA

10 9 8 7 6 5 4 3 2 1

CONTENTS

Maps & Charts

CloseUps

ON THE ROAD WITH FODOR'S

A trip takes you out of yourself. Concerns of life at home completely disappear, driven away by more immediate thoughts—about, say, what marvels will beguile the next day, or where you'll have dinner. That's where Fodor's comes in. We make sure that you know all your options, so that you don't miss something that's around the next bend just because you didn't know it was there. Because the best memories of your trip might well have nothing to do with what you came to Switzerland to see, we guide you to sights large and small all over the region. You might set out to see the Matterhorn and feast on fondue, but back at home you find yourself unable to forget hiking to a crystalline lake or stumbling upon an eclectic museum. With Fodor's at your side, serendipitous discoveries are never far away.

Our success in showing you every corner of Switzerland is a credit to our extraordinary writers. Although there's no substitute for travel advice from a good friend who knows your style, our contributors are the next best thing—the kind of people you would poll for travel advice if you knew them.

Australian-born **Sue Birrer** has lived and worked in Switzerland since 1981, and in Fribourg since 1988. Originally a physiotherapist, she gave up her practice in 1991 to concentrate on freelance writing (and her two young children). Sue considers her work for Fodor's a professional vacation from her primary enterprise—writing a series of science fiction novels for young adults.

Nancy Coons has been tracing ancestral trails in Switzerland since moving to Europe in 1987, when she also began covering Luxembourg, Belgium, Provence, and much of northeastern France for Fodor's. Based in her 300-year-old farmhouse in Lorraine, she has written on European culture and food for the *Wall Street Journal, International Herald Tribune, Opera News,* and *National Geographic Traveler.*

Katrin Gygax was born in Zürich. She moved to California when she was four and to Vancouver when she was six, and she didn't stop traveling for the next 28 years. Now based in Zürich with her own translating business, she's also writing movie reviews for a Swiss fashion magazine, working on a mystery-novel series, and singing whenever possible. For this edition she updated the Zürich, Eastern Switzerland, Luzern and Central Switzerland, Ticino, and Basel chapters.

Freelance restaurant reviewer and former Fodor's editor **Tania Inowlocki** returned to Europe—where she was raised—in early 2002. From her home in Geneva she has explored every corner of Switzerland, making full use of her language skills, which she describes as "fluent in French, fluent in German, and enterprising in Italian." A Belgian-American by birth, Tania has contributed to *Fodor's Belgium* as well as *Fodor's Switzerland.*

Geneva updater **Jennifer McDermott** moved to Geneva in 1984 and can't quite imagine living anywhere else. Trained as a geographer/anthropologist, she has written about Greek wine, Irish roots, and Geneva's history, opera, and regional museums. She teaches theater at the International School of Geneva, lends her voice to language tapes, and travels whenever she can.

Marton Radkai, journalist and translator, was born in New York City and raised in France, England, and Switzerland. His enthusiasm for Graubünden dates to a school field trip in 1974; when he laid eyes on the region's gorgeous mountains, it was love at first sight. Marton took up residence in Geneva in 2002, after seven years of living in Bavaria and writing for *Fodor's Germany.*

Sharon-Anne Wilcox has worked as a journalist and editor for a wide-range of popular magazines in the UK and Europe. A Londoner by birth, she enjoys reporting on city life throughout the world. Now settled in Zürich, she's become an aficionado of Switzerland's wonderful mountains and valleys.

Vaud, Bern, and Valais updater Kay Winzenried made her first visit to Switzerland in 1980 and has returned every year since. Now a dual citizen by marriage, she has lived in both the French- and German-speaking regions. She's used the centrally located country as a base for travels throughout Europe and a solo trip around the world, and as a training site for high-altitude trekking. Hiking with friends, exploring vineyards, and dining—be it rustic or haute cuisine—are her pleasures.

We'd also like to thank the staff of the Swiss regional tourist offices, as well as Evelyne Mock of the Switzerland Tourism office in New York, for their help with questions big and small.

You can rest assured that you're in good hands—and that no property mentioned in the book has paid to be included. Each has been selected strictly on its merits, as the best of its type in its price range.

ABOUT THIS BOOK

The best source for travel advice is a like-minded friend who's just been where you're headed. But with or without that friend, you'll be in great shape to find your way around your destination once you learn to find your way around your Fodor's guide.

SELECTION

Our goal is to cover the best properties, sights, and activities in their category, as well as the most interesting communities to visit. We make a point of including local food-lovers' hot spots as well as neighborhood options, and we avoid all that's touristy unless it's really worth your time. You can go on the assumption that everything in this book is recommended wholeheartedly by our writers and editors. Flip to On the Road with Fodor's to learn more about who they are. It goes without saying that no property pays to be included.

RATINGS

Orange stars ★ denote sights and properties that our editors and writers consider the very best in the area covered by the entire book. These, the best of the best, are listed in the Fodor's Choice section in the front of the book. Black stars ★ highlight the sights and properties we deem Highly Recommended, the don't-miss sights within any region. In cities, sights pinpointed with numbered map bullets ❶ in the margins tend to be more important than those without bullets.

SPECIAL SPOTS

Pleasures & Pastimes and text on chapter-title pages focus on experiences that reveal the spirit of the destination. Also watch for Off the Beaten Path sights. Some are out of the way, some are quirky, and all are worthwhile. When the munchies hit, look for Need a Break? suggestions.

TIME IT RIGHT

Check On the Calendar up front and chapters' Timing sections for weather and crowd overviews and best days and times to visit.

SEE IT ALL

Use Fodor's exclusive Great Itineraries as a model for your trip. Either follow those that begin the book, or mix regional itineraries from several chapters. In cities, Good Walks guide you to important sights in each neighborhood; ▶ indicates the starting points of walks and itineraries in the text and on the map.

BUDGET WELL

Hotel and restaurant price categories from ¢ to $$$$ are defined in the opening pages of each chapter—expect to find a balanced selection for every budget. For attractions, we always give standard adult admission fees; reductions are usually available for children, students, and senior citizens. Look in Discounts & Deals in Smart Travel Tips for information on destination-wide ticket schemes. Want to pay with plastic? AE, D, DC, MC, V following restaurant and hotel listings indicate whether American Express, Discover, Diners Club, MasterCard, or Visa are accepted.

BASIC INFO

Smart Travel Tips lists travel essentials for the entire area covered by the book; city- and region-specific basics end each chapter. To find the best way to get around, see the transportation section; see individual modes of travel ("Car Travel," "Train Travel") for details.

ON THE MAPS

Maps throughout the book show you what's where and help you find your way around. Black and orange numbered bullets ❶ ❶ in the text correlate to bullets on maps.

BACKGROUND

We give background information within the chapters in the course of explaining sights as well as in CloseUp boxes and in Understanding Switzerland at the end of the book. To get in the mood, review the Books & Movies section. The glossary can be invaluable.

FIND IT FAST

Within the book, chapters are arranged in a roughly clockwise direction starting with Zürich. Chapters are divided into small regions, within which towns are covered in logical geographical order; attractive routes and interesting places between towns are flagged as En Route. Heads at the top of each page help you find what you need within a chapter.

DON'T FORGET

Restaurants are open for lunch and dinner daily unless we state otherwise; we mention dress only when there's a specific requirement and reservations only when they're essential or not accepted—it's always best to book ahead. Hotels have private baths, phone, TVs, and air-conditioning and operate on the European Plan (aka EP, meaning without meals). We always list facilities but not whether you'll be charged extra to use them, so when pricing accommodations, find out what's included.

SYMBOLS

Many Listings

★ Fodor's Choice
★ Highly recommended
⊠ Physical address
✛ Directions
⌁ Mailing address
☎ Telephone
🖷 Fax
⊕ On the Web
✉ E-mail
🎟 Admission fee
☉ Open/closed times
⚑ Start of walk/itinerary
Ⓜ Metro stations
⊟ Credit cards

Outdoors

🏌 Golf
⛺ Camping

Hotels & Restaurants

🏨 Hotel
⇋ Number of rooms
⌂ Facilities
🍽 Meal plans
✗ Restaurant
⌁ Reservations
🏛 Dress code
⤄ Smoking
🍸 BYOB
✗🏨 Hotel with restaurant that warrants a visit

Other

☺ Family-friendly
🈁 Contact information
⇨ See also
⊠ Branch address
☞ Take note

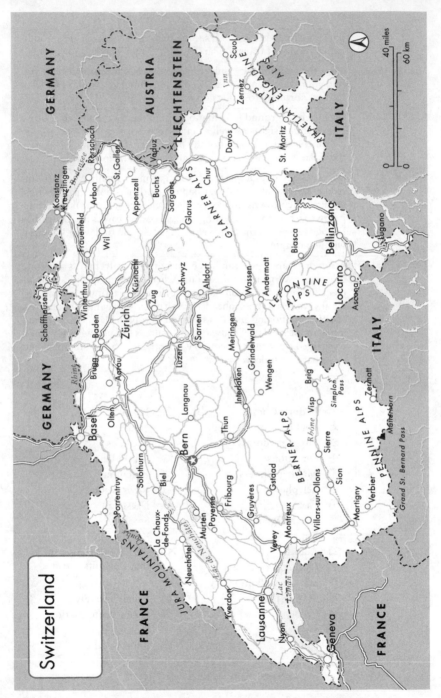

Switzerland

The geographical organization of the following paragraphs mirrors the organization of the book. Beginning with Zürich, the coverage follows a roughly clockwise path around the country, finishing in Geneva.

① Zürich

Given that it is one of the world's leading financial centers, Zürich is surprisingly small, but its wealth of cultural and material riches more than makes up for its size. Straddling the Limmat River, Zürich's center is made up primarily of medieval churches, guildhalls, and town houses, today providing homes for a charming mix of restaurants and hotels. The former moat-turned-main-road, the Bahnhofstrasse, boasts an array of luxury shops leading to the pristine lake, where residents and tourists alike cool off on hot summer afternoons. The city has shaken off most of its Old World cobwebs in favor of a young and refreshing air. Its social venues are varied and numerous—from the renowned opera to outdoor techno parties held on the surrounding hilltops; from see-and-be-seen cafés and sidewalk barbecues to the starched linens of the guilds' dining halls; from outdoor flea markets to the stylish haute couture boutiques in the Old Town. Snow-clad peaks in the distance oversee the hustle and bustle below.

② Eastern Switzerland

East of Zürich, the Rhine snakes through and around the cantons of Glarus, Schaffhausen, Thurgau, St. Gallen, and Appenzell, as well as the independent principality of Liechtenstein. The eastern cantons make up one of the quietest and most untouched regions of Switzerland, which is nevertheless chock-full of baroque churches, monasteries, and a wide variety of museums. In tiny towns and small cities, you'll find everything from wood-shingle farmhouses to town houses adorned with oriel windows and frescoes. Hills dotted with fruit trees and munching cows rise upward from the Bodensee toward Mt. Säntis, an imposing 8,000-foot peak with views of nearby Germany and Austria.

③ Graubünden

It's the stark geography of what used to be called Rhaetia in the Middle Ages that has determined the spirit of Graubünden and its people. The mountains made the region difficult to conquer, while the passes reaped profits from Europe's south–north traffic. Emperors, kings, and lesser lieges attempted to woo or coerce the Rhaetians for centuries, but they remained fiercely independent, thanks in part to clever alliances between noblemen and yeomen, notably the *Graubünden*, or "Grey Confederation," founded in 1395. Economic decline followed the Napoleonic wars, especially after the opening of new transalpine routes. But by the mid-19th century, the romantic landscapes were attracting new conquerors: tourists. And the Rhaetians have been giving them the warmest of welcomes ever since. No wonder it boasts some of Europe's finest resorts—St. Moritz, Davos, Klosters, Arosa, Pontresina. It is also the site of Switzerland's only national park, probably the only place in the country where skiing is forbidden.

(4) The Ticino

Italian in language, culture, and spirit, the Ticino is an irresistible combination of Mediterranean pleasures and Swiss efficiency. With its yacht-filled waterfront promenades of Locarno and Lugano and its constantly sunny climate, the Ticino is a canton set apart. Its hills preserve UNESCO World Heritage sites—the 15th-century castles of Bellinzona and the fossil-bearing strata of Monte San Giorgio—whereas its vibrant piazzas draw ever more aficionados to a variety of cutting-edge film and music festivals. The region's sinuous lakes, perhaps its greatest attraction, extend the promise of a relaxing stroll along fashionable waterfront promenades or a drawn-out lunch in a secluded grotto reachable only by boat. The local tradition of playing cards may have been overshadowed by a more sophisticated, touristic gallivanting, but the rustic feel, relaxed mood, and *italianità* (Italian flair) of the Ticino have not lost their hold.

(5) Luzern & Central Switzerland

Blessed with a sophisticated transportation system that easily gets you into almost every little town and onto every mountain, central Switzerland is the most visited region in the country. Lush green hillsides dotted with cows and chalets surround the Vierwaldstättersee, the "lake of the four forest cantons." Luzern itself, with its medieval Old Town so cleanly refurbished that it could be mistaken for a museum exhibit, is one of the country's major draws. As you stroll along the city's magnificent lakefront promenade, many Alpine views will look familiar, as this is where all those travel poster photos originate. Central Switzerland is steeped in history: the Oath of Eternal Alliance was renewed here, and it's also the home of the legend of Wilhelm Tell.

(6) Basel

Its position at the corner of three countries, the so-called *Dreilaendereck* where Switzerland meets Germany and France, puts Basel at the very center of Europe. This German-speaking city's motto, Basel beats differently, is a reference to the drums of its infamous carnival. Every year during *Fasnacht,* the city shows a boisterousness unrivaled by other Swiss towns. And it's not just during this festival that the population pours out into the streets. In the 15th century, the city won the right to hold an unlimited number of fairs, and has been doing its best to throw a year-round party ever since. The third largest city in Switzerland, Basel is home to people from 150 nations, all of whom help the city retain its cosmopolitan feel. Boasting more than 30 museums, Basel is a cultural capital that manages to retain a sense of fun.

(7) Fribourg, Neuchâtel & the Jura

Largely undiscovered, the cantons of Fribourg, Neuchâtel, and the Jura represent three very different worlds in western Switzerland. Fribourg, part German and part French, is overwhelmingly rural, its hills divided into a checkerboard of fields with a neatness only the Swiss can achieve. The abundance of castles and walled medieval villages attest to its less peaceful past, the ubiquitous religious buildings to Roman Catholic determination in the face of Protestant Bern. Neuchâtel, fiercely French in language and culture, exudes a sunny, holiday atmosphere, with its yellow sandstone buildings, stunning views of the alps and a pristine lakefront promenade refurbished for the Swiss Expo in 2002. The isolated Jura Mountains are more reminiscent of rural France than Switzerland; the plateau farmland is laced with horse-riding trails and cleft with deep forested gorges. The locals are hardy: temperatures can plummet to -30°F in winter, and snow lies on the ground for six months a year.

⑧ Bern

Humble and down-to-earth, Bern is a city of broad medieval streets, farmers' markets, and friendly, slow-spoken people. A dominant political center since the 12th century, Switzerland's federal capital sits in the country's largest canton (state) sharing name and coat of arms. Its size and influence mirror the pride, and on occasion, the boastfulness of its citizens. As a World Cultural Heritage city, its sandstone arcades, painted fountains, and performing mechanical clock, the Zytglogge, are as ardently protected as the country's neutrality.

Surrounding the capital city is a swath of productive farmland, the Emmental, famous for its holey cheese, and the best place to see the country's traditional agrarian way of life sheltered beneath the sweeping tile roof of a family homestead. Sectioned into tidy working plots, the region displays every possible shade of green in the growing season, its vertical hillsides and dairy cattle tended by hand. Rising behind them are snowcapped peaks with recognizable names—Jungfrau, Monch, and Eiger.

⑨ Berner Oberland

The Berner Oberland is among the most popular destinations in Switzerland, and with good reason. Here you'll find panoramas of the Eiger, Mönch, and Jungfrau mountains; crystalline lakes and waterfalls; and emerald slopes dotted with cattle and gingerbread chalets—not to mention some of the best skiing in the world. But the thrills aren't confined to the outdoors; there are many cultural events on offer, from world-class tennis matches and classical music concerts to family-friendly parks and an international country music festival.

⑩ Valais

Alpine villages, famous peaks (the Matterhorn, most notably), and world-class resorts (Zermatt, Saas-Fee, Crans-Montana, Verbier, Leukerbad) are all reasons to visit the valley of the Rhône. On one of the country's most fertile plains, fruit production and grape cultivation make full use of the intensely sunny environment. Once producers of quantity rather than quality, the focus on varietals thought to be nearly extinct and high altitude cultivation have elevated the reputation of Valaisan wines. Romans and other travelers through the ages have breached the mountain passes and settled in the valley leaving ruins and artifacts, dialects and bloodlines. Remote reaches like Iserables and Lotschental hold to their traditions and folk stories in celebrations and storytelling. This is the Switzerland of tumbledown huts, raclette eaters, winemakers, and yodelers.

⑪ Vaud

Lausanne, Montreux, and the Alpes Vaudoises constitute one of Switzerland's most diverse regions. Centered around Lac Léman (Lake Geneva), this French-speaking canton harbors some of the country's most famous cathedrals and castles, as well as Alpine villages, balmy lake resorts, gastronomic restaurants, and above all, its verdant vineyards. A heritage built on Roman foundations is evident in tumbledown ruins and restored fortifications strung along the waterfront. Territorial conflicts and Reformation struggles left their brand on the individual—slightly contrarian to the dictates of central authority and resistant to groupthink. Outside the commercial and academic centers, the rhythm of life remains tied to the cycles of the vineyards previously under the domain of monastic orders. The term *le quart d'heure Vaudois*, a 15-minute grace period for punctuality, affirms a more leisurely approach that needles its Germanic neighbors and time-pressed tourists.

⑫ Geneva

As the birthplace of Calvinism and the International Red Cross, home to the European headquarters of the United Nations, and a stronghold of private banks and exclusive boutiques, Geneva is, in many ways, a paradox. It's geographic positioning early on established the city's outsize importance; originally the guardian of a river crossing, then a market town straddling major trade routes, then a safe haven for Protestant refugees, now a neutral space where governments meet to negotiate everything from disarmament to the politics of AIDS, it is, today, home to only 185,000 people. Its manageable size is a blessing for visitors—any point in the city is accessible on foot from almost anywhere else. Look for superb private museums, immaculate public gardens, outstanding seasonal cooking, breathtaking views, and that uncanny Genevois knack for pointing out what's wrong.

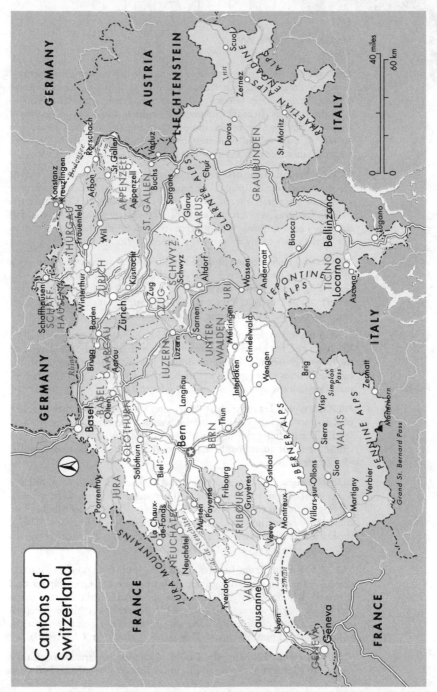

Cantons of
Switzerland

Swiss Gastronomy
9 Days

This food-intensive itinerary offers aficionados an opportunity to travel from one great dining experience to another, sampling the very finest *haute gastronomie* at one stop, the most authentic regional classics— even the earthiest peasant cuisines—at another. Incidental pleasures— wandering in the Alps, for example, or strolling through medieval town centers in Switzerland's greatest cities—can be squeezed in between meals. Remember that reservations must be made well in advance.

GENEVA 2 nights. Your first night, indulge in a hearty Lyonnaise meal at the Bistrot du Bœuf Rouge. For lunch the next day, head out into the vineyards for exquisite seasonal cuisine at the Domaine de Châteauvieux. Back in Geneva, have a relatively light Ticinese supper at La Favola. Fill the time between meals with a brisk stroll along the quais or a visit to one of the city's many museums. ⇨ *Chapter 12.*

LAUSANNE 1 night. Testing Phillipe Rochat's mettle at Restaurant de l'Hôtel de Ville in nearby Crissier may be the triumph of the trip—but reserve judgment for after Basel and Zürich. At night, head down to the waterfront at Ouchy and have a chic, light supper at the Café Beau-Rivage. ⇨ *La Côte & Lausanne in Chapter 11.*

BASEL 1 night. Two hours north, lunch at Bruderholz, which gives Phillipe Rochat a run for his money. Then, after visiting, say, the Münster and the history museum, relax in the downstairs bistro at the Teufelhof: the light specialties are prepared by Michael Baader, who is chef for the top-notch restaurant upstairs as well. ⇨ *Chapter 6.*

ZÜRICH 2 nights. Have lunch at Petermann's Kunststuben, in the suburb of Küssnacht, where the gastronomy vies for the title "best in Switzerland." Then, after a thorough walking tour of Zürich's Old Town, you can settle in for an atmospheric, old-world evening at the Kronenhalle. ⇨ *Chapter 1.*

LUZERN 1 night. For a total contrast and perhaps the most authentically *Swiss* meal of your tour, head for Galliker and a lunch of real farm food. Having absorbed the Lion Monument, crossed the Kapellbrücke, and toured the history museum, you can think about the evening meal: a light, sophisticated river-fish meal at Rotes Gatter, in Des Balances hotel, affords waterfront views. ⇨ *Luzern in Chapter 5.*

SAAS-FEE 1 night. From Luzern allow for a full day's scenic mountain drive south over the Brünigpass, then on over the Grimselpass and down the Rhône Valley to Brig and the spectacular little resort of Saas-Fee. Once there, retreat to the isolated Waldhotel Fletschhorn for a sophisticated dinner by chef Irma Dütsch and a bare minimum of one night to take in the mountain air. ⇨ *Zermatt & Saas-Fee in Chapter 10.*

VERBIER 1 night. Following the Rhône back west toward Geneva, take one more Alpine side trip up to this famous ski resort to feast and sleep at Rosalp, the popular rustic-chic inn in the village center. ⇨ *Val d'Entremont to the Col du Grand St-Bernard in Chapter 10.*

By Public Transportation Each of the stopovers is accessible by train, though some of the restaurants may require cabs or tram rides; a rental car will give you more flexibility for reaching country inns.

Castles & Cathedrals
8 Days

Romantics, history buffs, and architecture fans can circle western Switzerland to take in some of the country's best medieval and Gothic landmarks.

GENEVA 1 night. The excavations immediately below the 12th-century Cathédrale St-Pierre, open to the public as the *site archéologique,* have yielded two 4th-century sanctuaries, Roman mosaics, and an 11th-century crypt. ⇨ *Chapter 12.*

MONTREUX 1 night. The Château de Chillon, partially surrounded by the waters of Lac Léman (Lake Geneva), may be the most completely and authentically furnished in Switzerland, with tapestries, carved fireplaces, ceramics, and painted wooden ceilings. Lord Byron signed the pillar where his "Prisoner of Chillon" was manacled. ⇨ *Lavaux Vignobles & Montreux in Chapter 11.*

GRUYÈRES 1 night. This craggy castle-village draws crowds to its ancient central street, souvenir shops, quaint inns, and frescoed castle, complete with dungeon and spectacular views. ⇨ *Fribourg in Chapter 7.*

FRIBOURG 1 night. This bilingual city is the last Catholic stronghold of western Switzerland, rooted in its single-tower Cathédrale St-Nicolas. The cathedral's Last Judgment tympanum and art nouveau stained-glass windows deserve attention—but leave time to explore the Old Town, with its multilevel fortifications constructed for the ubiquitous Zähringens. ⇨ *Fribourg in Chapter 7.*

THUN 1 night. If you're driving, cut across the rolling verdure of canton Fribourg toward Thun (by train, connect through Bern), where you'll see the Bernese Alps looming in all their splendor. Schloss Zähringen, which dates from 1191, features a knights' hall, tapestries, local ceramics, and an intimidating collection of weapons. ⇨ *Thunersee in Chapter 9.*

BERN 1 night. The Zähringens fortified this gooseneck in the River Aare; its 15th-century Münster features a restored (full-color, painted) main portal. ⇨ *Chapter 8.*

BASEL 1 night. In this historic, cosmopolitan city is a Münster with a lovely Romanesque portal and the tomb of the great humanist Erasmus. ⇨ *Chapter 6.*

By Public Transportation The complete itinerary works by rail, with most sites accessible on foot from the station; Gruyères has bus connections to the elevated castle and the Old Town.

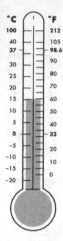

°C		°F
100		212
40		105
37		98.6
30		90
25		80
20		70
15		60
10		50
5		40
0		32
–5		20
–10		10
–15		0
–20		

In July and August Switzerland's best weather coincides with the heaviest crowds. June and September are still pleasant, and hotel prices can be slightly lower, especially in resorts. In May and June the mountains are at their loveliest, with Alpine flowers blooming and the peaks capped with snow; however, as ski season is over and high summer hasn't begun, this is often considered low season, and many resort hotels close down. Those that remain open reduce their prices considerably. Another low-season disadvantage: some cable car and cogwheel train operations take a break between the midwinter and midsummer rushes; some must wait for snow to clear before reopening. The most prestigious ski resorts charge top prices during the Christmas–New Year holidays but reduce them slightly in early January. February through Easter is prime time again. Many of the family-run traditional hotels fill up a year ahead, and you'll have to settle for less appealing lodgings. Also, check with the resort for exact dates of high seasons: they vary slightly from region to region. Late autumn—from mid-October through early December—is the least appealing season for visiting the Alps because there's usually little snow, no foliage, and a tendency toward dampness and fog. If you're sticking to the cities to shop and tour museums, you won't notice the doldrums that take over the resorts. The exception to the above rules of thumb: the Ticino, the only portion of Switzerland south of the Alps, boasts a Mediterranean climate and declares high season from April through October. Many of its hotels close down altogether from November through March.

Climate

Summer in Switzerland generally lasts from July to September and tends to be mild, although night temperatures can be chilly in some locations. At high altitudes, the air remains crisp through the hottest summer days. Beautiful fall foliage begins to lose its grip on the trees by the end of October, when the autumn rains usually sweep through the country. Snow can make its first appearance in November, which is usually foggy. Cold temperatures kick in from January to March, often dropping below the freezing point. In spring the trees begin to bloom again and as soon as temperatures rise enough, cafés open their outdoor seating areas as people gear up for the summer.

🔎 Forecasts **Weather Channel** ⊕ www.weather.com.

BERN

Jan.	36F	2C	May	65F	18C	Sept.	67F	19C
	25	– 4		47	8		50	10
Feb.	40F	4C	June	70F	21C	Oct.	56F	13C
	27	– 3		52	11		41	5
Mar.	49F	9C	July	74F	23C	Nov.	45F	7C
	34	1		56	13		34	1
Apr.	58F	14C	Aug.	72F	22C	Dec.	38F	3C
	40	4		56	13		29	– 2

GENEVA

Jan.	40F	4C	May	67F	19C	Sept.	70F	21C
	29	− 2		49	9		54	12
Feb.	43F	6C	June	74F	23C	Oct.	58F	14C
	31	− 1		56	13		45	7
Mar.	50F	10C	July	77F	25C	Nov.	47F	8C
	36	2		59	15		38	3
Apr.	59F	15C	Aug.	76F	24C	Dec.	40F	4C
	41	5		58	14		32	0

LUGANO

Jan.	43F	6C	May	70F	21C	Sept.	74F	23C
	29	− 2		50	10		56	13
Feb.	49F	9C	June	77F	25C	Oct.	61F	16C
	31	− 1		58	14		47	8
Mar.	56F	13C	July	81F	27C	Nov.	52F	11C
	38	3		61	16		38	3
Apr.	63F	17C	Aug.	81F	27C	Dec.	45F	7C
	45	7		59	15		32	0

ST. MORITZ

Jan.	29F	− 2C	May	50F	10C	Sept.	58F	14C
	11	−12		32	0		38	13
Feb.	34F	1C	June	59F	15C	Oct.	50F	10C
	13	−11		40	4		31	− 1
Mar.	38F	3C	July	63F	17C	Nov.	38F	3C
	18	− 8		41	5		22	− 6
Apr.	45F	7C	Aug.	61F	16C	Dec.	31F	− 1C
	25	− 4		41	5		14	10

ZÜRICH

Jan.	36F	2C	May	67F	19C	Sept.	68F	20C
	27	− 3		47	8		52	11
Feb.	41F	5C	June	74F	23C	Oct.	58F	14C
	29	− 2		54	12		43	6
Mar.	50F	10C	July	77F	25C	Nov.	45F	7C
	34	1		58	14		36	2
Apr.	59F	15C	Aug.	76F	24C	Dec.	38F	3C
	40	4		56	13		29	− 2

ON THE CALENDAR

Top events in Switzerland include Fasnacht celebrations in February and March, the Landsgemeinde open-air vote in Appenzell in April, the Montreux International Jazz Festival in July, the Menuhin Festival in Gstaad from mid-July through early September, Luzern's International Festival of Music from mid-August to mid-September, and the Fête de l'Escalade in Geneva in December. Events are named below as publicized by the host region, usually in the local language.

SPRING

March–May	The **Lugano Festival** is an annual spring concert series.
March	Villages throughout the Engadine and the Albula and Mustair valleys celebrate the **Chalanda Marz** children's festival on the first day of the month. Kids in costume parade and sing, ringing bells to chase away winter.
	The **Engadine Ski Marathon** covers the 42 km (26 mi) between Zuoz and Maloja.
	During St. Moritz's **Snow & Symphony Music Festival,** top classical and jazz musicians perform in luxury hotels and on mountaintops.
April	**Sechseläuten,** in Zürich, shows all its medieval guilds on parade and climaxes in the burning of the Böögg, a straw scarecrow representing winter.
	Small towns throughout the Valais hold a **Combat de Reines,** or cow fight, where female cows are pitted against each other in a head-butting contest to choose the "queen" who will lead the herds to higher pastures for the summer.
	Good Friday processions take place in several southern villages, including Mendrisio in the Ticino, where the procession derives from a medieval Passion Play that is performed on Maundy Thursday as well.
	Luzern's **Osterfestspiele** celebrates Easter with sacred music. International music stars perform at the **Spring Festival** in Samnaun.
	The lovely lake town of Morges draws a crowd to its annual **Fête de la Tulipe** (Tulip Festival).
	Landsgemeinde takes place in the town of Appenzell on the last Sunday of the month punctually at noon, with all citizens voting on cantonal issues by public show of hands.
May	The **International Jazz Festival—Bern** lasts five days in the federal capital.

SUMMER	
June—August	In Interlaken, an outdoor play about *Wilhelm Tell* is an epic-scale production with a huge cast of locals. For more than six weeks, the Yehudi Menuhin Festival in Gstaad showcases world-class musicians. Lugano's Blues to Bop Festival brings authentic blues to the lakefront.
June	The Grindelwald Country-Festival brings American country-and-western groups to this mountain resort.
	The Zürich Festival hosts dance, opera, theater, and more in several venues throughout the city.
July	World-class artists perform at the Montreux International Jazz Festival.
	In Leukerbad, the Clown & Cabaret Festival is an international congregation of clowns and street performers.
	The British Classic Car Meeting brings antique and classic autos to St. Moritz.
	During the Paléo Festival Nyon, international musicians play a multistage outdoor concert.
	The Shepherds Festival is a gathering of shepherds and their flocks at the Daubensee in Leukerbad.
	Engadiner Concert Weeks bring outdoor classical music events to resorts throughout the region.
	The Festival International de l'Orgue Ancien, at Valère in Sion, honors the 13th-century instrument within the church.
	In Vevey, the Marchés Folkloriques (Folkloric Markets) feature wine tasting.
	For more than two weeks the Verbier Festival & Academy hosts a classical music festival with an impressive guest roster.
August	Swiss National Holiday celebrates the confederation's birth in 1291 with fireworks and bonfires on the first of the month.
	Locarno's International Film Festival unveils top new movies in the Piazza Grande.
	The Fêtes de Genève packs Geneva's waterfront for 10 days of food and entertainment plus fireworks.
	In Zürich, the Street Parade, a huge techno music party, thumps its way through Zürich's lakefront district.
	The International Folklore Festival occurs in Fribourg.
	Zürich's Theaterspektakel showcases avant-garde and mainstream playwrights as well as theater troupes from around the world.

The world-renowned **Internationale Musikfestwochen,** in Luzern, combines concerts, theater, and art exhibitions.

Davos's **Young Artists in Concert** features tomorrow's classical music stars.

The **Vevey-Montreux Music Festival** invites important artists to these twin lake resorts.

FALL	
June—August	The multimedia **Images** festival in Vevey features cinema, video, and photography.
September	**Knabenschiessen** takes place in Zürich with a folk festival and fair.
	Bénichon, a traditional autumn Fribourg feast, is held during the second week of September.
	The **Neuchâtel Wine Festival** is the biggest in the country.
	L'Etivaz Cheese Sharing celebrates the division of spoils from the cheese cooperative with yodeling, wrestling, and other activities.
	Fribourg Braderie combines a citywide sidewalk sale, folk festival, and onion market.
	The small Vaud town of St-Cergue has an annual **Fête Désalpe,** a ritual for the cows coming down from the mountains. It lasts all of a Saturday morning, allowing hundreds of cows to parade the streets in amazing floral headgear. Another *désalpe* festival is held in October in Charmey, near Gruyères in Fribourg.
October	In Lugano a traditional **Wine Harvest Festival** is held at the Piazza della Riforma and on the lakeside.
	On the middle two Saturdays, **horse races** are held in Maienfeld.
	Olma Schweizer Messe für Land- und Milchwirtschaft (agricultural and dairy fair), in St. Gallen, gathers representatives of the farming industry from across Switzerland.
November	Bern's **Zwiebelemärit** (Onion Market) celebrates the open market established for area farmers in gratitude for aid they gave Bern after the great fire of 1405.
WINTER	
December	Geneva's **Fête de l'Escalade** commemorates the city's 1602 defeat of the Duke of Savoy. Local myth has it that one woman fought off the soldiers scaling the walls by dumping hot soup on their heads.
January	**Vogel Gryff Volksfest** is a colorful Basel tradition, with a costumed Griffin, a Lion, and a Wild Man of the Woods floating down the Rhine and dancing on the Mittlere Rheinbrücke. Winter golf tournaments happen in Silvaplana, Vulpera, and Disentis.

	Schlittedas Engiadinaisa is an Engadine tradition in which couples ride horse-drawn sleighs from village to village.
	The Château-d'Oex Hot-Air Balloon Week showcases the Vaud resort's specialty.
	St. Moritz hosts a blizzard of special events. The Gourmet Festival draws top-tier chefs. Several uncommon sports competitions take place on snow, such as the annual polo and cricket matches, and the White Turf horse races.
February	Hom Strom, at Scuol in the Lower Engadine, observes the burning of Old Man Winter. On the second weekend in February, dogsled races run from Maloja to Sils.
	Les Sommets Musicaux de Gstaad presents two weeks of varied classical music with outstanding performers.
	Fasnacht is observed in different locales throughout Switzerland, but most festively in Basel, where it begins at 4 AM on the Monday after Ash Wednesday, with a costume parade.
	Luzern celebrates on the Thursday before Ash Wednesday, with a traditional Fritschi procession.
	On the same day Schwyz celebrates Blätzli with a mummers' procession of harlequins.
	Lugano and other towns in the Ticino celebrate Carnevale with risotto and sausages served in the streets.

PLEASURES & PASTIMES

Dining

If you're looking for diverse dining experiences, you can't do much better than Switzerland, where French, Italian, or German cuisine may dominate, depending on which cantons you visit. In French areas (roughly Vaud, Geneva, Jura, Neuchâtel, and western parts of Fribourg and Valais) the cuisine is clearly Gallic, and wine stews, organ meats, and subtle sausages appear alongside standard *cuisine bourgeoise:* thick, rare beef entrecôte with a choice of rich sauces and *truite meunière* (trout dredged in flour and sizzled in butter). In the Ticino, the Italian canton, Italian cuisine appears virtually unscathed, particularly the Alpine-forest specialties of Piedmont and Lombardy (risotto, gnocchi, polenta, porcini mushrooms). The German cantons serve more pork than their neighbors and favor another standard dish that represents Switzerland: *Rösti,* a broad patty of hash brown potatoes crisped in a skillet and often flavored with bacon, herbs, or cheese. Beyond the obvious cultural differences, Swiss cuisine is also influenced by the terrain: mountain farmers have traditionally subsisted on such basic foods as raclette (cheese melted over boiled potatoes and garnished with pickled vegetables) or thin slices of air-dried beef, whereas cities nurtured wealthy burghers and noblemen with the cream of the crops of outlying lands—milk-fed veal, fruits from low-lying orchards. And anywhere near a lake there is plentiful fresh or smoked fish on the table.

Hiking

When the snow melts and the mountain streams start to flow, Switzerland takes to the hills. That the Swiss Alps are the ultimate in hiking is no secret: on a sunny day in high season in the more popular vacation areas, footpaths can be almost as crowded as a supermarket checkout line. On narrow trails hikers walk in single file, and the more aggressive pass on the left as if on the autobahns of Germany. However, there is an almost infinite quantity of quiet, isolated routes to be explored; if you prefer to hike in peace, head for one of the less-inhabited Alpine valleys—to be found in any of the cantons with the help of the local tourist office—and strike out on your own. Each of the regional tourist departments publishes suggested hiking itineraries along with lists of huts for overnight stays, and major map publishers distribute excellent topographical maps of wilderness trails.

Regional Celebrations

Basel's extravagant pre-Lenten observance of Fasnacht (Carnival)—in which up to 20,000 costumed revelers fill the streets with the sounds of fifes and drums—is only one of the hundreds of festivals that the Swiss celebrate during the year. Almost every Swiss canton hosts its own popular celebration of one event or another. Geneva's Festival of the Escalade commemorates the city's 1602 victory over the invading Duke of Savoy. Lesser-known festivals range from the frivolous—in the Schlitteda Engiadinaisa, young unmarried men and women ride decorated sleighs through the villages of the Engadine—to the symbolic—in the Landsgemeinde, the citizens of Appenzell pay homage to their country's democratic tradition by conducting the local vote by a public show of hands.

Shopping
Though you won't find many bargains in Switzerland, you will find some uniquely Swiss treasures. Some of the best souvenirs of this pragmatic country are typically practical, such as watches, clocks, and Swiss Army knives. (Do remember to pack knives in your checked luggage, or your souvenirs will be confiscated by airport security.) Others are more luxurious, such as chocolate; you'll be on the home turf of major manufacturers: Lindt, Nestlé, and Tobler. But you should also try small local chocolate shops, where the candy is made on the premises. Marvelous music boxes from the watchmaking country around Lake Neuchâtel are sold in specialty shops all over the country. Linens and good cottons are another Swiss specialty, as are pottery and ceramics—most of them dark-glazed and hand-painted with simple designs. Decoupage is the Swiss art of intricate silhouette paper cutting. It's traditionally done with black paper, but it can also be found in color.

Skiing
Switzerland is Europe's winter playground, and its facilities are as technically advanced as its slopes are spectacular. As one recent skier put it, "There's just *more*"—more slopes, longer runs, more stunning, crisp scenery than you'll find in U.S. resorts. Any level of skier can find a resort to meet his or her needs, from a cozy family-oriented village with easy and moderate slopes to the world-class challenges at Crans-Montana, Verbier, Wengen, St. Moritz, and Zermatt. Most resorts publish an area map showing their slopes and rating the trails for difficulty. Familiarize yourself with the resort's signs, including those warning of avalanche zones, before you set out.

Spectator Sports
If awards were given to countries with the most unusual sports competitions, Switzerland would win hands down. In the winter the action centers around St. Moritz, where a frozen lake provides a novel setting for polo, cricket, and horse races. The resort also has the world's only Cresta run; toboggan riders zip headfirst down a winding ice channel, accelerating to 90 mph. *Skikjöring,* which involves skiers being pulled by galloping horses, can be watched in February as part of the White Turf racing on the lake. Cows are the players in another, nonwinter event: in April small towns throughout the Valais hold a *combat de reines,* or cow fight. Female cows head-butt each other (though some contestants have been known to just placidly chew their cud); the winner, *la reine* (the queen), is crowned with flowers and given the honor of leading the parade of cows to their Alpine pastures. *Hornuss* is played in rural areas of the French-speaking cantons, particularly Fribourg and Vaud. Players wield wooden placards on sticks, tossing the placards into the air to stop a ball that is launched by a person wielding an extremely long, flexible implement that looks roughly like a golf club.

FODOR'S CHOICE

Fodor's Choice
★

The sights, restaurants, hotels, and other travel experiences on these pages are our editors' top picks—our Fodor's Choices. They're the best of their type in the area covered by the book—not to be missed and always worth your time. In the destination chapters that follow, you will find all the details.

LODGING

$$$$	**Des Bergues, Geneva.** Extraordinarily plush beds, complete 24-hour room service, discreetly helpful staff, and a seamless mastery of detail distinguish this historically gracious hotel.
$$$$	**Giardino, Ascona, the Ticino.** You'll find decadence in this small Ticinese village, from the pure linen sheets to the chauffeured Bentley.
$$$$	**Hotel Bellevue Palace, Bern.** Hard to imagine that the federal government is the landlord at this top-drawer hotel (run by hospitality professionals) where you are likely to see members of parliament dining.
$$$$	**L'Hostellerie du Pas de l'Ours, Valais.** A nine-room prototypical inn, it fulfills all dreams of what an Alpine hideaway should be.
$$$$	**Le Montreux Palace, Montreux, Vaud.** A grand hotel, residence to world-renowned thinkers and artists, preserves its belle epoque beauty while gently staying current with modern attributes demanded by globe-trotting guests.
$$$$	**Palace, Gstaad, Berner Oberland.** Satisfy your every whim at this hotel in Switzerland's top luxury destination. Enjoy every possible amenity: an elaborate health club, the best dance club in town, and world-class chefs imported for special occasions.
$$$$	**Widder, Zürich.** Made up of 10 former medieval town houses, this hotel is a perfect blend of history and luxury.
$$$$	**Zum Storchen, Zürich.** A 600-year-old structure on the banks of the Limmat, this is one of the city's most atmospheric hotels.
$$$–$$$$	**Bürgenstock Hotels and Resort, Bürgenstock, Central Switzerland.** From its perch high above Lake Luzern, this lodging offers breathtaking views of the surrounding mountains.
$$–$$$	**Krafft, Basel.** Try for a Rhine-side room at this elegant waterfront inn; it has a mosaic-tiled entrance hall, elaborate moldings and a sinuous atrium stairwell.
$$–$$$	**Ruedihus, Kandersteg, Berner Oberland.** Go for a full chalet experience here; with leaded-glass windows, homespun linen, and pewter pitchers, the all-wood building re-creates the atmosphere of the 1753 original.

$	**Bel'Espérance,** Geneva. The piano in the salon, the roof terrace views of the lake, and the bright, airy rooms add up to outstanding value for money.
$$$$	**Le Pont de Brent,** Brent, Vaud. Legendary chef Philippe Rochat's protégée, chef Gérard Rabaey shows off his culinary mettle in an understated villa in this tiny hamlet above Montreux.
$$$$	**Restaurant de l'Hôtel de Ville–Philippe Rochat,** Crissier, Vaud. Enjoy the fruits of Philippe Rochat's work with legendary chef Girardet at this refined star just outside Lausanne. Rochat spent nearly 20 years with his mentor, and he maintains the restaurant's stellar standards.
$$$$	**Restaurant Fischerzunft,** Schaffhausen, Eastern Switzerland. French nouvelle cuisine meets Asian simplicity in the eclectic kitchen of this eatery. The riverside location is enhanced by a shaded terrace in summer.
$$$–$$$$	**Domaine de Châteauvieux,** Geneva. Local vintners save their best wines for Philippe Chevrier's cellars at this hilltop country manor with sweeping vine-and-mountain views, charming guest rooms, and exquisite seasonal cuisine.
$$$–$$$$	**Hôtel-Restaurant Georges Wenger,** Le Noirmont, the Jura. You'll have to go off the beaten track, practically to the French border, in fact, to find one of the best chefs in Switzerland. It's well worth the trek, as chef Georges Wenger adapts local Jura ingredients to sophisticated, seasonal cuisine.
$$$–$$$$	**Schultheissenstube,** Bern. Without its refined service and stellar menu, this paneled dining room in the Hotel Schweizerhof could be a Stübli in a country inn: instead it is one of the city's top restaurants.
$$–$$$$	**Teufelhof,** Basel. Inside what was once a mansion, the Teufelhof now offers two excellent restaurants, a chic Weinstube, trendy bar—there are even medieval ruins in the basement wine shop. The menus are always intriguing.
$$–$$$	**Bistrot du Bœuf Rouge,** Geneva. The classics of the Lyonnaise table are prepared and presented with loving care at this tongue-in-cheek bistro two blocks from the Right Bank waterfront.
$$–$$$	**Des Trois Tours,** Bourguillon, near Fribourg. One of Switzerland's best chefs is busy delighting customers with his constantly changing, always delicious, regional cuisine.
$$–$$$	**Stern,** Chur, Graubünden. This 1677 inn at the hub of town carries on the age-old tradition of Graubündner culture, complete with waitresses in folk costumes.

$–$$$	**Findlerhof,** Valais. You must walk or ski to this enchanted hut above Zermatt where decks are filled with hearty folk savoring the sunshine, exceptional food and a view of the Matterhorn that could not be more perfect.
$–$$$	**Kronenhalle,** Zürich. The 20th-century art collection is as plentiful as the food; the robust cooking in hearty portions draws a genial crowd.
$–$$$	**Lorenzini,** Bern. An eclectic crowd of politicians, literati and business types share the upper and lower floors of this spectacular Italian restaurant.
$$	**Della Casa,** Bern. For typical regional food and a slightly irreverent staff, you will get a double serving of Swiss cuisine and urban chatter at this local favorite.
$$	**Le Relais de l'Entrecôte,** Geneva. Perfectly grilled cuts of beef, a secret house herb sauce, thin golden fries, and the restaurant's refusal to take reservations guarantee you will wait (briefly) for a table at this popular downtown spot.
$–$$	**Bierhalle Kropf,** Zürich. Under a giant boar's head and century-old murals, businesspeople, workers, and shoppers share crowded tables to feast on hearty cuisine.
¢–$	**Hotel Navegna,** Locarno, the Ticino. This hotel restaurant stands out for its phenomenally delicate homemade pastas.

CASTLES & MANSIONS

Château de Chillon, Veytaux, Vaud. Appearing adrift on the lake, the fundamentals of castle life and harshness of imprisonment emerge in the stone chambers and vaulted halls of Switzerland's best known fortresses.
Gruyères, Fribourg. This medieval fortress-town, complete with château, sits on a hill in front of a stunning backdrop of Alpine foothills.
Ital-Redinghaus, Schwyz. This magnificently preserved 17th-century home has period furnishings and a luxurious garden.

DRIVES

Corniche de la Vaud, Vaud. In the winemaking region of Vaud, this scenic road joins cobblestone villages and beckoning vineyards. The lake and mountain views—and the tastings of fruity, local wine—make for a memorable experience.
Emmental region, near Bern. Famous for its huge wheels of the buttery cheese with the holes, the agricultural region on the outskirts of the capital provides a close-up of farmstead life, folkloric traditions and natural beauty.

CHURCHES

Cathédrale de Notre-Dame, Lausanne, Vaud. Switzerland's largest church is a Burgundian Gothic treasure; its towers and spires crown one of the hilltops on which the city was founded.

Grossmünster, Zürich. Zürich's primary church offers excellent views of the city from its towers and fanciful Romanesque details on the columns of its cloister.

Jesuitenkirche, Luzern. This church's incredible 17th-century interior makes this one of the country's most popular sights.

Münster, Bern. The city's (and on state occasions, the country's) place of worship. Its 328-foot steeple, a city landmark, is an awesome lookout.

FOUNTAINS & WATERFALLS

Brunnen (fountains), Bern. In a city of more than 100 fountains, 11 medieval designs have become architectural icons. Placed along the main streets and plazas, they portray characters in allegory from the city's founder Berchtold V to an ogre taunting children.

Jet d'Eau, Geneva. The city's symbolic equivalent of the Eiffel Tower sends a huge, graceful, and perfectly placed plume of water up over the harbor, then lets it feather gently back to earth.

Rheinfall, Eastern Switzerland. With its mists, roaring water, jutting rocks, and bushy crags, this waterfall appears truly Wagnerian from the Neuhausen side.

HISTORY

Bundeshaus (parliament house), Bern. The domed parliament building stoically perched above the Aare represents the confederation's unity and neutrality; all four official languages are spoken in its chambers.

Monument de la Réformation, Geneva. The complex history of the Protestant Reformation as it unfolded across Europe is boldly rendered in granite.

Old Town, Basel. When the sound of fife-and-drum music drifts from upstairs windows of guild houses of Basel's Old Town, you'll think the Middle Ages have dawned once again.

Site archéologique, Geneva. An underground warren of excavated stone walls, spot-lit displays, mosaics, and metal walkways meanders through history underneath the Cathédrale St-Pierre.

Tellfreilichtspiele, Interlaken, Berner Oberland. For a festive evening, rent a lap blanket and settle in to watch a grand retelling of the life of Wilhelm Tell, performed under the stars.

MUSEUMS

Fondation Martin Bodmer, Geneva. A spectacular hilltop setting adds to the pleasure of this museum dedicated to text in all forms, from cuneiform tablets to Lord Byron manuscripts.

Fondation Pierre Gianadda, Valais. A cultural complex built by one brother to honor another, world-class art exhibitions and concerts are held on the site of Roman ruins. The surrounding sculpture garden and adjacent car museum assure something for everyone.

Kunsthaus, Zürich. A high-quality permanent collection of works from the 18th century onward is complemented by superb special exhibitions.

Musée International de la Croix-Rouge et du Croissant-Rouge, Geneva. The Red Cross Movement, and the historical need for it, are given scrupulously even-handed treatment in an intensely focused space.

Musée Olympique, Lausanne, Vaud. The spirit and accomplishment that drive world attention to athletic competition every four years are captured in the interactive exhibits and collections of memorabilia in the city that is home to the International Olympic Committee.

SWISS TIME

Patek Philippe Museum, Geneva. Fantastical creations, brilliant colors, lifelike detail, and awe-inspiring workmanship leave little doubt that watchmaking is about much more than time.

Zytglogge, Bern. Crowds gather at four minutes before the hour to watch the figures dance and play on this historical clock tower with gilded dials and astronomical settings.

TOWNS & VILLAGES

Appenzell, Eastern Switzerland. A town alive with traditional festivals still taken seriously by its citizens, and not just put on for the tourists.

Gandria, the Ticino. Clinging vertiginously to a hillside, its flower-filled balconies overlooking the lake, the tiny town of Gandria retains the ambience of an ancient fishing village.

Guarda, Graubünden. This federally protected hamlet in the Lower Engadine is full of architectural photo-ops, with cobblestone streets and flower boxes filled with red geraniums.

Morcote, the Ticino. This old resort village below Lugano has clay-color Lombard-style houses and arcades that look out on the waterfront.

Murten, Fribourg. This ancient town in western Switzerland near Avenches is a popular lake resort with a superbly preserved medieval center.

Stein-am-Rhein, Eastern Switzerland. A nearly perfectly preserved medieval village, replete with shingled, half-timber town houses boasting ornate oriels and flamboyant frescoes.

Zermatt, Valais. The car-free village of mazots and first-class inns shares top billing with the summit that captures the essence of the Alps.

VIEWS

Aletsch Glacier, Valais. As a World Heritage Nature site the wilds of the glacier and its expansive surroundings provide jaw-dropping views and unique experiences for the day-tripper or hiker.

Glacier 3000, Les Diablerets, Vaud. A two-part lift to the top of the Alpes Vaudoises is filled with nonstop, spine-tingling, 360-degree vistas. An additional reward is architect Mario Botta's glorious station restaurant.

Jungfraujoch, Berner Oberland. From the top of this 11,395-foot peak, the Aletsch Glacier looks like a vast sea of ice.

Matterhorn, Valais. Switzerland's snaggletooth summit stands alone in myth and grandeur.

Wengen, Berner Oberland. The sunset from this south-facing hilltop resort is a sublime way to end a day of skiing.

SMART TRAVEL TIPS

The organizations in this section can provide information to supplement this guide; contact them for up-to-the-minute details, and consult the A to Z sections that end each chapter for facts on the various topics as they relate to Switzerland's many regions. Happy landings!

ADDRESSES

Addresses in Switzerland sometimes list the street number followed by the street name. Officially, the number should follow the street name, as when it is used in a mailing address. You may see two-letter canton abbreviations in some addresses; Geneva is GE, Bern is BE, and Zürich is ZH.

AIR TRAVEL

BOOKING

When you book, look for nonstop flights and remember that "direct" flights stop at least once. Try to avoid connecting flights, which require a change of plane. Two airlines may operate a connecting flight jointly, so ask whether your airline operates every segment of the trip; you may find that the carrier you prefer flies you only part of the way. To find more booking tips and to check prices and make online flight reservations, log on to www.fodors.com.

CARRIERS

Swiss Air Lines, the national carrier more commonly known as Swiss, flies from Boston, Chicago, Los Angeles, and New York to Zürich, as well as from New York to Geneva. Continental flies from New York to Geneva and Zürich. Swiss flies from London to Geneva and Zürich, as does British Airways. From Australia and New Zealand, connections to Switzerland are available via Frankfurt or Bangkok. Air Canada connects major Canadian cities to Basel, Geneva and Zürich via Frankfurt or Munich. American and Delta fly from New York, Miami and Los Angeles to Zürich.

Low-cost airlines flying into Geneva include bmi Baby (from Birmingham and other cities in the United Kingdom), easyJet (from London and other European cities), fly Baboo (from Lugano, Florence, Venice, Prague), flybe (from Southampton), Hapag Lloyd Express (from Cologne-Bonn), and Jet 2 (from Leeds-Bradford). If you're headed to Zürich, Helvetic (from London) and Belair (from Mediterranean islands as well as Dubrovnik and other cities) are among the low-cost carriers.

⚑ Major Airlines Aer Lingus ☎ 0845/0844444 in U.K., 0818/365000 in Ireland, 01/2869933 in Switzerland ⊕ www.aerlingus.com. **Air Canada** ☎ 888/247-2262 ⊕ www.aircanada.com. **American** ☎ 800/433-7300 ⊕ www.aa.com. **British Airways** ☎ 0870/850-9850 in U.K. ⊕ www.britishairways.com. **Continental** ☎ 800/231-0856, 01/8009214 in Switzerland ⊕ www.continental.com. **Delta** ☎ 800/221-1212 ⊕ www.delta.com to Zürich. **Swiss** ☎ 877/359-7947, 0848/852000 in Switzerland ⊕ www.swiss.com.

⚑ Low-cost Carriers Belair ☎ 043/2118120 in Switzerland ⊕ www.belair-airlines.com. **bmi Baby** ☎ 0870/264-2229 ⊕ www.bmibaby.com. **easyJet** ☎ 0870/600-0000 ⊕ www.easyjet.com. **fly Baboo** ☎ 0848/445445 in Switzerland, 0800/4454-4545 in Europe ⊕ www.flybaboo.com. **flybe** ☎ 0871/700-0535 ⊕ www.flybe.com. **Hapag Lloyd Express** ☎ 0870/606-0519 in U.K., 0848/848553 in Switzerland ⊕ www.hlx.com. **Helvetic** ☎ 0207/026-3464 in the U.K., 043/5579099 in Switzerland ⊕ www.helvetic.com. **Jet 2** ☎ 0871/226-1737 in the U.K., 0848/000016 in Switzerland ⊕ www.jet2.com.

CHECK-IN & BOARDING

Always **find out your carrier's check-in policy.** Plan to arrive at the airport about two hours before your scheduled departure time for domestic flights and 2½ to 3 hours before international flights. You may need to arrive earlier if you're flying from one of the busier airports or during peak air-traffic times. In Switzerland, you will not usually need to check in more than an hour before boarding. If you are catching a connecting flight, make sure you have at least an hour to transfer, especially on Sunday in Zürich, where delays are frequent. To avoid delays at airport-security checkpoints, try not to wear any metal. Jewelry, belt and other buckles, steel-toe shoes, barrettes, and underwire bras are among the items that can set off detectors. Be sure to check your airline's limit on checked and carry-on luggage;

Swiss and other airlines often accept one carry-on item.

Assuming that not everyone with a ticket will show up, airlines routinely overbook planes. When everyone does, airlines ask for volunteers to give up their seats. In return, these volunteers usually get a several-hundred-dollar flight voucher, which can be used toward the purchase of another ticket, and are rebooked on the next flight out. If there are not enough volunteers, the airline must choose who will be denied boarding. The first to get bumped are passengers who checked in late and those flying on discounted tickets, so get to the gate and check in as early as possible, especially during peak periods.

Always **bring a government-issued photo ID** to the airport; even when it's not required, a passport is best.

For 20 SF per bag round-trip, passengers on Swiss and partner airlines with tickets on Swiss Federal Railways can forward their luggage to their final destination, allowing them to travel unencumbered. The baggage is retrieved from the train station at the final destination. Baggage check-in and airline boarding passes can be arranged at more than 100 train stations around Switzerland. An English-language "Fly-Rail Baggage" brochure is available free of charge from the Swiss Federal Railways.

CUTTING COSTS

The least expensive airfares to Switzerland are priced for round-trip travel and must usually be purchased in advance. Airlines generally allow you to change your return date for a fee; most low-fare tickets, however, are nonrefundable. It's smart to call a number of airlines and check the Internet; when you are quoted a good price, book it on the spot—the same fare may not be available the next day, or even the next hour. Always check different routings and look into using alternate airports. Also, price off-peak flights, which may be significantly less expensive than others. Travel agents, especially low-fare specialists (⇨ Discounts & Deals), are helpful.

Consolidators are another good source. They buy tickets for scheduled flights at reduced rates from the airlines, then sell them at prices that beat the best fare available directly from the airlines. Sometimes you can even get your money back if you need to return the ticket. Carefully read the fine print detailing penalties for changes and cancellations, purchase the ticket with a credit card, and confirm your consolidator reservation with the airline.

When you fly as a courier, you trade your checked-luggage space for a ticket deeply subsidized by a courier service. There are restrictions on when you can book and how long you can stay. Some courier companies list with membership organizations, such as the Air Courier Association and the International Association of Air Travel Couriers; these require you to become a member before you can book a flight.

Many airlines, singly or in collaboration, offer discount air passes that allow foreigners to travel economically in a particular country or region. These visitor passes usually must be reserved and purchased before you leave home. Information about passes often can be found on most airlines' international Web pages, which tend to be aimed at travelers from outside the carrier's home country. Also, try typing the name of the pass into a search engine, or search for "pass" within the carrier's Web site. EuropebyAir offers passes for travel that connects Basel, Geneva, and Zürich to other European destinations.

7 Consolidators **AirlineConsolidator.com** ☎ 888/468-5385 ⊕ www.airlineconsolidator.com, for international tickets. **Best Fares** ☎ 800/880-1234 or 800/576-8255 ⊕ www.bestfares.com; $59.90 annual membership. **Cheap Tickets** ☎ 800/377-1000 or 800/652-4327 ⊕ www.cheaptickets.com. **Expedia** ☎ 800/397-3342 or 404/728-8787 ⊕ www.expedia.com. **Hotwire** ☎ 866/468-9473 or 920/330-9418 ⊕ www.hotwire.com. **Now Voyager Travel** ✉ 45 W. 21st St., Suite 5A, New York, NY 10010 ☎ 212/459-1616 🖶 212/243-2711 ⊕ www.nowvoyagertravel.com. **Onetravel.com** ⊕ www.onetravel.com. **Orbitz** ☎ 888/656-4546 ⊕ www.orbitz.com. **Priceline.com** ⊕ www.priceline.com. **Travelocity** ☎ 888/709-5983, 877/282-2925 in Canada, 0870/876-3876 in U.K. ⊕ www.travelocity.com. **7** Courier Resources **Air Courier Association/Cheaptrips.com** ☎ 800/280-5973 or 800/282-1202 ⊕ www.aircourier.org or www.cheaptrips.com; $34

annual membership. **International Association of Air Travel Couriers** ☎ 308/632-3273 ⊕ www.courier.org; $45 annual membership. **Now Voyager Travel** ✉ 45 W. 21st St., Suite 5A, New York, NY 10010 ☎ 212/459-1616 🖶 212/243-2711 ⊕ www.nowvoyagertravel.com. **7** Discount Passes **EuropebyAir** ☎ 888/321-4737 ⊕ www.europebyair.com.

DOMESTIC FLIGHTS

The entire country of Switzerland is smaller in area than the state of West Virginia, so flying from one region to another is a luxury that, considering how efficient the trains are, few travelers require—unless there's a convenient connection from your intercontinental arrival point (Geneva, Zürich) to a smaller airport (Basel, Bern, Lugano, and Sion).

ENJOYING THE FLIGHT

State your seat preference when purchasing your ticket, and then repeat it when you confirm and when you check in. For more legroom, you can request one of the few emergency-aisle seats at check-in, if you're capable of moving obstacles comparable in weight to an airplane exit door (usually between 35 pounds and 60 pounds)—a Federal Aviation Administration requirement of passengers in these seats. Seats behind a bulkhead also offer more legroom, but they don't have underseat storage. Don't sit in the row in front of the emergency aisle or in front of a bulkhead, where seats may not recline.

Ask the airline whether a snack or meal is served on the flight. If you have dietary concerns, request special meals when booking. These can be vegetarian, low-cholesterol, or kosher, for example. Note that Swiss and many budget airlines such as easyJet charge for food and drink during flights. It's a good idea to pack some healthful snacks and a small (plastic) bottle of water in your carry-on bag. On long flights, try to maintain a normal routine, to help fight jet lag. At night, get some sleep. By day, eat light meals, drink water (not alcohol), and **move around the cabin** to stretch your legs. For additional jet-lag tips consult *Fodor's FYI: Travel Fit & Healthy* (available at bookstores everywhere).

Smoking policies vary from carrier to carrier. Many airlines prohibit smoking on all of their flights; others allow smoking only on certain routes or certain departures. Ask your carrier about its policy. Swiss, which does not allow smoking, stocks Nicorette gum.

FLYING TIMES

Flying time to Geneva or Zürich is just under 2 hours from London, 7 hours from New York, 10 hours from Chicago, 14 hours from Los Angeles, and 23 to 25 hours from Sydney.

HOW TO COMPLAIN

If your baggage goes astray or your flight goes awry, complain right away. Most carriers require that you **file a claim immediately.** The Aviation Consumer Protection Division of the Department of Transportation publishes *Fly-Rights,* which discusses airlines and consumer issues and is available online. You can also find articles and information on mytravelrights.com, the Web site of the nonprofit Consumer Travel Rights Center.

F Airline Complaints **Aviation Consumer Protection Division** ⊠ U.S. Department of Transportation, Office of Aviation Enforcement and Proceedings, C-75, Room 4107, 400 7th St. SW, Washington, DC 20590 ☎ 202/366-2220 ⊕ airconsumer.ost.dot.gov. **Federal Aviation Administration Consumer Hotline** ⊠ for inquiries: FAA, 800 Independence Ave. SW, Washington, DC 20591 ☎ 800/322-7873 ⊕ www.faa.gov.

RECONFIRMING

Check the status of your flight before you leave for the airport. You can do this on your carrier's Web site, by linking to a flight-status checker (many Web booking services offer these), or by calling your carrier or travel agent. In Switzerland, there is no longer a need to reconfirm your flight, though it won't hurt to do so. Swiss and other airlines now send electronic delay messages to passengers who provide cell phone numbers.

AIRPORTS

The major gateways are the Unique Zürich Airport (ZRH) and Geneva's Cointrin Airport (GVA). Most Swiss flights will fly via Zürich Airport, the airline's hub. Be sure to allot yourself at least an hour to transfer to your connecting flight. Delays are especially common on Sunday.

F International Airports Geneva: **Cointrin Airport** ☎ 022/7177111. Zürich: **Unique Zürich Airport** ☎ 01/8121212.

F Regional Airports Basel: **EuroAirport** ☎ 061/3253111. Bern: **Belp** ☎ 031/9602111. Lugano: **Aeroporto Lugano-Agno** ☎ 091/6101111. Upper Engadine: **Engadine Airport** ⊠ Samedan ☎ 081/8510851.

BIKE TRAVEL

Switzerland makes it easy to hop off a train and onto a bike, as you can rent bikes at some 100 train stations. Helmets are not included, however. Bikes can be returned to any station, but if you drop off a bike at a different station from where you picked it up, there's a service charge (7 SF if you arrange it in advance, double that if you don't). Rates for standard and mountain bikes are 30 SF per day. Groups get reductions according to the number of bikes. Individuals must make a reservation by 6 PM the day before they plan to use the bike, groups a week in advance. A daily train pass for a bike costs 15 SF (10 SF with a half-price pass). The Swiss Federal Railways baggage office can provide detailed information, as will all train stations.

You can also rent bikes—and helmets—at more affordable (and sometimes state-subsidized) rates in shops. In Geneva, several outlets even have bikes available free of charge during summer.

Throughout the country, the nine national bike routes are indicated with light blue signs displaying a white route number, and other recommend routes are marked with red signs showing a white bike symbol. Biking on major highways is not allowed. Local tourist offices are the best places to get bike maps for specific areas; you can also contact the Association for Transport & Environment or purchase their local and national cycling maps at a post office or newspaper shop. These maps provide information on where to rent bikes and what hotels welcome cyclists. The Cycling in Switzerland Foundation is another helpful resource; it publishes guides with maps to the national biking routes.

🚲 Bike Maps Association for Transport & Environment ✉ Lagerstrasse 18/Postfach, CH-3360 Herzogenbuchsee ☎ 062/9565656 ⎏ 062/9565699 ⊕ www.vcs-ate.ch and www.swisstravelcenter.ch. **Cycling in Switzerland Foundation** 🖂 Box 8275, CH-3001 Bern ☎ 031/3074740 ⎏ 031/3074748 ⊕ www.cycling-in-switzerland.ch. **🚲 Bike Rental Information Swiss Federal Railways** ☎ 0512/203461 ⊕ www.rail.ch.

BIKES IN FLIGHT

Most airlines accommodate bikes as luggage, provided they are dismantled and boxed; check with individual airlines about packing requirements. Some airlines sell bike boxes, which are often free at bike shops, for about $20 (bike bags can be considerably more expensive). International travelers often can substitute a bike for a piece of checked luggage at no charge; otherwise, the cost is about $100. Most U.S. and Canadian airlines charge $40–$80 each way.

BOAT & FERRY TRAVEL

All of Switzerland's larger lakes are crisscrossed by elegant steamers, some of them restored paddle steamers. Their café-restaurants serve drinks, snacks, and hot food at standard mealtimes; toilet facilities are provided. Service continues year-round but is greatly reduced in winter. Unlimited travel is free to holders of the Swiss Pass. The Swiss Card and the Flexipass (⇨ Train Travel) may also be used for boat travel.

FARES & SCHEDULES

Tickets can be purchased at ticket booths near the docks before departure; for some shorter boat rides, tickets are also sold at a counter on board before departure. Tourism offices usually have the latest schedules, though it may be better to check with the boat companies. Credit cards are generally accepted, as are Swiss francs and euros.

The Compagnie Générale de Navigation offers excursion boat rides on Lake Geneva for about 20 SF to 70 SF, depending on the distances covered. In the Ticino, the Navigazione Lago di Lugano and Nav-

igazione Lago Maggiore-Bacino Svizzero run frequent daily boat trips. In Zürich, boat rides of 1½ to 7 hours are available in summer. In winter, the number of boat rides dwindles.

🚢 Boat & Ferry Information Compagnie Générale de Navigation ✉ Rhodanie 17, Lausanne CH-1000 ☎ 0848/811848 ⊕ www.cgn.ch. **Navigazione Lago di Lugano** ✉ Casella Postale 56, CH-6906 Lugano ☎ 091/9715223 ⊕ www.lakelugano.ch. **Navigazione Lago Maggiore-Bacino Svizzero** ✉ Lungolago Motta, CH-6600 Locarno ☎ 091/7511865 ⊕ www.navlaghi.it.

BUSINESS HOURS

BANKS & OFFICES

Most businesses still close for lunch in Switzerland, generally from noon or 12:30 to 1:30 or 2, but this is changing, especially in larger cities. All remain closed on Sunday. Banks are open weekdays from 8:30 to 4:30 or 5. Post offices are generally open limited hours on Saturday.

GAS STATIONS

Gas station kiosks are usually open daily from 6:30 AM until 9 PM. Automatic pumps, which accept major credit cards and Swiss bank notes, are in service 24 hours a day.

MUSEUMS & SIGHTS

Museums generally close on Monday. There is, however, an increasing trend toward staying open late one night a week, usually on Thursday or Friday evening.

PHARMACIES

Pharmacies are generally open weekdays from 9 to 1 and 2 to 6, and Saturday 9 to 1. In cities, they tend to stay open through the lunch hour. To find out which pharmacy is covering the late-night shift, check listings posted near or on the window of any pharmacy.

SHOPS

Shops are generally open every day except Sunday. They usually close early (4 or 5 PM) on Saturday except in larger cities, where they stay open until 6 on Saturday and often stay open until 8 or 9 one day a week. Smaller stores close for an hour or two for lunch. Stores in train stations often stay open until 9 PM; in the

Geneva and Zürich airports, shops are open on Sunday.

BUS TRAVEL

Switzerland's famous yellow postbuses (called *Postautos* or *postcars*), with their stentorian tritone horns, link main cities with villages off the beaten track and even crawl over the highest mountain passes. Both postbuses and city buses follow posted schedules to the minute: you can set your watch by them. You can pick up a free schedule for a particular route in most postbuses; full schedules are included in train schedule books. You can also check the Swiss Post Web site. Watch for the yellow sign with the picture of a bus. Postbuses cater to hikers: walking itineraries are available at some postbus stops.

There's also a special scenic postbus route, the *Palm Express*. This route goes from St. Moritz to Lugano via the Maloja Pass. The buses run daily from mid-June through mid-October and, weather permitting, from late December through mid-June Friday to Sunday. Reservations can be made at any train station or tourist office.

DISCOUNT PASSES

The Swiss Pass (⇨ Train Travel) gives unlimited travel on the postbuses. You may have to pay a supplement of 5 SF to 10 SF on some of the Alpine routes; check in the timetables or ask the staff.

RESERVATIONS

Be sure to ask whether reservations are required, as is the case for some Alpine pass routes.
🚹 **Bus Information Swiss Post** ☎ 0900/300300, 1.19 SF per min ⊕ www.swisspost.com.

CAMERAS & PHOTOGRAPHY

Particularly when snapping mountain scenery, **include something of known size in the picture** to give a sense of scale. Also, **consider the light**; at sunrise or sunset you can capture spectacular colors, while the effects of storm clouds can be very dramatic. And if you find yourself itching to photograph those black-and-white cows? Remember to show them in context in order to make it an evocative travel picture.

The *Kodak Guide to Shooting Great Travel Pictures* (available at bookstores everywhere) is loaded with tips.
🚹 **Photo Help Kodak Information Center** ☎ 800/ 242-2424 ⊕ www.kodak.com.

EQUIPMENT PRECAUTIONS

Don't pack film or equipment in checked luggage, where it is much more susceptible to damage. X-ray machines used to view checked luggage are extremely powerful and therefore are likely to ruin your film. Try to ask for hand inspection of film, which becomes clouded after repeated exposure to airport X-ray machines, and keep videotapes and computer disks away from metal detectors. Always keep film, tape, and computer disks out of the sun. Carry an extra supply of batteries, and be prepared to turn on your camera, camcorder, or laptop to prove to airport security personnel that the device is real.

FILM & DEVELOPING

Major film brands are available in most newspaper and photo shops, and Advantix film is easy to find. You may have trouble finding 24-hour film developing in smaller towns and villages.

VIDEOS

The standard for videotapes in Switzerland is the PAL format.

CAR RENTAL

If booked from overseas, rates in Zürich and Geneva begin at around $50 a day and $200 a week for an economy car with air-conditioning, a manual transmission, and unlimited mileage. This does not include the 7.6% tax on car rentals. Try to arrange for a rental before you go; rentals booked in Switzerland are considerably more expensive. European companies like Europcar and Sixt often have better deals.
🚹 **Major Agencies Alamo** ☎ 800/522-9696 ⊕ www.alamo.com. **Avis** ☎ 800/331-1084, 800/ 879-2847 in Canada, 0870/606-0100 in U.K., 02/ 9353-9000 in Australia, 09/526-2847 in New Zealand ⊕ www.avis.com. **Budget** ☎ 800/527- 0700, 0870/156-5656 in U.K. ⊕ www.budget.com. **Dollar** ☎ 800/800-6000, 0800/085-4578 in U.K. ⊕ www.dollar.com. **Hertz** ☎ 800/654-3001, 800/ 263-0600 in Canada, 0870/844-8844 in U.K., 02/ 9669-2444 in Australia, 09/256-8690 in New

Zealand ⊕ www.hertz.com. **National Car Rental** ☎ 800/227-7368, 0870/600-6666 in the U.K. ⊕ www.nationalcar.com. **⚡ Local Agencies Europcar** ☎ 0848/808099 ⊕ www.europcar.ch. **Sixt** ☎ 0848/884444 ⊕ www.sixt.ch.

CUTTING COSTS

Eurailpass and Europass (⇨ Train Travel) both offer discount passes combining rail travel and car rental. For a good deal, book through a travel agent who will shop around.

Do look into wholesalers, companies that do not own fleets but rent in bulk from those that do and often offer better rates than traditional car-rental operations. Prices are best during off-peak periods. Rentals booked through wholesalers often must be paid for before you leave home. **⚡ Wholesalers Auto Europe** ☎ 207/842-2000 or 800/223-5555 🖷 207/842-2222 ⊕ www.autoeurope.com. **Destination Europe Resources (DER)** ✉ 9501 W. Devon Ave., Rosemont, IL 60018 ☎ 800/782-2424 🖷 800/282-7474 ⊕ www.der.com. **Europe by Car** ☎ 212/581-3040 or 800/223-1516 🖷 212/246-1458 ⊕ www.europebycar.com. **Kemwel** ☎ 877/820-0668 or 800/678-0678 🖷 207/842-2147 ⊕ www.kemwel.com.

INSURANCE

When driving a rental car you are generally responsible for any damage to or loss of the vehicle. Collision policies that car-rental companies sell for European rentals typically do not cover stolen vehicles. Before you rent—and purchase collision or theft coverage—see what coverage you already have under the terms of your personal auto-insurance policy and credit cards.

RULES & RESTRICTIONS

Your own driver's license is acceptable in Switzerland, but an International Driving Permit—available from the American and Canadian automobile associations and, in the United Kingdom, from the Automobile Association and Royal Automobile Club—is a good idea in case of emergency. The minimum age is generally 20, and you must have possessed a valid driver's license for at least one year.

Note that some agencies do not allow you to drive cars into Italy.

SURCHARGES

Before you pick up a car in one city and leave it in another, ask about drop-off charges or one-way service fees, which can be substantial. Also inquire about early-return policies; some rental agencies charge extra if you return the car before the time specified in your contract while others give you a refund for the days not used. To avoid a hefty refueling fee, fill the tank just before you turn in the car, but be aware that gas stations near the rental outlet may overcharge. It's almost never a deal to buy the tank of gas that's in the car when you rent it; the understanding is that you'll return it empty, but some fuel usually remains.

In Switzerland, some rental agencies charge daily fees of about 25 SF for drivers under 25. If you wish to pay cash, agencies may request a deposit.

CAR TRAVEL

EMERGENCY SERVICES

All road breakdowns should be called in to the central Switzerland-wide emergency number, 140. If you are on an expressway, pull over to the shoulder and look for arrows pointing you to the nearest orange radio-telephone, called Bornes SOS; use these phones instead of a mobile phone because they allow police to find you instantly and send help. There are SOS phones every kilometer (½ mi), on alternate sides of the expressway. **⚡ Emergencies** ☎ 140.

FROM THE U.K. BY FERRY

In addition to the relatively swift (and expensive) Channel Tunnel, on which cars piggyback on trains to cross the channel from Dover to Boulogne, there are many drive-on/drive-off car ferry services across the Channel, but only a few are suitable as a means of getting to Switzerland. The situation is complicated by the different pricing systems operated by ferry companies and the many off-peak fares, and by the tolls charged by France on some of its motorways; these add up, particularly if you drive long distances. To avoid the tolls, **take a northerly route through Belgium or the Netherlands and Germany,** where motorways are free. The crossings for this route are Felixstowe or Dover to Zeebrugge; Sheerness to Vlissingen; and Ramsgate to Dunkirk. All these continental ports have good road connections, and Switzerland can be reached in a day of hard driving.

GASOLINE
If there's one thing that's generally cheaper in Switzerland than elsewhere in Western Europe, it's gasoline. If you are crossing borders, try to fill the tank in Switzerland rather than in neighboring countries. Regular unleaded (*bleifrei* in German, *sans plomb* in French) gas costs just over 1.30 SF per liter. Leaded fuel is no longer available. Prices are slightly higher in mountain areas. **Have some 10 SF and 20 SF notes available,** as many gas stations (especially in the mountains) have vending-machine pumps that operate even when they're closed. Simply slide in a bill and fill your tank. Many of these machines also accept major credit cards with precoded PIN numbers. You can request a receipt (*Quittung* in German, *quittance* in French) from the machine.

PARKING
Parking areas are clearly marked. In blue or red zones a *disque* (provided in rental cars or available free from banks, tourist offices, or police stations) must be placed clearly in the front window noting the time of arrival. These zones are slowly being replaced by metered-parking white zones. Each city sets its own time allotments for parking; the limits are posted. Metered parking is often paid for at communal machines that vary from city to city. Some machines simply accept coins and dispense tickets. At others you'll need to punch in your parking space or license plate number, then add coins. The ticket for parking may or may not have to be placed in your car window; this information is noted on the machine or ticket. Parking in public lots normally costs 2 SF for the first hour, increasing by 1 SF every half hour thereafter.

ROAD CONDITIONS
Swiss roads are well surfaced but wind around considerably—especially in the mountains—so **don't plan on achieving high average speeds.** When estimating likely travel times, look carefully at the map: there may be only 32 km (20 mi) between one point and another—but there may be an Alpine pass in the way. There is a well-developed highway network, though some notable gaps still exist in the south along an east–west line, roughly between Lugano and Sion. Road signs throughout the country use a color-coding system, with the official route numbers in white against a colored background. Expressway signs are green and highway signs are blue (unlike in the rest of Europe, where expressway signs are blue and highway signs are green). Signs for smaller roads are light blue. All signage indicates the names of upcoming towns as well, and it is generally easiest to use these names for navigating. A combination of steep or winding routes and hazardous weather means some roads will be closed in winter. Signs are posted at the beginning of the climb.

To find out about road conditions, traffic jams, itineraries, and so forth, you can turn to two places: the Swiss Automobile Club has operators standing by on weekdays from 8 to 5 to provide information in all languages. Dues-paying members of the Touring Club of Switzerland may contact the organization for similar information. Note that neither of these numbers gets you breakdown service. For frequent and precise information in Swiss languages, you can dial 163, or tune in to local radio stations.
🚗 **Swiss Automobile Club** ☎ 031/3283111. **Touring Club of Switzerland** ☎ 022/4172424.

ROAD MAPS
You can supplement the road maps provided by the rental car agency with city, regional, or national maps that are on sale in newspaper shops and post offices.

RULES OF THE ROAD
As in most of the rest of Europe, driving is on the right. Vehicles on main roads have priority over those on smaller roads. At intersections, priority is given to the driver

on the right except when merging into traffic circles, when priority is given to the drivers coming from the left. In urban areas the speed limit is 50 kph (30 mph); on main highways, it's 80 kph (50 mph); on expressways, the limit is 120 kph (75 mph). Pass only on the left. It is illegal to make a right-hand turn on a red light. The blood-alcohol limit is 0.08.

Children under age seven are not permitted to sit in the front seat. **Use headlights** in heavy rain, in poor visibility, or in tunnels—they are compulsory. Always **carry your valid license and car-registration papers;** there are occasional roadblocks to check them. **Wear seat belts** in the front- and backseats—they are mandatory.

There are no tolls in Switzerland. To use the main highways, you must display a sticker, or *vignette*, on the top-center or lower corner of the windshield. You can buy one at the border or in post offices, gas stations, and garages. A vignette costs 40 SF or the equivalent in euros; you can only pay cash. Driving without a vignette puts you at risk for getting a 100 SF fine. Cars rented within Switzerland already have these stickers; if you rent a car elsewhere in Europe, **ask if the rental company will provide the vignette for you.**

Traffic going up a mountain has priority except for postbuses coming down. A sign with a yellow post horn on a blue background means that postbuses have priority. On winding mountain roads, a brief honk as you approach a curve is a good way of warning any oncoming traffic.

In winter **be sure your car has snow tires and snow chains.** The latter are mandatory in some areas and advisable in most. Snow-chain service stations have signs marked SERVICE DE CHAÎNES À NEIGE or SCHNEEKETTENDIENST; snow chains are available for rent.

If you have an accident, even a minor one, you must call the police.

CHILDREN IN SWITZERLAND

If you are renting a car, don't forget to arrange for a car seat when you reserve. For general advice about traveling with children, consult *Fodor's FYI: Travel*

with Your Baby (available in bookstores everywhere).

CAMPS & HOLIDAY COURSES

Every summer some 120 private schools in Switzerland offer leisurely language study and recreation courses for primary and secondary school-age children from around the world. Summer camps similar to those in the United States are also available. Ask Switzerland Tourism for a copy of "Holiday and Language Courses," a list of camps and summer programs in Switzerland.

FLYING

If your children are two or older, ask about children's airfares. As a general rule, infants under two not occupying a seat fly at greatly reduced fares or even for free. But if you want to guarantee a seat for an infant, you have to pay full fare. Consider flying during off-peak days and times; most airlines will grant an infant a seat without a ticket if there are available seats. When booking, confirm carry-on allowances if you're traveling with infants. In general, for babies charged 10% to 50% of the adult fare you are allowed one carry-on bag and a collapsible stroller; if the flight is full, the stroller may have to be checked or you may be limited to less.

Experts agree that it's a good idea to use safety seats aloft for children weighing less than 40 pounds. Airlines set their own policies: if you use a safety seat, U.S. carriers usually require that the child be ticketed, even if he or she is young enough to ride free, because the seats must be strapped into regular seats. And even if you pay the full adult fare for the seat, it may be worth it, especially on longer trips. Do **check your airline's policy about using safety seats during takeoff and landing.** Safety seats are not allowed everywhere in the plane, so get your seat assignments as early as possible.

When reserving, request children's meals or a freestanding bassinet (not available at all airlines) if you need them. But note that bulkhead seats, where you must sit to use the bassinet, may lack an overhead bin or storage space on the floor.

FOOD

Children's menus are available in many restaurants around Switzerland; otherwise, you can usually request a child-size portion and the prices will be adjusted accordingly.

LODGING

Most hotels in Switzerland allow children under a certain age to stay in their parents' room at no extra charge, but others charge for them as extra adults; be sure to find out the cutoff age for children's discounts. The Swiss Hotel Association (⇨ Hotels *in* Lodging) has listings of family-friendly hotels throughout the country.

Supervised playrooms are available in some of the better hotels, and many winter resorts provide lists of reliable babysitters. For recommended local sitters, **check with your hotel.**

SIGHTS & ATTRACTIONS

Places that are especially appealing to children are indicated by a rubber-duckie icon (🐥) in the margin.

The Adult Plus version of the Swiss Museum Passport (⇨ Discounts & Deals) allows free entrance for up to five children under 16 at participating museums.

TRANSPORTATION

Families traveling together in Switzerland should **buy an STS Family Card,** a special pass (20 SF if purchased in Switzerland or free with the purchase of a Swiss Pass or Europass) that allows each child under 16 to travel free on trains, postbuses, and boats when accompanied by ticket-holding parents or guardians. Nonfamily members between the ages of 6 and 16 receive a 50% discount if they travel with STS Family. Adults must hold a valid Swiss Pass, Swiss Card, or Eurail tariff ticket to obtain the STS Family Card, available at any train station (⇨ Train Travel).

COMPUTERS ON THE ROAD

Some hotels now have in-room modem connections; ask about rates before you plug in. You will also find Internet terminals in airports and train stations in many cities and towns. If you are using your own computer, you will need an adapter plug and should use a surge protector.

CONSUMER PROTECTION

Whether you're shopping for gifts or purchasing travel services, **pay with a major credit card** whenever possible, so you can cancel payment or get reimbursed if there's a problem (and you can provide documentation). If you're doing business with a particular company for the first time, contact your local Better Business Bureau and the attorney general's offices in your state and (for U.S. businesses) the company's home state as well. Have any complaints been filed? Finally, if you're buying a package or tour, always consider travel insurance that includes default coverage (⇨ Insurance).

🔳 **BBBs Council of Better Business Bureaus** ⊠ 4200 Wilson Blvd., Suite 800, Arlington, VA 22203 ☎ 703/276-0100 🖷 703/525-8277 ⊕ www.bbb.org.

CUSTOMS & DUTIES

When shopping abroad, keep receipts for all purchases. Upon reentering the country, **be ready to show customs officials what you've bought.** Pack purchases together in an easily accessible place. If you think a duty is incorrect, appeal the assessment. If you object to the way your clearance was handled, note the inspector's badge number. In either case, first ask to see a supervisor. If the problem isn't resolved, write to the appropriate authorities, beginning with the port director at your point of entry.

IN AUSTRALIA

Australian residents who are 18 or older may bring home A$400 worth of souvenirs and gifts (including jewelry), 250 cigarettes or 250 grams of cigars or other tobacco products, and 1,125 ml of alcohol (including wine, beer, and spirits). Residents under 18 may bring back A$200 worth of goods. Members of the same family traveling together may pool their allowances. Prohibited items include meat products. Seeds, plants, and fruits need to be declared upon arrival.

🔳 **Australian Customs Service** ⌀ Regional Director, Box 8, Sydney, NSW 2001 ☎ 02/9213-2000 or 1300/363263, 02/9364-7222 or 1800/020-504 quarantine-inquiry line 🖷 02/9213-4043 ⊕ www.customs.gov.au.

IN CANADA

Canadian residents who have been out of Canada for at least seven days may bring in C$750 worth of goods duty-free. If you've been away fewer than seven days but more than 48 hours, the duty-free allowance drops to C$200. If your trip lasts 24 to 48 hours, the allowance is C$50. You may not pool allowances with family members. Goods claimed under the C$750 exemption may follow you by mail; those claimed under the lesser exemptions must accompany you. Alcohol and tobacco products may be included in the seven-day and 48-hour exemptions but not in the 24-hour exemption. If you meet the age requirements of the province or territory through which you reenter Canada, you may bring in, duty-free, 1.5 liters of wine *or* 1.14 liters (40 imperial ounces) of liquor *or* 24 12-ounce cans or bottles of beer or ale. Also, if you meet the local age requirement for tobacco products, you may bring in, duty-free, 200 cigarettes and 50 cigars. Check ahead of time with the Canada Customs and Revenue Agency or the Department of Agriculture for policies regarding meat products, seeds, plants, and fruits.

You may send an unlimited number of gifts (only one gift per recipient, however) worth up to C$60 each duty-free to Canada. Label the package UNSOLICITED GIFT—VALUE UNDER $60. Alcohol and tobacco are excluded.

⑦ Canada Customs and Revenue Agency ⊠ 2265 St. Laurent Blvd., Ottawa, Ontario K1G 4K3 ☎ 800/461-9999 in Canada, 204/983-3500, 506/636-5064 ⊕ www.ccra.gc.ca.

IN NEW ZEALAND

All homeward-bound residents may bring back NZ$700 worth of souvenirs and gifts; passengers may not pool their allowances, and children can claim only the concession on goods intended for their own use. For those 17 or older, the duty-free allowance also includes 4.5 liters of wine or beer; one 1,125-ml bottle of spirits; and either 200 cigarettes, 250 grams of tobacco, 50 cigars, *or* a combination of the three up to 250 grams. Meat products, seeds, plants, and fruits must be declared upon arrival to the Agricultural Services Department.

⑦ New Zealand Customs ⊠ Head office: The Customhouse, 17–21 Whitmore St., Box 2218, Wellington ☎ 09/300–5399 or 0800/428–786 ⊕ www.customs.govt.nz.

IN SWITZERLAND

Entering Switzerland, a visitor who is 17 years or older and is arriving from Europe may bring in 200 cigarettes or 50 cigars or 250 grams of tobacco; 2 liters of alcohol up to 15 proof and 1 liter over 15 proof; if the visitor arrives from elsewhere, the quantities are doubled. Visitors over 17 may bring gifts valued at up to 100 SF. Medicine, such as insulin, is allowed for personal use only.

⑦ Federal Customs Administration ⊕ www.zoll.admin.ch/e/private/rv/reisen_einkaufen.php.

IN THE U.K.

From countries outside the European Union, including Switzerland, you may bring home, duty-free, 200 cigarettes, 50 cigars, 100 cigarillos, or 250 grams of tobacco; 1 liter of spirits or 2 liters of fortified or sparkling wine or liqueurs; 2 liters of still table wine; 60 ml of perfume; 250 ml of toilet water; plus £145 worth of other goods, including gifts and souvenirs. Prohibited items include meat and dairy products, seeds, plants, and fruits.

⑦ HM Customs and Excise ⊠ Portcullis House, 21 Cowbridge Rd. E, Cardiff CF11 9SS ☎ 0845/010–9000 or 0208/929–0152 advice service, 0208/929–6731 or 0208/910–3602 complaints ⊕ www.hmce.gov.uk.

IN THE U.S.

U.S. residents who have been out of the country for at least 48 hours may bring home, for personal use, $800 worth of foreign goods duty-free, as long as they haven't used the $800 allowance or any part of it in the past 30 days. This exemption may include 1 liter of alcohol (for travelers 21 and older), 200 cigarettes, and 100 non-Cuban cigars. Family members from the same household who are traveling together may pool their $800 personal exemptions. For fewer than 48 hours, the duty-free allowance drops to $200, which may include 50 cigarettes, 10 non-Cuban cigars, and 150 ml of alcohol (or 150 ml of perfume containing alcohol). The $200 allowance cannot be combined with other individuals' exemptions, and if you exceed it, the full value of all the goods will be taxed. Antiques, which U.S. Customs and Border Protection defines as objects more than 100 years old, enter duty-free, as do original works of art done entirely by hand, including paintings, drawings, and sculptures. This doesn't apply to folk art or handicrafts, which are in general dutiable.

You may also send packages home duty-free, with a limit of one parcel per addressee per day (except alcohol or tobacco products or perfume worth more than $5). You can mail up to $200 worth of goods for personal use; label the package PERSONAL USE and attach a list of its contents and their retail value. If the package contains your used personal belongings, mark it AMERICAN GOODS RETURNED to avoid paying duties. You may send up to $100 worth of goods as a gift; mark the package UNSOLICITED GIFT. Mailed items do not affect your duty-free allowance on your return.

To avoid paying duty on foreign-made high-ticket items you already own and will take on your trip, register them with Customs before you leave the country. Consider filing a Certificate of Registration for laptops, cameras, watches, and other digital devices identified with serial numbers or other permanent markings; you can keep the certificate for other trips. Otherwise, bring a sales receipt or insurance form to show that you owned the item before you left the United States.

For more about duties, restricted items, and other information about international travel, check out U.S. Customs and Border Protection's online brochure, *Know Before You Go*.

⚑ U.S. Customs and Border Protection ✉ For inquiries and equipment registration, 1300 Pennsylvania Ave. NW, Washington, DC 20229 ⊕ www.cbp.gov ☎ 877/287–8667 or 202/354–1000 ✉ For complaints, Customer Satisfaction Unit, 1300 Pennsylvania Ave. NW, Room 5.2C, Washington, DC 20229.

DISABILITIES & ACCESSIBILITY

Cantonal legislation ensures that people with disabilities can access public transportation, public buildings, and the like. Other helpful facilities, such as designated parking spaces for people with disabilities, are common.

Contact Mobility International Schweiz for information on accessible tours, restaurants, and hotels. Their Web site has information about venues that can easily be accessed by people in wheelchairs, but the information is only in German.

⚑ Local Resources Mobility International Schweiz ✉ Froburgstr. 4, CH-4600 Olten ☎ 062/2068835 🖶 062/2068839 ⊕ www.mis-ch.ch.

RESERVATIONS

When discussing accessibility with an operator or reservations agent, ask hard questions. Are there any stairs, inside *or* out? Are there grab bars next to the toilet *and* in the shower/tub? How wide is the doorway to the room? To the bathroom? For the most extensive facilities meeting the latest legal specifications, opt for newer accommodations. If you reserve through a toll-free number, consider also calling the hotel's local number to confirm the information from the central reservations office. Get confirmation in writing when you can.

TRANSPORTATION

Foreign visitors with either the Disabled Badge of their country or the International Wheelchair Badge mounted inside the windshield of their car are entitled to use parking spaces reserved for people with disabilities throughout the country. Motorists who cannot walk unaided can obtain a special permit for parking privileges, as well as the international badge mentioned above, from the local police authority.

Throughout the Swiss Federal Railways, wheelchairs are often available; inform the particular station ahead of time that you will need one. In addition, ramps or lifts and wheelchair-accessible toilets have been installed in more than 100 stations. All Inter-City and long-distance express trains and more than two-thirds of the country's regional shuttle trains now have wheelchair compartments. A brochure describing services for disabled travelers is available (in French, German, and Italian) from the Swiss Federal Railways. Use the Call Center Handicap to arrange for assistance at more than 160 support stations in the Swiss rail system.

⏃ Complaints Aviation Consumer Protection Division (⇨ Air Travel) for airline-related problems. **Departmental Office of Civil Rights** ⊠ For general inquiries, U.S. Department of Transportation, S-30, 400 7th St. SW, Room 10215, Washington, DC 20590 ☎ 202/366-4648 ᕦ 202/366-9371 ⊕ www.dot. gov/ost/docr/index.htm. **Disability Rights Section** ⊠ NYAV, U.S. Department of Justice, Civil Rights Division, 950 Pennsylvania Ave. NW, Washington, DC 20530 ᕦ ADA information line 202/514-0301, 800/ 514-0301, 202/514-0383 TTY, 800/514-0383 TTY ⊕ www.ada.gov. **U.S. Department of Transportation Hotline** ᕦ For disability-related air-travel problems, 800/778-4838 or 800/455-9880 TTY. **⏃ Call Center Handicap** ☎ 0800/007-102 ⊕ www.rail.ch/pv/mobil_e.htm#1.

TRAVEL AGENCIES

In the United States, the Americans with Disabilities Act requires that travel firms serve the needs of all travelers. Some agencies specialize in working with people with disabilities.

⏃ Travelers with Mobility Problems Access Adventures/B. Roberts Travel ⊠ 206 Chestnut Ridge Rd., Scottsville, NY 14624 ☎ 585/889-9096 ⊕ www.brobertstravel.com ✎ dltravel@prodigy. net, run by a former physical-rehabilitation counselor. **CareVacations** ⊠ No. 5, 5110-50 Ave., Leduc, Alberta, Canada, T9E 6V4 ☎ 780/986-6404 or 877/ 478-7827 ᕦ 780/986-8332 ⊕ www.carevacations. com, for group tours and cruise vacations. **Flying Wheels Travel** ⊠ 143 W. Bridge St., Box 382, Owatonna, MN 55060 ☎ 507/451-5005 ᕦ 507/451-1685 ⊕ www.flyingwheelstravel.com.

🄳 DISCOUNTS & DEALS

Besides the various discount transportation passes (⇨ Train Travel), there's a discount pass for Swiss museums. For a fee of 30 SF per month, the Swiss Museum Passport grants free entrance to more than 300 museums throughout the country. You can buy the passports at the participating museums and at many local tourist offices.

Be a smart shopper and compare all your options before making decisions. A plane ticket bought with a promotional coupon from travel clubs, coupon books, and direct-mail offers or purchased on the Internet may not be cheaper than the least expensive fare from a discount ticket agency. And always keep in mind that what you get is just as important as what you save.

⏃ Discount Museum Pass Swiss Museum Passport Office ⊠ Hornbachstr. 50, CH-8034 Zürich ☎ 01/3898456 ᕦ 01/3898400 ⊕ www.museums. ch/pass.

DISCOUNT RESERVATIONS

To save money, look into discount reservation services with Web sites and toll-free numbers which use their buying power to get a better price on hotels, airline tickets (⇨ Air Travel), even car rentals. When booking a room, always **call the hotel's local toll-free number** (if one is available) rather than the central reservations number—you'll often get a better price. Always ask about special packages or corporate rates.

When shopping for the best deal on hotels and car rentals, look for guaranteed exchange rates, which protect you against a falling dollar. With your rate locked in, you won't pay more, even if the price goes up in the local currency.

⏃ Airline Tickets Air 4 Less ☎ 800/AIR4LESS; low-fare specialist.

⏃ Hotel Rooms Accommodations Express ☎ 800/444-7666 or 800/277-1064. **Hotels.com** ☎ 800/246-8357 ⊕ www.hotels.com. **Steigenberger Reservation Service** ☎ 800/223-5652 ⊕ www.srs-worldhotels.com. **Turbotrip.com** ☎ 800/473-7829 ⊕ www.turbotrip.com.

PACKAGE DEALS

Don't confuse packages and guided tours. When you buy a package, you travel on your own, just as though you had planned the trip yourself. Fly/drive packages, which combine airfare and car rental, are often a good deal. In cities, ask the local visitor's bureau about hotel and local transportation packages that include tickets to major museum exhibits or other special events. If you **buy a rail/drive pass,** you may save on train tickets and car rentals. All Eurail-pass holders get a discount on Eurostar fares through the Channel Tunnel and often receive reduced rates for buses, hotels, ferries, sightseeing cruises, and car rentals.

EATING & DRINKING

The restaurants we list are the cream of the crop in each price category. Properties indicated by an ✗⊡ are lodging establishments whose restaurant warrants a special trip (and will accommodate nonhotel guests). In regional chapters price charts appear in the dining subsection of the Pleasures & Pastimes section, which follows each chapter introduction. In chapters devoted to a single city, price charts appear in the introductions to the dining section. Please note that the price charts reflect the cost of only the main dish at dinner and that two- and three-course menus are offered in many restaurants, representing a better value than the à la carte price charts would indicate. Unless otherwise noted, the restaurants listed in this guide are open daily for lunch and dinner.

MEALS & SPECIALTIES

Breakfast in Switzerland tends to be little more than coffee with bread, butter, and marmalade. If you prefer a lot of milk in your coffee, ask for a *renversé* in French (literally, *upside-down*) or a *Milchkaffee* in German. The signature Bircher muesli—invented by Dr. Maximilian Oskar Bircher-Benner at his diet clinic at the end of the 19th century—is available in most supermarkets (such as Migros and Coop) and can make a hearty lunch, especially when served with plain or fruit yogurt instead of milk.

For lunch or dinner, most regions offer cheese specialties such as fondue (literally, "melted" in French), which originated in the western part of Switzerland and comes in regional varieties, of which the Neuchâtel preparation is the most famous (combining equal portions of Gruyère and Vacherin). Raclette is a cheese specialty from the Valais canton. Traditionally, the cut surface of half a cheese is exposed to a fire and the melted cheese is consistently scraped off (*racler* means "to scrape") and

eaten with baked potatoes, pickled white onions, and other condiments. Another cheesy dish is a *Malakoff*, a chunk of Gruyère that is pressed onto a piece of toast and then deep-fried. You may order only one Malakoff at a time (which may be a blessing in disguise to those who tend to bite off more than they can chew). A crisp wine as you dine or a shot of kirsch after a meal can help soothe your over-taxed stomach.

The French-speaking cantons pride themselves on *filets de perche* (fried perch fillets), possibly the most popular dish in the region. A few variations on the theme exist—some with herbs or cognac sauce—but the traditional version is served with lemon and french fries on the side. German-speaking Switzerland made its mark in culinary history with the ubiquitous *Rösti,* a grated potato pancake—often spruced up with herbs, bacon, or cheese—that is served with nearly any meat or fish. Competing with Rösti for most popular side dish, *Spätzli* (egg-flour dumplings) continue to be fashioned according to age-old local traditions (though toss-in-boiling-water-and-serve packets have a strong following). The Ticino, to the south, has preserved its penchant for Italian cuisine, with risotto, gnocchi, polenta, and pasta dishes appearing on most menus.

Besides these staples, you are likely to encounter a variety of stews, organ meats, and sausages. Classics such as *truite meunière* (trout rolled in flour, fried in butter, and served with lemon and parsley) are also standard fare.

MEALTIMES

Many restaurants close after lunch (as of 3 PM) and reopen for dinner (about 6 PM). In remote regions it may prove difficult to find kitchens open past 9 or 10 PM, so plan ahead. Many restaurants are closed on Sunday and many close for the month of August or even longer. Bars often close at 1 or 2 AM, although clubs continue serving into the wee hours.

PAYING

Credit cards are widely accepted, and euros often accepted, especially in areas that border on the European Union. Note that service is included unless indicated on the menu. It is customary to leave a small tip in cash (up to 10% depending on how pleased you are with the service).

RESERVATIONS & DRESS

Reservations are always a good idea; we mention them only when they're essential or not accepted. Book as far ahead as you can, and reconfirm as soon as you arrive. (Large parties should always call ahead to check the reservations policy.) We mention dress only when men are required to wear a jacket or a jacket and tie.

WINE, BEER & SPIRITS

Quality and diversity are the hallmarks of Swiss wine, celebrated in annual festivals where everyone samples the year's harvest. They may not be widely exported, but Swiss wines are generally available in restaurants, and you can also get to know them in wine cellars (often with delicious local cheese). All of Switzerland's 23 cantons produce wines, but six areas outdo the rest: the Valais, Vaud, Geneva, the Three Lakes region in western Switzerland, the German-speaking region of eastern Switzerland, and the Ticino. The Chasselas is by far the most successful among white grapes, and pinot noir among the reds. Other top white grape varieties include Müller-Thurgau and Sylvaner; reds feature gamay and merlot. You can get more information from the Swiss Wine Exporters' Association (⊕ www. swisswine.ch).

Switzerland counts more than 120 official active breweries that regularly produce *Lager*, *Spezialbier* (slightly stronger and a touch more bitter than the lager), and *Festbier* (strong, dark holiday beer produced at Easter and Christmas and sometimes sold as *Bockbier* or *Märzenbier*). Specialty beer includes the amber *Altbier*, the corn-infused *Maisbier*, and *Weizenbier* (wheat beer). A bit of trivia: the strongest beer ever brewed is said to have been the now-retired Samichlaus brand from the Feldschlösschen Brewery; with a whopping 14% alcohol content, it had no head and an aroma akin to molasses.

Switzerland is brimming with spirits. Most notably, *kirsch* (cherry spirit) from Zug and the Lake Luzern region has gained worldwide recognition. Plums are used to make *Zwetschgenwasser*. The tiny damassine plum, reportedly brought back from Damascus by a crusading knight, is distilled into the delightfully fragrant *Damassine*, available in Saignelégier. The many apple spirits include *Träsch* and *Gravensteiner*; pears from the Valais give their spirit to the redolent *Williamine*. A unique variety of grappas are up for grabs in the grottoes of the Ticino; this potent firewater gets its name and taste from the skins of the grape. Now that vodka is gaining popularity among consumers around the globe, the Swiss have begun to promote their own designer spirit: Xellent, which entered the market in its sleek red bottle in 2003.

ELECTRICITY

To use electric-powered equipment purchased in the U.S. or Canada, **bring a converter and adapter.** The electrical current in Switzerland is 220 volts, 50 cycles alternating current (AC); wall outlets take plugs that have two or three round prongs. The two-pronged continental-type plugs can be used throughout the country.

If your appliances are dual-voltage, you'll need only an adapter. Don't use 110-volt outlets marked FOR SHAVERS ONLY for high-wattage appliances such as blow-dryers. Most laptops operate equally well on 110 and 220 volts and so require only an adapter.

EMBASSIES

🇦🇺 **Australia Consulate** ⊠ chemin des Fins 2 ⌂ Case Postale 172, CH-1211 Geneva ☎ 022/7999100

🇨🇦 **Canada Embassy** ⊠ Kirchenfeldstr. 88, CH-3005 Bern ☎ 031/3573200.

🇬🇧 **United Kingdom Embassy** ⊠ Thunstr. 50, CH-3005 Bern ☎ 031/3597700.

🇺🇸 **United States Embassy** ⊠ Jubiläumsstr. 93, CH-3001 Bern ☎ 031/3577011, 031/3577344 24-hour emergency hotline.

EMERGENCIES

🆘 **Police** ☎ 117. **Ambulance** ☎ 144.

ENGLISH-LANGUAGE MEDIA

BOOKS

It's quite easy to find English-language books, especially in major cities. Most bookstores have a selection of fiction and nonfiction; kiosks at train stations and airports stock some as well.

NEWSPAPERS & MAGAZINES

You can find the *International Herald Tribune* at newsstands and kiosks throughout Switzerland. *USA Today* and some British newspapers are also often available.

RADIO & TELEVISION

BBC World, BBC Prime, CNN, and CNBC are generally available on cable channels in hotels. Switzerland's only English-language radio station is WRG-FM (at 88.4 FM).

ETIQUETTE & BEHAVIOR

In Switzerland it's polite to **say hello and good-bye** (*bonjour, au revoir; grüezi, auf Wiedersehen; buon giorno, arrivederci*) to everyone you speak to, from police officers to cashiers. The standard gesture for each is a simple handshake. In the French- and Italian-speaking cantons, it is standard for friends to greet each other with three kisses on the cheek. In the German-speaking areas, kissing is much less common, as is hugging.

BUSINESS ETIQUETTE

When doing business, use your counterpart's first name only after he or she has used yours. Always shake hands when you greet and say good-bye.

GAY & LESBIAN TRAVEL

For resources in Switzerland, a good starting point is Dialogai, which has a library, tearoom, and bar. You can pick up a copy of its guide, which lists gay-friendly contacts for Switzerland's French-speaking region and in neighboring France (it's in French only). The English-speaking staff can also direct you to organizations in other major Swiss cities. For the latest parties in Zürich as well as information about clubs and events in Bern, Basel, Geneva, Luzern, and Lausanne, try www.gay.ch.

✈ Dialogai ✉ 11–13 rue de la Navigation, CH-1211 Geneva ☎ 022/9064040 🖷 022/9064044 ⊕ www. dialogai.org.

✈ Gay- & Lesbian-Friendly Travel Agencies Different Roads Travel ✉ 8383 Wilshire Blvd., Suite 520, Beverly Hills, CA 90211 ☎ 323/651-5557 or 800/429-8747 (Ext. 14 for both) 🖷 323/651-5454 ✉ lgernert@tzell.com. **Kennedy Travel** ✉ 130 W. 42nd St., Suite 401, New York, NY 10036 ☎ 212/840-8659, 800/237-7433 🖷 212/730-2269 ⊕ www. kennedytravel.com. **Now, Voyager** ✉ 4406 18th St., San Francisco, CA 94114 ☎ 415/626-1169 or 800/ 255-6951 🖷 415/626-8626 ⊕ www.nowvoyager. com. **Skylink Travel and Tour/Flying Dutchmen Travel** ✉ 1455 N. Dutton Ave., Suite A, Santa Rosa, CA 95401 ☎ 707/546-9888 or 800/225-5759 🖷 707/636-0951; serving lesbian travelers.

HEALTH

Switzerland's reputation for impeccable standards of cleanliness is well earned. But even at the foot of an icy-pure 6,560-foot glacier, you'll find the locals drinking bottled mineral water; you'll have to wrangle with the waiter if you want tap water with your meal. This is as much a result of the tradition of expecting beverages in a café to be paid for as it is a response to health questions. If you're traveling with a child under two years old, you may be advised by locals not to carry him or her on excursions above 6,560 feet; check with your pediatrician before leaving home. Adults should limit strenuous excursions on the first day at extra-high-altitude resorts, those at 5,248 feet and above. Adults with heart problems may want to avoid all excursions above 6,560 feet.

Europe has been plagued in recent years by what has now become an agricultural problem. The first cases of bovine spongiform encephalopathy (BSE), commonly known as "mad cow disease," surfaced in Great Britain in the mid-1980s. BSE is a fatal degenerative disease contracted by cattle. When contaminated beef is eaten by humans, it can result in Creutzfeldt-Jakob Disease (CJD), an extremely rare brain-wasting illness fatal to humans.

Europe reacted swiftly to the threat, placing a ban on all beef exported from Great Britain for a short period and immediately banning all use of feed prepared with animal by-products. People are still wary, but the risk of contracting the disease is considered extremely remote. The **Centers for**

Disease Control & Prevention (⊕ www.cdc.gov) reported, "the current risk for infection with the BSE agent among travelers to Europe is extremely small, if it exists at all." But, as always, stay informed.

OVER-THE-COUNTER REMEDIES

Basic over-the-counter medicines are available from pharmacies (*pharmacie, Apotheke, farmacia*), which are recognizable from afar thanks to signs with green crosses.

PESTS & OTHER HAZARDS

When hiking or skiing in the mountains, **be aware of the dangers of altitude sickness,** as well as other afflictions such as heat stroke, dehydration, sunstroke, frostbite, snow blindness. Symptoms of altitude sickness, which occurs in some individuals who ascend rapidly to high altitudes, include numbness, tingling, nausea, drowsiness, headaches, and vision problems. If you experience discomfort, return to a lower altitude as soon as possible. You should **wear sunscreen** all through the year; many different brands are available at ski shops near the slopes. If you plan to spend extended periods in rural areas, **take precautions against ticks,** especially in spring and summer. Wear long sleeves, long pants, and boots, and apply insect repellent containing the powerful repellent DEET. Two vaccines against tick-borne infections are available in Europe: TicoVac (also known as FSME Immun) and Encepur, but neither has been approved in the United States. Remove ticks with tweezers, grasping the insect by the head.

HOLIDAYS

National holidays include January 1 (New Year), Good Friday (March or April), Easter Sunday and Monday (March or April), May 1 (Labor Day), Ascension Day (May), Whitsunday and Whitmonday (May), August 1 (Swiss National Holiday), and December 25–26 (Christmas and Boxing Day).

INSURANCE

The most useful travel-insurance plan is a comprehensive policy that includes coverage for trip cancellation and interruption, default, trip delay, and medical expenses (with a waiver for preexisting conditions).

Without insurance you'll lose all or most of your money if you cancel your trip, regardless of the reason. Default insurance covers you if your tour operator, airline, or cruise line goes out of business—the chances of which have been increasing. Trip-delay covers expenses that arise because of bad weather or mechanical delays. Study the fine print when comparing policies.

If you're traveling internationally, a key component of travel insurance is coverage for medical bills incurred if you get sick on the road. Such expenses aren't generally covered by Medicare or private policies. U.K. residents can buy a travel-insurance policy valid for most vacations taken during the year in which it's purchased (but check preexisting-condition coverage). British and Australian citizens need extra medical coverage when traveling overseas.

Always **buy travel policies directly from the insurance company;** if you buy them from a cruise line, airline, or tour operator that goes out of business you probably won't be covered for the agency or operator's default, a major risk. Before making any purchase, review your existing health and home-owner's policies to find what they cover away from home.

🔢 Travel Insurers In the U.S.: **Access America** ✉ 2805 N. Parham Rd., Richmond, VA 23294 ☎ 800/284-8300 🖷 804/673-1491 or 800/346-9265 ⊕ www.accessamerica.com. **Travel Guard International** ✉ 1145 Clark St., Stevens Point, WI 54481 ☎ 715/345-0505 or 800/826-1300 🖷 800/955-8785 ⊕ www.travelguard.com.

🔢 Insurance Information In the U.K.: **Association of British Insurers** ✉ 51 Gresham St., London EC2V 7HQ ☎ 020/7600-3333 🖷 020/7696-8999 ⊕ www.abi.org.uk. In Canada: **RBC Insurance** ✉ 6880 Financial Dr., Mississauga, Ontario L5N 7Y5 ☎ 800/668-4342 or 905/816-2400 🖷 905/813-4704 ⊕ www.rbcinsurance.com. In Australia: **Insurance Council of Australia** ✉ Insurance Enquiries and Complaints, Level 12, Box 561, Collins St. W, Melbourne, VIC 8007 ☎ 1300/780808 or 03/9629-4109 🖷 03/9621-2060 ⊕ www.iecltd.com.au. In New Zealand: **Insurance Council of New Zealand** ✉ Level 7, 111–115 Customhouse Quay,

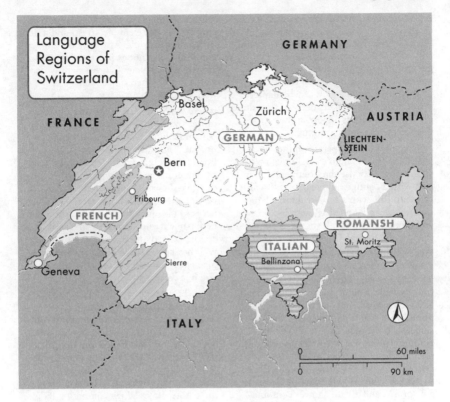

Language Regions of Switzerland

GERMANY

Basel

Zürich

FRANCE

GERMAN

AUSTRIA

LIECHTEN-
STEIN

Bern

Fribourg

FRENCH

ROMANSH

St. Moritz

ITALIAN

Bellinzona

Sierre

Geneva

ITALY

0   60 miles
0   90 km

Box 474, Wellington ☎ 04/472-5230 🖷 04/473-3011 ⊕ www.icnz.org.nz.

LANGUAGE

Nearly 70% of the population of Switzerland speaks one dialect or another of German; Swiss German can be a far cry from high German, although standard German is generally understood. French is spoken in the southwest, around Lake Geneva, and in the cantons of Fribourg, Neuchâtel, Jura, Vaud, and most of the Valais. Italian is spoken in the Ticino. In the Upper and Lower Engadines, in the canton of Graubünden, the last gasp of a Romance language called Romansh is still in daily use. There are several dialects of Romansh—five, in fact—so there's not much point in trying to pick up a few phrases. If you want to attempt communicating with the locals there, venture a little Italian. In the areas most frequented

by English-speaking tourists—Zermatt, the Berner Oberland, the Engadine, Luzern—people in the tourist industry usually speak English. Elsewhere, you might not be as lucky. See the vocabulary section at the back of the book for helpful words and phrases.

LANGUAGES FOR TRAVELERS

A phrase book and language-tape set can help get you started. *Fodor's French for Travelers, Fodor's German for Travelers, and Fodor's Italian for Travelers* (available at bookstores everywhere) are excellent.

LODGING

The lodgings we list are the cream of the crop in each price category. We always list the facilities available—but we don't specify whether they cost extra: when pricing accommodations, always ask what's included and what costs extra. In addition, assume that all rooms have a private bath unless otherwise noted. Properties indicated by an ✕▣ are lodging establishments whose restaurant warrants a special trip (and will accommodate nonhotel guests). In regional chapters price charts appear in the lodging section of Pleasures & Pastimes, which follows each chapter introduction. In chapters devoted to a single city, price charts appear in the introductions to the lodging section.

Assume that hotels operate on the European Plan (EP, with no meals) unless we specify that they use the Continental Plan (CP, with a continental breakfast), Breakfast Plan (BP, with a full breakfast), Modified American Plan (MAP, with breakfast and dinner), or the Full American Plan (FAP, with all meals).

Switzerland is as famous for its hotels as it is for its mountains, watches, and chocolates; its standards in hospitality are extremely high. Rooms are impeccably clean and well maintained, and they are furnished with comforts ranging from the simplest to the most deluxe. Prices are accordingly high: you will pay more for minimal comforts here than in any other European country. Americans accustomed to spacious motels with two double beds, a color TV, and a bath-shower combination may be disappointed in their first venture into the legendary Swiss hotel: spaces are small, bathtubs cost extra, and single rooms may have single beds. What you're paying for is service, reliability, cleanliness, and a complex hierarchy of amenities you may not even know you need.

Where no address is provided in the hotel listings, none is necessary: In smaller towns and villages, a postal code is all you need. To find the hotel on arrival, watch for the official street signs pointing the way to every hotel that belongs to the local tourist association.

Some things to bear in mind when you check in: the standard double room in Switzerland has two prim beds built together, with separate linens and, sometimes, sheets tucked firmly down the middle. If you prefer more sociable arrangements, ask for a "French bed," or *lit matrimonial*—that will get you a single-mattress double. Some hotels may offer extra beds—for example, to expand a double room to a triple. Also note that air-conditioning is not as prevalent as in the United States; evenings are generally cool, so Alpine air often stands in for a/c.

Particularly in ski resorts or in hotels where you'll be staying for three days or more, you may be quoted a room price per person including *demipension* (half board). This means that you've opted for breakfast included and to eat either lunch or dinner in the hotel, selecting from a limited, fixed menu. Unless you're holding out for gastronomic adventure, your best bet is to take half board. Most hotels will be flexible if you come in from the slopes craving a steaming pot of fondue, and they will then subtract the day's pension supplement from your room price, charging you à la carte instead.

Price charts are based on the cost of a standard double room during peak season, including tax, service, and breakfast only. Note that a hotel's prices may vary widely during the rest of the year and that the half board available at many hotels, for only slightly more than our listed room cost, significantly increases the value of these hotel stays. When comparing lodging options, **check hotels' low season rates and meal plans.**

APARTMENT & VILLA RENTALS

If you want a home base that's roomy enough for a family and comes with cooking facilities, consider a furnished rental. These can save you money, especially if you're traveling with a group. Home-exchange directories sometimes list rentals as well as exchanges.

Most resort tourist offices have lists of apartments for rent.

🔁 International Agents **Drawbridge to Europe** ✉ 98 Granite St., Ashland, OR 97520 ☎ 541/482–7778 or 888/268–1148 🖶 541/482-7779 ⊕ www. drawbridgetoeurope.com. **Hideaways International** ✉ 767 Islington St., Portsmouth, NH 03801 ☎ 603/430-4433 or 800/843-4433 🖶 603/430-4444 ⊕ www.hideaways.com, annual membership $145. **Hometours International** ✉ 1108 Scottie La., Knoxville, TN 37919 ☎ 865/690-8484 or 866/367-4668 ⊕ thor.he.net/~hometour/. **Interhome** ✉ 1990

N.E. 163rd St., Suite 110, North Miami Beach, FL 33162 ☎ 305/940-2299 or 800/882-6864 🖶 305/940-2911 ⊕ www.interhome.us. **Villas and Apartments Abroad** ✉ 183 Madison Ave., Suite 201, New York, NY 10016 ☎ 212/213-6435 or 800/433-3020 🖶 212/213-8252 ⊕ www.vaanyc.com. **Villas International** ✉ 4340 Redwood Hwy., Suite D309, San Rafael, CA 94903 ☎ 415/499-9490 or 800/221-2260 🖶 415/499-9491 ⊕ www.villasintl.com.

BED & BREAKFASTS

You can order brochures and get information about B&Bs from the user-friendly site of Bed & Breakfast Switzerland, ⊕ www.bnb.ch. You can make reservations online through the site.

CAMPING

Switzerland is ideal for campers, with approximately 450 sites throughout the country. All are classified with one to five stars according to amenities, location, and so on. The rates vary widely but average around 15 SF per night for a family of four, plus car or camper. For further details see the *Swiss Camping Guide,* published by the Swiss Camping Association, available at bookshops for 15 SF or from the Camping & Caravaning Association. Listings are also available from the Touring Club of Switzerland. To stay in most European campsites, you must have an International Camping Carnet verifying your status as a camper. This is available from any national camping association within Europe or from the National Campers & Hikers Association. Camping on public property is not allowed; to camp on private land, such as farmland, you must have the permission of the owner, but this is generally not done.

🚩 **Camping & Caravaning Association** ✍ Box 24, CH-6000 Luzern ☎ 041/3702190 🖶 041/3702146 ⊕ www.swisscamps.ch. **National Campers & Hikers Association** ✉ 4804 Transit Rd., Bldg. 2, Depew, NY 14043 ☎ 716/668-6242. **Touring Club of Switzerland** ✉ Ch. de Blandonnet 4, CH-1214 Vernier ☎ 022/4172727 🖶 022/4172020 ⊕ www.tcs.ch.

FARM STAYS

An unusual option for families seeking the local experience: Stay on a farm with a Swiss family, complete with children, animals, and the option to work in the fields.

Participating farm families register with the Schweizerischer Bauernverband (Swiss Farmers Association), listing the birth dates of their children, rooms and facilities, and types of animals your children can see. Prices are often considerably lower than those of hotels and vacation flats. You should be reasonably fluent in French or German, depending on the region of your stay. More information is available through Switzerland Tourism.

🚩 **Organizations Schweizerischer Bauernverband** (Swiss Farmers Association) ✉ Laurstr. 10, CH-5200 Brugg ☎ 056/4625111 🖶 056/4415348. **Verein Ferien auf dem Bauernhof** (Swiss Holiday Farms Association) ✉ Feierlenhof, CH-8595 Altnau ☎ 071/6952372 🖶 071/6952367 ⊕ www.bauernhof-ferien.ch.

HOME EXCHANGES

If you would like to exchange your home for someone else's, join a home-exchange organization, which will send you its updated listings of available exchanges for a year and will include your own listing in at least one of them. It's up to you to make specific arrangements.

🚩 **Exchange Clubs HomeLink International** 🏠 Box 47747, Tampa, FL 33647 ☎ 813/975-9825 or 800/638-3841 🖶 813/910-8144 ⊕ www.homelink.org; $110 yearly for a listing, online access, and catalog; $70 without catalog. **Intervac U.S.** ✉ 30 Corte San Fernando, Tiburon, CA 94920 ☎ 800/756-4663 🖶 415/435-7440 ⊕ www.intervacus.com; $125 yearly for a listing, online access, and a catalog; $65 without catalog.

HOSTELS

No matter what your age, you can save on lodging costs by staying at hostels.

In some 4,500 locations in more than 70 countries around the world, Hostelling International (HI), the umbrella group for a number of national youth-hostel associations, offers single-sex, dorm-style beds and, at many hostels, rooms for couples and family accommodations. Membership in any HI national hostel association, open to travelers of all ages, allows you to stay in HI-affiliated hostels at member rates; one-year membership is about $28 for adults (C$35 for a two-year minimum membership in Canada, £14 in the U.K.,

A\$52 in Australia, and NZ\$40 in New Zealand); hostels charge about \$10–\$30 per night. Members have priority if the hostel is full; they're also eligible for discounts around the world, even on rail and bus travel in some countries.

Individual members of Swiss Youth Hostels save 6 SF on accommodations (a family saves 12 SF). You can become a member for one year for 22 SF if you are under 18, 33 SF if you're older. Families can join for 44 SF. Order a membership card online or at any STA Travel agency.

🛈 International Organizations Hostelling International–USA ✉ 8401 Colesville Rd., Suite 600, Silver Spring, MD 20910 ☎ 301/495-1240 🖷 301/495-6697 ⊕ www.hiusa.org. **Hostelling International–Canada** ✉ 205 Catherine St., Suite 400, Ottawa, Ontario K2P 1C3 ☎ 613/237-7884 or 800/663-5777 🖷 613/237-7868 ⊕ www.hihostels.ca. **YHA England and Wales** ✉ Trevelyan House, Dimple Rd., Matlock, Derbyshire DE4 3YH, U.K. ☎ 0870/870-8808, 0870/770-8868, or 0162/959-2600 🖷 0870/770-6127 ⊕ www.yha.org.uk. **YHA Australia** ✉ 422 Kent St., Sydney, NSW 2001 ☎ 02/9261-1111 🖷 02/9261-1969 ⊕ www.yha.com.au. **YHA New Zealand** ✉ Level 1, Moorhouse City, 166 Moorhouse Ave., Box 436, Christchurch ☎ 03/379-9970 or 0800/278-299 🖷 03/365-4476 ⊕ www.yha.org.nz.

🛈 Swiss Organizations Swiss Youth Hostels ✉ Schaffhauserstr. 14, CH-8042 Zürich ☎ 01/3601414 🖷 01/3601460 ⊕ www.youthhostel.ch.

HOTELS

When selecting a place to stay, an important resource can be the Swiss Hotel Association (SHA), a rigorous and demanding organization that maintains a specific rating system for lodging standards. Four out of five Swiss hotels belong to this group and take their stars seriously. In contrast to more casual European countries, stars in Switzerland have precise meaning: a five-star hotel is required to have a specific staff–guest ratio, a daily change of bed linens, and extended hours for room service. In contrast, a two-star hotel must have telephones in the rooms, soap in the bathrooms, and fabric tablecloths in the restaurant. But the SHA standards cannot control the quality of the decor and the grace of service. Thus you may find a five-

star hotel that meets the technical requirements but has shabby appointments, leaky plumbing, or a rude concierge, or a good, family-run two-star pension that makes you feel like royalty.

Some rules of thumb: if you are looking for American-style chain-motel comfort—a big bed, color TV, minibar, safe—you will probably be happiest in four-star business-class hotels. A number of four-star hotels in Switzerland are part of the Best Western chain. If you are looking for regional atmosphere, family ownership (and the pride and care for details that implies), and moderate prices, but don't care about a TV or minibar, look for three stars: nearly all such rooms have showers and toilets. Two stars will get you tidy, minimal comfort with about a third of the rooms having private toilet and bathing facilities. One-star properties are rare: they have only shared facilities and no phone available in-house and generally fall below the demanding Swiss national standard. Several hotels in the SHA are specially rated *Landgasthof* or *relais de campagne,* meaning "country inn." These generally are rustic-style lodgings typical of the region, but they may range from spare to luxurious and are rarely set apart in deep country; some are in the midst of small market towns or resorts. The SHA distinguishes them as offering especially high-quality service, personal attention, and parking.

Many hotels close for a short period during their region's off-season. Closing dates often vary from year to year, so be sure to call ahead and check.

🛈 Organizations Swiss Hotel Association ✉ Monbijoustr. 130, CH-3001 Bern ☎ 031/3704111 ⊕ www.swisshotels.ch.

INNS

Travelers on a budget can find help from the *Check-in E & G Hotels* guide (E & G stands for *einfach und gemütlich:* roughly, "simple and cozy"), available through Switzerland Tourism. These comfortable little hotels have banded together to dispel Switzerland's intimidating image as an elite, overpriced vacation spot and offer simple two-star standards in usually very atmospheric inns.

Other organizations can help you find unusual properties: the Relais & Châteaux group seeks out manor houses, historic buildings, and generally atmospheric luxury, with most of its properties falling into the $$$ or $$$$ range. A similar group, Romantik Hotels and Restaurants, combines architectural interest, historic atmosphere, and fine regional food. Relais du Silence hotels are usually isolated in a peaceful, natural setting, with first-class comforts.

⁊ Organization Contacts Relais & Châteaux ✉ 15 rue Galvani, 75017 Paris, France ☎ 33/ 1/45-72-90-00 ⊕ www.relaischateaux.ch. **Relais du Silence** ✉ 17 rue d'Ouessant, 75015 Paris, France ☎ 33/1/44-49-90-00 ⊕ www.silencehotel. com. **Romantik Hotels and Restaurants** ☎ 49/69/ 661-2340 ⊕ www.romantikhotels.com.

RESERVING A ROOM

A few useful phrases in French, German, and Italian: a room with a bath (*une chambre avec salle de bain, ein Zimmer mit Bad, una camera con bagno*; a room with a view (*une chambre avec vue, ein Zimmer mit Aussicht, una camera con vista*); a quiet room (*une chambre calme, ein ruhiges Zimmer, una camera tranquilla.*)

⁊ Toll-Free Numbers Best Western ☎ 800/528-1234 ⊕ www.bestwestern.com. **Choice** ☎ 800/424-6423 ⊕ www.choicehotels.com. **Comfort Inn** ☎ 800/424-6423 ⊕ www.choicehotels.com. **Hilton** ☎ 800/445-8667 ⊕ www.hilton.com. **Holiday Inn** ☎ 800/465-4329 ⊕ www.ichotelsgroup.com. **Inter-Continental** ☎ 800/327-0200 ⊕ www. ichotelsgroup.com. **Marriott** ☎ 800/228-9290 ⊕ www.marriott.com. **Le Meridien** ☎ 800/543-4300 ⊕ www.lemeridien.com. **Radisson** ☎ 800/ 333-3333 ⊕ www.radisson.com. **Ramada** ☎ 800/ 228-2828, 800/854-7854 international reservations ⊕ www.ramada.com or www.ramadahotels.com. **Renaissance Hotels & Resorts** ☎ 800/468-3571 ⊕ www.renaissancehotels.com/. **Sheraton** ☎ 800/ 325-3535 ⊕ www.starwood.com/sheraton.

MAIL & SHIPPING

Airmail letters and postcards generally take two business days to reach the United Kingdom from Switzerland, at least four days to reach the United States, and a few days more to reach Australia and New Zealand.

OVERNIGHT SERVICES

FedEx and UPS operate out of Basel, Bern, Geneva, Lugano, and Zürich, although overnight service is only guaranteed to selected European destinations. An envelope weighing up to 1.1 lb will cost about 70 SF to the United States and Canada, 87 SF to the United Kingdom, 90 SF to Australia and New Zealand.

⁊ Major Services FedEx ☎ 0800/123800 ⊕ www.fedex.com/ch. **UPS** ☎ 0800/558833 ⊕ www.ups.com.

POSTAL RATES

Mail rates are divided into first-class "A" (airmail) and second-class "B" (surface). Letters and postcards to North America weighing up to 20 grams (about .7 oz) cost 1.80 SF and 1.40 SF; to the United Kingdom, 1.30 SF and 1.20 SF.

RECEIVING MAIL

If you're uncertain where you'll be staying, you can have your mail, marked *poste restante* or *postlagernd*, sent to any post office in Switzerland. It needs the sender's name and address on the back, and you'll need proof of identity to collect it. You can also have your mail sent to American Express for a small fee; if you are a cardholder or have American Express traveler's checks, the service is free. Postal codes precede the names of cities and towns in Swiss addresses.

MONEY MATTERS

Despite increased competition across Europe, the recent decrease in the Swiss franc's value against other currencies, and the negligible inflation rate over the past several years, Switzerland remains one of the most expensive countries on the Continent for travelers, and you may find yourself shocked by the price of a light lunch or a generic hotel room. If you are traveling on a tight budget, avoid staying in well-known resorts and the most sophisticated cities; Geneva, Zürich, Zermatt, Gstaad, and St. Moritz are especially expensive. If you are traveling by car, you have the luxury of seeking out small family hotels in villages, where costs are relatively low. Unless you work hard at finding budget accommodations, you will average more than 150 SF a night for two—more if you stay in business-class hotels.

A cup of coffee or a beer costs about 3 SF in a simple restaurant; ordinary open wines, sold by the deciliter ("deci"), start at about 3 SF. All three beverages cost sometimes double that in resorts, city hotels, and fine restaurants. A plain, one-plate daily lunch special averages 14–18 SF. A city bus ride costs between 1.50 SF and 2.20 SF, a short cab ride 15 SF. Prices throughout this guide are given for adults. Substantially reduced fees are almost always available for children, students, and senior citizens.

ATMS

You can withdraw money from ATMs in Switzerland as long as your card is properly programmed with your personal identification number (PIN). For use in Switzerland, your PIN number must be four digits long. If your PIN is longer than four digits, you may want to change it before leaving home. Banks offer good wholesale exchange rates.

CREDIT CARDS

Throughout this guide, the following abbreviations are used: **AE**, American Express; **D**, Discover; **DC**, Diners Club; **MC**, MasterCard; and **V**, Visa.

🔢 **Reporting Lost Cards** American Express ☎ 0800/550100. **Diners Club** ☎ 01/8354545. **MasterCard** ☎ 0800/897092 toll-free. **Visa** ☎ 0800/892733.

CURRENCY

The unit of currency in Switzerland is the Swiss franc (SF), available in notes of 10, 20, 50, 100, 200, and 1,000. Francs are divided into centimes (in Suisse Romande) or rappen (in German Switzerland). There are coins for 5, 10, 20, and 50 centimes or rappen. Larger coins are the 1-, 2-, and 5-franc pieces.

CURRENCY EXCHANGE

At press time the Swiss franc stood at 1.16 to the U.S. dollar, 0.94 to the Canadian dollar, and 2.22 to the pound sterling.

For the most favorable rates, **change money through banks.** Although ATM

transaction fees may be higher abroad than at home, ATM rates are excellent because they're based on wholesale rates offered only by major banks. You won't do as well at exchange booths in airports or rail and bus stations, in hotels, in restaurants, or in stores. To avoid lines at airport exchange booths, get a bit of local currency before you leave home.

In terms of convenience, train stations have the edge; more than 300 stations have currency exchange offices that are open daily, including lunch hours, when many banks are closed. These booths swap currency, buy and sell traveler's checks in various currencies, and cash Eurocheques.

🔢 **Exchange Services** International Currency Express ✉ 427 N. Camden Dr., Suite F, Beverly Hills, CA 90210 ☎ 888/278-6628 orders 🖷 310/278-6410 ⊕ www.foreignmoney.com. **Travel Ex Currency Services** ☎ 800/287-7362 orders and retail locations ⊕ www.travelex.com.

TRAVELER'S CHECKS

Do you need traveler's checks? It depends on where you're headed. If you're going to rural areas and small towns, go with cash; traveler's checks are best used in cities. Lost or stolen checks can usually be replaced within 24 hours. To ensure a speedy refund, buy your own traveler's checks—don't let someone else pay for them: irregularities like this can cause delays. The person who bought the checks should make the call to request a refund. Note that there is a limit (300 SF) on the cashing of Eurocheques drawn on European banks.

PACKING

In most of Switzerland the dress is casual. City dress is more formal. Men would be wise to pack a jacket and tie if dining in some of the expensive restaurants, even in mountain resorts; otherwise, a tie and sweater are standard at night. Women wear skirts more frequently here than in America, though anything fashionable is fine. Except at the most chic hotels in international resorts, you won't need formal evening dress.

Even in July and August the evening air grows chilly in the mountains, so **bring a**

warm sweater. And **take along a hat or sunscreen,** as the atmosphere is thinner at high altitudes. Glaciers can be blinding in the sun, so **be sure to bring sunglasses, especially for high-altitude hiking or skiing.** Good walking shoes or hiking boots are a must, whether you're tackling medieval cobblestones or mountain trails.

To ensure comfort, **budget travelers should bring their own washcloth and soap,** not always standard in one- and two-star-rated Swiss hotels. If you're planning on shopping and cooking, a tote bag will come in handy: most groceries do not provide sacks, but sturdy, reusable plastic totes can be bought at checkout. Coin-operated laundries are rare, so laundry soap is useful for hand washing.

In your carry-on luggage, pack an extra pair of eyeglasses or contact lenses and enough of any medication you take to last a few days longer than the entire trip. You may also ask your doctor to write a spare prescription using the drug's generic name, as brand names may vary from country to country. In luggage to be checked, **never pack prescription drugs, valuables, or undeveloped film.** And don't forget to carry with you the addresses of offices that handle refunds of lost traveler's checks. Check *Fodor's How to Pack* (available at online retailers and bookstores everywhere) for more tips.

To avoid customs and security delays, carry medications in their original packaging. Don't pack any sharp objects in your carry-on luggage, including knives of any size or material, scissors, nail clippers, tweezers, or corkscrews, or anything else that might arouse suspicion.

To avoid having your checked luggage chosen for hand inspection, don't cram bags full. The U.S. Transportation Security Administration suggests packing shoes on top and placing personal items you don't want touched in clear plastic bags.

CHECKING LUGGAGE

You're allowed to carry aboard one bag and one personal article, such as a purse or a laptop computer. Make sure what you carry on fits under your seat or in the overhead bin. Get to the gate early, so you can board as soon as possible, before the overhead bins fill up.

Baggage allowances vary by carrier, destination, and ticket class. On international flights, you're usually allowed to check two bags weighing up to 70 pounds (32 kilograms) each, although a few airlines allow checked bags of up to 88 pounds (40 kilograms) in first class. Some international carriers don't allow more than 66 pounds (30 kilograms) per bag in business class and 44 pounds (20 kilograms) in economy. On domestic flights, the limit is usually 50 to 70 pounds (23 to 32 kilograms) per bag. In general, carry-on bags shouldn't exceed 40 pounds (18 kilograms). Most airlines won't accept bags that weigh more than 100 pounds (45 kilograms) on domestic or international flights. Expect to pay a fee for baggage that exceeds weight limits. Check baggage restrictions with your carrier before you pack.

Airline liability for baggage is limited to $2,500 per person on flights within the United States. On international flights it amounts to $9.07 per pound or $20 per kilogram for checked baggage (roughly $640 per 70-pound bag), with a maximum of $634.90 per piece, and $400 per passenger for unchecked baggage. You can buy additional coverage at check-in for about $10 per $1,000 of coverage, but it often excludes a rather extensive list of items, shown on your airline ticket.

Before departure, itemize your bags' contents and their worth, and label the bags with your name, address, and phone number. (If you use your home address, cover it so potential thieves can't see it readily.) Include a label inside each bag and **pack a copy of your itinerary.** At check-in, make sure each bag is correctly tagged with the destination airport's three-letter code. Because some checked bags will be opened for hand inspection, the U.S. Transportation Security Administration recommends that you leave luggage unlocked or use the plastic locks offered at check-in. TSA screeners place an inspection notice inside searched bags, which are re-sealed with a special lock.

If your bag has been searched and contents are missing or damaged, file a claim with the TSA Consumer Response Center as soon as possible. If your bags arrive damaged or fail to arrive at all, file a written report with the airline before leaving the airport.

F Complaints U.S. Transportation Security Administration Contact Center ☎ 866/289-9673 ⊕ www.tsa.gov.

PASSPORTS & VISAS

When traveling internationally, carry your passport even if you don't need one (it's always the best form of ID) and **make two photocopies of the data page** (one for someone at home and another for you, carried separately from your passport). If you lose your passport, promptly call the nearest embassy or consulate and the local police.

U.S. passport applications for children under age 14 require consent from both parents or legal guardians; both parents must appear together to sign the application. If only one parent appears, he or she must submit a written statement from the other parent authorizing passport issuance for the child. A parent with sole authority must present evidence of it when applying; acceptable documentation includes the child's certified birth certificate listing only the applying parent, a court order specifically permitting this parent's travel with the child, or a death certificate for the nonapplying parent. Application forms and instructions are available on the Web site of the U.S. State Department's Bureau of Consular Affairs (⊕ travel.state.gov).

ENTERING SWITZERLAND

Australian, British, Canadian, New Zealand, and U.S. citizens need only a valid passport to enter Switzerland for stays of up to 90 days.

PASSPORT OFFICES

The best time to apply for a passport or to renew is in fall and winter. Before any trip, check your passport's expiration date, and, if necessary, renew it as soon as possible.

F Australian Citizens Passports Australia Australian Department of Foreign Affairs and Trade ☎ 131-232 ⊕ www.passports.gov.au.

F Canadian Citizens Passport Office ⊠ to mail in applications: 200 Promenade du Portage, Hull, Québec J8X 4B7 ☎ 819/994-3500 or 800/567-6868 ⊕ www.ppt.gc.ca.

F New Zealand Citizens New Zealand Passports Office ☎ 0800/22-5050 or 04/474-8100 ⊕ www.passports.govt.nz.

F U.K. Citizens U.K. Passport Service ☎ 0870/521-0410 ⊕ www.passport.gov.uk.

F U.S. Citizens National Passport Information Center ☎ 877/487-2778, 888/874-7793 TDD/TTY ⊕ travel.state.gov.

RESTROOMS

Restroom standards are high even for public toilets, such as those in train stations, where you sometimes have to pay a small fee. It is appropriate to buy a drink in a bar when you want to use the facilities. Basel has made waves with its public toilets with one-way glass—no one see you when you're inside, but you have a view of the entire street.

SAFETY

Don't wear a money belt or a waist pack, both of which peg you as a tourist. Distribute your cash and any valuables (including your credit cards and passport) between a deep front pocket, an inside jacket or vest pocket, and a hidden money pouch. Do not reach for the money pouch once you're in public.

Use common sense, especially after dark, and particularly in large cities. Walk on well-lit, busy streets. **Look alert and aware;** a purposeful pace helps deter trouble wherever you go. Store valuables in a hotel safe or, better yet, leave them at home. Keep a sharp eye (and hand) on handbags and backpacks; do not hang them from a chair in restaurants. Carry wallets in inside or front pockets rather than hip pockets. Use ATMs in daylight, at an indoor location when possible.

WOMEN IN SWITZERLAND

If you carry a purse, choose one with a zipper and a thick strap that you can drape across your body; adjust the length so that the purse sits in front of you at or above hip level. (Don't wear a money belt or a waist pack.) Store only enough money in the purse to cover casual spending.

Distribute the rest of your cash and any valuables between deep front pockets, inside jacket or vest pockets, and a concealed money pouch.

SENIOR-CITIZEN TRAVEL

Women over 62 and men over 65 qualify for special seasonal (and in some cases year-round) discounts at a variety of Swiss hotels. With married couples, at least one spouse must fulfill these conditions. Prices include overnight lodging in a single or double room, breakfast, service charges, and taxes. Arrangements can also be made for extended stays. Senior citizens are entitled to discounts on trains, buses, and boats, at all movie theaters in Switzerland, and, where posted, at museums and attractions.

To qualify for age-related discounts, mention your senior-citizen status up front when booking hotel reservations (not when checking out) and before you're seated in restaurants (not when paying the bill). Be sure to have identification on hand. When renting a car, ask about promotional car-rental discounts, which can be cheaper than senior-citizen rates.

A special guide to hotels that offer senior discounts, *Season for Seniors,* is available from the Swiss Hotel Association (⇨ Hotels *in* Lodging) or from Switzerland Tourism.

🚩 **Educational Programs Elderhostel** ✉ 11 Ave. de Lafayette, Boston, MA 02111-1746 ☎ 877/426-8056, 978/323-4141 international callers, 877/426-2167 TTY 🖨 877/426-2166 ⊕ www.elderhostel.org. **Interhostel** ✉ University of New Hampshire, 6 Garrison Ave., Durham, NH 03824 ☎ 603/862-1147 or 800/733-9753 🖨 603/862-1113 ⊕ www.learn.unh.edu.

SHOPPING

From outdoor farmers' markets and flea markets to haute couture boutiques, Switzerland offers myriad shopping opportunities.

KEY DESTINATIONS

Zürich's Bahnhofstrasse is teeming with impeccable shopwindows that will tempt you to purchase watches, chocolate, antiques, and designer clothing. Shop under the eaves, rain or shine, in Bern's historical center, where luxury boutiques squat next

to bakeries and butcher shops. In Geneva, chic shops line the Rue du Rhône, the Rue de la Confédération, and the nearby side streets. Italian flair defines shopping in Lugano, whose piazzas attract fans of the world's major brands.

The factory outlet FoxTown—in Mendrisio, Villeneuve, and Zürich—counts Versace, Polo Ralph Lauren, Gucci, Max Mara, Yves Saint Laurent, and other big names among its draws.

SMART SOUVENIRS

Cheese is an obvious souvenir, but as it can no longer be imported into the United States, Americans might consider buying a *caquelon,* the pot in which fondue is made. Caquelons are available in department stores as well as larger supermarkets for anywhere from 15 to 200 SF; note that the cast-iron ones are very heavy. Swiss army knives, a bottle of kirsch, or a designer watch also make good souvenirs, as does a traditional decorative cut-out made of leather, parchment, or paper and usually reflecting a silhouetted landscape with cows.

SPORTS & OUTDOORS

GOLF

There are 80 golf courses throughout Switzerland. Usually you can rent clubs and play on a daily greens fee basis, especially on weekdays, although some clubs restrict visitors to the driving range. For more information contact the Swiss Golf Network, which has a directory of all courses. It can also provide specific information, such as course fees and conditions, but bookings must be made through the individual club.

🚩 **Swiss Golf Network** ✉ pl. Croix-Blanche 19, CH-1066 Epalinges ☎ 021/7843531 ⊕ www.asg.ch.

HIKING

The Swiss Alps are riddled with hiking trails; yellow trail indicators are standard all over the country. Hiking is an especially popular pastime in the German-speaking areas, such as the Berner Oberland. For suggested hiking itineraries including lists of huts for overnight stays, contact regional tourist offices or the the Fédération Suisse de Tourisme Pédestre

(Swiss Hiking Federation); many news-paper stands, kiosks, train stations, and bookstores also carry detailed topographi-cal maps with marked trails.

⏚ Fédération Suisse de Tourisme Pédestre (Swiss Hiking Federation) ✉ Im Hirshalm 49, CH-4125 Riehen ☎ 061/6069340 ⊕ www.swisshiking.ch.

SKIING

Switzerland's legendary phenomenal ski slopes are bolstered by excellent trans-portation networks, plentiful vacation packages, and visitor facilities.

Slope difficulty levels are indicated with color codes. A black slope is the most dif-ficult; red indicates intermediate levels; blue is for beginners. A daily bulletin of ski and weather conditions throughout Switzerland is available by calling ☎ 0900/162333 (0.86 SF per min); re-ports are in the local language.

Serious skiers may want to join the Swiss Alpine Club. Applications should be ad-dressed to Mr. Edmond F. Krieger at the Sektion Zermatt branch. Remember to in-clude a passport-size photo. Excursions in-volve much climbing. It's not necessary to be fluent in German. For a booklet of mountain-club huts, contact the Swiss Alpine Club in Bern. A hut directory called "Hütten der Schweizer Alpen," complete with color photos, can be ordered for 44 SF from the club's office in Verlag.

⏚ Swiss Alpine Club ✉ Sektion Zermatt, Haus Dolomit, CH-3920 Zermatt ☎☎ 027/9672610 ✉ Monbijoustr. 61, Postfach, CH-3000 Bern ☎ 031/3701880 ☎ 031/3701890 ⊕ www.sac-cas.ch or www.sac-verlag.ch.

STUDENTS IN SWITZERLAND

Reduced student fees are often available for individual admission tickets, trans-portation, and so forth. An International Student Identification Card (ISIC), avail-able through the Council on International Educational Exchange, is generally ac-cepted. The Swiss Museum Passport (⇨ Discounts and Deals) has a reduced student fee. Rail Europe offers a special pass for people under 26 and a reduced fee for people between ages 12 and 25.

⏚ IDs & Services STA Travel ✉ 10 Downing St., New York, NY 10014 ☎ 212/627-3111, 800/777-0112

24-hr service center ☎ 212/627-3387 ⊕ www.sta.com. **Travel Cuts** ✉ 187 College St., Toronto, On-tario M5T 1P7, Canada ☎ 800/592-2887 in U.S., 416/979-2406 or 866/246-9762 in Canada ☎ 416/979-8167 ⊕ www.travelcuts.com.

TAXES

What you see is what you pay in Switzer-land: restaurant checks and hotel bills in-clude all taxes.

VALUE-ADDED TAX

If your purchases in a shop amount to 400 SF and the goods are exported within 30 days of the purchase date, you may reclaim the V.A.T. (7.6% in Switzerland). This tax is included in the sales price of most items.

When making a purchase, **ask for a V.A.T. refund form** and find out whether the mer-chant gives refunds—not all stores do, nor are they required to. Have the form stamped like any customs form by customs officials when you leave the country or, if you're visiting several European Union countries, when you leave the EU. Be ready to show customs officials what you've bought (pack purchases together, in your carry-on luggage); budget extra time for this. After you're through passport control, take the form to a refund-service counter for an on-the-spot refund, or mail it to the address on the form (or the enve-lope with it) after you arrive home.

A service processes refunds for most shops. You receive the total refund stated on the form. Global Refund is a Europe-wide ser-vice with 210,000 affiliated stores and more than 700 refund counters—located at major airports and border crossings. Its re-fund form is called a Tax Free Check. The service issues refunds in the form of cash, check, or credit-card adjustment. If you don't have time to wait at the refund counter, you can mail in the form instead.

⏚ V.A.T. Refunds Global Refund ✉ 99 Main St., Suite 307, Nyack, NY 10960 ☎ 800/566-9828 ☎ 845/348-1549 ⊕ www.globalrefund.com.

TELEPHONES

Cellular phones (*natels*) may be rented at either the Geneva or Zürich airports from Rent@phone. You can arrange for a rental on a daily, weekly, or monthly basis. The Rent@phone desks are clearly indicated in each airport.

F Cell-Phone Rental Rent@phone ☎ 022/7178263 in Geneva, 01/8165063 in Zürich ⊕ www.rentaphone.ch.

AREA & COUNTRY CODES

The country code for Switzerland is 41. When dialing a Swiss number from abroad, drop the initial 0 from the local area code. The country code is 1 for the United States and Canada, 61 for Australia, 64 for New Zealand, and 44 for the United Kingdom.

INFORMATION & OPERATORS

Dial 111 for information within Switzerland (1.60 SF for two requests 24 hours a day). All telephone operators speak English, and instructions are printed in English in all telephone booths.

INTERNATIONAL CALLS

You can dial most international numbers direct from Switzerland, adding 00 before the country code. If you want a number that cannot be reached directly, dial 1141 for a connection. Dial 1159 for international numbers and information. (Neighboring countries have their own information numbers: 1151 for Austria; 1152 for Germany; 1153 for France; and 1154 for Italy.) It's cheapest to use the booths in train stations and post offices: calls made from your hotel cost a great deal more. For precise information on the cost of any call, dial 0800/868788. Current rates for calls to the United States, United Kingdom, and Canada are 0.12 SF per minute weekdays and 0.10 SF per minute on weekends and Swiss holidays. Calls to Australia and New Zealand cost 0.25 SF a minute weekdays and 0.20 SF per minute on weekends and Swiss holidays.

LOCAL CALLS

Dial the local area code (including the 0) when calling any local number.

LONG-DISTANCE CALLS

There's direct dialing to everywhere in Switzerland. For local area codes consult the pink pages and for international country and city codes, consult the green-banded pages at the front of the telephone book. Include the area code preceded by 0 when dialing anywhere within Switzerland.

LONG-DISTANCE SERVICES

AT&T, MCI, and Sprint access codes make calling long-distance relatively convenient, but you may find the local access number blocked in many hotel rooms. First ask the hotel operator to connect you. If the hotel operator balks, ask for an international operator, or dial the international operator yourself. One way to improve your odds of getting connected to your long-distance carrier is to travel with more than one company's calling card (a hotel may block Sprint, for example, but not MCI). If all else fails, call from a pay phone.

F Access Codes AT&T Direct ☎ 0800/890011. **MCI WorldPhone** ☎ 800/444-4141. **Sprint International Access** ☎ 800/877-4646 for other areas.

PHONE CARDS

A variety of international phone cards in denominations of 10 to 50 SF are available in newspaper shops. You can use the code on the card until you run out of units.

PUBLIC PHONES

To make a local call on a pay phone, pick up the receiver, insert a phone card, and dial the number. A local call costs 0.50 SF plus 0.10 SF for each additional unit. Toll-free numbers begin with 0800. Swisscom phone cards are available in 5 SF, 10 SF, or 20 SF units; they're sold at post offices, train stations, airports, and kiosks. Slip a card into an adapted public phone, and a continual readout will tell you how much money is left on the card. The cost of the call will be counted against the card, with any remaining value still good for the next time you use it. If you drain the card and still need to talk, the readout will warn you: you can either pop in a new card or make up the difference with coins, although very few phones still accept coins. Many phone booths now also accept Visa, MasterCard, and American Express cards, but be sure to have a four-digit PIN code (⇨ Credit Cards *in* Money Matters).

TIME

Switzerland is six hours ahead of New York, nine hours ahead of Los Angeles, one hour ahead of London, and nine hours behind Sydney.

TIPPING

Despite all protests to the contrary and menus marked *service compris,* the Swiss *do* tip at restaurants, giving quantities anywhere from the change from the nearest franc to 10 SF or more for a world-class meal that has been exquisitely served. Unlike American-style tipping, calculated by a percentage, usually between 10% and 20%, a tip is still a tip here: a nod of approval for a job well done. If, in a café, the waitress settles the bill at the table, fishing the change from her leather purse, give her the change on the spot—or calculate the total, including tip, and tell her the full sum before she counts it onto the tabletop. If you need to take more time to calculate, leave it on the table, though this isn't common practice in outdoor cafés. If you're paying for a meal with a credit card, try to tip with cash instead of filling in the tip slot on the slip: not all managers are good about doling out the waiters' tips in cash. Bartenders are also tipped along these lines. Tipping porters and doormen is easier: 2 SF per bag is adequate in good hotels, 1 SF per trip in humbler lodgings (unless you travel heavy). A fixed rate of 5 SF per bag applies to porter fees at the Geneva and Zürich airports. Tip taxi drivers the change or an extra couple of francs, depending on the length of the drive and whether they've helped with your bags. To tip other hotel personnel, you can leave an appropriate amount with the concierge or, for cleaning staff, with a note of thanks in your room.

TOURS & PACKAGES

Because everything is prearranged on a prepackaged tour or independent vacation, you spend less time planning—and often get it all at a good price.

BOOKING WITH AN AGENT

Travel agents are excellent resources. But it's a good idea to collect brochures from several agencies, as some agents' suggestions may be influenced by relationships with tour and package firms that reward them for volume sales. If you have a special interest, find an agent with expertise in that area; the American Society of Travel Agents (ASTA; ⇨ Travel Agencies) has a database of specialists worldwide. You can log on to the group's Web site to find an ASTA travel agent in your neighborhood.

Make sure your travel agent knows the accommodations and other services of the place being recommended. Ask about the hotel's location, room size, beds, and whether it has a pool, room service, or programs for children, if you care about these. Has your agent been there in person or sent others whom you can contact?

Do some homework on your own, too: local tourism boards can provide information about lesser-known and small-niche operators, some of which may sell only direct.

BUYER BEWARE

Each year consumers are stranded or lose their money when tour operators—even large ones with excellent reputations—go out of business. So check out the operator. Ask several travel agents about its reputation, and try to **book with a company that has a consumer-protection program.** (Look for information in the company's brochure.) In the United States, members of the United States Tour Operators Association are required to set aside funds ($1 million) to help eligible customers cover payments and travel arrangements in the event that the company defaults. It's also a good idea to choose a company that participates in the American Society of Travel Agents' Tour Operator Program; ASTA will act as mediator in any disputes between you and your tour operator.

Remember that the more your package or tour includes, the better you can predict the ultimate cost of your vacation. Make sure you know exactly what is covered, and beware of hidden costs. Are taxes, tips, and transfers included? Entertainment and excursions? These can add up.

⑦ **Tour-Operator Recommendations American Society of Travel Agents** (⇨ Travel Agencies). **National Tour Association (NTA)** ⊠ 546 E. Main St.,

Lexington, KY 40508 ☎ 859/226-4444 or 800/682-8886 🖷 859/226-4404 ⊕ www.ntaonline.com. **United States Tour Operators Association (USTOA)** ✉ 275 Madison Ave., Suite 2014, New York, NY 10016 ☎ 212/599-6599 🖷 212/599-6744 ⊕ www.ustoa.com.

TRAIN TRAVEL

The Swiss Federal Railways, or SBB/CFF/FFS, has a very extensive network; trains and stations are clean, and as you'd expect, service is extremely prompt. The cleanliness extends to restrooms—in most countries these are grim affairs, but in Switzerland's large city stations, look for "McClean" restrooms. They have nothing to do with the red-and-yellow hamburger chain; instead, they're immaculate, sleekly designed spaces, with bathrooms, changing stations, showers, and a toiletries kiosk. Entrance is about 2 SF.

Trains described as Inter-City or Express are the fastest, stopping only in principal towns. *Regionalzug/Train Régional* means a local train. If you're planning to use the trains extensively, get the official timetable ("Kursbuch" or "Horaire") for 16 SF; the portable pocket version is called "Reka" and costs 12 SF.

In addition to the federal rail lines there are some private rail lines, such as the Montreux-Oberland-Bernois line and the Rhätische Bahn. These private lines generally accept discount rail passes (⇨ Cutting Costs) for a surcharge.

If your itinerary requires changing trains, **bear in mind that the average connection time is six to eight minutes.** 🚆 Swiss Federal Railways ☎ 0900/300300, 1.19 SF per min ⊕ www.rail.ch.

CLASSES

Consider a first-class ticket only if the extra comfort is worth the price. The principal difference between first and second class is more space, as the first-class cars are less crowded. Seat size is the same, upholstery fancier, and you usually will be delivered to the track position closest to the station.

You can rely on the Swiss rail service to provide clean, timely service in both first and second class. If you are eager to read or get some work done on the train, try the Quiet Area compartments available in first and second class on a number of routes in Switzerland. Travelers are asked not to use cell phones, listen to music, or engage in loud conversation. The upper decks of some first-class cars also offer business compartments or seats; they are designated with the laptop icon and are equipped with power outlets.

CUTTING COSTS

To save money, **look into rail passes.** But be aware that if you don't plan to cover many miles, you may come out ahead by buying individual tickets. If Switzerland is your only destination in Europe, there are numerous passes available for visitors. The **Swiss Pass** is the best value, offering unlimited travel on Swiss Federal Railways, postbuses, lake steamers, and the local bus and tram services of 36 cities. It also gives reductions on many privately owned railways, cable cars, and funiculars. Available from Switzerland Tourism and from travel agents outside Switzerland including Rail Europe and Europe On Rail, the card is valid for four days (240 SF second class; 360 SF first class); eight days (340 SF second class; 510 SF first class); 15 days (410 SF second class; 615 SF first class), 22 days (475 SF second class; 715 SF first class); or one month (525 SF second class; 790 SF first class). There's also a three-day **Flexipass** (230 SF second class; 345 SF first class), which offers the same unlimited-travel options as a regular Swiss Pass for any three days within a 30-day period. There's a 15% discount on the Swiss Pass and the Flexipass for two or more people. The **STS Family Card** is issued to nonresidents of Switzerland and Liechtenstein, upon request. For information on the Family Card, *see* Children in Switzerland.

Within some popular tourist areas, **Regional Holiday Season Tickets** are available. Their discount offers vary; prices vary widely, too, depending on the region and period of validity. Passes are available from Switzerland Tourism and local tourist boards, but to be on the safe side, inquire well in advance.

The **Swiss Card,** which can be purchased in the United States through Rail Europe, Europe On Rail, and at train stations at the Zürich and Geneva airports and in Basel, is valid for 30 days and grants full round-trip travel from your arrival point to any destination in the country, plus a half-price reduction on any further excursions during your stay (170 SF second class; 242 SF first class). For more information about train travel in Switzerland, get the free "Swiss Travel System" or "Discover Switzerland" brochures from Switzerland Tourism.

Switzerland is one of 17 countries in which you can **use Eurailpasses,** which provide unlimited first-class rail travel, in all of the participating countries, for the duration of the pass. If you plan to rack up the miles, get a standard pass. These are available for 15 days ($572), 21 days ($740), one month ($918), two months ($1,298), and three months ($1,606). If your plans call for only limited train travel, **look into a Europass,** which costs less money than a Eurailpass. Unlike with Eurailpasses, however, you get a limited number of travel days, in a limited number of countries, during a specified time period. For example, a two-month pass allows between 5 and 15 days of rail travel; costs range between $360 and $710. Keep in mind that the basic Europass is good only in France, Germany, Italy, Spain, and Switzerland, though you have the option of adding two "associate countries" (Austria, Hungary, the Netherlands, Belgium, Luxembourg, Greece, or Portugal). Or **consider the Eurail Selectpass,** which allows for a certain number of train-travel days over a two-month period in any three adjoining Eurail countries that are connected by train or ship. Costs range from $346 for 5 travel days to $502 for 10 travel days.

In addition to standard Eurailpasses, **ask about special rail-pass plans.** Among these are the Eurail Youthpass (for those under age 26), the Eurail and Europass Saver-passes (which give a discount for two or more people traveling together), the Euraildrive Pass and the Europass Drive (which combine travel by train and rental car). Whichever pass you choose, remember that you must **purchase your pass before you leave** for Europe.

Many travelers assume that rail passes guarantee them seats on the trains they wish to ride. Not so. You need to **book seats ahead even if you are using a rail pass;** seat reservations are required on some European trains, particularly high-speed trains, and are a good idea on trains that may be crowded—particularly in summer on popular routes. You will also need a reservation if you purchase sleeping accommodations.

FROM THE U.K.

With the Channel Tunnel completing a seamless route, you can leave London around noon on the Eurostar and (thanks to connections via Paris–Lyon on the French *train à grande vitesse*) have a late supper in Geneva. Note that the TGV tracks connecting Geneva and Paris are a bit bumpy, which can be unsettling for sensitive passengers.

The *Venice–Simplon–Orient Express* stops in Luzern between London and Venice. Information is also available from the tour company Abercrombie & Kent.

🚄 Train Information **Abercrombie & Kent** ✉ 1520 Kensington Rd., Oak Brook, IL 60521-2141 ☎ 630/954-2944 or 800/323-7308 🖷 630/954-3324 ⊕ www.abercrombiekent.com. **Europe On Rail** ✉ 725 Day Ave., Suite 1, Ridgefield, NJ 07657 ☎ 877/667-2457 🖷 866/329-7245 ⊕ www.europeonrail.com. **Rail Europe** ✉ 500 Mamaroneck Ave., Harrison, NY 10528 ☎ 914/682-5172 or 800/438-7245 🖷 800/432-1329 ✉ 2087 Dundas E, Suite 106, Mississauga, Ontario L4X 1M2 ☎ 800/361-7245 🖷 905/602-4198 ⊕ www.raileurope.com. *Venice–Simplon–Orient Express* ✉ 20 Upper Ground, London SE1 9PD ☎ 020/7928-6000 ⊕ www.orient-express.com.

FARES & SCHEDULES

The Swiss Federal Railways has a user-friendly site that lets you check fares and schedules. You can also call its hotline, which has information in English. Most rail stations let you purchase tickets from machines that accept cash and major credit cards.

🚄 Train Information **Swiss Federal Railways** ☎ 0900/300300, 1.19 SF per min ⊕ www.rail.ch.

RESERVATIONS

Make seat reservations for trips during rush hours and in high season, especially on international trains. Reservations are compulsory for accompanied bikes on Inter-City trains. A bicycle reservation costs 5 SF up to 15 minutes before departure; if you board without a reservation, you will be asked to pay a 10 SF surcharge.

SCENIC ROUTES

Switzerland makes the most of its Alpine rail engineering, which cuts through the icy granite landscape above 6,560 feet, by offering special trains that run from one tourist destination to another, crossing over spectacular passes with panoramic cars. The *Glacier Express,* for example, connects the two glamorous resorts of Zermatt and St. Moritz, crawling over the Oberalp Pass and serving lunch in a burnished-wood period dining car; the *Wilhelm Tell Express* combines a rail crossing of the Saint Gotthard Pass with a cruise down the length of Lake Luzern. The *Golden Pass/Panoramic Express* climbs from the balmy waterfront of Montreux into the Alpine terrain through Gstaad to Interlaken and rolls on to Luzern via the Brünig Pass. (Note that this is not a direct trip; it involves several train changes.) The *Bernina Express* ascends from Chur to St. Moritz, then climbs over the magnificent Bernina Pass into Italy, where visitors can connect by postbus to Lugano. These sightseeing itineraries take 4–11 hours' travel time. For information on these and other scenic routes, contact Swiss Federal Railways or Railtour Suisse, Switzerland's largest train-tour company.

🚆 Scenic Route Information Railtour Suisse ✉ Chutzenstr. 24, CH-3000 Bern 🕾 031/3780101 🖷 031/3780108 ⊕ www.railtour.ch. **Swiss Federal Railways** 🕾 0900/300300, 1.19 SF per min ⊕ www.rail.ch.

TRANSPORTATION AROUND SWITZERLAND

Switzerland offers perhaps the best transit network in Europe: impeccable expressways studded with emergency phones; trams and buses snaking through city streets; steamers crisscrossing blue lakes; and, of course, the famous trains, whose wheels roll to a stop under the station clock just as the second hand sweeps to 12.

Once at the station, a web of transportation options gets you even closer to those spectacular views: cogwheel trains grind up 45-degree slopes, lifts and gondolas sail silently to vantage points, tiny Alpine Metros bore through granite up to green tundra above 8,000 feet.

Traveling by car is the surest way to penetrate the Swiss landscape, but if you invest in a rail pass (⇨ Train Travel), you will not feel cut off. Most Swiss trains intersect with private excursion networks and allow for comfortable sightseeing itineraries without huge layovers. And there's always a sturdy yellow postbus, following its appointed rounds at minimal cost; connections to obscure villages and trails are free to holders of the Swiss Pass.

TRAVEL AGENCIES

A good travel agent puts your needs first. Look for an agency that has been in business at least five years, emphasizes customer service, and has someone on staff who specializes in your destination. In addition, **make sure the agency belongs to a professional trade organization.** The American Society of Travel Agents (ASTA)—the largest and most influential in the field with more than 20,000 members in some 140 countries—maintains and enforces a strict code of ethics and will step in to help mediate any agent-client disputes involving ASTA members if necessary. ASTA (whose motto is "Without a travel agent, you're on your own") also maintains a Web site that includes a directory of agents. (If a travel agency is also acting as your tour operator, *see* Buyer Beware *in* Tours & Packages.)

🚆 Local Agent Referrals American Society of Travel Agents (ASTA) ✉ 1101 King St., Suite 200, Alexandria, VA 22314 🕾 703/739-2782 or 800/965-2782 24-hr hotline 🖷 703/684-8319 ⊕ www.astanet.com. **Association of British Travel Agents** ✉ 68-71 Newman St., London W1T 3AH 🕾 020/7637-2444 🖷 020/7637-0713 ⊕ www.abta.com. **Association of Canadian Travel Agencies** ✉ 130 Albert St., Suite 1705, Ottawa, Ontario K1P 5G4 🕾 613/237-3657 🖷 613/237-7052 ⊕ www.acta.ca. **Australian Federation of Travel Agents** ✉ Level 3,

309 Pitt St., Sydney, NSW 2000 ☎ 02/9264-3299 or 1300/363-416 🖷 02/9264-1085 ⊕ www.afta.com. au. **Travel Agents' Association of New Zealand** ✉ Level 5, Tourism and Travel House, 79 Boulcott St., Box 1888, Wellington 6001 ☎ 04/499-0104 🖷 04/499-0786 ⊕ www.taanz.org.nz.

VISITOR INFORMATION

Learn more about foreign destinations by checking government-issued travel advisories and country information. For a broader picture, consider information from more than one country.

AngloPhone (☎ 0900/576444) is an English-language information service giving details on hotels, restaurants, museums, nightlife, skiing, what to do in an emergency, and more. Lines are open weekdays 9–noon and 2–7. Calls cost 3.13 SF per minute.

🚹 Tourist Information **Australia** ✉ Swiss Travel Centre, Reid House Level 8, 75 King St., Sydney NSW 2000 ☎ 800/251-911 🖷 02/9475-1255 ⊕ www. sydneytravel.com.au/swiss.

U.K. ✉ Switzerland Travel Centre, 1 New Coventry St., London W1V 8EE ☎ 020/7734-1921 🖷 020/7437-4577.

U.S. (nationwide) ✉ 608 5th Ave., New York, NY 10002 ☎ 212/757-5944 🖷 212/262-6116 ⊕ www. myswitzerland.com.

🚹 Government Advisories **U.S. Department of State** ✉ Overseas Citizens Services Office, 2100 Pennsylvania Ave. NW, 4th fl., Washington, DC 20520 ☎ 202/647-5225 interactive hotline or 888/407-4747 ⊕ www.travel.state.gov. **Consular Affairs Bureau of Canada** ☎ 800/267-6788 or 613/944-6788 ⊕ www.voyage.gc.ca. **U.K. Foreign and Commonwealth Office** ✉ Travel Advice Unit, Consular Division, Old Admiralty Building, London SW1A 2PA ☎ 0870/606-0290 or 020/7008-1500 ⊕ www.fco. gov.uk/travel. **Australian Department of Foreign Affairs and Trade** ☎ 300/139-281 travel advice,

02/6261-1299 Consular Travel Advice Faxback Service ⊕ www.dfat.gov.au. **New Zealand Ministry of Foreign Affairs and Trade** ☎ 04/439-8000 ⊕ www.mft.govt.nz.

WEB SITES

Do check out the World Wide Web when planning your trip. You'll find everything from weather forecasts to virtual tours of famous cities. Be sure to visit Fodors.com (⊕ www.fodors.com), a complete travel-planning site. You can research prices and book plane tickets, hotel rooms, rental cars, vacation packages, and more. In addition, you can post your pressing questions in the Travel Talk section. Other planning tools include a currency converter and weather reports, and there are loads of links to travel resources.

For more specific information on Switzerland, visit **Switzerland Tourism** (⊕ www. myswitzerland.com), which allows travelers to customize a vacation in Switzerland and even to book it through an interactive travel planner.

Go Ski (⊕ www.goski.com) lists the country's top resorts and hosts a skiing-focused forum. **Great Outdoor Recreation Pages** (GORP; ⊕ www.gorp.com) has information on trekking and walking in the Alps. **Pro Helvetia** (⊕ www.pro-helvetia.ch), a Swiss arts group, promotes arts events and publishes books and brochures on all aspects of Swiss cultural life. The **Swiss Broadcasting Corporation** (⊕ www. swissinfo.org) highlights top news stories involving Switzerland. **Swissart Network** (⊕ www.swissart.ch) has links to several museums, city art associations, and galleries; some information is in English. **Swissworld** (⊕ www.swissworld.org) posts general information on a host of topics ranging from politics to Christmas carols.

ZÜRICH

GILD THE LILY
at the guildhalls along the Limmatquai ➪ *p.10*

THAT'S SO GROSS!
The Grossmünster takes Gothic to the
extreme ➪ *p.12*

GO FOR BAROQUE
at the extravagant 16th-century Rathaus ➪ *p.13*

YOU SAY YOU WANT A REVOLUTION?
See the café where Lenin fretted and
fumed ➪ *p.22*

DINE AND DASH
with a sausage on a roll—Zürich's
fast food ➪ *p.5*

HAVE ARTISTIC VISIONS
of Miró and Matisse while you dine ➪ *p.20*

Updated by
Katrin Gygax

WHEN THE POUND STERLING sagged in the 1960s, the English coined the somewhat disparaging term "the gnomes of Zürich," which evoked images of sly little Swiss bankers rubbing their hands and manipulating world currencies behind closed doors. Yet the spirit that moves the Züricher doesn't come out of folkloric forests but rather from the pulpit of the Grossmünster, where the fiery Reformation leader Ulrich Zwingli preached sermons about idle hands and the devil's playthings. It's the Protestant work ethic that has made Zürich one of the world's leading financial centers. One Zwingli lesson stressed the transience of wealth, and Zürichers show native caution in enjoying their fabulous gains. Nor have they turned their backs on their humbler heritage: on a first visit you might be surprised to see a graceful jumble of shuttered Gothic buildings instead of cold chrome-and-glass towers.

Zürich is, in fact, a beautiful city, sitting astride the Limmat River where it emerges from the Zürichsee (Zürich Lake). Its charming *Altstadt* (Old Town), making up a substantial part of the city center, is full of beautifully restored historic buildings and narrow, hilly alleys. In the distance, snowy mountains overlook the lake, and the shores are dominated by century-old mansions. Very few high-rise buildings disturb the skyline, and even they are small by U.S. standards. There are not even any dominating castles to haunt the Züricher with memories of imperialism: in keeping with its solid bourgeois character, Zürich has always maintained a human scale.

The earliest known Zürichers lived around 4500 BC in small houses perched on stilts by the lakeside. The remains of 34 Stone Age and Bronze Age settlements are thought to be scattered around the lake. Underwater archaeologists have discovered a wealth of prehistoric artifacts dating back thousands of years, from Stone Age pottery to Bronze Age necklaces; many relics are on display at the Schweizerisches Landesmuseum (Swiss National Museum) near the main train station.

In the 1st century BC the Romans, attracted by Zürich's central location, built a customhouse on a hill overlooking the Limmat River. In time the customhouse became a fortress, the remains of which can be seen on the Lindenhof, a square in the city center. The Romans were also accommodating enough to provide Zürich with its patron saints. Legend has it that the Roman governor beheaded the Christian brother and sister Felix and Regula on a small island in the river. The martyred siblings then picked up their heads, waded through the water, and walked up a hill before collapsing where the Grossmünster now stands.

When the Germanic Alemanni, ancestors of the present-day Zürichers, drove out the Romans in the 5th century, the region gradually diminished in importance until the Carolingians built an imperial palace on the Limmat four centuries later. Louis the German, grandson of Charlemagne, then founded an abbey here, appointing his daughter the first abbess; it was built on the site of what is now the Fraumünster, near the Bahnhofstrasse.

By the 12th century Zürich had already shown a knack for commerce, with its diligent merchants making fortunes in silk, wool, linen, and leather.

If you have 1 day

Start in the small but luxuriously gentrified Altstadt and window-shop along the Bahnhofstrasse. Wind through the medieval streets toward the pretty Limmat River, looking into the Fraumünster to see the Chagall stained-glass windows. Then cross over to the bustling Oberdorf and Niederdorf areas to see the Grossmünster and the Rathaus. If you're in the mood for a museum, choose from three excellent, varied collections: Asian art at the Museum Rietberg, historic and cultural artifacts at the Swiss National Museum, or paintings at the Kunsthaus.

If you have 3 days

In three days you can take fuller advantage of Zürich's cultural offerings. Start with the introductory walk outlined above; also consider ordering opera or concert tickets on your first day. The next afternoon can be spent visiting another museum or two, or one of the contemporary arts centers in Zürich West. In good weather take a boat trip on the Zürichsee. Or, better yet, rent a bicycle, ride downriver, then pick a spot on the wide grassy riverbank to relax and have a picnic.

If you have 5 days

For a taste of backcountry Switzerland, drive north through the scenic countryside up to Schaffhausen, passing the Rhine Falls and a slew of wood-shingle farmhouses. If art is more your interest, visit the Am Römerholz collection in the nearby art town of Winterthur.

By 1336 this merchant class had become too powerful for an up-and-coming band of tradesmen and laborers who, allied with a charismatic aristocrat named Rudolf Brun, overthrew the merchants' town council and established Zürich's famous guilds. Those 13 original guilds never really lost their power until the French Revolution—and have yet to lose their prestige. Every year prominent Zürich businessmen dress up in medieval costumes for the guilds' traditional march through the streets, heading for the magnificent guildhalls.

If the guilds defined Zürich's commerce, it was the Reformation that defined its soul. From his pulpit in the Grossmünster, Zwingli galvanized the region, and he ingrained in Zürichers their devotion to thrift and hard work—so successfully that it ultimately led them into temptation: the temptations of global influence and tremendous wealth. The Zürich stock exchange is the fourth-largest in the world, after those of New York, London, and Tokyo.

However, Zürich is far from a cold-hearted business center. In 1916 the avant-garde Dadaist movement started here, when a group of artists and writers, including Tristan Tzara, Jean Arp, and Hugo Ball, rebelled against traditional artistic expression. Zürich also drew in Irish author James Joyce, who spent years here re-creating his native Dublin in his *Ulysses* and *A Portrait of the Artist as a Young Man*. Now the city's extraordinary museums and galleries and luxurious shops along the Bahnhofstrasse, Zürich's 5th Avenue, attest to its position as Switzerland's cultural—if not political—capital.

The latest addition to the city's profile is Zürich West, an industrial neighborhood that's quickly being reinvented. Amid the cluster of cranes, former factories are being turned into spaces for restaurants, bars, art galleries, and dance clubs. Construction and restoration will most likely be ongoing well into 2008.

EXPLORING ZÜRICH

From the northern tip of the Zürichsee, the Limmat River starts its brief journey to the Aare and, ultimately, to the Rhine—and it neatly bisects Zürich at the starting gate. The city is crisscrossed by lovely, low bridges. On the left bank are the Altstadt, the grander, genteel section of the old medieval center; the Hauptbahnhof, the main train station; and Bahnhofplatz, a major urban crossroads and the beginning of the world-famous luxury shopping street, Bahnhofstrasse. The right bank constitutes the livelier old section, divided into the Oberdorf (Upper Village) toward Bellevueplatz, and the Niederdorf (Lower Village), from Marktgasse to Central and along Niederdorfstrasse, which fairly throbs on weekends. Most streets around the Rathausbrücke and the Grossmünster are pedestrian-only zones.

Scattered throughout the town are 13 medieval guildhalls, or *Zunfthäuser,* that once formed the backbone of Zürich's commercial society. Today most of these house atmospheric restaurants where high ceilings, leaded-glass windows, and coats of arms evoke the mood of merchants at their trade. Often these restaurants are one floor above street level because in the days before flood control the river would rise and inundate the ground floors.

Zürich is officially divided into a dozen numbered *Kreis* (districts), which spiral out clockwise from the center of the city. Kreis 1, covering the historic core, includes the Altstadt, Oberdorf, and Niederdorf. Zürich West is part of Kreis 5. Most areas in the city are commonly known by their Kreis, and a Kreis number is generally the most helpful in giving directions.

Numbers in the text correspond to numbers in the margin and on the Zürich map.

Bahnhofstrasse & the Altstadt

Zürich's Altstadt (Old Town) is home to several of Zürich's most important landmarks—the Lindenhof, St. Peters, the Fraumünster, and the Stadthaus—as well as the shop-lined Bahnhofstrasse.

a good walk

Begin at the **Hauptbahnhof** ❶ ▶, a massive 19th-century edifice. Directly behind the Hauptbahnhof is the **Schweizerisches Landesmuseum** ❷, housed in an enormous 19th-century neo-Gothic mansion; behind that is a shady green park. Walk northward to the tip of the park, cross on the left-hand side of the bridge, turn south a bit along Sihlquai, and head up Ausstellungsstrasse to the **Museum für Gestaltung** ❸, which holds an impressive collection of 20th-century graphic art. Back at the train station, look across Bahnhofplatz, and you'll see traffic careen-

Dining

Since the mid-1990s, Zürich's restaurant trade has boomed. The new establishments, both Swiss and international, tend to favor lighter, leaner meals served in bright spaces that are often open to the street. The traditional cuisine, no longer ubiquitous but still easily found, is called *nach Zürcher Art*, meaning "cooked in the style of Zürich." Think meat, mushrooms, potatoes, butter, cream—an extremely rich cuisine, perfectly suited to the leaded-glass and burnished-oak guildhalls. The signature dish, which you'll encounter throughout both French and German Switzerland, is *geschnetzeltes Kalbfleisch*, or in French *émincé de veau*: bite-size slices of milky veal (and sometimes veal kidneys) sautéed in butter and swimming in a rich brown sauce thick with cream, white wine, shallots, and mushrooms. Its closest cousin is *Geschnetzeltes Kalbsleber* (calves' liver), in similar form. Both are often served in hefty portions; you'll clean your plate only to have a fresh one appear with the second half of your serving. The inevitable accompaniment is *Rösti* (hash brown potatoes), served in portions of equal scale. You may also find *Spätzli*, flour-egg dough fingers, either pressed through a sieve or snipped, gnocchi-style, and served in butter. Another culinary must is Zürich's favorite portable food, sausage and *Bürli* (a roll). The best are to be had at the Hintere Sterne at Bellevueplatz, an outdoor stand run by gruff men who are a tradition in themselves. *Kalbsbratwurst* (veal) is mild, the smaller *Cervelat* (pork) saltier. Join the locals and munch away while waiting for a tram.

Zürichers also have a definite sweet tooth: refined cafés draw crowds for afternoon pastries, and chocolate shops vie for the unofficial honor of making the best chocolate truffles in town.

Guildhalls

In exploring Zürich's core, you will want to enter at least one of the famous medieval union clubhouses scattered along the riverfront neighborhoods; the best way is to dine in one, as all but the Zunfthaus zur Meisen have been converted into restaurants. Having polished off a traditionally meat-heavy meal, ask if you can have a peek into the other dining rooms—they are, for the most part, museum-perfect in their leaded-glass and Gothic-wood detail.

Museums

The wealth of Zürich bankers and industrialists gave rise to private art collections that are now part of the public art scene. Among the best is the Kunsthaus, with one of the world's best collections of Swiss art, and the Museum Rietberg is famous for its East Asian collections. Many local museums host temporary design exhibitions, since Zürich was one of the centers of the graphic design industry early in the 20th century; the Museum für Gestaltung is devoted to all types of design.

Shopping

Many of Zürich's designer boutiques lie hidden along the narrow streets between the Bahnhofstrasse and the Limmat River. Quirky bookstores and antiques shops lurk in the sloping cobblestone alleyways leading off Niedorfstrasse and Oberdorfstrasse. The fabled Bahnhofstrasse—famous because it's reputedly the most expensive street in the world—is dominated by large department stores and extravagantly priced jewelry shops.

ing around a statue of Alfred Escher, the man who brought Zürich into the modern age.

Cross the square to the Bahnhofstrasse, Zürich's principal business and shopping boulevard. A quarter of the way up the street—about five blocks—veer left into the Rennweg and left again on Fortunagasse, an atmospheric medieval street well removed from the contemporary elegance of the Bahnhofstrasse. Climb up to the **Lindenhof** ❹, a quiet, grassless square with a view across the river to the Niederdorf. From here a maze of medieval alleys leads off to your right. Nestled among them is **St. Peters Kirche** ❺, whose tower has the largest clock face in Europe.

From St. Peters Kirche bear right on Schlüsselgasse and duck into a narrow alley, Thermengasse, which leads left; you'll walk directly over excavated ruins of Roman baths. At Weinplatz, turn right on Storchengasse, where some of the most elite boutiques are concentrated, and head toward the delicate spires of the **Fraumünster** ❻. In the same square, you'll see two of Zürich's finest guildhalls, the **Zunfthaus zur Waag** ❼ and **Zunfthaus zur Meisen** ❽.

Wind left up Waaggasse past the Hotel Savoy to the **Paradeplatz** ❾. From here you can take a quick side trip to the art collection at **Haus Konstruktiv** ❿ by going up Talackerstrasse to Sihlstrasse, turning left onto Selnaustrasse. Back at Paradeplatz, continue south on Bahnhofstrasse, which, as it nears the lake, opens onto a vista of boats, wide waters, and (on a clear day) distant peaks. At the Bürkliplatz, look to your right: those manicured parks are the front lawn of the Hotel Baur au Lac, the aristocrat of Swiss hotels. Beyond, you'll see the modern structure of the Kongresshaus and the Tonhalle, where the Zürich Tonhalle Orchestra resides. Across General-Guisan-Quai is one of the local swans' favorite hangouts: the boat dock, which is the base for trips around the Zürichsee.

Here you can take General-Guisan-Quai west to Seestrasse to the **Museum Rietberg** (about a 25-minute walk) or turn left and cross the Quaibrücke (Quay Bridge) for one of the finest views in town, especially at night, when the floodlit spires are mirrored in the inky river, whose surface is disturbed only by drifting, sleeping swans.

TIMING   The area is surprisingly compact; half a day is enough time for a cursory visit. If you're planning on museum hopping, the Schweizerisches Landesmuseum and Museum Rietberg merit at least two hours apiece.

Sights to See

Alfred Escher. Leave it to Zürich to have a statue that honors not a saint, not a poet or artist, but rather the financial wizard who single-handedly dragged Zürich into the modern age back in the mid-19th century. Escher (1819–82) established the city as a major banking center, championed the development of the federal railways and the city's university, and pushed through the construction of the tunnel under the St. Gotthard Pass. ⊠ *In the middle of Bahnhofpl., Kreis 1.*

Bahnhofstrasse. Zürich's principal boulevard offers luxury shopping and hulking department stores, whereas much shifting and hoarding of the world's wealth takes place discreetly behind the banks' upstairs windows. However, the long-standing story of the treasure trove below the Bahnhofstrasse was quashed—the subterranean vaults that once stored great piles of gold and silver now lie empty. In 1998 a local journalist was allowed access to the vaults; at the end of the dark labyrinths the scribe found nothing but empty rooms, the precious metals having been moved to a site near the airport several years earlier. ⊠ *Runs north–southwest of Limmat River, Kreis 1.*

★ ❻ **Fraumünster** (Church of Our Lady). Of the church spires that are Zürich's signature, the Fraumünster's is the most delicate, a graceful sweep to a narrow spire. It was added to the Gothic structure in 1732; the remains of Louis the German's original 9th-century abbey are below. Its Romanesque choir is a perfect spot for meditation beneath the ocher, sapphire, and ruby glow of the 1970 stained-glass windows by the Russian-born Marc Chagall, who loved Zürich. The Graubünden sculptor Alberto Giacometti's cousin, Augusto Giacometti, executed the fine painted window, made in 1930, in the north transept. ⊠ *Stadthausquai, Kreis 1* ☉ *Daily 10–4.*

off the beaten path

MUSEUM RIETBERG – A prodigious gathering of art from India, China, Africa, Japan, and Southeast Asia is displayed in the neoclassical Villa Wesendonck, once home to Richard Wagner (it was for the lady of the house that he wrote his *Wesendonck Songs*). The rich collection ranges from Cambodian Khmer sculptures and jade Chinese tomb art to Japanese Noh masks and Tibetan bronzes. From the city center follow Seestrasse south about 1¼ km (1 mi) until you see signs for the museum; or take Tram 7 to the Rietberg Museum stop. ⊠ *Gablerstr. 15, Kreis 2* ☎ *01/2063131* ⊕ *www.rietberg.ch* ☎ *6 SF* ☉ *Tues. and Thurs.–Sun. 10–5, Wed. 10–8.*

▶ ❶ **Hauptbahnhof** (Main Railway Station). From the bustling main concourse of this immaculate 19th-century edifice you can watch crowds rushing to their famously on-time trains. Beneath lies a shopping mall, open daily from 8 to 8 (an exception to the closed-on-Sunday rule), with everything from grocery stores to clothing boutiques and bookshops. ⊠ *Between Museumstr. and Bahnhofpl., Kreis 1.*

❿ **Haus Konstruktiv** (Museum of Constructive Art). A permanent collection and special exhibits trace the history of constructive art, including minimal art, concept art, and neo geo work (a style based on Japanese animation). Featured artists include Sophie Taeuber-Arp, Paul Klee, and Max Bill. ⊠ *Selnaustr. 25, Kreis 1* ☎ *01/2177080* ⊕ *www. hauskonstruktiv.ch* ☎ *14 SF* ☉ *Wed. and Fri. noon–6, Thurs. noon–8, weekends 11–6.*

❹ **Lindenhof** (Linden Court). On the site of this quiet square, overlooking both sides of the river, a Roman customhouse and fortress and a Carolingian palace once stood. The fountain was erected in 1912, commemorating the day in 1292 when Zürich's women saved the city from the Habsburgs. As the story goes, the town was on the brink of defeat as the Habsburg aggressors moved in. Determined to avoid this humil-

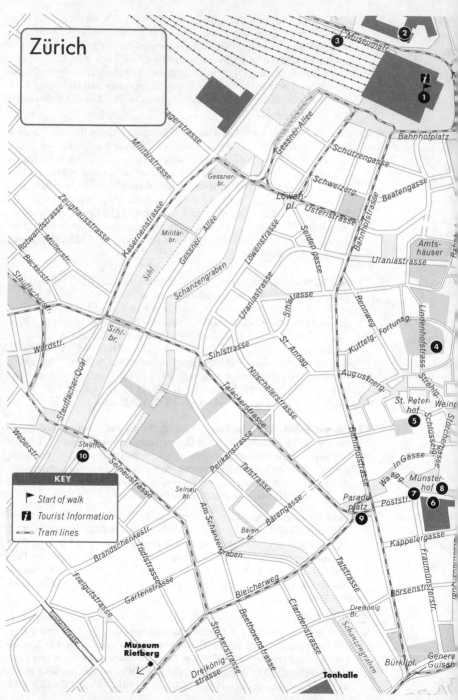

Zürich

KEY

🚩 Start of walk

ℹ️ Tourist Information

⋯⋯ Tram lines

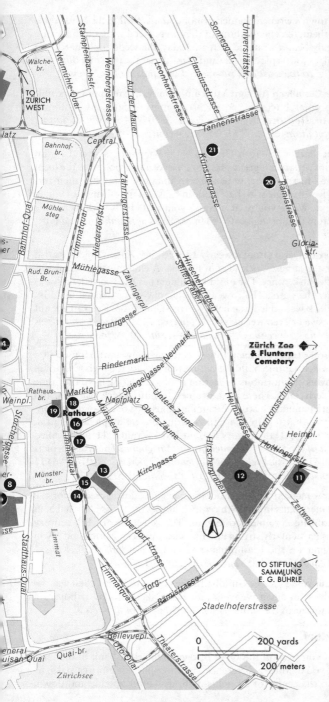

iation, the town's women donned armor and marched to the Lindenhof. On seeing them, the enemy thought they were faced with another army and promptly beat a strategic retreat. Today, the scene could hardly be less martial, as locals play boccie and chess under the trees. ⊠ *Bordered by Fortunag. to the west and intersected by Lindenhofstr., Kreis 1.*

❸ Museum für Gestaltung (Design Museum). Innovative temporary exhibitions focus on architecture, poster art, graphic design, and photography. ⊠ *Ausstellungstr. 60, Kreis 5* ☎ *01/4466767* ⊕ *www. museum-gestaltung.ch* ⊑ *7 SF* ⊙ *Tues.–Thurs. 10–8, Fri.–Sun. 11–6.*

❾ Paradeplatz (Parade Square). The hub of the Bahnhofstrasse and a tram junction, this square is a great place to observe a microcosm of the local upper crust—furrowed-brow bankers striding to work while their fur-trimmed wives struggle with half a dozen bags and the dilemma of where to shop next. While you're at it, spoil your taste buds with incredible chocolate from the Sprüngli café. ⊠ *Intersection of Bahnhofstr. and Poststr., Kreis 1.*

★ **❺ St. Peters Kirche.** Dating from the early 13th century, Zürich's oldest parish church has the largest clock face in Europe. A church has been on this site since the 9th century. The existing building has been considerably expanded over the years. The tower, for example, was extended in 1534, when the clock was added; the nave was rebuilt in 1705. Keep an eye out for inexpensive or even free classical concerts. ⊠ *St. Peterhofstatt, Kreis 1* ☎ *No phone* ⊙ *Weekdays 8–6, Sat. 9–4, Sun. 10 AM for services.*

★ **❷ Schweizerisches Landesmuseum** (Swiss National Museum). Housed in a gargantuan neo-Gothic building dating from 1889, the Swiss National Museum owns an enormous collection of objects dating from the Stone Age to modern times. There are costumes, furniture, early watches, and a great deal of military history, including thousands of toy soldiers reenacting famous battles. In the hall of arms there's a splendid mural, painted by the late-19th-century Bernese artist Ferdinand Hodler, called *The Retreat of the Swiss Confederates at Marignano.* The work depicts a defeat in 1515 by the French. ⊠ *Museumstr. 2, Kreis 5* ☎ *01/2186511* ⊕ *www.musee-suisse.ch* ⊑ *5 SF* ⊙ *Tues.–Sun. 10–5.*

❽ Zunfthaus zur Meisen. This aristocratic baroque edifice, erected for the city's wine merchants in the 18th century, houses the Swiss National Museum's exquisite ceramics collection. The selection of 18th-century porcelain is particularly strong and includes works by Zürich and Nyon makers. Enter on the Fraumünster side. ⊠ *Münsterhof 20, Kreis 1* ☎ *01/2212807* ⊑ *3 SF* ⊙ *Tues.–Sun. 10:30–5.*

❼ Zunfthaus zur Waag (Scales Guildhall). This circa-1637 guildhall was the meeting place for linen weavers and hat makers. Today it houses a lovely restaurant of the same name. ⊠ *Münsterhof 8, Kreis 1.*

Niederdorf & Oberdorf

As soon as you step off the Quai Bridge on the right bank of the Limmat River, you'll notice a difference: the atmosphere is more casual. The area is also the center of Zürich's nightlife—both upscale and down, with the city's opera house and its historic theater, as well as plenty of bars and clubs.

As you explore the area along Münstergasse to Marktgasse, parallel to the river, you'll notice a less Calvinistic bent. Each of the narrow streets and alleys that shoot east off Marktgasse (which quickly becomes Niederdorfstrasse) offers its own brand of entertainment. Niederdorfstrasse eventually empties onto the Central tram intersection, across the river from the main train station; from there it's easy to catch a tram along the Bahnhofstrasse or the Limmatquai.

a good walk

Start at the Quai Bridge and head up Rämistrasse to Heimplatz, where you'll find the **Schauspielhaus Pfauenbühne** ⓫ ▶. Across Heimplatz is the **Kunsthaus** ⓬, indispensable for art lovers. Head back down Rämistrasse to Bellevueplatz—where you can catch a tram to the impressive private **Stiftung Sammlung E. G. Bührle** collection—and follow Limmatquai downstream to the gaunt, imposing **Grossmünster** ⓭, with its distinctive stout twin towers.

Head back down the steps to the banks of the Limmat, where you'll find the 18th-century **Helmhaus** ⓮. Now an art museum, the Helmhaus is attached to the late-15th-century **Wasserkirche** ⓯, one of Switzerland's most delicate late-Gothic structures. Along the Limmatquai a series of former guildhalls houses popular restaurants, the 13th-century **Zunfthaus zum Rüden** ⓰, **Zunfthaus zur Zimmerleuten** ⓱, and the **Zunfthaus zur Saffran** ⓲ among them. Across the Limmatquai, the striking baroque **Rathaus** ⓳ seems to rise up from the river.

Head back across the Limmatquai and up into the Niederdorf streets, which meander past tiny houses, art galleries, antiques shops, and neo-punk boutiques. Follow Marktgasse to **Rindermarkt,** which joins the picturesque Neumarkt and Spiegelgasse streets at a tiny medieval square where you'll see a fine early Gothic tower, the Grimmenturm. There's another Gothic tower farther down Spiegelgasse at Napfplatz, used during the 14th century by Zürich bankers. Several artistic and political figures made their homes on narrow Spiegelgasse—Lenin lived at No. 14, just before the Russian Revolution, and at No. 12 the exiled revolutionary German playwright Georg Büchner (1813–37) wrote *Woyzeck* before dying of typhoid. At the foot of the street a plaque marks the site of the Cabaret Voltaire, where the Dadaist movement took shape, conceived in Zürich by French exile Hans Arp, who in the 1920s proclaimed the new movement one that could "heal mankind from the madness of the age."

From Napfplatz take Obere Zäune up to the broad medieval **Kirchgasse,** packed with antiques shops, galleries, and bookstores. From here you can either return to the Grossmünster or venture north to see the **Graphische Sammlung** ⓴, with its woodcuts, etchings, and engravings; or head to the **Zoologisches Museum** ㉑.

TIMING A quick overview of the Niederdorf and Oberdorf won't take more than a half day, but it's the kind of area where there's always something new to discover, no matter how often you come back. Leave yourself extra time if you'd like to window-shop or invest a couple of hours in one of the galleries or museums, especially the Kunsthaus.

Sights to See

❷⓿ Graphische Sammlung (Graphics Collection). The impressive collection of the Federal Institute of Technology includes a vast library of woodcuts, etchings, and engravings by such European masters as Dürer, Rembrandt, Goya, and Picasso. Pieces from the permanent collection are often arranged in thematic exhibitions. Take Tram 6 or 10 from the Bahnhofplatz or Central stops or Tram 9 from Bellevue to the ETH/ Universitätsspital stop. ✉ *Rämistr. 101, Kreis 1* ☎ *01/6324046* ☕ *Free* ◷ *Mon., Tues., Thurs., and Fri. 10–5, Wed. 10–7.*

⓭ Grossmünster (Great Church). This impressive cathedral is affectionately
Fodor$Choice known to English speakers as the "Gross Monster." Executed on the
★ plump twin towers (circa 1781) are classical caricatures of Gothic forms bordering on the comical. The core of the structure was built in the 12th century on the site of a Carolingian church dedicated to the memory of martyrs Felix and Regula, who allegedly carried their severed heads to the spot. Charlemagne is said to have founded the church after his horse stumbled over their burial site. On the side of the south tower an enormous stone Charlemagne sits enthroned; the original statue, carved in the late 15th century, is protected in the crypt. In keeping with what the 16th-century reformer Zwingli preached from the Grossmünster's pulpit, the interior is spare, even forbidding, with all luxurious ornamentation long since stripped away. The only artistic touches are modern: stained-glass windows by Augusto Giacometti, and ornate bronze doors in the north and south portals, dating from the late 1940s. ✉ *Zwinglipl., Kreis 1* ☎ *01/2525949* ◷ *Mid-Mar.–Oct., daily 9–6; Nov.–mid-Mar., daily 10–5.*

⓮ Helmhaus. The open court of this museum once served as a linen market. Inside, there are changing exhibitions of contemporary, often experimental, art by Zürich-based artists. In spring the museum hosts an exhibition of works from the city's annual competition for young artists. ✉ *Limmatquai 31, Kreis 1* ☎ *01/2516177* ☕ *Free* ◷ *Tues., Wed., and Fri.–Sun. 10–6, Thurs. 10–8.*

Kirchgasse. Antiques, art, and book enthusiasts will delight in the shops on this street. No. 13 was Zwingli's last home before he was killed in battle (1531) while defending the Reformation.

⓬ Kunsthaus (Museum of Art). With a varied and high-quality permanent
Fodor$Choice collection of paintings—medieval, Dutch and Italian baroque, and im-
★ pressionist—the Kunsthaus is possibly Zürich's best art museum. The collection of Swiss art includes some fascinating works; others might be an acquired taste. Besides works by Ferdinand Hodler, with their mix of realism and stylization, there's a superb room full of Johann Heinrich Füssli paintings, which hover between the darkly ethereal and the grotesque. Otherwise, Picasso, Klee, Degas, Matisse, Kandinsky, Chagall, and Munch are all satisfyingly represented. ✉ *Heimpl. 1, Kreis 1* ☎ *01/2538484* ⊕ *www.kunsthaus.ch* ☕ *Varies with exhibition* ◷ *Tues.–Thurs. 10–9, Fri.–Sun. 10–5.*

off the beaten path

STIFTUNG SAMMLUNG E. G. BÜHRLE – One of Switzerland's best private art collections is owned by the E. G. Bührle Foundation. Though it's highly regarded for its impressionist and post-impressionist works, the collection also includes religious sculptures as well as Spanish and Italian paintings from the 16th to 18th centuries. Take Tram 11 from Bellevueplatz, then Bus 77 from Hegibachplatz to the Altenhofstrasse stop. ⊠ *Zollikerstr. 172, Kreis 8* ☎ *01/4220086* ⊕ *www.buehrle.ch* ⊠ *9 SF* ⊙ *Tues., Fri., and Sun. 2–5, Wed. 5–8.*

★ ⑲ **Rathaus** (Town Hall). Zürich's striking baroque government building dates 1694–98. Its interior remains as well preserved as its facade: there's a richly decorated stucco ceiling in the banquet hall and a fine ceramic stove in the council room. ⊠ *Limmatquai 55, Kreis 1* ☎ *043/2596801* ⊠ *Free* ⊙ *By appointment only.*

Rindermarkt. Fans of Gottfried Keller, commonly considered Switzerland's national poet and novelist, will want to visit this street. The 19th-century writer's former home, at No. 9, became famous thanks to his novel *Der Grüne Heinrich* (*Green Henry*). Opposite is the restaurant, Zur Oepfelchammer, where Keller ate regularly. ⊠ *Street between Marktg. and Neumarkt, Kreis 1.*

▶ ⑪ **Schauspielhaus Pfauenbühne** (Peacock Theater). During World War II this was the only German-language theater in Europe that wasn't muzzled by the Nazis, and it attracted some of the Continent's bravest and best artists. It has been presenting plays ever since it was built in 1884; today its productions aren't always so risky, but they are stunningly mounted and performed, in German of course. There are no tours, so to see the interior you must see a show. ⊠ *Rämistr. 34, Kreis 1* ☎ *01/2587777.*

⑮ **Wasserkirche** (Water Church). One of Switzerland's most delicate late-Gothic structures, this church displays stained glass by Augusto Giacometti. Both the church and the Helmhaus once stood on the island on which martyrs Felix and Regula supposedly lost their heads. ⊠ *Limmatquai 31, Kreis 1* ⊙ *Tues. and Wed. 2–5.*

🔆 ㉑ **Zoologisches Museum.** Engaging and high-tech, the Zoological Museum allows you a close look in its accessible displays on Swiss insects, birds, and amphibians. You can examine butterflies and living water creatures through microscopes and listen to birdcalls as you compare avian markings. ⊠ *Karl Schmid-Str. 4, Kreis 1* ☎ *01/6343838* ⊠ *Free* ⊙ *Tues.–Fri. 9–5, weekends 10–4.*

⑯ **Zunfthaus zum Rüden.** Now housing one of Zürich's finest restaurants, this 13th-century structure was the noblemen's guildhall. Peek inside at the barrel-vaulted ceiling and 30-foot beams; or better yet, stop for a meal. ⊠ *Limmatquai 42, Kreis 1.*

⑱ **Zunfthaus zur Saffran.** Portions of this guildhall for haberdashers date from as early as 1389. The restaurant downstairs has outdoor seating underneath medieval arches facing the river. ⊠ *Limmatquai 54, Kreis 1.*

⑰ Zunfthaus zur Zimmerleuten. Dating from 1708, this was the carpenters' guild. Its main restaurant draws business groups to a number of lovely dark-wood halls; its former storage cave houses a cozy restaurant of the same name. ⊠ *Limmatquai 40, Kreis 1.*

off the beaten path

WINTERTHUR – A wealth of fine art was donated to the textile town Winterthur by prosperous local merchants. One such denizen was Oskar Reinhart, whose splendid home on the hill overlooking the town now contains the huge Am Römerholz collection of paintings from five centuries, including works by Rembrandt, Manet, Renoir, and Cézanne. Winterthur is a half hour from Zürich by train, on the main rail route to St. Gallen; fast trains depart daily from the main train station, about every 15 minutes. From the train station, take Bus 10 to Haldengut or Bus 3 to Spital and follow the Römerholz sign up the hill. By car, follow the autobahn signs for Winterthur–St. Gallen. Take the Winterthur-Ohringen exit onto Schaffhauserstrasse into town, then left on Rychenbergstrasse to Haldenstrasse. ⊠ *Haldenstr. 95, Winterthur* ☏ *052/2692740* ⊡ *8 SF* ⊙ *Tues.–Sun. 10–5.*

ZÜRICH ZOO – This is one of Europe's outstanding zoos, with more than 1,500 animals, including Asian elephants, black rhinos, seals, and big cats. One of the more unusual attractions is a huge dome stocked with flora and fauna you might encounter in a jungle in Madagascar. Set in a tree-filled park, the zoo is just east of the city center and easily reached by Trams 5 and 6. ⊠ *Zürichbergstr. 221, Kreis 6* ☏ *01/2542505* ⊡ *14 SF* ⊙ *Mar.–Oct., daily 9–6, Nov.–Feb., daily 9–5.*

JAMES JOYCE'S GRAVE – The inimitable Irish author not only lived and wrote in Zürich, but died here as well. The city's most famous literary resident is buried in the Friedhof Fluntern (Fluntern Cemetery); atop his grave sits a contemplative statue of the writer, complete with cigar. A few steps away is the grave of another renowned author, Nobel Prize winner Elias Canetti. The cemetery is adjacent to the Tram 6 terminus. ⊙ *Mar., Apr., Sept., and Oct., daily 7–7; May–Aug., daily 7 AM–8 PM; Nov.–Feb., daily 8–5.*

Zürich West

Although banking is an important part of Zürich's economy, it's not the only one; starting around 1860, the city was a major center for the machine industry, supplying transportation companies with ball bearings, cables, and the like. With this industry in a decline since the early 1990s there has been a shift toward information technology and the service industry, leaving a great swath of land downstream from the city center with empty warehouses. Today these cavernous spaces are being snatched up by young entrepreneurs. The result, these days anyway, is part construction chaos, part swinging cultural center. Bars, restaurants, and dance clubs sprout up almost daily. The area is loosely bordered by Hardstrasse, Hardturmstrasse, and Pfingstweidstrasse; to get there by public transportation, take Tram 4 or 13 to Escher Wyss Platz. It's a roughly 10-minute trip from the Hauptbahnhof. The character of this area is developing—stay tuned.

Sights to See

Kunsthalle (Center of Contemporary Art). One of two major art venues on the top floors of a former brewery, the Kunsthalle presents new local and international artists in huge, stark, white rooms. A survey of Richard Prince's paintings and Keith Tyson's installations mixing objects, paintings, and photography have drawn large crowds of modern art lovers in the past few years. Works are always cutting edge: you can say you saw it here first. There are four smaller galleries and a well-stocked art bookstore in the same building. ⊠ *Limmatstr. 270, Kreis 5* ☎ *01/2721515* ⊕ *www.kunsthallezurich.ch* ⊠ *8 SF* ⊙ *Tues., Wed., Fri. noon–6, Thurs. noon–8, weekends 11–5.*

Migros Museum für Gegenwartskunst (Migros Museum of Contemporary Art). One floor below the Kunsthalle, this airy, white loft has the same focus—up-and-coming contemporary artists—but is privately funded by Switzerland's largest department store chain, Migros. Shows of recent work are interspersed with exhibitions from the extensive Migros collection, which includes works by Andy Warhol. The museum sponsors regular discussions with the artists, often in English. ⊠ *Limmatstr. 270, Kreis 5* ☎ *01/2772050* ⊕ *www.migrosmuseum.ch* ⊠ *8 SF* ⊙ *Tues., Wed., Fri. noon–6, Thurs. noon–8, weekends 11–5.*

Turbinenplatz. This sprawling space bordered by the Stadttheater Schiffbauhalle is a great place to collapse on a bench and take in the surrounding architecture, a mixture of 19th-century industrial buildings of brick and rusty iron and modern glass structures encased in polished steel. The former shipyards' enormous metal casting bay makes up the main hall of a nearby shopping mall. ⊠ *Josefstr. and Technoparkstr., Kreis 5.*

WHERE TO EAT

Zürich's inflated cost of living is reflected in its restaurants. There's a shortage of truly budget options, but keep in mind that daily prix-fixe menus are considerably cheaper and that even the glossiest places have business-lunch menus—your best bet for sampling Zürich's highest cuisine at cut rates. If you're on a tight budget, watch for posted *Tagesteller* offerings. These daily specials, with meat, potatoes, and possibly a hot vegetable, can still be found in the Niederdorf for under 20 SF.

WHAT IT COSTS In Swiss francs				
$$$$	**$$$**	**$$**	**$**	**¢**
MAIN COURSE over 60	40–60	25–40	15–25	under 15

Prices are per person for a main course at dinner.

$$$-$$$$ ✕ **Casa Ferlin.** The crimson velvet curtains may be over-the-top for some, but the quality of what may be Zürich's best fresh pasta keeps regulars coming back. This family-run establishment, in business for al-

CloseUp
ULRICH ZWINGLI, FREEDOM FIGHTER

VISITORS TO ZÜRICH SOON HEAR about Ulrich Zwingli, the no-nonsense (and, one suspects, humor-free) religious reformer who taught the city to buckle down, work hard, and fear the Lord. But who was this much revered man of the cloth, and why is he depicted holding a huge sword in the statue that stands in front of the Wasserkirche?

In 1484 Zwingli was born in the tiny village of Wildhaus in the canton of St. Gallen. He entered the priesthood, eventually rising to the head position at the Grossmünster in the city of Zürich. He had no problem declaring publicly where he differed with the teachings of the Catholic Church. His first quarrel, around 1512, was over the evils of the Swiss mercenary service propagated by the Pope. A few years later, around 1519, he joined the fight against the church's growing practice of exacting payment for the forgiving of sins.

Taking a closer look at the New Testament, Zwingli came up with his own very simple theology: If it's not in the Bible, it doesn't apply. This focus on both the Old and New Testaments soon spread throughout the Christian world, affecting Protestant congregations all the way to the English colonies in America. While Martin Luther's form of protest was largely peaceful, Zwingli was not above getting into the fray. As people took up arms over their right to worship as they saw fit, Zwingli suited up and went to battle. He died in 1531, along with 500 of his compatriots, clutching that very big sword at the Battle of Kappel am Albis in the canton of Zürich.

most a century, offers excellent traditional Italian dishes such as beef ravioli, veal fillet in lemon-sage sauce and zabaglione marsala. The lunch crowd is mostly financial bigwigs, while evenings attract entire local families. ⊠ *Stampfenbachstr. 38, Kreis 1* ☎ *01/3623509* ♤ *Reservations essential* ▤ *AE, DC, MC, V* ⊘ *Closed weekends and mid-July–mid-Aug.*

$$$–$$$$ ✕ **Haus zum Rüden.** The most culinarily ambitious of Zürich's many Zunfthaus dining places, this fine restaurant is also the most architecturally spectacular, combining a barrel-vaulted ceiling and 30-foot beams. Slick modern improvements—including a glassed-in elevator—manage to blend intelligently with the ancient decor. Innovative entrées might include perch with red lentils in a curry-ginger sauce or honey peppered chicken. The river views are especially impressive at night; ask for a window table. ⊠ *Limmatquai 42, Kreis 1* ☎ *01/2619566* ▤ *AE, DC, MC, V.*

$$$–$$$$
Fodor'sChoice
★
✕ **Petermann's Kunststuben.** Serious and chic, this is one of Switzerland's gastronomic meccas. Though it's south of city center, sitting on the lake's eastern shore, this formal restaurant is more than worth the investment of time, effort, and travel budget. Chef Horst Petermann never rests on his laurels: the ever-changing menu may include scrambled eggs with

truffles and foie gras or lobster in anise sauce. ✉ *Seestr. 160, Küssnacht* ☎ *01/9100715* ⚲ *Reservations essential* ☰ *AE, DC, MC, V* ☉ *Closed Sun. and Mon., 2 wks in Feb., and 3 wks in late summer.*

$$$ ✕ **Veltliner Keller.** Though its rich, carved-wood decor borrows from Graubündner Alpine culture, this dining spot is no tourist trap. The house, built in 1325 and functioning as a restaurant since 1551, has always stored Italian-Swiss Valtellina wines, which were carried over the Alps to Zürich. There is a definite emphasis on the heavy and the meaty, but the kitchen is flexible and reasonably deft with more modern favorites as well: veal steak with Gorgonzola, grilled salmon, and dessert mousses. ✉ *Schlüsselg. 8, Kreis 1* ☎ *01/2254040* ☰ *AE, DC, MC, V* ☉ *Closed weekends.*

$$–$$$ ✕ **Baur au Lac Rive Gauche.** Though it has traded its self-important neo-Gothic decor for a lighter Mediterranean look, business executives still revel in the clublike atmosphere. The cuisine is lighter and trendier now, a mix of Asian and European influences, but the wine list still taps Hotel Baur au Lac's impressive cave. ✉ *Talstr. 1, Kreis 1* ☎ *01/2205060* ⚲ *Reservations essential* ☰ *AE, DC, MC, V.*

$$–$$$ ✕ **Kindli.** In compliance with the kitchen's ban on the use of packaged foods, the meals served at this warm, inviting restaurant are prepared with seasonal ingredients. The results are such innovative dishes as crumbed fried chicken with a bean salad and lamb cutlets with pesto-tossed tomatoes. There is also a five-course meal accompanied by a glass or two of wine preselected for each course. ✉ *Pfalzg. 1, Kreis 1* ☎ *043/ 8887678* ☰ *AE, DC, MC, V.*

$$–$$$ ✕ **La Salle.** This is a favorite haunt of theatergoers heading for the Schauspielhaus Schiffbauhalle—it conveniently shares the same building. The glass, steel, and concrete interior mixes well with the brick elements left from the original factory building. Beneath an enormous Murano glass chandelier, elegantly dressed patrons enjoy delicate dishes such as rabbit fillet with tarragon and fish with artichoke sauce. The hefty wine list can be sampled at the apricot-color bar, where a smaller version of the menu is available. ✉ *Schiffbaustr. 4, Kreis 5* ☎ *01/ 2587071* ☰ *AE, DC, MC, V.*

$$–$$$ ✕ **Zunfthaus zur Schmiden.** The sense of history and the decor alone—a magnificent mix of Gothic wood, leaded glass, and tile stoves—justify a visit to this popular landmark, the guild house of blacksmiths and barbers since 1412. All the Zürich meat classics are available in enormous portions (steaming double helpings of Geschnetzeltes, whole skillets of crisp Rösti), and there's a considerable selection of alternatives, fish among them. The guild's own house-label wine is fine. ✉ *Marktg. 20, Kreis 1* ☎ *01/2505848* ☰ *AE, DC, MC, V.*

$$–$$$ ✕ **Zunfthaus zur Waag.** An airy guildhall, its woodwork whitewashed, its leaded-glass windows looking out to the Fraumünster, this lovely dining spot offers generous portions of the local classics like grilled perch in butter and calves' liver with sage. A second portion waits at a side table in a chafing dish. ✉ *Münsterhof 8, Kreis 1* ☎ *044/2169966* ☰ *AE, DC, MC, V.*

★ **$$–$$$** ✕ **Zunfthaus zur Zimmerleuten/Küferstube.** Although the pricier Zunfthaus upstairs is often overwhelmed with large banquets, at substreet level a cozy, candlelit haven called the *Küferstube* (Coopers' Pub) serves

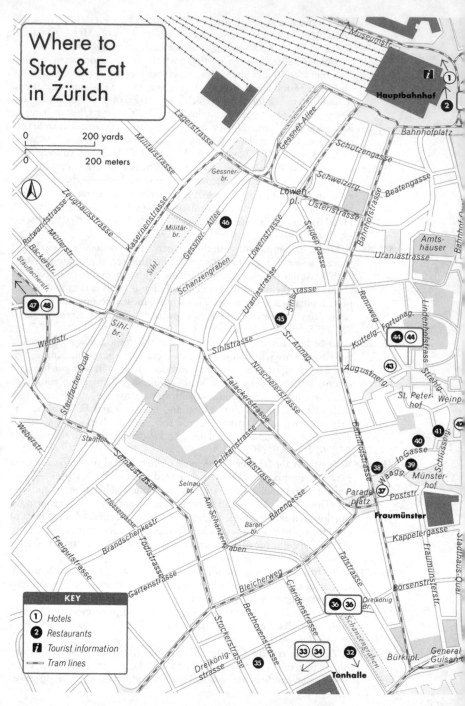

Where to Stay & Eat in Zürich

0 ⟍ 200 yards
0 ⟍ 200 meters

KEY

① Hotels
② Restaurants
𝒊 Tourist information
— Tram lines

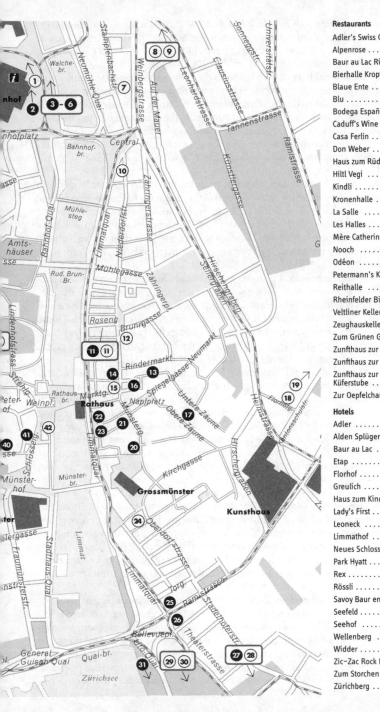

atmospheric meals in a dark-beamed Old Zürich setting. Sumptuous traditional standards include dishes using all parts of the animal, such as tripe in tomato sauce and sweetbreads in Riesling butter. ⊠ *Limmatquai 40, Kreis 1* ☎ *01/2505361* ☱ *AE, DC, MC, V.*

$–$$$ ✕ **Blaue Ente.** Part of a chic shopping gallery in a converted mill south of the city center, this modern bar-restaurant draws well-dressed crowds from the advertising and arts scene. In a setting of whitewashed brick and glass, with jazz filtering through from the adjoining bar, guests sample duck breast with raspberries, headcheese with spinach, and veal cutlets with gnocchi. Take the No. 2 or 4 tram toward Wildbachstrasse. Reservations are advised. ⊠ *Seefeldstr. 223, Kreis 8* ☎ *01/3886840* ☱ *AE, DC, MC, V.*

$–$$$ ✕ **Blu.** For breathtaking views of the lake, this understated dining room is the next best thing to being outside. Filled with linen-covered tables, it looks out onto a small sailboat harbor and the mountains beyond through a trio of 20-foot glass walls. The kitchen whips up delicious Italian favorites, from sea bass in a salt crust to rack of lamb with olives. In summer the tables spill out onto the square outside. ⊠ *Seestr. 457, Kreis 2* ☎ *01/4888585* ☱ *AE, DC, MC, V.*

$–$$$ ✕ **Bodega Española.** The coats of arms of old Spanish provinces and garlands of onions and garlic encircle the dark-paneled interior of this upstairs Niederdorf restaurant. It specializes in big steaks, seafood, omelets, and paella. Be sure to sample the excellent house rioja (a Spanish wine specialty shop adjoins, so the choice is extensive) and crown your meal with a Cuban cigar. Downstairs is a smoky bar that serves amazing tapas. ⊠ *Münsterg. 15, Kreis 1* ☎ *01/2512310* ☱ *AE, DC, MC, V.*

$–$$$ ✕ **Kronenhalle.** From Stravinsky, Brecht, and Joyce to Nureyev, Deneuve,
Fodor'sChoice and Saint-Laurent, this beloved landmark has always drawn a stellar crowd.
★ The atmosphere is genial, the cooking hearty, and the collection of 20th-century art astonishing. Every panel of gleaming wood wainscoting frames works by Picasso, Braque, Miró, or Matisse, collected by patroness-hostess Hulda Zumsteg, who owned the restaurant from 1921 until her death in 1985. Her son, Gustav, carries on the tradition, serving robust cooking in hefty portions: fish in sage butter, veal steak in morel sauce, duck *à l'orange* with red cabbage, and Spätzli. ⊠ *Rämistr. 4, Kreis 1* ☎ *01/ 2516669* ⚹ *Reservations essential* ☱ *AE, DC, MC, V.*

★ **$–$$$** ✕ **Zum Grünen Glas.** This French-inclined restaurant in a quiet corner of the Niederdorf is part of the trend toward lighter food and portions that don't overflow your plate. You might try angler fish with tomatoes and pine nuts or lamb with rosemary, then finish with a lemon sorbet. Wainscoting, parquet floors, and crisp white tablecloths make for a comfortable dining room; an outside courtyard is open in summer. ⊠ *Untere Zäune 15, Kreis 1* ☎ *01/2516504* ☱ *AE, DC, MC, V.*

★ **$–$$$** ✕ **Zur Oepfelchammer.** Dating from 1801, this was once the haunt of Zürich's beloved writer Gottfried Keller. One section is a dark and heavily graffitied bar, with sagging timbers and slanting floors; there are also two welcoming little dining rooms with coffered ceilings and plenty of carved oak and damask. Traditional meat dishes—calves' liver, Geschnetzeltes Kalbfleisch, tripe in white-wine sauce—come in generous portions; salads are fresh and seasonal. The place is always packed, and service can be slow, so stake out a table and plan to spend the evening. ⊠ *Rindermarkt 12, Kreis 1* ☎ *01/2512336* ☰ *MC, V* ☉ *Closed Sun. and Mon.*

★ ¢–$$$ ✗ **Caduff's Wine Loft.** In a 19th-century whitewashed former warehouse, industrial lighting, parquet floors, and the occasional strategically placed cactus set the minimalist tone for the kitchen's delicious, simple cuisine. The market determines the menu, which could be anything from tuna with tomatoes and baby asparagus to meat loaf. If you can't decide on a wine, you're welcome to browse downstairs in the candlelit cellar— there are only about 1,000 bottles to choose from. ⊠ *Kanzleistr. 126, Kreis 4* ☎ *01/2402255* ☰ *AE, DC, MC, V.*

$$ ✗ **Alpenrose.** It doesn't get more Swiss than this: the ingredients, the recipes, the wines, and the decor are all Helvetian. (The cook is German, but never mind.) This former local greasy spoon has been buffed to an elegant shine, keeping the wainscotting and etched glass windows, adding linen tablecloths, a stuffed chamois head, and paintings of the Matterhorn and other well-known landmarks. Enjoy *engadiner pizokel* (flour dumplings) with ham, mushrooms, spinach, and pears. ⊠ *Fabrikstr. 12, Kreis 5* ☎ *01/ 2713919* ☰ *MC, V* ☉ *Closed Mon. and mid-July–mid-Aug.*

★ $–$$ ✗ **Adler's Swiss Chuchi.** Right on the Niederdorf's main square, Hirschenplatz, this squeaky-clean Swiss-kitsch restaurant has an airy, modern decor, with Alpine-rustic chairs, and Big Boy–style plastic menus. It serves good home-cooked national specialties; the fondue is reputedly the best in Zürich. Excellent lunch menus are rock-bottom cheap and served double quick. ⊠ *Roseng. 10, Kreis 1* ☎ *01/2669666* ☰ *AE, DC, MC, V.*

$–$$ ✗ **Bierhalle Kropf.** Under the mounted boar's head and restored century-
Fodor'sChoice old murals depicting gallivanting cherubs, businesspeople, workers, and
★ shoppers share crowded tables to feast on generous hot dishes and a great selection of sausages. The *Leberknödli* (liver dumplings) are tasty, the potato croquettes are filled with farmer's cheese and garnished with a generous fresh salad, and the *Apfelküechli* (fried apple slices) are tender and sweet. The bustle and clatter provide a lively, sociable experience, and you'll more than likely get to know your neighbor. ⊠ *In Gassen 16, Kreis 1* ☎ *01/2211805* ☰ *AE, DC, MC, V* ☉ *Closed Sun.*

$–$$ ✗ **Hiltl Vegi.** Founded in 1898, when vegetarians were regarded as "grass eaters," this restaurant has more than proved its staying power. It was taken over in 1904 by Bavarian Ambrosius Hiltl, who married the cook; the current patron, Rolf Hiltl, is their great-grandson. The lunchtime salad bar has plenty of flavorful options; at night there is an all-you-can-eat Indian buffet as well as a menu. ⊠ *Sihlstr. 28, Kreis 1* ☎ *01/2277000* ☰ *AE, DC, MC, V.*

$–$$ ✗ **Les Halles.** This old warehouse space in Zürich West hasn't been renovated so much as cleaned up and then highlighted with an eclectic mix of antiques and '50s collectibles, all of which are for sale. The fare is health conscious—made from organic ingredients sold in the attached health food store—and includes couscous with vegetables, chicken with peppers, and tomatoes and eggplant. In summer, snag a table on the multitiered veranda out back. ⊠ *Pfingstweidstr. 6, Kreis 5* ☎ *01/2731125* ☰ *AE, DC, MC, V.*

$–$$ ✗ **Mère Catherine.** This popular bistro with a Provençal veneer presents blackboard specials, with the chef turning out onion soup, duck-liver terrine, seafood, and a few meat dishes—even Canadian-raised *steak de cheval* (horse steak). The young, bohemian clientele also enjoys the restaurant's small, hipster-packed Philosophe bar next door. On warm evenings, opt for courtyard seating. ⊠ *Nägelihof 3, Kreis 1* ☎ *01/ 2505940* ⊟ *AE, MC, V.*

★ **$–$$** ✗ **Reithalle.** In a downtown theater complex behind the Bahnhofstrasse, this old military riding stable now does its duty as a noisy and popular restaurant. Its past is plain to see, as candles are perched on the mangers and beams. Young locals share long tables arranged mess-hall-style to sample French and Italian specialties, many vegetarian, as well as an excellent international list of open wines listed on the blackboard. In summer the courtyard is lined with communal tables. ⊠ *Gessnerallee 8, Kreis 1* ☎ *01/2120766* ⊟ *AE, MC, V.*

$–$$ ✗ **Rheinfelder Bierhaus.** Locals know this dark, smoky Niederdorf institution by its unsettling nickname, Bluetig Tuume or the Bloody Thumb. It is famous locally for its *entrecôte café de Paris* (steak with herb butter), sausage standbys, and the pride of the Spanish/Romansch owners: an incongruous but freshly homemade paella, which must be ordered in advance. ⊠ *Marktg. 19, Kreis 1* ☎ *01/2512991* ⊟ *No credit cards.*

★ **$–$$** ✗ **Zeughauskeller.** Built as an arsenal in 1487, this enormous stone-and-beam hall offers hearty meat platters and a variety of beers and wines in comfortable Germanic chaos. The waitstaff is harried and brisk, especially at lunchtime, when crowds are thick. Unlike the shabbier beer halls in Niederdorf, this one is clean and bourgeois, reflecting its Paradeplatz location. They're not unaccustomed to tourists—menus are posted in English, Japanese, and at least 10 other languages—but locals consider this their home away from home. ⊠ *Bahnhofstr. 28, at Paradepl., Kreis 1* ☎ *01/2112690* ⊟ *AE, DC, MC, V.*

$ ✗ **Don Weber.** In summer, the tables of this Zürich West hot spot sometimes spill so far off the sidewalk that the few nearby parking spaces disappear. Ceiling fans, tropically themed paintings, and a large beer selection play up the holiday ambience. Service is fast and charming, and the Tex-Mex fare—beef fajitas, chicken tostadas, veggie burritos, and the like—is very good. Later in the evening the kitchen closes and the place goes into serious party mode. ⊠ *Hardstr. 316, Kreis 5* ☎ *01/ 2720540* ⊟ *AE, DC, MC, V.*

$ ✗ **Nooch.** Zürich's first Japanese noodle bar is spacious and uncluttered, and tables are large enough for sharing without cramping your style or compromising your privacy. Hearty but health-conscious soups made with ramen, soba and udon noodles are the specialty. The kitchen's pledge is to use fresh seasonal ingredients without preservatives, MSG, cream, or butter, and to add as little animal fat as possible. The restaurant also has what may be the city's largest gastronomic smoke-free zone: only 4 tables out of 26 have been set aside for smokers. ⊠ *Heinrichstr. 267, Kreis 5* ☎ *043/3668535* ⊟ *AE, DC, MC, V.*

★ **$** ✗ **Odéon.** This historic café-restaurant was once frequented by the pre-Revolution Lenin, who nursed a coffee while he read the daily papers. These days, an air of countercultural chic mixes with the cigarette smoke. You can nurse a coffee, too, or choose from a menu of burgers,

BLTs, and bratwurst. ✉ *Limmatquai 2, Kreis 1* ☎ *01/2511650* ▤ *AE, DC, MC, V.*

WHERE TO STAY

Spending the night in Zürich is as expensive as eating out, though the options are no more outlandishly priced than those in the prestigious ski resorts. Deluxe hotels—the five-star landmarks—average between 450 SF and 600 SF per night for a double, and you'll be lucky to get a shower and toilet in your room for less than 140 SF. Yet a full (if top-heavy) range of choices is available in the city center, so even if you're flying into Zürich on your way to a mountain retreat, don't shy away from a stopover of a day or two. Luckily, almost all the hotels that cater to businesspeople during the week offer significantly cheaper weekend rates.

WHAT IT COSTS In Swiss francs				
$$$$	**$$$**	**$$**	**$**	**¢**
DOUBLE ROOM over 350	250–350	175–250	100–175	under 100

Prices are for two people in a standard double room in high season, including breakfast, tax, and service charge.

$$$$ 🏨 **Alden Splügenschloss.** Constructed at the turn of the 20th century as luxury apartments, this Relais & Châteaux property consists entirely of suites, all done in beige with chocolate leather accents and filled with such amenities as flat-screen televisions. Each sleek marble bath has its own whirlpool. The location—in a spare banking district—may be a little out of the way for sightseeing, but if you're looking for peace and quiet, this hotel is worth the effort. ✉ *Splügenstr. 2, Kreis 1, CH-8002* ☎ *01/2899999* 🖷 *01/2899998* ⊕ *www.alden.ch* ⬓ *22 suites* ⚭ *2 restaurants, in-room data ports, bar* ▤ *AE, DC, MC, V* ⓄⓁ *BP.*

★ **$$$$** 🏨 **Baur au Lac.** This highbrow patrician of Swiss hotels turns its broad back to the commercial center; its front rooms overlook the lake, the canal, and the manicured lawns of its own private park. The signature classic room decor gleams with rich fabrics and such ultramodern comforts as triple-glazed windows and CD players. Lakeside corner junior suites (priced as deluxe doubles) are a relatively good value. In summer, meals (including breakfast) are served in the glassed-in pavilion along the canal; in winter, in the glowing Restaurant Français. ✉ *Talstr. 1, Kreis 1, CH-8022* ☎ *01/2205020* 🖷 *01/2205044* ⊕ *www.bauraulac. ch* ⬓ *107 rooms, 18 suites* ⚭ *2 restaurants, café, in-room data ports, in-room safes, minibars, gym, hair salon, bar, dance club, meeting rooms* ▤ *AE, DC, MC, V.*

★ **$$$$** 🏨 **Florhof.** This is an anti-urban hotel, a gentle antidote to the bustle of downtown commerce. In a dreamily quiet residential area by the Kunsthaus, this Romantik property pampers guests with its polished wood, blue-willow fabric, and wisteria-sheltered garden. The restaurant serves light, seasonal menus, and meals on the terrace on a summer's night are positively rhapsodical. ✉ *Florhofg. 4, Kreis 1, CH-8001* ☎ *01/2614470* 🖷 *01/2614611* ⊕ *www.romantikhotels.com/zuerich* ⬓ *33 rooms, 2 suites*

   ⟨ *Restaurant, in-room safes, minibars; no a/c in some rooms* ▤ *AE, DC, MC, V* � *BP.*

★ **$$$$** ⊞ **Park Hyatt.** Just a few blocks from the lake, the wide open spaces of the city's first American-style luxury hotel are accented in black marble, rich maple, and lots of gleaming glass. Rooms have parquet floors with soft carpets, burgundy and beige fabrics on the furnishings, and floor-to-ceiling windows. Locals frequent the restaurant, which uses only local seasonal ingredients for dishes such as caramelized halibut with pine nuts and beef tenderloin with white truffle risotto. ⊠ *Beethovenstr. 21, Kreis 1, CH-8002* ☎ *043/8831234* ⊜ *043/8831235* ⊕ *www.hyatt.ch* ⇘ *142 rooms, 12 suites* ⟨ *Restaurant, café, room service, in-room data ports, in-room safes, minibars, in-room DVD players, health club, massage, sauna, bar, lounge, babysitting, dry cleaning, laundry service, Internet, business services, meeting rooms, airport shuttle, no-smoking rooms* ▤ *AE, DC, MC, V.*

 $$$$ ⊞ **Savoy Baur en Ville.** The city's oldest hotel perennially improves itself, regularly sprucing up its rooms and amenities to maintain its conservative sleekness. The rooms, with gray-stone bathrooms, walk-in closets, and period furniture, typify what the hotel calls its "past-modern" decor. There are two fine restaurants—one French, one Italian—as well as a slick café-bar. The hotel is directly on the Paradeplatz, at the hub of the banking, shopping, and sightseeing districts. ⊠ *Am Paradepl., Poststr. 12, Kreis 1, CH-8022* ☎ *01/2152525* ⊜ *01/2152500* ⇘ *112 rooms, 8 suites* ⟨ *2 restaurants, in-room data ports, bar, meeting rooms; no a/c* ▤ *AE, DC, MC, V* ⦿I *BP.*

 $$$$ ⊞ **Widder.** Zürich's most captivating hotel was created when 10 adjacent medieval houses were gutted and combined—now steel fuses with ancient stone and timeworn wood. Behind every door is a fascinating mix of old and new; a guest room could mix restored 17th-century frescoes and stone floors with a leather bedspread and halogen bell jars. Four suites have private roof terraces; in the basement you can mosey into the wine cellar to sample and discuss the vintages. ⊠ *Rennweg 7, Kreis 1, CH-8001* ☎ *01/2242526* ⊜ *01/2242424* ⊕ *www.widderhotel.ch* ⇘ *42 rooms, 7 suites* ⟨ *2 restaurants, in-room data ports, in-room fax, bar, library, meeting rooms* ▤ *AE, DC, MC, V* ⦿I *BP.*

Fodor's Choice ★

 $$$$ ⊞ **Zum Storchen.** The central location of this airy 600-year-old structure—tucked between the Fraumünster and St. Peters Kirche on the gull-studded bank of the Limmat River—is stunning. The modern hotel is impeccable and intimately scaled. It has warmly appointed rooms, some with French windows that open over the water. Deluxe corner rooms, with views toward both river and lake, are worth fighting for. ⊠ *Weinpl. 2, Kreis 1, CH-8001* ☎ *01/2272727* ⊜ *01/2272700* ⊕ *www.storchen.ch* ⇘ *75 rooms* ⟨ *Restaurant, café, in-room data ports, in-room fax, in-room safes, minibars, refrigerators, bar, business services, no-smoking rooms* ▤ *AE, DC, MC, V* ⦿I *BP.*

Fodor's Choice ★

$$$–$$$$ ⊞ **Haus zum Kindli.** This charming little bijou hotel could pass for a 3-D Laura Ashley catalog, with every cushion and bibelot as artfully styled as a magazine ad. The result is welcoming, intimate, and less contrived than many hotels' cookie-cutter decors. Even the restaurant downstairs is filled with English bookcases and floral prints. Guests earn

10% off menu prices, though they must vie with crowds of locals for a seat near the cabaret stage. ⊠ *Pfalzg. 1, Kreis 1, CH-8001* ☎ *01/2115917* 🖨 *01/2116528* 📞 *16 rooms* ⚓ *Restaurant, minibars; no a/c* ▤ *AE, DC, MC, V* ⦿ *BP.*

$$$–$$$$ 🏨 **Seefeld.** In the heart of the lakeside district—close to restaurants, the opera, and movie theaters—this friendly, no-nonsense hotel is a real find. The guest rooms are comfortable, with hardwood floors, sleek furnishings, and sparkling bathrooms. Thanks to double-glazed windows, they are also quite quiet. The king-size beds are a treat not usually found in this country. ⊠ *Seefeldstr. 63, Kreis 8, CH-8008* ☎ *01/3874141* 🖨 *01/3874151* ⊕ *www.hotel-seefeld.ch* 📞 *64 rooms* ⚓ *In-room fax, in-room safes, minibars, gym, bar, dry cleaning, laundry service, Internet, no-smoking rooms; no a/c* ▤ *AE, DC, MC, V* ⦿ *BP.*

$$$–$$$$ 🏨 **Wellenberg.** This Niederdorf hotel makes a definite retro statement with its burled wood, black lacquer, art deco travel posters, and Hollywood photos. Guest rooms are relatively spacious, the central location is superb, and if you're somehow feeling cut off from the outside world, you can bring your laptop and modem—or rent one of theirs— get a password at reception, and plug into the Internet. An air circulation system pumps fresh air throughout the hotel. ⊠ *Niederdorfstr. 10, Kreis 1, CH-8001* ☎ *01/2624300* 🖨 *01/2513130* ⊕ *www.hotel-wellenberg.ch* 📞 *45 rooms* ⚓ *In-room data ports, in-room safes, minibars; no a/c* ▤ *AE, DC, MC, V* ⦿ *BP.*

$$–$$$$ 🏨 **Neues Schloss.** Managed by the Arabella-Sheraton chain, this intimate hotel in the business district, just a few minutes' walk from Paradeplatz, offers a warm welcome, good service, and classic decor. Its Le Jardin restaurant (closed Sunday) is popular with theatergoers for its preperformance menu. ⊠ *Stockerstr. 17, Kreis 1, CH-8022* ☎ *01/2869400* 🖨 *01/2869445* 📞 *58 rooms* ⚓ *Restaurant, in-room data ports, in-room fax, in-room safes, minibars* ▤ *AE, DC, MC, V.*

$$$ 🏨 **Greulich.** The uncluttered rooms at this out-of-the-way designer hotel underscore the quietness of the neighborhood. Bathrooms are sunny and separated from the rooms by milky glass, making both spaces seem larger. The hotel wraps around a birch tree-filled courtyard, which in summer acts as the ground floor restaurant's main dining room. The kitchen offers Spanish-Swiss specialties, taking its mandate from the slow-food movement. ⊠ *Herman-Greunlichstr. 56, Kreis 4 CH-8004* ☎ *043/2434243* 🖨 *043/2434200* ⊕ *www.greulich.ch* 📞 *10 rooms, 8 suites* ⚓ *Restaurant, in-room data ports, Internet; no a/c* ▤ *AE, DC, MC, V.*

★ $$$ 🏨 **Rössli.** Ultrasmall but friendly, this hotel is in the heart of Oberdorf. The chic white-on-white decor mixes stone and wood textures with bold textiles and mosaic tiles. Extras include safes and bathrobes—unusual in this price range. Some singles are tiny, but all have double beds. The suite on the top floor has a roof terrace with a marvelous view of the Limmat and the Altstadt. ⊠ *Rösslig. 7, Kreis 1, CH-8001* ☎ *01/2567050* 🖨 *01/2567051* ⊕ *www.hotelroessli.ch* 📞 *16 rooms, 1 suite* ⚓ *In-room data ports, in-room safes, minibars, bar; no a/c* ▤ *AE, DC, MC, V* ⦿ *BP.*

$$$ 🏨 **Seehof.** Offering the best of both worlds, this lodging is in a quiet neighborhood, yet is conveniently close to the opera, movie theaters, and the lake. It's a favorite of hip business executives and travelers looking for seclusion. The bright rooms' parquet floors and white walls and furnishings give them a fresh, crisp look. The bar downstairs has a good selection of wines; in summer a garden terrace adds to the charm. ⊠ *Seehofstr. 11, Kreis 1, CH-8008* ☎ *01/2545757* 🖷 *01/2545758* ⊕ *www.hotelseehof.ch* ⤴ *19 rooms* ♻ *In-room data ports, in-room fax, in-room safes, minibars, bar; no a/c* ⊟ *AE, DC, MC, V* ⑩ *BP.*

$$–$$$ 🏨 **Lady's First.** Once a rooming house for country girls attending school in the big city, this boutique hotel has two floors that cater exclusively to women—a first in Switzerland. A stylish palette and steel furnishings join the original 1900 parquet floors and high stuccoed ceilings. The extensive wellness center offers saunas, massages, and various treatments, and the use of the facilities is included in the room rate. (Nonguests can also book spa time.) ⊠ *Mainaustr. 24, Kreis 8, CH-8008* ☎ *01/3808010* 🖷 *01/3808020* ⊕ *www.ladysfirst.ch* ⤴ *28 rooms* ♻ *In-room data ports, sauna, spa, steam room; no a/c* ⊟ *AE, DC, MC, V* ⑩ *BP.*

$$–$$$ 🏨 **Zürichberg.** The view from atop the prestigious hill that gives its name to both the neighborhood and the hotel is the flashiest thing about this down-to-earth property. Its rooms, all with parquet floors, are crisply furnished. In the Schneckenhaus (Snail House) annex, rooms radiate outward from a central, oval atrium and are done in deep orangey reds. Tram 6 heads straight to the hotel from the Hauptbahnhof. Locals flock to the excellent restaurant to gaze down at the city from the outdoor terrace. ⊠ *Orellistr. 21, Kreis 7, CH-8044* ☎ *01/2683535* 🖷 *01/2683545* ⊕ *www.zuerichberg.ch* ⤴ *66 rooms* ♻ *2 restaurants, café, in-room data ports, in-room fax, in-room safes, minibars, dry cleaning, laundry service, meeting rooms; no a/c* ⊟ *AE, DC, MC, V* ⑩ *BP.*

$$ 🏨 **Adler.** This once-shabby place, smack in the middle of Niederdorf, has metamorphosed into a smart, state-of-the-art hotel. From the gleaming lobby to the sleek, modular rooms, the ash-and-granite decor makes the most of tight spaces. Hand-painted murals of city landmarks remind you you're in Zürich. The hotel does not add a surcharge to phone calls made from the rooms. The restaurant off the lobby, Adler's Swiss Chuchi, is known locally as a great place for fondue. ⊠ *Roseng. 10, Kreis 1, CH-8001* ☎ *01/2669696* 🖷 *01/2669669* ⊕ *www.hotel-adler. ch* ⤴ *52 rooms* ♻ *Restaurant, in-room data ports, in-room safes, minibars; no a/c* ⊟ *AE, DC, MC, V* ⑩ *BP.*

$–$$ 🏨 **Leoneck.** From the cowhide-covered front desk to the edelweiss-print curtains, this budget hotel wallows in its Swiss roots but balances this indulgence with no-nonsense conveniences such as built-in pine furniture and tile baths (albeit with cow-print shower curtains). There isn't much space to stretch out, though, and the furnishings sometimes show their age. The adjoining restaurant, Crazy Cow, slings out its own Swiss kitsch (Rösti-burgers) in an over-the-top decor of milk cans, miniature Matterhorns, and the ubiquitous black-and-white bovines. ⊠ *Leonhardstr. 1, Kreis 1, CH-8001* ☎ *01/2542222* 🖷 *01/2542200* ⊕ *www.leoneck. ch* ⤴ *78 rooms* ♻ *Restaurant, in-room data ports, in-room fax, no-smoking rooms; no a/c* ⊟ *AE, DC, MC, V* ⑩ *BP.*

$–$$ 🏨 **Rex.** Its parking-garage architecture brightened up with assertive colors and jazz posters, this foursquare property has some businesspeople's necessities (computer connections, desks big enough to spread out your papers), without the depth of service offered by more expensive hotels. Its restaurant, the Blauer Apfel, draws a loyal, young-professional lunch clientele to its cool, blue-halogen-lit tables. It's three stops from the Central heading north on Tram 7 or 15. ✉ *Weinbergstr. 92, Kreis 6, CH-8006* 🕾 *01/3602525* 🖶 *01/3602552* 📠 *37 rooms* 🛎 *Restaurant, in-room data ports, in-room safes, minibars; no a/c* 🖃 *AE, DC, MC, V* 🍴 *BP.*

$ 🏨 **Limmathof.** This spare but welcoming hotel inhabits a handsome, historic building and is ideally placed on the Limmatquai, minutes from the Hauptbahnhof and steps from the Limmatquai and Central tram stops. All rooms have tile bathrooms and plump down comforters. There's an old-fashioned wood-paneled Weinstube (wine bar) and a bright vegetarian restaurant that doubles as the breakfast room. ✉ *Limmatquai 142, Kreis 1, CH-8023* 🕾 *01/2676040* 🖶 *01/2620217* ⊕ *www. limmathof.com* 📠 *62 rooms* 🛎 *Restaurant, in-room data ports, Weinstube; no a/c* 🖃 *AE, DC, MC, V* 🍴 *BP.*

$ 🏨 **Zic-Zac Rock Hotel.** Perfectly set in the lively Niederdorf, this hotel lets you indulge your inner groupie. All rooms are named after rock personalities, from Bryan Adams to Led Zeppelin, and decorated accordingly. Framed albums, portraits, and gold records hang on the pastel yellow walls. Furnishings are no-frills but comfortable; most rooms share showers and toilets. The American restaurant and bar downstairs draw plenty of nonguests and on weekends the hotel fairly throbs with bass. ✉ *Marktg. 17, Kreis 1, CH-8001* 🕾 *01/2612181* 🖶 *01/2612175* ⊕ *www.ziczac. ch* 📠 *49 rooms, 7 with bath, 2 suites* 🛎 *2 restaurants, bar, airport shuttle; no a/c* 🖃 *AE, DC, MC, V.*

¢ 🏨 **Etap.** Working on the principle that cheap should only mean inexpensive, this chain hotel is a dependable pick. Every room around the world is exactly the same: violet-and-gray walls and carpeting, one double bed, a single bunk set above it, and shower and toilet in separate, immaculate fiberglass modules. The rate for two is always the same. The location gives this branch an edge—it's in the hip, industrial Zürich West neighborhood. Take Tram 4 or 13 from the Hauptbahnhof to Escher Wyss Platz; the Etap is within easy walking distance from there. ✉ *Technoparkstr. 2, Kreis 5, CH-8005* 🕾 *01/2762000* 🖶 *01/2762001* ⊕ *www.etaphotel.com* 📠 *160 rooms* 🛎 *No a/c, no room phones* 🖃 *AE, MC, V.*

NIGHTLIFE & THE ARTS

Nightlife

Of all the Swiss cities, Zürich has the liveliest nightlife. The Niederdorf is Zürich's nightlife district, with cut-rate hotels, strip joints, and bars crowding along Marktgasse, which becomes Niederdorfstrasse. On Thursday and weekend nights, the streets flow with a rowdy crowd of club and bar hoppers. In Zürich West, the locales are all a shade hipper. In winter things wind down between midnight and 2 AM, but come summer most places stay open until 4 AM.

CloseUp
SOMETHING'S ALWAYS GOING ON

IF YOU SEE AN ELEPHANT *wandering around the streets of Zürich, don't worry: it just means the circus is in town. In the winter months, a series of circuses—with acrobats, fire-eaters, and lion tamers—travels throughout the country in red-and-white caravans, each stopping along the way in Zürich. In addition to the usual opera, theater and concert seasons, the city holds a variety of events throughout the year.*

One of Zürich's most important festivals is Sächsilüüte, a kind of Groundhog Day in which descendents of medieval guild members circle a burning snowman until its head blows off (how long this takes determines whether spring will come early or late). The annual debate has become almost as interesting as the event itself, as the male-only guilds refuse to let women participate.

When spring finally arrives, so does Jazznojazz, with jazz musicians playing at venues all over town. Summer is time for Christopher Street Day, a huge celebration of gay pride. Even if you don't speak German, you should still attend the Theater Spektakel, a two-week outdoor theater festival, for the excellent food. Sensuous dancing marks the nine days of Tangowoche, while techno music is the sound track for the lovefest called Street Parade.

Fall arrives with the Lange Nacht der Museen, when museums leave their doors open all night. Knabenschiessen, a country fair held on the outskirts of the city, lets youngsters test their aim at shooting competitions. Toward the end of the year is Expovina, a wine exhibition held on boats moored at Bürkliplatz, and then there's that elephant again.

Bars

DOWNTOWN A welcoming bar that tips a wink to Spain's most famous film director, **Almodobar** (✉ Bleicherweg 68, Kreis 1 ☎ 043/8444488) is as eclectic as its clientele. Sitting on the zebra-skin stools in the bar you'll probably spy young designers in leather pants and faux-fur jackets. **Barfüsser** (✉ Spitalg. 14, Kreis 1 ☎ 044/2514064), established in 1956, claims to be one of the oldest gay bars in Europe. It has comfortable lounge chairs and space to mix and mingle. There's also excellent sushi. **Barrique** (✉ Marktg. 17, Kreis 1 ☎ 01/2525941) is a vinotheque featuring a world-renowned wine list. **Café Central Bar** (✉ Central 1, Kreis 1 ☎ 01/2515555), in the Hotel Central, is a popular neo–art deco café by day and a piano bar by night.

Cranberry (✉ Metzgerg. 3, Kreis 1 ☎ 01/2612772) stocks broad selections of rum and port; it also has an upstairs cigar room. The **James Joyce Pub** (✉ Pelikanstr. 8, off Bahnhofstr., Kreis 1 ☎ 01/2211828) is a beautifully paneled Irish pub where the wood is as dark as the Guinness. The **Jules Verne Panorama Bar** (✉ Uraniastr. 9, Kreis 1 ☎ 043/8886666) is a wine bar with a wraparound view of downtown.

The narrow bar at the **Kronenhalle** (✉ Rämistr. 4, Kreis 1 ☏ 01/2511597) draws mobs of well-heeled locals and internationals for its prize-winning cocktails. Serving a young, arty crowd until 4 AM, **Odéon** (✉ Limmatquai 2, Kreis 1 ☏ 01/2511650) is a cultural icon, a place where Mata Hari danced, Lenin and Trotsky plotted the revolution, and James Joyce scrounged drinks. It's mostly gay, but everyone goes because the place is so chic. At **Purpur** (✉ Seefeldstr. 9, Kreis 2 ☏ 01/4192066), a Morrocan-style lounge, you can take your drinks lying down on a heap of throw pillows while DJs mix ambient sound.

ZÜRICH WEST At **Basilica** (✉ Heinrichstr. 237, Kreis 5 ☏ 043/3669383), hipsters lounge in an Italianate decor of red velvet and marble statues. Once you get past the name, you'll find that **Hard One** (✉ Heinrichstr. 269, Kreis 5, ☏ 01/4441000) has great views of Zürich West and good selection of champagnes.

Not just for intellectuals, **I.Q.** (✉ Hardstr. 316, Kreis 5 ☏ 01/4407440) has a good selection of whiskeys. **Spheres** (✉ Hardturmstr. 66, Kreis 5 ☏ 01/4406622) is a bar and bookstore with a great selection of international magazines.

Dancing

The medieval-theme **Adagio** (✉ Gotthardstr. 5, Kreis 1 ☏ 01/2063666) books classic rock, jazz, and tango musicians for well-dressed thirtysomethings. Zürich's exclusive set meets at **Indochine** (✉ Limmatstr. 275, Kreis 5 ☏ 01/4481111), whose gorgeous interior evokes Southeast Asia. The music floats between pop, disco, house, and techno. **Kaufleuten** (✉ Pelikanstr. 18, Kreis 1 ☏ 01/2253333) is a local landmark that draws a well-dressed, upwardly mobile crowd. It's a popular performance space for established artists such as Prince and Nina Hagen who are looking for an intimate venue. The Rolling Stones once showed up unannounced for an impromptu concert.

Mascotte (✉ Theaterstr. 10, Kreis 1 ☏ 01/2524481), blasting everything from funk and soul to house and techno, is popular with all ages. A legendary techno club, **Oxa Dance Hall** (✉ Andreastr. 70, Oerlikon, Kreis 1 ☏ 01/3116033) draws thousands of casual young Swiss who dance all night (and often well into the next day). Take Tram 14 from the Hauptbahnhof to the Oerlikon terminus.

Jazz Clubs

Casa Bar (✉ Münsterg. 30, Kreis 1 ☏ 01/2612002), long the sole bastion of jazz here, now has excellent competition. **Moods** (✉ Schiffbaustr. 6, Kreis 5 ☏ 01/2768000) hosts international and local acts in the hip Zürich West district. The popular **Widder Bar** (✉ Widderg. 6, Kreis 1 ☏ 01/2242411), in the Widder Hotel, attracts local celebrities with its 800-count "library of spirits" and top-name acts.

The Arts

Despite its small population, Zürich is a big city when it comes to the arts; it supports a top-rank orchestra, an opera company, and a theater. Check *Zürich News,* published weekly in English and German, or

"Züri-tipp," a German-language supplement to the Friday edition of the daily newspaper *Tages Anzeiger*. The city's annual **Züricher Festspiele**— a celebration of opera, ballet, concerts, theater, and art exhibitions— runs from late June through mid-July. You'll need to book well ahead for this—details are available from the tourist office or **Info- und Ticketoffice** (✆ Postfach, CH-8023 ☎ 01/2699090). Tickets to opera, concert, and theater events can also be bought from the tourist office. Tickets for almost any event can be purchased in advance by telephone from **Ticketcorner** (☎ 0900/800800). Depending on the event, **Musik Hug** (✉ Limmatquai 28–30, Kreis 1 ☎ 01/2694100) makes reservations. The music store **Jecklin** (✉ Rämistr. 30, Kreis 1 ☎ 01/2537676) promotes and sells tickets for various music events.

Film

Movies in Zürich are serious business, with films presented in the original language. Check newspapers and the ubiquitous posters, and watch for the initials *E/d/f*, which means an English-language version with German (Deutsch) and French subtitles. **Metropole** (✉ Badenerstr. 16, Kreis 4 ☎ 0900/556789) has a great sound system and the largest screen in Zürich.

Music

The Zürich Tonhalle Orchestra, named for its concert hall, the **Tonhalle** (✉ Claridenstr. 7, Kreis 1 ☎ 01/2063434), which was inaugurated by Brahms in 1895, enjoys international acclaim. There are also solo recitals and chamber programs here. The season runs from September through July; tickets sell out quickly, so book through the Tonhalle.

Opera

The permanent company at the **Opernhaus** (✉ Theaterpl., Kreis 1 ☎ 01/2686666) is widely recognized and difficult to drop in on if you haven't booked well ahead, but single seats can sometimes be secured at the last minute. Performances are held from September through July.

Theater

The venerable **Schauspielhaus Pfauenbühne** (✉ Rämistr. 34, Kreis 7 ☎ 01/2587777) has a long history of cutting-edge performances with a strong inventive streak; during World War II this was the only German-language theater in Europe that remained independent. Nowadays its main stage presents finely tuned productions (in German), while experimental works are given in the Keller (cellar). Its sister stage, the **Schauspielhaus Schiffbauhalle** (✉ Schiffbaustr. 4, Kreis 1 ☎ 01/2587777), is home to large-scale productions, also in German.

During late August and early September the **Theaterspektakel** takes place, with circus tents housing avant-garde theater and experimental performances on the lawns by the lake at Mythenquai.

SPORTS & THE OUTDOORS

Bicycling

You don't get much for free in Switzerland, but one exception is Zürich's free bike-rental program. For a refundable deposit of 20 SF and your passport you can borrow a bike. More than 300 bikes are available from six pickup points; scooters, skateboards, children's bicycles, and child seats are also available. The most central pickup points are at Platform 18 of the Hauptbahnhof, the Globus department store on the Bahnhofstrasse and Löwenplatz, and at Theaterplatz/Stadelhofen. Bikes are available from the train station year-round; other locations distribute bikes between early May and the end of October. A great place to bike is the path along the river; it starts at the Hauptbahnhof and runs along the left bank of the Limmat, heading downriver. You can reach Kloster Fahr, the last Catholic monastery in the canton of Zürich, in under an hour. A yellow hiking trail sign will point you in the right direction.

Golf

The 9-hole **Dolder Golf Club** (☎ 01/2615045) is near the Dolder Grand Hotel at Kurhausstrasse 65. **Golf & Country Club Zürich** (☎ 01/9180050), with 18 holes, is near the city center in Zumikon, a suburb of Zürich.

Running

The track closest to the center is at **Allmend Sportplatz** (✛ Take Tram 13 to last stop in the direction of Albisgütli ⊠ Kreis 1). The **Dolder Grand** hotel at Kurhausstrasse 65 has a running path that winds through the forest; it's open to nonguests.

SHOPPING

The store-lined **Bahnhofstrasse** concentrates much of Zürich's most expensive (from elegant to gaudy) goods at the Paradeplatz end. There's another pocket of good stores around **Löwenstrasse,** southwest of the Hauptbahnhof. The **Niederdorf** offers less expensive, younger fashions, as well as antiques and antiquarian bookshops. The west bank's Altstadt, along **Storchengasse** near the Münsterhof, is a focal point for high-end designer stores.

Many city-center stores are open weekdays 9–8, Saturday 8–4. Most close on Sunday, with the exception of the shops at the Hauptbahnhof and the Stadelhofen train station. Many smaller shops, particularly in the Niederdorf area, open later in the morning or the early afternoon and are closed entirely on Monday.

Department Stores

COOP (⊠ Bellevuepl., Kreis 1 ☎ 043/2688700) is cheap and cheerful. **Globus** (⊠ Bahnhofstr. and Löwenpl., Kreis 1 ☎ 01/2266060) sells men's and women's designer clothes and housewares. There is also a pricey but irresistible delicatessen in the basement. **Jelmoli** (⊠ Bahnhofstr. and Seideng., Kreis 1 ☎ 01/2204411) has top-notch brand-name merchandise and swarms of staffers. **Manor** (⊠ Bahnhofstr. 75, Kreis 1 ☎ 01/2295699) is dependable and affordable.

Markets

At **Bürkliplatz** (⊠ Lake end of Bahnhofstr., Kreis 1), there's a flea market from 6 to 3:30 every Saturday from May to October. There's a curio market on the **Rosenhof** (⊠ Niederdorfstr. and Marktg., Kreis 1) every Thursday from 10 to 9 and Saturday from 10 to 4 between April and Christmas.

Specialty Items

Books

The antiquarian bookshops in the upper streets of the Niederdorf area are rich with discoveries—and most have selections of books in English. **Biblion** (⊠ Kirchg. 40, Kreis 1 ☎ 01/2613830) specializes in antique books and binding. The **EOS Buchantiquariat Benz** (⊠ Kirchg. 17 and 22, Kreis 1 ☎ 01/2615750) is a superb general bookshop spread over two storefronts. Both sell secondhand books as well as antiquarian tomes. The eclectic **medieval art & vie** (⊠ Spiegelg. 29, Kreis 1 ☎ 01/2524720), sells books, music, and replicas of medieval artifacts, including reproduction medieval shoes, jewelry, and water bottles.

Chocolate

Sprüngli (⊠ Paradepl., Kreis 1 ☎ 01/2244711 ⊠ Hauptbahnhof, Kreis 1 ☎ 01/2118483 ⊠ Löwenpl., Kreis 1 ☎ 01/2119612), the landmark chocolatier and café for wealthy Bahnhofstrasse habitués, concocts heavenly truffles and *Luxembourgli*, small cream-filled cookies that require immediate eating. Good, plain hot lunches and salads are also served. **Teuscher** (⊠ Storcheng. 9, Kreis 1 ☎ 01/2115153 ⊠ Bahnhofstr. 46, Kreis 1 ☎ 01/2111390 ⊠ Jelmoli, Bahnhofstr. at Seidengasse, Kreis 1 ☎ 01/2204387 ⊠ Cafe Schober, Napfg. 4, Kreis 1 ☎ 01/2518060) specializes in champagne truffles.

Collectibles

In the center of town virtually every street has some kind of antiques or collectibles shop. Especially intriguing are "modern antiques" shops, which carry odds and ends from recent decades. **Eselstein** (⊠ Stadelhoferstr. 42, Kreis 1 ☎ 01/2611056) stocks items from the 1950s through the 1970s ranging from lamp shades to standing ashtrays, plus such finds as Russian samovars. **Hannibal** (⊠ St. Jakobstr. 39, Kreis 4 ☎ 01/2426044) is a delightful lumber room of postwar vases, chairs, pedal-operated trash bins, and rotary-dial telephones (remember them?).

Food

Inhale tempting smells from around the world at **H. Schwarzenbach** (⊠ Münsterg. 19, Kreis 1 ☎ 01/2611315), an old-style, open-bin shop with oak shelves lined with coffee, dried fruits, nuts, and grains. Whet your palate at **Scot & Scotch** (⊠ Wohllebg. 7, Kreis 1 ☎ 01/2119060) with any one of 400 whiskeys from around the globe (nosings and tastings on request).

Men's Clothes

Zürich's most elegant department store, **Grieder** (⊠ Bahnhofstr. 30, Kreis 1 ☎ 01/2243636), carries designs by Armani and Zegna, among others. **Trois Pommes** (⊠ Storcheng. 6, Kreis 1 ☎ 01/2124710) is the central boutique of a series of designer shops scattered through the Storchengasse area; the racks are heavily stacked with such high-profile international designers as Jil Sander, Versace, Donna Karan, and Dolce & Gabbana.

Toys

AHA (✉ Spiegelg. 14, Kreis 1 ☎ 01/2510560) sells hypnotic optical-illusion gifts in styles and sizes to suit all ages. **Pastorini Spielzeug** (✉ Weinpl. 3, Kreis 1 ☎ 01/2287070) is a four-story mother lode of original and creative playthings, many hand-carved.

Women's Clothes

Beatrice Dreher Presents (✉ Gassen 14, Kreis 1 ☎ 01/2115548) carries Chloë and Krizia. You can snag some of last season's fashions at deep discounts at Trois Pommes' bargain-basement **Check Out** (✉ Tödistr. 44, Kreis 1 ☎ 01/2027226), where DKNY, Calvin Klein, and Dolce & Gabbana are jumbled on the racks. **En Soie** (✉ Strehlg. 26, Kreis 1 ☎ 01/2115902) stocks gleaming, sometimes raw-textured silks, but although the fabrics are sophisticated, there's still an element of whimsy. At **Sonja Rieser** (✉ Froschaug. 2, Kreis 1 ☎ 01/2513847) the selection of gorgeous handmade hats runs from elegant to wild. For the absolute latest, go to the main **Trois Pommes** (✉ Storcheng. 6, Kreis 1 ☎ 01/2110621) for Jil Sander, Alaïa, and Comme des Garçons.

ZÜRICH A TO Z

To research prices, get advice from other travelers, and book travel arrangements, visit www.fodors.com.

AIR TRAVEL

CARRIERS Some 60 airlines, including American, United, and, of course, Swiss Air Lines, known as Swiss, serve the Unique Zürich Airport. You can also catch domestic and European flights out of Unique on Swiss.
⛐ Airlines & Contacts Swiss ☎ 0848/852000.

AIRPORTS & TRANSFERS

Unique Zürich Airport is Switzerland's most important airport and the 10th-busiest in the world. It's 11 km (7 mi) north of the city.
⛐ Airport Information Unique Zürich Airport ☎ 0900/300313.

AIRPORT It's easy to take a Swiss Federal Railways feeder train directly from the
TRANSFERS airport to Zürich's Hauptbahnhof (main station). Tickets cost 5.40 SF one way, and trains run every 10–15 minutes, arriving in 10 minutes. Taxis cost dearly in Zürich. A ride into the center costs 50 SF–60 SF and takes around 20 minutes. Most larger hotels have their own shuttles to and from the airport.
⛐ Train Information Hauptbahnhof ☎ 0900/300300.

CAR TRAVEL

The A2 expressway from Basel to Zürich leads directly into the city. A1 continues east to St. Gallen. Approaching from the south and the St. Gotthard route, take A14 from Luzern (Lucerne); after a brief break of highway (E41) it feeds into A3 and approaches the city along the lake's western shore. You can take A3 all the way up from Chur in Graubünden.

EMERGENCIES

Dial ☎ 117 for the police in case of an emergency, or ☎ 144 for an ambulance. Doctors and dentists can be referred in case of emergency by the English-speaking operators who staff the *Notfalldienst* (Emergency Service) phones. In Kreis 1, the pharmacy Bellevue Apotheke is open 24 hours.

☎ **Bellevue Apotheke** ⊠ Theaterstr. 14, Kreis 1 ☎ 01/2525600. **SOS Aerzte** (Emergency House Calls) ☎ 01/3604444. **Zürich Universitätsspital** ⊠ Schmelzbergstr. 8, Kreis 1 ☎ 01/2551111.

ENGLISH-LANGUAGE MEDIA

The Bookshop has a wide selection of new books in English. Payot carries a good stock of English fiction despite the store's French focus.

☎ **Bookstores The Bookshop** ⊠ Bahnhofstr. 70, Kreis 1 ☎ 01/2110444. **Payot** ⊠ Bahnhofstr. 9, Kreis 1 ☎ 01/2115452.

TAXIS

Taxis are very expensive, with an 8 SF minimum but no charge for additional passengers. An available taxi is indicated by an illuminated rooftop light. You can order a cab by calling Züri Taxi or Alpha Taxi.

☎ Taxi Companies **Alpha Taxi** ☎ 01/7777777. **Züri Taxi** ☎ 01/2222222.

TOURS

BICYCLE TOURS From May to September, Wednesday through Sunday at 10:30 AM, you can take a 2½-hour bike tour from the opera house for 25 SF. The tour is given in German and English; bikes are supplied; no reservations are necessary.

BUS TOURS Three introductory bus tours with English commentary are offered by the tourist office. Cityrama's daily tour covers the main city sights and then goes on to Rapperswil to see the rose gardens and castle. The trip lasts three hours, leaving at 11 AM; it costs 45 SF. The Zürich Trolley Experience (32 SF) gives a good general idea of the city in two hours; it leaves at 9:45 AM, noon, and 2 PM, though there's no tour at 9:45 in winter. The Combo Tour goes farther and includes a train trip to the top of the nearby Üetliberg. This is also a daily tour, given at 9:45 AM, noon, and 2 PM; it takes four hours and costs 40 SF. All tours start from the Hauptbahnhof.

The tourist bureau also offers day trips by coach to Luzern, up the Rigi, Titlis, or Pilatus mountains, and the Jungfrau.

WALKING TOURS Daily from June to October, the tourist office offers two-hour walking tours (20 SF) that start at the Hauptbahnhof. You can join a group with English-language commentary, but the times vary, so call ahead.

TRAIN TRAVEL

There are straightforward connections and several express routes leading directly into Zürich from Basel, Geneva, Bern, and Lugano. All roads lead to the Hauptbahnhof in the city center.

☎ Train Information **Hauptbahnhof** ☎ 0900/300300.

TRAM TRAVEL

ZVV, the tram service in Zürich, is swift and timely. It runs from 5:30 AM to midnight, every six minutes at peak hours, every 12 minutes at other times. All-day passes cost 7.20 SF and can be purchased from the same vending machines at the stops that post maps and sell one-ride tickets; you must buy your ticket before you board. Free route plans are available from VBZ offices, located at major crossroads (Paradepl., Bellevue, Central, Kluspl.). Stops are clearly signposted.

🛈 ZVV ☎ 0848/988988.

TRAVEL AGENCIES

🛈 Local Agent Referrals **Imholz Reisen** ✉ Central 12, Kreis 1 ☎ 01/2675500. **Kuoni Travel** ✉ Bahnhofpl. 7, Kreis 1 ☎ 01/2243333.

VISITOR INFORMATION

🛈 Tourist Information **Hotel reservations** ✉ Hauptbahnhof, Kreis 1 CH-8023 ☎ 01/2154040 🖷 01/2154044. **Tourist information** ✉ Hauptbahnhof, Kreis 1 CH-8023 ☎ 01/2154000.

EASTERN SWITZERLAND
APPENZELL, LIECHTENSTEIN, SCHAFFHAUSEN, ST. GALLEN

SAVE ROOM FOR DESSERT
if it's a cream-filled *Biber* ⇨*p.47*

OPEN A NEW WINDOW
in Schaffhausen, known for its ornate oriels ⇨*p.38*

MARVEL AT THE MEDIEVAL
in perfectly preserved Stein-am-Rhein ⇨*p.48*

HIT THE BOOKS
at St. Gallen's magnificent rococo library ⇨*p.52*

DOUBLE YOUR PLEASURE
as Urnäsch celebrates the new year twice ⇨*p.58*

SEAL IT WITH A KISS
and a stamp from philately-mad
Liechtenstein ⇨*p.60*

Updated by
Katrin Gygax

DESPITE ITS PROXIMITY TO ZÜRICH, this Germanic region, with Germany to the north and Austria to the east, maintains a personality apart—a personality that often plays the wallflower when upstaged by more spectacular touristic regions. Lush with orchards and gardens, its north dominated by the romantic Rhine, with a generous share of mountains (including Mt. Säntis, at roughly 8,200 feet) and lovely hidden lakes, as well as the enormous Bodensee (Lake Constance), the region does not lack for variety. Because the east draws fewer crowds, those who do venture in find a pleasant surprise: this is Switzerland sans hard sell, where the people live out a natural, graceful combination of past and present. And although it's a prosperous region, with its famous textiles and fruit industry, its inns and restaurants cost noticeably less than those in regions nearby.

The region covers a broad sociological spectrum, from the thriving city of St. Gallen, with its magnificent baroque cathedral, to the plateau valley of Appenzell, where women couldn't vote in cantonal elections until the federal court intervened on their behalf in 1991 (federal law had granted women the national vote in 1971). On the last Sunday in April in Appenzell city, you still can witness the *Landsgemeinde,* an open-air election for cantonal issues counted by a show of hands.

Architecture along the Rhine resembles that of old Germany and Austria, with half-timbers and rippling red-tile roofs. In cities like Schaffhausen, masterpieces of medieval frescoes decorate town houses, many of which have ornate first-floor bays called oriels. In the country, farmhouses are often covered with fine, feathery wooden shingles as narrow as Popsicle sticks and weathered to chinchilla gray. Appenzell has its own famous architecture: tidy narrow boxes painted cream, with repeated rows of windows and matching wood panels. The very countryside itself—conical green hills, fruit trees, belled cows, neat yellow cottages—resembles the naive art it inspires.

Exploring Eastern Switzerland

The cantons of Glarus, Schaffhausen, Thurgau, St. Gallen, and Appenzell harbor some of Switzerland's oldest traditions. Although the cities have plenty of energy, the countryside of this region changes little over the years. In the northern part of the region are the old Rhine city of Schaffhausen, the dramatic Rheinfall, and the preserved medieval town of Stein-am-Rhein. The Bodensee occupies the northeastern corner of Switzerland, just below Germany. Farther south are the textile center of St. Gallen, the hilly Appenzell region, and the resort area of the Toggenburg Valley. The tiny principality of Liechtenstein lies just across the eastern border, within easy driving distance.

About the Restaurants & Hotels

Eastern Switzerland is the home of the leisurely meal. After setting out on a Sunday walk, many families sit down for a three-hour lunch or dinner. Most towns have at least one restaurant with outside seating, often a gravel-lined yard with red metal chairs and tables under a stand of chestnut trees. Traditional local takeout consists of "fist" food: sausages from an outside barbecue accompanied by a crusty bun. Wander around the sights as you munch. More and more hotels in this region are throwing away their Formica and commissioning hand-painted furniture to complement the beams they've so carefully exposed. However, bargain renovations tend toward the crisp if anonymous look of light tongue-in-groove pine paneling and earth-tone ceramic baths. The prices are somewhat lower on average here, with only slight variations from high to low season. Half board is rarely included.

WHAT IT COSTS In Swiss francs					
	$$$$	**$$$**	**$$**	**$**	**¢**
RESTAURANTS	over 60	40–60	25–40	15–25	under 15
HOTELS	over 350	250–350	175–250	100–175	under 100

Restaurant prices are per person for a main course at dinner. Hotel prices are for two people in a standard double room in high season, including tax and service.

Timing

Summers in eastern Switzerland provide the best weather and activities but also the greatest traffic, both on roads and in towns; spring and fall are good alternatives. Though most places in this region are not too terribly crowded even in summer, Stein-am-Rhein is an exception. It receives enough coach tours to virtually paralyze the village with pedestrians during high season; if you go, arrive earlier in the day or come on a weekday when crowds are a bit thinner.

SCHAFFHAUSEN & THE RHINE

Known to many Swiss as Rheinfallstadt (Rhine Falls City), Schaffhausen is the seat of the country's northernmost canton, which also shares its name. To gaze upon the grand mist-sprayed Rheinfall, arguably the most famous waterfall in Europe, is to look straight into the romantic past of Switzerland. Goethe and Wordsworth were just two of the world's best-known wordsmiths to immortalize the falls' powerful grandeur.

Schaffhausen

▶ ★   *48 km (29 mi) northeast of Zürich, 20 km (12 mi) west of Stein-am-Rhein.*

A city of about 74,000, Schaffhausen was, from the early Middle Ages on, an important depot for river cargoes, which—effectively stopped by the rapids and waterfall farther along—had to be unloaded there. The name *Schaffhausen* is probably derived from the skiff houses along the riverbank. The city has a small but beautiful *Altstadt* (Old Town), whose charm lies in its extraordinary preservation; examples of late Gothic, baroque, and rococo architecture line the streets. It doesn't feel like a museum, though; these buildings are very much in use, often as shops or restaurants, and lively crowds of shoppers and strollers throng the streets. Many streets (including Vorstadt, Fronwagplatz, Vordergasse, and Unterstadt) are pedestrian-only.

Numbers in the text correspond to numbers in the margin and on the Eastern Switzerland and Liechtenstein and Schaffhausen maps.

Although eastern Switzerland is topographically the country's lowest region, it's still fairly rugged. It won't take long to see the major sights, but they are spread throughout the region, so leave time each day to be in transit. Train travel here is more complicated than in neighboring areas, requiring more intercity changes, so plan your itinerary accordingly. If you want to go up into the Appenzell hills, though, you should rent a car. St. Gallen is a good base for visiting the Bodensee, Appenzell, Mt. Säntis, and the principality of Liechtenstein; farther west, Schaffhausen offers easy access to the magnificent Rheinfall, medieval Stein-am-Rhein, and the Bodensee, as well.

2

If you have 1 or 2 days

If you are coming from Zürich, enter the region at its northernmost tip and start with the old Rhine city of ▦ **Schaffhausen ❶–❿** ▸, known for its medieval frescoes and baroque oriel windows. From there it's an easy excursion to the nearby **Neuhausen am Rheinfall ⓫**, the city known for its broad, dramatic series of falls. Just on the other side of Schaffhausen, spend an hour or two in tiny **Stein-am-Rhein ⓬**, a medieval gem situated on the river. Then dip south to ▦ **St. Gallen ⓱**, a busy textile center with an active Old Town beside its grand baroque cathedral. From St. Gallen you can explore the picture-pretty **Appenzell ⓲**.

If you have 4 or 5 days

With a little more time, you can spend your first two days in the northernmost areas, visiting ▦ **Schaffhausen ❶–❿**, **Neuhausen am Rheinfall ⓫**, and **Stein-am-Rhein ⓬**; then make your way south, starting below Germany's Konstanz and following the southern coast of the Bodensee, a popular spot for local resorters. See the twin cities of **Kreuzlingen and Konstanz ⓯** (the latter is in Germany) and ▦ **Gottlieben ⓮**. Visit ▦ **St. Gallen ⓱** and ▦ **Appenzell ⓲**, then trace the **Toggenburg Valley ㉒**, which runs in a great curve between Mt. Säntis and Wildhaus and draws Swiss tourists to its resorts and spas. Head to the tiny principality of Liechtenstein to see the royal castle and explore its art and stamp museums. Finally, go west to the Walensee, whose shores are flanked by a series of lovely villages.

a good walk

Upon entering the Old Town, it becomes obvious why Schaffhausen is also known as the *Erkerstadt*—the City of Oriel Windows. Begin your walk at the north end of the Old Town at the **Schwabentorturm ❶** ▸, where one of the two remaining defense towers houses one of the gates to the town. Continue along Vorstadt, glancing at the oriel windows, many dating from the 17th century. If you cast your gaze up above the houses every now and then, you can see the other tower peek out above the rooftops. The brilliantly painted facade of **Zum Goldenen Ochsen ❷** will be on your right—its oriel window is striking. Vorstadt then leads into **Fronwagplatz ❸**, with its clock tower and the Mohrenbrunnen and Metzgerbrunnen fountains at its north and south ends.

Continue east along the Vordergasse, where on your right you'll find the fine mansion **Haus zum Ritter** ❹, followed by the **Schmiedstube** ❺, the Smiths' Guild House. Farther up the street to your left is the imposing St. Johannkirche. To the right of the church lies the Haus zum Sittich, a bright yellow structure with Renaissance oriel windows and relief sculpture. Take a left at the fork in the road up ahead to see the duplex **zur Wasserquelle** and **zur Zieglerburg** ❻. Across from the duplex stands the Tellenbrunnen fountain.

Double back to the fork in the road and stroll down the tail end of Vordergasse. As you wait at the pedestrian crossing at Bachstrasse, the gray-and-white **Gerberstube** ❼ welcomes you to this quieter part of town. Farther along the Unterstadt looking north is a group of odd houses with crooked and sharp angles. This is the entrance to the **Munot** ❽. The meandering steps that lead to the tower are flanked by vineyards. Having enjoyed the view from the tower, double back to the pedestrian crossing at Bachstrasse. Cross the street and take the first left. You will come upon a cluster of large buildings that house the city library and the **Münster zu Allerheiligen** ❾. Head west on Münsterplatz. This leads you straight to the entrances of the Münster and the **Museum zu Allerheiligen** ❿. Now head up the hill to the government buildings on your left. The Altes Zeughaus (Old Armory), built by Johannes Jacob Meyer, is regarded as a good example of Swiss Renaissance architecture.

TIMING The entire walk takes about two hours, including the hike up to the Munot. You may want to linger at the Munot if the weather is clear and the view particularly good. A visit to the Museum zu Allerheiligen will add another hour. Keep in mind that the museum and cathedral are closed on Monday and open late on weekdays.

Sights to See

❸ **Fronwagplatz.** Lined with shops and cafés, this square is a favorite place for young people to stroll, especially in the evening. A large 16th-century fountain-statue of a prosperous burgher, the **Metzgerbrunnen**, watches over the marketplace. The **clock tower** once held the market scales; its astronomical clock (1564) records not only the time but also eclipses, seasons, and the course of the moon through the zodiac. Across the square, a reproduction of the 1535 **Mohrenbrunnen** (Moor's Fountain) represents Kaspar of the Three Kings. The original fountain is stored in the Museum zu Allerheiligen.

❼ **Gerberstube** (Tanners' Guild House). A pair of lions frames the doorway of the remarkable baroque building. A two-handled tanner's knife used to stretch between the lions, but unfortunately it collapsed when nearby roadworks shook the neighborhood. A restaurant now occupies the building. ⊠ *Bachstr. 8.*

❹ **Haus zum Ritter** (Knight's House). The city's finest mansion dates from 1492. Its fresco facade was commissioned by the resident knight, Hans von Waldkirch. Tobias Stimmer covered all three stories with paintings on classical themes, which are now displayed in the Museum zu Allerheiligen; the reproduction of the original was made in the 1930s. ⊠ *Vorderg. 65.*

2

Dining Your plate will feel the weight of German and Austrian influence in this most Teutonic of Swiss regions: portions are hearty, and pork appears often. A side of *Spätzli* (exact translation: little sparrows) or *Knöpfli* (little buttons) adds further heft: these are flour-egg dough fingers, either pressed through a sieve or snipped, gnocchi-style, and served in butter. Another favorite side dish is *Hörnli* (little horns), crescent-shape pasta with butter and cheese. You can also can order a full-meal portion of *Käseknöpfli* (cheese dumplings), which come smothered in a pungent cheese sauce.

All across Switzerland you'll find the St. Gallen bratwurst, which is called *Olma Bratwurst* on its home turf. In restaurants it's served with thick onion sauce and *Rösti* (hash brown potatoes), but in St. Gallen itself the locals eat it on the go, lining up at lunchtime at one of many outdoor stands, then holding the thick white-veal sausage in a napkin with one hand and a round, chewy chunk of whole-grain *Bürli* bread in the other.

The famous Appenzeller cheese deserves its stardom, as among the fine hard cheeses of Switzerland it has the most complex, spicy flavor, with traces of nutmeg. Other Appenzeller treats include a variation of Graubünden's famous air-dried beef, here called *Mostbröckli* and steeped in sweet apple cider before drying. It is served in translucent slices, its moist, mildly sweet flavor countered with bits of pickled onion. *Bauernschüblig* are dark dried-blood sausages. If you've got a sweet tooth, try two regional specialties: Appenzeller *Biber* (honey cakes filled with almond and stamped with a design) and *Birnebrot* (thick dried-pear puree wrapped in glazed dough). *Chäsmagarone* is a rich, plain dish of large macaroni layered with butter, grated Appenzeller cheese, and butter-fried onions—it's often eaten with *Apfelmus* (applesauce).

Eastern Switzerland is the country's orchard region, especially the Thurgau area. There are several fine fruit juices made here, as well as *Most* (sweet cider) and some good fruit schnapps. Among area wines, Berneck comes from the Rhine Valley, Hallau from near Schaffhausen, and crisp whites from Stein-am-Rhein.

Hiking Uncrowded hiking trails lead through all kinds of terrain, from rolling vineyards along the Rhine to isolated, rugged mountain wilderness above the Toggenburg Valley. This is a region of unspoiled nature, well-preserved villages, and breathtaking scenery.

---

need a break? Snag an outdoor table at **Restaurant zur Alten Post** (⊠ Schwertstr. 1 ☎ 052/6252255) for one of many spaghetti dishes offered, from the classic garlic and olive oil to chicken with Chinese vegetables.

8 Munot. Built between 1564 and 1585 in full circle form based on an idea by Albrecht Dürer, the massive stone ramparts served as a fortress allowing the defense of the city from all sides. From its top are splendid

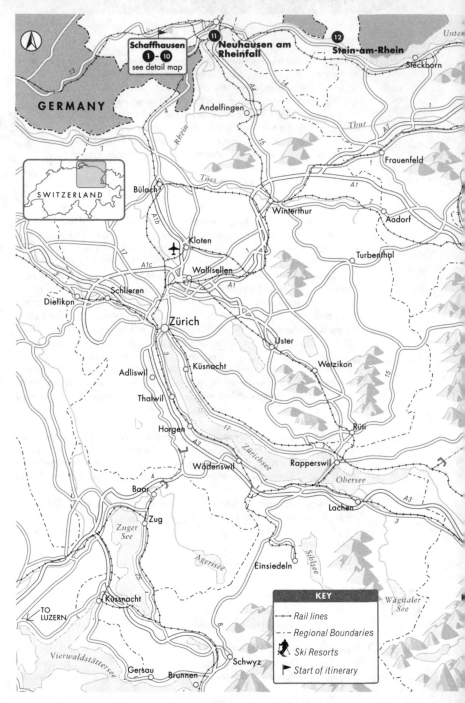

Schaffhausen
1–**10**
see detail map

11 Neuhausen am
Rheinfall

12 Stein-am-Rhein

Unter

Steckborn

Andelfingen

Thur

Frauenfeld

Töss

Bülach

Winterthur

Aadorf

Kloten

Turbenthal

Wallisellen

Schlieren

Dietikon

Zürich

Uster

Wetzikon

Adliswil

Küsnacht

Thalwil

Horgen

Rüti

Wädenswil

Zürichsee

Rapperswil

Obersee

Baar

Lachen

Zug

Zuger
See

Ägerisee

Einsiedeln

Sihlsee

TO
LUZERN

Küssnacht

Wägitaler
See

Vierwaldstättersee

Gersau

Brunnen

Schwyz

KEY	
⊢—•→	Rail lines
—·—·—	Regional Boundaries
🎿	Ski Resorts
⊢	Start of itinerary

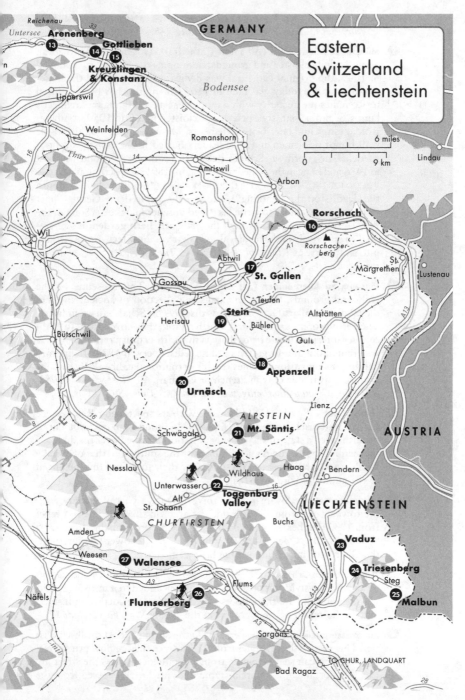

Eastern Switzerland & Liechtenstein

Schaffhausen and Rhine Valley views. ⊠ *Munotstieg* ⊠ *Free* ⊙ *May–Sept., daily 8–8; Oct.–Apr., daily 9–5.*

⑨ Münster zu Allerheiligen (All Saints Cathedral). This beautiful cathedral, along with its cloister and grounds, dominates the lower city. Founded in 1049, the original cathedral was dedicated in 1064, and the larger one that stands today was built in 1103. Its interior has been restored to Romanesque austerity with a modern aesthetic (hanging architect's lamps, Scandinavian-style pews). The **cloister**, begun in 1050, combines Romanesque and later Gothic elements. Memorial plates on the inside wall honor noblemen and civic leaders buried in the cloister's central garden. The enormous **Schiller Bell** in the courtyard beyond was cast in 1486 and hung in the cathedral tower until 1895. Its inscription, VIVOS—VOCO/MORTUOS—PLANGO/FULGURA—FRANGO ("I call the living, mourn the dead, stop the lightning"), supposedly inspired the German poet Friedrich von Schiller to write his "Lied von der Glocke" ("Song of the Bell"). You'll also pass through the aromatic **herb garden**; it's re-created so effectively in the medieval style that you may feel you've stepped into a tapestry. ⊠ *Klosterpl. 1* ⊠ *Free* ⊙ *Tues.–Fri. 10–noon and 2–5, weekends 10–5.*

⑩ Museum zu Allerheiligen (All Saints Museum). This museum, on the cathedral grounds, houses an extensive collection of ancient and medieval historical artifacts, as well as displays on Schaffhausen industry. The period rooms are definitely worth a look; they cover 15th- to 19th-century interiors. The best of these is the 15th-century refectory, which was rented out and forgotten until its rediscovery in 1924. Temporary exhibitions on various themes reach international caliber. Museum literature is available only in French or German. ⊠ *Klosterpl. 1* ☎ *052/6330777* ⊕ *www.allerheiligen.ch* ⊠ *Free* ⊙ *Tues.–Sun. 11–5.*

⑤ Schmiedstube (Smiths' Guild House). With its spectacular Renaissance portico and oriel dating from 1653, this building is an embodiment of Schaffhausen's state of suspended animation. Framed over the door are the symbols of the tongs and hammer for the smiths and that of a snake for doctors, who depended on smiths for their tools and thus belonged to the guild. ⊠ *Vorderg. 61.*

► **① Schwabentorturm** (Swabian Gate Tower). Once a part of the city wall, the tower dates from 1370. Inside the arch on the keystone is a relief from 1933 that bears a wise caution for anyone crossing the street: LAPPI TUE D'AUGE UF ("Open your eyes, you idiot!"). The tower's counterpart, the **Obertorturm**, lies just off the Fronwagplatz.

② Zum Goldenen Ochsen (At the Golden Ox). This late-Gothic building had a Renaissance-style portico and oriel window added to it in 1609. Flanking the windows are three floors of exterior frescoes depicting historic and mythological figures, most from the Trojan War. ⊠ *Vorstadt 17.*

⑥ Zur Wasserquelle and Zur Zieglerburg (At the Spring and At the Brick Castle). This rococo duplex dates from 1738; since they're now private residences, you can see them only from the outside. Across the street are the **Tellenbrunnen**, a fountain-statue of Wilhelm Tell copied from the

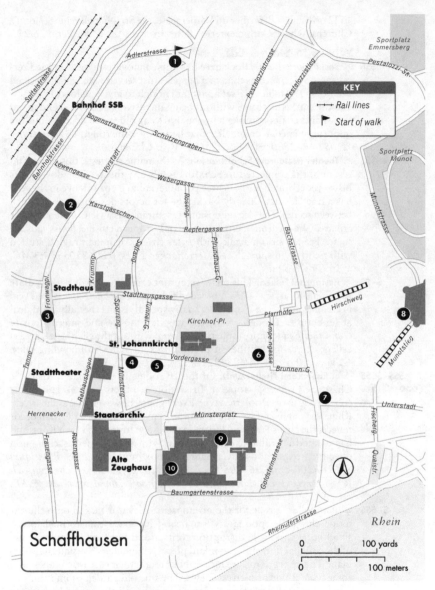

KEY
+—+ Rail lines
► Start of walk

Schaffhausen

0   100 yards

0   100 meters

1522 original, and, farther up Vordergasse, the **St. Johannkirche** (St. John's Church), whose Gothic exterior dates from 1248. ⊠ *Vorderg. 26/28.*

Where to Stay & Eat

$$$ ✕ **Beckenburg.** Locals flock here to sample innovative twists on Mediterranean staples, such as tuna in a pepper crust served with vanilla mashed potatoes. The tables are set apart far enough to give you lots of privacy, and the staff is attentive without being intrusive. Beechwood and metal tables and chairs complement the 300-year-old wood accents and the imposing Venetian chandelier that hangs over the room. ⊠ *Neustadt 1* ☎ *052/6252820* ⊟ *AE, DC, MC, V* ⊘ *Closed Sun.*

$–$$$ ✕ **Theater Restaurant Schaffhausen.** As the name suggests, this bistro and restaurant is connected to Schaffhausen's city theater. The downstairs bistro is decorated with theater paraphernalia; a cozy alcove in the rear has a door leading directly backstage for actors desiring a quick snack between scenes. The elegant upstairs restaurant has a view of Herrenacker Square. Choose from a cross section of European cuisine: Swiss sausage salad, French sirloin steak with *frites* (fries), or Italian ravioli stuffed with ricotta and spinach. ⊠ *Herrenacker 23* ☎ *052/6250558* ⊟ *MC, V* ⊘ *Closed Sun.*

$–$$ ✕ **Restaurant Falken.** This busy restaurant caters to crowds with a palate for simple local fare—Rösti, breaded fish, and *Geschnetzeltes* (sliced veal in cream sauce). The *Tagesteller* (daily special) is an especially good deal at lunchtime. Though plain, the wooden facade and interior create *Gemütlichkeit* (comfortable friendliness) without the clichés. It's an excellent choice for families; it even houses its own small bowling alley. ⊠ *Vorstadt 5* ☎ *052/6253221* ⊟ *AE, DC, MC, V.*

$$$–$$$$ ✕▥ **Rheinhotel Fischerzunft.** Of the 10 rooms in this modern Relais &
Fodor'sChoice Châteaux property—some in fussy florals, others in sleek jewel-tone
★ solids—seven overlook the river. Every guest, however, shares the lovely Rhine view at breakfast. The restaurant's mixed nautical and Asian decor reflects the chef's Franco-Chinese leanings: he trained in Hong Kong and has created a brilliant, eclectic menu with such dishes as cinnamon dove breast with goose liver pâté on an ox mouth salad. ⊠ *Rheinquai 8, CH-8200* ☎ *052/6320505* ⊜ *052/6320513* ⊕ *www.fischerzunft.ch* ⟿ *6 rooms, 4 suites* ⚅ *Restaurant, in-room safes, minibars; no a/c* ⊟ *AE, DC, MC, V* ⦿*l BP.*

$–$$$ ▥ **Park-Villa.** Except for the no-nonsense elevator tacked onto the exterior, this belle epoque–style mansion has been transformed into a small hotel with little disruption to its grand but familial style. Many of the original furnishings—inlaid pieces, chandeliers, Persian rugs—remain. The upper floors are modern but retain their eccentric shapes, and some have Rhine or fortress views. The fine old garden room is luxurious and a steal (the toilet is down the hall); all the other rooms have full baths. The hotel sits slightly apart, and uphill, from the Old Town. ⊠ *Parkstr. 18, CH-8200* ☎ *052/6252737* ⊜ *052/6241253* ⊕ *www. parkvilla.ch* ⟿ *21 rooms, 4 suites* ⚅ *Restaurant, tennis court, bar; no a/c* ⊟ *AE, DC, MC, V* ⦿*l BP.*

$$ ▥ **Kronenhof.** This fine, quiet city hotel in the heart of Schaffhausen's Old Town has a traditional, shutter- and flower-trimmed facade. Rooms have a crisp look, with birch furniture and abstract prints. The main

FIST FOOD

St. Gallen is almost as famous for its Olma Bratwurst as for the textiles it used to manufacture for shipment throughout the world. But while the textile industry is in decline, there's no chance the cream-color sausage with its sides crisply browned to perfection will be disappearing from the region anytime soon. Locals get theirs from **Gemperli** (Schmidg. 34), the butcher, who makes them from a recipe that dates back to 1438. You'll be offered mustard or even ketchup, but aficionados eat theirs plain—

there's more than enough taste, thanks to the many spices mixed in with the ground veal. If sweets are more your thing, try a St. Galler Biber—a gingerbread patty with almond paste filling—from **Konfiserie Scherrer** (Marktg. 28). One Biber can replace a whole meal; they are so rich you may find yourself living on lettuce and water for the next 24 hours.

restaurant serves excellent, refined versions of local dishes, including fresh fish and rich soups. ⊠ *Kirchhofpl. 7, CH-8200* ☎ *052/6357575* 🖷 *052/ 6357565* ⊕ *www.kronenhof.ch* 🖙 *38 rooms, 2 suites* ⚬ *Restaurant, café, in-room data ports, in-room safes, minibars, bar; no a/c* ⊟ *AE, DC, MC, V* ⧉ *BP.*

$$ 🏨 **Promenade.** This solid, simple, Edwardian hotel, on the same set-apart residential hill as the Park-Villa, offers spare Formica-and-beige rooms, a garden restaurant, and modest fitness equipment. There's a pretty walk through a nearby park to the Old Town. ⊠ *Fäsenstaubstr. 43, CH-8200* ☎ *052/6307777* 🖷 *052/6307778* 🖙 *37 rooms* ⚬ *Restaurant, minibars, gym, sauna, meeting rooms; no a/c* ⊟ *AE, DC, MC, V.*

$ 🏨 **Löwen.** At the edge of suburban Herblingen, where the bedroom community seems to melt back into its origins as a half-timber country town, this quintessential old guesthouse still draws the locals to its pub and serves regional standards in its restaurant. Rooms, however, are all modern, with ceramic tile and modern pine paneling. ⊠ *Im Höfli 2, CH-8207 Herblingen* ☎ *052/6432208* 🖷 *052/6432288* 🖙 *7 rooms* ⚬ *Restaurant, pub; no a/c* ⊟ *No credit cards.*

Sports &the Outdoors

Bicycles are a popular mode of transportation. They can be rented at the **train station** (☎ 051/2234217) in Schaffhausen.

Neuhausen am Rheinfall

⓫ *3 km (1¾ mi) south of Schaffhausen.*

FodorsChoice
★

Adjacent to Neuhausen, on the north bank of the Rhine, a series of magnificent waterfalls powers the city's industry (arms, railroad cars, aluminum). The **Rheinfall** is 492 feet wide, drops some 82 feet in a series of three dramatic leaps, and is split at the center by a bushy crag straight out of a 19th-century landscape painting. The effect—mists, roaring water, jutting rocks—is positively Wagnerian; Goethe saw in the falls the "ocean's source." There's a footpath, Rheinuferweg, that leads from Schaffhausen's Old Town along the river to the falls (a 25- to 35-minute walk). It's marked with the standard yellow hiking-trail signs. From Neuhausen there's a good view toward **Schloss Laufen,** a 12th-century castle that overlooks the Rheinfall.

Stein-am-Rhein

⑫ *20 km (13 mi) east of Schaffhausen.*

Fodor'sChoice ★

Stein-am-Rhein, a nearly perfectly preserved medieval village and one of Switzerland's loveliest towns, lies at the point where the Rhine leaves the Bodensee. Crossing the bridge over the river, you see the village spread along the waterfront, its foundations and docks rising directly out of the water. Here, restaurants, hotels, and shops occupy 16th- and 17th-century buildings, and the Rhine is calm and lazy—nothing like the sprawling industrial trade route it becomes farther downstream.

The **Rathausplatz** (Town Hall Square) and main street, Understadt, are flanked by tight rows of shingled, half-timber town houses, each rivaling the next for the ornateness of its oriels, the flamboyance of its frescoes. The elaborate decor usually illustrates the name of the house: Sonne (Sun), Ochsen (Ox), Weisser Adler (White Eagle), and so on. Most of the artwork dates from the 16th century. The **Rathaus** (Town Hall) itself was built between 1539 and 1542, with the half-timber upper floors added in 1745; look for its fantastical dragon waterspouts, typical of the region.

The Benedictine **Kloster St. Georgen** (Monastery of St. George), a half-timber structure built in 1007, houses a cloister and a small museum of woodwork and local paintings. ✛ *Edge of Old Town, just upstream from the last bridge over the Rhine before the Bodensee* ☎ *052/7412142* ▧ *3 SF* ☉ *Museum: Apr.–Oct., Tues.–Sun. 10–5.*

Directly above the town atop vineyards and woods stands the 12th-century hilltop castle of **Hohenklingen,** which now houses a restaurant and offers broad views of the Rhine Valley and the lake beyond.

Where to Stay & Eat

★ **\$\$–\$\$\$** ✕ **Sonne.** Upstairs, you'll find a formal dining room (ceiling beams, damask, and Biedermeier) where chef Philippe Combe's inventive, contemporary dishes—Rhine fish, rack of lamb in a thyme crust—command top prices. Downstairs in the *Weinstube* (wine parlor), he offers a Tagesteller, simple light lunches, and selections from the fine wine list, dished up in a spare, chic, gentrified pub: more beams, stone, stucco, and parquet. ✉ *Rathauspl.* ☎ *052/7412128* ▤ *AE, DC, MC, V* ☉ *Closed Tues. and Wed.*

¢–\$ ✕ **Der Rote Ochse.** The beautiful frescoed facade invites its admirers into this warm little Weinstube, where dark antiques surround a *Kachelofen* (tile stove) and candles glow on the tables. The simple menu is thick with hearty cuisine—a variety of sausages such as *Rauchwurst* (smoked sausage), local cheeses, and delicious homemade pastas. When they say the food is regional, they mean it: all ingredients are obtained from the village and the surrounding areas. ⊠ *Rathauspl. 129* ☎ *052/7412328* ▤ *No credit cards.*

$$$ ▦ **Chlosterhof.** Its brick-and-angled-glass exterior seems utterly misplaced in this medieval setting, but this hotel worked hard to face as many rooms as possible toward the Rhine. Inside, the look is modern, suburban, and business-class despite token vaulting in the lobby and scattered antiques; the focus is on entertaining conference groups. The rooms have sleek dark-pine cabinetry and some four-poster beds, but the creamy pastels and carpets say upscale international chain. Suites claim the best river views. ⊠ *Oehningerstr. 201, CH-8260* ☎ *052/ 7424242* ⊞ *052/7411337* ⊕ *www.chlosterhof.ch* ⊅ *44 rooms, 26 suites* ⚫ *3 restaurants, in-room data ports, minibars, in-room VCRs, pool, gym, sauna, bar, dance club, meeting rooms; free parking; no a/c* ▤ *AE, DC, MC, V* ⧠ *BP.*

★ $$-$$$ ▦ **Adler.** With one of the most elaborately frescoed 15th-century facades on the Rathausplatz, this hotel has a split personality. On the outside it's flamboyant, but inside it's no-nonsense. The decor is airy, slick, and immaculate, with gray industrial carpet, white stucco, and blond wood throughout. Double-glaze windows cut the noise from the square. A local family runs the hotel, so other families will fit right in. The cheerful restaurant serves excellent regional cooking, along with some French dishes. ⊠ *Rathauspl. 15, CH-8260* ☎ *052/7426161* ⊞ *052/7414440* ⊕ *www. adlersteinamrhein.ch* ⊅ *25 rooms* ⚫ *Restaurant; no a/c* ▤ *AE, DC, MC, V* ⊗ *Closed Jan. and Feb.* ⧠ *BP.*

★ $$ ▦ **Rheinfels.** Even some of the bathrooms have ceiling beams in this fine old waterfront landmark, which was built between 1508 and 1517. The public spaces have creaking pine-plank floors and suits of armor on display, and every room—modernized in beige and rose tones—has a Rhine view. The hotel's suite is in essence an apartment; it has its own separate entrance, a one-car garage, and a boat jetty. The restaurant specializes in top-quality freshwater fish. Both the hotel and the restaurant are closed on Wednesday. ⊠ *Rhig. 8, CH-8260* ☎ *052/7412144* ⊞ *052/7412522* ⊅ *16 rooms, 1 suite* ⚫ *Restaurant, minibars, meeting rooms; no a/c* ▤ *MC, V* ⧠ *BP.*

$ ▦ **Zur Rheingerbe.** Right on the busy waterfront promenade, this small inn has wood-panel ceilings and big furniture reminiscent of Sears (sculptured carpet, spindle beds). Some rooms overlook the Rhine. The excellent first-floor restaurant has a full-length bay window along the riverfront. The hotel and restaurant are closed on Wednesday. ⊠ *Schifflände 5, CH-8260* ☎ *052/7412991* ⊞ *052/7412166* ⊅ *7 rooms* ⚫ *Restaurant* ▤ *AE, DC, MC, V.*

en route   Fourteen kilometers (9 mi) east of Stein-am-Rhein, the town of **Steckborn** has some fine old houses, including the Baronenhaus and the Gerichtshaus. It's also home to **Turmhof Steckborn,** a half-timber waterfront castle built in 1320 that currently houses a small local museum containing artifacts from prehistoric times through the Roman and Alemannic settlements. ☎ *052/7612903* ⊡ *5 SF* ⊗ *Mid-May–mid-Oct., Wed., Thurs., and weekends 3–5, or by appointment.*

Arenenberg

⑬ *20 km (12 mi) east of Stein-am-Rhein, 40 km (25 mi) east of Schaffhausen.*

East of Stein-am-Rhein, the Rhine opens up into the Untersee, the lower branch of the Bodensee. In its center lies the German island of Reichenau. Charles the Fat, great-grandson of Charlemagne, was buried here.

The villages on either side of the Untersee are dominated by castles. On the Swiss side, behind the village of Mannenbach (nearly opposite Reichenau), the **castle** was once home to the future Napoléon III and serves today as a museum with furnishings and artwork from the Second Empire. ⊠ *Behind Mannenbach* ☎ *071/6643260* 🖾 *10 SF* ⊙ *Tues.–Sun. 10–6, Mon. 2–6.*

Gottlieben

⑭ *5 km (3 mi) east of Arenenberg, 45 km (28 mi) east of Schaffhausen.*

The village of Gottlieben has a Dominican monastery-castle, where the Protestant reformers Jan Hus and Jerome of Prague were imprisoned in the 15th century by order of Emperor Sigismund and antipope John XXIII, who was himself confined in the same castle a few years later. Today, though the castle can be viewed only from the outside, Gottlieben offers a romantic, half-timber waterfront promenade—and two fine old hotels—before you reach the urban complex of Kreuzlingen and Germany's Konstanz.

Where to Stay

$$–$$$
🏠 **Drachenburg und Waaghaus.** On the misty bank of the Rhine between the Bodensee and the Zellersee rises this half-timber cluster of onion domes, shutters, and gilt gargoyles. The original early-18th-century Drachenburg lies across the way from the second building, the Waaghaus. A third house catches the overflow. All three have gleaming old staircases, four-poster beds, brocade, chaise longues, and crystal sconces throughout the labyrinth of rooms and parlors. The scale is grand but cozy, and Rhine-view rooms are furnished like honeymoon suites. Its restaurants vary in ambience; the most sophisticated is the one in the original house. ⊠ *Am Schlosspark, CH-8274* ☎ *071/ 6667474* 🖨 *071/6691709* ⊕ *www.drachenburg.ch* ⌁ *58 rooms, 2 suites* ♨ *2 restaurants, in-room safes, minibars, bar; no a/c* ⊟ *AE, DC, MC, V* ⭐ *BP.*

$–$$
🏠 **Krone.** Immediately downstream from the Drachenburg und Waaghaus lodging, this member of the Romantik chain is smaller, cheaper, and more discreet than its flamboyant neighbor, though it dates from the same era. Standard doubles are done in mild, classic beiges; the suites are quite baroque and have lake views. Breakfast is served in a beam-and-herringbone-ceiling hall overlooking the Rhine. The glowing dark-wood restaurant offers nouvelle-influenced seafood as well as lake fish. ⊠ *Seestr., CH-8274* ☎ *071/6698060* 🖨 *071/6668069* ⊕ *www. romantikhotel.ch/krone* ⌁ *22 rooms, 3 suites* ♨ *Restaurant, minibars, meeting rooms; no a/c* ⊟ *AE, DC, MC, V* ⭐ *BP.*

BODENSEE TO ST. GALLEN

Along the shores of the Bodensee, orchards stripe rolling hills that slowly rise to meet the foothills of the Alps around St. Gallen. About 2,000 years ago this region lay on the northeastern border of the Roman Empire, Arbon (Arbor Felix) being the first stop on the trade route for goods coming into the empire from points east. Today the region is mostly rural, with clusters of farmhouses dotting the grassy slopes. In summer the lake teems with vacationers, but otherwise it's a distinctly tranquil area.

Bodensee

Known in English as Lake Constance, the Bodensee is about 65 km (40 mi) long and 15 km (9 mi) wide, making it second in size in Switzerland only to Lac Léman (Lake Geneva). The strong German flavor of the towns on its Swiss edge is seasoned with a resort-village mellowness; palm trees fringe the waterfront. This isn't the Mediterranean, though; as the lake is not protected by mountains, it is turbulent in stormy weather and even on fine days is exposed to the wind. Nonetheless, it draws European vacationers in summer for swimming, windsurfing, and fishing. Many Swiss have built tidy homes along the lakefront.

Sports & the Outdoors

HIKING As a summer resort destination, the area around the Bodensee is usually thronged with hikers. For timed hiking itineraries, topographical maps, and suggestions on the areas best suited to your style of wandering, consult the Tourismusverband Ostschweiz (Tourist Association of Eastern Switzerland).

SWIMMING People do swim in the Bodensee; there are several public beaches, usually more grass than sand. Most have changing rooms and concession stands. **Arbon** (☎ 071/4461333) has a gravel beach—getting into the water can be a little rough on tender feet. **Kreuzlingen** (☎ 071/6881858) has some sand at the water's edge, though you'll be spreading your towel on the grass. **Romanshorn** (☎ 071/4631147) is also mostly grass.

Kreuzlingen & Konstanz

🕕 *7 km (4 mi) east of Gottlieben, 46 km (28 mi) east of Schaffhausen.*

The German city of Konstanz, with its Swiss twin of Kreuzlingen, dominates the straits that open into the Bodensee. Though Kreuzlingen itself offers little of interest to travelers, Konstanz has a lovely, concentrated *Altstadt* (Old Town) area. It's easily accessible from the Swiss side, though your passport may be checked even if you pass on foot. Konstanz belonged to Switzerland until 1805; today the two border towns share the dominant German influence.

en route About halfway between Kreuzlingen and Rorschach (follow Highway 13 east along the Bodensee), you'll come to the small town of **Romanshorn.** An industrial town and an important ferry port for Friedrichshafen in Germany, this is also a surprisingly enjoyable resort with fine views of the Swiss and Austrian mountains.

Between Romanshorn and Rorschach on Highway 13, **Arbon** (known to the Romans as Arbor Felix) lies on a little promontory jutting out into the Bodensee, surrounded by lovely meadows and orchards. It was a Celtic town before the Romans came in 60 BC and built military fortifications. Evidence of the Romans can be found in an interesting collection of relics in the late-Gothic St. Martinskirche.

Rorschach

⑯ *41 km (25 mi) southeast of Kreuzlingen, 80 km (49 mi) southeast of Schaffhausen.*

The lake resort of Rorschach, a port on the Bodensee, lies on a protected bay at the foot of the Rorschacherberg, a 2,896-foot mountain covered with orchards, pine forests, and meadows. For generations, Rorschach has carried on a thriving grain trade with Germany, as the imposing baroque **Kornhaus** (Granary), built in 1746, attests.

Sports & the Outdoors

SAILING   There are several sailing schools along the lake near Rorschach, including **Segel & Motorbootschule Rorschach** (☎ 071/8448989).

SWIMMING   In Rorschach there is a pocket-size public **beach** (☎ 071/8411684).

St. Gallen

⑰ *14 km (9 mi) southwest of Rorschach, 94 km (59 mi) southeast of Schaffhausen.*

Switzerland's largest eastern city, bustling St. Gallen is dominated by students during the school year. The narrow streets of the *Altstadt* (Old Town) are flanked by a wonderful variety of boutiques and antiques shops. The city has been known for centuries as both an intellectual center and the source of some of the world's finest textiles. St. Gallus, an Irish missionary, came to the region in 612 to live in a hermit's cell in the Steinach Valley. In 719 an abbey was founded on the site where he died. Soon a major cultural focus in medieval Europe, the abbey built a library of awesome proportions.

Fodor'sChoice   The abbey was largely destroyed in the Reformation and was closed ★ down in 1805, but its magnificent rococo **Stiftsbibliothek** (Abbey Library), built between 1758 and 1767, still holds a collection of more than 100,000 books and manuscripts. The library hall itself is one of Switzerland's treasures. You enter behind the cathedral and change into the provided large, gray carpet slippers to protect the magnificently inlaid wood flooring. The hall is a gorgeous explosion of gilt, frescoes, and undulating balconies, but the most striking aspect by far is the burnished woodwork, all luminous walnut and cherry. Its contents, including incunabula and illuminated manuscripts that are more than 1,200 years old, constitute one of the world's oldest and finest scholarly collections. Also on display, incongruously, is an Egyptian mummy dating from 700 BC. ⊠ *Klosterhof 6c* ☎ *071/ 2273416* ⊠ *7 SF* ☉ *Apr.–Nov., Mon.–Sat. 10–5, Sun. 10–4; Dec.–Mar., Mon.–Sat. 10–noon and 1:30–5, Sun. 10–noon and 1:30–4.*

★ The **Kathedrale** (Cathedral) is an impressive sight. Begun in 1755 and completed in 1766, it is the antithesis of the library, though the nave and rotunda are the work of the same architect, Peter Thumb. The scale is outsize and the decor light, bright, and open despite spectacular excesses of wedding-cake trim. ⊠ *Klosterhof* ☎ *071/2273381* ☉ *Daily 9–6, except during services.*

need a break?

Café Seeger (⊠ Oberer Graben 2 ☎ 071/2229790) is a relaxing Viennese-style café and restaurant. You can put your feet up in the lounge while you read the paper.

The grounds of the abbey and the cathedral border the **Old Town,** which demonstrates a healthy symbiosis between scrupulously preserved Renaissance and baroque architecture and a thriving modern shopping scene. The best examples of oriel windows, half-timbering, and frescoes can be seen along Gallusstrasse, Schmiedgasse, Marktgasse, and Spisergasse, all pedestrian streets. For a good picnic spot, head to the **Mühleggbahn,** a self-service funicular that runs up the hillside to a lovely view of St. Gallen and the Bodensee. Once up top, take two immediate right turns to the wooden stairs leading to a paved path with park benches. ⊠ *Off the abbey end of the Old Town* ☎ *071/2439595* 💺 *1.70 SF* ☉ *Daily 6 AM–11:30 PM.*

St. Gallen's history as a textile capital dates from the Middle Ages, when convent workers wove linen toile of such exceptional quality that it was exported throughout Europe. The industry expanded into cotton and embroidery, before collapsing in 1918. Today, St. Gallen dominates the small luxury market for fine handmade textiles and embroidery. To enjoy some marvelous old embroidery, visit the **Textilmuseum** (Textile Museum). Its lighting is dim to protect the delicate fabrics and its captions are all in German, but the work speaks for itself. ⊠ *Vadianstr. 2* ☎ *071/2221744* ⊕ *www.textilmuseum.ch* 💺 *5 SF* ☉ *Mon.–Sat. 10–noon and 2–5, Sun. 10–5, 1st Wed. of each month 10–5.*

Where to Stay & Eat

$$$ ✕ **Am Gallusplatz.** This is St. Gallen's grandest restaurant both in terms of cuisine and decor. The menu is based on market-fresh ingredients and may include such favorites as beef Stroganoff with basmati rice. There's also an enormous wine list. The dining room impresses with its cross-vaulted ceilings and heavy chandeliers. ⊠ *Gallusstr. 24* ☎ *071/2233330* 🗃 *AE, MC, V* ☉ *Closed Mon.*

$–$$$ ✕ **Concerto.** The glassed-in terrace of the Tonhalle concert hall provides a year-round spring setting and a beautiful view of its park. The all-day kitchen serves up inventive twists on local standards—fish wrapped in bacon with tomato sauce, for example—and has dishes for all appetites and pocketbooks. ⊠ *Museumstr. 25* ☎ *071/2420777* 🗃 *AE, MC, V.*

$–$$$ ✕ **Netts Schützengarten.** In the corner of the local brewery, this bistro polishes a 19th-century industrial look, with copper pipes, exposed brick, and hardwood floors. Owner Köbi Nett's travels have resulted in a far-reaching menu: Spanish tapas, Indonesian shrimp curry, Olma Bratwurst. The beer is tapped directly from the vats next door. ⊠ *St. Jakobstr. 35* ☎ *071/2426677* 🗃 *AE, MC, V* ☉ *Closed Sun.*

★ **$-$$$**   ✕ **Schlössli.** Tidy, bright, and modern despite its setting in a historic building, this first-floor (second-floor to Americans) landmark has a less woody atmosphere than its peers, the Bäumli and the Schäfli, but better cooking. Look for inventive dishes such as poached mixed seafood in saffron sauce. The café draws casual family groups and locals at lunch; businesspeople choose the slightly more formal dining room that adjoins it. ⊠ *Am Spisertor, Zeughausg. 17* ☎ *071/2221256* ▤ *AE, DC, MC, V* ⊘ *Closed weekends.*

$-$$$ ✕ **Weinstube zum Bäumli.** All dark, glossy wood and leaded glass, this 500-year-old first-floor (second-floor to Americans) beauty serves classic local fare (veal, bratwurst, Rösti) to tourists, businesspeople, and workers, who share tables comfortably in the midst of the noisy bustle. ⊠ *Schmiedg. 18* ☎ *071/2221174* ▤ *MC, V* ⊘ *Closed Sun. and Mon.*

$-$$$ ✕ **Zum Goldenen Schäfli.** Of the first-floor (second-floor to Americans) restaurants that are St. Gallen's trademark, this is the most popular, and its slanting floors groan under crowds of locals and tourists. The low ceiling and walls are all aged wood. The menu offers regional standards lightened up for modern tastes. Crabs with paprika, for example, are a favorite. ⊠ *Metzgerg. 5* ☎ *071/2233737* ▤ *AE, DC, MC, V* ⊘ *Closed Sun. No lunch Sat.*

$$$-$$$$ ☷ **Einstein.** Tucked back into a slope at the edge of the Old Town, this former embroidery factory is now an upscale business-class hotel, with sleek interiors (polished cabinetry, subdued floral fabrics), a uniformed staff, and a five-star attitude. The generous breakfast buffet, laid out in the skylighted top-floor loft, is not included in the room price. A modern glass-and-steel annex holds additional rooms and a business center. ⊠ *Berneggstr. 2, CH-9001* ☎ *071/2275555* ☐ *071/2275577* ⊕ *www.einstein.ch* ☜ *62 rooms, 3 suites* ♨ *Restaurant, in-room data ports, in-room fax, minibars, bar, meeting rooms; no a/c* ▤ *AE, DC, MC, V.*

$$-$$$ ☷ **Radisson SAS.** A 10-minute walk from the Old Town, this glass-and-steel business hotel has crisp, stylish rooms with spacious baths. The hotel staff is outgoing and extremely accommodating. Many locals and tourists come to try their luck at the casino. ⊠ *St. Jakobstr. 55, CH-900* ☎ *071/2421212* ☐ *071/2421200* ⊕ *www.tagungen-st-gallen.ch* ☜ *105 rooms, 15 suites* ♨ *Restaurant, in-room data ports, in-room fax, minibars, gym, sauna, casino, business services, meeting rooms, no-smoking rooms* ▤ *AE, DC, MC, V.*

$$ ☷ **Weissenstein.** With as quiet a location as you can get in the heart of the city, this hotel is all about relaxation. Comfy Swedish feather duvets cover large double beds; a rarity in a region where "double" usually means two singles pushed together. Bathrooms are small but up-to-date. In summer you can take your breakfast on the shady terrace. ⊠ *Davidstr. 22, CH-9000* ☎ *071/2280628* ☐ *071/2260630* ⊕ *www.cityweissenstein.ch* ☜ *20 rooms* ♨ *Restaurant, in-room data ports, in-room safes, minibars* ▤ *AE, DC, MC, V* ⊙I *BP.*

$-$$ ☷ **Vadian.** A narrow town house tucked behind half-timber landmarks in the Old Town, this is a discreet and tidy little place with an alcohol-free policy. Most of its tiny rooms have beige stucco walls, knotty pine furniture, and modern tile baths. Rooms without bath are a better bargain. ⊠ *Gallusstr. 36, CH-9000* ☎ *071/2281878* ☐ *071/2281879*

⊕ *www.hotel-vadian.com* ⚘ *13 rooms, 6 with bath* ⚘ *No a/c* ⊟ *AE, DC, MC, V* ⌖ *BP.*

$ ⊞ **Elite.** The decor may be functional but the staff is friendly at this lodging in Old Town. Its style harkens back to 1950s modern deco. Half the rooms have baths; the others have only sinks and thus cost less. The rooms away from the street are quieter. ⊠ *Metzgerg. 9/11, CH-9004* ☎ *071/ 2221236* ⊟ *071/2222177* ⊕ *www.hotel-elite-sg.com* ⚘ *26 rooms, 13 with bath* ⚘ *No a/c* ⊟ *AE, DC, MC, V* ⌖ *BP.*

Sports & the Outdoors

Ⓒ **Säntispark.** Just outside St. Gallen lies this year-round, family-friendly sports and spa park. There is something to please (and exhaust) everyone—racquet sports, bowling, miniature golf, billiards. Children can dive into the wave pool at the water park and enjoy the rides and playgrounds. For relaxing, there's a solarium, sauna, and massage center. Equipment can be rented; most activities cost under 20 SF. ⊹ *From main train station in St. Gallen, 15 min by Bus 7 (Abtwil), or by car along Hwy. A1, exit Winkeln* ☎ *071/3131515* ⊕ *www.saentispark.ch* ▱ *Free* ☉ *Weekdays 9 AM–10 PM, weekends 8 AM–10 PM.*

Shopping

ANTIQUE PRINTS   An outstanding assortment of antique prints of Swiss landscapes and costumes is sold at a broad range of prices at **Osvald Oliver** (⊠ Marktg. 26 ☎ 071/2235016). The pictures are cataloged alphabetically by canton for easy browsing.

TEXTILES &   Although the region's textile industry has now shrunk substantially, it's
EMBROIDERY   still world renowned for its quality. You'll find some fine examples at **Rocco Textil** (⊠ Spiserg. 41 ☎ 071/2222407), which has a small but wonderful selection of embroidery, linens, and lace. The shop is an especially good source for custom work. **Sturzenegger** (⊠ Marktg. 21 ☎ 071/ 2224576), the better-known embroidery firm, established in 1883, sells its own line of linens and lingerie, designed and manufactured in the factory a block away.

Appenzell

⓲ *20 km (12 mi) south of St. Gallen, 98 km (60 mi) southeast of*
Fodor'sChoice *Schaffhausen.*
★

Isolated from St. Gallen by a ridge of green hills, Appenzell is one of Switzerland's quieter regions. The city of St. Gallen melts away into undulating hills spotted with doe-eyed cows, a steep-pastured, isolated verdure reminiscent of the Ozarks. Prim, symmetrical cottages inevitably show rows of windows facing the valley. Named Appenzell after the Latin *abbatis cella* (abbey cell), the region served as a sort of colony to the St. Gallen abbey, and its tradition of fine embroidery dates from those early days. The perfect chance to see this embroidery is during a local festival, such as the Alpfahrten, when cows are herded down the mountains. Women's hair is coiffed in tulle, and their dresses have intricate embroidery and lace, often with an edelweiss motif; men wear embroidered red vests and suspenders decorated with edelweiss or cow figures. These traditional costumes are taken very seriously; they can cost thousands of francs, but in this case, pride supersedes economy. A small highway (No. 3) leads into the hills through Teufen; the quaint Appenzell–Teufen–Gais rail line also serves the region.

The town of Appenzell blends some of the best and worst of the region, offering tourists a concentrated and somewhat self-conscious sampling of the culture. Its streets lined with bright-painted homes, bakeries full of Birnebrot and souvenir Biber, and shops full of machine-made embroidery, Appenzell seems to watch the tourists warily and get on with its life while profiting from the attention. Its **Landsgemeindeplatz** in the town center is the site of the famous open-air elections (until 1991, for men only), which take place the last Sunday in April. Embroidery is big business here, but it's rare to find handmade examples of the local art; though women still do fine work at home, it's generally reserved for gifts or heirlooms. Instead, large factories have sprung up in Appenzell country, and famous fine-cotton handkerchiefs sold in specialty shops around the world are made by machine here at the Dörig, Alba, and Lehner plants.

The **Museum Appenzell** showcases handicrafts and local traditions, regional history, and an international embroidery collection—it's a good general overview of the area's history and culture. The building itself dates from 1560. An English-language guide is available. ✉ *Hauptg. 4* ☎ *071/7889631* 🌐 *www.museum.ai.ch* 🎫 *5 SF* ⏲ *Apr.–Oct., daily 10–noon and 2–5; Nov.–Mar., Tues.–Sun. 2–5.*

Where to Stay & Eat

$–$$ ✕ **Traube.** The traditional interior here may be understated, but in summer the outside terrace overlooks a lovely landscaped garden hidden from major streets. The menu leans to pork and potatoes; fondue and Appenzeller *Chäshörnli* (cheese and macaroni) round out the mostly heavy offerings. The daily lunch special is usually under 20 SF. ✉ *Marktg. 7* ☎ *071/7871407* 💳 *MC, V* ⏲ *Closed Mon.*

★ **$$** ✕🏨 **Appenzell.** This comfortable lodging has all the gabled Gemütlichkeit of its neighbors, with a view over the Landsgemeindeplatz. Homey rooms, warmed with polished wood, owe their airiness to the traditional rows of windows. The fine woodwork and antiques in the breakfast room are remnants of the previous house on the property. The brightly lit restaurant offers fresh interpretations of regional fare, such as the *Hauptgass* (an Appenzeller cheese gratin with pork, prosciutto, and tomato), plus a selection of healthful and vegetarian dishes. ✉ *Landsgemeindepl., CH-9050* ☎ *071/7881515* 📠 *071/7881551* 🌐 *www.hotel-appenzell.ch* 🛏 *16 rooms* 👍 *Restaurant, café, patisserie, in-room data ports, Internet, no-smoking rooms; no a/c* 💳 *AE, DC, MC, V* 🍽 *BP.*

★ **$** ✕🏨 **Hof.** One of Appenzell's most popular restaurants serves hearty regional meats and cheese specialties, such as *Käseschnitte* (cheese toast) and *Käsespätzli* (Spätzli with cheese), to locals and tourists who crowd elbow to elbow along shared tables and talk over the clatter from the bar. The rustic-wood decor, ladder-back chairs, and the display of sports trophies add to the local atmosphere. If you can still move after all that cheese, play skittles at the in-house lanes after dinner. The furnishings, walls, and floors of the rooms upstairs are all blond wood, making them resemble saunas. ✉ *Engelg. 4, CH-9050* ☎ *071/7874030* 📠 *071/*

7875883 ⊕ *www.gasthaus-hof.ch* ⟿ *17 rooms* ⟳ *Restaurant; no a/c* ▭ *AE, DC, MC, V* ⊺⊙⊺ *BP.*

$$–$$$ ⊞ **Säntis.** A member of the Romantik hotel group, this prestigious hotel has a crisp and formal ambience, though the earliest wing has been a hotel-restaurant since 1835. Old-style touches—inlaid wood furnishings, painted beams—mix comfortably with the jewel-tone rooms and gleaming walnut cabinetry; some rooms have four-poster or canopy beds. The first-floor restaurant serves slightly Frenchified regional specialties in either of two wood-lined dining rooms, one Biedermeier, the other a folksy Appenzeller style. Guests can borrow bikes for free. ✉ *Landsgemeindepl., CH-9050* ☎ *071/7881111* 🖷 *071/7881110* ⊕ *www.romantikhotels.com/Appenzell* ⟿ *31 rooms, 6 suites* ⟳ *Restaurant, in-room safes, minibars, sauna, bar, no-smoking rooms; no a/c* ▭ *AE, DC, MC, V* ☉ *Closed early Jan.–early Feb.* ⊺⊙⊺ *BP.*

$–$$ ⊞ **Löwen.** Wising up to travelers' quests for "typical" local decor, the owners of this renovated 1780 guest house furnished several rooms in authentic Appenzeller style, with embroidered linens and built-in armoires painted with bright designs and naive local scenes—some actually reflecting the views from the window. Standard rooms in dormitory-style oak also are available for a slightly lower price. ✉ *Hauptg. 25, CH-9050* ☎ *071/7888787* 🖷 *071/7888788* ⊕ *www.loewen-appenzell.ch* ⟿ *19 rooms, 9 suites* ⟳ *Restaurant, in-room safes, minibars, sauna, bar, meeting rooms; no a/c* ▭ *AE, DC, MC, V* ⊺⊙⊺ *BP.*

$ ⊞ **Freudenberg.** With its vantage point on a velvety green hillside overlooking town, this modern chalet with gray and blue trim is the most scenic and tranquil hotel you'll find in the area. Rooms are bright and airy, with Appenzeller murals and modern, white-tile bathrooms. Four rooms have balconies, and the broad, shaded café shares the pretty views. ✉ *Riedstr. 57, CH-9050* ☎ *071/7871240* 🖷 *071/7878642* ⊕ *www.hotelfreudenberg.ch* ⟿ *7 rooms* ⟳ *Restaurant, café; no a/c* ▭ *AE* ⊺⊙⊺ *BP.*

Shopping

CHEESES   Picnickers can sample the different grades of Appenzeller cheese and its unsung mountain rivals at **Mösler** (✉ Hauptg. 25 ☎ 071/7871317). **Sutter** (✉ Marktstr. 8 ☎ 071/7871333) has a good selection of locally made cheeses.

EMBROIDERY   True, locally made hand embroidery is rare in Appenzell. Many handkerchiefs that beautifully reproduce the blindingly close work that locals no longer pursue have been hand-stitched in Portugal. Though an odd souvenir, they capture the spirit of Appenzell handwork better than much of the pretty, though broad, machine work available in the stores. **Margreiter** (✉ Hauptg. 29 ☎ 071/7873313) carries a large stock of machine-made handkerchiefs from the local Dörig, Alba, and Lehner factories, many decorated with edelweiss or other Alpine flowers. **Trachtenstube** (✉ Hauptg. 23 ☎ 071/7871606) offers high-quality local handiwork—lace, embroidery, and crafts.

LIQUEURS   Butchers, bakers, and liquor shops up and down the streets offer souvenir bottles of Appenzeller Bitter (Alpenbitter), a very sweet aperitif made in town. A well-balanced eau-de-vie called Appenzeller Kräuter, made of blended herbs, is another specialty.

CloseUp

THE BEST OFFENSE?

There is an article in Liechtenstein's constitution that states that every able-bodied man up to 60 years old must be prepared to defend his country at a moment's notice, but there hasn't been an official army since 1868. It wasn't always so: Liechtenstein was treaty-bound in the 18th century to contribute five men to the army of the Holy Roman Empire, as well as to cover the expenses of "half a cavalryman." This was increased to 80 men when Liechtenstein joined the German Confederation in 1814, but the expense of keeping an armed force was so steep that it was disbanded after the Austro-Prussian War came to a close. Since then, the only peacekeepers in the country have been the police force, which is augmented whenever necessary by a contingent of auxiliary service members. When all else fails, Switzerland has been known to offer its troops for civil service, such as helping to combat floods or mountain slides.

Stein

⑲ *13 km (8 mi) northwest of Appenzell, 94 km (58 mi) southeast of Schaffhausen.*

The quiet village of Stein (not to be confused with Stein-am-Rhein) consists of little more than sturdy old farmhouses and red-roof homes with the obligatory geraniums in window boxes. At the **Schaukäserei** (showcase dairy), modern cheese-making methods are demonstrated. Note that cheese is made 9–2 only. ☎ *071/3685070* ⊕ *www.showcheese.ch* ⊠ *Free* ⊙ *Mon.–Sat. 9–5, Sun. 8–7.*

The **Appenzeller Volkskunde Museum** (Folklore Museum) displays Appenzell arts and crafts, local costumes, and hand-painted furniture. ☎ *071/ 3685056* ⊕ *www.appenzeller-museum-stein.ch* ⊠ *7 SF* ⊙ *Mon. 1:30–5, Tues.–Sat. 10–noon and 1:30–5, Sun. 10–5.*

Urnäsch

⑳ *10 km (6 mi) west of Appenzell, 110 km (68 mi) southeast of Schaffhausen.*

If you're interested in a traditional festival, you'll want to head to this modest countryside town on December 31 or January 13. New Year's and Old New Year's (according to the Julian calendar) are both celebrated with an early morning parade of *Chläuse,* men done up in amazingly complicated masks, huge headpieces, and costumes made of bark, moss, and branches. Some of them wear enormous cowbells around their necks as well. It's a good idea to reserve a table for lunch at one of the local restaurants so you don't get left out in the cold— the parade draws crowds of spectators. Contact the Urnäsch tourist office for more information.

The **Museum für Appenzeller Brauchtum** (Museum of Appenzeller Tradition) displays costumes, cowbells, a cheese wagon, and examples of farmhouse living quarters. ☎ *071/3642322* ⊕ *www.museum-urnaesch.ch* ✉ *6 SF* ⊘ *Apr.–Oct., daily 1:30–5; Nov.–Mar., by appointment only.*

Mt. Säntis

㉑ *11 km (7 mi) southeast of Urnäsch, 121 km (75 mi) southeast of Schaffhausen.*

For a pleasurable high-altitude excursion out of Appenzell southwest to the hamlet of Schwägalp, a cable car that departs every 30 minutes carries you up to the peak of Mt. Säntis, at 8,209 feet the highest in the region and with beautiful views of the Bodensee as well as of the Graubünden and Bernese Alps. The very shape of the summit—an arc of jutting rock that swings up to the jagged peak housing the station—is spectacular. ☎ *071/3656565* ✉ *34 SF round-trip* ⊘ *Mid-June–Oct. Sun.–Thurs. 7:30–6, Fri. and Sat. 7:30–6:30; Nov.–mid-June, daily 8:30–5.*

Toggenburg Valley

㉒ *Entrance 11 km (7 mi) south of Mt. Säntis, 132 km (82 mi) southeast of Schaffhausen.*

A scenic pre-Alpine resort area popular with locals but relatively unexplored by outsiders, this is an ideal place for skiers and hikers who hate crowds. In the rugged Upper Toggenburg, weather-boarded dwellings surround the neighboring resorts of Wildhaus (birthplace of religious reformer Huldrych Zwingli), Unterwasser, and Alt-St. Johann. As they lie within shouting distance of each other, the ski facilities can be shared, and the jagged teeth of the mountains behind provide a dramatic backdrop.

If you're interested in the Reformation, you may want to make a pilgrimage to Wildhaus's **Zwinglihaus,** the farmhouse where Huldrych Zwingli was born in 1484. His father was president of the village's political commune, and the house was used as a meeting place for its council. A small museum within displays some restored furniture from his time, though not from his family, and an impressive collection of period Bibles. The fire-and-brimstone preacher celebrated his first mass in the town's now-Protestant church and went on to lead the Protestant Reformation in Zürich. ⊠ *Schönenboden, Wildhaus/Lisighaus* ☎ *071/9991625* ✉ *Free* ⊘ *June–mid-Nov. and Jan.–mid-Apr., Tues.–Sun. 2–4.*

Skiing

Equally popular with locals, the triplet ski resorts of **Wildhaus, Unterwasser, and Alt-St. Johann** combine forces to draw visitors into the Churfirsten "paradise" in the Toggenburg Valley. Here you'll find altitudes and drops to suit even jaded skiers, the most challenging starting on the 6,809-foot-high Gamserrugg and winding down 3,280 feet to Wildhaus itself; a medium-difficult rival winds from Chäserrugg (7,419 feet) all the way down to Unterwasser. A one-day pass for all three resorts costs 47 SF; a five-day pass costs 180 SF; a seven-day pass costs 225 SF. There are ski schools in all three resorts. For reservations, call the **Wildhaus chamber of commerce** (☎ 071/9999911).

Alt-St. Johann, at 2,952 feet, has one chairlift and two T-bars. Unterwasser, at 2,985 feet, has one funicular railway, one cable car, four T-bars, 50 km (31 mi) of downhill runs, 45 km (28 mi) of cross-country trails, and 27 km (17 mi) of ski-hiking trails. At 3,601 feet, Wildhaus offers skiers four chairlifts, five T-bars, 50 km (31 mi) of downhill runs, 45 km (28 mi) of cross-country trails, and 27 km (17 mi) of ski-hiking trails.

Sports & the Outdoors

RACQUET SPORTS **Wildhaus** (☎ 071/9991211) has two outdoor tennis courts. **Unterwasser** (☎ 071/9993030) has three outdoor tennis courts and a tennis and squash center.

LIECHTENSTEIN & THE WALENSEE

When you cross the border from Switzerland into the principality of Liechtenstein, you will see license plates marked FL: this stands for Fürstentum Liechtenstein (Principality of Liechtenstein). You are leaving the world's oldest democracy and entering a monarchy that is the last remnant of the Holy Roman Empire—all 160 square km (59 square mi) of it.

This postage-stamp principality was created at the end of the 17th century, when a wealthy Austrian prince, Johann Adam von Liechtenstein, bought out two bankrupt counts in the Rhine Valley and united their lands. In 1719 he obtained an imperial deed from Emperor Karl VI, creating the principality of Liechtenstein. The noble family poured generations of wealth into the new country, improving its standard of living, and in 1862 an heir, Prince Johann the Good, helped Liechtenstein introduce its first constitution as a "democratic monarchy" in which the people and the prince share power equally.

Today the principality's 32,000 citizens enjoy one of the world's highest per-capita incomes and pay virtually no taxes. Its prosperous (though discreet) industries range from making jam to molding false teeth.

Back in Switzerland, the Walensee and Flumserberg region is sparsely populated, with a long lake flanked on both sides by steep mountains with beginner to intermediate ski areas. In summer the action moves downhill, where swimmers enjoy the cool water at several beaches along the lake.

Vaduz (Liechtenstein)

❷❸ *15 km (9 mi) southeast of the Toggenburg Valley, 159 km (98 mi) southeast of Schaffhausen.*

Arriving in downtown Vaduz (there are exits from the A13 expressway from both the north and the south), a visitor could make the mistake of thinking Liechtenstein's only attraction is its miniature scale. Liechtenstein's small **Briefmarkenmuseum** (Stamp Museum) demonstrates the principality's history as a maker of beautifully designed, limited-edition postage stamps. Have your passport stamped for 2 SF at the **Fremdenverkehrszentrale** (tourist office) in the same building. ⊠ *Städtle 37* ☎ *423/2366105* 🎫 *Free* ☉ *Daily 10–noon and 1:30–5.*

The **Kunstmuseum Liechtenstein** (Liechtenstein Museum of Art) offers ever-changing exhibitions, showing at any time only a fraction of the country's extraordinary art collection. The museum's holdings include items from the prince's world-famous art collection, ranging from paintings by Rembrandt and Rubens to Greek and Roman mythological art. ⊠ *Städtle 32* ☎ *423/2350300* ⊕ *www.kunstmuseum.li* 🖾 *12 SF* ⊘ *Tues., Wed., and Fri.–Sun., 10–5, Thurs. 10–8.*

The **Liechtensteinisches Landesmuseum** (National Museum), in a former tavern and customhouse with a modern annex built into the cliff, covers the geology, history, and folklore of the principality. ⊠ *Städtle 43* ☎ *423/2396820* ⊕ *www.landesmuseum.li* 🖾 *8 SF* ⊘ *Tues., Wed., and Fri.–Sun., 10–5, Thurs. 10–8.*

The **Ski Museum Vaduz** is a small shrine to Switzerland's preferred pastime. Here you'll find numerous variations on the Alpine theme, including skis, sleds, ski fashion, and literature. ⊠ *Fabrikweg 5* ☎ *423/2321502* ⊕ *www.skimuseum.li* 🖾 *6 SF* ⊘ *Weekdays 2–6, or by appointment.*

At the top of a well-marked hill road (you can climb the forest footpath behind the Engel hotel) stands **Vaduz Castle**. Here, His Serene Highness Hans–Adam II, reigning prince of Liechtenstein, duke of Troppau and Jaegerndorf, reigns in a gratifyingly romantic fortress-home with striped medieval shutters, massive ramparts, and a broad perspective over the Rhine Valley. Originally built in the 12th century, the castle was burned down by troops of the Swiss Confederation in the Swabian Wars of 1499 and partly rebuilt during the following centuries, until a complete overhaul that started in 1905 gave it its present form. It is not open to the public, as Hans-Adam II enjoys his privacy. He is the son of the late, beloved Franz Josef II, who died in November 1989 after a more than 50-year reign. Franz Josef's birthday, August 15, is still celebrated as the Liechtenstein national holiday. Hans-Adam II has been known to join the crowds below to watch the fireworks while wearing jeans.

Where to Stay & Eat

★ $ ✕ **Wirthschaft zum Löwen.** Though there's plenty of French, Swiss, and Austrian influence, Liechtenstein has a cuisine of its own, and this is the place to try it. In a wood-shingle landmark farmhouse on the Austrian border, the friendly Biedermann family serves tender homemade *Schwartenmagen* (the pressed-pork mold unfortunately known as headcheese in English), pungent *Sauerkäse* (sour cheese), and Käseknöpfli, plus lovely meats and the local crusty, chewy bread. Be sure to try the region's distinctive wines. When driving here on Route 16, keep an eye out for Schellenberg, posted to the left; if you zip past it, you'll end up in Austria. ⊠ *FL-9488 Schellenberg, 10 km (6 mi) north of Vaduz off Rte. 16* ☎ *423/3731162* ▤ *AE, MC, V.*

$$$$ ✕▣ **Park-Hotel Sonnenhof.** With a superb view over the valley and mountains beyond, this hillside retreat offers understated luxury minutes from downtown Vaduz. The clean, comfortable rooms are decorated in bright colors. The public areas are full of antiques, rugs, woodwork, and familial touches. The restaurant serves excellent, unstodgy French food, such as duck *à l'orange* with green beans and soybean sprouts.

⊠ *Mareestr. 29, FL-9490* ☎ *423/2390202* 🖷 *423/2390203* ⊕ *www.
sonnenhof.li* ⇗ *17 rooms, 12 suites* ⚒ *Restaurant, in-room safes, minibars, pool, sauna, meeting rooms; no a/c* ⊟ *AE, DC, MC, V* ⊘ *Closed
late Dec.–early Jan.* ⦿| *BP.*

★ **$$–$$$** ✕⊞ **Real.** Here you'll find rich, old-style Austrian-French cuisine pre-
pared by Martin Real, son of the unpretentious former chef, Felix
Real—who still presides over the 20,000-bottle wine cellar. There's an
abundance of game in season, richly sauced seafood, and soufflés.
Downstairs, the more casual Stübli atmosphere is just right for *Geschnetzeltes mit Rösti* (veal in cream sauce with hash brown potatoes). Upstairs in this Relais & Châteaux establishment, the guest rooms are small
but airily decorated. ⊠ *Städtle 21, FL-9490* ☎ *423/2322222* 🖷 *423/
2320891* ⊕ *www.hotel-real.li* ⇗ *11 rooms, 2 suites* ⚒ *Restaurant,
Stübli, in-room safes, minibars; no a/c* ⊟ *AE, DC, MC, V* ⦿| *BP.*

$–$$ ✕⊞ **Engel.** This elegant, centrally located hotel-restaurant has a com-
fortable local ambience despite the tour-bus crowds. The restaurant downstairs dishes up home cooking, and there's a *Biergarten* (beer garden)
where Liechtensteiners meet. Upstairs, the more formal restaurant serves
Chinese cuisine. The guest rooms are in fresh colors, with tile bathrooms.
⊠ *Städtle 13, FL-9490* ☎ *423/2361717* 🖷 *423/2331159* ⇗ *20 rooms*
⚒ *Restaurant, minibars, pub; no a/c* AE, DC, MC, V.

Sports & the Outdoors

BICYCLES & In Triesen (4 km [2½ mi] south of Vaduz), bikes can be rented from **Bike**
MOTORCYCLES **Garage** (⊠ Landstr. 256 ☎ 423/3900390).

TENNIS **Vaduz** (☎ 423/2327720) has public covered courts on Schaanerstrasse.
Covered courts are also accessible in nearby **Schaan** (☎ 423/2332343).
Rental equipment is available.

Shopping

POTTERY Though shops on the main street of Vaduz carry samples of the local
dark-glaze pottery, painted with folksy flowers and figures, the central
source is 8 km (5 mi) north of Vaduz at **Schaedler Keramik** (⊠ Rte. 16,
Nendeln ☎ 423/3731414). Simpler household pottery is available for
sale as well as the traditional and often ornate hand-painted pieces. Pottery making is demonstrated daily. The shop is open weekdays 8–5.

STAMPS Liechtenstein is sometimes called the unofficial, per capita world champion of stamp collecting. To buy some of its famous stamps, whether
to send a postcard to a philatelist friend or to invest in limited-issue commemorative sheets, you must line up with the tour-bus crowds at the
popular **post office** (⊠ Städtle).

Triesenberg (Liechtenstein)

㉔ *3 km (2 mi) southeast of Vaduz, 162 km (100 mi) southeast of
Schaffhausen.*

This cluster of pretty chalets clings to the mountainside, with panoramic
views over the Rhine Valley. Triesenberg was settled in the 13th century
by immigrants from the Valais in southwestern Switzerland. The **Walser
Heimatmuseum** (Valais Heritage Museum) traces the culture of these im-

migrants. Furnishings and tools from farmers and craftsmen are displayed, and an entertaining 20-minute slide show (in English) illustrates their Alpine roots. ⊠ *Dorfenzentrum* ☎ *423/2621926* ⊕ *www.triesenberg. li* ⊠ *2 SF* ⊘ *Sept.–May, Tues.–Fri. 1:30–5:30, Sat. 1:30–5; June–Aug., Tues.–Fri. 1:30–5:30, Sat. 1:30–5, Sun. 2–5.*

Malbun (Liechtenstein)

㉕ *5 km (3 mi) southeast of Triesenberg, 167 km (103 mi) southeast of Schaffhausen.*

In winter this 5,250-foot-high mountain resort near the Austrian border draws crowds of local families who come for the varied slopes, many of which are well suited to beginners. England's Prince Charles and Princess Anne learned to ski here while visiting the Liechtenstein royal family in Vaduz. In summer Malbun becomes a quiet, unpretentious resort with reasonable prices.

Skiing

Malbun is a sunny, natural bowl with low, easy slopes and a couple of difficult runs; you can ride a chairlift to the top of the Sareiserjoch and experience the novelty of skiing from the Austrian border back into Liechtenstein. Facilities are concentrated at the center, including hotels and cafés overlooking the slopes. The resort also has a **ski school** (☎ 423/2639770). One-day lift tickets cost 37 SF; five-day passes cost 150 SF.

Where to Stay

$–$$$ ⊡ **Alpenhotel.** The Vögeli family's welcoming smiles and good food have made this remodeled chalet a Liechtenstein institution. The old rooms are small, with creaky pine trim; the higher-priced rooms are modern stucco. ⊠ *Malbun FL-9490* ☎ *423/2631181* 🖨 *423/2639646* ◄╝ *21 rooms* ⚂ *Restaurant, café, minibars, pool* ☰ *AE, DC, MC, V.*

Sports & the Outdoors

Liechtenstein has a 162-km (100-mi) network of Alpine hiking trails, and another 243 km (150 mi) of valley hiking. Malbun and Steg are ideal starting points for mountain hikes. You can get trail maps at the tourist office or at magazine kiosks.

Flumserberg

㉖ *25 km (15 mi) west of Malbun, 122 km (75 mi) southeast of Schaffhausen.*

On the windswept, timberless slopes overlooking the Walensee and the Churfirsten Mountains, this resort is the site of one of the world's longest cableways. Over a distance of about 3 km (2 mi), a procession of little four-seater cabins reaches up to the rocky summit at **Leist,** 6,743 feet up.

Skiing

Flumserberg, spanning 3,936 feet–7,288 feet, has five cable cars, 10 chairlifts, four T-bars, 60 km (40 mi) of downhill runs, 21 km (13 mi) of cross-country trails, and 20 km (12 mi) of mountain trails. The runs are suitable for beginner to intermediate skiers. You can also endeavor to skate, skibob, night ski, or snowboard in the Funpark, where snow is molded into jumps and half pipes. A **ski school** (☎ 081/7333939) provides help for the less proficient. The German-only *Schneebericht* (☎ 081/7201510) gives current information on snow conditions. One-day lift tickets cost 49 SF; six-day passes are 221 SF.

Walensee

㉗ *5 km (3 mi) northwest of Flumserberg, 127 km (78 mi) southeast of Schaffhausen.*

Between Liechtenstein and Zürich, the spectacular, mirrorlike lake called the Walensee is a deep emerald gash that stretches 16 km (10 mi) through the mountains, reflecting the jagged Churfirsten peaks. At the western end of the Walensee, **Weesen** is a quiet, shady resort noted for its mild climate and lovely lakeside walkway. Six kilometers (4 mi) north of Weesen on a winding mountain road lies **Amden,** perched 3,116 feet above the Walensee in the relatively undiscovered region south of the Churfirsten Mountains.

Skiing

Despite its small size, **Amden** is a major winter sports center, offering modest skiing in a ruggedly beautiful setting. Easy and medium slopes with unspectacular drops and quick, short-lift runs provide good weekend getaways for crowds of local Swiss families. The highest trails start at 5,576 feet; there are a chairlift, three T-bars, one children's lift, 25 km (16 mi) of downhill runs, and 8 km (5 mi) of cross-country trails. You can also take advantage of the **ski school** (☎ 055/6111560), a natural ice rink, and walking paths. One-day lift tickets cost 29 SF; six-day passes cost 125 SF.

Sports & the Outdoors

For sports enthusiasts, **Amden** also has a public **open-air skating rink,** the heated indoor pool **Hallenbad Amden** (☎ 055/6111588), and an **outdoor tennis court** (☎ 055/6112089). There are also many **public beaches** that dot the southern shore of the Walensee.

off the
beaten
path

RAPPERSWIL – Between the Walensee and Zürich, about 36 km (22 mi) northwest of Weesen and 40 km (24 mi) southeast of Zürich, this small town on Zürichsee (Lake Zürich) offers pleasant views and summertime waterfront strolls. Three rose gardens in the town center, including one for people with disabilities, account for Rapperswil's claim as the "Swiss City of Roses." A forbidding 13th-century **SCHLOSS RAPPERSWIL –** looks like part of a Gothic novel, with a trio of grave towers. Inside the castle is the small **Polenmuseum** (☎ 055/2101862), which highlights the history of Polish immigrants to Switzerland. It's open weekends from 1 to 5 in November, December, and March, and daily from 1 to 5 from April to October; admission is 4 SF. The castle's walkway faces a small deer park and affords a view of Zürich; from the terrace you'll see the Glarus Alps. At the **Knie's Kinderzoo** (☎ 055/2206760), there are dolphin shows, 70 types of animals from around the world, elephant and pony rides, and plenty of creatures to feed and pet. It's open mid-March through October Monday through Saturday from 9 to 6, Sunday from 9 to 7, and admission is 10 SF. Follow signs; it's near the train station.

EASTERN SWITZERLAND A TO Z

To research prices, get advice from other travelers, and book travel arrangements, visit www.fodors.com.

AIRPORTS

Unique Zürich Airport, just north of Zürich, is about 48 km (30 mi) south of Schaffhausen, about 75 km (46 mi) west of St. Gallen, and 130 km (81 mi) northwest of Liechtenstein.

🛪 Airport Information **Unique Zürich Airport** ☎ 0900/300313.

BOAT & FERRY TRAVEL

Swiss Federal Railways provides regular year-round service on the Bodensee through Schweizer Bodensee Schiffahrtgesellschaft (Swiss Bodensee Cruiseline Co.), though fewer boats run in winter. The Schweizerisches Schiffahrtgesellschaft Untersee und Rhein ship company offers a winning combination of a boat ride on the Rhine with romantic views of storybook castles, citadels, and monasteries. Boats run regularly up- and downstream, docking at Schaffhausen, Stein-am-Rhein, Gottlieben, Konstanz, and Kreuzlingen. Prices vary according to the distance traveled. A one-way trip from Schaffhausen to Kreuzlingen takes about 4½ hours. On both boat lines, you'll travel free if you have a Swiss Pass.

🛪 Boat & Ferry Information **Schweizer Bodensee Schiffahrtgesellschaft** ☎ 071/4667888. **Schweizerisches Schiffahrtgesellschaft Untersee und Rhein** ✉ Freierpl. 7, CH-8202 Schaffhausen ☎ 052/6340888.

BUS TRAVEL

The famous yellow postbuses provide much of the public transport in areas not served by trains, particularly to smaller towns and Liechtenstein, which has no rail service. The bus schedules are usually posted outside the town post office, but you can also obtain information from any train station. The smallest towns have one bus in the morning and one in the evening. In larger towns, buses run several times a day.

CAR TRAVEL

The A1 expressway from Zürich heads for St. Gallen through Winterthur. To reach Schaffhausen from Zürich, take A1 to Winterthur, then head north on the cantonal highway E41/15. You also can leave Zürich by way of the A4 expressway past Unique Zürich Airport, crossing through Germany briefly and entering Schaffhausen through Neuhausen am Rheinfall. From the south, the A13 expressway, shared with Austria, leads you from Chur along Liechtenstein to the east end of the Bodensee; from there, you take A1 into St. Gallen. Liechtenstein is best reached by car; from Zürich, take the A1 expressway to Sargans, then change to the A13 heading north and take the Vaduz exit. From St. Gallen, follow the A1 northeast to the Bodensee, where it changes into the A13. Follow this south approximately 50 km (31 mi) to the Vaduz exit.

Driving in eastern Switzerland allows you to see the best of this region; Highway 13 goes along the south shores of the Untersee and Bodensee and continues up through the hills to Appenzell. Neither St. Gallen nor Schaffhausen is a big enough city to warrant all-out panic, although you'll find it easiest to head directly for the center and abandon the car for the duration of your visit. Try to get into a parking lot, as finding a spot on the street can be difficult. In Schaffhausen, there's underground parking at the Stadttheater underneath Herrenacker. In St. Gallen, the Old Town is surrounded by underground parking lots. You'll find entrances on Burggraben, Oberergraben, and, most conveniently, on St. Georgenstrasse, right by the abbey.

EMERGENCIES

⌗ Police ☎ 117. Ambulance ☎ 144. Doctor, dentist, late-night pharmacies ☎ 111. Medical assistance St. Gallen ☎ 071/4941111.

TOURS

The Schaffhausen tourist office gives daily guided walking tours with English commentary of the Old Town, the monastery, and the Munot. For a unique take on the city, try one of the nighttime guided walks which focus on murders, pestilence, public hangings, and other dark events, available in English on request.

⌗ Tours **Schaffhausen tourist office** ✉ Herrenacker 15, CH-8201 ☎ 052/6324020 ⊕ www. schaffhausen-tourismus.ch.

TRAIN TRAVEL

A connection by train from the Zürich Hauptbahnhof into the SBB Bahnhof Schaffhausen takes about 40 minutes; into SBB Bahnhof St. Gallen or Sargans, about an hour. Connections from the south (Graubünden) are more difficult, as both Austria and the Alps intervene.

Rail connections are somewhat complicated in this area, especially if you want to visit more of Appenzell than its major towns. Schaffhausen and St. Gallen are the main hubs from which regional trains head into the countryside and along the Bodensee. The only railroads into the canton are the narrow-gauge line between St. Gallen and the town of Appenzell, which passes Teufen and Gais, and the Gossau–Appenzell–Wasserauen line. To see more of the territory, you may return to St. Gallen on this same line by way of Herisau.

Although there is no regional rail pass available for eastern Switzerland, the general Swiss Pass rail pass (available from Switzerland Tourism and from travel agents outside Switzerland) includes St. Gallen and Schaffhausen city transit as well as overall rail privileges. You cannot enter Liechtenstein by rail; the international express train that passes between Switzerland and Austria doesn't bother to stop in Liechtenstein. From the train stations at Buchs or Sargans, you can catch a postbus into Vaduz.

⌗ Train Information **SBB Bahnhof Schaffhausen** ☎ 051/2234500. **SBB Bahnhof St. Gallen** ☎ 051/2280280.

VISITOR INFORMATION

The tourist office for all of eastern Switzerland is based in St. Gallen. There are small regional visitor information offices throughout eastern Switzerland. Liechtenstein's office is in its capital.

🛈 **Main Tourist Offices Tourismusverband Ostschweiz** (Tourist Association of Eastern Switzerland) ✉ Bahnhofpl. 1a, St. Gallen CH-9001 ☎ 071/2273737 🖷 071/2273767 ⊕ www.ostschweiz-i.ch. **Liechtenstein** ✉ Städtle 37, FL-9490 Vaduz ☎ 423/2396300 🖷 423/2396301 ⊕ www.tourismus.li.

🛈 **Regional Tourist Offices Appenzellerland** ✉ Hauptg. 4, CH-9050 Appenzell ☎ 071/7889641 ⊕ www.appenzell.ch. **Schaffhausen** ✉ Herrenacker 15, CH-8201 ☎ 052/6324020 ⊕ www.schaffhausen-tourismus.ch. **Stein-am-Rhein** ✉ Oberstadt 3, CH-8260 ☎ 052/7422090 ⊕ www.stein-am-rhein.ch. **Thurgau** ✉ Arbonerstr. 2, CH-8580 Amriswil ☎ 071/4118181 ⊕ www.thurgau-tourismus.ch. **Urnäsch** ✉ Dorf 78, CH-9107 ☎ 071/3642640 ⊕ www.urnaesch.appenzell.ch.

GRAUBÜNDEN
AROSA, DAVOS, ST. MORITZ

3

Updated by
Marton Radkai

THOUGH THE NAMES OF ITS RESORTS—St. Moritz, Davos, Klosters, Arosa—register almost automatic recognition, the region wrapped around them remains surprisingly little known. Resort life in winter contrasts sharply with the everyday existence of the native mountain farmers.

Graubünden is the largest canton in Switzerland, covering more than one-sixth of the entire country. As it straddles the continental divide, its rains pour off north into the Rhine, eastward with the Inn to the Danube and Black Sea, and south to the River Po. The landscape is thus riddled with bluff-lined valleys, and its southern half basks in crystalline light: except for the Italian-speaking Ticino, it receives the most sunshine in the country. Its 150 valleys and 615 lakes are flanked by 937 peaks, among them Piz Buin (10,867 feet) in the north and Piz Bernina (13,307 feet) in the south, the canton's highest mountain.

Like many Swiss Cantons, Graubünden is culturally diverse. To the north it borders Austria and Liechtenstein, and in the east and south it abuts Italy. Swiss-German and Italian are widely spoken. The ancient Romansh language (literally, "Roman") is still predominant in the Lower Engadine and Surselva; it is estimated that 30% of Graubünden residents can speak it. The language dates back to the 1st century BC, when the area was conquered by the Romans and became a province called Rhaetia Prima. Some say the tongue predates the Romans and originated as long ago as 600 BC, when an Etruscan prince named Rhaetus invaded the region.

Anyone versed in a Latin language can follow Romansh's simpler signs (*abitaziun da vacanzas,* for example, is a vacation apartment), but Romansh is fragmented into five dialects, which developed separately in formerly isolated valleys, so that depending on where you are, the word for *house* can be seen written on the facades of homes as *casa, chasa, chesa, tga/tgesa, or tgea.* The name *Graubünden*—Grisons (French), Grigioni (Italian), and Grischun (Romansh)—originates from the "Gray Confederation," one of three leagues that joined together in 1471 to resist the feudal Habsburg rulers. After a period as a "free state," Graubünden became a Swiss canton in 1803.

Exploring Graubünden

The region is fairly neatly bisected by a spine of 9,800-foot peaks into two very different sections connected by the Julier, Albula, and Flüela passes. In the north is the region's capital, Chur; to the west lies Surselva; and farther east are the famous ski resorts of Arosa, Klosters, and Davos. The southern part of the canton includes the Engadine, with its lakes, sophisticated resorts, and the National Park. The canton extends east to Austria and south toward Italy from the valleys of Bergell, Müstair, and Puschlav.

About the Restaurants & Hotels

Hoteliers in Graubünden invest fortunes in preserving Alpine coziness on both the outside and *inside* of their lodgings, which is not always the case in other parts of Switzerland. Wood is commonly used to soften interiors, and the source is often *Arvenholz*, the prized Swiss stone pine that grows here. Its wood is thick with knots and rich in natural color, which deepens over the years.

Tourism is one of the economic mainstays of Graubünden and therefore restaurants tend to stay open throughout the day for the hungry visitor. The way to be sure is to look for a sign that bears the word *durchgehend*, meaning without a stop. Some places, however, will serve only snacks—or close entirely—between around 2:30 and 5:30. If traveling in the low season (November or April), you may encounter quite a few closed doors. If you're on the move, you may want to avoid restaurants altogether and simply opt for a visit to the butcher, the cheese shop, and the baker to pick up some regional specialties to enjoy as a picnic. Finally, the rugged and remote mountainscape is deceiving. Hikers and skiers will frequently encounter a cozy *Bergbeizli*, literally a mountain inn, where fine locally grown food is served up in a most congenial atmosphere.

Prices in this popular region are comparatively high. Even higher prices can be charged for the winter holiday period and in February; during the rest of winter you may find special lower-priced packages that include ski tickets. Summer rates are also generally lower. Many hotels close between seasons, from April to mid-June and from mid-October to mid-December, but the dates and months vary each year, so be sure to check. In a few winter resorts there are hotels that stay closed all summer; we have not included these in our listings. Hotels publish tariffs in various ways; double-check to see whether you're paying per person or per room, as well as whether you have *demipension* (half board). If you plan to stay in one place for more than a day or two, half board can cut costs. You may also want to ask about *GästeKarte* (guest cards), small booklets given by hotels that provide various deals on local transit or attractions. These are distributed in some resort towns, including Klosters, Davos, and Flims/Laax.

WHAT IT COSTS In Swiss francs					
	$$$$	$$$	$$	$	¢
RESTAURANTS	over 60	40–60	25–40	15–25	under 15
HOTELS	over 350	250–350	175–250	100–175	under 100

Restaurant prices are per person for a main course at dinner. Hotel prices are for two people in a standard double room in high season, including tax and service.

Timing
Graubünden's resorts fill to capacity in winter. Thanks to a score of warm-weather sports such as hiking, biking, golfing, horseback riding, sailing, windsurfing, and even hot-air ballooning, there's a lot going on in summer as well. In early fall the weather is generally mild, with clear skies. Avoid visiting mountain resorts between mid-October and early December and between mid-April and mid-June; during these off-seasons, most hotels and cable cars close (exact dates vary from year to year, depending on factors such as planned renovations, snowfall, and the Easter holiday).

Numbers in the text correspond to numbers in the margin and on the Graubünden map.

If you have 2 days

If you approach Graubünden from the north on A13, begin by exploring the capital, **Chur ②**. Then take the train to 🚆 **Arosa ③** to ski or hike; it's a gorgeous trip in winter or summer. To see the countryside with its perched villages and tiny wooden chalet stations, sit on the right side of the train. To see the engine and first coaches winding ahead of you, take a seat between the middle or rear of the train. Alternatively, head 20 km (12½ mi) west from Chur, to **Flims ④** and the neighboring villages of Laax and Falera, to ski in winter or, in summer, to white-water raft or see the Hinterrhein gorge and the Alps from the basket of a balloon.

If you have 3 or 4 days

From **Chur ②** ☛ travel through the Prättigau valley, passing through the canton's wine-producing area around **Maienfeld ①**. Make 🚆 **Klosters ⑤** your base if you want peace and quiet, or drive over the Wolfgang Pass to 🚆 **Davos ⑥** if you're looking for an action-oriented trip.

If you have 5 or more days

Head for the Lower and Upper Engadine. The **Parc Naziunal Svizzer ⑩** ☛ (open June to October) is a magnificent federally protected nature reserve. If you're traveling by car, detour to visit the pretty village of **Guarda ⑦**. Spend a night in 🚆 **Scuol ⑧** or nearby Tarasp-Vulpera. To explore the Upper Engadine, aim for 🚆 **St. Moritz ⑭** or 🚆 **Sils ⑮**. You may want to take one of the Rhätische Bahn's special train trips (open carriages in summer, at the back of a snowplow in winter) over the Bernina Pass to Poschiavo. Or you can loop back to Chur, going over the Julier or the Albula pass (the latter is open in summer only).

HEIDI COUNTRY

The Maienfeld region, with its hills and craggy peaks sloping down to sheltered vineyards, is the gateway from the north into Graubünden, but its claim to fame is that the legendary Heidi lived here. To the west in Surselva, the villages of Flims, Laax, and Falera together form the Alpine Arena, Graubünden's biggest connected ski area. Arosa, to the east in the Schanfigg valley, is a quieter resort village that lies at the end of a spectacular, steep, winding road.

Maienfeld

① *17 km (11 mi) north of Chur.*

Surrounded by vineyards, the charming small towns of Maienfeld and Jenins provided the setting for Johanna Spyri's much-loved *Heidi*—a children's story of an orphan who grows up with her grandfather on an isolated Alpine farm. You can hike from Maienfeld along the Heidi-Weg (Heidi Path), either on the short circular route or continuing across steep open meadows and through thick forest to what have now been designated Peter the Goatherd's Hut and the Alm-Uncle's Hut. Here you might meet today's version of that character, who enjoys a chat and can answer Heidi-related questions in English. On both routes, you pass through **Heididorf** (Heidi Village), in reality the hamlet of Oberrofels. Here you can find the house that was used as a model for the illustrations in the original *Heidi* books. It now houses Heidi-appropriate furnishings and life-size models of Heidi, Grandfather, and Peter. ☎ *081/ 3301912* ⊕*www.heididorf.ch* ☜*5 SF* ⊘ *Mid-Mar.–mid-Nov., daily 10–5.*

As an alternative to walking the route, you can take a two-hour tour in a **horse-drawn carriage** (☎ 081/3301912). The cost is 30 SF per person. At the **Heidihof Hotel** (☎ 081/3004747), an extended farmhouse, have a snack and take in the view or spend the night. For the total "Heidi experience" you can sleep in straw at a nearby farm.

In Maienfeld, visit a few of the two dozen local wine merchants or have a meal in the Knight's Hall of **Schloss Brandis,** a castle whose earliest portions date from the 10th century. ☎ *081/3022423* ⊘ *Closed mid-July–mid-Aug.*

Across the river (and cantonal border), just three minutes by train, you can visit the famous spa center at **Bad Ragaz** with its indoor-outdoor warm pools. ☎ *081/3032741* ☜ *17 SF* ⊘ *Daily 7:30 AM–9 PM.*

Chur

▶ ❷ *17 km (11 mi) south of Maienfeld.*

A small city (and cantonal capital) of 35,000, with a modern downtown and a busy rail crossroads, Chur is actually the oldest continuously settled site north of the Alps. Recent discoveries of Stone Age tools put Chur's origins back to roughly 11,000 BC. The Romans founded Curia Raetorium on the rocky terrace south of the river; from here, they protected the Alpine routes that led to the Bodensee. By AD 284 the town served as the capital of the flourishing Roman colony Rhaetia Prima. Its heyday was during the Middle Ages, when it was ruled by bishops and bishop-princes. Narrow streets, cobblestone alleys, hidden courtyards, and ancient shuttered buildings still abound.

The **Rathaus** (Town Hall) was built as two structures in 1464 and connected in 1540. At ground level, under the arches, is the old marketplace. In the open hall on the second floor is a model of the Old Town, which can help you plan a tour of the city. The Grosser Ratsaal (Council Chamber) has a timber ceiling dating from 1493; the Bürgerratskammer (Citizens' Council Chamber) has wall panels from the Renaissance. Both chambers have old ceramic stoves, the one in the Ratsaal depicting the various deadly sins. Embedded in the wall beside the door opening onto Reichsgasse is a rod of iron about a foot long—the standard measure of a foot or shoe before the metric system was introduced. Although both chambers are generally closed to the public, very small groups can contact the tourist office to arrange a visit. ⊠ *Poststr.*

3

Dining

Graubünden, with its myriad dialects and potent blend of Latin and German blood, has a cuisine as novel and unexpected as its culture. The Graubünden idea of fast food is a *salsiz* (a kind of small, rectangular-shape salami) and a piece of bread. Besides regional specialties like the ubiquitous *Bündner-fleisch* (air-dried beef pressed into rectangular loaves and shaved into translucent slices), *Gerstensuppe* (barley soup), and *Nusstorte* (short-bread with a chewy walnut-and-caramel filling), you will find a broad range of international cooking, notably in the larger resorts. Italian influence is strong and the Germanic *Spätzli* (tiny flour dumplings) coexist with gnocchi, risotto, and polenta.

You may feel you've stepped back into the Middle Ages when you sit down to *pizzoccheri neri* (buckwheat noodles with greens and potatoes, swimming in garlic butter and melted cheese) or to *maluns* (grated potatoes stirred in pools of butter until they form crisp balls). *Capuns* or *chrutcapuns* are bundles of Swiss chard smothered in butter and cheese and flavored with dried meat. These down-to-earth treats are making a comeback in either traditional or more modern interpretations. Year-round, but especially in fall, many menus feature wild game: the centuries-old hunting tradition is especially strong in this canton. Look for *Reh* or *Hirsch* (roe or red deer) and *Gems* (chamois), usually served with red cabbage, fruits, and chestnuts or in a *Pfeffer* (strongly flavored, peppery stew).

Most restaurants' wine lists include a selection of the red pinot noir and white Riesling Sylvaner from the Bündnerherrschaft region around Maienfeld, Jenins, and Malans as well as the hearty red Nebbiolo of the Veltlin. The latter is actually grown over the southern border in Valtellina, which was ceded to Italy in 1815, but some quantities have always been brought in bulk into the canton for bottling and can be considered, at least in spirit, to be Swiss. As an alternative to wine, try one of the regional mineral waters: Valser, Passugger, or Rhäzünzer.

Many restaurants in resort towns close from the end of April to mid-June and October to December; there are variations and exceptions, of course, so if you plan a visit in the off-season, check in advance.

Skiing

With Davos, site of the world's first ski lift, St. Moritz, arguably the world's ritziest resort, and a host of other hot spots within its confines, Graubünden has earned its reputation as the ultimate winter destination. You'll find downhill skiing and snowboarding for all skill levels, as well as miles of *Langlauf* (cross-country skiing) trails prepared for both the classic and skating techniques. You can participate in moonlight or torchlight skiing at almost all of the resorts, usually followed by a get-together with your fellow travelers. Sports shops can outfit you with the necessary equipment; in Davos and Flims-Laax you can even rent ski clothing. If you plan to spend a few days in one resort, check with local tourist offices for special packages. If you want to spend a day in a different resort within Graubünden, buy the lift ticket with your train ticket and the return fare will be just 1 SF.

Trains The Rhätische Bahn, the network of trains that traverse Graubünden, is tailor-made for sightseeing. Its 400 km (248 mi) of narrow-gauge tracks run through some of Switzerland's most spectacular scenery. Special short trips for rail enthusiasts include excursions on three remaining steam locomotives and trips in open carriages over the Bernina Pass. The legendary *Glacier Express* from St. Moritz to Zermatt and trains throughout the region traverse spectacular terrain, the bright-red cars crossing bridges built unbelievably high over gorges and cutting through mountainsides.

The **Kirche St. Martin** (St. Martin's Church) was built in 1491 after a fire destroyed the original dating from the 8th century. Since 1526 it has been Protestant. On your right as you enter are three stained-glass windows created in 1919 by Augusto Giacometti, the father of the Graubünden sculptor Alberto Giacometti. The steeple dates from 1917; with permission from the sacristan, you can climb to the top to see the bells. ✉ *Evangel. Kirchgemeinde, Kirchg. 12* ☎ *081/2522292* ⊙ *Weekdays 8:30–11:30 and 2–5.*

The **Rätisches Museum** provides a thorough, evocative overview of the canton's development. Displayed in a 1675 mansion, the collection includes not only furnishings and goods from the period, but also archaeological finds from the region, both Roman and prehistoric. ✉ *Hofstr. 1* ☎ *081/2572889* 💶 *5 SF* ⊙ *Tues.–Sun. 10–noon and 2–5.*

Opposite the Rätisches Museum, a stone archway under the **Hof-Torturm** (Citadel Gate Tower) leads into the court of the strong bishop-princes of Chur, once hosts to Holy Roman emperors who passed through on their way between Italy and Germany—sometimes with whole armies in tow. The bishops were repaid for their hospitality by imperial donations to the people. The thick fortifications of the residence demonstrate the disputed powers of the bishops; by the 15th century, irate inhabitants who rebelled again and again were rebuffed and punished with excommunication. By 1526 the Reformation had broken the domination of the Church, although the city remains a Catholic bishopric today. The Hofkellerei Stübli is now at the base of the tower. Head up to the second floor and you can have a drink in the paneled room, dating from 1522, once used for church meetings. There's a good view of the city from this vantage point. ✉ *Hof 1.*

The **Kathedrale St. Maria Himmelfahrt** (Cathedral of the Assumption) was built between 1151 and 1272, drawing on stylistic influences from across Europe. The structure on this site in prehistoric times was supplanted by a Roman castle, a bishop's house in the 5th century, and a Carolingian cathedral in the 8th century. The capitals of the columns are carved with fantastical beasts; at their bases are clustered less threatening animals such as sheep and marmots. In the choir is a magnificent 15th-century, three-sided altar in gilded wood. The comprehensive restoration of the cathedral, now under way, is scheduled for completion by 2007. The cathedral's treasures can be viewed by appointment. ✉ *Hof* ☎ *081/2529250* ⊙ *Daily 8–7.*

Obere Gasse, once the main street through Chur and a major route between Germany and Italy, is now lined with small shops and cafés. At the end stands the 16th-century Obertor (Upper Gate), guarding the bridge across the Plessur River. ⊠ *Old Town, between the Obertor and Arcaspl.*

Collections at Graubünden's art museum, the **Bündner Kunstmuseum,** include works by well-known artists who lived or worked in the canton, including Angelika Kauffmann, Giovanni Segantini, Giovanni and Alberto Giacometti, and Ernst Kirchner. The building itself is a majestic neoclassical structure erected in 1875 as a private residence. ⊠ *Postpl.* ☎ *081/2572868* ☎ *7 SF* ☉ *Tues., Wed., and Fri.–Sun. 10–noon and 2–5, Thurs. 10–noon and 2–8.*

off the
beaten
path

VIA MALA – Heading toward the San Bernardino pass on the A13, turn off at Thusis and follow the sign for the Via Mala (the "bad road"), which was used by the Romans and traders over centuries. It runs about 6 km (3½ mi) alongside the narrow Hinterrhein gorge. Shortly after the beginning of the gorge, you can climb down 321 steps (for a fee of 5 SF) to view the river, rock formations, a mid-18th-century bridge, and old road itself. Continue to **Zillis** to see the church's renowned 12th-century painted wood ceiling, whose 153 panels mostly depict stories from the Bible. It is one of the world's oldest original artistic works from the Romanesque era.

Where to Stay & Eat

$–$$ ✕ **Controversa.** This modern brasserie-style restaurant and bar offers a wide choice of salads (self-service or made to order) and more than a dozen original pasta dishes, such as tagliatelle with chicken and mango in a curry sauce. If your appetite isn't up to the heaping servings, you can order half portions. ⊠ *Steinbruchstr. 2* ☎ *081/2529944* ☰ *AE, DC, V* ☉ *Closed Sun. and Mon.*

$$–$$$ ✕ ▦ **Stern.** For a dip into authentic local flavors, head to this historic
FodorsChoice inn, built in 1677. The restaurant serves local wines and moderately priced,
★ regional dishes such as *Z'Marend im Schtärna* (a platter of meats and cheeses). The family-owned and -run hotel neighbors the town's main church, but don't worry about lost sleep; its bells don't chime at night. Rooms are modern and wood-clad; you can relax on a rooftop terrace or in the fireplace lounge. Note that the elevator goes only to the third floor. ⊠ *Reichg. 11, CH-7000* ☎ *081/2585757* ☎ *081/2585758* ⊕ *www.stern-chur.ch* ⇋ *58 rooms* ♿ *Restaurant, cable TV; no a/c* ☰ *AE, DC, MC, V* ❢❢ *BP.*

$$ ▦ **ABC Terminus.** This *garni* (without a restaurant) business hotel is just yards from the train station. (Luckily, there are no night trains to keep you awake.) It occupies five floors of a corporate metal-and-glass box; the entry is hidden between shops. Amenities and rooms are state-of-the-art. ⊠ *Bahnhofpl., CH-7000* ☎ *081/2526033* ☎ *081/2525524* ⊕ *www.hotelabc.ch* ⇋ *36 rooms* ♿ *Cable TV, sauna, business services, meeting rooms, no-smoking floor; no a/c* ☰ *AE, DC, MC, V* ❢❢ *BP.*

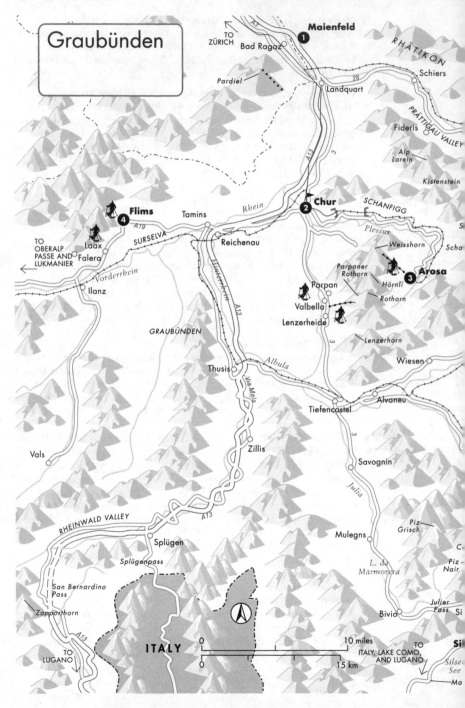

Graubünden

TO ZÜRICH

Maienfeld ❶

Bad Ragaz

RHÄTIKON

Schiers

Landquart

Pardiel

28

PRÄTTIGAU VALLEY

Fideris

Alp Larein

Kistenstein

Chur ❷

SCHANFIGG

Rhein

Plessur

Tamins

A19

Reichenau

Weisshorn

Scha

SURSELVA

Flims ❹

Laax

Falera

TO OBERALP PASSE AND LUKMANIER

Vorderrhein

Ilanz

Parpaner Rothorn

Parpan

Hörnli

Arosa ❸

Rothorn

Valbella

Lenzerheide

GRAUBÜNDEN

Lenzerhorn

Wiesen

Thusis

Albula

Via Mala

Tiefencastel

Alvaneu

Vals

Zillis

Savognin

Julia

Piz Grisch

RHEINWALD VALLEY

A13

Splügen

Splügenpass

Mulegns

L. da Marmorera

Piz Nair

C

San Bernardino Pass

Zapporthorn

A13

TO LUGANO

ITALY

Bivio

Julier Pass

Si

0   10 miles

0   15 km

TO ITALY, LAKE COMO, AND LUGANO

Si

Silse See

Ma

Nightlife

The futuristic **Giger Bar** (✉ Comercialstr. 23 ☎ 081/2537506) is a strange space created by Academy Award winner H. R. Giger, a Chur native who designed the sets for the film *Alien*.

Sports & the Outdoors

GOLF The 27-hole **Domat-Ems** (☎ 081/6503500) golf course is 15 minutes by bus or train from Chur.

SWIMMING Chur has indoor and outdoor **swimming pools** (✉ Sportanlagen Obere Au ☎ 081/2544288).

Arosa

★ ❸ *29 km (18 mi) southeast of Chur.*

Although high-altitude Arosa (5,900 feet) is a well-known winter and summer sports center, its modest size, isolated location, quiet atmosphere, and natural beauty set it apart. On a winter walk, you are more likely to be overtaken by sleds and horse-drawn carriages than by cars. "I spent weeks up there," wrote author Hermann Hesse in 1934, "and I found a level of vigor and youth I would never have thought possible." Arosa lies at the end of a beautiful, winding 30-km (19-mi) road with grades of more than 12% and more than 360 turns. Taking the train from Chur is less nerve-wracking than driving, and affords some wonderful views.

The town has two sections: Inner-Arosa, where the Walsers ("immigrants" from the Valais) built their wooden chalets in the 14th century, is at the end of the valley; Ausser-Arosa is near the train station and the Obersee (Upper Lake). Between the two is the impossible-to-miss casino, with its mosaic facade of screaming colors. A convenient free bus shuttles through the town, and traffic is forbidden between midnight and 6 AM. After you deliver your luggage to your hotel, you probably won't be using your car again while in town.

Don't miss the light, water, and music show on the lake at 9:50 PM every Saturday from mid-June to mid-October (except in the event of heavy rain or wind). Drop into the **Schanfigger Heimatmuseum** to see a slide show and learn about local history. The museum building itself, a mid-16th century wooden farmhouse, is a sight to behold. ✉ *Poststr., Inner-Arosa* ☎ *No phone* 💰 *3 SF* ☉ *Late Dec.–early Apr., Tues. and Fri. 2:30–4:30; mid-June–mid-Oct., Mon., Wed., and Fri. 2:30–4:30.*

Skiing

Arosa's ski area is small compared with those of the Upper Engadine, Davos-Klosters, and the Alpine Arena (Flims-Laax). Closely screened in by mountains, the 5,900-foot-high resort has runs suitable for every level of skier. Its 15 lifts serve 70 km (43 mi) of trails. The slopes can be accessed directly from the valley at three points: the top of the village; behind the train station; and Prätschli, a "feeder" lift to the main ski area. The black piste on the **Weisshorn** (8,700 feet) is challenging, but most of the runs there, as well as on **Hörnli** (8,200 feet), are easy to intermediate. You can get snow-sports instruction at the official **Swiss Ski School** (☎ 081/3771150). Another option for ski lessons is the **ABC**

Snowsport School (☎ 081/3565660). For snowboarding lessons, try **Bananas Swiss Snowboard School** (☎ 081/3774008). All schools have English-speaking instructors. A one-day lift ticket costs 55 SF; a six-day pass costs 256 SF. For cross-country skiing or snowshoeing the Maran and Isla trails have 30 km (18 mi) of groomed trails. There are three official sled runs: Tschuggen, Prätschli, and Untersee. You can rent sleds at the train station or at **Stivetta Sport** (⊠ Innere Poststr. ☎ 081/3772181).

Where to Stay & Eat

$$–$$$ ✗ **Le Bistro.** The decor fits the name, with tile floor, old French posters and newspaper cuttings on the walls, and masses of dried flowers hanging from the ceiling. Start with oysters or truffles and fried duck liver with apple and celery purée. The menu emphasizes fish dishes such as monkfish and crawfish casserole and salmon lasagna. For something more local, try the sauerkraut garnished with meat and sausages. Some fish and pasta dishes are offered in smaller portions, which are perfectly adequate for most appetites. ⊠ *Hotel Cristallo, Poststr.* ☎ *081/3786868* ▤ *AE, DC, MC, V* ⊘ *Closed mid-Apr.–late June and late Sept.–early Dec.*

$–$$$ ✗ **Hold.** This busy family restaurant sits literally at the foot of the slopes. The menu is mostly traditional fare, including a range of fondues that will put an end to the greatest hunger pangs. A trio of advantages makes it an especially good place to bring kids: there are children's meals for under 10 SF; it's adjacent to the children's ski school; and it has a small playroom. ⊠ *Poststr.* ☎ *081/3771408* ▤ *AE, DC, MC, V* ⊘ *Closed Easter–mid-June and mid-Oct.–early Dec.*

$$$ ✗▥ **Waldhotel National.** At this peaceful retreat, set in its own wooded grounds above the village, you can ski or sled home in winter. North-facing rooms look over the forest, and south-facing ones look over Arosa and the mountains. All are tastefully decorated and have touches of golden pine. The Kachelofa-Stübli serves local and French specialties. Hotel residents enjoy their meals in the airy Thomas Mann Restaurant. Reservations are essential for this popular restaurant. It's closed on Sunday evenings in summer. ⊠ *CH-7050* ☎ *081/3785555* ▤ *081/3785599* ⊕ *www.waldhotel.ch* ⤶ *79 rooms, 14 junior suites, 1 apartment* ⟂ *2 restaurants, Stübli, in-room safes, minibars, cable TV, pool, hair salon, massage, sauna, piano bar* ▤ *AE, DC, MC, V* ⊘ *Closed mid-Apr.–mid-June and mid-Sept.–early Dec.* ¶ *BP.*

$$ ✗▥ **Arve Central.** There are flowers in the window boxes here year-round—in winter, wooden blooms replace the real thing. The flower theme is carried through the whole hotel, from the deep-pile carpet to the room key rings and the staff's uniforms. There are good views on the south side; the rooms in back have neither balcony nor view. The wood-clad Arve and the Enzian restaurants offer some of the best food in town with eclectic, changing menus. Herbs gathered from the kitchen's garden appear in dishes such as bream baked in a salt crust. The restaurants close on Monday and Tuesday in May. ⊠ *Off Poststr., CH-7050* ☎ *081/3785252* ▤ *081/3785250* ⊕ *www.arve-central.ch* ⤶ *45 rooms, 2 suites, 1 apartment* ⟂ *2 restaurants, pool, hot tub, sauna, bar; no a/c* ▤ *AE, DC, MC, V.*

★ **$$$$**   ▥ **Kulm.** Twenty-eight cowbells hanging above the reception desk are all that recall the hotel's past as a 19th-century wooden chalet. The current modern structure is a sporty luxury hotel. Its position on the farthest edge of town, at the base of the slopes, is its biggest draw; from its wraparound windows you can take in acres of green hills or snowy slopes (south-facing rooms have balconies). Rooms have soft prints and neutral tones; bathrooms are tile and stone. In winter an Italian trattoria and a Thai restaurant join the main restaurants (jacket requested). ✉ CH-7050 ☎ 081/3788888 🖷 081/3788889 ⊕ www.arosakulm.ch ⤴ 122 rooms, 15 suites ⚖ 5 restaurants, in-room safes, minibars, cable TV, putting green, 2 tennis courts, pool, health club, spa, bowling, squash, bar, piano bar, dance club, babysitting, free parking, parking (fee) 🖃 AE, DC, MC, V ⊘ Closed late Sept.–early Dec. and mid-Apr.–mid-June ⬥ BP.

$$ 🏨 **Alpensonne.** Family owned and run, this hotel is only about 200 yards from the ski lifts of Inner-Arosa. The public spaces are light and bright. Guest rooms are in soft colors with lots of wood. Some have showers only, and some of these are not yet tiled, so be sure to specify. Several family rooms are available, with multiple beds. Rooms facing south have great views. The café-Stübli serves meat and cheese fondues daily. Half board is available for an additional 25 SF per person. ✉ Poststr., CH-7050 ☎ 081/3771547 🖷 081/3773470 ⊕ www.hotelalpensonne.ch ⤴ 35 rooms, 3 apartments ⚖ Restaurant, café, Stübli, minibars, cable TV, sauna, steam room, bar, recreation room; no a/c 🖃 AE, DC, MC, V ⊘ Closed late Apr.–late June and mid-Oct.–early Dec. ⬥ BP.

★ $–$$ 🏨 **Sonnenhalde.** The automatic heavy pine door that welcomes you to this chalet hotel garni is your first sign of its happy marriage of charm and modern comfort. The sizable rooms are bright, with wall-to-wall wood and rustic decor. Some rooms easily accommodate extra beds (for an additional fee). Bathrooms have showers instead of tubs; the lowest-price rooms have only sinks and share the other facilities. ✉ CH-7050 ☎ 081/3771531 🖷 081/3774455 ⊕ www.sonnenhalde-arosa.ch ⤴ 21 rooms, 14 with bath ⚖ Cable TV, sauna, steam room; no a/c 🖃 AE, DC, MC, V ⊘ Closed late Apr.–late June and mid-Oct.–early Dec. ⬥ BP.

Nightlife & the Arts

BARS At the Hotel Eden, the **Kitchen Club** (✉ Jory-Jenny-Str. ☎ 081/3787106) is a disco inside an kitchen dating back to 1907. A young crowd dances among old pots and pans while the DJ perches above antique refrigerators. The après-ski crowd here is chic—you should change out of your ski bibs first. In the casino, **Nuts** (✉ Poststr. ☎ 081/3773940) plays the latest tunes for young people.

MUSIC From Christmas to mid-April and during the summer, concerts are given at 5 PM on Tuesday on the hand-painted organ in Arosa's 500-year-old, wooden-roof **Bergkirchli** (mountain chapel). A yodeling festival takes place in July, and music courses are given from June through October; get the program from **Kulturkreis Arosa** (☎ 081/3538747 🖷 081/3538750).

Sports & the Outdoors

GOLF Europe's highest tee (6,209 feet) is on hole number 8 of Arosa's 18-hole course at **Maran** (☎ 081/3774242).

HIKING & BIKING	The **Davos tourist office** (☎ 081/4152121) can arrange four-day walking or biking trips from Davos to Arosa.
HORSEBACK RIDING	Call **L. Messner** (☎ 081/3774196) for guided horseback tours and horse-drawn carriage rides in summer and sleigh rides in winter.
PARAGLIDING & BALLOONING	Weather permitting, the **Paragliding Taxi** (☎ 079/4498813) arranges daily paragliding flights from December to March. For a balloon flight over Arosa or the Graubünden Alps, call **Walter Vollenweider** (☎ 01/3913714). A special ballooning week is held each January.
SKATING & CURLING	Arosa has several skating rinks. At the indoor **Eissporthalle** (☎ 081/3771745) you can watch ice hockey as well as take skating or curling lessons; there's an open-air rink alongside. Another option is the **Inner-Arosa rink** (☎ 081/3772930).
SWIMMING	If you can take cold water, you can have a free swim in the lakes. Some hotels open their pools to the public; check with the tourist office. The **Clubhotel Altein** (☎ 081/3773151) has a warm saltwater pool.
TENNIS	There are 15 hotel-owned courts, all of which are open to the public; contact the tourist office for details. You can rent equipment from the hotels.

Flims

❹ *49 km (30 mi) west of Arosa.*

Travelers in search of a mountain resort warm enough to sit outside on summer evenings started coming to Flims in 1877. The village extends along a terrace above a Rhine gorge and has two sections: the lively Dorf and the quieter Waldhaus, the old Romansch center. Houses and hotels are mostly chalet-style, with no concrete high-rises marring the views. The neighboring villages of Laax and Falera link together with Flims and make up the "Alpine Arena," the largest connected ski area in Graubünden.

In **Laax,** (*Ils lags,* Romansch for "the lakes"), 3 km (2 mi) from Flims, you can stay in the old village or the newer center of Murschetg. Murschetg sprouted up in the late 1960s with hotels, discos, and ski lifts and grew through the '70s to become a distinct area. A shuttle bus connects the two centers.

In homey **Falera,** you can visit the site of 26 menhirs near the church of St. Remigius. These huge stones are mysteriously arranged geometrically and date back to the time the village was first settled, in roughly 1500 BC. The church itself is a perfect setting for a summer chamber music concerts.

> **off the beaten path**
>
> **VALS –** For a dose of stellar contemporary architecture, take an hour's drive via Illanz down a dead-end valley to this otherwise traditional village. Acclaimed Swiss architect Peter Zumthor designed the elegant, minimalist baths of **FELSEN-THERME –** using locally quarried stone. ☎ 081/9268080 ⊕ *www.therme-vals.ch* ☽ *Late May–early Nov. and mid-Dec.–late Apr., Mon. 11–9, Tues.–Sun. 11–8.*

Skiing

The Alpine Arena covers 100 square km (39 square mi). From the Crap Sogn Gion valley stations in Flims, Laax, and Falera you can access 220 km (137 mi) of easy, intermediate, difficult, and off-trail runs, most of which are above 4,920 feet. The run from the Vorab glacier to Flims village is 14 km (9 mi). The valley stations of Crap Sogn Gion have 28 (mostly high-speed) lifts and New Technology Centers, rental centers for equipment and ski clothing (including goggles and glove rental). The arena has great facilities for snowboarders, including three half pipes and a boarder park. World championships for snowboarding, the Boardercross World Tour Finals, are held in April in Laax. For snow-sports instruction, contact the **Swiss Ski School** (☎ 081/9277171) in Laax or Flims. The **Snowboard Fahrschule** (☎ 081/9277155) in Laax teaches snowboarding and skiing. Lift tickets are 59 SF for one day, 301 SF for six days. Transport between the villages is free. Cross-country skiers and winter walkers have roughly 50 km (31 mi) of prepared trails. The **Langlauf Center** (☎ 081/6351688) in Flims offers cross-country skiing lessons.

Where to Stay & Eat

$$$$ ╳▨ **Park Hotels Waldhaus.** Scattered around extensive, wooded grounds, the various buildings of this spa center are connected by walkways and tunnels. For belle epoque comfort, choose the main building; for modern rooms, try the Belmont. The Villa Silvana has less expensive rooms and, with its children's club and children's restaurant, is especially welcoming to families. The restaurant complex includes La Cena, an Italian spot with seasonal specialties such as truffle risotto and rabbit with mushroom sauce. Barbecues are held on the large terrace in summer. A free hotel bus service takes guests to the slopes and into town. ✉ CH-7018 Flims Waldhaus ☎ 081/9284848 ☎ 081/9284858 ⊕ www.park-hotels-waldhaus.ch ➭ 145 rooms, 10 suites ♻ 4 restaurants, minibars, cable TV, driving range, putting green, 10 tennis courts, indoor pool, hair salon, massage, sauna, 3 bars, children's programs (ages 2–10); no a/c ▤ AE, DC, MC, V ⊘ Closed mid-Apr.–late May and mid-Oct.–mid-Dec. ⌾ MAP.

Sports & the Outdoors

BALLOONING   Around 30 balloons participate in the annual Flims Balloon Festival, held over the course of a week in early October. Year-round you can go aloft with **Swissraft** (☎ 081/9115250).

BIKING   In summer the slopes are turned over to mountain bikers. A total of 237 km (148 mi) of trails have been opened to bikers of all skill levels. There are several annual events, including the Red Bull Trailfox competition for the two-wheeler acrobats in June and the Fat Tire competition for motorbikers in early August. In Laax Murschetg, there's a mountain-bike freestyle park. The **Tacho School** (☎ 081/9277155) in Laax gives mountain-bike coaching and organizes excursions.

HIKING   Hikers enjoy seemingly endless well-tended paths that offer gorgeous views of the valleys and surrounding mountains. A special treat is the **Kulinarik Trail** (☎ 081/9209200), which lets you taste a three- or four-course gourmet meal as you hike.

SWIMMING   In summertime take a dip in the **Laaxersee** (🖾 5 SF), a lake in Laax. The 21°C (70°F) **Caumasee** (🖾 6 SF) is an azure lake in the forest below Flims.

WHITE-WATER   White-water raft down the Rhine gorge through spectacular scenery with
RAFTING   **Swissraft** (☎ 081/9115250).

PRÄTTIGAU & DAVOS

The name "Prättigau" means "meadow valley," and it's just that—a lush landscape of alternating orchards, pastures, and pine-covered mountains (though the main highway is a very busy route). The predominant language is German, brought by "immigrants" from the Valais in the 13th century, though most villages still have Romansch names. Prättigau's most renowned ski resort is Klosters. Its equally famous neighbor and ski-region partner, Davos, lies in the Landwasser Valley, over the Wolfgang Pass. If you prefer an urban experience, head to Davos; for a quieter village experience, look to Klosters.

Klosters

⑤ *26 km (19 mi) southeast of Landquart.*

Once a group of hamlets, Klosters has become a small but chic resort, made up mostly of weathered-wood and white-stucco chalets. The village has two districts: Platz, which is older and busier, and Dorf, which lies on the main road toward Landquart. Klosters is famed for its skiing—British royal family members are faithful visitors—and makes the most of its access to the slopes of the Parsenn, above Davos. In Klosters Platz, the church of **St. Jacob**, dating from 1492, is the only remnant of the medieval monastery from which the village took its name. Its windows were painted by Augusto Giacometti.

A brief visit to the folk museum **Nutli-Hüschi** shows the resort's evolution from its mountain roots: a pretty wood-and-stone chalet, built in 1565, has been restored and fitted with the spare furnishings of its day, including kitchen tools and a bed that could be expanded as the child grew. ✉ *Monbielerstr. at Talstr.* ☎ *081/4102020* 🖾 *2 SF* ⊘ *Dec.–mid-Apr. and late June–mid Oct., Wed. and Fri. 3–5.*

Skiing

Klosters is known for its vast range of downhill runs, which, together with those of Davos, total 320 km (200 mi). These are divided almost equally among easy, moderate, and difficult pistes. From the Gotschnagrat (7,494 feet), skiers can connect to the Parsenn slopes, and try, for example, the famous Weissflüh run down to the village of Küblis. The sunny Madrisa slopes above Klosters Dorf offer relatively easy skiing and snowboarding. For instruction or to go on a snowshoe trek, contact the **Swiss Ski & Snowboard School** (☎ 081/4102828), which has a branch in both Platz and Dorf. Lift tickets to the combined Davos/Klosters area cost 57 SF for one day and up to 279 SF for six days, depending on how many and in which areas you want to ski. Train or bus transport back to Klosters from other villages within the ski area is included in the price of the regional ski ticket. There are 35 km (22 mi) of cross-country tracks and you can get lessons at the **Nordic Ski School** (☎ 081/4102020 or 081/4221040).

Where to Stay & Eat

$$-$$$ ✕ **Alte Post.** In this warm local favorite, pleasantly cluttered with ceramics and game trophies, choose from a straightforward menu thick with old-style dishes: thyme-flavored rabbit, *tête de veau* (veal head) vinaigrette, beef with marsala and risotto, and lots of and lamb. If you like salmon, a special menu features the fish in every dish but the sorbet. (They smoke their own Norwegian salmon.) The restaurant is about a mile out of town but worth the trip. ✉ *Doggilochstr. 136, Klosters-Aeuja* ☎ *081/4221716* ▭ *DC, MC, V* ⊗ *Closed Mon. and Tues. and May and Nov.*

$-$$$ ✕ **Höhwald.** This is a friendly, touristy restaurant up the hill from Klosters in Monbiel, with a large, open terrace that takes in valley and mountain views. Try their special plate of mixed Graubünden specialties, which includes Capuns, Prättigauer *Knödlis* (dumplings), and *Chäsgatschäder* (a mixture of bread, milk, and cheese). ✉ *Klosters-Monbiel* ☎ *081/4223045* ▭ *AE, MC, V* ⊗ *Closed Tues. and mid-Apr.–May and late Oct.–Dec.*

★ $$$-$$$$ ✕▩ **Walserhof.** The most sophisticated establishment in Klosters, Walserhof was built in 1981 with the weathered boards from an old farmhouse. The only drawback is its location on the main road through town; the best views take in either the street or fairly well-developed fields behind. Its restaurant and café are paneled with ancient carved wood; stone, stucco, and quarry tile are used elsewhere. The superb restaurant serves regional dishes, such as trout in cider and lamb stew with polenta. ✉ *Landstr., CH-7250 Klosters-Platz* ☎ *081/4102929* 🖶 *081/4102939* ⊕ *www. walserhof.ch* ⇒ *11 rooms, 3 suites* ⟂ *Restaurant, café, minibars, cable TV, gym, sauna; no a/c* ▭ *AE, DC, MC, V* ⊗ *Closed Easter–late June and mid-Oct.–early Dec.* ❍❘ *BP.*

$-$$$ ✕▩ **Rustico.** Good things come in small packages here—guest rooms are on a petite scale but are very attractive. Each has a hand-painted flower on its door. Inside are parquet floors, country cottons, and white tile showers. The lounge area has a fireplace and leads out to a summer terrace. In the restaurant, hung with original art, a seasonal menu caters to both omnivores and vegetarians with dishes such as roast chamois with chestnuts and deep-fried mushrooms. The restaurant is closed on Thursday in summer. ✉ *Landstr., CH-7250 Klosters-Platz* ☎ *081/4221212* 🖶 *081/4225355* ⊕ *www.swiss-lifestyle.com* ⇒ *12 rooms* ⟂ *Restaurant, in-room safes, minibars, cable TV, sauna, billiards, bar; no a/c* ▭ *DC, MC, V* ⊗ *Closed June and Nov.* ❍❘ *BP.*

$-$$$$ ▩ **Chesa Grischuna.** Although it's directly in the town center at the crossroads, this creaky 1890 mountain farmhouse qualifies as a country inn—and is one of the region's most popular places to stay. Every room, including those in the nearby annex, is full of old carved wood, and some have balconies. There are antiques throughout, and plenty of public spaces, as this is a sociable place. Whether you bowl in the vaulted cellar, play cards, or dance to the piano music at happy hour, you'll be surrounded by the coveted social mix of Klosters regulars. ✉ *Bahnhofstr., CH-7250 Klosters-Platz* ☎ *081/4222222* 🖶 *081/*

4222225 ⊕ *www.chesagrischuna.ch* ⇝ *25 rooms, 23 with bath* ⚹ *Restaurant, in-room data ports, cable TV, bowling, bar; no a/c* ⊟ *AE, MC, V* ⊘ *Closed late May–early July and mid-Oct.–mid-Dec.* ⦿ *BP.*

$$–$$$ ⊞ **Albeina.** This large and luxurious chalet-style hotel has easy access to the Madrisa slopes. In summer you can join special tennis or horseback-riding weeks. Rooms are tastefully decorated, with floral details. Rooms for a lower rate are available in summer or early December; they're on the north side of the building or in the Chesa Albeina guesthouse. The popular Dörfji Bar draws regulars. ⊠ *CH-7252 Klosters-Dorf* ☎ *081/4232100* 🖷 *081/4232121* ⊕ *www.albeinahotel.ch* ⇝ *64 rooms* ⚹ *2 restaurants, minibars, cable TV, 2 tennis courts, pool, massage, sauna, steam room, billiards, boccie, bar, playground; no a/c* ⊟ *AE, DC, MC, V* ⊘ *Closed mid-Apr.–mid-June and mid-Oct.–mid-Dec.* ⦿ *BP.*

$$ ⊞ **Silvapina.** This delightful hotel in an old chalet-style building, is family-run and family-welcoming. It is right by the station (trains don't run at night) and a few minutes' walk from the slopes. Rooms are done either all in wood or in white with touches of pine. Bathrooms have showers instead of tubs; south-facing rooms have balconies. Half board is offered in winter for an additional 25 SF. ⊠ *CH-7252 Klosters-Dorf* ☎ *081/4221468* 🖷 *081/4224078* ⊕ *www.silvapina.ch* ⇝ *15 rooms, 3 apartments* ⚹ *Restaurant, Stübli, cable TV, sauna, billiards, Ping-Pong, bar; no a/c* ⊟ *AE, MC, V* ⊘ *Closed May and Nov.* ⦿ *BP.*

Fodor's Choice
★

Nightlife
Revelers dance late into the night at the **Casa Antica** (⊠ Landstr. 176 ☎ 081/4221621), in a 300-year-old converted barn. A popular after-dinner spot, **Chesa Bar** (⊠ Bahnhofstr. 12 ☎ 081/4222222) has piano music and several intimate bar areas. In the Silvretta Parkhotel there's the **Kir Royal** (⊠ Landstr. 190 ☎ 081/4233435) disco and a piano bar.

Sports & the Outdoors

BIKING & HIKING The Klosters area has plenty of trails for exploring the countryside. The 250 km (155 mi) of summer hiking routes are reduced to 30 km (19 mi) of prepared paths in winter. There are 120 km (74½ mi) of mountain-biking routes. To rent mountain bikes, try the **Hew Bike Shop** (⊠ Klosters-Dorf ☎ 081/4223942). Another source for mountain bikes is **Andrist Sport** (⊠ Klosters-Platz ☎ 081/4102080).

HORSEBACK For horseback riding excursions, contact **Jürg Marugg** (☎ 081/4221463).
RIDING For summer or winter carriage or sleigh rides call **C. Flütsch** (☎ 081/4221873). **Joh Marugg** (☎ 081/4222429) also offers carriage and sleigh rides.

PARAGLIDING **Grischa Flying Center** (☎ 081/4222070 or 079/3361919) will sign you up for introductory sessions in summer or winter. Flights start at 160 SF per person.

SKATING Klosters's **Sportszentrum** (⊠ Doggilochstr. 11, Klosters-Platz ☎ 081/4102131) has rinks for skating, hockey, curling, and ice bowling in season. Skate rentals are available.

SLEDDING The area has three sled runs: Gotschna-Klosters, Alpenrösli, and Mälcheti-Aeuja. Sleds are available for rental at **Andrist Sport** (⊠ Klosters-Platz

☏ 081/4102080). **Sport Gotschna** (✉ Klosters-Platz ☏ 081/4221197) also rents sleds.

SWIMMING The town's heated **outdoor swimming pool** (✉ Doggilochstr. ☏ 081/ 4221524) is open all summer. The indoor pool of the **Hotel Pardenn** (☏081/ 4232020) is open to the public. The indoor pool at the **Hotel Sport** (☏ 081/4233030) has a wall of windows. The 14 meter indoor pool at the **Silvretta Parkhotel** (☏ 081/4233435) is open to the public as well.

TENNIS There are seven sand courts (five are lighted for nighttime play) to reserve at the **Sportszentrum** (✉ Doggilochstr. 11, Klosters-Platz ☏ 081/ 4102131). You can rent equipment at the Sportszentrum's **Tennis School Kämpf** (☏ 081/4102141).

Davos

❻ *11 km (7 mi) southwest of Klosters.*

Davos, at 5,116 feet is considered to be the highest town in Europe. It's famous for its ice sports and skiing and hosts the annual World Economic Forum. The town and its lake lie in the Landwasser Valley, which runs parallel to the Upper Engadine, though they're separated by the vast Albula chain, reaching to more than 9,840 feet. On the opposite side of the valley stands the Strela chain, dominated by the Weissfluh.

This is a capital for action-oriented sports enthusiasts and not necessarily for anyone seeking a peaceful, rustic mountain retreat (especially at the end of December when there's an invasion of ice hockey fans for the international Spengler Cup). Davos is divided into the Platz and the Dorf (village), which together are one noisier-than-average urban strip, though Dorf is calmer. The town's first visitors came to take cures for lung diseases in the bracing mountain air. Now, except for a few token historic structures and brightly painted buildings, the town is modern and architecturally undistinguished. But no matter how densely populated and fast-paced the town becomes, the slopes are still spectacular and the regulars return.

Davos was once famous as a retreat for people suffering from respiratory problems such as tuberculosis. It was the inspiration for Thomas Mann's novel *The Magic Mountain.* Recalling the days when the streets were lined with spittoons is the **Museum of Medicine,** which exhibits old-fashioned medical equipment. ✉ *Platzstr. 1, Davos-Platz* ☏ *081/ 4135210* 🖾 *3 SF* ☉ *Thurs. 5–7, and by appointment.*

Among the town's few architectural highlights, the late-Gothic **Kirche St. Johann** (Church of St. John the Baptist) stands out by virtue of its windows by Augusto Giacometti. Nearby is the 17th-century Rathaus (Town Hall). ✉ *Rathausstutz 2.*

The **Kirchner Museum** boasts the world's largest collection of works by the German artist Ernst Ludwig Kirchner, founder of the expressionist movement. He traveled to Davos in 1917 for health reasons and stayed until his death in 1938. ✉ *Promenade 82, Davos-Platz* ☏ *081/4132202* ⊕ *www.kirchnermuseum.ch* 🖾 *10 SF* ☉ *Easter–mid-July and*

INSPIRING GRAUBÜNDEN

NIETZSCHE'S FAMOUS philosophical work Thus Spoke Zarathustra opens it's second part with Zarathustra returning to the mountains "to seek the solitude of his cave." While the author's thinking may have been abstract, the cave and the mountains were probably quite real. For it was in Sils Maria, in the summer of 1883, that Nietzsche began writing this lengthy treatise on man and superman. His fundamental concept of recurrence came to him during a walk around nearby Silverplaner Lake.

For those seeking inspiration, Graubünden has always been a natural high. Countless artistic personalities have come to the canton for rest and relaxation and left with some great work of literature or art in their bags (or at least their heads, waiting to be created). Something in the clarity of the air and proximity to the sky seems to dispel all the cares and worries of the daily grind and set creative juices flowing. For some, like Marcel Proust, it was the "bracing air, the aroma of hay and the sound of the brooks." For others, such as Hermann Hesse, the "powerful, severe beauty" of the mountains around Arosa provided the vim and vigor to edit his novel about religion and salvation, Narcissus and Goldmund. (He had been immobilized by a skiing accident, making it easier to devote himself to his work.) Nietzsche, for his part, felt he had arrived in the "Promised Land" on his first trip to the Engadin in 1879.

The gentle meadows and mysterious, aromatic forests of pine embraced by rugged snow-tipped mountains have all done their part to enthrall visitors. Goethe, Germany's greatest poet and writer, traveled through the hair-raising Via Mala gorge on his way back from Italy and had to stop for a while to draw some sketches of the almost eerie sights. Decades later he recalled the trip: "The road over the Splügen mountains is indescribably beautiful, the Via Mala is the most frightening rocky pass in all of Switzerland."

Perhaps a similar thrill was felt by Robert Louis Stevenson when he came to vacation in Davos during the winter season of 1881–82. What the foggy and damp landscape of his native Scotland failed to do, Graubünden accomplished, enabling him to finish Treasure Island. (One might wonder about the connection between the South Seas setting of the novel and the snow covered landscape around Davos, but inspiration does move in strange ways.)

Davos also sparked the imagination of novelist Thomas Mann. In June 1912, he accompanied his wife Katja on a cure in the comfortable, belle-epoque rooms of the Schatzalp sanatorium. There he saw the first outlines of his novel The Magic Mountain, symbolizing Europe and its political and social choices: either to bask in illness and submit to death, or to choose life and social commitment. Needless to say, his depiction of such an indolent society living in a morbid expectation of death—"flirting and taking their temperature"—did not please the people of Davos, whose community had made a name for itself as a serious spa for curing, or a least alleviating, tuberculosis. The fame of The Magic Mountain, however, has long made up for any acrimony, and now healthy and positive-minded guests can stay at the Schatzalp, which has become a fine hotel.

At times, of course, the inspiration went in a different direction. Sir Arthur Conan Doyle may have come up with a new case for Sherlock Holmes during his sojourn in Davos in 1892, but there is no record of it. He did, however, astonish the locals with his idea of a good time, introducing golf to the region.

Oct.–Christmas, Tues.–Sun. 2–6; mid-July–Sept. and Christmas–Easter, Tues.–Sun. 10–6.

The **Wintersportmuseum** has a collection of equipment from sleds to ski bindings. ✉ *Promenade 43, Davos-Platz* ☎ *081/4132484* 🖃 *5 SF* ☉ *Late June–mid-Oct., Tues. and Thurs. 4:30–6:30; Dec.–Apr., Tues., Thurs., and Sat. 4:30–6:30.*

Skiing

Davos can accommodate some 24,000 visitors on 325 km (202 mi) of runs. The steepish slopes of the **Parsenn-Gotschna** are accessed from town by the Schatzalp or Parsenn funiculars. When lines for the Parsenn are off-puttingly long, try the **Rinerhorn**, a 15-minute ride by bus or train. Here the slopes lead to the hamlet of **Glaris**, 7 km (4½ mi) from Davos. A must for the skilled skier is the descent from **Weissfluhgipfel** (9,330 feet) to **Küblis**, in the Prättigau. This magnificent, 13-km (8-mi) piste has a vertical drop of 6,560 feet and is classified as difficult at the top but moderate for most of its length. A real challenge for experts is the three-hour tour across the mountains to Arosa—which requires a guide and good weather conditions. An easy 2-km (1-mi) run is number 11, the Meierhofer Tälli, which Davosers renamed the Hillary Clinton run, as it's her favorite here. **Jakobshorn**, a ski and snowboard area on the west-facing side, is reached by cable car and lift from Davos-Platz. The **Pischa** ski area, on the Flüela Pass road, and the **Bünda** slope, in Davos-Dorf, are especially suitable for children and families.

Lift tickets to the combined Davos–Klosters area cost up to 57 SF for one day, 279 SF for six days—depending on which areas you choose to ski—and include transport between the ski areas. The **Snowsports School Davos** (✉ Promenade 157, Davos-Dorf ☎ 081/4162454) gives skiing, cross-country, snowboard, and telemark lessons. If you need to get outfitted for skiing, including clothing, go to **PaarSenn** (✉ Promenade 159, Davos-Dorf ☎ 081/4101013). For the expert skier (freestyle, off-piste, and the like) the place to go is **New Trend Skischool** (✉ Brämabüelstr. 11, Davos-Platz ☎ 081/4132040).

There are more than 75 km (47 mi) of prepared cross-country ski trails, for which there is no charge. The **cross-country ski school** (☎ 081/4162454) is in Davos-Platz.

Where to Stay & Eat

$–$$ ✕ **Bistro Angelo.** If you have had enough Bündner specialties, try this restaurant, which doubles as a store selling wines and spirits, pasta and honey. The menu changes every few days depending on what produce is available. Fresh- and saltwater fish are the specialty here, as are affordable prices. ✉ *Promenade 119, Davos-Platz* ☎ *081/4165979* 🖃 *AE, DC, MC, V* ☉ *Closed Sun. in summer.*

★ **$$–$$$** ✕🖭 **Hubli's Landhaus.** Though it's on the busy mountain highway between Davos and Klosters, this country inn is quiet as well as comfortable and attractive with its rustic decor. The strong point by far is the food. Chef Felix Hubli prepares sophisticated fare (goose liver pâté served on creamed onions, Scottish salmon in a balsamic vinaigrette) and serves it in two lovely dining rooms: one for visitors, one for demipension guests, who—considering the à la carte prices—get a terrific deal. The guest rooms are modestly priced, especially the ones with a sink and shared bathroom down the hall. ⊠ *Kantonstr., CH-7265 Davos-Wolfgang* ☎ *081/4171010* 🖷 *081/4171011* ⊕ *www.hublis.ch* ⮧ *20 rooms* ♿ *2 restaurants, minibars, cable TV, sauna, bar; no a/c* ▤ *AE, DC, MC, V* ⊙ *Closed Mon. and late Apr.–early June and mid-Oct.–mid-Dec.* ꙩ *BP.*

$$$–$$$$ ▦ **Schatzalp.** About 950 feet above town on a quiet, car-free slope, this expansive hotel will transport you back to the grand spa days of Davos. It served once as a sanatorium, and is described in Mann's *Magic Mountain.* The rooms, lobby, foyer and dining room are all decorated in elegant belle epoque style. Spend summer afternoons enjoying the breeze on the long veranda or visiting the hotel's botanical garden featuring high-altitude plants from five continents. The hotel is only accessible by its own funicular, the Schatzalp-Bahn, in Davos-Platz near the Hotel Europe. ⊠ *Mattastr., CH-7270 Davos-Platz* ☎ *081/4168131* 🖷 *081/4163939* ⮧ *47 rooms* ♿ *Restaurant, piano bar, minibars, cable TV, pool, sauna; no a/c* ▤ *AE, DC, MC, V* ꙩ *MAP.*

$$$–$$$$ ▦ **Steigenberger Belvedere.** With its neoclassical stone fireplace, wedding-cake white plaster, and period details, this is a grand hotel in every sense of the word. The enormous gray building with south-facing balconies is just above the main street. Rooms are decorated in woods ranging from rustic Arvenholz to classic mahogany. If it's cold outside, the murals of tropical birds and plants around the pool provide a comforting contrast. ⊠ *Promenade 89, CH-7270 Davos-Platz* ☎ *081/4156000* 🖷 *081/4156001* ⊕ *www.davos.steigenberger.ch* ⮧ *144 rooms, 27 suites* ♿ *3 restaurants, minibars, cable TV, pool, hair salon, massage, sauna, steam room, bar; no a/c* ▤ *AE, DC, MC, V* ⊙ *Closed late Apr.–late June and late Oct.–early Dec.* ꙩ *BP.*

$$–$$$ ▦ **Bünda.** This hotel is right by the beginners' ski slope and a ski school branch, as well as on the cross-country ski track. The Parsenn cable car is only a few minutes' walk. Rooms in the main building are smaller, some with showers instead of a tub. Two share a bathroom. Larger, more expensive rooms are in the Residenz, connected to the hotel by an underground passage. ⊠ *Museumstr., CH-7260 Davos-Dorf* ☎ *081/4171819* 🖷 *081/4171820* ⊕ *www.buenda.ch* ⮧ *31 rooms, 29 with bath* ♿ *2 restaurants, minibars, cable TV, gym, sauna, steam room; no a/c* ▤ *AE, DC, MC, V* ⊙ *Closed mid-Apr.–early June* ꙩ *BP.*

$–$$$ ▦ **Ochsen.** An ambitious young team runs this modest hotel. A few of the rustic rooms take in views of the Jakobshorn (the Jakobshorn station is just a few minutes' walk). ⊠ *Talstr. 10, CH-7270 Davos-Platz* ☎ *081/4149020* 🖷 *081/4149021* ⮧ *47 rooms* ♿ *Restaurant, Stübli, in-room data ports, minibars, cable TV, bar; no a/c* ▤ *AE, DC, MC, V* ⊙ *Closed May* ꙩ *BP.*

Nightlife & the Arts

BARS In the Hotel Europe, the **Ex Bar** (⊠ Promenade 63, Davos-Platz ☎ 081/4154141) is where hipsters gather to listen to live music.

DANCING The **Cabanna Club** (⊠ Promenade 63, Davos-Platz ☎ 081/4154141) lures an energetic crowd with techno music. The **Pöstli Club** (⊠ Promenade 42, Davos-Dorf ☎ 081/4154500) is a winter-only institution with a dance floor and music ranging from rock to folk and pop. In the Hotel Davoserhof, the **Rotliechtli Music Club** (✉ Berglistutz 15, Davos-Dorf ☎ 081/4156666) attracts a young—or at least young at heart—crowd with somewhat traditional tastes in music.

MUSIC The annual Young Artists in Concert festival is held from mid-July to early August. Young musicians from all over the world practice and perform in churches and in the Congress Center.

Sports & the Outdoors

GOLF **Golf Club Davos** (☎ 081/4165634) has 18 holes that range from easy to quite tricky. The course, designed by Don Harradine, has been perfectly integrated into the town and the surrounding landscape.

HIKING & BIKING Davos is threaded with more than 450 km (280 mi) of well-marked trails perfect for hiking or biking in winter and summer. Mountain bikes can be rented at the train station or at **Ettinger Sport** (✉ Talstr. 6, Davos-Dorf ☎ 081/4135410 ✉ Promenade 61, Davos-Platz ☎ 081/4106161).

PARAGLIDING **Delta- und Gleitschirmschule Davos** (☎081/4136043 or 079/3572050) gives lessons and offers tandem flights during the summer and winter seasons.

RACQUET SPORTS **Tennis & Squash Center Davos** (✉ Clavadelerstr. ☎ 081/4133131) has four indoor and five outdoor tennis courts, plus two squash and four badminton courts. Rental equipment is available.

SAILING & WINDSURFING Sailing and windsurfing are popular on Davos Lake. To rent boats or take a lesson with a sailing school, call **Segelschule Davosersee** (☎ 081/4161577). **Hans Heierling** (☎ 081/4165918) offers lessons and rents boats as well.

SKATING Davos has a long reputation as an important ice-sports center, with its enormous **Sports Center Davos** (✉ Talstr. 41 ☎ 081/4153600) and speed-skating rink, the biggest natural ice track in Europe. The Ice Stadium maintains one indoor and two outdoor rinks; rental skates are available.

SWIMMING Davos has an indoor-outdoor **swimming pool complex** (✉ Promenade 90 ☎ 081/4136463) that is open to the public. You can also swim at the **Strandbad** (open beach) in Davos Lake.

en route The main road from Davos leads into the Engadine by way of the bleak and spectacular **Flüelapass** (Flüela Pass), which is open in summer and only during the day in winter, if at all. (The Vereina tunnel provides year-round train service from Klosters to Sagliains, near Susch–Lavin.)

LOWER ENGADINE

The lower Inn valley is one of Graubünden's most picturesque. Houses typically have deep Etruscan-arch doors, thick walls, and sunken windows. Look for built-in wooden benches at the front entrances and triangular windows from which grandparents can watch what is going on in the street. Decorative sgraffiti designs—a signature of the Engadine—are produced by whitewashing a layer of dark stucco, then scraping designs or words into the paint, revealing the color underneath.

"Allegra!" is the proper Romansh greeting on the street in these parts. You'll hear people talk of Schellenursli, a little boy with a big bell who is featured in a popular children's story about the festival of Chalanda Marz, which the whole of Engadine celebrates on March 1. It was the first day of the year in the Roman calendar, but now is supposed to mark the end of winter. The Lower Engadine—more enclosed than its upper counterpart—shares the region's crisp "champagne" climate.

Guarda

❼ *34 km (21 mi) east of Davos.*

FodorsChoice
★

Traveling down the valley toward Austria in summer, stop off in Guarda, one of a pleasant chain of small villages that include Ardez and Ftan. Each has fine sgraffitied homes, but Guarda, where the architecture is government-protected, is particularly well suited for a leisurely exploration along its steep, cobbled streets. The dark-on-light etchings on the facades (contrasting sharply with the bright flowers on the windowsills) draw pedestrians from one photo stop to the next. As its name implies, Guarda ("watch") sits high on a hillside looking out over the valley and the peaks to the south, which reach up to 9,840 feet.

Where to Stay & Eat

$–$$$ ✕🏨 **Meisser.** This picturesque, family-owned hotel, made up of three ancient farmhouses, has sgraffiti and flower boxes on the outside, antiques and honey-color pine inside. Have a drink in the stable bar, then choose among such dishes as chamois with a walnut crust and elderberry sauce or *Güggeli auf Alpenheu* (chicken roasted in hay) in the Veranda restaurant. Rooms are simple and modern, though you can have a splendid carved-pine room if you pay a bit more. An adjacent, renovated 17th-century farmhouse has a half-dozen suites. ✉ CH-7545 ☎ 081/8622132 🖷 081/8622480 ⊕ *www.hotel-meisser.ch* ⤙ *21 rooms, 6 suites* ♿ *2 restaurants, in-room data ports, minibars, bar, playground; no TV in some rooms* ⊟ *AE, DC, MC, V* ⊗ *Closed mid-Apr.–late May and early Nov.–late Dec.* ⏀ *BP.*

Scuol

❽ *13 km (8 mi) east of Guarda.*

The villages of Scuol and Tarasp-Vulpera effectively form one big resort. The area owes its popularity to the 20 mineral springs (traditionally used for liver cures), the beautiful surroundings (mountains and dense forests), and the proximity of the Parc Naziunal Svizzer. Previously popular only in summer, the villages now fill up in winter, thanks to skiing on the south-facing slopes of Motta Naluns.

A small town, Scuol has a petite but exemplary old town, with five fountains from which you can do a taste-test comparison of normal tap water against spring water. For the inside-and-out spa experience,

CloseUp

THE BELLS OF CHALANDAMARZ

OLD MAN WINTER is an especially tough customer in Graubünden, but the locals, going back to Roman days, have a one-day festival to spook him out of his snowshoes and send him packing. On March 1, the youngest schoolchildren (six- to eight-year-olds) gather in the village squares of the Engadin and many other towns and villages in other valleys to celebate Chalandamarz. The name derives from the Latin calendae martius, literally the March calendar. Dressed in traditional costumes, the girls with a riot of silk and paper flowers in their hair, the children march through the villages ringing bells of all sizes (known as talocs) and singing songs. In the old days, they would stop at houses to collect food or other gifts that would be brought home to the families. Now cash is the preferred gift, used to fund the evening Chalandamarz dances.

The Chalandamarz procession in Guarda is special for two reasons. First, it takes place on the last day of February and only boys participate. Secondly, the town is the setting for the story "Schellenursli" ("A Bell for Ursli"), written by Selina Chönz with wonderful illustrations by Alois Carigiet. It tells of a young and poor goatherd named Ursli who, after many trials and tribulations, acquires the largest bell in town and is allowed to lead the procession. Within Switzerland, Schellenursli is as well known as Heidi. Graubünden has several Schellenursli trails. The one in St. Moritz, oddly, leads up to the "Heidihütte" where the 1970s TV series was shot.

head for the **Bogn Engiadina Scuol,** one of Europe's most modern spas. The calming blue interior, fantastic aquatic murals, and shifting reflections from backlighted pools start relaxing you before your toes even touch the water. Six pools, both indoor and outdoor, range in temperature from 60°F to 90°F. There are also saunas, solariums, steam rooms, and a massage area. A special Roman-Irish ritual treatment alternates between moist and dry heat, massage, and mineral baths. A therapy center offers mud baths, gymnastics, thalassotherapy, and electrotherapy (if you have a doctor's prescription). In addition to steeping in mineral water, you can drink it from four different sources. Reservations must be made at least 24 hours ahead. ⊠ Town center ☎ 081/ 8612002 ⊠ 25 SF for bathing area; 66 SF with Roman-Irish baths ⊙ June–Apr., daily 9 AM–10 PM.

The other two villages lie on the opposite side of the river from Scuol. **Vulpera,** whose permanent residents number just five, has a 1876 Trinkhalle with its spring pumping out water rich in minerals said to be good for the digestive tract. From Vulpera you can take a 15-minute bus ride up to **Tarasp,** a cluster of houses, inns, and farms around a tiny lake. The village is dominated by the impressive stronghold **Schloss Tarasp,** perched 500 feet above. The main tower and chapel date from the 11th century, when the castle was built by the leading family of Tarasp. Tarasp became part of Austria in 1464; the imperial eagle still can be seen on the castle walls. In the early 1800s, Napoléon gave Tarasp to the canton Graubünden, newly part of the Swiss federation. The castle went through several owners and subsequent neglect before passing into private hands in the early 20th century. You must join a tour to see the interior; the schedule varies quite a bit, so call ahead for tour times. Special midnight tours are conducted during the full moon. The bus from Vulpera departs roughly every hour. It's a 1½ hour walk from Scuol, following a well marked path that goes over the Punt'Ota (high bridge). ☎ 081/8649368 ☒ 10 SF ☉ June–Oct., daily; Christmas–Easter, Tues. and Thurs.

Skiing & Snowboarding

The region's ski area centers around 14 gondolas and lifts going up Scuol's **Motta Naluns,** at elevations between 4,100 and 9,184 feet. The 80 km (50 mi) of trails include the 12-km (7½-mi) Traumpiste (Dream Run), a good run of medium difficulty, with a few tough areas. There is a wide range of ski passes available for an equally wide range of prices beginning at 50 SF for a day pass. Some passes even include use of the Bogn Engiadina Scuol spa. Tarasp has one short ski lift for beginners. Bus transport between Scuol/Sent and Scuol/Tarasp-Vulpera is free of charge if you have a ski pass.

Snowboarding is extremely popular on these broad, sunny slopes. Scuol's snowboard school, **The School** (☎ 081/8641723), is the oldest in Europe. You could also sign up with **Schweizer Schneesportschule Scuol** (☎ 081/ 8641723) for instruction in Alpine and cross-country skiing. There are 60 km (37 mi) of prepared cross-country tracks around Scuol. Rental equipment is available at sports shops in Scuol and next to the Motta Naluns cable-car station.

Where to Stay & Eat

★ $$$$ ✕▦ **Schlosshotel Chastè.** This Relais & Châteaux treasure has been in the Pazeller family's care for 500 years. It started as a farm, then supplied provisions to builders of Tarasp Castle, which looms above. It eventually drew overnight guests—and today it's an impeccable, welcoming inn. The exterior has been preserved, but behind the magnificently carved wood door are modern comforts. Each room varies a bit from the others: a canopy bed here, an antique trunk there. Rudolf Pazeller himself is the chef and offers a small but sophisticated menu; his fish dishes, such as the bouillabaisse, are outstanding. ☒ CH-7553 Tarasp ☎ 081/8613060 ☎ 081/8613061 ⊕ www.relaischateaux.ch/ chaste ⇨ 20 rooms ⚹ Restaurant, Stübli, minibars, cable TV, hot tub, massage, sauna, steam room, bar; no a/c ⊟ AE, DC, MC, V ☉ Closed early Apr.–late May and mid-Oct.–mid-Dec. ⅠⓄⅠ BP.

$$$ ✕▦ **Villa Maria.** Family-owned and -run, this hillside retreat is particularly well situated for golfers; it's next to the golf course on the road to Tarasp and has its own putting green. The interior is homey, with Oriental rugs on the quarry tile floors and a fireplace in the main dining room. Some rooms have balconies overlooking the forested valley. The main restaurant's kitchen takes advantage of market produce

and the chef's homegrown vegetables. The huge Sunday brunch is a culinary event. ⌧ *CH-7552 Vulpera* ☎ *081/8641138* 🖷 *081/8649161* ⊕ *www.villamaria.ch* ⇝ *15 rooms* ⚴ *2 restaurants, bar, cable TV; no a/c* ▤ *AE, DC, MC, V* ⊘ *Closed Easter–late May and late Oct.–late Dec.* ⎥◎⎮ *BP.*

$$–$$$ 🖾 **Hotel Villa Post.** The former post office provides simply and tastefully decorated rooms and a friendly ambience. Guests are welcomed with a drink in the hotel's own museum, which displays vintage tableware from the grand days of tourism in the early 20th century. The familial atmosphere is ideal for those seeking a peaceful home away from home. The pine-panel restaurant serves local specialties made from market-fresh ingredients. A nightcap in front of the fireplace on winter evenings rounds off a perfect experience. ⌧ *CH-7552 Vulpera* ☎ *081/8641112* 🖷 *081/8649585* ⊕ *www.villa-post.ch* ⇝ *25 rooms* ⚴ *Restaurant, minibars, cable TV; no a/c* ▤ *AE, MC, V* ⊘ *Closed May and Nov.* ⎥◎⎮ *MAP.*

★ $–$$ 🖾 **Engiadina.** This 16th-century typical Engadine house has rooms done in beige tones touched with bright reds or blues, and four older units (with showers only) done in Swiss pine. An apartment for four can be rented in a second house. The main restaurant and the Bündner Stübli have a welcoming, country feel, with light wood, blue linens, and cushions. The restaurant is closed Sunday and Monday. ⌧ *Rablüzza, CH-7550* ☎ *081/8641421* 🖷 *081/8641245* ⊕ *www.engiadina-scuol.ch* ⇝ *10 rooms, 1 apartment, 1 suite* ⚴ *2 restaurants, minibars, cable TV; no a/c* ▤ *MC, V* ⊘ *Closed late Apr.–mid-June and mid-Oct.–mid-Dec.*

$–$$ 🖾 **Villa Engiadina.** This folly of towers and gables standing guard over Vulpera was built in 1902 and was transformed into a hotel in the late 1990s. Owing to the architecture, each room has a different shape and has been individually furnished. The rooms in the towers are especially attractive, offering a sprawling view of the valley. A no-smoking restaurant offers (among other things) fresh vegetables from the hotel's own garden. The homemade cakes have earned a reputation throughout the valley. A surcharge of 40 SF gives you half-board privileges. ⌧ *CH-7552 Vulpera* ☎ *081/8612244* 🖷 *081/8612266* ⊕ *www.villa-engiadina.ch* ⇝ *19 rooms* ⚴ *Restaurant, minibars, cable TV; no a/c* ▤ *DC, MC, V* ⊘ *Closed Apr. and Nov.* ⎥◎⎮ *BP.*

¢ 🖾 **Element Igloos.** Here's an alternative to the usual pine guest room: an igloo perched on Motta Naluns. The igloos are ready at the beginning of January and, depending on the weather, are habitable until mid-April. The price includes extra-thick sleeping bags; a hot evening meal of soup, fondue, and goulash; and a hot breakfast in the morning. One thing's for sure: you'll beat everyone else to the slopes. ⌧*CH-7550* ☎*081/8600777* 🖷 *081/8600778* ⊕ *element-scuol.ch* ⇝ *25 spots in 5 igloos* ▤ *No credit cards* ⎥◎⎮ *BP.*

Sports & the Outdoors

BIKING Rental bicycles are available at sports shops and the Motta Naluns cable-car station. For the adventurous, bikes can be taken on the cable car; once on the mountain, you can explore on your own or join a guided tour. Contact the tourist office for details.

GOLF There is a **9-hole course** (☎ 081/8649688) and driving range open in Vulpera from late May to early October. Winter golf is played in Tarasp beginning late January. Contact **Herr Jäger** (☎ 081/8641138) at the Hotel Villa Maria.

HORSEBACK A great way to explore this rugged part of Graubünden is on horseback.
RIDING **Reitstall San Jon** (☎ 081/8641062) organizes horseback riding tours of the region. In winter you can see the countryside from horse-drawn sleds.

ICE SPORTS Open-air ice rinks for hockey, curling, and skating are available in Scuol from early December to early March at **Sportanlage Trü** (☎ 081/8612006). **Eishalle Gurlaina** (☎ 081/8640272), in Scuol, has indoor skating facilities. There are three main sled runs, between 2½ and 7 km (1½ and 4½ mi) long. You can rent a sled at the Motta Naluns mountain station or from **Sport Conradin** (☎ 081/8641410). **Sport Heinrich** (☎ 081/8641956) rents sleds in Scuol.

TENNIS Reserve sand courts through **Tennis Gurlaina** (☎ 081/8640643); the courts are available from mid-May to mid-October. **Robinsons Club Schweizerhof** (✉ Vulpera ☎ 081/8611700) has two indoor courts and two outdoor sand courts. You can also rent equipment.

WHITE-WATER **Swissraft** (☎ 081/9115250) organizes daily white-water rafting expedi-
RAFTING tions in rubber dinghies on the River Inn from late May to early October. **Engadin Adventure** (☎ 081/8611419) runs rafting and canoeing excursions from early June to mid-September.

off the beaten path

SAMNAUN – About 23 kilometers (14 mi) toward the Austrian border, a road leads up from the hamlet of Vinadi to the isolated duty-free area around Samnaun, which shares its vast ski area with Ischgl in Austria. The 41 modern ski lifts with a capacity of 69,000 passengers per hour include the world's only double-decker lift, which carries 180 people. The local Boarders' Paradise is Europe's biggest snowboarders' park. For information contact the Samnaun tourist office. ✉ *CH-7563 Samnaun-Dorf* ☎ *081/8685858* ⊕ *www. samnaun.ch.*

Zernez

❾ *27 km (17 mi) southwest of Scuol.*

This small town lies at the crossroads of the Lower Engadine and the route over the Ofen Pass to the Val Müstair and Italy. Serious hikers sporting loden hats, knickers, and sturdy boots come to stock up on picnic goods and topographical maps before setting off for the Parc Naziunal Svizzer. In winter, there are cross-country trails. The alpine skiing areas of the Lower and Upper Engadine are accessible by public transport.

Where to Stay

$ 🏨 **Bär-Post.** This lodging, now family-run, started out as a stagecoach stop in the late 1800s. The rustic, wood-clad rooms all have baths with either tub or shower. The main difference between the higher- and lower-price rooms is size. Half board, at 25 SF per day, is available if you stay three days or more. The meals, using ingredients from the hotel's own gardens, include many Graubünden specialties. ✉ *CH-7530* 🖷 *081/ 8515500* 🖶 *081/8515599* 🌐 *www.forum.ch/baer-und-post* 🖙 *46 rooms* ♨ *Restaurant, minibars, cable TV, 2 tennis courts, pool, sauna; no a/c* 🖃 *AE, DC, V* ⊙ *Closed late Oct.–late Dec.* ⭐| *BP.*

$ 🏨 **Chasa Veglia.** "The old house" with its converted barn is down a
Fodor's Choice quiet side street. The owner's wood-carving skills are on display at every
★ turn, from the doors and chairs to ceilings and fretwork panels over the lighting fixtures. Rugs on parquet floors and a display of old farm and kitchen implements add to the atmosphere. One room is an exception, painted pink and decorated in an ultramodern style. Rooms are small; those without a bathtub have a shower, except for two rooms with only a toilet and sink. ✉ *CH-7530* 🖷🖷 *081/2844868* 🌐 *www.infoart.ch/cv* 🖙 *11 rooms, 9 with bath* ♨ *Cable TV; no a/c* 🖃 *No credit cards* ⊙ *Closed early May–mid-June and early Nov.–late Dec.* ⭐| *BP.*

$ 🏨 **Piz Terza.** This hotel is completely modern behind its traditional facade; its rooms have a utilitarian look, but the back rooms have balconies with flower boxes. The public pool is across the street. ✉ *CH-7530* 🖷 *081/8561414* 🖶 *081/8561415* 🖙 *23 rooms* ♨ *Cable TV; no a/c* 🖃 *No credit cards* ⊙ *Closed mid-Mar.–early June and late Oct.–Christmas* ⭐| *BP.*

Parc Naziunal Svizzer

🔟 ☛ *Access roads from Zernez, Scuol, S-Chanf, and the Ofen Pass.*
Fodor's Choice
★ The Swiss National Park, established in 1914, is a magnificent nature reserve. Its 173 square km (107 square mi) area (which includes the Macun lakes near Lavin) is minute compared with a U.S. or Canadian national park. It has no amenities such as campgrounds and picnic sites. Dead wood is left to rot and insects to multiply. Rangers see that rules are obeyed—no fires, dogs, bikes, skis, or tents are allowed, and picking plants is forbidden. Although the last bear was shot in the Lower Engadine in 1904, the park is home to large herds of ibex (the heraldic animal on the Graubünden flag), chamois, red and roe deer, and marmots. Don't forget binoculars; without them you might not see much fauna—the animals give a wide berth to the 80 km (50 mi) of marked paths. If big game make no appearance, you can just enjoy the scenery and watch out for a bearded vulture overhead. Before heading into the park, visit the **Nationalpark-Haus** in Zernez, where you can watch a video in English, stock up on maps, and enjoy the natural history exhibit, which includes a "marmot underground experience." Guided walks in English are available on Tuesday and Thursday; reserve one to two days in advance to join a group (10 SF for adults) or book a private guided walk.

Trails start out from parking lots off the park's only highway (visitors are encouraged to take buses back to their starting point)—a series of wild, rough, and often steep paths. Visitors are restricted to the trails except at designated resting places. The Il Fuorn–Stabelchod–Val dal

Botsch trail marks botanical and natural phenomena with multilingual information boards and leads to a spectacular barren ridge at 7,672 feet; the round-trip journey takes about four hours.

A three-hour route from picturesque S-chanf (pronounced sss-*chanff*) takes you into a deep glacial valley where ibex and chamois often gather; the return, by a riverside trail, passes a snack bar—just across the park border and thus permitted. ✉ *Nationalpark-Haus, CH-7530 Zernez, leaving the village toward Ofenpass* ☎ *081/8561378* 🖷 *081/ 8561740* ⊕ *www.nationalpark.ch* ✑ *Free* ⊙ *June–Oct., Wed.–Mon. 8:30–6, Tues. 8:30* AM–10 PM.

Where to Stay

$–$$ 🏨 **Il Fuorn.** This century-old mountain inn in the Swiss National Park is on the highway and makes an ideal base for hikers. Choose from either old-style rooms without bath or pine-and-stucco rooms with bath. Multibed rooms are available for groups. The plain Swiss cooking is augmented by some game specialties. ✉ *CH-7530* ☎ *081/8561226* 🖷 *081/8561801* 🛏 *32 rooms, 12 with bath* ♨ *Restaurant, Stübli; no a/c, no TV in some rooms* ☰ *AE, DC, MC, V* ⊙ *Closed late Oct.–mid-May* ⦿ *BP.*

---

off the beaten path

MÜSTAIR – If you continue through the National Park over the Ofen Pass to the Münster valley and Italy, you can visit the UNESCO World Heritage site convent church of St. John in Müstair, on the Italian border. The Benedictine convent is still active and even offers fasting weeks in spring and fall. Take time to wonder at the Romanesque frescoes AD 800–1170; further paintings are being uncovered using laser technology. Admission is free. The appealingly simple convent complex also houses a small **museum** (🖾 3 SF ⊕ www.muestair.ch) with baroque statues and Carolingian works.

---

en route

Driving south along the River Inn from the Swiss National Park toward its source in the Upper Engadine Valley, you will pass **Zuoz**, one of the valley's most attractive villages, with its small, uncrowded ski area and cross-country trails in winter and its fountains, water troughs, and overflowing flower boxes in summer. It's a peaceful, Romansh-flavored stop before reaching the busier resorts farther up the valley.

UPPER ENGADINE

Stretching from Brail to Maloja and with a gate to the Swiss National Park at S-chanf, this is one of the country's highest regions—the highest settlement is at 6,710 feet—and one of its most dazzling. From mountain peaks, such as Piz Corvatsch or Piz Nair, you can swoosh down world-class slopes or simply take in the dizzying view over the lakes and mountains. Besides summer and winter sports, both seasons are packed tight with cultural programs and events. Summer is also when the lowland farmers send their cows up to the high alpine pastures so they can have a relaxing mountain holiday, too.

Samedan

① *27 km (17 mi) southwest of Zernez, 10 km (6 mi) northeast of St. Moritz.*

This small, if less prestigious, resort is the administrative capital of the Upper Engadine; it was once its largest community. There are magnificent views of the awe-inspiring Bernina chain to the south, including the permanently snowcapped Piz Bernina (13,300 feet), Graubünden's highest peak, and Piz Palü (12,808 feet). The town has several good sports facilities, from a rollerblading track to a small ski area. Host to the Upper Engadine's airfield, it has a popular gliding center that's open in summer. The 18-hole golf course in nearby St. Moritz is the highest in Europe, but with hardly any noticeable gradients. Transport to the Upper Engadine's main ski areas is provided by the Engadin Bus service, which is included in the price of a regional ski ticket.

Where to Eat

★ **$$–$$$** ✕ **Berghotel Muottas Muragl.** For a meal with a truly spectacular view, reserve a window table at this mountainside restaurant outside town. The menu covers national and regional specialties, such as Capuns with smoked ham. The international wine list is the result of the English manager's worldwide winery visits. There's a "smoker's den," where you can enjoy a cigar and a whiskey after your meal. Bright, very simple guest rooms ($) are available if you'd like to spend a night in total peace and quiet. ✉ *Punt Muragl* ☎ *081/8428232* 🖃 *AE, DC, MC, V* ☻ *Closed mid-Apr.–late May and mid-Oct.–mid-Dec.*

en route

★ At **Punt Muragl,** off the highway between Samedan and Pontresina, you'll find the funicular for Muottas Muragl at 8,055 feet. Up here, summer or winter, walkers can take the Philosophers' Path, which is dotted with quotations from famous minds such as Socrates and Descartes, as well as more modern observations about life. Following the three circular paths takes about 2½ hours. Two lifts give access to easy skiing. These, together with a playground, make Muottas a good excursion for children. An alternative way back down to the valley is the 4-km (2½-mi) sled run. Sleds can be rented at the valley station. The funicular fare is 26 SF, 15 SF for an evening round-trip.

Pontresina

② *5 km (3 mi) south of Samedan.*

On a south-facing shelf along the Flaz Valley, Pontresina grew by converting its farmhouses to pensions and hotels for use by summer tourists. Today its climbing school is making a name for itself, and the village has become a popular hiking center. From here you can see clear across to the Roseg Valley, once filled with a glacier that has retreated to the base of Piz Roseg itself. The river Flaz winds through the valley from the Morteratsch glacier, which oozes down from Piz Bernina. Although the main street is built up with restaurants and shops, the resort still has a relaxed atmosphere. Every second Thursday in July and August, there's a street market in the lower part of the village, with locals selling fresh produce and handmade crafts.

The **Museum Alpin** gives some local history and documents the region's flora and fauna; be sure to check out the room full of birds whose recorded songs can be heard at the push of a button. There's also an exhibit on mining in the Engadine. ⊠ *Via Maistra* ☎ *081/8427273* ≥*5 SF* ⊙ *Mid-June–mid-Oct. and late Dec.–mid-Apr., Mon.–Sat. 4–6.*

Skiing

There's a small beginners' slope in the village at San Spiert. The compact ski areas of Diavolezza (9,768 feet) and, on the other side of the road, Lagalb (9,705 feet), on the Bernina pass, complement the much more extensive ones of St. Moritz. All three are about 20 minutes away by bus. Lift tickets cost 69 SF for one day, 332 SF for a six-day regional ticket. Rides on the Engadin bus service are included in the price of a regional ski ticket. Newcomers can learn the basics at the **Ski and Snowboard School** (☎ 081/8388383). Below the village, on the Engadine Marathon Trail, is the **Tolais Cross-Country Ski Center** (☎ 081/8426844).

Where to Stay & Eat

$–$$$ ✗**Steinbock.** Owned by the Walther family, proprietors of the neighboring Hotel Walther, this 17th-century house has been modernized in keeping with Engadine style—lots of wood and warm colors. The Colani Stübli serves regional and seasonal specialties, such as polenta *cun crema*, a filling cornmeal dish. The game dishes served in autumn are exceptional, especially the *Gemspfeffer* (chamois ragout cooked in wine) with hazelnut Spätzli and red cabbage. For dessert you might try *Nusskrapfen* (puff pastry with a sticky nut filling). ⊠ *Via Maistra* ☎ *081/8393626* ▭ *AE, DC, MC, V.*

★ $ ✗**Café Puntschella.** Either way you look here, you can't go wrong: your chair will face either the Roseg Valley or the spread of fresh-made pastries. The menu can satisfy all kinds of cravings, from bowls of breakfast muesli to plates of *Rösti* (pan-fried potatoes). Locals know to ask for the beignetlike *Quarkinis* with vanilla sauce—as well as a seat on the terrace. ⊠ *Via Mulin* ☎ *081/8388030* ▭ *V* ⊙ *Closed Mon. and Tues. in May.*

$$$$ ✗▤ **Grand Hotel Kronenhof.** This breathtaking building was completed
Fodor'sChoice   in 1898, and the exterior has changed little since. The lobby and din-
★   ing rooms, with elaborate moldings, pink cherubs, and heavy chandeliers, are dazzling. The guest rooms are tastefully done with Biedermeier furniture. The lawn that sprawls out toward the Roseg Valley is a social center in summer and winter, with tennis courts doubling as an ice rink. A gourmet restaurant serves international cuisine, including specialties such as roast lamb with an olive crust. The Kronenstübli offers simpler regional fare. ⊠ *CH-7504* ☎ *081/8303030* ᐕ *081/8303031* ⊕ *www.kronenhof.com* ➥ *93 rooms* ⚹ *2 restaurants, café, minibars, cable TV, 2 tennis courts, pool, hair salon, massage, sauna, steam room, bowling, ice-skating, bar; no a/c* ▭ *AE, DC, MC, V* ⊙ *Closed mid-Apr.–mid-June and mid-Sept.–mid-Dec.* ⎪⎤⎪ *BP.*

★ **$$$$** ✗▦ **Walther.** Though it was built in 1907, this hotel's interior is contemporary, save for a few moldings; the look is gracious without being overly formal. The decor is strictly classical, with discreet blues and yellows in public rooms. Guest rooms have pastel color schemes and modern baths; some have south-facing balconies. The restaurant serves beautifully presented international dishes. A jacket is requested here: for a more casual meal you can eat at the Steinbock next door. The pool is in a pavilion that opens on to a wooded garden. ⊠ *CH-7504* ☎ *081/8393636* 🖷 *081/8393637* ⊕ *www.hotelwalther.ch* 🛏 *62 rooms, 9 suites ⚐ 2 restaurants, minibars, cable TV, driving range, 3 tennis courts, pool, health club, massage, bicycles, piano bar; no a/c* ▭ *AE, DC, MC, V* ⊘ *Closed Easter–mid-June and mid-Oct.–Christmas* ▯◻ *BP.*

★ **$$$–$$$$** ✗▦ **Saratz.** This 19th-century grand hotel has a spacious lobby with huge windows and a new wing that extends the building lengthwise. All interiors are done in warm, vibrant colors. The views of the Roseg Valley, from anywhere on the hotel's extensive grounds, are inspiring. Try a special Engadine dish such as *Chapunets* (chicken) with Parmesan in the Saratz restaurant; the Pitschna Scena Stüblis serves international specialties, including a luscious Thai curry. The hotel's family-friendly amenities include a kindergarten and a kid-size breakfast bar. ⊠ *CH-7504* ☎ *081/8394000* 🖷 *081/8394040* ⊕ *www.saratz.ch* 🛏 *73 rooms, 19 suites ⚐ 2 restaurants, minibars, cable TV, in-room data ports, pool, massage, sauna, Turkish bath, 2 bars; no a/c* ▭ *AE, DC, MC, V* ⊘ *Closed early Apr.–early June and mid-Oct.–early Dec.* ▯◻ *BP.*

$ ✗▦ **Roseggletscher.** You can reach this isolated hotel on foot or by horse-drawn carriage or sleigh (it's about 7½ km [4½ mi] up the ruggedly beautiful Roseg Valley). The restaurant offers simple regional favorites throughout the year; in fall there's wild game. This is a very popular lunch spot for hikers, bikers, and cross-country skiers, who reward themselves with a selection from the massive dessert buffet. The rooms are spartan but fresh; you pay a little more for a private shower. ⊠ *CH-7504* ☎ *081/8426445* 🖷 *081/8426886* 🛏 *13 rooms, 5 with bath, 3 dorm rooms ⚐ Restaurant, cafeteria, minibars, cable TV; no a/c* ▭ *AE, V* ⊘ *Closed mid-Oct.–early Dec. and late Apr.–mid-June* ▯◻ *BP.*

$$–$$$ ▦ **Bernina.** This elegant, symmetrical building at the foot of Bernina mountain has simple, solid rooms at affordable prices. Half board is well worth the 30 SF or 50 SF for a three- or five-course meal. Services include free transfer to and from the train station. ⊠ *CH-7504* ☎ *081/8388686* 🖷 *081/8388687* ⊕ *www.hotelbernina.ch* 🛏 *70 rooms ⚐ 2 restaurants, minibars, cable TV, sauna, steam room; no a/c* ▭ *AE, DC, MC, V* ⊘ *Closed Easter–late June and mid-Oct.–mid-Dec.* ▯◻ *BP.*

$ ▦ **Bahnhof.** Next to the entrance to the Roseg Valley, the cross-country skiing center, and the train station, the hotel offers dependable, low-key accommodations. Rooms have sinks with bathrooms down the hall; one room in an adjoining house has a shower. The restaurant, with its pink linen and flowers, offers simple fare at reasonable prices. ⊠ *CH-7504* ☎ *081/8388000* 🖷 *081/8388009* ⊕ *www.hotel-bahnhof.ch* 🛏 *21 rooms, 1 with bath ⚐ Restaurant, café; no a/c, no room TVs* ▭ *AE, DC, MC, V* ▯◻ *BP.*

Nightlife & the Arts

BARS & LOUNGES At Hotel Müller, **Cento Bar** (✉ ☎ 081/8393000) is a local hangout with rustic furnishings. **Bar Pitschna Scena** (✉ Hotel Saratz ☎ 081/8394000) has live music Thursday nights in summer and winter seasons. **Piano-Bar** (✉ Sporthotel ☎ 081/8389400) is a cozy, blond-wood bar.

MUSIC The **Kurorchester Pontresina** plays chamber concerts daily between mid-June and mid-September at 11 AM in the Tais forest. Check with the tourist office for more information.

Sports & the Outdoors

BICYCLING Touring and mountain bikes can be rented at the **Fähndrich Sport** (☎ 081/8427155). **Bollinger Bike Shop** (☎ 081/8426262) rents all kinds of bikes and can suggest scenic routes. To take on steep mountain descents like Lagalb–Poschiavo, contact **Engadin Ferien** (☎ 081/8300001).

CARRIAGE & Horse-drawn carriages and sleighs can be booked through **M. Kaiser**
SLEIGH RIDES (☎ 081/8426274). **V. Rietberger** (☎ 081/8428353) is another vendor offering sleigh and carriage rides. The Roseg Valley "horse omnibus" is run by **L. Costa** (☎ 081/8426057) as a scheduled service in summer and winter. The trip is very popular, so be sure to make a reservation.

FISHING Trout fishing in the Lej Nair and Lej Pitschen mountain lakes is free for Pontresina guests in season, from mid-June to mid-September. For information about obtaining a license, contact the tourist office.

HIKING Pontresina and the top of the Alp Languard chairlift (open only in summer) are good starting points for hikers. The Diavolezza and Lagalb cable cars, which run in summer, also bring you to good hiking trails. For information on a variety of guided excursions, including mushroom hunting and glacier hiking, contact the tourist office. If you're staying overnight in Pontresina, the tours are free; day visitors pay a small fee.

ICE SPORTS There's a large **natural ice-skating rink** (☎ 081/8427341) off the main street; rental skates and instruction are available. From December through March, 10 curling rinks with instructors are available at **Sport-pavilion Roseg** (✉ Via Maistra ☎ 081/8426346 or 081/8426349).

MOUNTAIN **Bergsteigerschule Pontresina** (✉ Via Maistra ☎ 081/8388333), the biggest
CLIMBING mountain climbing school in Switzerland, offers instruction in rock and ice climbing for people of all skill levels. The company also leads guided tours in English.

SWIMMING In addition to an indoor pool, **Pontresina Hallenbad** (✉ Via Maistra ☎ 081/8427341 or 081/8428257) offers a sauna, a solarium, and a sunbathing terrace.

TENNIS More than a dozen public tennis courts are available in Pontresina at different hotels. Inquire at the tourist office. **Gruber Sport** (✉ Via Maistra ☎ 081/8426236) rents rackets.

WHITE-WATER For white-water rafting excursions on the Flaz River, contact **Michel Massé**
RAFTING (☎ 081/8426824).

Celerina

⑬ *2 km (1 mi) south of Samedan, 3 km (1¼ mi) northeast of St. Moritz.*

Celerina (Schlarigna in Romansh) lies just below St. Moritz, at the foot of that resort's bobsled runs. Even though it may seem overshadowed by its more famous neighbor, Celerina is a first-rate resort in its own right; not only does it share the ski area of Corviglia-Marguns with St. Moritz, but it's reputed to be the sunniest place in the valley. A cluster of Engadine houses characterizes its oldest neighborhood. Celerina's most striking landmark stands just outside the village. The 15th-century church of **San Gian** (St. John) has a richly painted wooden ceiling. The church lost its spire in a lightning strike in 1682. Many years later an offer to replace the spire was turned down, as locals thought the church looked more impressive without it. ⊙ *Mid-June–mid-Oct., Mon. 2–4, Wed. 4–5:30, and Fri. 10:30–noon.*

Where to Eat

$ ⊞ **Zur Alten Brauerei.** A young and youth-oriented crowd fills this conveniently located house, once the highest-altitude brewery in Europe. The only clue to its past life is the huge brewing vessel lid above the bar. Cheerful rooms are white-walled and simply furnished; all come with showers. The self-service restaurant serves mostly Italian fare, but the fondue and raclette draw people from far and wide. The cable-car station for the St. Moritz–Celerina Corviglia slopes is nearby. ⊠ *CH-7505* ☎ *081/8321874* 🖷 *081/8321877* ⊕ *www.alte-brauerei.ch* ⇆ *63 rooms* ⚘ *Restaurant, cable TV, sauna, steam room, gym, billiards, bar; no a/c* ⊟ *No credit cards* ⦿| *BP.*

St. Moritz

★ ⑭ *5 km (3 mi) west of Pontresina, 85 km (53 mi) southeast of Chur.*

St. Moritz is one of the world's best-known winter resorts—so famous, in fact, that its name is a registered trademark. It has had longer than most to burnish its reputation, as winter tourism began here in 1864. The town has been a favorite among celebrities, blue bloods, tycoons, and wannabes for generations, and it shows in the sometimes snooty attitudes you encounter in local establishments. Nevertheless, the crowds do include nature lovers and outdoors enthusiasts. Fur coats, anoraks, and colorful cross-country ski outfits are all acceptable attire.

The resort stands at the edge of a lake; the original center around the Bad (spa) is at lake level, with the Dorf (village) above. At the top of the Dorf is St. Moritz's answer to Pisa—a leaning tower, all that's left of a 13th-century church. Other than that, don't expect a picturesque village that might appear on the lid of a chocolate box. St. Moritz has its fair share of unattractive buildings and, in winter, traffic snarls. But the latter have improved quite a bit since the creation of a pedestrian-only zone in the village. It's also a place that's difficult to see if you're on a budget. If you'd rather not splurge on luxury accommodations, you can enjoy scenery—and the scene—without digging too deeply into your pocket. You can window-shop the designer boutiques from A(rmani) to Z(egna), relax with coffee and cake on a sunny café terrace, and take a 1½-hour local tour by car or van.

The resort's events calendar is especially impressive. This is the place to see winter sports that were, or still are, found only here, such as polo and cricket played on snow, bobsledding on natural ice, and horse racing on snow, which includes *skikjöring* (skiers pulled by riderless horses). The frozen lake acts as the "white arena" for some events and provides the backdrop for others. A tent village complete with grandstands, palm trees, restaurants, bars, and art exhibitions is installed on the lake from late January through February. Watch for the annual winter Gourmet Festival in St. Moritz, when world-renowned chefs serve their specialties in local restaurants and hotels. The Grand Gourmet Finale is a gargantuan feast prepared by about 25 chefs and their assistants, usually presented on the frozen lake.

Besides challenging sports, the town offers relaxation at the **St. Moritz Bad** (spa complex). The local mineral springs have been known for more than 3,000 years; in 1535 the physician and alchemist Paracelsus praised the water, which is the richest in iron and carbonic acid in Europe. Massages and most treatments are done in individual cabins with private baths. Peat baths and packs need a doctor's prescription, but you can take a mineral bath anytime; try one with natural aromas such as pine or rosemary (35 SF). ☎ 081/8333062 ☉ *Weekdays 8–7, Sat. 8–noon.*

Get a glimpse of the old way of life in the **Engadine Museum,** housed in a building dating from 1906. The museum has displays of furniture, tools, and pottery in rooms decorated in styles from different periods. ✉ *Via dal Bagn 39* ☎ *081/8334333* 🎫 *5 SF* ☉ *June–Oct., weekdays 9:30–noon and 2–5, Sun. 10–noon; Dec.–Apr., weekdays 10–noon and 2–5, Sun. 10–noon.*

The somewhat forbidding stone structure that houses the **Segantini Museum** showcases the work of Italian artist Giovanni Segantini (1858–99). His huge triptych *La Vita, La Natura, La Morte* hangs in the domed upper floor. Take a seat on the bench to absorb his meditations on life, nature, and death. ✉ *Via Somplaz* ☎ *081/8334454* ⊕ *www.segantini-museum.ch* 🎫 *10 SF* ☉ *June–mid-Oct. and early Dec.–late Apr., Tues.–Sun. 10–noon and 3–6.*

Skiing
Don't let the whirlwind of activities at St. Moritz make you forget that its raison d'être is skiing. You can reach the **Corviglia–Piz Nair, Suvretta,** and **Marguns** slopes, immediately above St. Moritz, from the Chantarella–Corviglia funicular in Dorf, the Signal cableway in Bad, the Suvretta chairlift, and the Marguns gondolas in Celerina. There are 80 km (50 mi) of difficult, intermediate, and easy runs and a half pipe for snowboarders. The Upper Engadine ski region offers 350 km (217 mi) of prepared trails. The views from Corviglia, Piz Nair, and the Suvretta Paradise run are magnificent.

Descents behind Piz Nair (10,026 feet) eventually lead down to Marguns; they are often in shadow in early winter but have the best snow up to the end of the season. With the help of snowmaking equipment, conditions usually remain excellent until late April. The sunny Suvretta slopes are usually less crowded but do not benefit from snowmaking equipment. For instruction there are a number of choices, including the **Suvretta Snowsports School** (☎ 081/8363600). The **St. Moritz Ski School** (☎ 081/8300101 in town, 081/8335553 on Corviglia) is the oldest in Switzerland. You can join a group and go with an instructor on a free "ski safari," offered by any ski school, which begins in Sils and ends in St. Moritz Bad. Rental equipment is available at **Ski Service Corvatsch** (☎ 081/8387788) at the Corviglia valley and mountain stations. One-day tickets for St. Moritz are between 49 SF and 64 SF; for the whole Upper Engadine region a one-day pass costs between 56 SF and 69 SF. Six-day regional passes run between 262 SF and 332 SF. Prices include transportation between ski stations on the Engadin bus service and free entry to the public swimming pools in St. Moritz and Pontresina. For reports on daily snow conditions, call the **hotline** (☎ 0844/844944); the English-language version comes last.

Cross-country skiing has its base in St. Moritz Bad, where the **Langlauf school** (✉ Parkhotel Kurhaus ☎ 081/8336233) offers lessons and excursions. You can try out the close-by Engadine Marathon track or the many side valleys. Near the school is a lighted circular trail of 3 km (2 mi) open from 5 PM to 9:30 PM.

Where to Stay & Eat

$$$–$$$$ ✕ **Jöhri's Talvò.** Roland Jöhri's restaurant, in a 17th-century Engadine house, marries the best of Graubünden tradition with classic French elegance. Both the cooking and decor reflect this philosophy, from the delicate linens softening weathered woodwork to the light sauces that curb the heaviness of local dishes. A popular fish menu could include a house-style bouillabaisse or shellfish risotto. The desserts are elaborate works of art. But be prepared to spend as much on a meal as on a hotel room. ✉ *Champfèr, 3 km (2 mi) southwest of St. Moritz* ☎ *081/8334455* ⚠ *Reservations essential* ▤ *AE, DC, MC, V* ☾ *Closed mid-Apr.–mid-June and mid-Oct.–mid-Dec.*

$–$$$ ✕ **Engiadina.** With its plain linoleum and pine trim, this could pass for a St. Moritz diner, though its raison d'être is fondue; champagne fondue is the house specialty. Other favorites are *steak-frîtes* (steak with french fries) and escargots. It's a popular oddity in this ritzy resort. ✉ *Schulhauspl.* ☎ *081/8333265* ▤ *AE, DC, MC, V.*

★ $–$$ ✕ **Meierei.** You reach this country inn via a private forest road or, in winter, across the lake—on foot or by horse-drawn carriage or sleigh. In the 17th century this was a farm and there's still a *Meierei* (tenant farm) attached to it. Today the restaurants draw people for such modern combinations as pumpkin gnocchi with lobster. If you don't want a full meal, you can have just coffee and *Apfelstrudel* or Bündnerfleisch and a glass of wine. The sun terrace is a popular meeting spot for walkers, cross-country skiers, and horseback riders. ✉ *Via Dimlej* ☎ *081/8333242* ▤ *AE, DC, MC, V* ☾ *Closed late Mar.–mid-June and mid-Oct.–mid-Dec.*

★ **$–$$** ✕ **Veltlinerkeller.** This bright, genial restaurant has nothing swanky about it—just lots of wood and a welcoming fire where the meat is roasted while you and an enormous elk (one of the owner's hunting trophies) look on. In addition to grilled meats and whole trout, there are tasty pastas and other Italian specialties. ⊠ *Via dal Bagn* ☎ *081/8334009* 🖃 *AE, DC, MC, V.*

$$$–$$$$ ✕🖬 **Schweizerhof.** Built in 1896, this family-owned hotel has slick guest rooms with burled-wood cabinets and contemporary color schemes. The painted ceiling of the main dining room depicts a glittering birch forest. The informal Acla restaurant serves up solid meals such as chateaubriand and Wiener schnitzel. An outdoor restaurant opens in summer, and the hotel has its own mountain hut on the Suvretta slope. The rooftop wellness center offers saunas, steam baths, massages, and superb views over the lake. ⊠ *Via dal Bagn, CH-7500* ☎ *081/8370707* 🖨 *081/8370700* ⊕ *www.schweizerhofstmoritz.ch* ⇆ *73 rooms, 10 junior suites* ⌂ *2 restaurants, in-room safes, minibars, cable TV, health club, massage, 4 bars; no a/c* 🖃 *AE, DC, MC, V* ⦿⦿ *BP.*

$$$–$$$$ ✕🖬 **Steffani.** Not only does this hotel stay open all year, but it hasn't closed its doors for one day since 1930. Built in 1869, it's owned and run by the third generation of the Märky family. There's a lively, cosmopolitan atmosphere, with young skiers congregating in the Cava bar and the English-speaking Cresta crowd meeting in the first-floor bar. The decor has been dubbed by regulars (and accepted with good humor by the management) as "Austrian-yodel-baroque." The Corviglia funicular station and the shops are just a few steps away. ⊠ *Via Traunter Plazzas, CH-7500* ☎ *081/8369696* 🖨 *081/8369717* ⊕ *www.steffani.ch* ⇆ *59 rooms, 5 suites* ⌂ *3 restaurants, Stübli, minibars, cable TV, pool, hair salon, hot tub, massage, sauna, 3 bars, dance club; no a/c* 🖃 *AE, DC, MC, V* ⦿⦿ *BP.*

$$$$ 🖬 **Carlton.** If you won't miss having hotel grounds for outdoor activities, consider this luxurious hotel, which was built in 1913 for the last czar of Russia. It's bright and modern, without a scrap of pine: its white-marble lobby resembles a performing-arts center. Some guest rooms are designed along contemporary lines and are filled with leather furniture; others evoke eras gone by with crystal chandeliers. The baths are white marble. The pool and south-facing rooms have views over the lake. Ties are requested in the dining room. ⊠ *Via J. Badrutt, CH-7500* ☎ *081/8367000* 🖨 *081/8367001* ⊕ *www.carlton-stmoritz.ch* ⇆ *99 rooms, 6 suites* ⌂ *2 restaurants, cable TV, pool, hair salon, massage, sauna, bar; no a/c* 🖃 *AE, DC, MC, V* ⊘ *Closed late Mar.–mid-June and late Sept.–early Dec.* ⦿⦿ *BP.*

$$$$ 🖬 **Kulm.** The Kulm claims some important firsts. It was the first luxury lodging in St. Moritz (1856), and the first hotel in Switzerland to have electricity (1878). In keeping with its pedigree, its interiors are opulent, its rooms spacious. The health club is truly superlative; besides the pool and saunas, there are a saltwater grotto, a thalassotherapy area, and a fitness room with a lake view. In the Rôtisserie (open only in winter) and the main dining room, jacket and tie are a must, but more casual dining options are also available. A steeply priced half board is mandatory over the winter holidays. ⊠ *Via Maistra, CH-7500* ☎ *081/8368000*

🛏 *081/8368001* ⊕ *www.kulmhotel-stmoritz.ch* ⤴ *139 rooms, 41 suites* ⑂ *4 restaurants, in-room data ports, minibars, cable TV, putting green, 3 tennis courts, health club, hair salon, ice-skating, 2 bars; no a/c* ⊟ *AE, DC, MC, V* ☉ *Closed early Apr.–late June and mid-Sept.–mid-Dec.* ⑩ *MAP.*

★ **$$$$** 🏨 **Suvretta House.** The hotel has many assets: a unique location outside the village with stupendous views of Piz Corvatsch and the Silvaplana Lake, a private ski school, and access to the Corvilgia slopes just outside the front door. In the health complex you can soak in an outdoor hot tub (even in winter) or dream under the sauna's night sky reproduced with tiny lights. Jacket and tie are requested after 7 PM in the lobby and main dining room, but a casual downstairs area reserved for guests has English-style lounges, an informal restaurant, and even a children's restaurant. ⊠ *Via Chasellas 1, CH-7500 St. Moritz-Suvretta* 🕾 *081/ 8363636* 🖷 *081/8363737* ⊕ *www.suvrettahouse.ch* ⤴ *170 rooms, 10 junior suites* ⑂ *4 restaurants, cable TV, in-room data ports, in-room safes, driving range, 3 tennis courts, pool, health club, hair salon, massage, ice-skating, 2 bars, shops; no a/c* ⊟ *AE, DC, MC, V* ☉ *Closed mid-Apr.–late June and early Sept.–mid-Dec.* ⑩ *BP.*

$$$–$$$$ 🏨 **Badrutt's Palace.** The world's first Palace hotel is now under the management of Rosewood Hotels & Resorts but remains in Badrutt family hands. Major renovations of the public areas and guest rooms are ongoing. The cathedral-like lobby hints at the hotel's impressive facilities and services: private ski school, an in-house bridge hostess, complete fitness facilities, a driving range, a disco in winter, and a barbecue in summer, to name a few. Jacket and tie are required in the main restaurant and in public areas after 7:30 PM. ⊠ *Via Serlas, CH-7500* 🕾 *081/ 8371000* 🖷 *081/8372999* ⊕ *www.badruttspalace.com* ⤴ *170 rooms, 39 suites* ⑂ *3 restaurants, in-room data ports, minibars, room TVs with video games, driving range, 4 tennis courts, pool, gym, hair salon, hot tub, massage, sauna, ice-skating, 3 bars, dance club, nightclub; no a/c* ⊟ *AE, DC, MC, V* ☉ *Closed mid-Apr.–early July and early Sept.–mid-Dec.* ⑩ *BP.*

★ **$$$–$$$$** 🏨 **Laudinella.** Here you'll find the facilities of a top hotel at a reasonable price—with cultural offerings to boot. An in-house arts center hosts more than 50 courses each year for writers and music lovers. Your stay might coincide with that of an orchestra, an alphorn group, or a choir, allowing you to attend an informal concert. The hotel is a short walk from cross-country trails and from the Signal cable car. The good-size rooms are white with pine furniture; those in the newer wing have primary-color accents, whereas the older rooms are done in pastels and have shower only. The bar is open in high season only. ⊠ *Via Tegiatscha 17, CH-7500* 🕾 *081/8360000* 🖷 *081/8360001* ⊕ *www. laudinella.ch* ⤴ *170 rooms, 10 suites* ⑂ *3 restaurants, café, in-room data ports, in-room safes, minibars, cable TV, massage, sauna, bar, library; no a/c* ⊟ *AE, DC, MC, V* ⑩ *BP.*

$$–$$$$ 🏨 **Languard.** This small, family-owned garni hotel is on a side street in the town center. Details like sgraffiti, carved ceilings, and fine darkened pine in some rooms preserve the best from its earlier days. The big corner rooms deserve their higher price; back rooms are small, but all have tile baths. Front rooms have mountain and lake views. In the small sitting area, check out the collection of skiing trophies won by the owner's father, who used to run St. Moritz's ski school. ✉ *Off Via Maistra, CH-7500* ☎ *081/8333137* 🖷 *081/8334546* ⊕ *www. languard-stmoritz.ch* ➳ *22 rooms* ♿ *In-room safes, minibars, cable TV; no a/c* 🖃 *AE, DC, MC, V* ⊗ *Closed late Apr.–early June and mid-Oct.–early Dec.* ⏀ *BP.*

$$–$$$$
Fodor$Choice
★
🏨 **Waldhaus am See.** With a big, sunny terrace, and a clientele ranging from family clans to seniors, this hotel is geared to leisurely stays. It's perched on the edge of the lake, a good walk from the center of town. Rooms are plain with pine trim and tile baths. According to the *Guinness Book of World Records*, the Devil's Place bar holds the record for the world's largest selection of whiskies. In winter and summer half board is included in the price; in May and November prices include breakfast only. ✉ *Via Dimlej, CH-7500* ☎ *081/8366000* 🖷 *081/8366060* ⊕ *www. waldhaus-am-see.ch* ➳ *51 rooms, 2 apartments* ♿ *Restaurant, Stübli, cable TV, gym, sauna, bar; no a/c* 🖃 *AE, DC, MC, V* ⏀ *BP.*

Nightlife & the Arts

To find out what's happening, check the English-language section in the weekly *Engadin Information* brochure, available at the tourist office, hotels, and shops.

BARS & LOUNGES   The après-ski clique favors the Steffani Hotel's **Cava** (✉ Via Traunter Plazzas ☎ 081/8369696). Choose from the world's largest selection of whiskies at the **Devil's Place** (✉ Via Dimlej ☎ 081/8366000). This bar in the Waldhaus am See is mentioned in the *Guinness Book of World Records*. For elegant but informal surroundings try the **Grischuna** (✉ Schulhauspl. ☎ 081/8370404). Hotel Hauser's open-air **Roo** (✉ Via Traunter Plazzas ☎ 081/8334402) attracts those who've spent the day on the slopes.

CASINOS   The **Casino St. Moritz** (✉ Via Veglia 15/Via Maistra 28 ☎ 081/8321080) supplements its roulette with 59 slot machines. It's open Sunday through Thursday until 2 AM, Friday and Saturday until 3 AM. It closes in May and November.

DANCING   **Anton's Bar** (✉ Via Chasellas 1 ☎ 081/8363636), a winter-season spot at the Suvretta House, is jacket-and-tie formal. In Badrutt's Palace, the **King's Club** (✉ Via Serlas ☎ 081/8371000), has a Moorish decor. Open only in the winter, it has a steep cover charge on weekends. For more formal dancing to live music, try the winter-only **Sunny Bar** (✉ Via Maistra ☎ 081/8368000). This old-style dance hall is in the Kulm. In the basement of the Steffani Hotel is **Vivai** (✉ Via Traunter Plazzas ☎ 081/ 8336939), which opens for both the winter and summer seasons.

MUSIC   The musical highlight in St. Moritz is the **Snow & Symphony Music Festival** (☎ 081/8344646), which takes place over 10 days in early spring. Prize-winning classical and jazz musicians, chamber orchestras, and a symphony orchestra give roughly 20 concerts. The performances are held in hotels and on mountaintops. The **Engadine Concert Weeks** (☎ 081/ 8426573) take place from mid-July to late August, with smaller-scale performances throughout the Upper Engadine. The **St. Moritz Chamber**

Orchestra gives free daily concerts in summer at 10:30 AM in the spa center's hall or park. Contact the tourist office for more information.

Sports & the Outdoors

BICYCLING   Maps of biking routes (3 SF) are available at the tourist office. Mountain-bike rentals cost about 25 SF a day at **Scheuing Sport** (✉ Schulhauspl. ☎ 081/8333170).

BOBSLEDDING   In 1890 and 1891, the first bobsled races were held on the road between St. Moritz and Celerina. The present-day run, built each year from natural ice, follows roughly the same course; it's the only one of its kind in the world. You can watch the **Olympia Bob Run** (☎ 081/8300200) races for around 5 SF. Or you can tear along the run yourself by riding behind an experienced pilot. The ride costs 210 SF; book well in advance. The run is open from late December through early March.

CRESTA   On the world's only Cresta Run, riders on skeletons (a metal toboggan) rush headfirst down a winding ice channel from St. Moritz to Celerina, accelerating to about 90 mph. You can watch the runs every morning from the path or the roof of the Junction Hut. If you'd like to try the run, contact the **St. Moritz Tobogganing Club** (☎ 081/8334609). It's a private club, but they do allow temporary memberships (for a steep fee). The Cresta is open from late December to the last day of February. Note that the run is not open to women.

GOLF   Samedan's 18-hole **Engadine Golf Course** (☎ 081/8510466) is about 10 minutes by car from St. Moritz. It's open from late May to early October. The **St. Moritz Golf Club** (☎ 081/8368236) has a 9-hole course in the Kulm Park.

HIKING   There are dozens of hiking and walking routes around St. Moritz, all well signposted. Maps are available at the tourist office. Most cable cars, funiculars, and some chairlifts run in summer, providing access to higher trails, including the magnificent Via Engiadina path along the mountainside at roughly 6,560 feet to the beginning of the valley. The full walk takes about six hours, but you can descend to valley level earlier if you are tuckered out.

HORSEBACK RIDING   At the **Riding Resort Seaside Stables** (✉ Via Ludains ☎ 081/8335733), you can take a group lesson or go on an excursion for 50 SF an hour. The **Hossmann Stables** (✉ Champfèr, 3 km [2 mi] southwest of St. Moritz ☎ 081/8337125) specialize in Western-style riding; a group lesson or excursion costs 40 SF for one hour, 70 SF for two hours.

For horse-drawn sleigh or carriage rides, contact **M. Giovanoli** (☎ 081/8331279). You could also schedule a carriage or sleigh ride with **A. Lampert** (☎ 081/8333235). **A. Melcher** (☎ 081/8337457) is another resource. **D. Motti** (☎ 081/8333768) is available as well. A popular winter route is the ride across the frozen lake.

ICE-SKATING & CURLING   The lakeside **Ludains Skating Rink** (✉ St. Moritz-Bad ☎ 081/8335030) is open from mid-July to late April. Skate rentals are available. The skating and curling rinks at the **Kulm** hotel (☎ 081/8368000) are open to the public in winter; rental skates and curling lessons are available.

PARAGLIDING   **H. Zwyssig** (☎ 081/8332416 or 079/3532159) offers flights with an experienced pilot from the top station of the Corviglia funicular from mid-December through late March. The cost is 230 SF per person.

TENNIS   The **Corviglia Tennis Center** (✉ St. Moritz-Bad ☎ 081/8331500) has four indoor and four outdoor tennis courts, as well as a couple of squash courts. It's open year-round except from late May to early June.

WALKING   **S. Lareida** (☎ 081/8334465) leads botanical and mineralogical walks in the region around St. Moritz.

en route   Between St. Moritz and Sils lies the lakeside village of **Silvaplana**. Its attractions include sailing and kite-surfing (a sport that has been gaining popularity over the past few years) in summer, and snowshoeing and a snow golf tournament in winter. The **Piz Corvatsch** (11,319 feet) ski area adjoins that of Sils; together they share 45 km (28 mi) of runs. The gorgeous views from the top are worth the trip in summer or winter—on a clear day you can see as far as Monte Rosa, the Jungfrau, and the Austrian Alps.

Sils

⑮ *13 km (8 mi) southwest of St. Moritz.*

The village of Sils (in Romansh, Segl) sits in the meadows between the lakes of Silvaplana and Sils, just by the road leading to Italy over the Maloja Pass. It has two sections: Sils Maria, at the foot of the mountains, and Sils Baselgia. Access to Sils Baselgia is over the Inn River just by the tiny church of St. Lorenz; a barrier prevents through traffic to Sils Maria, so if you're driving, leave your car in Sils Maria's underground parking lot.

Sils smoothly mixes old and new. There are many examples of Engadine architecture; often the older houses have roofs of slate from the nearby Fex Valley. The awe-inspiring views from Sils Baselgia over the lake are still a favorite subject for artists. Friedrich Nietzsche, who spent seven summers in Sils Maria, called the lakeside region "the land of silver colors." The philosopher wrote about a dozen books, including *Also Sprach Zarathustra (Thus Spake Zarathustra),* while living in what is now the **Nietzsche Haus** museum. The house displays a collection of his original manuscripts and photographs. You can also see photos and mementos of other literati who put their thoughts on paper while vacationing in the village—from Thomas Mann to Anne Frank. ☎ 081/8265369 ✉ 5 SF ☉ *Mid-June–mid-Oct. and late Dec.–mid-Apr., Tues.–Sun. 3–6.*

Skiing

Sils was a predominantly summer resort until the Sils Furtschellas cableway opened in 1972. The Furtschellas slopes join those of Corvatsch, and skiing on this north side of the valley is especially popular at the beginning and end of the season. Lessons are available through Sils's **Swiss Ski School** (☎ 081/8385055). One-day passes for Furtschellas-Corvatsch cost 64 SF.

Where to Stay & Eat

$$$ ✕🖃 **Margna.** Named after the mountain above Sils, this hotel, originally a private house, still has an intimate atmosphere. Oriental rugs, antiques, paintings, and flowers fill the public spaces, and guest rooms are done in Engadine style (white walls with pine accents or all pine). The brightest rooms face the garden. Request a room with a fully modern bath, as not all have been renovated. The main restaurant serves Italian specialties; simpler pastas or Engadine specialties are served in the Stüva. The hotel has its own small golf course and driving range, with resident English pro. ✉ *CH-7515 Sils Baselgia* ☎ *081/8384747* ☎ *081/8384748* ⊕ *www.margna.ch* ↯ *64 rooms, 5 suites* ♨ *3 restaurants, minibars, cable TV, driving range, 6-hole golf course, pool, massage, sauna, steam room, bar; no a/c* ⊟ *MC, V* ☉ *Closed early Apr.–mid-June and early Oct.–mid-Dec.* ⵟⵔ *BP.*

★ **$$** ✕🖃 **Pensiun Andreola/Chesa Marchetta.** For a special regional experience, try this pension and restaurant run by two sisters. The guesthouse and its dining room are furnished in pine and cotton prints, and the neighboring Chesa Marchetta is an Arvenholz gem, perfectly preserved since 1671 with its tiny (really tiny—there are only four tables) restaurant. The menu is limited to a salad and one main dish, such as homemade pasta with lamb, with the permanent option of fondue *chinoise* (paperthin sliced meat cooked in bouillon). Meals are served evenings only; snacks are served from 3:30 on. Restaurant reservations are essential; the hotel rates include half board. ✉ *CH-7514 Sils Maria* ☎ *081/8265232* ☎ *081/8266260* ↯ *10 rooms, 4 with bath* ♨ *Restaurant, Stübli, minibars, cable TV; no a/c* ⊟ *MC, V* ☉ *Closed mid-Apr.–mid-June and mid-Oct.–mid-Dec.*

★ **$$$–$$$$** 🖃 **Waldhaus.** Approaching Sils, you'll spot this hotel perched like a castle above the village. Its guests have included Hermann Hesse, Marc Chagall, Albert Einstein, and Richard Strauss. In the same family since it opened in 1908, it has been continually updated, with an eye to tradition. The understated rooms, all with magnificent views and shiny antique fixtures in the baths, come in a wide range of sizes, and are priced accordingly. The large bar glows with walnut walls and subtle halogen lighting over its fireplace. The Waldhaus stays open longer than other luxury hotels in the valley. ✉ *CH-7514 Sils Maria* ☎ *081/8385100* ☎ *081/8385198* ⊕ *www.waldhaus-sils.ch* ↯ *140 rooms* ♨ *3 restaurants, Stübli, minibars, cable TV, miniature golf, 3 tennis courts, pool, hair salon, massage, steam room, bar, parking (fee); no a/c* ⊟ *AE, DC, MC, V* ☉ *Closed late Apr.–early June and late Oct.–mid-Dec.* ⵟⵔ *BP.*

$$–$$$ 🖃 **Chesa Randolina.** The main attraction of this hotel, which used to be a farm and horse-drawn coach business with a guesthouse, is its unobstructed view over the lake. The rooms are mostly furnished in pine; the best have balconies facing the lake. There's a spacious lounge with a stone fireplace and a restaurant done in soft greens and yellows, plus a Stübli serving a range of fondues (reservations required for nonguests). ✉ *CH-7515 Sils Baselgia* ☎ *081/8265151* ☎ *081/8265600* ⊕ *www. randolina.ch* ↯ *37 rooms* ♨ *Restaurant, Stübli, bar; no a/c, no room TVs* ⊟ *MC, V* ☉ *Closed mid-Apr.–early June and mid-Oct.–mid-Dec.* ⵟⵔ *MAP.*

Nightlife & the Arts

Small **chamber ensembles** perform from late June through September at 4 or 4:30 on the Konzertplatz in Sils Maria; in inclement weather, they move to the nearby church.

Sports & the Outdoors

BOATING Rowboats can be rented from **Schiffahrtgesellschaft Silsersee** (☎ 081/8265343) in Sils Maria. **F. Gianni** (☎ 081/8265343 or 079/4243227) runs the only motorboat allowed on the Engadine lakes; he takes you around the lake, stopping in tiny communities like Isola.

DOGSLEDDING Contact **Sämy Stöckli** (☎ 079/4404166) to have huskies pull you across extraordinary frozen landscapes near Sils. There are races across the lakes in mid-February.

HIKING Sils has 90 km (55 mi) of trails, including the popular walk into the Fex Valley, where you can visit a frescoed 16th-century church; the key is at the Hotel Sonne or the Pension Crasta, opposite. Maps are available at the tourist office and train station.

HORSE-DRAWN CARRIAGES From June to October a scheduled "bus service" travels from the Hotel Maria in Sils Maria to the end of the valley for 25 SF round-trip. Private carriages or sleighs head to the valley from the village square in both summer and winter. You can arrange a trip with **Mr. Clalüna** (☎ 081/8265286). **G. Coretti** (☎ 081/8265673) also drives a carriage and sleigh.

ICE-SKATING The **Muot Marias** (☎ 079/6550207) ice rink is open daily in winter. On Tuesday and Thursday it's lighted for evening skating. Skate rentals and lessons are available.

TENNIS Sils has six courts open to the public. Four are at the **Waldhaus Hotel** (☎ 081/8385100). The other two are outdoor courts that can be booked through the tourist office.

WINDSURFING Two **Windsurf Centers** (Sils ☎ 081/8265786 ☒ Silvaplana ☎ 081/8289229) operate on Silvaplana lake. Both give lessons and rent equipment; they're run by a former world champion windsurfer.

GRAUBÜNDEN A TO Z

To research prices, get advice from other travelers, and book travel arrangements, visit www.fodors.com.

AIRPORTS

Engadin Airport is used mainly by private planes. At 5,600 feet, it's the highest airport in Europe. The closest international airports are Zürich (about 2 hours from Chur) and Lugano (about 2½ hours from St. Moritz).

🚺 Airport Information **Engadin Airport** ☒ Samedan, 5 km [3 mi] from St. Moritz ☎ 081/8525433.

BUS TRAVEL

You can take the Swiss postbus (postauto) system's *Palm Express* from Lugano in the Ticino to St. Moritz. The 4½-hour trip passes through a corner of Italy and over the Maloja Pass. The bus runs twice daily from mid-June through mid-October; reservations are essential.

Postautos are a good way to wind your way up Alpine switchbacks over the region's great passes—that is, if you're not inclined to motion sickness. You can also use them to make circle tours with some careful study of the schedule. Information is available at all post offices. The main ski resorts have "sport bus" shuttles, which connect the villages and mountain stations. The service is usually included in the price of your lift ticket or on presentation of a "guest card" (check to see if your hotel offers these discount booklets).

🔁 Bus Information *Palm Express* ☎ 081/8376764 or 091/8078520 ⊕ www.swisspost.com.

CAR TRAVEL

Graubünden is mountainous with few major highways. Drivers can enter either by way of the San Bernardino Pass from the south or from the north on A13, the region's only expressway. Coming from Austria and Munich, the A27 leads into the Lower Engadine; roads over the Ofen and Bernina passes lead into the Engadine from the South Tyrol and Veltline areas of Italy respectively, and the approach to the Upper Engadine from Italy is over the Maloja Pass. The Oberalp and Lukmanier passes lead from Uri and Ticino respectively to the Surselva region to join A13.

The A13 expressway cuts a swift north–south route through Graubünden. A car is definitely necessary if you want to explore deeper into the countryside. Fine valley roads connect the rest of the area, though to move from one resort to another you may have to crawl over a mountain pass. If you're traveling in winter, make sure to check the status of the passes beforehand. The San Bernardino old road and the Oberalp, Albula, and Flüela passes close, but the San Bernardino Tunnel and the Maloja, Bernina, Julier, and Ofen passes are usually open to traffic. Local road condition information is generally broadcast in German, French, and Italian, but you could also ask for the latest reports at the tourist offices. The Lukmanier will stay open in winter for a five-year trial period that started in 2001. Trains through the Vereina tunnel shuttle cars between Klosters and Sagliains (Susch–Lavin). The tunnel cuts the travel time from Zürich from 5 hours to just 2¾ hours. Cars can also be taken by rail from Thusis to Samedan; the service is limited and reservations are essential. Tickets are between 35 SF and 40 SF.

🔁 Car Transport/Rail Reservation ☎ 081/6511113.

EMERGENCIES

There are national lines and many local lines for emergencies in Graubünden. For the general line for the criminal **police**, dial ☎ 117. The general number for an **emergency doctor or ambulance** is ☎ 144. Klinik Gut in St. Moritz specializes in urgent care. **Doctors, dentists, and emergency pharmacies** are listed in resort tourist periodicals or can be requested by calling information at ☎ 111.

🔁 Doctors **Arosa** ☎ 081/3772728. **Chur** ☎ 081/2523636. **Klosters** ☎ 081/3080808. **Pontresina** ☎ 081/8427766 or 081/8426268. **St. Moritz** ☎ 081/8330033. **Zernez** ☎ 081/8561215 or 081/8561616.

🔒Local Ambulances Chur ☎081/3533535. **Davos** ☎081/4101111. **Klosters** ☎081/4221713.
Upper Engadine ☎ 081/8518888. **🔒 Local Hospitals Chur** ☎ 081/2566111. **Davos** ☎ 081/4148888. **Klinik Gut, St. Moritz** ☎ 081/8334141. **Upper Engadine/Samedan** ☎ 081/8518111. **Scuol** ☎ 081/8611000. **🔒 Local Police Arosa** ☎ 081/3771938. **Chur** ☎ 081/2544341. **Davos** ☎ 081/4137622. **Flims** ☎ 081/9111164. **Klosters** ☎ 081/4221236. **Pontresina** ☎ 081/8426271. **St. Moritz** ☎ 081/8322727. **Scuol** ☎ 081/8641414. **Zernez** ☎ 081/8561212.

SPORTS & THE OUTDOORS

HIKING   Arosa, Davos, and Lenzerheide-Valbella offer special hiking packages. You can walk from Davos to Arosa one day and from Arosa to Lenzerheide the next. No need to worry about booking a hotel or transporting your luggage, as it's all taken care of. A seven-day program lets you spend more time in each resort. Contact local tourist offices or the regional tourist office, Graubünden Holidays. Similar arrangements can be made in the Engadine; call Engadin Ferien for information.
🔒 Engadin Ferien ☎ 081/8300001 ⊕ www.engadinferien.ch.

WALKING   The Arosa tourist office offers guided tours and nature walks daily from June through October; you can visit a cheese maker, a regional museum, and a 15th-century chapel. The Davos and Klosters tourist offices arrange guided walks at least once a week from July to September. The Chur tourist office arranges guided tours from April to October every Wednesday at 2:30. To explore on your own, pick up a map from the tourist office and follow the green and red footprints on the pavement. The Pontresina tourist office offers guided walking tours of its Old Town from mid-June to mid-October. It also offers guided botanical excursions, glacier treks, and hiking trips to the Swiss National Park, plus mushroom-picking outings in season (usually August–September). If you are staying in Pontresina, these trips are free; day visitors pay a small fee. Guides for all of the above tours speak English.

TRAIN TRAVEL

The Swiss Federal Railway trains that enter Graubünden only travel as far as Chur. From there the fine local Rhätische Bahn (RhB) takes over. The *Bernina Express* runs from Chur to St. Moritz via the Albula route and on to Italy past the spectacular Bernina peaks, lakes, and glaciers. The *Engadine Star,* which began service in 2000, makes its way from Klosters to St. Moritz in a couple of hours. The glamorous *Glacier Express,* billed as "the slowest express in the world," connects St. Moritz with Zermatt via the Oberalp Pass, crossing 291 bridges during its 7½-hour journey. The train includes an antique burnished-wood dining car; you can book a table through Passaggio Rail. Reservations for these trains are mandatory and can be made at almost any European rail station. As on the federal railways, a variety of reduced-price passes are available. For information on the local train network, contact Rhätische Bahn or the regional tourism office, Graubünden Holidays.
🔒 Train Information Passaggio Rail ✉ CH-7000 Chur ☎ 081/2521425. **Rhätische Bahn** ☎ 081/2549100 ⊕ www.rhb.ch. **Swiss Federal Railway** (SBB/CFF/FFS) ☎ 0900/ 300300 ⊕ www.rail.ch.

VISITOR INFORMATION
The canton's tourist information center is Graubünden Holidays. Although a few of the local tourism Web sites do not have English translations yet, all tourist offices have English-speaking staff and plenty of printed information in English.

🚹 Local Tourist Offices **Arosa** ✉ CH-7050 ☎ 081/3787020 ⊕ www.arosa.ch. **Bündner Herrschaft/Maienfeld** ✉ CH-7304 Maienfeld ☎ 081/3301912 or 081/3025858 ⊕ www.buendnerherrschaft.ch. **Chur** ✉ Grabenstr. 5, CH-7002 ☎ 081/2521818 🖶 081/2529076 ⊕ www.churtourismus.ch. **Davos** ✉ Promenade 67, CH-7270 ☎ 081/4152121 ⊕ www.davos.ch. **Flims-Laax** ✉ Alpenarena, CH-7032 ☎ 081/9209200 🖶 081/9209201 ⊕ www.alpenarena.ch. **Klosters** ✉ Alte Bahnhofstr. 6, CH-7250 ☎ 081/4102020 ⊕ www.klosters.ch. **Pontresina** ✉ Rondo Center, CH-7504 ☎ 081/8388300 ⊕ www.pontresina.ch. **St. Moritz** ✉ Via Maistra, CH-7500 ☎ 081/8373333 ⊕ www.stmoritz.ch. **Scuol & Tarasp-Vulpera** ✉ CH-7550 ☎ 081/8612222 ⊕ www.scuol.ch. **Sils** ✉ CH-7514 Sils Maria ☎ 081/8385050 ⊕ www.sils.ch. **Zernez** ✉ CH-7530 ☎ 081/8561300 ⊕ www.zernez.ch.

🚹 Regional Tourist Office **Graubünden Holidays** ✉ Alexanderstr. 24, CH-7001 Chur ☎ 081/2542424 🖶 081/2542400 ⊕ www.graubuenden.ch.

THE TICINO
LOCARNO, LUGANO

Updated by
Tania Inowlocki

NEWCOMERS A BIT WEAK ON THEIR GEOGRAPHY might hear the names Lugano, Ascona, Locarno, and Bellinzona and assume—quite naturally—they're in Italy. Color photographs of the region might not set them straight: nearly every publicity shot shows palm trees and mimosas, azure waters and indigo skies. Surely this is the Italian Mediterranean or the coast of the Adriatic. But behind the waving date palms are telltale signs: fresh paint, manicured gardens, punctual trains. There's no mistake about it: it's a little bit of Italy, but the canton Ticino is decidedly Swiss.

For the German Swiss, it's a little bit of paradise. They can cross over the St. Gotthard or San Bernardino passes and emerge in balmy sunshine, eat gnocchi and polenta in shaded *grotti* (rustic outdoor restaurants), drink merlot from ceramic bowls, gaze at the waters of Lago Maggiore (Lake Maggiore)—and still know their lodging will be strictly controlled by the Swiss Hotel Association. They don't even have to change currency. The combination is irresistible, and so in spring, summer, and fall they pour over the Alps to revel in low-risk Latin delights.

And the Ticinese welcome them like rich, distant cousins, to be served and coddled and—perhaps just a bit—despised. For the Italian-speaking natives of the Ticino—a lonely 8% of the Swiss population—are a minority in their own land, dominated politically by the German-speaking Swiss, set apart by their language as well as by their culture. Their blood and their politics are as Mediterranean as their climate: in a battle over obligatory seat belts, the Ticinese consistently voted to reject the federal intrusion. They were voted down by their Germanic neighbors—a 70% majority—and they protested. It was brought to vote again, and again they were defeated. Nowadays the Ticinese defy the federal law—and their policemen, Ticinese themselves, of course, turn a blind and supportive eye.

Their Italian leanings make perfect sense: an enormous mountain chain cuts them off from the north, pushing them inexorably toward their lingual roots. Most of the territory of the Ticino belonged to the pre-Italian city-states of Milan and Como until 1512, when the Swiss Confederation took it over by force. It remained a Swiss conquest—oppressed under the then-tyrannical rule of Uri, Schwyz, and Unterwalden, the very cantons now revered for forming the honorable Confederation of Switzerland—until 1798, when from the confusion of Napoléon's campaigns it emerged a free canton, and in 1803 it joined the confederation for good.

It remains a canton apart nonetheless, graceful, open, laissez-faire. Here you'll instantly notice differences in manner and body language among Ticinese engaged in conversation; you'll also notice fewer English-speaking Swiss. The climate, too, is different: there's an extraordinary amount of sunshine here, more than in central Switzerland and even sunny Italy immediately across the border. Mountain-sports meccas aside, this is the most glamorous of Swiss regions: the waterfront promenades of Lugano, Locarno, and Ascona, lined with pollards, rhododendrons, and bobbing yachts, blend a rich social mix of jet-set resorters. A few miles' drive brings

Lugano and Locarno alone provide an overview of the region, but completing the picture requires forays to the less touristy waterfront village of Ascona, the mountain stronghold of Bellinzona, and the rural, rugged mountain valleys beyond.

Numbers in the text correspond to numbers in the margin and on the Ticino and Lugano maps.

4

If you have
1 or 2
days

Concentrate on ⊡ **Lugano** ➐–➒ ▶, exploring the waterfront shops, venturing east to the Villa Favorita, and riding a funicular up Monte Brè. On the second day, take in the sights of the serene hillside city ⊡ **Locarno** ➌ and the former fishing village of **Ascona** ➏, both on the shore of Lago Maggiore.

If you have
3 or 4
days

In addition to all of the above, explore the medieval fortifications of **Bellinzona** ➊, the canton's capital, and tiny **Campione** ㉑, an Italian enclave on Swiss territory. Also take a drive through the wilds of the Ticino, into any of the numerous rugged valleys, and discover tiny ancient villages perched on the mountainsides. A perfect sample would be a drive through **Valle di Blenio** ➋.

the canton's impoverished past into view—the foothill and mountain villages are still scattered with low-roof stone cabins, but nowadays those cabins often prove to have been gentrified as chic vacation homes.

Although they're prosperous, with Lugano standing third in banking, after Zürich and Geneva, the Ticinese hold on to their past, a mountain-people culture that draws them to hike, hunt, and celebrate with great pots of risotto stirred over open outdoor fires. It's that contrast—contemporary glamour, earthy past—that grants travelers a visit that's as balanced and satisfying as a good merlot.

Exploring the Ticino

The canton is divided into two geographic regions by the small mountain range (1,817 feet) called Monte Ceneri, which rises up south of the valley below Bellinzona. Extending northeast and northwest of Monte Ceneri in the windswept Sopraceneri region are several mountainous valleys, including Valle di Blenio, Valle Maggia, Valle Verzasca, and Valle Leventina. Included in this region north of or, literally, above Monte Ceneri are Locarno and Ascona, which share a peninsula bulging into Lago Maggiore. The more developed southern region, Sottoceneri ("below Ceneri"), is home to business and resort towns, notably Lugano.

About the Restaurants & Hotels

The best place to sample the canton's down-to-earth delicacies is in a grotto, one of the scores of traditional country restaurants scattered across the region. Some of them are set deep in the mountains and forests, others can be reached only by boat and have little more than a few rows of picnic tables and a string of festive lights. Some serve only cold meats, but a few offer one or two hot dishes each day. To experience an authentic grotto, avoid the ones with *ristorante* in their names; the categories of eating establishments are carefully regulated, so these will always be pricier—and not the real thing. The better restaurants of the Ticino tend to stop serving between 3 and 7 or thereabouts, but pizzerias are usually open nonstop.

The hotel industry of this Mediterranean region of Switzerland capitalizes on its natural assets, with lakeside views of Lago Maggiore and Lago di Lugano, and swimming pools and terraces that pay homage to the omnipresent sun. As the Ticino is at its best in spring and fall, and packed with sunseekers in summer, many hotels close down for the winter. Tourist offices often publish lists of those remaining open, so if you're planning to come in low season—and even in January the lake resorts can be balmy—check carefully. Keep in mind that most hotels are not air-conditioned, in spite of hot spells in July and August. Vacation resorts don't depend on the *demipension* (half board) system as much as their mountain counterparts, but arrangements can be made.

WHAT IT COSTS In Swiss francs				
$$$$	**$$$**	**$$**	**$**	**¢**
RESTAURANTS over 60	40–60	25–40	15–25	under 15
HOTELS over 350	250–350	175–250	100–175	under 100

Restaurant prices are per person for a main course at dinner. Hotel prices are for two people in a standard double room in high season, including tax and service.

Timing

Lush and Mediterranean, the Ticino is gorgeous in springtime; the season starts as early as mid-March here, making the region a popular late-winter escape. In summertime, lakeside activity surges, and the weather can at times be hot. Warm summer nights are incredibly romantic, particularly on the Lago di Lugano. Crowds fill the promenades at Lugano and Locarno throughout the summer, but neither waterfront becomes unpleasantly jammed—although the road from Bellinzona to Locarno and Lugano is usually packed.

SOPRACENERI

The mountainous valleys of Valle di Blenio, Valle Maggia, Valle Verzasca, and Valle Leventina reach like the fingers of a hand south from the Alps into the basin of Lago Maggiore and Monte Ceneri, in the Sopraceneri. At the tips are the sun-kissed resorts of Locarno and Ascona, both on the northern edge of Lago Maggiore. Here the true spirit of the canton is still evident in the numerous small valley communities, some with fewer than 100 inhabitants—although each, nonetheless, is politically autonomous. The Sopraceneri reveals a slightly slower-paced, homier side of the Ticino, leaving the flashier offerings to Lugano in the south.

Italian with an accent

Of all the Swiss regions, Ticino can be the most pleasurable in which to eat, as the stylish and simple cuisine of Italy has been adopted virtually intact. Because the Ticinese were once a poor mountain people, their everyday cooking shares the earthy delights of another once-poor mountain people, the Piedmontese, whose steaming polenta and rib-sticking gnocchi break bread with game and meaty porcini mushrooms. *Manzo brasato* (savory braised beef with vegetables), *busecca* (vegetable soup with tripe), and osso buco are standards, as are any number of variations on risotto. Game offerings usually include *coniglio* (rabbit), *lepre* (hare), and *capretto* (roast kid). Wherever you eat, *il piatto del giorno* (the daily special) can help you economize.

4

As in the rest of Switzerland, local cold meats come in a broad variety, from myriad salamis to prosciutto *crudo*, the pearly pink cured raw ham made famous in Parma. Any food product made locally is called *nostrano*, and the prosciutto crudo nostrano is worth asking for, as you won't find a match for its forthright, gamey flavor back home. Eat it with bread and sweet butter to balance the salt. Most cooks import Italian cheeses—Parmigiano-Reggiano, sharp pecorino—though there are good, hard, white mountain varieties (Piora, Gesero) in most shops. Tiny *formaggini*—little molds of ultrafresh goat cheese—taste best with coarsely ground black pepper and olive oil. Or try the *zincarlin*, a fresh cheese mixed with parsley, garlic, and pepper.

The local wine is merlot; a warm, generous wine counted as one of the top Swiss reds. The wine is poured into an individual *boccalino*, a traditional ceramic pitcher, or a small ceramic bowl, to be drunk from like a cup. Instead of beer to quench locals' thirsts, a mix of *gazosa* (lemon-lime soda) and *vino nostrano* (the house red wine) is de rigueur. If you want a real Italian-style espresso, one-finger deep and frothing with golden foam, ask for *un liscio*. Otherwise they'll serve it with cream, Swiss style, and might even charge you extra. If you want a shot of grappa (grape brandy) thrown in, ask for it *corretto*—literally, "correct." Or finish off your meal with a shot of *Nocino*, a traditional walnut liqueur also known as *Ratafiá* (from *rata fiat*, meaning "it's done"). Walnuts picked before San Giovanni's day (June 25) are soaked in grappa and mixed with a secret combination of herbs and spices. Most Nocino is produced privately from closely guarded recipes—no two taste alike.

Mountain Valleys

Valle di Blenio, Valle Maggia, Valle Verzasca, Valle Leventina, and other mountain valleys a short distance from the major cities are rugged reminders of the region's modest history. Stone homes, called *rustici*, dot the valleys, some cut so deeply into the land that the sun never quite reaches bottom. Driving through these valleys can be disorienting, for time seems to have stopped; you'll encounter whole villages perched on craggy mountainsides in apparent defiance of gravity.

Waterfront Promenades Switzerland's sunniest water-
fronts—with boating, swimming, charming cafés, fine dining, and shops of all
sorts—are in the Ticino. Palm-lined promenades in Lugano, Locarno, and Ascona offer tremendous views overlooking the formidable Italian Alps. Locals
still turn out for the *passeggiata*—the afternoon stroll along the water.

Bellinzona

❶ *128 km (79 mi) south of Luzern, 150 km (93 mi) south of St. Moritz.*

FodorśChoice
★
All roads lead to Bellinzona, the fortified valley city that guards the important European crossroads of the St. Gotthard and San Bernardino
routes. Its importance through the ages makes itself evident: massive fortified castles—no fewer than three—rise over its ancient center. As the
only example of late medieval military architecture preserved along the
Alpine range, the castles and fortifications have been named a World
Heritage site by UNESCO. They were built by the noble Sforza and Vis-
conti families, the dukes of Milan who ruled northern Italy and environs for centuries and held this crucial juncture until 1422, when the
Swiss Confederates began a violent century of battling for its control.
Bellinzona passed to the Swiss Confederation in 1503. Ironically, the
names of the castles built in part to keep the Swiss at bay were then
changed to Schwyz, Uri, and Unterwalden—the three core cantons of
the Swiss Confederation. Eventually the names were changed again, and
the fortresses are known today as Castelgrande, Castello di Montebello,
and Castello di Sasso Corbaro.

The three castles have been exceptionally well restored, and each merits a visit (a walk along the ramparts at night is particularly appealing),
but the city itself should not be overlooked: it's a classic Lombard town,
with graceful architecture, red cobblestones, and an easy, authentically
Italian ambience. It's relatively free of tourists and thus reveals the Ticino way of life, complete with a lively produce market on Saturday featuring boar salami, wild mushrooms, and local cheeses.

The **centro storico** (Old Town), with its heavy-column arcades, wrought-
iron balconies, and shuttered facades, exhibits the direct influence of
medieval Lombardy. It's a small area, distinguished by red cobblestones.

The **Palazzo Civico,** located in the Old Town on the Piazza Nosetto, is
a splendid Renaissance structure that was heavily rebuilt in the 1920s.
Its courtyard is framed by two stacked rows of delicate vaulted arcades,
with airy loggias at the top. The **Castelgrande** was begun in the 6th century, though the current structure dates from the 1200s. The massive
exterior is dominated by two heavy, unmatched towers and the remaining portion of a crenellated wall that once stretched all the way to
the river. Renovations have added an elaborate modern complex of restaurants and museums, including historical and archaeological exhibitions.
The 14th-century ceiling murals, created to embellish the wooden ceiling of a local villa (now demolished), offer a peek at privately commissioned decorative art. ⊠ *Monte San Michele* ☎ *091/8258145* 🗺 *4 SF,*

8 SF combination ticket for Castelgrande, Castello di Montebello, and Castello di Sasso Corbaro ☉ Daily 10–6.

The imposing late-Renaissance facade of the **Chiesa Collegiata di San Pietro e San Stefano** (Church of St. Peter and St. Stephen), begun in the 16th century, stands across from the Castelgrande. Its interior is lavishly frescoed in the baroque style by late-18th-century Ticino artists. ☒ *Piazza Collegiata* ☎ *091/8252131.*

The most striking of Bellinzona's three castles is the **Castello di Montebello.** The center portion, its oldest section, dates from the 13th century; the palace and courtyard are from the 15th century, with spectacular walkways around the top of the encircling walls. The center structure houses an attractive, modern Museo Civico (Civic Museum) and the Museo Archeologico (Archeological Museum), with exhibits on local history and architecture, including an impressive collection of Gothic and Renaissance stone capitals. ☒ *Salita ai Castelli* ☎ *091/8251342* ☒ *4 SF, 8 SF combination ticket for Castelgrande, Castello di Montebello, and Castello di Sasso Corbaro ☉ Mar.–Nov., daily 10–6.*

The lofty **Castello di Sasso Corbaro** looks like it was constructed from square and rectangular building blocks; the almost complete absence of curvature is typical of Sforza design. It was designed by a Florentine military engineer and built in 1479 for the duke of Milan, who insisted the work be completed in six months. Temporary art exhibitions are held in the Belvedere and the Emma Paglia Room. Ambitious walkers can reach the castle in about 45 minutes by traveling uphill from the Castello di Montebello along a switchback road through woods; if you're driving, follow the signs. ☎ *091/8255906* ☒ *4 SF, 8 SF combination ticket for Castelgrande, Castello di Montebello, and Castello di Sasso Corbaro ☉ Apr.–Nov., daily 10–6.*

Chiesa San Biagio (Church of St. Biagio), one of Bellinzona's two Italianate churches, is a spare medieval treasure guarded on the exterior by an outsize fresco of a soldierly Christ. The 12th-century late-Romanesque structure suggests a transition into Gothic style. Natural alternating redbrick and gray stone complement fragments of exquisitely colored 14th-century frescoes. ☒ *Via San Biagio 13, Bellinzona-Ravecchia* ☎ *091/8252131.*

The city's art gallery, **Museo Villa dei Cedri,** sporadically dips into its coffers—made up of a donated private collection—and hangs worthwhile exhibits. Behind the garden and grounds, the city maintains a tiny vineyard used to produce its very own merlot, available for sale inside. ☒ *Piazza San Biagio 9* ☎ *091/8218520* ⊕ *www.villacedri.ch* ☒ *8 SF ☉ Tues.–Fri. 9–noon and 4–7, weekends 11–6.*

Where to Stay & Eat

★ **$$–$$$** ✕ **Castelgrande.** Don't expect a quick buffet lunch served to shorts-clad tourists here: this chic restaurant is a serious experience, with a daringly cool decor and sophisticated efforts from the Italian chef, such as goose liver with blueberries or pigeon and pearl onions in a sweet-and-sour sauce. The wine list flaunts more than 70 Ticino merlots. With a lighter

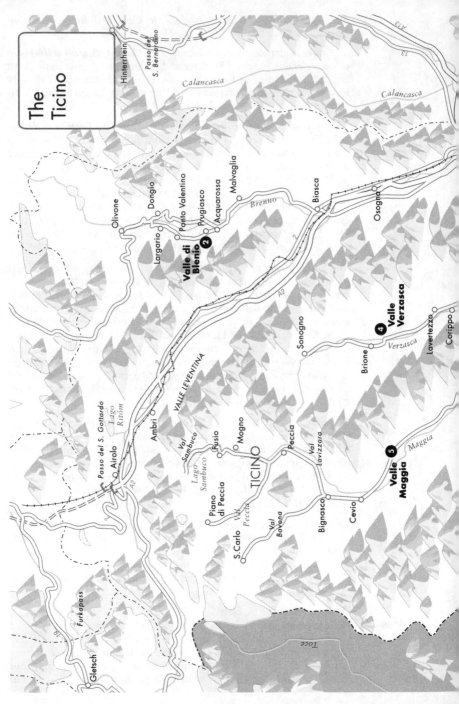

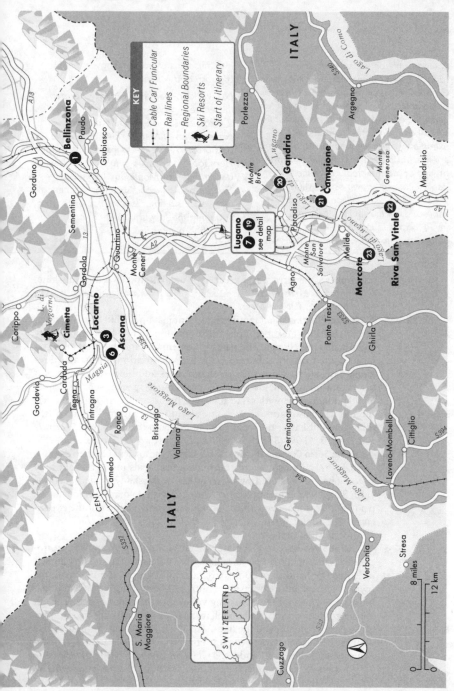

CloseUp

TICINO'S FOSSIL TROVE

Rooted firmly on the southern shores of Lago di Lugano, the 3,595-foot Monte San Giorgio has been an irresistible draw for paleontologists since the mid-19th century. Scientific excavations in its five successive strata have regularly churned out extremely well preserved fossils, allowing scientists to study the evolution of various groups of marine creatures of the geological era known as the Middle Triassic (245–230 million years ago). Thousands of the reptiles, fish, and invertebrates found here—some of them unique specimens—have made their way into museums of paleontology in Zürich, Lugano, and Milan.

No wonder, then, that UNESCO added the entire region—an area measuring 2,098 acres and extending across the communities of Meride, Riva San Vitale, and Brusino Arsizio—to the list of World Heritage natural sites in July 2003. This designation for Monte San Giorgio is Switzerland's second such honor, coming two years after that for the glaciers spanning the Jungfrau, Aletsch, and Bietschhorn summits.

atmosphere, the terrace is a great spot to soak up views and sunshine. ⊠ *Monte San Michele* ☎ *091/8262353* ⊕ *www.castelgrande.ch* ⊟ *AE, DC, MC, V* ⊘ *Closed Mon.*

★ **$$–$$$** ✕ **Malakoff.** In this small family restaurant just up the hill from the town center, chef Rita Fuso prepares traditional Italian fare from impeccably high-quality ingredients. The pasta is homemade, and the vegetables and meats come from local farms. Try seasonal variations on standard regional fare, such as risotto with chanterelles and blueberries. The best bet (and a great value) is the daily two-course special, such as home-made rabbit terrine with salad followed by osso buco and buttered fettuccine. The Fusos are so passionate about food that smokers are asked to abstain until after the meal so as not to ruin their palate. ⊠ *Carrale Bacilieri 10* ☎ *091/8254940* ⊟ *AE, DC, MC, V* ⊘ *Closed Sun.*

$–$$ ✕ **Osteria Sasso Corbaro.** From the heights of the ancient Castello di Sasso Corbaro, this atmospheric restaurant serves meals inside a beautifully restored hall or outside, at wooden tables, in the shady, walled-in courtyard. The cooking is simple and regional, with cold and grilled meats, trout, and seasonal vegetables. Good local wines round out the experience. ⊠ *Castello Sasso Corbaro* ☎ *091/8255532* ⊟ *AE, DC, MC, V* ⊘ *Closed Mon. and Dec.–Feb.*

¢–$ ✕▣ **Grotto Paudese.** Immaculate, friendly, and family-run, this grotto-cum-bed-and-breakfast perches high above the town in the tiny hamlet of Paudo. Its handful of rooms are tastefully simple, if a bit small; the owners squeeze in the occasional antique chest of drawers. There's an unsurpassed view of the twinkling valley and the Alps beyond. The adjoining grotto is warmly traditional, turning out a robust daily meal (homemade pasta, polenta, and the like). The inn is roughly a 15-minute drive up from Bellinzona. Going east into the Val Morobbia, follow signs for Pianezzo and then for Paudo. ⊠ *CH-6582 Paudo* ☎☎ *091/8571468* ⊷ *4 rooms* ⚐ *Restaurant, bar; no a/c, no room phones, no room TVs* ⊟ *V* ⊘ *Closed mid-Dec.–Feb.* ⦿l *BP.*

en route

To see the deep countryside of the Ticino—beyond its resorts and cities—follow the A2 expressway north from Bellinzona toward St. Gotthard; after 17 km (11 mi), exit at **Biasca,** a miniature Bellinzona itself, as it guards two major access roads from the north.

Valle di Blenio

2 *17 km (11 mi) north of Bellinzona, 80 km (49 mi) north of Lugano.*

North of Biasca toward Olivone is the Valle di Blenio, a characteristic Ticinese valley cutting deeper and higher into wild, rocky country. Its villages mingle tidy suburban cottages with the architectural signature of Ticino life: ancient stone houses, some little more than huts, with ramshackle roofs of odd-size slabs. These homes are the rustici once inhabited by mountain people starving under the harsh rule of the Swiss-German confederates. Today the heirs of both those ancient lines happily profit from a new twist: the Ticinese now rent their abodes to wealthy tourists—most of them Swiss-German—seeking to escape the pressures of urban prosperity. In these villages—Largario, Ponto Valentino, Prugiasco—you'll see the real, rural Ticino.

Locarno

3 *21 km (13 mi) west of Bellinzona, 39 km (24 mi) northwest of Lugano.*

Superbly placed on the sheltered curve of the northernmost tip of Lago Maggiore and surrounded on all sides by mountains, Locarno is Switzerland's sunniest town. Subtropical flora flourish here, with date palms and fig trees, bougainvillea and rhododendron, and even aloe vera burgeoning on the waterfront. Its fauna are no less colorful: every spring, summer, and fall the arcaded streets and cafés teem with exotic characters in fur coats and T-shirts, lamé, and leather. Don't forget your sunglasses—you don't show your face in Locarno without a stylish set of shades.

In August, Locarno makes worldwide news with its film festival, showcasing the latest cinema on an outdoor screen in the Piazza Grande; it also hosts international artists in concert. The facilities haven't drawn just culture hounds: In 1925, Briand, Stresemann, Mussolini, and Chamberlain initialed the Locarno Pact, securing the peace—albeit temporarily—in Europe.

Modern Locarno is actually made up of three communities so tiny and close together that you often don't notice you've moved from one to another: Locarno, Muralto, and Minusio. The town's raison d'être is its waterfront, which has a graceful promenade curving around the east flank of the bay and a beach and public pool complex along the west. Its clear lake is often still as glass, reflecting the Ticinese Alps across to the south. Locarno's Lombard-style arcades and historic landmarks continually draw visitors inland as well. There are a few pedestrians-only streets in the heart of the Old Town.

★ The **Piazza Grande** is the heart of the Old Town and its social center, too: from under the crowded arcades shoppers spill onto the square to lounge in cafés and watch each other drink, smoke, and pose. **Chiesa**

Nuova (New Church; ⊠ Via Cittadella) is an exuberantly decorated baroque church (1630) with an enormous statue of St. Christopher on the facade. Down the street from the New Church, the **Casa dei Canonici** (House of the Canons; ⊠ Via Cittadella) dates from the same period. Note the lovely interior courtyard; it's now a private house.

The heavy, frescoed **Chiesa di San Francesco** (Church of St. Francis; ⊠ Via S. Francesco) and its convent date from the mid-15th century; legend has it that it was founded by St. Anthony of Padua. The emblems on its Renaissance facade show Locarno's social distinctions of the era: the eagle represents the aristocrats; a lamb, the country folk; and the ox (unkind, surely), the citizens. In its sanctuary, concerts are performed every spring and fall; contact the tourist office for more information. The 17th-century **Chiesa di Sant'Antonio** (Church of St. Anthony; ⊠ Via Sant'Antonio) lies at the end of a fine, narrow street lined with splendid old houses in both medieval and flamboyant baroque styles.

Immediately to the right of the Church of St. Anthony stands the **Casa Rusca,** an 18th-century residence that now serves as the city art gallery. Its permanent collections include the work of Jean Arp, and temporary exhibits highlight both Swiss and international artists. ⊠ *Via Sant'Antonio* ☎ *091/7563185* ⊠ *7 SF* ⊙ *Tues.–Sun. 10–5.*

Built in 1300 as a stronghold of the dukes of Milan, Castello Visconteo was soon virtually destroyed by the invading Swiss Confederates. Today it contains a **Museo Civico e Archeologico** (Municipal and Archaeological Museum), with Roman relics—including a major glass collection—and Romanesque sculpture. ⊠ *Piazza Castello 2* ☎ *091/ 7563180* ⊠ *5 SF* ⊙ *Apr.–Oct., Tues.–Sun. 10–5.*

★ You can get to the **Santuario della Madonna del Sasso** (Sanctuary of the Madonna of the Rock) via a five-minute funicular ride to a high plateau (the funicular is close to the train station). The sprawling church complex is where, in 1480, Brother Bartolomeo da Ivrea saw a vision of the Virgin Mary; the sanctuary was begun seven years later and was gradually enlarged to include a convent, a museum, and side galleries. Within the sanctuary, you'll find Bramantino's 1520 *The Flight into Egypt* and *Christ Carried to the Sepulcher,* a dramatic, Caravaggesque procession scene painted in 1870 by Antonio Ciseri, from nearby Ascona. You'll also see naive-art votive gifts to the Madonna from individuals who have survived everything from family tragedies to fender benders. Call for an appointment; admission rates depend on the number of visitors. ⊠ *Via Santuario 2, Orselina* ☎ *091/7436265* ⊠ *By appointment only.*

off the beaten path | **CIMETTA** – A winter-sports center with views of Monte Rosa, the Swiss Alps, and the Italian Apennines, Cimetta (5,482 feet) can be reached only by chairlift; first you must catch a cable car (near the train station) to Cardada, then a chairlift to the resort. But don't be put off; the ride is part of the fun: as the lake falls away below, you'll sail over meadows and wooded hills. Cimetta is also a hiker's paradise. The trip costs 25 SF in winter and 33 SF in summer. ☎ *091/7353030* ⊙ *Apr.–Oct., daily 8–8; late Dec.–Mar., Mon.–Thurs. 9–6, Fri.–Sun. 8–8.*

Where to Stay & Eat

$$$ ✕ **Centenario.** Across from the waterfront east of the town center, this
Fodor'sChoice gracious *ristorante* serves innovative Franco-Italian cuisine that's
★ unashamedly nouvelle and absolutely top quality, from its moderately
priced business lunch to the all-out *menu de dégustation* (sampling
menu). Specialties include seafood ravioli and roasted foie gras with cel-
ery root and apples. You can have an aperitif on the lakefront terrace
before sitting down to a meal surrounded by quarry tile, gleaming sil-
ver, and Persian rugs. ⊠ *Lungolago 13, Locarno-Muralto* ☎ *091/
7438222* ⊟ *AE, DC, MC, V* ⊘ *Closed Sun. and Mon., last 3 wks in
July and first 3 wks in Feb.*

$–$$ ✕ **Casa del Popolo.** Although the politics might lean left at this popular
restaurant, the Italian favorites are done just right. Try the amazingly
delicate *piccata alla Milanese* (veal cutlets pounded thin, coated in egg,
and sautéed), the spicy *penne all'arrabbiata* (pasta with red pepper and
tomato sauce), or any of the 20 types of pizza. Red-check tablecloths
and occasional appearances by the local politico round it all out. ⊠ *Piazza Corporazione* ☎ *091/7511208* ⊟ *No credit cards.*

$$$–$$$$ ✕▥ **Reber au Lac.** This richly landscaped oasis at the end of the wa-
terfront row dates from 1886 and has been continuously run by the
Reber family. The interiors exude patrician calm with pleasing touches
such as antique Venetian glass lamps, lacy duvet covers, and the oc-
casional bit of gilt or wrought iron. Awning-shaded balconies over-
look the lake or pool, and interiors are done in tasteful pastels—no
two rooms are alike. The Grill Room has a good reputation among
locals for its Franco-Italian cuisine and creative fish menus served in
a Spanish setting. ⊠ *Viale Verbano 55, CH-6602 Locarno-Muralto*
☎ *091/7358700* 🖶 *091/7358701* ⊕ *www.hotel-reber.ch* ⤶ *61 rooms,
9 suites* ♨ *3 restaurants, in-room safes, minibars, tennis court, pool,
sauna, beach, bar, business services, no-smoking rooms; no a/c in
some rooms* ⊟ *AE, DC, MC, V* ⊘ *Closed late Oct.–Feb.* ▮❍▮ *BP.*

$$–$$$ ✕▥ **Belvedere.** Well above the city, this hotel has gone all out, with
interiors in postmodern beech, lacquer, and marble. All rooms face south,
and the suites in the wing on the hill have particularly breathtaking
views. The elegant dining hall, with its frescoes, elaborately trimmed
vaults, and a massive stone fireplace, is all that remains of the origi-
nal building, a private home built in 1680. L'Affresco, the formal restau-
rant, serves upscale Italian specialties; look for turbot in a potato crust
and homemade pastas. You can reach the Belvedere by funicular from
the train station or on foot in a five-minute uphill walk. ⊠ *Via ai Monti
della Trinità 44, CH-6600* ☎ *091/7510363* 🖶 *091/7515239* ⊕ *www.
belvedere-locarno.com* ⤶ *75 rooms, 5 suites, 1 apartment* ♨ *2 restau-
rants, in-room safes, minibars, 2 pools (1 indoors), health club, bicy-
cles, 2 bars, playground, meeting rooms, no-smoking rooms; no a/c
in some rooms* ⊟ *AE, DC, MC, V* ▮❍▮ *BP.*

$ ✕▥ **Cittadella.** This popular dining spot in the Old Town offers inex-
pensive regional food—pizzas, pastas, simply prepared fish—in its ca-
sual downstairs trattoria, and fancier fish dishes in the more formal
restaurant upstairs. The preparation is light, the flavors subtle with oils
and herbs. Upstairs are a handful of pleasing rooms, some up under the

rafters, all with classic stone-tile floors in cream and red. They may be simple, but they're a great bargain. ⊠ *Via Cittadella 18, CH-6600* ☎ *091/7515885* 🖷 *091/7517759* 🖅 *11 rooms ♨ 2 restaurants; no a/c, no room phones* 🖶 *AE, DC, MC, V* ⵙ *BP.*

¢–$ ✕🖭 **Hotel Navegna.** It may not look like much from the outside, but this
Fodor'sChoice is a true diamond in the rough, right on the lake farther up the shore
★ from the promenade. The rooms are simply furnished in bright florals, and there's a fireplace in the living room for damp days. But it's the inventive Ticinese cooking that earns raves for gregarious owner Enrico Ravelli, who supplies the kitchen with fresh poultry, eggs, vegetables, and herbs from his own farm in the hills. The phenomenally delicate homemade pastas shouldn't be missed. It's easiest to reach the hotel via the Minusio exit from the A13 highway. ⊠ *Via alla Riva 2, CH-6648 Locarno-Minusio* ☎ *091/7432222* 🖷 *091/7433150* ⊕ *www.navegna. ch* 🖅 *20 rooms ♨ Restaurant, bicycles; no a/c* 🖶 *MC, V* ☉ *Closed late Dec.–Easter* ⵙ *BP.*

$$ 🖭 **Du Lac.** A terrific location makes this friendly hotel a particularly good base. It's at the east end of the Old Town's nerve center, the Piazza Grande, but thanks to the pedestrians-only zone and the nearby public gardens, it's relatively quiet. The rooms are done in refreshing cool greens, yellows, and blues; many have balconies. There's a lovely terrace for breakfast, and public parking is close by. ⊠ *Via Ramogna 3, CH-6600* ☎ *091/7512921* 🖷 *091/7516071* ⊕ *www.du-lac-locarno.ch* 🖅 *30 rooms ♨ In-room safes, minibars, no-smoking rooms; no a/c* 🖶 *AE, DC, MC, V* ⵙ *BP.*

Nightlife & the Arts

BARS The smoky **Bar Lungolago** (⊠ Via Bramantino 1, Locarno ☎ 091/ 7515246) draws a stylish crowd. **Simba Bar** (⊠ Lungolago Motta 3a ☎ 091/7523388) is very popular with a young crowd of Swiss and Italians.

CASINO The **Casinò di Locarno** (⊠ Via Largo Zorzi 1, Piazza Grande ☎ 091/ 7511535) has 195 slot machines and *boule* (a type of roulette). It's open every day from noon to 2 AM, until 4 AM on Friday and Saturday nights.

FILM The **Locarno International Film Festival** (⊠ Via B. Luini 3a ☎ 091/7562121 ⊕ www.pardo.ch), gaining ground on the prestige front because of the caliber of the films it premieres, takes place every August in the Piazza Grande.

MUSIC The **Back Home Again–American Music Festival Locarno** (⊠ Via B. Luini 3 ☎ 091/7910091 ⊕ www.pardo.ch) takes place in late May 2005. The musical menu has a little of everything, from Cajun and country to bluegrass and the blues.

THEATER The **Teatro di Locarno** (⊠ Palazzo Kursaal, Via Largo Zorzi 1 ☎ 091/ 7561093) hosts international theatrical companies from October through May. For tickets contact the Locarno tourist office.

Valle Verzasca

④ *12 km (7 mi) north of Locarno, 25 km (15½ mi) north of Lugano.*

A short drive along Route 13 through the wild and rugged mountain gorge of the Valle Verzasca leads to Corippo, where a painterly composition of stone houses and a 17th-century church are all protected as architectural landmarks. The mountain village of Sonogno lies at the end of the 26-km (16-mi) valley.

About 12 km (7 mi) north of Corippo, in the town of Lavertezzo, you'll find a graceful double-arch stone bridge, the **Ponte dei Salti**, dating from 1700.

Valle Maggia

⑤ *4 km (2 mi) northwest of Locarno, 30 km (19 mi) northwest of Lugano.*

A drive through this rugged agricultural valley that stretches northwest from Locarno will give you a sense of the tough living conditions endured for centuries by Ticinese farmers, who today mine granite. The valley is cut so far into the earth that sunlight in winter never seems to reach bottom—a stark contrast to sunny Locarno, only a short distance south. Until the 1920s, many Valle Maggia natives immigrated to the United States; some returned, bringing with them several English phrases that still pepper the local dialect. As you pass through Gordevio, Maggia, Someo, and Cevio—the latter, the valley's main village—you feel as if you're in a time capsule. There's little commercialization, and the mostly 17th-century houses call to mind a movie set. Bignasco, just beyond Cevio, is the last village before the valley splits in two continuing north.

off the beaten path **MOGNO –** Beyond Bignasco, to the east, lies the Val Lavizzara. At Peccia the road splits again, with Val Sambuco to the east. Nearly at the end of this valley, in tiny Mogno, stands a beautiful modernist chapel built in 1994 by world-renowned Ticinese architect Mario Botta, who designed the San Francisco Museum of Modern Art.

Ascona

⑥ *3 km (1¾ mi) west of Locarno.*

Though it's only a few minutes from Locarno, tiny Ascona has a life of its own. Little more than a fishing village until the end of the 19th century, the town was adopted by a high-minded group of northerners who arrived to develop a utopian, vegetarian artists' colony on **Monte Verità**, the hillside park behind the waterfront center. Influenced by Eastern and Western religions as well as the new realms of psychology, its ideals attracted thousands of sojourners, including dancer Isadora Duncan and psychologist C. G. Jung. You can visit the group of Monte Verità buildings, including the unusual flat-roof, wooden Casa Anatta, and view papers and relics of the group's works. ☎ *091/7910327* 🖼 *6 SF* ⊘ *Apr., May, and Sept., Tues.–Sun. 2:30–6:30; July and Aug., Tues.–Sun. 3–7.*

Monte Verità's influence spread and its reputation grew throughout the world. Today the still-small village of 5,000 attracts artists, art restorers, and traditional bookbinders to its ancient, narrow streets. On the waterfront, however, it's a sun-and-fun scene, with the pedestrian-only ★ **Piazza Motta** crowded with sidewalk cafés and the promenade on the water's edge swarming with boats. Behind Piazza Motta, a charming labyrinth of lanes leads uphill past art galleries (not all showing gallery-quality work) to **Via Borgo**, lined with contemporary shops and galleries.

BRISSAGO ISLANDS – Federally preserved as botanical gardens, the Brissago Islands teem with more than 1,000 species of subtropical plants. Plaques identify the flora in Italian, German, and French; an English guide to the plants is for sale at the gate (8 SF). Have lunch or drinks at the restaurant, in a beautifully restored 1929 villa that now doubles as a seminar center. Boats bound for the islands depart regularly from Brissago, Porto Ronco, Ascona, and Locarno. You must leave with the last boat back to the mainland—usually around 6 PM—so check the schedule carefully when plotting out your excursion. Purchase your ticket at the entrance to the gardens or when you book your boat trip; Swiss Boat Pass discounts apply. *☎ 091/7511865 for boat, 091/7914361 for tour ☎ Boat: 13 SF round-trip from Ascona, 22 SF round-trip from Locarno; gardens: 7 SF ☉ Daily 9–6.*

Where to Stay & Eat

$–$$$ ✕ **San Pietro.** Tucked away in a maze of tiny streets, this little gem offers creative Italian-influenced pasta and fish dishes. Sample its local fish fillet in lemon basil sauce, ravioli with vegetables and almonds, or any of the grilled specialties. The most romantic tables are in the intimate garden, slipped between the walls of neighboring houses. ⊠ *Passagio S. Pietro 6 ☎ 091/7913976 ☰ AE, DC, MC, V ☉ Closed Mon. and Jan.*

$–$$ ✕ **Grotto du Rii.** On your way to or from Italy, this beautiful stone grotto with lush flowers pouring out of its windows is straight out of a fairy tale. Before your meal, enjoy the rosemary-infused wine on the terrace at the foot of Intragna's vineyards. Mainstays such as osso buco with polenta may be followed with the more daring *dolcesorpresa* (surprise dessert). On Tuesday night, the four-course meal accompanied by Ticinese musicians is a good deal. The restaurant is a short walk from the Centovalli train station. Intragna, whose church tower is the tallest in the Ticino, is a good spot from which to start hikes into the hills. ⊠ *Via Cantonale, Intragna ☎ 091/7961861 ⊕ www.grottodurii.ch ☉ Closed Wed.*

$–$$ ✕ **Osteria Nostrana.** The tables of this bustling restaurant spread into the piazza overlooking the lake. Inside, rough wooden ceilings, marble-top tables, chandeliers, and a hodgepodge of photos and posters add to its charm. Look for the spaghetti Enzo (with porcini mushrooms, bacon, and cream) along with daily and seasonal specials. The wine list deserves consideration; it has more than 100 Italian and Swiss vintages. ⊠ *Piazza Motta ☎ 091/7915158 ☰ AE, DC, MC, V.*

★ $$$$ ✕⌂ **Eden Roc.** Two hotels were combined to create this modern luxury resort; the result has double the usual number of facilities, including a private boat jetty. Marble floors, walls, and even ceilings gleam throughout the common areas, where inventive furniture adds a funky spark. Guest rooms give you plenty of space to stretch out, with huge white marble and tile bathrooms and lots of closet space. Best of all are the front rooms with balconies almost the size of the rooms themselves. The two lakeside restaurants spill out onto the terrace in warm weather. ⊠ *Via Albarelle 16, CH-6612* ☎ *091/7857171* 🖶 *091/ 7857143* ⊕ *www.edenroc.ch* ⇗ *50 rooms, 32 suites* 🖒 *3 restaurants, in-room data ports, in-room safes, minibars, 3 pools, health club, hair salon, massage, waterskiing, bicycles, bar, Internet* 🖃 *AE, DC, MC, V* †⊙† *BP.*

$$$$ ✕🖾 **Giardino.** Luxury borders on decadence at this glamorous villa.
Fodor's Choice Interiors make the most of Portuguese ceramics, Veronese marble, and
★ della Robbia–style room-number plaques; beds are encased in pure linen sheets. Ground-floor rooms have small private gardens; a beautifully landscaped pool, chauffeured Bentley, antique-bus shuttle, and pink bicycles are available for guest use. The staff is extraordinary, the highly rated restaurants excellent, serving Italian, vegetarian, and regional cuisine. Weekly events range from hiking and picnics to dinner theater with singing waiters or opera. Prepare to be spoiled. ⊠ *Via Segnale 10, CH-6612* ☎ *091/7858888* 🖶 *091/7858899* ⊕ *www.giardino. ch* ⇗ *54 rooms, 18 suites, 5 apartments* 🖒 *2 restaurants, café, in-room safes, minibars, pool, gym, hair salon, sauna, steam room, bicycles, piano bar, wine bar, babysitting* 🖃 *AE, DC, MC, V* ⊘ *Closed mid-Nov.–mid-Mar.* †⊙† *MAP.*

★ **$$$** 🖾 **Castello Seeschloss.** Built in 1250, this castle hotel on the waterfront square has an interior rich with frescoes, beams, vaults, and heavy masonry, lightened with a contemporary touch. Each room is different: a wrought-iron bed in the back tower, a blue wooden canopy bed in Room 205, or a loft in the lavish front tower. Most impressive are the lakeside rooms, which have original 16th- to 18th-century frescoes. There's a private courtyard for summer-night dining, a huge garden in back, and an isolated pool. Honeymooners, take note: deluxe rooms in the towers start at prices not much higher than standard doubles. Ask for an air-conditioned room in summer. ⊠ *Piazza Motta, CH-6612* ☎ *091/7910161* 🖶 *091/7911804* ⊕ *www.castello-seeschloss.ch* ⇗ *45 rooms* 🖒 *3 restaurants, minibars, pool, bar; no a/c in some rooms* 🖃 *AE, DC, MC, V* ⊘ *Closed Jan. and Feb.* †⊙† *BP.*

$$–$$$ 🖾 **Schiff.** You're assured of a good view at this family-owned and -run hotel; the front rooms face the bustling piazza and the placid lake, and back rooms look over the rooftops. All are pretty and bright, with spring-green decor and white-tile baths. Look into the excellent low- and off-season deals. ⊠ *Lungolago G. Motta 21, CH-6612* ☎ *091/ 7912533* 🖶 *091/7921315* ⊕ *www.hotel-schiff-ascona.ch* ⇗ *16 rooms* 🖒 *Restaurant, café, bicycles; no a/c in some rooms* 🖃 *AE, DC, MC, V* ⊘ *Closed Jan.–mid-Feb.* †⊙† *BP.*

$ 🖾 **Tamaro.** The shuttered windows of this 18th-century patrician house look out on the waterfront; inside, you can lounge in sitting rooms richly furnished with antiques, books, and even a grand piano. The rooms range from lavish corner doubles with lake views and reproduction antiques to tiny quarters overlooking the courtyard that are an excellent value. There's a private sun terrace high over the street with fine lake views. ✉ *Piazza G. Motta 35, CH-6612* ☎ *091/7854848* 🖷 *091/7912928* ⊕ *www.hotel-tamaro.ch* ⤴ *51 rooms* ☾ *3 restaurants, café, in-room safes, minibars, pool, bicycles, meeting rooms, no-smoking rooms; no a/c* ☐ *AE, DC, MC, V* ☺ *Closed mid-Nov.–Feb.* ❁❘ *BP.*

Nightlife & the Arts

The ideals that brought Isadora Duncan here still bring culture to Ascona: every year it hosts a series of world-class jazz and classical music concerts. The lakefront piazza serves as an open-air stage for almost daily summer entertainment, with mime, theater, and live pop bands. Locarno's August film festival is only a cab ride away across the peninsula.

BARS & DANCING   In Hotel Eden Roc, **La Brezza** (✉ Via Albarelle 16 ☎ 091/7857171 ⊕ www.edenroc.ch) is the place to sip bellinis (peach liqueur with champagne) and listen to live music.

MUSIC   **JazzAscona New Orleans & Classics** (☎ 091/7910091 ⊕ www.jazzascona. com) seeks out performers a cut above standard Dixieland and swing groups and brings an amazing international selection of them to its open-air bandstands in June and July. The **Settimane Musicali** (☎ 091/7910091 ⊕ www.settimane-musicali.ch) bring in orchestras, chamber groups, and top-ranking soloists to Ascona and Locarno. Events run from late August to mid-October.

SOTTOCENERI

Although Monte Ceneri is no Everest, it marks the borderline between the Sopraceneri with its vastly different southern cousin "below" the Ceneri. The Sottoceneri is the Ticino with attitude, where culture and natural beauty join forces with business and commerce. The resort town of Lugano is an international glamour magnet, but even there the incredible scenery and traditional warmth haven't been completely upstaged.

Lugano

➤ *45 km (28 mi) southeast of Ascona, 39 km (24 mi) southeast of Locarno.*

Strung around a sparkling bay like Venetian glass beads, with dark, conical mountains rising primordially out of its waters and icy peaks framing the scene, Lugano earns its nickname as the Rio of the Old World. Of the three world-class waterfront resorts, Lugano tops Ascona and Locarno for architectural style, sophistication, and natural beauty. This isn't to say that it has avoided the pitfalls of a successful modern resort: there's thick traffic right up to the waterfront, much of it manic Italian style, and it has more than its share of concrete waterfront high-rise hotels with balconies skewed to produce "a room with a view" regardless of aesthetic cost. Yet the sacred passeggiata—the afternoon stroll to see and be seen that winds down every Italian day—asserts the city's true personality as a graceful, sophisticated resort. It's not Swiss, not Italian. . . just Lugano.

a good
walk

Begin at the **Piazza della Riforma** ❼ ▶, which is dominated by the **Palazzo Civico** ❽, or town hall. Look up to the gable above the clock to see the city's coat of arms. (The building also houses the tourist office, whose entrance is on the lake side.) On the western side of the square the Piazza della Riforma bleeds into the **Piazza Rezzonico**, which contains a large fountain by Otto Maraini dating from 1895.

Heading out of the Piazza della Riforma on the north side, onto the Via Luvini, you come to the **Piazza Dante,** which is dominated by a large department store and a bank. From here, if you pop over one street east to the busy Via Pretorio, you can get a look at Lugano's oldest building, the Pretorio (1425), at No. 7. Back at Piazza Dante, turn left down Via Pessina, which leads you into the **Piazza Cioccaro**, on your right. Here the funicular from the train station terminates and the typical *centro storico* (Old Town) begins, its narrow streets lined with chic clothing shops and small markets offering pungent local cheeses and porcini mushrooms.

From the Piazza Cioccaro walk up the shop-lined staircase street of Via Cattedrale. The street curves left, ending at the **Cattedrale di San Lorenzo** ❾. Take a moment to enjoy the view from the church square. Continue up to the right of the church on Via Paolo Ragazonni to the Hotel Federale; there you can leave the road and take the footpath through the gardens on the slope below the train station. Go up the steps but don't cross over to the station. Turn left and follow the Via Maraini south to the end of the parking lot. Cross over the tracks at the marked crossing and turn onto the path that will lead you to **Parco del Tassino** ❿.

Retrace your steps back to the station and on the way down just near the cathedral, explore the Salita Chiattone, another street of steps and shops near Via Cattedrale. Before reaching the bottom, turn right to connect with Piazza Cioccaro and the funicular. Turn right onto the Via Pessina and follow it into the lively **Piazza Maraini.** Here you can start a leisurely stroll down the **Via Nassa,** which runs between the Piazza della Riforma and the Piazza Luini. It's characterized by a long row of porticos, many housing chic designer clothing shops. Nestled among the medieval and modern buildings on the right, between Piazza San Carlo and Piazza Battaglini, is the 17th-century baroque church San Carlo Borromeo. The street ends at the **Chiesa di Santa Maria degli Angioli** ⓫, facing the lake at the Piazza Luini.

Across the road, spreading south along the lakefront promenade, is the **Giardino Belvedere** ⓬. At the southwest end of the gardens, an incongruous bust of George Washington stands on the lake promenade in its own little gazebo. "Georgio" never visited Lugano, of course; this image was erected in 1859 by a grateful Swiss engineer who had made his fortune in America. A little farther south, directly across the Riva Antonio Caccia, is the **Museo d'Arte Moderna** ⓭.

Head back northeast along the waterfront promenade known as **Il Lungolago** ⓮, and at the Imbarcadero Centrale (Central Wharf) take the underpass to cross the road, coming back up at the Piazza della Riforma. Leave the piazza at the northeast side through a portico onto

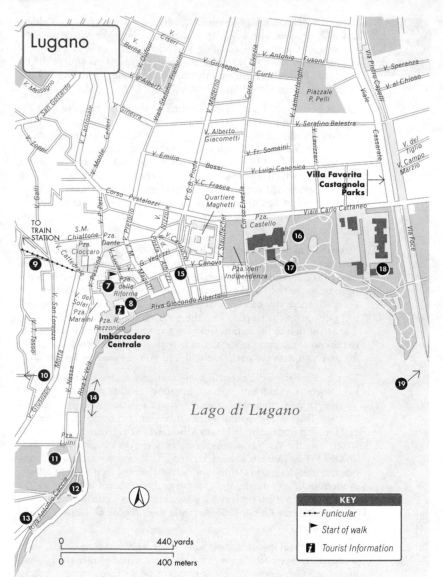

Lugano

Villa Favorita
Castagnola
Parks

Piazzale
P. Pelli

TO TRAIN STATION

Imbarcadero
Centrale

Lago di Lugano

KEY

•••• Funicular

▶ Start of walk

🛈 Tourist Information

0 ——— 440 yards
0 ——— 400 meters

the Via Canova. After crossing over the Via della Posta/Via Albrizzi, you come to the **Museo Cantonale d'Arte** ⑮, on your right. Continue straight ahead to the 17th-century church of San Rocco, with its neo-baroque facade. Turn left onto Via Carducci before you reach the church and you'll find a small orange-tile pedestrian entranceway into the **Quartiere Maghetti**—a town within a town. It's a tangle of streets full of porticoes, little squares, shops, and offices, a modern take on old forms, created in the early 1980s by the architects Camazind, Brocchi, and Sennhauser. Exit the Quartiere Maghetti onto Via Canova (you'll be behind the church now) and continue east, crossing Via Stauffacher. On your left is the open **Piazza dell'Independenza**. Cross over the wide Corso Elvezia to enter the **Parco Civico** ⑯. Inside the grounds, in addition to the nearly 15 acres of greenery, you'll find the **Museo Civico di Belle Arti** ⑰ and **Museo Cantonale di Storia Naturale** ⑱. From here you can opt to spend the afternoon at the **Lido** ⑲, the city's public beach and pool, just east of the park across the River Cassarate. Or you can head back to town along the waterfront promenade, and take in the stunning mountain views: straight ahead, the rocky top of Monte Generoso (5,579 feet), and flanking the bay at right and left, respectively, Monte San Salvatore and Monte Brè.

TIMING   It's best to walk through the city in the morning, before it gets too hot. A quick overview, without much time in the museums or parks, would take a couple of hours. Or make a day of it, taking in the main sights in the morning, stopping for lunch, and then spending the afternoon in the museums or on the Lido. Remember that the museums are closed on Monday.

What to See

⑨ **Cattedrale di San Lorenzo** (Cathedral of St. Lawrence). Behind this church's early Renaissance facade is a richly frescoed baroque interior with a baptismal font dating from 1430. The church has premedieval origins: it became a collegiate church in 1078. Eight centuries later it became a cathedral. ⊠ *Via Cattedrale, Old Town.*

★ ⑪ **Chiesa di Santa Maria degli Angioli** (Church of St. Mary of the Angels). The simple facade doesn't prepare you for the riches within. Begun in the late 15th century, the church contains a magnificent fresco of the *Passion and Crucifixion,* as well as *The Last Supper* and *Madonna with the Infant Jesus,* all by Bernardino Luini (1475–1532). ⊠ *Piazza Luini, Old Town.*

⑫ **Giardino Belvedere** (Belvedere Gardens). This lakefront sculpture garden frames a dozen modern works with palms, camellias, oleanders, and magnolias. At the far west end there's a public swimming area. ⊠ *On lake side of Quai Riva Antonio Caccia near Piazza Luini, Old Town* ▧ *Free* ☉ *Daily 24 hrs.*

⑲ **Lido.** The city's public beach has two swimming pools and a restaurant. To reach it, you'll have to cross the Cassarate River. Heading east from the Parco Civico, cross Viale Castagnola and then turn toward the lake. The main swimming-area entrance is just ahead on the right. Everyone from families to scenesters comes here to cool off. ⊠ *Via Cassarate 6*

☎ *091/9714041* 🏖 *Beach 6 SF, changing cabins 6 SF* ⊘ *May and Sept., daily 9–7; June–Aug., daily 9–7:30.*

★ ⑭ **Il Lungolago** (lake promenade). This 2-km (1-mi) waterfront path lined with pollarded lime trees, funereal cypresses, and graceful palm trees stretches from the Lido all the way to the Paradiso neighborhood. Il Lungolago is the place to see and be seen—while taking in the views, of course. At night luminous fountains turn the lake near the Parco Civico into a special attraction.

⑬ **Museo d'Arte Moderna** (Museum of Modern Art). Consistently outstanding temporary exhibitions are the hallmark of this museum, whose permanent collection includes Chagall, Monet, Pissarro, Rousseau, and Futurist artist Umberto Boccioni. Brochures are available in English. ✉ *Villa Malpensata, Riva Antonio Caccia 5, Lungolago* ☎ *091/9944370* ⊕ *www.museodartemoderna-lugano.ch* 🏷 *11 SF.*

⑮ **Museo Cantonale d'Arte** (Cantonal Art Museum). A group of three palaces dating from the 15th to the 19th centuries was adapted for this museum. Its exhibits include paintings, sculpture, and photography, including some important avant-garde works. The permanent collection holds works by Klee, Turner, Degas, Renoir, and Hodler as well as contemporary Ticinese artists. Descriptive material is available in English. ✉ *Via Canova 10, Old Town* ☎ *091/9104780* ⊕ *www.museo-cantonale-arte.ch* 🏷 *Permanent collection 7 SF, temporary exhibits 3 SF* ⊘ *Tues. 2–5, Wed.–Sun. 10–5.*

⑱ **Museo Cantonale di Storia Naturale** (Cantonal Museum of Natural History). A museum since 1854, it contains exhibits on fossils, animals, and plants (there's a large section on mushrooms), mostly those typical of the region. ✉ *Viale Cattaneo 4, Parco Civico* ☎ *091/9115380* 🏷 *Free* ⊘ *Tues.–Sat. 9–noon and 2–5.*

⑰ **Museo Civico di Belle Arti** (Municipal Art Museum). The restored Villa Ciani, with its lofty vaulted ceilings and tile floors, displays hundreds of works by Swiss and European artists from the 15th to the 20th centuries. Especially noteworthy is the extensive collection of paintings by Futurist artist Umberto Boccioni, Cesare Tallone, and impressionists Monet, Rousseau, and Matisse. English-language brochures are available. ✉ *Villa Ciani, Parco Civico* ☎ *091/8007196* 🏷 *5 SF* ⊘ *Tues.–Sun. 10–noon and 2–6.*

⑧ **Palazzo Civico** (Town Hall). This neoclassical Lombard structure dates from 1844. Inside there's a large inner yard surrounded by a four-sided arcade, with a wide vestibule on the piazza side. It houses the town council and tourist office. ✉ *Piazza della Riforma, Old Town.*

⑯ **Parco Civico** (City Park). A green oasis in the city center, the park has cacti, exotic shrubs, and more than 1,000 varieties of roses, as well as an aviary, a tiny deer zoo, and a fine view of the bay from its peninsula. ✉ *South of Viale Carlo Cattaneo, east of Piazza Castello.*

☾ ⑩ **Parco del Tassino** (Tassino Park). On a plateau just behind and south of the train station, this park offers lovely bay views from its rose gardens.

A small deer park and playground make it very child-friendly. ⊕ *Take Bus 2 east to San Domenico stop in Castagnola, or use funicular from Old Town to train station* 🎟 *Free.*

► ★ **❼** **Piazza della Riforma** (Reformation Square). In the early 19th century, several buildings were removed in order to enlarge the square—providing more room for the present-day café tables. Commonly referred to simply as "la Piazza," it's the social and cultural heart of the city and the site of markets and open-air music performances. ⊠ *Just north of the Imbarcadero Centrale, Old Town.*

---

off the beaten path

VILLA FAVORITA – This splendid 17th-century mansion in Castagnola houses a portion of the extraordinary private art collection of the Baron von Thyssen-Bornemisza. Although, after a scandalous international divorce battle, portions of the collection were transferred to Spain, a significant display of 19th- and 20th-century paintings and watercolors from Europe and America remains. Artists represented include Giorgio de Chirico, Frederick Church, Lucien Freud, Edward Hopper, Jackson Pollock, and Andrew Wyeth. The villa gardens are also worth a stroll; they're planted with native and exotic flora. Take Bus 1 in the direction of Castagnola (ask to be let off at the villa), or take the 40-minute walk from town, heading east along the lake on Viale Castagnola, which turns into Via Riviera past the Castagnola Wharf. Call ahead, as opening hours often change during special exhibitions. ⊠ *Via Rivera 14, Castagnola* 🕾 *091/ 9721741* 🎟 *10 SF* ⊙ *Easter–Oct., Fri.–Sun. 10–5.*

CASTAGNOLA PARKS – For an idyllic daytime excursion, combine a trip to the Villa Favorita with one or both of the parks adjacent to it. The **Parco degli Ulivi** (Olive Park) spreads over the lower slopes of Monte Brè and offers a romantic landscape of silvery olive trees mixed with cypress, laurel, and wild rosemary; you enter it from the Sentiero di Gandria (Gandria Footpath). **Parco San Michele** (St. Michael Park), also on Monte Brè, has a public chapel and a broad terrace that overlooks the city, the lake, and the Alps. From Cassarate, walk up the steps by the lower terminus of the Monte Brè funicular.

MONTE BRÈ, MONTE SAN SALVATORE & MONTE GENEROSO – The serious view hound may want to reach the top of one of the three peaks that define the landscape around Lugano. **Monte Brè** (🕾 091/ 9713171 ⊕ www.montebre.ch 🎟 Funicular 20 SF round-trip ⊙ Daily 9:15–12:15 and 2–6:45) has a funicular that departs every 30 minutes from the east end of Lugano in Cassarate. It's also possible to drive, cycle, or hike to the crest. At the top are several well-marked hiking trails, as well as an "art trail" in the summit village of Brè, a path studded with pieces of sculpture. A guided tour of the art trail can be booked at the funicular station. **Monte San Salvatore** (🕾 091/9852828 ⊕ www.montesansalvatore.ch 🎟 Funicular 20 SF round-trip ⊙ Mid-Sept.–mid-May, daily 9–6:30; mid-May–mid-June, daily 8:30–6:30; mid-June–mid-Sept., daily

8:30–11 PM) can be reached via the funicular in Paradiso. At the top are a huge relief model of the entire Sottoceneri region, marked "nature itinerary" paths, which have signs pointing out flower and tree specimens, and other marked hikes down and around the area. For yet more spectacular views take a boat from Lugano across to Capolago, where you can take the 40-minute cogwheel train up **Monte Generoso** (☎ 091/6481105 🌐 www.montegeneroso.ch 🎫 Train 36 SF round-trip ⏲ Mid-Mar.–early Nov., trains run daily 10:15–3:15). Trains depart every hour. At the top are a restaurant, café, and lots of marked hiking trails.

HERMANN HESSE MUSEUM – In the tower of the Casa Camuzzi, a fabulous jumble of old houses on a hilltop in Montagnola, is this tiny but impressive museum dedicated to Hermann Hesse. The Nobel Prize–winning author lived here the last 43 years of his life, writing most of his important works, including *Siddhartha* and *Steppenwolf*. The rooms in which he lived and worked have been meticulously preserved; you can see his papers, books, desk, glasses, even his straw hat. Take the postbus marked Agra-Montagnola from Lugano's train station for the 10-minute ride to Montagnola. Once there, walk down past the parking lot, going straight between the old houses (and sometimes actually through them, via passageways) to the Casa Camuzzi. ✉ *Montagnola* ☎ *091/9933770* 🌐 *www.hessemontagnola.ch* 🎫 *6 SF* ⏲ *Mar.–Oct., Tues.–Sun. 10–12:30 and 2–6:30; Nov.–Feb., weekends 10–12:30 and 2–6:30.*

Where to Stay & Eat

★ **$$$–$$$$** ✕ **Al Portone.** Silver and lace dress up the stucco and stone here, but the ambience is strictly casual. Chef Roberto Galizzi pursues *nuova cucina* (contemporary Italian cuisine) with ambition and flair. You might choose duck liver with mango chutney and pears, lobster in squid-ink sauce, or lamb with eggplant and zucchini stew. Or you could *lascia fare a Roberto* (leave it to Robert)—as he calls his menu de dégustation. ✉ *Viale Cassarate 3, Lugano/Cassarate* ☎ *091/9235511* 💳 *AE, DC, MC, V* ⏲ *Closed Sun., Mon., and first 2 wks in Aug.*

★ **$$$** ✕ **Santabbondio.** Ancient stone and terra-cotta blend with pristine pastels in this upgraded grotto, where subtle, imaginative, new Franco-Italian cuisine *du marché* (based on fresh produce) is served in intimate little dining rooms and on a shady terrace. Watch for perch with mango and sage or beef fillet with figs in balsamic vinegar to confirm the local opinion: chef Martin Dalsass is the canton's best. There's a good selection of open wines. You'll need a cab to get here, but it's worth the trip. ✉ *Via Fomelino 10, Lugano/Sorengo* ☎ *091/9932388* 💳 *AE, DC, MC, V* ⏲ *Closed Sun., Mon., first wk of Jan., and last wk of Feb.*

$–$$$ ✕ **Da Raffaele.** Having a meal in this family-run Italian restaurant feels like being let in on a neighborhood secret. Start with a pasta, like the marvelous homemade orecchiette (ear-shape pasta) or *mezzelune* (half moons) stuffed with ricotta and spinach, then try something from the grill, like *gamberoni alla griglia* (grilled shrimp). The staff doesn't speak English, but their warmth needs no translation. The restaurant is just outside the city in a residential neighborhood, but is easily reached by car or bus (take Bus 8 or 9 from the train station to the last stop, Viganello). ✉ *Contrada dei Patrizi 8/Via Pazzalino, Viganello* ☎ *091/ 9716614* ⊟ *AE, MC, V* ☺ *Closed Sun., last wk of July, first 2 wks of Aug. No lunch Sat.*

★ $–$$$ ✕ **Locanda del Boschetto.** Tucked away at the end of a cul-de-sac in a residential neighborhood, the grill is the first thing you see in this grotto-style ristorante, a specialist in pure and simple seafood *alla griglia* (grilled). The decor is a study in linen and rustic wood, and the service is helpful and down-to-earth. ✉ *Via Boschetto 8, Paradiso* ☎ *091/9942493* ⊟ *AE, DC, MC, V* ☺ *Closed Mon., Aug., and first 2 wks of Nov.*

$–$$$ ✕ **Orologio.** Snowy tablecloths and chairs stand out against dark hardwood floors in this open, minimalist restaurant. The attentive staff is quick to bring you modern Italian dishes such as thinly sliced octopus with olive oil, jumbo shrimp with saffron and fresh garlic, or lamb cutlets with carrots and baby potatoes—but they retreat to let you linger over coffee. ✉ *Via Nizzola 2, Old Town* ☎ *091/9232338* ⊟ *AE, DC, MC, V* ☺ *Closed Sun. and 2 wks in Aug.*

★ ¢–$$ ✕ **La Tinera.** Tucked down an alley off Via Pessina, this cozy basement taverna squeezes loyal locals and tourists onto wooden benches for authentic regional specialties, hearty meats, and pastas. Local wines are served in traditional ceramic bowls. ✉ *Via dei Gorini 2, Old Town* ☎ *091/ 9235219* ⊟ *AE, DC, MC, V* ☺ *Closed Sun. and Aug.*

$ ✕ **Grotto Figini.** Absolutely authentic, this grotto pulls in a rowdy local crowd for a boccalino of good merlot and a satisfying, rib-sticking meal of polenta and grilled meats. Don't expect English or other tourists, and don't take personally the stares you'll receive when you first walk in. It's in a short stretch of woods on a hill in Gentilino, above Lugano-Paradiso. After your meal you can stroll down the shady road to see old *grotti* hidden in the overgrown hillside. ✉ *Via ai Grotti, Gentilino* ☎ *091/9946497* ⊟ *V* ☺ *Closed Mon. and mid-Dec.–Feb.*

★ $$$$ ✕▦ **Ticino.** In this 500-year-old former monastery (protected as a historical monument), shuttered windows look out from every room onto a glassed-in garden. The vaulted halls are lined with art and antiques; rooms are unpretentious yet elegant, with pleasing details such as embroidered towels and special orthopedic mattresses. The formal restaurant is full of dark-wood wainscoting and leather banquettes. The menu blends Ticinese and French cuisine; it's famous for its fresh seafood and rack of lamb with herbs. The hotel is steps from the funicular to the train station. ✉ *Piazza Cioccaro 1, Old Town, CH-6901* ☎ *091/9227772* 🖷 *091/9236278* ⊕ *www.romantikhotels.com/lugano* ⤴ *18 rooms, 2 suites* ⚭ *Restaurant, bar, library, no-smoking rooms; no a/c in some rooms* ⊟ *AE, DC, MC, V* ☺ *Closed Jan. No lunch weekends* ⫣⃝ *BP.*

$$$$
Fodor'sChoice
★ ✕▦ **Villa Principe Leopoldo & Residence.** This extravagantly furnished mansion, perched on a hillside high over a lake, offers old-world service with splendor to match. The villa was built in 1868 on behalf of Prince Leopold of Hohenzollern. There's a stunningly arranged pool-and-terrace complex encircled by a double staircase—a slightly baroque touch of Bel Air. The rooms in both the villa and the adjacent build-

ing are gracefully lush in muted tones and marble. Fabulous creations from chef Dario Ranza, such as pink grapefruit risotto with shrimp or sea bass baked in a salt crust, make dining here a notable experience. ⊠ *Via Montalbano 5, Collina d'Oro, CH-6900* ☎ *091/9858855* 🖷 *091/9858825* ⊕ *www.leopoldohotel.com* ⤳ *67 rooms, 24 suites* ♨ *2 restaurants, minibars, 2 tennis courts, 2 pools, health club, massage, 2 bars, Internet, meeting rooms, no-smoking rooms* ⊟ *AE, DC, MC, V* ⦿| *BP.*

$–$$ ✗⊡ **Delfino.** A four–minute stroll up from the lake, the Delfino is perched in a quiet residential area and offers all of its guests balconies, most of them with a view of the lake. Family-run since 1970, this unpretentious lodging prides itself on seasonal specialties prepared by a former sous-chef of Ascona's redoubtable Eden Roc. A tempting proposition: mango leaves with pan-fried goose liver dumplings with fennel and dried grapes to start, followed by veal steak with rosemary foam, and rounded out with strawberry soup with freshly made lavender ice cream. ⊠ *Via Casserinetta 6, Paradiso, CH-6902* ☎ *091/9859999* 🖷 *091/9859900* ⊕ *www.delfinolugano.ch* ⤳ *50 rooms* ♨ *Restaurant, minibars, pool, hot tub, bar, Internet, meeting rooms; no a/c* ⊟ *AE, DC, MC, V* ⦿| *BP.*

★ $$$$ ⊡ **Splendide Royale.** This landmark villa was first converted into a hotel in 1887. Much of the Victorian luster of its public spaces—with their marble, pillars, terrazzo, and antiques—has been respectfully preserved, as it is one of the last palace-style hotels in Ticino. Since a wing was added in the '80s, you can choose between discreetly modern rooms decorated in beech, beige, and gold or more florid period rooms in the original wing complete with chandeliers and ceiling murals. All rooms have heated floors in the bathrooms; the balconies and terraces open onto lake or garden views. ⊠ *Riva A. Caccia 7, CH-6900* ☎ *091/9857711* 🖷 *091/9857722* ⊕ *www.splendide.ch* ⤳ *88 rooms, 8 suites* ♨ *Restaurant, in-room safes, minibars, pool, massage, sauna, piano bar, business services, meeting rooms* ⊟ *AE, DC, MC, V* ⦿| *BP.*

$$$–$$$$ ⊡ **Du Lac.** This comfortable, bright hotel offers more lakefront luxury than many of the glossier hotels farther down the same beach. Owned by the same family since it was founded in 1920, this lodging has been regularly renovated. Huge, impressive needlework tapestry art reproductions, handmade by the owner's father, cover the walls of the generously sized lobby and restaurant. The rooms are all spacious and face the lake; those on the sixth floor are the quietest. There's a private swimming area on the lake. ⊠ *Riva Paradiso 3, Lugano-Paradiso, CH-6902* ☎ *091/9864747* 🖷 *091/9864748* ⊕ *www.dulac.ch* ⤳ *52 rooms, 1 suite* ♨ *Restaurant, minibars, pool, health club, massage, beach, waterskiing, bar, Internet, meeting rooms, no-smoking rooms; no a/c* ⊟ *AE, DC, MC, V* ☉ *Closed Jan. and Feb.* ⦿| *BP.*

$$–$$$ ⊡ **International au Lac.** Next to the Church of St. Mary of the Angels, this big, friendly hotel is just a stone's throw from the lake. The interiors are floridly decorated, with many paintings, antiques, and heavy, sumptuous furniture. The large garden and pool in the back make you forget you're downtown. Rooms on the side are quieter. ⊠ *Via Nassa 68, Old Town, CH-6901* ☎ *091/9227541* 🖷 *091/9227544* ⊕ *www.*

hotel-international.ch ⤷ *80 rooms* ⚗ *Restaurant, in-room safes, pool, bar, parking (fee); no a/c in some rooms* ▭ *AE, DC, MC, V* ☺ *Closed Nov.–Easter* ⦿l *BP.*

$$ ⊞ **Park-Hotel Nizza.** Tucked into the dense tropical foliage of the lower slopes of Monte San Salvatore, this former villa mixes old and modern comforts. Most rooms are small, but all are quiet and comfortable; panoramic views of the lake below don't cost extra. The hotel has its own farm and vineyards on the hill behind—the source of the organic produce used by the kitchen. The restaurant makes its own wine, with some very original labels designed by the owner. Summer meals are served in the garden; there's a special farmer's breakfast on Tuesday and a cocktail party on Friday evening. ✉ *Via Guidino 14, Lugano-Paradiso, CH-6902* ☎ *091/9941771* ⎙ *091/9941773* ⊕ *www.villanizza.com* ⤷ *28 rooms* ⚗ *Restaurant, in-room safes, minibars, pool, hot tub, bar, Internet, playground, no-smoking rooms; no a/c* ▭*AE, MC, V* ☺ *Closed late Oct.–3 wks before Easter* ⦿l *BP.*

$–$$ ⊞ **Zurigo.** Close to parks, shops, and the waterfront promenade, this hotel offers bright, modern rooms with pale lemon linoleum floors, light wood furnishings, shiny white-tile baths, and a shady front garden. Formerly for the budget-minded, it has taken a step up, but still offers decent value for the money. North-facing rooms are the quietest. ✉ *Corso Pestalozzi 13, Old Town, CH-6900* ☎ *091/9234343* ⎙ *091/9239268* ⤷ *48 rooms* ⚗ *Internet, parking (fee); no a/c in some rooms* ▭ *AE, DC, MC, V* ☺ *Closed Dec. and Jan.* ⦿l *BP.*

$ ⊞ **San Carlo.** Ideally located on the main shopping street, this friendly hotel is one of the best deals in town. It's near the funicular and a block from the waterfront. The rooms are tiny, but clever carpentry makes the most out of small spaces, creating niches for a mirror, a television, or a hideaway bed. The breakfast room is small, so breakfast in bed is encouraged. ✉ *Via Nassa 28, Old Town, CH-6900* ☎ *091/9227107* ⎙ *091/9228022* ⤷ *22 rooms* ⚗ *No-smoking rooms; no a/c* ▭ *AE, DC, MC, V* ⦿l *BP.*

Nightlife & the Arts

BARS Just off the Piazza delle Riforma, **Bottegone del Vino** (✉ Via Magatti 3, Old Town ☎ 091/9227689) has a great selection of wine accompanied by good local cheeses and tapas. It's closed on Sunday. **Hotel Eden** (✉ Riva Paradiso 1, Old Town ☎ 091/9859200) has a popular piano bar. For a refined place to enjoy a cocktail, head to the palatial **Splendide Royale** (✉ Riva A. Caccia 7, Lungolago ☎ 091/9857711).

CASINO In addition to slot machines and gaming tables, the three-floor **Casinò Lugano** (✉ Via Stauffacher 1, Old Town ☎ 091/9737111) has a bar and restaurant.

DANCING On Friday and Saturday nights, **Dancing Morandi** (✉ Via Trevano 56, Molino Nuovo ☎ 091/9712291) is a great place to dance to songs from the '70s and '80s. The lively **Disco Prince** (✉ Via Stauffacher 1, Old Town ☎ 091/9233281) has a DJ and attracts a younger crowd. With three dance floors, **Titanic** (✉ Via Cantonale, Pambio-Noranco ☎ 091/9856010) is the region's biggest disco.

MUSIC   The free **Blues to Bop Festival** livens up the Piazza della Riforma at the end of August. In July, **Estival Jazz** brings jazz and world music to the Piazza della Riforma. From April to June, the city hosts its **Lugano Festival,** which draws world-class orchestras and conductors.

Shopping

Cute novelty shops and antiques stores line the staircase street of **Via Cattedrale.** All the top designers can be found in the shops lining the pedestrian-only **Via Nassa.** If it's Italian and international designer clothing bargains you're after, explore the factory outlet store called **Fox Town** (⊠ Via Angelo Maspoli, Mendrisio ☎ 091/6405020). It's open daily from 11 to 5.

Gandria

㉒   *7 km (4 mi) southeast of Lugano.*

Fodor'sChoice
★

Although today its narrow waterfront streets are crowded with tourists, the tiny historic village of Gandria merits a visit, either by boat or by car. Gandria clings vertiginously to the steep hillside; a labyrinth of stairways and passageways lined with flower-filled balconies hangs directly over open water. Souvenir and crafts shops now fill its backstreet nooks, but the ambience of an ancient fishing village remains.

MUSEO DOGANALE – Across Lago di Lugano from Gandria—almost in Italy—is the small Customs Museum, casually known as the Smugglers' Museum. Displays of ingenious containers, weapons, and contraband explore the romantic history of clandestine trade. You can catch a boat from the jetty in Gandria. ☎ *091/9239843* ☒ *Free* ☉ *Apr.–Oct., daily 1:30–5:30.*

Campione

㉑   *18 km (11 mi) south of Gandria, 12 km (7 mi) south of Lugano.*

In the heart of Swiss Italy lies Campione. Here, in this southernmost of regions, the police cars have Swiss license plates but the police officers inside are Italian; the inhabitants pay their taxes to Italy but do it in Swiss francs. Its narrow streets are saturated with history, and the surrounding landscape is a series of stunning views of Lago di Lugano and Monte San Salvatore.

In the 8th century, the lord of Campione gave the tiny scrap of land, less than a square kilometer (½ square mi) in area, to the monastery of St. Ambrosius of Milan. Despite all the wars that passed it by, Campione remained Italian until the end of the 18th century, when it was incorporated into the Cisalpine Republic. When Italy unified in 1861, Campione became part of the new Kingdom of Italy—and remained so. There are no frontiers between Campione and Switzerland, and it benefits from the comforts of Swiss currency, customs laws, and postal and telephone services. Despite its miniature scale, it has exercised disproportionate influence on the art world: in the Middle Ages, a school of

A CENTURY OF WINE

Roughly 6,000 tons of wine grapes—about 7% of Switzerland's total production—are grown each year in the rolling hills of the Ticino. Leading the way is the popular merlot grape, introduced in 1905. It wasn't a success solely because it grows well in this region. An epidemic of phylloxera was destroying the country's vineyards, and the merlot grape proved to be the most resistant.

Merlot now accounts for 80% of the region's wine production. Thanks to technological advances, the Ticino also produces white and blush varieties. A sampling of merlot in the region's grotti, restaurants, and vineyards will reveal a wide range of wines, including some very fine vintages with top-quality barrel maturation. If you want to learn more about the wines of the region, you might wish to follow le strade del vino (the wine roads), which map out 69 restaurants, 43 wine producers, and five enotecas of note. For information, contact Ticinowine (☎ 091/6901353 ⊕ www.ticinowine.ch).

stonemasons, sculptors, and architects from Campione and the surrounding region worked on the cathedrals of Milan, Verona, Cremona, Trento, and Modena—even the Hagia Sophia in Istanbul.

Nightlife & the Arts

Campione is a magnet for gamblers, and at its glittering **Casino** (✉ Piazza Milano 1 ☎ 091/6401111), the sky's the limit. When you're not playing the tables you can have dinner in the restaurant or enjoy a show. Men are required to wear a jacket, but they don't have to wear a tie in summer.

Riva San Vitale

22 9 km (5½ mi) south of Campione, 13 km (8 mi) south of Lugano.

At the south end of Lago di Lugano sits Riva San Vitale, which rivals Campione for its odd history: in 1798 its people objected to new boundaries and declared themselves an independent republic. Their glory lasted 14 days before a small cantonal army marched in and persuaded them to rejoin Switzerland. A 5th-century **Battistèro** (baptistery) remains, still containing its original stone font.

About 4 km (2 mi) south of Riva San Vitale is little **Mendrisio,** cradle of the Ticinese wine industry. It's known for its medieval processions, held on the Thursday and Friday before Easter.

Morcote

23 6 km (4 mi) northwest of Riva San Vitale, 10 km (6 mi) south of Lugano.

FodorsChoice
★

At the southernmost tip of the glorious Ceresio Peninsula is the atmospheric village of Morcote, its clay-color houses and arcades looking directly over the waterfront. A steep and picturesque climb leads up to the **Chiesa di Madonna del Sasso** (Church of the Madonna of the Rock), with its well-preserved 16th-century frescoes; its elevated setting affords wonderful views.

Where to Stay & Eat

$$–$$$ ✕⊞ **Dellago.** Combining a soothing atmosphere, personal service, and
Fodor'sChoice unpretentious savoir faire, this stylish refuge right on the lake spoils
★ its guests. At dinnertime the casual lakeside terrace lures many locals, devotees of chef and co-owner Klaus Höckel, who whips up astounding entrées such as the gleaming buttermilk-port tower with smoked salmon cured in lemongrass, ginger, and honey or tiger prawns marinated in tamarind-garlic pesto and served on a sumptuous bed of leeks, shiitake mushrooms, and sprouts. Individually decorated rooms are equipped with a range of treats: ask for surround-sound stereo, a private rooftop hot tub, a DVD player, or a plasma TV. After a refreshing breakfast—replete with homemade jams, fine teas, and a selection of unusual breads—why not take the hotel paddle boat out for a spin? ⊠ *Lago di Lugano, CH-6815 Melide* ☎ *091/6497041* 🖷 *091/6498915* ⊕ *www.hotel-dellago.ch* ➦ *50 rooms* ⌂ *Restaurant, bar; no a/c in some rooms* ⊟ *AE, DC, MC, V* ⊫ *BP.*

★ **$–$$** ✕⊞ **Bella Vista.** High above Lago di Lugano, surrounded by vineyards, lies this outstanding getaway. A handful of superb rooms occupy two restored 17th-century houses; the decor is a mix of antique and ultramodern. One sleek room has the original fireplace; the tower suite's bathroom is done in granite and glass. All have beautiful views. The restaurant is equally luxe. The menu includes several lobster dishes, homemade pastas, and a heavenly potato gratin. In fine weather you'll be served on the outdoor terrace, which has a truly spectacular view. Vico Morcote is about 2 km (1¼ mi) south of Melide; follow the sign from the main road. ⊠ *Strada da Vigh 2, CH-6921 Vico Morcote* ☎ *091/9961143* 🖷 *091/9961288* ➦ *9 rooms, 2 suites, 1 apartment* ⌂ *Restaurant, bar; no a/c* ⊟ *AE, DC, MC, V* ⊫ *BP* ⊘ *Closed Jan.*

THE TICINO A TO Z

To research prices, get advice from other travelers, and book travel arrangements, visit www.fodors.com.

AIR TRAVEL

Swiss Air Lines, known as Swiss, Switzerland's domestic carrier, has direct connections to Lugano's airport, Aeroporto Lugano-Agno, from Unique Zürich Airport, Cointrin in Geneva, and other European destinations.

🖪 **Airlines & Contacts Swiss** ☎ 0848/852000.

AIRPORTS & TRANSFERS

The nearest international airport is in Italy. Malpensa, near Milan, is one of the biggest hubs in southern Europe.

🖪 **Airport Information Aeroporto Lugano-Agno** ⊠ 7 km [4½ mi] west of Lugano, Agno ☎ 091/6051226. **Linate** ✈ 10 km [6 mi] east of Milan ☎ 0039/274-852-200. **Malpensa** ✈ 50 km [31 mi] northwest of Milan ☎ 0039/274-852-200.

AIRPORT
TRANSFERS To get to Lugano from Aeroporto Lugano-Agno, contact Fly Car Lugano. Bus Express Chiasso connects Milan's Malpensa Airport with Lugano.
🛈 Taxis & Shuttles Bus Express Chiasso ☎ 091/9948878. **Fly Car Lugano** ☎ 091/8078520.

BOAT & FERRY TRAVEL

Lago di Lugano and Lago Maggiore are plied by graceful steamers that carry passengers from one waterfront resort to another, offering excellent views of the mountains. Steamer travel on Lago di Lugano is included in the Swiss Pass; tickets can be purchased near the docks before departure. On Lago di Lugano, the Navigazione Lago di Lugano (Navigation Company of Lake Lugano) offers excursions around the bay to Gandria and toward the Villa Favorita.

Boats owned by Navigazione Lago Maggiore-Bacino Svizzero (Swiss Navigation Company of Lake Maggiore) cruise Lago Maggiore. Discounts are given for Swiss and Swiss Boat passes.
🛈 Boat & Ferry Information Navigazione Lago di Lugano ✉ Casella Postale 56, CH-6906 Lugano ☎ 091/9715223 ⊕ www.lakelugano.ch. **Navigazione Lago Maggiore-Bacino Svizzero** ✉ Lungolago Motta, CH-6600 Locarno ☎ 091/7511865 ⊕ www.navlaghi.it.

BUS TRAVEL

The Palm Express scenic postbus route carries visitors from St. Moritz to Lugano via the Maloja Pass and Italy; reservations are strongly recommended. It takes about four hours and can be arranged at any train station or tourist office. You can also contact Railtour Suisse.

There's a convenient postbus sightseeing system here that you can use to get around the region, even into the backcountry. La Posta (post and telegraph office) publishes illustrated booklets with suggested itineraries and prices; you can get them through the Autopostale Ticino-Moesano or through local tourist and post offices. Postbus excursion prices are reduced with the Locarno or Lugano Holiday Passes and are free with the Swiss Pass.
🛈 Bus Information Autopostale Ticino-Moesano ✉ Via S. Balestra, CH-6900 Lugano ☎ 091/8078520 ⊕ www.post.ch. **Railtour Suisse** ☎ 031/3780000.

CAR TRAVEL

There are two major gateways into the Ticino: the St. Gotthard Pass, in the northwest, and the San Bernardino Pass, to the northeast. From the St. Gotthard Pass, the swift A2 expressway leads down the Valle Leventina to Bellinzona, where it joins with A13, which cuts south from the San Bernardino. A2 directs the mingled traffic flow southward past Lugano to Chiasso and the Italian border, where the expressway heads directly to Como and Milan. As an alternative, there's the St. Gotthard Tunnel—17 km (11 mi) of dense air and darkness speeding you through the Alps rather than over them. If traffic is light, it can cut an hour off your travel time, but if the passes are closed and it's holiday migration time, tunnel traffic can be nasty.

A car is a real asset here if you intend to see the mountain valleys—and a hindrance in the congested lakeside resorts. Lugano is particularly difficult to drive through, and the parking garages are usually packed. Traffic between Bellinzona and Locarno can move at a crawl during high season. There's a handful of main roads between towns, but secondary roads peter out. Wherever you are in the Ticino, the Italian (read: fast and risky) driving style dominates.

EMERGENCIES

🚩 ++CE: Contacts head does not appear in print++ **Police** ☎ 117. **Medical Assistance/ Ambulance** ☎ 144. **Lugano Civic Hospital** ☎ 091/8116111. **Lugano Dental Clinic** ☎ 091/9350180.

TOURS

The *Wilhelm Tell Express* carries you by paddle steamer and rail from Luzern over the St. Gotthard Pass and into Locarno and Lugano with a guide and running commentary in English. Inquire at any rail station for details. The *Bernina Express,* Europe's highest Alp-crossing railway, takes you from Chur to St. Moritz in the *Glacier Express;* then you cross the Alps over the Bernina Pass into Italy (in summer it's even possible in an open-air train car) and continue into Lugano. Several variations are possible. Both offer discounts for Swiss Pass and Swiss Boat Pass holders. Inquire at any railway station for information and reservations.

Guided walks are available in all areas covering cultural, historical, architectural, and natural interests. English-language brochures with maps are available from local tourist offices for both guided and self-guided tours.

TRAIN TRAVEL

The St. Gotthard route connects south from Zürich, cuts through the pass tunnel, and heads into Bellinzona and Lugano. Side connections lead into Locarno from Brig, crossing the Simplon Pass and cutting through Italy. Swiss Pass travelers do not have to pay Italian rail fares to cross from Brig to Locarno via Domodossola. Trains connect out of Zürich's airport and take about three hours to Lugano, Locarno, and Ascona; from Geneva, catch the Milan express, changing at Domodossola, Locarno, and Bellinzona. Trains do not go directly into Ascona but stop at Locarno: you must connect by taxi or local bus. For train information from Lugano, call the Swiss Federal Railway, here called the Ferrovie Federali Svizzere (FFS).

Secondary rail connections here are minimal and can make all but the most mainstream rail sightseeing a complicated venture; most excursions will require some postbus connections. Nevertheless, there is a regional discount pass called the Holiday Pass FART. The pass is valid for the Lugano and Locarno areas and gives you unlimited free travel for three or seven consecutive days on local transit routes (bus and train) and a 30% to 50% discount on others. Passes are available from the train station or tourist office.

🚩 **Train Information Ferrovie Federali Svizzere (FFS)** ☎ 0900/300300, 1.19 SF per min.

VISITOR INFORMATION

The principal tourist authority for the Ticino is Ticino Turismo.
⁊ Local Tourist Office Bellinzona ⊠ Viale Stazione 18, CH-6500 ☎ 091/8252131. **Biasca** ⊠ contrada Cav. Pellanda 4, CH-6710 ☎ 091/8623327. **Blenio** ⊠ CH-6716 Acquarossa ☎ 091/8721467. **Lago Maggiore (Locarno, Ascona, and Brissago Islands)** ⊠ Via Largo Zorzi 1, CH-6600 Locarno ☎ 091/7910091. **Lugano** ⊠ Piazza della Riforma, CH-6900 ☎ 091/9133232. **Mendrisiotto e Basso Ceresio** ⊠ Via Ang. Maspoli, CH-6850 Mendrisio ☎ 091/6465761.

⁊ Regional Tourist Offices Ticino Turismo ⊠ Viale Stazione 18, CH-6501 Bellinzona ☎ 091/8252131 🖷 091/8254120 ⊕ www.ticino-tourism.ch.

LUZERN & CENTRAL SWITZERLAND
LUZERN, ENGELBERG, WEGGIS, SCHWYZ, ZUG

5

PLEASE DON'T CRY
at the onion-domed Jesuitenkirche ⇨*p.157*

ON A CLEAR DAY
enjoy the view from Mt. Pilatus ⇨*p.167*

IT'S AN UPHILL CLIMB
to the downhill skiing at Mt. Rigi ⇨*p.172*

PREPARE FOR LANDING
at Bürgenstock's private helipad ⇨*p.171*

MAKE A PASS
over the mountains at St. Gotthard ⇨*p.176*

TELL TALES
about a certain rebellious archer ⇨*p.165*

Updated by
Katrin Gygax

WITH THE MIST RISING OFF THE WAVES and the mountains looming above the clouds, it's easy to understand how Wagner could have composed his *Siegfried Idyll* in his mansion beside the lake. This is inspiring terrain, romantic and evocative. When the waters roil up, you can hear the whistling chromatics and cymbal clashes of Gioacchino Rossini's thunderstorm from his 1829 opera, *Guillaume Tell*. It was on Lake Luzern, after all, that Wilhelm Tell—the beloved, if legendary, Swiss national hero— supposedly leapt from the tyrant Gessler's boat to freedom. And it was in a meadow nearby that three furtive rebels and their cohorts swore an oath by firelight and planted the seed of the Swiss Confederation.

The Rütli Meadow on the western shore of Lake Luzern is the very spot where the Confederates of Uri, Schwyz, and Unterwalden are said to have met on the night of November 7, 1307, to renew the 1291 Oath of Eternal Alliance—Switzerland's equivalent of the U.S. Declaration of Independence. With this oath, the world's oldest still-extant democracy was born, as the proud charter territories swore their commitment to self-rule in the face of the Habsburg's Holy Roman Empire. Every August 1, the Swiss national holiday, citizens gather in the meadow in remembrance of the oath, and the sky glows with the light of hundreds of mountaintop bonfires.

Wilhelm Tell played an important role in that early rebellion, and his story, especially as told by German poet and playwright Friedrich von Schiller in his play *Wilhelm Tell* (1805), continues to stir those with a weakness for civil resistance. Though there are no valid records of his existence, and versions of the legend conflict with historical fact, no one denies the reality of his times, when central Switzerland—then a feudal dependent of Austria but by its own independent will not yet absorbed into the Holy Roman Empire—suffered brutal pressures and indignities under its local rulers. The mythical Gessler was one of those rulers, and his legendary edict—that the proud Swiss should bow before his hat suspended from a pole in the village square at Altdorf—symbolizes much crueler oppressions of the time. Schiller's Tell was a consummate hero: brisk, decisive, a highly skilled helmsman as well as marksman, and not one for diplomatic negotiations. He refused to kneel and provoked his famous punishment: to shoot an apple off his young son's head before a crowd of fellow townsmen. If he refused, both would be killed. Tell quietly tucked an arrow in his shirt bosom, loaded another into his crossbow, and shot the apple clean through. When Gessler asked what the second arrow was for, Tell replied that if the first arrow had struck his child, the second arrow would have been for Gessler and would not have missed.

For this impolitic remark, Tell was sentenced to prison. While deporting him across Lake Luzern, the Austrians (including the ruthless Gessler) were caught in a violent storm (remember your Rossini) and turned to Tell, the only man on board who knew the waters, to take the helm. Unmanacled, he steered the boat to a rocky ridge, leapt free, and pushed the boat back into the storm. Later he lay in wait in the woods near Küssnacht and shot Gessler in the heart. This act of justified violence inspired the people to overthrow their oppressors and swear the Oath of Eternal Alliance around a roaring bonfire, laying the groundwork for the Swiss Confederation.

Pretty romantic stuff. Yet for all its potential for drama, central Switzerland and the area surrounding Lake Luzern are tame enough turf: neat little towns, accessible mountains, smooth roads, resorts virtually glamour-free—and modest, graceful Luzern (Lucerne) astride the River Reuss much as it has been since the Middle Ages.

An eminently civilized region, Zentralschweiz (Central Switzerland) lacks the rustic unruliness of the Valais, the spectacular extremes of the Berner Oberland, the eccentricity of Graubünden. Nor does it have the sophistication and snob appeal of jet-set resorts or the cosmopolitan mix of Geneva, Basel, and Zürich. Instead, villages range neatly around their medieval centers; houses are tidy, pastel, picture-book cottages, deep-roofed and symmetrical, each rank of windows underscored with flowers. Luzern, the capital, hosts arts festivals and great shopping but little native industry. Serene and steady as the Reuss that laps at the piers of its ancient wooden bridges, it's an approachable city in an accessible region.

Central Switzerland's popularity with tourists has spawned an infrastructure of hotels, restaurants, museums, excursions, and transportation that makes it one of the easiest places in Switzerland to visit, either by car or by rail—and one of the most rewarding. As Wagner exclaimed, "I do not know of a more beautiful spot in this world!"

Exploring Luzern & Central Switzerland

Called variously the Vierwaldstättersee or the Luzernersee—it depends at which end you are standing—Lake Luzern and its environs take in not only the four cantons that abut the lake—Luzern, Uri, Schwyz, and Unterwalden—but the canton of Zug as well. Unterwalden itself is divided politically into two half-cantons: Obwalden (upper) and Nidwalden (lower). It was the canton of Schwyz that gave Switzerland its name.

The narrow, twisting lake flows from Flüelen, where the Reuss opens into the Urnersee, its southernmost leg. This is the wildest end of the lake, where much of the Tell story was set. The north end of the lake is flanked by the region's highest points, Mt. Pilatus (6,953 feet) and Mt. Rigi (5,894 feet). Luzern lies in a deep bay at the lake's northwest extreme and at the point where the rivers Reuss and Emme part ways. Zug stands apart, on the northern shore of its own Lake Zug, which is divided from Lake Luzern by the mass of Mt. Rigi.

Numbers in the text correspond to numbers in the margin and on the Central Switzerland and Luzern (Lucerne) maps.

About the Restaurants & Hotels

Because this is a heavily visited region, most restaurants are open all day, sometimes with a more limited menu between lunch and dinner. Restaurant owners also take advantage of the love for outdoor dining common to locals and tourists alike—you'll find outside seating wherever possible, from huge gravel-strewn terraces shaded by magnificent chestnut trees to tiny sidewalk tables fighting for space with pedestrians. Un-

When visiting this area, you must change modes of transit frequently to see it all; part of the region's interest is the variety of boats, trains, and other less common modes of transportation you'll take to reach the sights. On any given day, you may walk through the lovely Old Town of Luzern, ascend Mt. Pilatus by cable car and descend by cogwheel train, take a lake steamer, or drive to the Rütli Meadow.

If you have 1 or 2 days

Take in the Old Town sights of ⬚ **Luzern** ❶–⓰ ⌐, then consider a half-day boat trip on Lake Luzern. With another day, consider spending half of it ascending **Mt. Pilatus** ⓱ to see central Switzerland's best mountaintop panoramas.

5

If you have 3 or more days

In addition to all of the above, take a trip to **Einsiedeln** ㉘, with its 9th-century Benedictine monastery. A combined train and cable-car trip from ⬚ **Weggis** ㉑ will take you to the summit of Mt. Rigi, where you can see as far as the Black Forest and Mt. Säntis and even spend the night in the hotel at the top. If you're traveling by car, you can follow the course of a lake steamer from Luzern, driving to the St. Gotthard Pass along the lakefront highway (A2).

---

less you're eating in one of the upscale hotels where "smart casual" clothing is a must, the unofficial dress code of the rest of the country applies: if you're clean, you're in. Fresh jeans are preferable to a dirty suit.

Luzern provides a convenient home base for excursions all over the region; it's also easy to find a countryside overnight spot among the many villages peppered with small, shuttered guesthouses. As the terrain and climate vary radically between balmy lakefronts and icy heights, check carefully for high and low seasons before booking ahead. Resorts such as Weggis and Vitznau cut back service considerably in winter, just when Engelberg comes alive. Luzern, unlike most Swiss urban areas, has high and low seasons, and prices drop by as much as 25% in winter, approximately November through March. Rates are often calculated on a per-person basis, so it's wise to confirm rates, particularly if you're traveling as anything other than a couple.

WHAT IT COSTS In Swiss francs					
	$$$$	$$$	$$	$	¢
RESTAURANTS	over 60	40–60	25–40	15–25	under 15
HOTELS	over 350	250–350	175–250	100–175	under 100

Restaurant prices are per person for a main course at dinner. Hotel prices are for two people in a standard double room in high season, including tax and service.

Timing

Summer is the ideal season for boat excursions and great views from the tops of Mt. Pilatus and Mt. Rigi. In fall, when the crowds thin, you'll find crisp weather around the mountains and the lake.

LUZERN

▶ *57 km (36 mi) southwest of Zürich.*

Luzern city is a convenient home base for excursions all over central Switzerland. The countryside here is tame, and the vast Vierwaldstättersee offers a prime opportunity for a lake steamer cruise.

Where the River Reuss flows out of Lake Luzern, Luzern's Old Town straddles the narrowed waters. There are a couple of discount passes available for museums and sights in the city. One is a museum pass that costs 29 SF and grants free entry to all museums for one month. If you're staying in a hotel, you may also want to pick up a special visitor's card; once stamped by the hotel, it entitles you to discounts at most museums and other tourist-oriented businesses. Both passes are available at the tourist office.

Old Town & Beyond

a good walk

Start at the **Kultur- und Kongresszentrum ❶** ▶, near the train station, which gives you a beautiful view of all the places you'll see in Luzern. Walk down Pilatusstrasse to see the city's latest addition to its cultural offerings, the **Sammlung Rosengart ❷**. Cut north to Bahnhofstrasse, taking a left to the modern bridge, the Rathaus-Steg, and head north to the **Altes Rathaus ❸**, across the bridge. This late-Renaissance building is on Rathausquai, the city's main avenue. Just to the right of the Rathaus is the **Am Rhyn-Haus ❹**, now a museum dedicated to Picasso. Turn left and climb the stairs past the ornately frescoed Zunfthaus zur Pfistern, a guildhall dating from the late 15th and early 16th centuries, to the Kornmarkt, where the grinding din of the grain market was once heard. Cut left to the **Weinmarkt ❺**. Leave the square from its west end, turn right on Kramgasse, and head west across the Mühlenplatz to the **Spreuerbrücke ❻**, an unlikely exhibition space for dark paintings of the medieval plague epidemic. Crossing the bridge to the left bank, you'll find a pair of museums, the **Natur-Museum ❼** and the **Historisches Museum ❽**. From the end of the Spreuerbrücke, cut back upriver along Pfistergasse, veer left on Bahnhofstrasse, and turn right into Münzgasse to the **Franziskanerkirche ❾**. Return to Bahnhofstrasse and head to the **Jesuitenkirche ❿**. Continuing east past the Rathaus-Steg Bridge, you'll see the **Kapellbrücke ⓫**, the oldest bridge of its kind in Europe.

After crossing the Kapellbrücke, break away from Old Town through thick pedestrian and bus traffic at Schwanenplatz to Schweizerhofquai. Double back and take the first right, St. Leodegarstrasse, to the **Hofkirche ⓬**. Go back down the church steps, doubling back on St. Leodegarstrasse, turn right, and continue on to Löwenstrasse. Turn right and walk up to Löwenplatz and the **Bourbaki-Panorama ⓭**, which dominates the square with its mix of Victorian and modern architecture. Beyond the plaza, up Denkmalstrasse, is the **Löwendenkmal ⓮**, called by Mark Twain "the most mournful and moving piece of stone in the world." Immediately adjoining the small park that shades the lion lies the **Gletschergarten ⓯**. Return down Denkmalstrasse and, at Löwen-

5

Dining

Rooted in the German territory of Switzerland and the surrounding farm-lands, central Switzerland's cuisine is down-home and hearty. In the mountains there are Alpine cheese specialties (*Aelpler Magrone*—pasta, butter, cheese, and fried onions); in the orchard country around Zug, there are such cherry specialties as *Zuger Kirschtorte*, a rich white cake soaked with cherry schnapps. Pears from the local orchards are dried, then spiced and poached in sweetened red *Dole* (wine). Luzern takes pride in its *Kügeli-paschtetli*, puff-pastry nests filled with tiny veal meatballs, chicken, or sweetbreads; mushrooms; cream sauce; and occasionally raisins.

But here the real *cuisine du marché*, based on fresh market ingredi-ents, focuses on lake fish. Lake Luzern and its neighboring Zugersee (Lake Zug) produce an abundance of *Egli* (perch), *Hecht* (pike), *Forellen* (trout), and *Felchen* (whitefish); Zug produces its own exclusive *Röteln*, a red-bellied relative of the trout. Restaurants—especially along waterfronts—trade heavily in these freshwater fish, whether they come from the region or not. Ask, and you may get an honest answer: the sources vary, but the style of prepa-ration remains local. In Zug whole fish may be baked with sage, bay leaves, shallots, cloves, and plenty of white wine and butter; a Luzern tradition has them sautéed with tomatoes, mushrooms, and capers.

Hiking

Since Switzerland's septicentennial, central Switzerland has marked and de-veloped a historic foot trail, the Swiss Path, which covers 35 km (21½ mi) of lakefront lore along the southernmost branch of Lake Luzern. You'll trace the mythical steps of Wilhelm Tell and the genuine steps of medieval forerunners, climb through steep forests and isolated villages, and visit the holiday resort of Brunnen. Complete information and maps can be requested through Zen-tralschweiz Tourismus (Central Switzerland Tourism).

Shopping

Although Luzern no longer produces embroidery or lace, you can find a wide variety of Swiss handiwork of the highest quality, crafts, and watches in all price categories. High-end watch dealers Gübelin and Bucherer offer in-expensive souvenirs to lure shoppers into their luxurious showrooms; smaller shops carry Tissot, Rado, Corum, and others—but prices are controlled by the manufacturers. Watch for closeouts on older models.

---

platz, turn right on Museggstrasse, which cuts through an original city gate and runs parallel to the watchtowers and crenellated walls of Luzern, constructed around 1400. The fifth tower is **Zytturm** ⑯.

TIMING The Old Town is easy to navigate and ideal for walking. You can take in the sights on this route in about three hours; to this add another hour each to see the Natur-Museum and Historisches Museum, and time to linger at the Kapellbrücke and the Löwendenkmal. Note that both the Natur-Museum and the Historisches Museum are closed Monday.

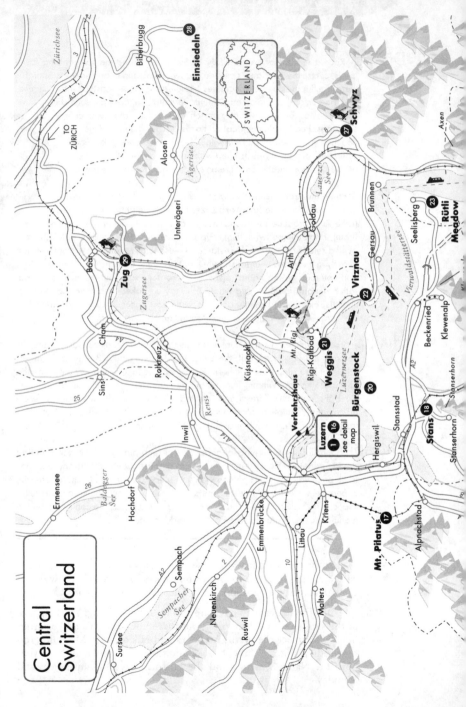

Central Switzerland

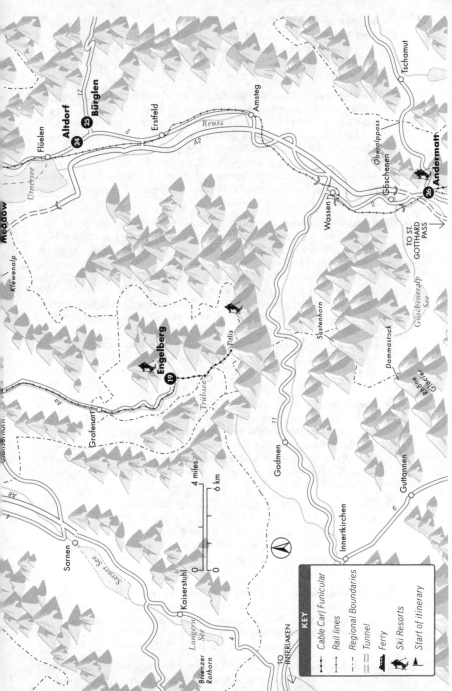

KEY

✚	Cable Carl Funicular
┿	Rail lines
– – –	Regional Boundaries
═	Tunnel
──	Ferry
⛷	Ski Resorts
▲	Start of itinerary

Tschamut

Andermatt **26**

Oberalppass

Göschenen

TO ST. GOTHARD PASS

Amsteg

Wassen

Reuss

Erstfeld

A2

Bürglen **25**

Altdorf **24**

Flüelen

Meadow

Urnersee

Klewenalp

Sustenhorn

Dammastock

Göscheneralp See

Rhône Glacier

Engelberg **19**

Titlis

Trübsee

Grafenort

Gadmen

Guttannen

Sarnen

Sarner See

Innertkirchen

Kaiserstuhl

Lungern See

Brienzer Rothorn

4 miles

6 km

TO INTERLAKEN

Sights to See

❸ Altes Rathaus (Old Town Hall). In 1606 the Luzern town council held its first meeting in this late-Renaissance-style building, built between 1602 and 1606. It still meets here today. ⊠ *Rathausquai, facing the north end of Rathaus-Steg.*

❹ Am Rhyn-Haus. Also known as the Picasso Museum, this spot contrasts a beautiful, 17th-century building with its modern holdings. The collection consists of Picasso drawings from the 1950s onward as well as some of his most important sculptures, including *Femme au chapeau.* There are also more than 100 photographs of the artist. For a choice selection of Picasso paintings, head to the affiliated collection, the Sammlung Rosengart. ⊠ *Furreng. 21* ☎ *041/4103533* 💷 *8 SF, 18 SF for combination ticket to Sammlung Rosengart* ⊙ *Apr.–Oct., daily 10–6; Nov.–Mar., daily 11–5.*

★ ⓭ Bourbaki-Panorama. The panorama was the IMAX theater of the 19th century; its sweeping, wraparound paintings brought to life scenes of epic proportions. The Bourbaki is one of only 30 remaining in the world. Painted by Édouard Castres between 1876 and 1878 (who was aided by many uncredited artists, including Ferdinand Hodler), it depicts the French Army of the East retreating into Switzerland at Verrières, a famous episode in the Franco-Prussian War. As you walk around the circle, the imagery seems to pop into three dimensions; in fact, with the help of a few strategically placed models, it does. There's a recorded commentary in English. Its conical wooden structure is surrounded by a modern glass cube filled with shops, movie theaters, and a restaurant. ⊠ *Löwenpl. 11* ☎ *041/4123030* ⊕ *www.panorama-luzern.ch* 💷 *8 SF* ⊙ *Daily 9–6.*

❾ Franziskanerkirche (Franciscan Church). Since its construction in the 13th century, this church has been persistently remodeled. It still retains its 17th-century choir stalls and carved wooden pulpit. The barefoot Franciscans once held a prominent social and cultural position in Luzern, which took a firm stance against the Reformation and today remains approximately 70% Roman Catholic. ⊠ *Franziskanerpl., just off Münzg.*

⓯ Gletschergarten (Glacier Garden). This 19th-century tourist attraction was excavated between 1872 and 1875 and has been dramatically pocked and polished by Ice Age glaciers. A private museum on the site displays impressive relief maps of Switzerland. ⊠ *Denkmalstr. 4* ☎ *041/4104340* ⊕ *www.gletschergarten.ch* 💷 *10 SF* ⊙ *Apr.–Oct., daily 9–6; Nov.–Mar., daily 10–5.*

❽ Historisches Museum (Historical Museum). Housed in the late-Gothic armory dating from 1567, this stylish institution exhibits numerous city icons, including the original Gothic fountain that stood in the Weinmarkt. Reconstructed rooms depict rural and urban life. ⊠ *Pfisterg. 24* ☎ *041/2285424* ⊕ *www.hmluzern.ch* 💷 *10 SF* ⊙ *Tues.–Sun. 10–5.*

⓬ Hofkirche. This sanctuary of St. Leodegar was first part of a monastery founded in 750. Its Gothic structure was mostly destroyed by fire in 1633 and rebuilt in late-Renaissance style, so only the towers of its predecessor were preserved. The carved pulpit and choir stalls date from the 17th century, and the 80-rank organ (1650) is one of Switzerland's finest. Outside, Italianate loggias shelter a cemetery for patrician families of old Luzern. ⊠ *St. Leodegarstr. 6* ☎ *041/4105241* ⊙ *Call for hrs.*

off the
beaten
path

VERKEHRSHAUS – Easily reached by steamer, car, or Bus 8 or 6, the Swiss Transport Museum is almost a world's fair in itself, with a complex of buildings and exhibitions both indoors and out, including live demonstrations, dioramas, and a "Swissorama" (360-degree screen) film about Switzerland. Every mode of transit is discussed, from stagecoaches and bicycles to jumbo jets and space capsules. The museum also houses the country's first IMAX theater. If you're driving, head east on Haldenstrasse at the waterfront and make a right on Lidostrasse. Signs point the way. ⊠ *Lidostr. 5* ☎ *041/ 3704444* ⊕ *www.verkehrshaus.org* 🎟 *24 SF* ⊙ *Apr.–Oct., daily 10–6; Nov.–Mar., daily 10–5.*

🔟 **Jesuitenkirche** (Jesuit Church). Constructed in 1666–77 this baroque church
Fodor's Choice with a symmetrical entrance is flanked by two onion-dome towers,
★ added in 1893. Inside, its vast interior, restored to its original splendor, is a rococo explosion of gilt, marble, and epic frescoes. Nearby is the Renaissance **Regierungsgebäude** (Government Building), seat of the cantonal government. ⊠ *Bahnhofstr., just west of Rathaus-Steg* ☎ *041/ 2100756* ⊕ *www.jesuitenkirche-luzern.ch* ⊙ *Daily 6 AM–6:30 PM.*

⑪ **Kapellbrücke** (Chapel Bridge). The oldest wooden bridge in Europe
Fodor's Choice snakes diagonally across the Reuss. When it was constructed in the early
★ 14th century, the bridge served as a rampart in case of attacks from the lake. Its shingle roof and grand stone water tower are to Luzern what the Matterhorn is to Zermatt, but considerably more vulnerable, as a 1993 fire proved. Almost 80% of this fragile monument was destroyed, including many of the 17th-century paintings inside. However, a walk through this dark, creaky landmark will take you past polychrome copies of 110 gable panels, painted by Heinrich Wägmann in the 17th century and depicting Luzern and Swiss history, stories of St. Leodegar and St. Mauritius, Luzern's patron saints, and coats of arms of local patrician families. ⊠ *Between Seebrücke and Rathaus-Steg, connecting Rathausquai and Bahnhofstr.*

▶ ★ ❶ **Kultur- und Kongresszentrum** (Culture and Convention Center). Architect Jean Nouvel's stunning glass-and-steel building manages to both stand out and fuse with its ancient milieu. The lakeside center's roof is an oversized, cantilevered, flat plane; shallow water channels thread inside, and immense glass plates mirror the surrounding views. The main draw is the concert hall, which opened in 1998. Although the lobbies are rich in blue, red, and stained wood, the hall itself is refreshingly pale, with acoustics so perfect you can hear the proverbial pin drop. Among the annual music events is the renowned International Music Festival. A museum focuses on rotating exhibits of new international artists. ⊠ *Europapl. 1* ☎ *041/2267070* ⊕ *www.kkl-luzern.ch.*

Luzern (Lucerne)

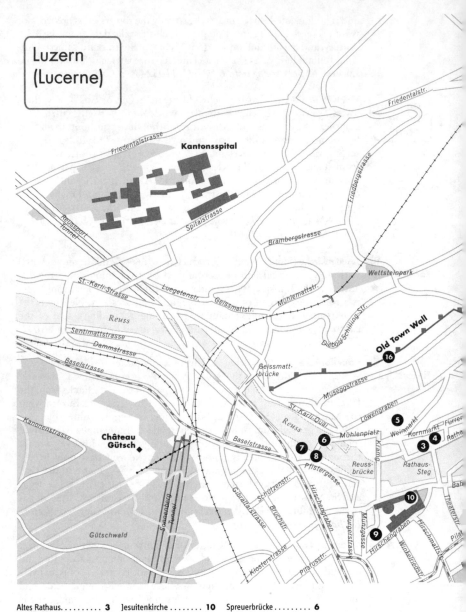

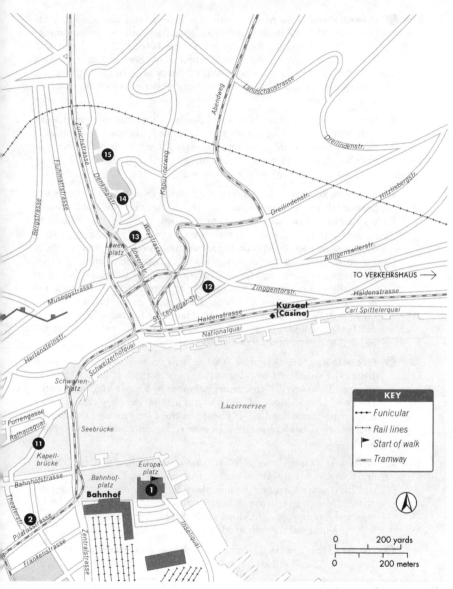

15

14

13

12

11

2

1

Zürichstrasse

Denkmalstr.

Fluhmattstrasse

Bergstrasse

Kapuzinerweg

Weystrasse

Löwen-
platz

Löwenstr.

Museggstrasse

Hertensteinstr.

St.-Leodegar-Str.

Haldenstrasse

Nationalquai

Schweizerhofquai

Schwanen-
Platz

Purrengasse

Rathausquai

Seebrücke

Kapell-
brücke

Bahnhofstrasse

Theaterstr.

Pilatusstrasse

Frankenstrasse

Zentralstrasse

Bahnhof-
platz

Bahnhof

Europa-
platz

Inseliquai

Abendweg

Landschaustrasse

Dreilindenstr.

Dreilindenstr.

Hitzlisbergstr.

Adligenswilerstr.

Zinggentorstr.

Haldenstrasse

Carl Spittelerquai

TO VERKEHRSHAUS →

**Kursaal
(Casino)**

Luzernersee

KEY

•••• *Funicular*

⊢⊢⊢ *Rail lines*

▶ *Start of walk*

⚌ *Tramway*

0		200 yards
0		200 meters

★ ⑭ **Löwendenkmal** (Lion Monument). The Swiss guards who died defending Louis XVI of France at the Tuileries in Paris in 1792 are commemorated here. Designed by Danish sculptor Berthel Thorwaldsen and carved out of a sheer sandstone face by Lucas Ahorn of Konstanz, this 19th-century wonder is a simple, stirring image of a dying lion. The Latin inscription translates, "To the bravery and fidelity of the Swiss." ⊠ *Denkmalstr.*

🖐 ⑦ **Natur-Museum** (Natural History Museum). Unusually modern display techniques bring nature lessons to life here. The museum focuses on local natural history, with panoramas of early Luzern settlers and live animals for children to meet. ⊠ *Kasernenpl. 6* ☎ *041/2285411* ⊕ *www. naturmuseum.ch* 🏷 *6 SF* ⊙ *Tues.–Sun. 10–5.*

❷ **Sammlung Rosengart** (Rosengart Collection). A father-and-daughter team amassed this amazing group of works by major late-19th- and 20th-century artists. Now housed in a former bank building, the collection, opened to the public in 2002, reveals their intensely personal approach; the Rosengarts acquired according to their own tastes instead of investment potential. Here you can see Miro's *Dancer,* Léger's *Contraste de formes,* and works by Cézanne, Monet, Matisse, Klee, and Chagall. There's an especially rich selection of Picassos; the artist painted the daughter, Angela Rosengart, five times. You can buy a combination ticket to see the Picasso drawings in the Am Rhyn-Haus. ⊠ *Pilatusstr. 10* ☎ *041/ 2201660* ⊕ *www.rosengart.ch* 🏷 *15 SF, 18 SF for combination ticket to the Am Rhyn-Haus* ⊙ *Daily 10–6.*

❻ **Spreuerbrücke** (Chaff Bridge). This narrow covered bridge dates from 1408. The weathered wood structure's interior gables hold a series of eerie, well-preserved 17th-century paintings by Kaspar Meglinger of the *Dance of Death.* Medieval in style and inspiration, they chronicle the plague that devastated all of Europe in the 14th century. ⊠ *Between Geissmattbrücke and Reussbrücke, connecting Zeughaus Reuss-Steg and Mühlenpl.*

❺ **Weinmarkt** (Wine Market). What is now the loveliest of Luzern's several fountain squares drew visitors from all across Europe in the 15th to 17th centuries with its passion plays. Its Gothic central fountain depicts St. Mauritius (patron saint of warriors), and its surrounding buildings are flamboyantly frescoed in 16th-century style. ⊠ *Square just west of Kornmarkt, north of Metzgerainli.*

⑯ **Zytturm** (Time Tower). The clock in this fifth watchtower was made in Basel in 1385 and still keeps time. ⊠ *North of and parallel to Museggstr.*

Where to Stay & Eat

★ **$$–$$$** ✕ **Galliker.** Step past the ancient facade and into a room roaring with local action. Brisk waitresses serve up the dishes *Mutti* (Mom) used to make: fresh *Kutteln* (tripe) in rich white wine sauce with cumin seeds; real *Kalbskopf* (chopped fresh veal head) served with heaps of green onions and warm vinaigrette; and authentic Luzerner Kügelipaschtetli. Occasional experiments in a modern mode—such as steak with wasabi sauce—prove that Peter Galliker's kitchen is no museum. Desserts may include raspberries with peppermint ice cream. ⊠ *Schützenstr. 1* ☎ *041/2401002* ⊟ *AE, DC, MC, V* ✆ *Closed Sun., Mon., and mid-July–mid-Aug.*

$$–$$$ ✕ **Old Swiss House.** This popular establishment pleases crowds with its beautifully contrived collection of 17th-century antiques, its leaded glass, and an old-world style now pleasantly burnished by more than 130 years of service. The standing menu includes specialties from around the country: cheese croquettes, veal and *Rösti* (fried shredded potatoes), lake fish, and chocolate mousse. ⊠ *Löwenpl. 4* ☎ *041/4106171* ⊟ *AE, DC, MC, V* ✆ *Closed Mon. and Feb.*

$–$$$ ✕ **Bodu.** A touch of Paris in the heart of Luzern. The darker, barlike entrance leads to the bright main room with a terrace overlooking the river. Advertising posters from the '20s and '30s look down on simple wooden tables and a green-and-yellow checkered floor. Sumptuous dishes are based on fresh market ingredients wherever possible: sea bass with thyme and wild rice, grilled corn-fed chicken with an olive-garlic baguette. ⊠ *Kornmarkt 5* ☎ *041/4100177* ⊟ *AE, DC, MC, V.*

$–$$ ✕ **Pfistern.** One of the architectural focal points of the Old Town waterfront, this floridly decorated guild house—the guild's origins can be traced back to 1341—provides an authentic medieval setting in which to sample reasonably priced local fare. Lake fish and *pastetli* (meat pies with puff pastry) are worthy local options. Inside, it's woody and publike, if slightly down-at-the-heels, but in summer the small first-floor balcony may provide the best seat in town. ⊠ *Kornmarkt 4* ☎ *041/4103650* ⊟ *AE, DC, MC, V.*

$–$$ ✕ **Rebstock/Hofstube.** Formerly a 16th-century tavern, this spot is now a meeting place for Luzern's art and media set. The lively brasserie hums with locals lunching by the bar, and the more formal old-style restaurant glows with wood and brass under a low-beamed parquetry ceiling. Fresh market ingredients are combined for modern, international fare, including rabbit and ostrich, as well as East Asian and vegetarian specialties. ⊠ *St. Leodegarpl. 3* ☎ *041/4103581* ⊟ *AE, DC, MC, V.*

★ $$$$ ✕⌸ **Palace Hotel.** This waterfront hotel drinks in the broadest possible lake views. Built in 1906, it has been brilliantly refurbished so that its classical look has a touch of postmodernism. Rooms are large enough for a game of badminton, and picture windows afford sweeping views of Mt. Pilatus. The hotel's elegance also seeps into its restaurant, Jasper ($$–$$$$). The contemporary cuisine—lamb with wild mushrooms and *capuns* (sausages and beet leaves wrapped in wheat flour dough)—is faultlessly prepared and formally presented. The bar has a clubby look—leather chairs, brass fixtures, and a long oak bar. ⊠ *Haldenstr. 10, CH-6002* ☎ *041/4161616* ⊟ *041/4161000* ⊕ *www.palace-luzern.com* ⇆ *178 rooms, 45 suites* ⚹ *2 restaurants, in-room data ports, in-room safes, health club, massage, bar, laundry service, meeting rooms, parking (fee); no a/c* ⊟ *AE, DC, MC, V.*

★ $$$–$$$$ ✕⌸ **Des Balances.** Built in the 19th century on the site of two ancient guildhalls, this waterfront property is full of style. State-of-the-art tile baths, up-to-date pastel decor, and one of the best sites in the heart of the Old Town make this the slickest in its price class. Rotes Gatter

($$–$$$$), the hotel's chic restaurant, has a combination as desirable as it is rare: soigné decor, shimmering river views, and a sophisticated menu with fish dishes such as perch with a mustard crust and champagne mousse, or the house specialty, meat and fish fondue. The restaurant has a more casual, less expensive bistro area as well. ⊠ *Weinmarkt, CH-6000* 🕾 *041/4182828* 🖷 *041/4182838* ⊕ *www.balances.ch* ⤶ *50 rooms, 7 suites* ⚹ *Restaurant, in-room safes, minibars, meeting rooms; no a/c* ⊟ *AE, DC, MC, V* ◯| *BP.*

★ **$$$–$$$$** ✕⊞ **Wilden Mann.** The city's best-known hotel creates a gracious and authentic experience of old Luzern, with stone, beams, brass, and burnished wood everywhere. (Even the street is atmospheric—across the way is a 16th-century pharmacy.) The hotel's reputation extends to its restaurants; the Burgerstube ($–$$$$) is cozy with its dark beams and family crests, whereas vaulting and candlelight make the Liedertafel ($–$$$$) more formal. Both menus strike a fine balance between old-style local cooking and savvy French cuisine, with dishes such as lamb fillet with tomatoes, beans, and bacon. ⊠ *Bahnhofstr. 30, CH-6003* 🕾 *041/2101666* 🖷 *041/2101629* ⊕ *www.wilden-mann.ch* ⤶ *35 rooms, 8 suites* ⚹ *2 restaurants, in-room data ports, minibars, library; no a/c* ⊟ *AE, DC, MC, V* ◯| *BP.*

$$$$ ⊞ **National Hotel.** This monumental landmark, founded in 1870, was once home base to Cesar Ritz, the man who invented the world's first modern luxury hotel. The inner sanctums of this lodging trumpet a florid splendor, down to the last cupola, crown molding, and Corinthian column. The hotel's mansarded facade stretches the length of two city blocks, dominating the lakeside promenade. The French provincial rooms have brass beds; the domed bar is decked with mahogany and aglitter with crystal; and the marble-columned breakfast hall may be the most splendid in Switzerland. ⊠ *Haldenstr. 4, CH-6003* 🕾 *041/4190909* 🖷 *041/4190910* ⊕ *www.national-luzern.ch* ⤶ *78 rooms, 10 suites* ⚹ *4 restaurants, café, in-room data ports, in-room safes, minibars, pool, health club, massage, piano bar, babysitting, parking (fee); no a/c* ⊟ *AE, DC, MC, V.*

$$$$ ⊞ **Schweizerhof.** Built in the 1840s and expanded in the 1860s, this imposing structure has hosted Napoléon III, Leo Tolstoy, and Mark Twain—and Richard Wagner lived here while his lakefront home at Tribschen was being completed. The rooms all have sweeping views of the lake and mountains. Their modern style has a modern twist: gilt mirrors, richly colored carpets, and marble-and-tile bathrooms cover the luxury bases, and Internet access and voice mail keep you connected. ⊠ *Schweizerhofquai 3, CH-6002* 🕾 *041/4100410* 🖷 *041/4102971* ⊕ *www. schweizerhof-luzern.ch* ⤶ *101 rooms, 6 suites* ⚹ *2 restaurants, café, in-room data ports, in-room safes, minibars, gym, bar, meeting rooms, free parking; no a/c* ⊟ *AE, DC, MC, V.*

$$$–$$$$ ⊞ **The Hotel.** Architect Jean Nouvel, who also designed Luzern's Kultur- und Kongresszentrum, focuses on ultrahip design; parquet floors are this lodging's only remaining old-world touch. Metal blocks act as cupboards, and mirrors, puffy chairs, and dark walls add to the look. But the highlight of each room is the enlarged movie still that covers the ceiling. Fellini, Wenders, and von Trier are represented, among others, and yes, the photograph is positioned so that you see it while lying on your bed. An Asian/French fusion restaurant attracts locals as well as hotel guests. ☒ *Sempacherstr. 14, CH-6000* ☎ *041/2268686* 🖷 *041/2268690* ⊕ *www.the-hotel.ch* 🛏 *10 rooms, 15 suites* ♨ *Restaurant, in-room data ports, minibars, bar* ☰ *AE, DC, MC, V.*

\$\$\$–\$\$\$\$ 🏨 **Montana.** This 1910 palace glows with beeswaxed beauty, its luxurious original woodwork, parquet, and terrazzo all in superb condition. The public rooms flank the ground floor's south side and on a clear day offer a magnificent view of the lake and the mountains. The guest rooms are decorated in art deco style, with bold patterns and funky furniture. Those in back overlook a hillside, while the front doubles (slightly costlier) have balconies overlooking the city and lake. The building is perched on a slope above town, accessible by funicular from the lakeshore Haldenstrasse or by car. ☒ *Adligenswilerstr. 22, CH-6002* ☎ *041/4190000* 🖷 *041/4190001* ⊕ *www.hotel-montana.ch* 🛏 *55 rooms, 10 suites* ♨ *Restaurant, in-room safes, minibars, bar, free parking; no a/c* ☰ *AE, DC, MC, V* ⃝ *BP.*

\$\$\$ 🏨 **Hofgarten.** This gracious 12th-century house has been artfully modernized with an eclectic mix of colors and themes. One room contains a 5-foot-tall antique stove (still operable), and another resembles the interior of a clipper ship. The Hofgarten has one of Luzern's best vegetarian restaurants, with dishes that could satisfy even a meat lover. ☒ *Stadthofdstr. 14, CH-6006* ☎ *041/4108888* 🖷 *041/4108333* ⊕ *www. hofgarten.ch* 🛏 *17 rooms, 1 suite* ♨ *Restaurant, parking (fee); no a/c* ☰ *AE, DC, MC, V* ⃝ *BP.*

\$\$\$ 🏨 **Krone.** Spotless and modern, this hotel softens its edges with pastel linens and walls; look in the recessed niche of one of the interior walls for a stone shrine retained from the original structure. The rooms facing the Weinmarkt have high ceilings and tall windows that let in lots of light. Rooms to the back have no direct sun but are still bright and a little larger. The restaurant has a no-alcohol policy. ☒ *Weinmarkt 12, CH-6004* ☎ *041/4194400* 🖷 *041/4194490* ⊕ *www.krone-luzern. ch* 🛏 *25 rooms* ♨ *Restaurant, café, minibars; no a/c* ☰ *AE, DC, MC, V* ⃝ *BP.*

\$\$ 🏨 **Des Alpes.** This historic hotel, with a terrific riverfront location in the bustling heart of the Old Town, has an interior resembling a laminate-and-vinyl chain motel. The rooms, however, are generously proportioned and tidy; front doubles, five with balconies, overlook the water and promenade. Cheaper back rooms face the Old Town; those on higher floors have rooftop views and plenty of light. ☒ *Furrergasse 3, CH-6003* ☎ *041/4105825* 🖷 *041/4107451* ⊕ *www.desalpes-luzern.ch* 🛏 *45 rooms* ♨ *Restaurant, café; no a/c* ☰ *AE, DC, MC, V* ⃝ *BP.*

\$–\$\$ 🏨 **Löwengraben.** For something completely different, spend a night in jail—which this hotel was until several years ago. Bright paint, comfortably simple beds, modular bathroom facilities, and the odd antique furnishing take the blues out of the jailhouse and replace it with funky charm. Although the rooms are small, the fun atmosphere that radiates from the bars and restaurants downstairs adds to the draw. ☒ *Löwengraben 18, CH-6004* ☎ *041/4171212* 🖷 *041/4171211* ⊕ *www.loewengraben. ch* 🛏 *51 rooms, 4 suites* ♨ *2 restaurants, 2 bars, nightclub, no-smoking rooms; no a/c, no room TVs* ☰ *AE, MC, V* ⃝ *BP.*

$–$$ ▦ **Schlüssel.** This spare, no-nonsense lodging on the Franziskanerplatz attracts young bargain hunters. It's a pleasant combination of tidy modern touches (quarry tile, white paint) and antiquity: you can have breakfast or a simple hot meal in a low, cross-vaulted "crypt" and admire the fine old beams in the lobby. Several of the rooms overlook the square's Franciscan church (be prepared for morning church bells). ⊠ *Franziskanerpl. 12, CH-6003* ☎ *041/2101061* 🖨 *041/2101021* ⬏ *10 rooms* ♿ *Restaurant; no a/c* ⊟ *AE, MC, V.*

★ ¢–$ ▦ **Tourist.** Despite its friendly, collegiate atmosphere, this cheery dorm-like spot is anything but a backpackers' flophouse. It has a terrific setting on the Reuss around the corner from the Old Town. Its spare, modern architecture is brightened with fresh, trendy colors and framed prints, and rooms that don't have a river view face the quiet backyard instead. The staff is young and helpful, and the coed four-bed dorms (sex-segregated in high season) draw sociable travelers with their rock-bottom prices. There are also seven private-bath doubles. Shared baths are well maintained. ⊠ *St. Karli Quai 12, CH-6004* ☎ *041/4102474* 🖨 *041/4108414* ⊕ *www.touristhotel.ch* ⬏ *11 rooms, 2 suites* ♿ *Bar, laundry facilities, Internet; no a/c, no room phones, no smoking* ⊟ *AE, DC, MC, V.*

Nightlife & the Arts

For information on goings-on around town, go to the tourist office for a copy of the German/English *Luzern City Guide*, published quarterly by the city. Get it stamped by your hotel for discounts on museums, public transit, and special events.

Nightlife

BARS & LOUNGES In the Hotel Montana, **Louis Bar** (⊠ Adligenwilerstr. 22 ☎ 041/4190000) offers live jazz in the style of Louis Armstrong. While you're there, sip one of the 80 Scotch whiskies behind the bar. The beautiful **Meridiani** (⊠ Klosterstr. 12 ☎ 041/2404344) bar pours everything from coffee to cognac. Students and young professionals mix and mingle at **Oops** (⊠ Zentralstr. 10 ☎ 041/2102255). If you need a jolt, choose from 60 different kinds of coffee.

Opus (⊠ Bahnhofstr. 16 ☎ 041/2264141) specializes in fine wines, many served by the glass. **P1** (⊠ Pilatusstr. 1 ☎ 041/2201315) is a drinks-and-dancing penthouse lounge with a fabulous view.

CASINO The most sophisticated nightlife in Luzern is found in the **Grand Casino Luzern** (⊠ Haldenstr. 6 ☎ 041/4185656 ⊕ www.grandcasinoluzern. ch), an early-20th-century building on the lake's northern shore near the grand hotels. You can play *boule* (a type of roulette) in the Gambling Room; dance in The Club; watch the cabaret in the Casineum; or have a meal in Olivio, a Mediterranean restaurant with views of the mountains and the lake.

The Arts

FILM Movie theaters, concentrated on the south bank along Pilatusstrasse and Bahnhofstrasse, usually screen films in their original language. You can also catch a show in the Bourbaki-Panorama development.

WAS WILHELM TELL NORWEGIAN?

ACCORDING TO an 18th-century story by Gilg Tschudi, Wilhelm Tell performed his heroic deeds in 1307. But that puts him several centuries behind two 11th-century Norwegians named Eindridi and Hemingr. To force Eindridi to accept Christianity, King Olaf is said to have ordered him to shoot a "writing plate" from his son's head. Eindridi's wife persuaded the king to drop the matter. Hemingr was not so lucky. After the hunter won several athletic challenges, an irate King Harald ordered him to shoot not a mere apple, but a hazelnut from his son's head. Hemingr made the shot and, like Tell, took his revenge on the ruler.

A century later, a tippler named Toko bragged about his skill with a bow. The Dane was forced by a king to shoot an apple off his son's head. As Tell would later do, Toko kept an arrow destined for the king should he fail. Toko was then forced to ski down a cliff into the North Sea, a feat he miraculously survived.

A 17th-century English ballad tells of Adam Bell, Clim of the Clough, and William of Cloudesley—outlaws who live off the king's deer, Robin Hood style. In the ballad, William of Cloudesley is the man with the bow:

"An apple upon his [son's] head he set,

And then his bowe he bent;

Syxe score paces they were outmet,

And therefore Cloudesley went . . .

Toko's story was in a book that includes the tale of Amleth, a Danish prince, which Shakespeare used for his play Hamlet. If Shakespeare had chosen Toko's story, who knows what form Tell's legend might have taken?

FOLKLORE The *Night Boat* (☎ 041/3194978) sails from the Landungsbrücke—a dock right on the Bahnhofplatz-Europlatz—every evening from May through September. This pleasant lake cruise has meals, drinks, and a folklore show. Performances at the **Stadtkeller** (✉ Sternenpl. 3 ☎ 041/4104733) come with yodelers, dirndled dancers, and more.

MUSIC Luzern, the cultural hub of central Switzerland, hosts the annual **Lucerne Festival** (✉ Hirschmattstr. 13, CH-6002 ☎ 041/2264480) from mid-August to mid-September in the Kultur- und Kongresszentrum. Outstanding performers come from all over the world; recent guests have included mezzo-soprano Cecilia Bartoli and the Berlin Philharmonic Orchestra with conductor Simon Rattle. Performing at the Kultur- und Kongresszentrum, the **Luzerner Symphonieorchester** (✉ Europapl. ☎ 041/2103060), the local orchestra in residence, has a season that runs from October through June.

THEATER The **Luzerner Theater** (✉ Theaterstr. 2 ☎ 041/2106618), directly on the waterfront on the Bahnhof side of town, is home to Luzern's principal theater group, which stages plays in German and operas in their original language.

Sports & the Outdoors

Bicycling

The standard Swiss practice of renting bicycles from the **train station** (✉ Bahnhofpl. ☎ 051/2273261) comes in handy here, as the lake-level terrain offers smooth riding.

Boating

Pedal-, motor-, and sailboats are available in Luzern through **Marina Charter** (✉ Alpenquai 13 ☎ 041/3607944). **SNG Luzern** (✉ Alpenquai 11 ☎ 041/3680808), open weekdays only, offers fair-weather boat rentals from April to October and year-round hour-long boat tours for 25 SF. **Werft Herzog AG** (✉ Nationalquai ☎ 041/4104333) specializes in motorboats for up to 10 passengers.

Golf

Just above Luzern, on the Dietschiberg, the **Lucerne Golf Club** (☎ 041/4209787) has an 18-hole course open to visitors.

Swimming

At the **Lido** (✉ Lidostr. ☎ 041/3703806), past the casino and near the Verkehrshaus, you can swim in Lake Luzern from May to September.

Water Sports

Contact **Dobler und Ingold** (✉ Alpenquai 13 ☎ 041/3608244) to rent windsurfing equipment. **Waterfun** (✉ Alpenquai/Tribschen dock ☎ 079/4177676) offers wakeboarding and waterskiing.

Shopping

The best shopping in the region is concentrated in Luzern, which, although it no longer produces embroidery or lace, still offers a wide variety of Swiss handicrafts as well as the luxury goods appropriate to its high profile. In summer most shops don't close in the evening until 9 and open on Sunday morning after 11. On Thursday night year-round, shops stay open until 9.

Department Stores

The main department store in town is **Globus** (✉ Pilatusstr. 4 ☎ 041/2270707); it's a good place to hunt for souvenirs. **Migros** (✉ Hertensteinstr. 9 ☎ 041/4170740) specializes in groceries and inexpensive items.

Embroidery

The main producer of Swiss embroidery is **Sturzenegger** (✉ Schwanenpl. 7 ☎ 041/4101958) of St. Gallen, which sells its own machine-made lace and embroidered goods as well as Hanro and Calida underwear. The store also stocks a conservative line of women's dresses and blouses.

Handicrafts & Gifts

Aux Arts du Feu (✉ Schweizerhofquai 2 ☎ 041/4101401) offers high-end china and crystal. **Bookbinders Design** (✉ Hertensteinstr. 3 ☎ 041/4109506), an upscale stationer, stocks precision writing instruments and brightly colored, handmade, recycled-paper products. **Schmid-Linder** (✉ Denkmalstr. 9 ☎ 041/4104346) carries an extensive line of Swiss embroidery and linen as well as cuckoo clocks, cowbells, and a large stock of wood carvings from Brienz, in the Berner Oberland.

Markets

From May to October, a **Flohmärt**, or flea market, takes place every Saturday from 8 to 4 at Untere Burgerstrasse, not far from the Franziskanerkirche. For locally made crafts, there's a **Handwerksmarkt** on the Weinmarkt. It takes place on the first Saturday of every month from April through December.

Watches

Competition is fierce, and the two enormous patriarchs of the watch business advertise heavily and offer inexpensive souvenirs to lure shoppers into their luxurious showrooms. **Bucherer** (⊠ Schwanenpl. 5 ☎ 041/ 3697700) represents Piaget and Rolex. **Gübelin** (⊠ Schweizerhofquai 1 ☎ 041/4105142) is the exclusive source for Audemars Piguet, Patek Philippe, and its own house brand.

Women's Clothing

The czarina of women's fashion in Luzern is Christina De Boer, who runs a group of designer boutiques. **Christina De Boer** (⊠ Werchlaubeg. 14 ☎ 041/4106239) is an exclusive boutique with cashmere fashions and high-end labels such as Jil Sander and Rena Lange. **Rive Gauche** (⊠ Pilatusstr. 14 ☎ 041/2108916) has a wide variety of mid-range labels such as Gabriele Seba.

LUZERN ENVIRONS

Since Luzern doesn't have the sprawling suburbs associated with most cities, bucolic landscapes are just a short day trip away. Craggy mountaintops, lush hills dotted with grazing cows, and peaceful lakeside villages are easily reached by boat, train, or car.

Mt. Pilatus

⑰ *10 km (6 mi) southwest of Luzern.*

This 6,953-foot mountain was named either from the Latin *pileatus* (wearing a cap), to refer to its frequent cloud covering, or, more colorfully, to the ghost of Pontius Pilate, which supposedly haunts the summit. (His body, it was said, was brought here by the devil.) For centuries it was forbidden to climb the mountain and enrage the ghost, who was said to unleash deadly storms. Unlike Queen Victoria, who rode to the summit by mule in 1868, you can travel there and back by cable car for a hefty 79 SF from Luzern.

Take a bus from the train station in Luzern to the suburb of Kriens, where you catch a tiny, four-seat cable car that flies silently up to Fräkmüntegg (4,600 feet); then change to the 40-seat cable car that sails through open air up the rock cliff to the summit station (5,560 feet). From here a 10-minute walk takes you to the **Esel**, at the center of Pilatus's multiple peaks, where views unfold over the Alps and the sprawling, crooked Lake Luzern.

A pleasant variation for the return trip to Luzern from Mt. Pilatus involves riding a steep cogwheel train, often down gradients inclined nearly 48%, through four tunnels that pierce sheer rock, to Alpnachstad. From there take the train or the ferry, which leaves from the jetty across from the train station, back to Luzern. To go on to Engelberg, get off the Luzern-bound train at Hergiswil, where you can cross the track and climb aboard the small, private Stans-Engelberg train that heads up the Engelbergertal (Engelberg Valley).

Stans

⑱ *10 km (6 mi) southeast of Mt. Pilatus, 10 km (6 mi) south of Luzern.*

In the heart of lush valley terrain and mossy meadows, Stans is an old village whose appealing Old Town center is dotted with the deep-roof houses typical of central Switzerland. This was the home of the beloved Heinrich Pestalozzi, the father of modern education. When the French army invaded the village in 1798, slaughtering nearly 2,000 citizens, it was Pestalozzi who gathered the orphaned children into a school, where he applied his progressive theories in the budding science of psychology to the practice of education. Instead of rote memorization and harsh discipline, Pestalozzi's teaching methods emphasized concrete examples (using plant specimens to teach botany, for example) and moral as well as intellectual development—quite a liberal education. He also championed the idea of fostering a child's individuality.

The bell tower of the **Pfarrkirche St. Peter und St. Paul** (Church of Sts. Peter and Paul) is in Italian Romanesque style with increasing numbers of arched windows as it rises. The incongruous steeple was added in the 16th century. ⊠ *Knirig. 1.*

On the town square stands a 19th-century **monument to Arnold von Winkelried,** a native of Stans who martyred himself to lead the Swiss Confederates to victory over the Austrians at the battle of Sempach in 1386. The Austrians, armed with long spears, formed a Roman square so that the Swiss, wielding axes and halberds, couldn't get in close enough to do any damage. Shouting, "Forward, confederates, I will open a path!" von Winkelried threw himself on the spears, clasping as many of them as he could to his breast—creating an opening for his comrades. ⊠ *Knirig., facing the Pfarrkirche St. Peter und St. Paul.*

en route   A two-part journey on a nostalgic 1893 funicular and an ultramodern cable car takes you to the **Stanserhorn** (6,200 feet), from whose peak you can see the Titlis, the highest point in central Switzerland. You can also see the Jungfrau. ⊠ *Stans* ☎ *041/6188040* 💳 *38 SF round-trip* ☉ *Apr.–Nov., daily 8:30–4:30.*

Engelberg

⑲ *12 km (8 mi) south of Stans, 27 km (17 mi) south of Luzern.*

At the top of the village of Obermatt, Engelberg (3,280 feet) is a popular resort for skiers from nearby Zürich, but its slopes are limited in comparison with those of St. Moritz, Wengen, and Zermatt. From Luzern, the resort is easily reached on an hourly train. Engelberg clusters at the foot of its Benedictine **Kloster** (monastery), founded in 1120; inside there's one of the largest organs in the country. Until the French invaded in 1798, massacring thousands, this monastery ruled the valley. Of the guided tours, those on Thursday and Saturday at 10 are in English. ☎ 041/6396161 ☒ 6 SF ☉ *Guided tours mid-Jan.–Apr. and July–mid-Oct., Wed.–Sat. 10 and 4; mid-Oct.–mid-Jan., May, and June, Wed.and Thurs. at 10, Fri., Sat. at 4.*

off the
beaten
path

MOUNT TITLIS – This is perhaps the most impressive of the many rocky peaks that surround the Obermatt's long, wide bowl. Thanks to a sophisticated transportation system that benefits skiers, hikers, climbers, and sightseers alike, it's possible to ride a small cable car up to the tiny mountain lake (and famous ski area) called Trübsee (5,904 feet). From there change and ascend to Stand to catch the Rotair cable car, which rotates to give 360-degree panoramas on its way up to the summit station on the Titlis. There's an ice grotto (serving drinks from a solid-ice bar) and a restaurant: whose views take in the Jura Mountains, the Graubünden and Bernese Alps, and what seems from this perspective like the puny Pilatus. ☒ *Engleberg* ☎ *041/6395060* ☒ *52 SF round-trip.*

Skiing

At the base of the 9,906-foot-high Titlis, **Engelberg** has two funicular railways, seven cable cars, 13 lifts, 45 km (28 mi) of downhill runs, 34 km (21 mi) of cross-country trails, 3½ km (2 mi) of toboggan runs, and ice-skating. About half the runs are intermediate level, and there are plenty of easy slopes as well; advanced skiers will have relatively slim pickings. A **ski school** (☎ 041/6395454) and **snowboard school** (☎ 041/6395455) are in the **Tourist Center** (☎ 041/6397777).

Where to Stay & Eat

★ $–$$ ✕**Bierlialp.** The delicious pizzas that come from this trattoria's stone oven are 18-inch extravaganzas—and that's a single serving. The modern decor is softened by warm candlelight and an even warmer welcome. For a more elaborate entrée, try the grilled pangasius (a kind of catfish) fillet with prosecco risotto or the truffle ravioli. ☒ *Dorfstr. 21* ☎ *041/6371717* ☰ *AE, MC, V.*

★ $–$$ ✕**Engelberg.** Rosmarie and Robert Infanger serve haute cuisine at prices that are refreshingly sane; favorites at this chalet include osso bucco with porcini mushroom risotto and curried pike perch. Linen tablecloths and candlelight mellow the traditional post-and-beam interior. ☒ *Dorfstr. 14* ☎ *041/6397979* ⊕ *www.hotel-engelberg.ch* ☰ *AE, MC, V.*

$$ ✕▥ **Spannort.** Regular renovations keep this 1970s version of a traditional hotel looking sharp. Pale wood is everywhere, from the beam ceilings to the heavy chalet-style furniture. An emphasis on light and innovative cuisine makes the restaurant a favorite of guests and locals alike; look for fresh choices such as butter-lettuce salad with shrimp and saffron vinaigrette. ☒ *Dorfstr. 26, CH-6390* ☎ *041/6372626* 🖨 *041/6374477* ⊕ *www.spannort.ch* ⇄ *16 rooms, 4 suites* ♨ *Restau-*

rant, in-room data ports, minibars, sauna, bar; no a/c ⊟ *AE, DC, MC, V* ⦿ *BP.*

★ $ ✕▣ **Alpenclub.** This is the real McCoy: an old-fashioned chalet, built in 1856, with every square inch pine paneled and dark timbered. It's got all the requisites, such as down-quilted beds, a glowing fondue Stübli, and a sunny terrace looking out on snowy peaks. It's lively, casual, and, above all, cheap. It draws mobs of young skiers to its disco bar and pizzeria, and families to its firelit restaurant (all serve à la carte only). Though it stands slightly beyond the urbanized center, it's not for quiet retreats, at least in ski season. ⊠ *Dorfstr. 5, CH-6390* ☎ *041/6371243* 🖷 *041/ 6370337* ⊕ *www.alpenclub.ch* ⇄ *9 rooms* ⚖ *Restaurant, pizzeria, Stübli, bar; no a/c* ⊟ *AE, DC, MC, V* ⊘ *Closed May and June.*

$$$–$$$$ ▣ **Ramada-Treff.** In a resort haunted by fading grand hotels from a bygone boom, this central high-rise, a little bit of Dallas in the Alps, strikes a jarring note. Built in 1983 on the ashes of its predecessor, it has fresh, solid rooms with warm wood accents, balconies with views, and generous facilities. If you're looking for quiet, reserve a room at the back of the hotel, away from the street. ⊠ *Dorfstr. 33, CH-6390* ☎ *041/ 6395858* 🖷 *041/6395859* ⊕ *www.ramada-treff.ch* ⇄ *97 rooms, 31 suites* ⚖ *2 restaurants, café, minibars, pool, gym, massage, sauna, bar, meeting rooms, parking (fee); no a/c* ⊟ *AE, DC, MC, V* ⦿ *BP.*

★ $$–$$$$ ▣ **Edelweiss.** Walk a few minutes uphill from the center of town to find this 1903 hotel. It's perfect if you're looking for organized activities: skiing, snowman building, and sleigh rides in winter; mountain biking, river rafting, and wellness courses in summer. Rooms are outfitted with modern, Scandinavian-style wood furniture, and some bathrooms have beautiful old fixtures. A four-course dinner is served nightly, although special needs (vegetarian, low sodium) can be accommodated. Children have a supervised playroom. ⊠ *Terracestr., CH-6390* ☎ *041/6397878* 🖷 *041/6397888* ⊕ *www.edelweissengelberg. com* ⇄ *50 rooms* ⚖ *Restaurant, sauna, bar, Internet, free parking; no a/c* ⊟ *AE, DC, MC, V* ⦿ *BP.*

$–$$$ ▣ **Schweizerhof.** Though the exterior suggests a once–grande dame, this lovely old fin de siècle structure has been attentively remodeled inside to combine a fresh, light, modern knotty-pine look with plush Edwardian comforts. Guest rooms are modern and airy. Bay-window corner doubles are worth asking for. Four family suites with separate bed- and living rooms make this a perfect option for families and small groups. ⊠ *Dorfstr. 42, CH-6390* ☎ *041/6371105* 🖷 *041/6374147* ⊕ *www.schweizerhof-engelberg.ch* ⇄ *30 rooms, 10 suites* ⚖ *Restaurant, some in-room data ports, in-room safes, gym, sauna, steam room; no a/c* ⊟ *AE, DC, MC, V* ⦿ *BP.*

$–$$ ▣ **Europe.** Built in 1908, this Jugendstil beauty offers modern amenities in a bright, elegant setting. Some of the rooms are simple to the point of being bland, but others have small chandeliers and beautifully detailed, mirrored wardrobes. Step onto the wrought-iron balconies and gaze up at the Titlis or down at the neighboring park; the rooms over the front entrance have especially incredible views. The hotel also houses a hotel management school, so you might find yourself being practiced on every now and then. ⊠ *Dorfstr. 40, CH-6390* ☎ *041/6397575*

🏛 *041/6397576* ⊕ *www.hoteleurope.ch* 🛏 *50 rooms, 13 suites* 🛁 *Restaurant, minibars, sauna, bar, Internet; no a/c* 🟰 *AE, DC, MC, V* 🍴 *BP.*

Sports & the Outdoors

MOUNTAIN BIKING — Mountain biking is very popular here; there's a well-traveled path from the Jochpass to the Trübsee. Free bike maps are available at the tourist office. You can rent bikes from **Bike 'n' Roll** (✉ Dorfstr. 31 🕾 041/6380255).

TENNIS — The **Sporting Park Engelberg** (✉ Engelbergstr. 11 🕾 041/6373494) has two indoor courts and six outdoor courts; the shop also rents equipment.

TO ST. GOTTHARD & EINSIEDELN

From Luzern you can take a lake steamer all the way down to the Urnersee, the southern leg of Lake Luzern, here called Vierwaldstättersee, or you can drive the same route along the northern lakefront highway to Brunnen, then head north for 30 km (19 mi) to the historic pilgrimage town of Einsiedeln. If you want to climb to Rigi Kulm, the summit of Mt. Rigi, the trip will involve switching to train or cable car. To visit the St. Gotthard Pass you'll need a car. Drive Route 2 all the way up the Reuss Valley to the pass and you'll be rewarded with a fabulous view of the Leventina Valley on the other side. Hannibal's elephants never had it so easy.

If you choose to take a lake cruise, depart at any convenient time (schedules are available at the ticket and tourist offices) from the main docks by the train station; the boat will be marked for Flüelen. First-class seats are on top; each level has a restaurant-café. The exterior seats are only slightly sheltered; if you want to sit inside, you may feel obligated to order a drink. Take advantage of the boat's many stops—you can get on and off at will.

Bürgenstock

❷⓿ *20 km (13 mi) southeast of Luzern.*

Most Flüelen-bound boats go to the base of the Bürgenstock, where visitors can take a funicular to the isolated resort at the top of a ridge. Though the plateau isn't terribly high—only 1,500 feet—it rises dramatically above the water and offers striking views over the region; that's why a small colony of luxury hotels has mushroomed here. Bürgenstock also can be approached by car, up a narrow, steep road, from Stansstad, on the road between Luzern and Stans.

Where to Stay

$$$–$$$$
Fodor'sChoice
★ — 🏨 **Bürgenstock Hotels & Resort.** This trio of luxury hotels—dating from 1873, 1904, and 1991—has everything from a 14th-century late-Gothic chapel to its own helicopter landing pad. Rooms in all three are spacious and understated. The friendly, accommodating staff has seen more than its share of VIPs, from Shirley MacLaine to Sergei Rachmaninoff. The full-service health club, with such spa services as aromatherapy and

massage, is a great place to get pampered. Bring along your hiking boots, as the hotel has a restaurant perched on top of the nearby Hammetschwand Peak. ✉ *Bürgenstock, CH-6363* ☎ *41/6129010* 🖶 *41/6129011* ⊕ *www.buergenstock-hotels.ch* ᗤ *183 rooms, 67 suites ⅚ 5 restaurants, in-room data ports, in-room safes, minibars, 9-hole golf course, tennis courts, 2 pools (1 indoor), lake, fitness classes, gym, hair salon, massage, bicycles, 2 bars, shop, laundry service, Internet, business services, convention center, meeting rooms, helipad; no a/c* ▤ *AE, DC, MC, V* 🍴 *BP.*

Weggis

★ ㉑ *25 km (15 mi) northeast and across the lake from Bürgenstock, 20 km (12 mi) northeast of Luzern.*

With a pretty waterfront park and promenade, Weggis is a summer resort town known for its mild, almost subtropical climate. It's far from the highway and accessible only by the secondary road, so you get a pleasant sense of isolation. The famed **Mt. Rigi** (1,798 m [5,900 feet]) is just a cable-car ride away from Weggis: follow signs for the Rigibahn, a station high above the resort (a 15-minute walk). From here you can ride a large cable car to **Rigi-Kaltbad**, a small resort on a spectacular plateau; walk across to the electric rack-and-pinion railway station and ride the steep tracks of the Vitznau–Rigi line to the summit of the mountain. Take an elevator to the **Rigi-Kulm** hotel to enjoy the views indoors or walk to the crest (45 minutes) to see as far as the Black Forest in one direction and Mt. Säntis in the other. Or consider climbing to the top, staying in the hotel, and getting up early to see the sun rise over the Alps—a view that astounded both Victor Hugo and Mark Twain. With Lake Luzern on one side and Lake Zug on the other, Mt. Rigi can seem like an island.

You have the option of returning to Luzern from Weggis by taking a different railway down, from Rigi to Arth-Goldau; the two lines were built by competing companies in the 1870s in a race to reach the top and capture the lion's share of the tourist business. The line rising out of the lakefront resort of Vitznau won, but the Arth-Goldau line gets plenty of business, as its base terminal lies on the mainstream St. Gotthard route. The round-trip fare from Vitznau or Arth-Goldau to Rigi-Kulm is 58 SF.

Skiing

Mt. Rigi, at 5,900 feet, has two funicular railways, three cable cars, seven lifts, 30 km (19 mi) of downhill runs, 14 km (9 mi) of cross-country trails, 14 km (9 mi) of ski-hiking trails, and curling.

Where to Stay & Eat

$$–$$$ ✕ **Renggli's.** This restaurant is ideally located on the waterfront, with its own private dock and a terrace overlooking the lake. The eclectic cuisine ranges from refined vegetarian dishes to more exotic fare, such as mango curry chicken and jumbo shrimp. Standards are jazzed up, too: pike perch with creole rice, for instance. ✉ *Seestr. 21* ☎ *041/3900170* ▤ *AE, DC, MC, V* ☉ *Closed Tues. and Wed.*

$$$–$$$$ ⊡ **Albana.** This lush Jugendstil hotel has fabulous lake and mountain views. The grand public areas are its best features, with 15-foot ceilings—one painted with cherubs and clouds and trimmed in gold leaf. A pair of antique Venetian chandeliers glistens over the restored period furniture. The dusty-pink-and-white rooms, however, have modern furniture; the white-tile bathrooms have spacious tubs. Eight rooms have the original parquet floors—these are the ones to ask for. The restaurant's menu is imaginative; try the "herb cappuccino" soup and lamb enveloped in Rösti with a white-bean ragout. ⊠ *Luzernerstr. 26, CH-6353* ☎ *041/ 3902141* ☐ *041/3902959* ⊕ *www.albana-weggis.ch* ⇨ *57 rooms* �ፊ *Restaurant, in-room safes, sauna, steam room, bar, meeting rooms; no a/c* ⊟ *AE, DC, MC, V* ⦿| *BP.*

★ **$$–$$$** ⊡ **Beau-Rivage.** Built in 1908 but much modernized, this attractive business-class resort concentrates its comforts on a small but luxurious waterfront site, with a restaurant above the manicured lawn, a small swimming pool with mountain views, and lounge chairs at the lake's edge. Its rooms glow with rosy wood, brass, and pastel fabrics. It's at the center of town, near the boat landing. ⊠ *Gotthardstr. 6, CH-6353* ☎ *041/3927900* ☐ *041/3901981* ⊕ *www.beaurivage-weggis.ch* ⇨ *40 rooms* �ፊ *Restaurant, in-room safes, minibars, pool, bar, meeting rooms; no a/c* ⊟ *AE, DC, MC, V* ⦿ *Closed Nov.–Mar.* ⦿| *BP.*

$–$$ ⊡ **Rigi-Kulm.** This high-altitude hotel is perfect for mountaintop stopovers; built in 1950 and rather generic, it still has the air of a rugged but genteel lodge. Southern rooms have rustic decor and great views. (Be warned, however: if it's raining during your stay, the views disappear.) A short walk from the summit, at 5,900 feet, it's accessible by cable car from Weggis to Rigi-Kaltbad, then by cogwheel rail; or by cogwheel from Vitznau or Arth-Goldau. Or you can climb up from Weggis, allowing either three hours or, as Mark Twain required, three days, depending on your penchant for resting. ⊠ *Rigi Kulm CH-6410* ☎ *041/8550303* ☐ *041/8550055* ⊕ *www.rigikulm.ch* ⇨ *40 rooms* �ፊ *Restaurant, café; no a/c, no room TVs* ⊟ *AE, DC, MC, V* ⦿| *BP.*

Sports & the Outdoors
The **tourist office** (☎ 041/3901155) at Weggis rents bicycles and has information about public tennis courts.

Vitznau

㉒ *4 km (2½ mi) southeast of Weggis, 26 km (16 mi) east of Luzern.*

For a quintessentially scenic, quiet spot, stop over in Vitznau, a tiny waterfront resort that competes with Weggis in balmy weather, although its main claim to fame is the palatial Park Hotel, built in 1902.

Where to Stay

★ **$$$$** ⊡ **Park Hotel.** This isolated but lavish retreat dominates the tiny lakefront village of Vitznau. Constructed in 1902 and enlarged in 1985, it's a vaulted and beamed Edwardian dream in impeccable modern form. Even the corridors are grand, with massive oak triple doors and Persian runners stretching over quarry tile. Rooms are decorated in timeless pastels, and lakefront rooms command dreamy Alpine views. The back rooms overlook the slopes of the Rigi, dotted with grazing cows.

With the hotel's restaurants and all the activities available, you could easily find yourself not wanting to budge. ⊠ *Kantonstr., CH-6354* ☎ *041/3996060* 🖷 *041/3996070* ⊕ *www.parkhotel-vitznau.ch* ⥲ *71 rooms, 33 suites ⚓ 2 restaurants, café, in-room safes, miniature golf, 2 tennis courts, indoor pool, health club, beach, dock, waterskiing, bicycles, bar, playground, meeting rooms; no a/c* ⊟ *AE, DC, MC, V* ⊙ *Closed Nov.–mid-Apr.* ⦿| *BP.*

$–$$ 🖾 **Rigi.** Less than a third the price of the grandiose Park Hotel, this solid lodging has modernized interiors and a welcoming atmosphere in its public areas. A dozen rooms have balconies with lake views; four have small kitchenettes. The hotel is one block from the boat landing and close to the Rigibahn (which means there's some traffic noise during the day). Both the restaurant and the Stübli serve good, simple fish dishes, and there's a pleasant garden terrace. ⊠ *Seestr., CH-6354* ☎ *041/3972121* 🖷 *041/3971825* ⊕ *www.rigi-vitznau.ch* ⥲ *36 rooms ⚓ Restaurant, Stübli, some kitchenettes, minibars; no a/c* ⊟ *AE, DC, MC, V* ⦿| *BP.*

★ ¢ 🖾 **Schiff.** Claiming much the same view as the Park, this old roadhouse is perched on the hill across the street and offers cheap rooms with shared bathrooms in '50s-style summer cottages. The vine-trellised terrace restaurant, wide open to the water and mountain skyline, serves inexpensive lake-fish dishes. It's down-to-earth here and decidedly friendly. ⊠ *Kantonstr., CH-6354* ☎ *041/3971357* 🖷 *041/3972498* ⥲ *5 rooms without bath ⚓ Restaurant; no a/c, no room phones, no room TVs* ⊟*AE, DC, MC, V* ⊙ *Closed Oct. and Nov.* ⦿| *BP.*

Sports & the Outdoors

SWIMMING Because of a quirk of climate, Vitznau's bay is naturally warmer than Luzern's Lido, making this a great place to swim.

TENNIS The **Arabella Sheraton Vitznauerhof** (⊠ Seestr. ☎ 041/3997777) has a tennis court and equipment to rent at 25 SF per hour.

en route | From Vitznau a boat tour will take you across Lake Luzern to **Beckenried,** from which a cable car leads up to Klewenalp (5,250 feet), a small resort overlooking the lake. The area is excellent for hiking, with breathtakingly panoramic views of the lake and mountains on clear days. You can get a hiking trail map from newsstands or from local tourist offices. If you're driving, you could also follow the north shore to Gersau, a tiny lake resort that was an independent republic— the world's smallest—from 1332 to 1798. From Gersau the boat snakes around the sharp peninsula of the Seelisberg; the 1980 completion of a 9¼-km (6-mi) tunnel through the peninsula, south of the lake, opened the way for even swifter north–south travel between Luzern and points north and the St. Gotthard route and points south.

At the south end of Lake Luzern, past the Seelisberg Peninsula, the narrow, majestic Urnersee is the wildest and most beautiful leg of the lake. Along its shores lie some of the most historic—or, at least, romantic—landmarks in the region. The Schillerstein, on the right as you cruise past the peninsula, is a natural rock obelisk extending nearly 85 feet up out of the lake; it bears this simple dedication: TO THE AUTHOR OF *WILHELM TELL*, FRIEDRICH VON SCHILLER. 1859.

Rütli Meadow

★ ㉓ *15 km (10 mi) northwest of Altdorf on Urnersee, 35 km (22 mi) southeast of Luzern.*

Perhaps the most historically significant site in central Switzerland, the Rütli Meadow, just above the Rütli dock, is where the confederates of Schwyz, Unterwalden, and Uri are said to have met in 1307 to renew the 1291 Oath of Eternal Alliance. The **Tellsplatte,** on the east side of the lake, at the foot of the Axen Mountain, is the rocky ledge onto which Tell, the legendary rebellious archer, leapt to escape from Gessler's boat, pushing it back into the stormy waves as he jumped. There's a small chapel here, built around 1500 and restored in 1881; it contains four frescoes of the Tell legend, painted at the time of restoration.

Another monumental event took place here centuries later: amid threats of a 1940 German invasion, General Guisan, Swiss army commander in chief, summoned hundreds of officers to the meadow to reaffirm their commitment to the Swiss Confederation in a secret, stirring ceremony.

Altdorf

㉔ *20 km (12 mi) south of Rütli Meadow, 35 km (22 mi) southeast of Luzern.*

Schiller's play *Wilhelm Tell* sums up the tale for the Swiss, who perform his play religiously in venues all over the country—including the town of Altdorf, just up the road from the Rütli Meadow. Leave the steamer at Flüelen, the farthest point of the boat ride around the lake, and connect by postbus to Altdorf, the capital of the canton Uri and, by popular if not scholarly consensus, the setting for Tell's famous apple-shooting scene.

There's an often-reproduced **Tell monument** in the village center, showing a proud father with crossbow on one shoulder, the other hand grasping his son's hand; it was sculpted by Richard Kissling in 1895.

Sports & the Outdoors

BIKING You can rent bikes at the **train station** (☎ 041/8701093) in Flüelen. Mountain bikes and motorbikes can be rented and serviced in Altdorf through **Zweirad Affentranger** (✉ Gotthardstr. 53 ☎ 041/8701315).

Bürglen

㉕ *3 km (1¾ mi) southeast of Altdorf, 40 km (25 mi) southeast of Luzern.*

Tell was supposedly from the tiny town of Bürglen, just up the road from Altdorf. The **Tell Museum** devoted to him displays documents and art related to the legend. ✉ *Postpl.* ☎ *041/8704155* 🖃 *5 SF* ☯ *Mid-May–June and Sept.–late Oct., daily 10–11:30 and 1:30–5; July–Aug., daily 9:30–5:30.*

CloseUp

WATCH YOUR STEP!

Dozens of people are injured or even killed while hiking in the Alps, many of them travelers who misjudge the steep inclines and unsteady ground. Although all of the trails are regularly maintained and most high-level walkways have railings, there are hazards every hiker should keep in mind. For example, slippery conditions in the loose gravel or on patches of grass after it rains or snows can often lead to a fall.

The best way to ward off injury is to bring a good pair of hiking boots, a walking

stick, and to maintain a slow and careful pace. Pay attention to weather conditions: summer storms can develop suddenly. These days locals take along a cell phone just in case; reception is good in almost every corner of the country.

Andermatt

26 *25 km (15 mi) south of Bürglen (exit the A2 expressway at Göschenen), 67 km (41 mi) southeast of Luzern.*

Andermatt serves as a crossroads for traffic arriving from the Furka Pass, the Oberalp Pass, and the St. Gotthard Pass. It's a relaxing little backwater (no tracts of condos here), with lovely hiking trails and, thanks to its level terrain, fine cross-country skiing. It's much more a local spot than a sunglasses-and-celebrities resort. From the top of **Gemsstock,** approached by cable car from the town, it's said you can see 600 Alpine peaks.

Skiing

A high, sheltered plateau at the crossroads of three passes—the Gotthard, the Furka, and the Oberalp—**Andermatt** (4,750 feet) is easily accessible from all directions. It has five cable cars, 10 lifts, 55 km (34 mi) of downhill runs, 20 km (12 mi) of cross-country trails, and a snowboard fun park. The ski runs are especially suited for intermediate to advanced skiers. The German-language **snow hotline** (☎ 041/8870181) reports on the latest conditions.

Sports & the Outdoors

MOUNTAIN BIKING Mountain biking is popular here; to rent bikes, call **Snow Limit** (✉ Gotthardstr. 41, CH-6490 ☎ 041/8870614). The shop also stocks ski equipment.

off the beaten path **ST. GOTTHARD PASS –** This ancient passage started as a narrow path in the 13th century; a railway tunnel was not completed until 1882, and the road tunnel was finished in 1980. In these bleak and icy heights, the watershed of both the Rhine and the Rhône, you may spot eerie, partially concealed military facilities dug deep into the rock:

these are former Swiss army bunkers built during WWII. One section today houses a hotel, but it's only for those who don't suffer from claustrophobia. The pass closes in winter, but in summer it's a great mountain-biking destination. Take the old road that's closed to traffic; it's known as Alte Gotthardstrasse and runs alongside the main road. There's a hotel at the top; you can gaze at the breathtaking views and have a simple meal at its terrace restaurant.

Schwyz

㉗ *30 km (20 mi) north of Andermatt (via Hwy. 8 or the A2 expressway—exit just past Altdorf), 44 km (27 mi) east of Luzern.*

This historic town is the capital of the canton Schwyz, root of the name Switzerland, and source of the nation's flag. Switzerland's most precious archives are stored here as well. Traces of an independent settlement at Schwyz have been found from as far back as the Bronze Age (2500 BC–800 BC), but it was its inhabitants' aid in the 1291 Oath of Allegiance that put Schwyz on the map. You can see the beautifully scripted and sealed original document as well as battle flags and paintings of the period in Schwyz's **Bundesbriefmuseum** (Federal Charters Museum). ⊠ *Bahnhofstr. 20* ☎ *041/8192064* ⊕ *www.bundesbriefmuseum.ch* ⌖ *4 SF* ۞ *May–Oct., Tues.–Fri. 9–11:30 and 1:30–5, weekends 9–5; Nov.–Apr., Tues.–Fri. 9–11:30 and 1:30–5, weekends 1:30–5.*

Schwyz has several notable baroque churches and a large number of fine old patrician homes dating from the 17th and 18th centuries, not least being the **Ital-Redinghaus** with its magnificent interior, antique stoves, and fine stained glass. A visit to this grand house includes a peek inside the neighboring **Bethlehemhaus,** the oldest wooden house in Switzerland, dating from 1287. ⊠ *Rickenbachstr. 24* ☎ *041/8114505* ⊕ *www.irh.ch* ⌖ *4 SF* ۞ *May–Oct., Tues.–Fri. 2–5, weekends 10–noon and 2–5.*

Fodor'sChoice
★

Curiously, many of Schwyz's splendid houses owe their origin to the battlefield. The men of Schwyz had a reputation as fine soldiers and were in demand in other countries as mercenaries during the 16th and 17th centuries. They built many of the houses you can see today with their military pay. Schwyz's most famous landmark is the **Rathaus** (Town Hall); its richly frescoed exterior (1891) depicts the Battle of Morgarten, where the Austrian army was defeated by the Swiss. The building is still used as the Town Hall. ⊠ *Hauptpl. 1.*

Einsiedeln

㉘ *27 km (18 mi) northeast of Schwyz, 69 km (43 mi) northeast of Luzern.*

A minor summer and winter resort, Einsiedeln has been a pilgrimage site since AD 946; it is the home of the **Black Madonna,** still on display in the Benedictine monastery after more than 1,000 years. The monastery was founded in Charlemagne's time, when Meinrad, a Hohenzollern count and monk, chose the remote site to pursue his devotions in solitude. The abbess of Zürich gave him an image of the Virgin Mary, for which he built a little chapel, and Meinrad lived in peace, brought food—the story goes—by two ravens. When he was murdered by brigands seeking treasure, the ravens followed the thieves to Zürich and shrieked over their heads until they were arrested. A monastery was built over Meinrad's grave. When it was completed, the bishop of Konstanz was invited to consecrate it, but as he began the ceremony, a voice was heard crying out in the chapel three times, "Brother, desist: God himself has consecrated this building." A papal bull acknowledged the miracle and promised a special indulgence to pilgrims.

Through the ages the monastery of Einsiedeln has been destroyed many times by fire, but the Black Madonna has always been saved. When Napoléon's armies plundered the church, hoping to carry off the sacred image, it had already been taken to the Tirol in Austria for safekeeping. Today the Black Madonna is housed in a black-marble chapel just inside the west entrance to the church. When seen from a distance, its color appears to be a rich bronze, not black, and there's something gentle about the figure despite its jeweled splendor. The present abbey structure was built by Caspar Moosbrugger in 1735 and decorated by the famous brothers Egid Quirid and Cosmos Damian Asam; it's one of the finest late-baroque churches of its kind, the impressive simplicity and grace of the exterior contrasting vividly with the exuberance of its ornate interior. In front of the church, a grand square surrounds a golden statue of the Virgin Mary with a large gilt crown. Around the base, water trickles from 14 spouts, and pilgrims, to be sure of good luck, traditionally drink from each one in turn.

Einsiedeln is just off the A3 autobahn that connects Zürich with eastern Switzerland. You can take this autobahn to return to Luzern, but a more interesting route is via Alosen and Unterägeri by the Ägerisee, to Zug, famous for its Old Town.

The Arts

Einsiedeln remains a center for religious ceremony and celebrates a Festival of the Miraculous Dedication every September 14. Every 5 to 10 years some 700 citizens, coached by the monks, perform *Das Grosse Welttheater* (*the Great World Drama*) before the abbey church. A religious drama on life and the problems of humankind, it was first performed before the Court of Spain in 1685. The next performance of this historic pageant is scheduled for summer 2007.

Zug

🕙 *27 km (17 mi) northwest of Einsiedeln, 28 km (18 mi) northeast of Luzern (via A14 and A4).*

Since the end of the last century, Zug has become a bustling, modern town full of multinational corporations, but its contemporary life unfurls around the remnants of ancient ramparts and its lakefront neighborhood seems frozen in another century. The most atmospheric streets of Zug are the Oberaltstadt and the Unteraltstadt, tight lanes closed in on each side by narrow, shuttered 16th-century town houses. From the train station area on Alpenstrasse you can head straight for the waterfront of the **Zugersee** (Lake Zug). This landscaped promenade and park has fine views of Mt. Rigi, Mt. Pilatus, and the Bernese Alps—including the Eiger, the Mönch, and the Jungfrau.

Zug's Old Town is dominated by the **Rathaus** (Town Hall), which was completed in the early 16th century. Inside, there are exhibits of gold and silver work as well as embroideries, wood carvings, stained glass, and the flag Peter Kolin held until he perished in the Battle of Arbedo (1422), when 3,000 Swiss tried valiantly to hold off 24,000 Milanese soldiers. Unfortunately, you'll get only a glimpse of these fine furnishings if you dine in the **Rathauskeller,** one of the best—but most expensive—restaurants in central Switzerland. Otherwise, the Rathaus is closed to the public. ✉ *Oberaltstadt 1.*

need a break? Stop at the patisserie-café **Meier** (✉ Alpenstr. 16 ☎ 041/7111049) for coffee and a slice of the famous Zug Kirschtorte—though called cherry cake, the only cherry you'll find is in the heavily alcoholic essence that soaks the delicate yellow cake and buttercream.

By passing through a gate under the Zytturm (Clock Tower), you'll come upon the waterfront **Kolinplatz,** dedicated to the prominent local Kolin family and decorated with a fountain topped by a statue of Wolfgang Kolin. South of the Kolinplatz, up a small hill, is the **Kirche St. Oswald** (Church of St. Oswald), built in the 15th and 16th centuries; its delicate spires rise high above the town.

The Burg, a former Habsburg residence, has a half-timber exterior so intensely restored it looks like a Disney set for *Snow White.* It now houses the **Burg-Museum,** focusing on archaeology, art, and the history of Zug. Admission is free on Sunday. ✉ *Kirchenstr. 11* ☎ *041/7283297* ⊕ *www.museenzug.ch* 🎫 *5 SF* ☉ *Tues.–Fri. 2–5, weekends 10–noon and 2–5.*

Where to Stay & Eat

$$–$$$$ ✕ **Rathauskeller.** Upstairs in this historic landmark you're surrounded by a museumlike collection of medieval regional treasures but are served cutting-edge cuisine. The emphasis is on seafood (poached lobster in cream sauce), meats (tender rabbit fillet with wild-mushroom risotto), and a minimum of visual fuss. Downstairs, in the bright, hip bistro, you can order simpler, cheaper dishes from the same kitchen. ✉ *Oberaltstadt 1* ☎ *041/7110058* ⊟ *AE, V* ☉ *Closed Sun. and Mon.*

$$–$$$ ✕ **Aklin.** This 500-year-old Altstadt landmark serves *Grossmutters Küche* (Grandmother's cooking)—*Kalbskopf* (chopped veal head), *Siedfleisch* (boiled beef), and lake fish—on candlelit wooden tables by a ceramic-tile stove in the upstairs restaurant or in the atmospheric, casual bistro downstairs. ✉ *Kolinpl. 10* ☎ *041/7111866* ⊟ *AE, DC, MC, V* ☉ *Closed Sun.*

$$–$$$ 🛏 **Ochsen.** Although the notch-gabled facade has been preserved at this 16th-century landmark, the interior is strictly upscale-chain. Hints of architectural detail have been sanded away, and the buffed wood of the restaurant looks more Scandi-sleek now than Swiss; it's hard to believe that Goethe was once a guest here. The rooms are high-tech chic; the best are at the far back (above a tiny courtyard) and—of course—look-

ing over the Kolinplatz fountain toward the lake. The restaurant deserves its good reputation for fine local dishes: meats, Rösti, and its specialty, lake fish. ☒ *Kolinpl. 11, CH-6301* ☎ *041/7293232* ☒ *041/7293222* ⊕ *www.ochsen-zug.ch* ⟳ *46 rooms* ⚮ *Restaurant, minibars; no a/c* ⊟ *AE, DC, MC, V* ⊚| *BP.*

Sports & the Outdoors

At 1,430 feet, Zug has 9 km (6 mi) of cross-country ski trails, 17 km (11 mi) of ski-hiking trails, and curling. You can rent bicycles from the **train station** (☎ 041/2268700).

LUZERN & CENTRAL SWITZERLAND A TO Z

To research prices, get advice from other travelers, and book travel arrangements, visit www.fodors.com.

AIR TRAVEL

Swiss Air Lines, known as Swiss, flies in most often from the United States and the United Kingdom.

🛂 **Airlines & Contacts Swiss** ☎ 877/359-7947 in U.S., 0845/601-0956 in U.K.

AIRPORTS

The nearest airport to Luzern is Unique Zürich Airport, which is approximately 54 km (33 mi) northeast of Luzern.

🛂 **Airport Information Unique Zürich Airport** ☎ 0900/300313.

BOAT & FERRY TRAVEL

It would be a shame to see this historic region only from the shore; some of its most impressive landscapes are framed along the waterfront, as seen from the decks of one of the cruise ships that ply the lake. Rides on these are included in a Swiss Pass or a Swiss Boat Pass. Individual tickets can be purchased at Luzern's departure docks; the fee is based on the length of your ride. You can arrange any combination of transportation, such as a leisurely cruise from Luzern to Flüelen at the lake's southernmost point, lasting about 3½ hours and costing 45 SF for second class, 69 SF for first class. A return train trip, via the Arth-Goldau railroad line, takes little more than an hour. The discount Tell Pass gives you free boat rides.

🛂 **Boat & Ferry Information Luzern departure docks** ☒ Near train station ☎ 041/3676767.

BUS TRAVEL

The postbus network carries travelers faithfully, if slowly, to the farthest corners of the region. It also climbs the St. Gotthard and the Furka passes (remember, these are closed in winter). For schedules and prices, check at the post office nearest your home base or pick up a copy of the *Vierwaldstättersee Fahrplan*, a booklet (2 SF) that covers cruise ships and private railways as well as postbuses, available at the local tourist office. If you're staying in a Luzern hotel, you'll be eligible for the special Guest-Ticket, offering unlimited rides for three days for a minimal fee of 8 SF. The Tell Pass includes postbus discounts.

CAR TRAVEL

It's easy to reach Luzern from Zürich by road, approaching from national expressway A3 south, connecting to A4 via the secondary E41 in the direction of Zug, and continuing on A4, which turns into the A14, to the city. A convenient all-expressway connection between the two cities is due to open in 2006. From Basel in the northwest, it's a clean sweep by the A2 to Luzern. Approaching from the south, take the A2 to Altdorf, where a tunnel sweeps you through to the shores of the lake. If you're heading for resorts on the north shore, leave the expressway at Flüelen and follow the scenic secondary route.

Although Mt. Rigi and Mt. Pilatus aren't accessible by car, nearly everything else in this region is. The descent from Andermatt past the Devil's Bridge, which once carried medieval pilgrims from the St. Gotthard Pass and drew thrill seekers during the 19th century, now exemplifies awe-inspiring Swiss mountain engineering: from Göschenen, at 3,627 feet, to the waterfront, it's a four-lane expressway.

EMERGENCIES

For medical emergencies or to contact the police, refer to the phone numbers listed below. If your car breaks down, contact the Swiss Automobile Club or the Touring Club of Switzerland.

🚑 **Medical Emergencies** ☎144. **Police** ☎117. **Swiss Automobile Club** ☎ 031/3283111. **Touring Club of Switzerland** ☎ 022/4172727.

TOURS

The Luzern tourist office offers English-language walking tours of the city daily from May to October and Wednesday and Saturday from November to April. Tours take about two hours and cost 18 SF. Schiffahrtsgesellschaft des Vierwaldstättersees offers historic and Alpine theme cruises with English commentary daily from May to October.

🚢 **Tour Operator Recommendations Schiffahrtsgesellschaft des Vierwaldstättersees** ✉ Werftestr. 5, CH-6002 Luzern ☎ 041/3676767.

TRAIN TRAVEL

Luzern functions as a rail crossroads, with express trains connecting hourly from Zürich, a 49-minute trip, and every two hours from Geneva, a 3½- to 4-hour trip changing at Bern. Trains enter from the south via the St. Gotthard Pass from the Ticino and via the Furka Pass from the Valais. For rail information, call the Bahnhof.

Swiss National Railways is enhanced here by a few private lines (to Engelberg, Pilatus, the Rigi Kulm) that make it possible to get to most sights. If you don't have a Swiss Pass, there's a central Switzerland regional discount pass, called the Tell Pass, on sale from April to October. The 15-day pass grants you five days of unlimited free travel on main routes, 10 days at half fare. The seven-day pass gives you two days free, five at half fare. (Besides the national lines, most private rail lines will also accept the pass.) The ticket can be bought at rail or boat ticket offices, on cruise boats, from travel agencies, or from tourist offices. The 15-day pass costs 184 SF second class, 213 SF first class; the seven-day pass costs 135 SF second class, 152 SF first class. Plan your itinerary carefully to take full advantage of all discount rates; before you buy a regional pass, add up your excursions à la carte. Remember that many routes always charge half price. All boat trips and the private excursions to Rigi and Pilatus are free to holders of regional passes—but getting to the starting point may cost you half the ususal price. If you plan to cover a lot of ground, however, you may save considerably. Choose your free days in advance: you must confirm them *all* with the first inspector who checks your pass.

🚆 Train Information **Bahnhof** ✉ Bahnhofpl. ☎ 0900/300300 ⊕ www.sbb.ch.

VISITOR INFORMATION

The principal tourist office for the whole of central Switzerland, including the lake region, is Zentralschweiz Tourismus (Central Switzerland Tourism). The main tourist office for the city of Luzern is in the Bahnhof, off Track 3. There are also local tourist offices and an accommodations service in many of the region's towns, often near the train station.

🚆 Local Tourist Information **Altdorf** ✉ Schützengasse., CH-6460 ☎ 041/8720450. **Andermatt** ✉ Offizieles Verkehrsbüro, Gotthardstr. 2, CH-6490 ☎ 041/8871454. **Einsiedeln** ✉ Hauptstr. 85, CH-8840 ☎ 055/4184488. **Engelberg** ✉ Klosterstr. 3, CH-6390 ☎ 041/6397777 ⊕ www.engelberg.ch. **Luzern** ✉ Bahnhof: Zentralstr. 5, CH-6002 ☎ 041/2271717 ⊕ www.luzern.com. **Schwyz** ✉ Obersteisteg 14, CH-6430 ☎ 041/8555950 ⊕ www.schwyz-tourismus.ch. **Stans** ✉ Bahnhofpl. 4, CH-6370 ☎ 041/6108833 ⊕ www.stans.ch. **Vitznau** ✉ Seestr., CH-6354 ☎ 041/3980035 ⊕ www.vitznau.ch. **Weggis** ✉ Seestr. 5, CH-6353 ☎ 041/3901155 ⊕ www.weggis.ch. **Zug** ✉ Bahnhofpl., CH-6300 ☎ 041/7110078 ⊕ www.zug-tourismus.ch.

🚆 Regional Tourist Information **Zentralschweiz Tourismus** ✉ Alpenstr. 1, Luzern CH-6002 ☎ 041/2271744 🖷 041/2271720 ⊕ www.centralswitzerland.ch.

BASEL

Updated by
Sharon-Anne
Wilcox

THOUGH IT LACKS THE GILT AND GLITTER of Zürich and the Latin grace of Geneva, in many ways Basel (Bâle in French) is the most sophisticated of Swiss cities. At the frontier between two of Europe's most assertive personalities, France and Germany, and tapped directly into the artery of the Rhein (Rhine), the city has flourished on the lifeblood of two cultures and grown surprisingly urbane, cosmopolitan, worldly wise. It is also delightfully eccentric, its imagination fed by centuries of intellectual input: Basel has been host to Switzerland's oldest university (1460) and patron to some of the country's—and the world's—finest minds. A northern center of humanist thought and art, it nurtured the painters Konrad Witz and Hans Holbein the Younger as well as the great Dutch scholar Erasmus. And it was Basel's visionary lord mayor Johann Rudolf Wettstein who, at the end of the Thirty Years' War, negotiated Switzerland's groundbreaking—and lasting—neutrality.

Each day, more than 30,000 French and German commuters cross into Basel. Banking activity here is surpassed only by that of Zürich and Geneva, and every month representatives of the world's leading central banks meet behind closed doors in the city center at the Bank for International Settlements. Enormous international pharmaceutical firms—Novartis and Roche—crowd the riverbanks. Yet Basel's population hovers around a modest 200,000; its urban center lies gracefully along the Rhine, no building so tall as to block another's view of the cathedral's twin spires. Two blocks from the heart of the thriving shopping district you can walk through medieval residential streets cloaked in perfect, otherworldly silence to Minster Mount, where the impressive Romanesque-Gothic cathedral offers superb views over the Old Town and River Rhine to the surrounding mountains.

The high number of museums per capita is a reflection of Basel's priorities: the city has more than 30, including the world-class Kunstmuseum, the Museum Tinguely, and the Fondation Beyeler. As high culture breeds good taste, Basel has some of the most varied, even quirky, shopping in Switzerland; antiquarian bookstores, calligraphers, and artisans do business next to sophisticated designer shops and famous jewelers. But you can still get a beer and a bratwurst here: Baslers almost exclusively speak German or their own local version of *Schwyzerdütsch,* called *Baseldütsch.* On the Marktplatz, hungry shoppers stand in front of a mobile kitchen, holding bare *Wienerli* (hot dogs) and dipping the pink tips into thick golden mustard. They also indulge in *Kaffe und Kuchen*—the late-afternoon coffee break the neighboring Germans live for—but Baslers do it differently. Instead of the large slices of creamy cake, they select tiny sweet gems—two or three to a saucer, but petite nonetheless—and may opt for a delicate Chinese tea.

The Celts were the first to settle here, around 500 BC, on the site of the Münsterhügel (cathedral mount). During the 1st century BC the Romans established a town at Augst, then called Colonia Augusta Raurica; the ruins and the theater can be visited today, 10 km (6 mi) outside town. By the 3rd century, the Romans had taken the present cathedral site in Basel proper, naming the town Basilia (royal stronghold). Germanic invaders banished them around 450, and it wasn't until the Holy Roman

If you have **1 or 2** **days**	Begin with a stroll through Basel's Old Town, making sure to see the Münster and the sweeping views from the terrace overlooking the Rhine. Art enthusiasts could decide to circle from here directly to the Kunstmuseum, and shoppers may want to head down one of the winding alleyways into the Freie Strasse or the Marktplatz. A leisurely late-afternoon walk across the Mittlere Rheinbrücke and upstream along the sunny Kleinbasel riverside promenade (Oberer Rheinweg) is a good way to see the town in its best light. On the following day take in some of the city's smaller museums, perhaps in the picturesque St. Alban quarter. From here take a ferryboat across the river and head east to the Museum Tinguely. Or organize your day around a trip to Riehen; the Fondation Beyeler's stunningly well-rounded (and beautifully presented) collection of 20th-century art can be reached in a mere 20 minutes by tram.
If you have **3 to 5** **days**	Given the luxury of several days, you can explore even more of Basel's museums. In summer you might opt to take a boat trip to the Roman ruins of Augusta Raurica, east of Basel. You could also take a driving tour of the small villages scattered south of Basel: Balsthal, Holderbank, Oberer Hauenstein, Langenbruck, and Liestal.

emperor Henry II took Basel under his wing in the 11th century that stability returned. His image and that of his wife, Kunegunde, adorn the cathedral and the Rathaus (Town Hall). Henry built the original cathedral—on the site of a church destroyed by a raiding band of Hungarian horsemen in 916—and established Basel as one of the centers of his court. In 1006 the bishop of Basel was made ruler of the town, and throughout the Middle Ages these prince-bishops gained and exerted enormous temporal and spiritual powers. Though the prince-bishops are no more, Basel still uses one of their symbols in its coat of arms—a striking black staff.

Yet Basel is first and foremost a Renaissance city in the literal sense of the word: a city of intellectual and artistic rebirth. In 1431 the Council of Basel, an ecumenical conference on church reform, was convened here, bringing in—over a period of 17 years—the great sacred and secular princes of the age. One of them, who later became Pope Pius II, granted permission for the founding of the university and established Basel as the cultural capital it remains today.

Art and academia over the ages haven't made Basel stuffy, however. The Baslers' Lenten celebration of Fasnacht (related to Mardi Gras, or Carnival) turns the city on its ear. The streets are filled with grotesquely costumed revelers bearing huge homemade lanterns scrawled with comments and caricatures relating to local current events. Although the festivities last only three days, you'll see masks displayed and sold everywhere all year long, and you'll hear strains of fife-and-drum marches wafting from the guild houses' upper windows; they're rehearsing for the celebration. Like confetti lodged between the cobblestones, there always seems to be a hint of Fasnacht, age-old and unpredictable, even in Basel's most sedate and cultivated corners.

EXPLORING BASEL

The Rhine divides the city of Basel into two distinct sections: on the southwestern bank lies Grossbasel (Greater Basel), the commercial, cultural, and academic center. Directly upriver from Grossbasel wind the quiet medieval streets of St. Alban, where you can stroll along the Rhine, peek into antique stores' windows, then have a quiet bistro meal. The opposite bank, to the northeast, is Kleinbasel (Little Basel), a Swiss enclave on the "German" side of the Rhine that is the industrial quarter of the city. Unless you're visiting on business and meeting at the convention center east of the river, your time on the right bank will probably be limited to a waterfront stroll and possibly a good night's sleep, as it does have some good hotels.

Numbers in the text correspond to numbers in the margin and on the Basel map.

Old Town

Standing in the middle of the Marktplatz or even watching river traffic from the Mittlere Rheinbrücke, it's easy to envision the Basel of centuries ago. On a bend of the Rhine, Basel's Old Town is full of majestic Gothic spires and side streets that have remained largely unchanged since the 1600s. Still, much of the delicately preserved architecture of the Old Town incorporates impressive, state-of-the-art museums and miles of shop-lined pedestrian zones.

a good walk

Six bridges link the two halves of the city; the most historic and picturesque is the **Mittlere Rheinbrücke ❶ ▶**. On the corner of what is now a chain restaurant at Schifflände, you can see a facsimile of the infamous **Lällekönig ❷**, a 17th-century gargoyle once mechanized to stick out his tongue and roll his eyes at his rivals across the river.

Walking across the bridge, you'll see Basel's peculiar, gondolalike ferryboats, attached to a high wire and angling silently from shore to shore, powered only by the swift current of the river (you can ride one for 1.20 SF). Across the Rhine, gaze at the seated **statue of Helvetia**, one of Basel's many tongue-in-cheek sculptures.

Back across the Mittlere Rheinbrücke in Grossbasel, turn left up a steep alley called the **Rheinsprung**, banked with 15th- and 16th-century houses. Turn right at Archivgässlein, and you'll come to the **Martinskirche ❸**, the city's oldest parish church, dating from 1288.

Continue along Martinsgasse to the elegant neighboring courtyards of the **Blaues und Weisses Haus ❹**, meeting place of kings. Just beyond, turn left and head toward the fountain adorned by a mythical green basilisk into the Augustinergasse. At No. 2 is the entrance to the **Naturhis-**

Dining When the Germanic hordes arrived here to rout the Romans, they brought their favorite foods along with them. When Baslers enjoy a home-cooked meal, it's inevitably sausage, schnitzel, and *Spätzli* (tiny flour dumplings) washed down with beer. The city's restaurants also pay more than a little homage to the cooking of the city's French neighbors. And being very cosmopolitan, there's an ever-changing—depending on what's in fashion—array of other cuisines available. The proximity of the Rhine means that most restaurants serve a variety of freshwater fish. If Basel could claim a regional specialty, it would be salmon. (These days much of it is shipped in from elsewhere, but the Rhine variety is making a comeback.) The meaty fish is best served *nach Basler-Art* (Basel-style), meaning in a white-wine marinade with fried onions on top. Try it with a bottle of the fruity local Riesling-Sylvaner.

Fasnacht Dating from the Middle Ages, Fasnacht, Switzerland's best-known festival, draws people from all over the world. Beginning at 4 AM on the Monday following Ash Wednesday, all lights are turned off and the city is illuminated by the lanterns of the *Cliques* (carnival associations). The event features a blast of fifes and drums, boisterous *Guggemusik* (played by enthusiastic, rather than talented, marching bands), and a covering of confetti. The streets are packed with onlookers who have fortified themselves against the cold morning with a bowl of the traditional *Mehlsuppe* (flour soup). A colorful masked procession traverses the Old Town until dawn, and continues for the next two days. Nearby Liestal stages its own spectacular ceremony during which burning stacks of wood are paraded through the town and finally heaped together.

Museums With a renowned collector's handpicked paintings (the Fondation Beyeler), an homage to unique mechanized art (the Museum Tinguely), and one of the world's oldest public art collections (the Kunstmuseum), Basel easily earns a high rank in the art world. There are many smaller museums of astounding variety, with collections highlighting paper, printing, and pharmaceutical history. The city's interest in art is evident each spring when it hosts one of Europe's largest art fairs. If you plan to visit many of the city's museums and galleries, the BaselCard is a good idea. It gives you unlimited admission to participating museums for one, two, or three days. It can be purchased at Basel Tourismus offices and most hotels.

---

torisches Museum ⑤ and the **Museum der Kulturen Basel** ⑥. Under one roof you'll find one of the world's foremost natural history and prehistory collections.

Augustinergasse leads into the Münsterplatz, dominated by the striking red-sandstone 12th-century **Münster** ⑦, burial place of Erasmus and Queen Anna of Habsburg. Walk around to the church's riverside to a terrace called the Pfalz, which affords wide views of the river, the Old Town, and, on a clear day, the Black Forest.

From the Münsterplatz, head down Rittergasse, past its elegant villas and courtyards, to the first busy cross street. Ahead of you is St. Alban-Vorstadt, which leads to the **St. Alban-Tor ❽**, one of the original 13th-century medieval city gates. St. Alban-Tal leads from St. Alban-Vorstadt down to St. Alban-Rheinweg on the Rhine to the **Basler Papiermühle/ Schweizer Papiermuseum und Museum für Schrift und Druck ❾** and the **Museum für Gegenwartskunst ❿**. Leaving the museums by way of the St. Alban-Rheinweg along the riverside, ascend the Wettstein Bridge stairs and head left onto St. Alban-Graben. Here is the imposing **Kunstmuseum ⓫**, home of one of Europe's oldest public collections.

Continue down St. Alban-Graben to the intersection of Steinenberg. A few blocks straight ahead into Elisabethenstrasse will take you to the **Haus zum Kirschgarten ⓬**, which has parts of the city's historical collections. To circle back into the Old Town, however, veer right on Steinenberg, which goes by the **Kunsthalle ⓭**. Just beyond the art gallery, the whimsical Tinguely-Brunnen, or **Fasnacht-Brunnen,** puts on a show on the Theaterplatz. (A Richard Serra sculpture, normally covered in graffiti, also punctuates the square.) Zoo enthusiasts may want to take advantage of the tram service along Steinentorstrasse to reach the **Zoologischer Garten ⓮**, west of the SBB train station.

Continue on Steinenberg until it opens out onto the bustling Barfüsserplatz. Here the **Puppenhaus Museum ⓯** displays toys from the 18th and 19th centuries, and the **Historisches Museum ⓰** exhibits annals and objects out of Basel's proud past in the mid-14th-century Franciscan Barfüsserkirche, or Church of the Shoeless Friars.

Behind the tram concourse on Barfüsserplatz, follow the pedestrian zone to Leonhardsberg, which leads left up the stairs to the late-Gothic **Leonhardskirche ⓱**. Continue along the church walk into Heuberg street, the spine of one of the loveliest sections of old Basel. A network of small streets threads through the quarter, lined with graceful old houses from many periods: Gothic, Renaissance, baroque, Biedermeier. Heuberg feeds into Spalenvorstadt, which will take you ahead two blocks to the **Holbeinbrunnen,** styled from a drawing by Hans Holbein.

The Spalenvorstadt stretches on to the impressive 14th-century **Spalentor ⓲**, another of Basel's medieval city gates. Spalengraben curves north from here past the buildings of the Universität, one of the six oldest universities in German-speaking Europe. Nearby Petersplatz is the site of the 13th-century **Peterskirche ⓳**.

Petersgasse, behind the Peterskirche, presents an exemplary row of houses, some only a single window wide. Several small streets scale downhill from here, among them the Totengässlein, which leads past the **Pharmazie-Historisches Museum ⓴**. The steep stairs wind on in the direction of the **Marktplatz ㉑**, the historic and modern heart of Basel, with its towering **Rathaus ㉒**.

Leading off the south end of the Marktplatz, main shopping streets Freie Strasse and Gerbergasse are lined with international shops and department stores. The north end heads toward **Fischmarkt ㉓**. Marktgasse leads to the historic **Drei Könige Hotel** ㉔. If you're feeling energetic, walk to the **Museum Tinguely** ㉕ by crossing over the Mittlere Rheinbrücke and heading east toward Solitude Park on Kleinbasel's sunny waterfront promenade Oberer Rheinweg. Or take a 20-minute tram ride (No. 6 from Barfüsserplatz, Marktplatz, or Schifflände) to the **Fondation Beyeler** ㉖, with its modern-art collection and green park.

TIMING Moving at a rapid clip you can see the major sights, as well as a cross section of the cultural and artistic collections, in four to six hours. A more leisurely itinerary, including strolling around the Old Town shops and visiting museums on the Kleinbasel side, will while away at least a whole day, if not two. If you're looking to save a few francs, many museums are free the first Sunday of the month and from Tuesday to Saturday between 4 and 5 PM. Most museums are closed Monday.

Sights to See

🖑 ❾ **Basler Papiermühle/Schweizer Papiermuseum und Museum für Schrift und Druck** (Basel Paper Mill/Swiss Museum for Paper, Writing and Printing). Though its name sounds esoteric, this museum, in a beautifully restored medieval waterfront mill with a functioning waterwheel, is surprisingly accessible. Demonstrations of papermaking, typesetting, and bookbinding reveal much about the ancient craft. You can participate in a 12-step papermaking process, beginning with the pulpy raw material simmering in the "visitors' vat." Kids can try out quills and ink or spell their names in pieces of type for printing. Most descriptions have an English translation, but some special exhibits are in German only. ⊠ *St. Alban-Tal 35/37, St. Alban* ☎ *061/2729652* ⊕ *www.papiermuseum.ch* ☒ *12 SF* ⊙ *Tues.–Sun. 2–5.*

❹ **Blaues und Weisses Haus** (Blue House and White House). Built between 1762 and 1768 for two of the city's most successful silk merchants, these were the residences of the brothers Lukas and Jakob Sarasin. In 1777 the emperor Joseph II of Austria was a guest in the Blue House and subsequent visitors—including Czar Alexander of Russia, Emperor Francis of Austria, and King Friedrich Wilhelm III of Prussia, who met for dinner here in 1814—take this historical site's guest book over the top. The restored houses are both white with blue trim, but they're distinguished by their gates: the Blue House is made of intricate iron, and the White House is stately wood. ⊠ *Martinsg., Grossbasel.*

㉔ **Drei Könige Hotel** (Three Kings Hotel). The statues on the facade depict three wise men who visited here nearly a millennium ago—in 1032 to be precise. Rodolphe III, king of Burgundy; Emperor Konrad II; and the latter's son, the future Heinrich III, held a meeting here that joined Burgundy to the Holy Roman Empire. The young general Napoléon Bonaparte stayed here in 1797 (a suite was named for him and decorated in opulent Empire style), followed by other stellar guests, including Princess Victoria, Charles Dickens and Picasso. In 1887 the great Hungarian-born Jewish writer Theodor Herzl stayed here during the first Zionist Congress, which laid the groundwork for the founding of the state of Israel. ⊠ *Blumenrain 8, Grossbasel.*

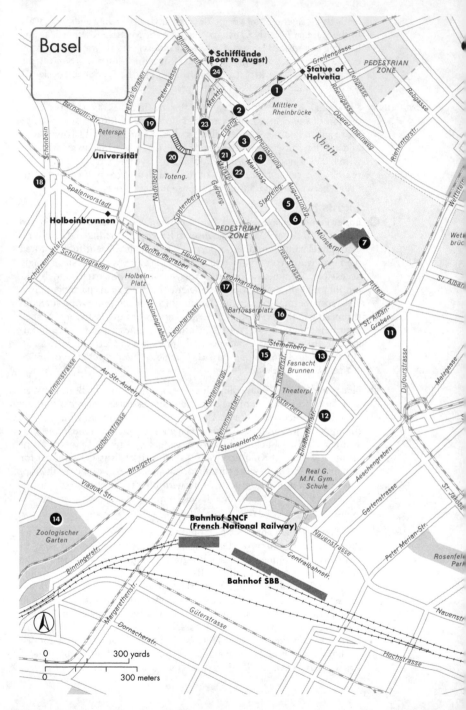

Basel

Schifflände
(Boat to Augst)

Statue of
Helvetia

PEDESTRIAN
ZONE

Greifengasse

Uferg.

Rheing.

Rebg.

Oberer Rheinweg

Rehentorstr.

Rhein

Wettste

Wett
brüc

Mittlere
Rheinbrücke

Bernoulli-Str.

Petersgraben

Petersgasse

Blumenrain

Martkt

Martkt

Eiseng.

Rheinsprung

Peterspl.

Universität

Nadelberg

Toteng.

Spalenberg

Gerberg.

Martkpl.

Martkgasse

Stapfelbg.

Augustinerg.

Münsterpl.

St. Alban

St. Albar

Holbeinbrunnen

Schönbein

Spalenvorstadt

Schützenmattstr.

Schützengraben

Leonhardsgraben

Heuberg

Freie Strasse

Münsterpl.

Ritterg.

Holbein-
Platz

Steinengraben

Leonhardstr.

Leonhardsberg

Barfüsserplatz

St. Alban-
Graben

Dufourstrasse

Metzgerg.

Leimenstrasse

Au Str. Auberg

Steinenberg

Steinenvorstadt

Kornberg

Theaterstr.

Fasnacht
Brunnen

Theaterpl.

Klosterberg

Elisabethenstr.

Aeschengraben

Gartenstrasse

St. Jakobs

Holbeinstrasse

Birsigstr.

Steinentorstr.

Real G.
M.N. Gym.
Schule

Nauenstrasse

Peter Merian-Str.

Viadukt Str.

Zoologischer
Garten

Bahnhof SNCF
(French National Railway)

Rosenfeld
Park

Binningerstr.

Margarethenstr.

Centralbahnstr.

Bahnhof SBB

Nauenstr.

Dornacherstr.

Güterstrasse

Hochstrasse

0   300 yards

0   300 meters

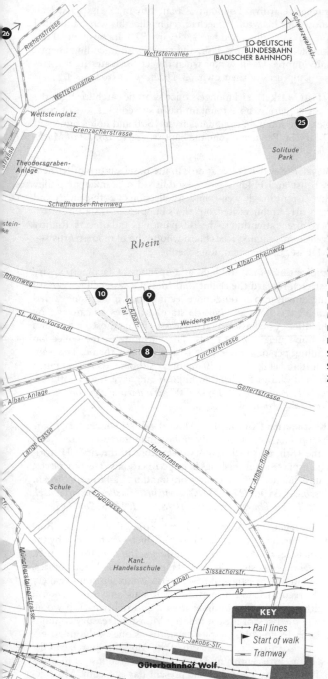

TO DEUTSCHE
BUNDESBAHN
(BADISCHER BAHNHOF)

Wettsteinallee

Riehenstrasse

Wettsteinallee

Wettsteinplatz

Grenzacherstrasse

Theodorsgraben-
Anlage

Schaffhauser Rheinweg

Solitude
Park

Rhein

St. Alban-Rheinweg

Rheinweg

St. Alban-Vorstadt

St. Alban-
Tal

Weidengasse

Zürcherstrasse

Gellertstrasse

Alban-Anlage

Lange Gasse

Hardstrasse

St. Alban-Ring

Schule

Engelgasse

Münchensteinerstrasse

Kant.
Handelsschule

Sissacherstr.

St. Alban

A2

St.-Jakobs-Str.

Güterbahnhof Wolf

KEY

┼┼ *Rail lines*
► *Start of walk*
══ *Tramway*

🕲 **Fasnacht-Brunnen** (Carnival Fountain). Created by the Swiss artist Jean Tinguely, known for his work in mechanized media, this witty, animated construction was commissioned by the city in 1977. Its busy metal figures, in whimsical style, churn, lash, and spray with unending energy. It is especially impressive in winter when the jets of water freeze, creating unique sculptures of their own. ⊠ *Theaterpl., Grossbasel.*

㉓ **Fischmarkt** (Fish Market). Fishmongers once kept the catch fresh for the market on this square, whose fountain basin served as a sort of communal cooler. The fountain itself dates from 1390 and holds figures of the Virgin Mary, St. Peter, and John the Baptist. ⊠ *Northwest of Marktpl., Grossbasel.*

㉖ **Fondation Beyeler** (Beyeler Foundation). In the Basel suburb of Riehen, **Fodor'sChoice** art dealers Ernst and Hildy Beyeler established a permanent public
★ home for their astonishingly well-rounded collection of 20th-century and contemporary art. Architect Renzo Piano's building uses simple, introverted lines to direct attention to the 200 paintings and objects. Rightly so, as the collection's catalog reads like a who's who of modern artists—Cézanne, Matisse, Lichtenstein, Rauschenberg.

In this limpid setting of natural light and openness, Giacometti's wiry sculptures stretch toward the ceiling and Monet's water lilies seem to spill from the canvas into an outdoor reflecting pool. Indigenous carved figures from New Guinea and Nigeria stare into faces on canvases by Klee and Dubuffet. A stellar selection of Picassos is juxtaposed with views of blue skies and neighboring fields. The harmony of the collection notwithstanding, personal preference is a perceivable theme. The tram trip from Schifflände takes about 20 minutes. Although there isn't much explanatory material in English, an English-language tour is offered. ⊠ *Baselstr. 101, Riehen* ☎ *061/6459700* ⊕ *www.beyeler.com* 🎟 *18 SF* ☉ *Thurs.–Tues. 10–6, Wed. 10–8.*

⑫ **Haus zum Kirschgarten** (Kirschgarten House). This 18th-century home was built as a palace for a young silk-ribbon manufacturer. Nowadays it contains the 18th- and 19th-century collections of the city's Historical Museum, displayed as furnishings in its period rooms. The timepieces, porcelain, and faience are especially outstanding. ⊠ *Elisabethenstr. 27–29, Grossbasel* ☎ *061/2711333* ⊕ *www.historischesmuseumbasel. ch* 🎟 *7 SF* ☉ *Tues., Thurs., Fri., Sun. 10–5, Wed. 10–8, Sat. 1–5.*

★ ⑯ **Historisches Museum** (Historical Museum). Housed within the **Barfüsserkirche** (Church of the Shoeless Friars), which was founded by the barefoot Franciscans in 1250 and rebuilt during the mid-14th century, the museum has an extensive collection of tapestries, wooden sculptures, coins, armor, and other vestiges of Basel's past. An underground gallery displays fully reconstructed **medieval and Renaissance guild rooms**, complete with stained glass, ceramic stoves, and richly carved wood. Downstairs, in the back of the church, the **Münster Treasury** contains priceless reliquaries in gold. Despite its status as one of the finest examples of Franciscan architecture north of the Alps, the church was deconsecrated in the 19th century and turned into a warehouse until it was rescued in 1894 and converted to the present-day museum. Most descriptions are in German only. ⊠ *Barfüsserpl., Steinenberg 4, Grossbasel* ☎ *061/2058600* ⊕ *www.historischesmuseumbasel.ch* ⊠ *7 SF* ⊘ *Wed.–Mon. 10–5.*

Holbeinbrunnen (Holbein Fountain). Created by an unknown 16th-century stonemason, this fanciful fountain was inspired by several other works. It depicts a group of dancing farmers, copied from a drawing by Hans Holbein; above stands a bagpiper, copied from a Dürer engraving. The fountain itself is a replica, the original having been moved to the Historical Museum. ⊠ *Spalenvorstadt, 2 blocks up the tram tracks toward Spalentor, Grossbasel.*

★ ⓭ **Kunsthalle** (Basel Art Gallery). Managed through Basel's community of artists, the Basler Kunstverein, this museum has hosted precedent-setting exhibits of contemporary art since 1872. In addition to showing several modern masters early in their careers (Klee and Picasso), the gallery was the first in Europe to display works by American Abstract Expressionists. Recent exhibits have featured Chuck Close and Martin Kippenberger. An on-site theater hosts video installations, performances, and local and foreign films. ⊠ *Steinenberg 7, Grossbasel* ☎ *061/2069900* ⊕ *www.kunsthallebasel.ch* ⊠ *10 SF* ⊘ *Tues., Wed., Fri. 11–6, Thurs. 11–8:30, weekends 11–7.*

⓫ **Kunstmuseum** (Museum of Fine Arts). In a city known for its museums, **Fodor'sChoice** the Kunstmuseum is Basel's heirloom jewel. It was built between 1932 ★ and 1936 to house one of the oldest public art collections in Europe, owned by the city since 1661; the imposing facade gives way to an inner courtyard studded with statues. Inside is the world's largest assemblage of paintings by the Holbein family, an exceptional group of works by Konrad Witz, and, in fact, such a thorough gathering of the works of their contemporaries that the development of painting in the Upper Rhine is strikingly illuminated. Other Swiss artists are well represented: from Basel's own Arnold Böcklin to Klimt-like Ferdinand Hodler. The museum's other forte is its international 20th-century collection, from Georges Braque to Jasper Johns. Most information is in German, but English descriptions are sometimes provided for special exhibits. ⊠ *St. Alban-Graben 16, Grossbasel* ☎ *061/2066262* ⊕ *www. kunstmuseumbasel.ch* ⊠ *10 SF, includes admission to Museum für Gegenwartskunst* ⊘ *Tues.–Sun. 10–5.*

★ ❷ **Lällekönig.** When a famous gate tower on the Grossbasel side was destroyed, with it went the notorious Lällekönig, a 15th-century gargoyle of a king once mechanized by clockwork to stick out his tongue and roll his eyes at the "lesser" citizens across the river. Kleinbasel residents seek symbolic revenge even today, though. Every year during the Vogel Gryff festival, a birdlike figure dances to the midpoint of the bridge, gives the Lällekönig a flash of his backside, and takes the party back to Kleinbasel. You can see a facsimile of the Lällekönig on the corner of what is now a chain restaurant at Schifflände 1. The original still ticks and taunts away in the nether regions of the Historical Museum. ⊠ *Schifflände, Grossbasel.*

⓱ **Leonhardskirche** (St. Leonard's Church). Like virtually all of Basel's churches, this one was destroyed in the 1356 earthquake and rebuilt in the Gothic style, although its Romanesque crypt remains. Its High Gothic wooden pulpit is distinctive. Free organ concerts are often held on Friday evening. ✉ *Heuberg, Grossbasel* ⊙ *Daily 10–5.*

㉑ **Marktplatz** (Marketplace). Flowers, fruits, and vegetables are sold most mornings from open stands in this central square, Basel's historic and modern heart. In fall and winter passersby purchase bags of hot roasted chestnuts, the savory scent of which wafts through the square. ⊹ *Tram crossroads at foot of Rathaus, south of Marktg.* ⊙ *Market: Mon., Wed., and Fri.* 6 AM–6:30 PM; *Tues., Thurs., and Sat.* 6 AM–1:30 PM.

❸ **Martinskirche** (St. Martin's Church). The excellent acoustics make this church popular for concerts, although it's rarely used for services. The lower portions of the tower date from 1288, making it the oldest parish church in town; the upper part was rebuilt after the earthquake of 1356. The fountain outside, with the statue of a warrior dressed for battle, dates from the 16th century. ✉ *Martinsg., Grossbasel.*

▶ ★ ❶ **Mittlere Rheinbrücke** (Middle Rhine Bridge). Basel's most historic bridge is a good metaphor for the city's successful mix of custom and commerce. It's used as a catwalk for many of Basel's centuries-old celebrations; bright banners seem to anticipate a passing parade. But underneath it's practical—processions of barges glide through its low-slung arches. First built around 1225, the bridge made possible the development of an autonomous Kleinbasel and the consequent rivalry that grew between the two half towns. A stone bridge replaced the wooden one at the turn of the 20th century, its 1478 chapel reconstructed at the center of the new bridge. ✉ *Schifflände, Grossbasel.*

★ ❼ **Münster** (Cathedral). Basel's cathedral evolved into its current form through a chance shift of nature and the changing whims of architects. The site started as a 9th-century Carolingian church, then became a cathedral, which was consecrated by Henry II in 1019. Additions, alterations, and reconstructions in late Romanesque–early Gothic style continued through the 12th and 13th centuries. When Basel's devastating earthquake destroyed much of the building in 1356, subsequent reconstruction, which lasted about a century, took on the dominant Gothic style. The facade of the north transept, the **Galluspforte** (St. Gall's Door), is a surviving remnant of the original Romanesque structure. It's one of the oldest carved portals in German-speaking Europe—and one of the loveliest. Slender, fine-tooled columns and rich high-relief and freestanding sculptures frame the door. Each of the evangelists is represented by his symbol: an angel for Matthew, an ox for Luke, a lion for Mark, and a bulbous-chested eagle for John. Above, around the window, a wheel of fortune flings little men off to their fates.

Inside on the left, following a series of tombs of medieval noblemen whose effigies recline with their feet resting on their loyal dogs, stands the strikingly simple **tomb of Erasmus.** Below the choir, you can see the delicately rendered death portraits on the double **tomb of Queen Anna of Habsburg** and her young son Charles, from around 1285. The vaulted **crypt** was part of the original structure and still bears fragments of murals from 1202.

The Münsterplatz square itself is one of the most satisfying architectural ensembles in Europe, its fine town houses set well back from the cathedral, the center filled with pollarded trees. ✉ *Münsterpl., Grossbasel* ⊕ *www.baslermuenster.ch* ⊙ *Easter–mid-Oct., Mon.–Sat. 10–5, Sun. 1–5; mid-Oct.–Easter, Mon.–Sat. 11–4, Sun. 2–4.*

> **need a break?** It's hard to beat the plaza tables of **Café zum Isaak** (✉ Münsterpl. 16, Grossbasel ☎ 061/2614712 ⊕ www.zum-isaak.ch) for scenic value; it has a direct view of the cathedral's towers. The café is closed Monday.

❻ Museum der Kulturen Basel (Basel Museum of Cultures). You'll experience a moment of extreme cultural contrast here—walk in from the cobblestone street, and you'll suddenly find yourself at a woven-palm "culthouse" from Papua, New Guinea. This is one of the world's foremost ethnographic collections, with 32,000 pieces from the far corners of the globe. The extensive ground-floor exhibits on Oceania and Melanesia include standing pole figures, dance staffs, and bristling headdresses. The museum shares its space with the Natural History Museum. Key parts of the collection have English-language information sheets. ✉ *Augustinerg. 2, Grossbasel* ☎ *061/2665500* ⊕ *www.mkb.ch* 🎫 *7 SF, includes admission to Naturhistorisches Museum* ⊙ *Tues.–Sun. 10–5.*

❿ Museum für Gegenwartskunst (Museum of Contemporary Art). Carrying Basel's art collections up to the present, this museum focuses on works from the 1960s on. The fittingly modern building looks as though it has shouldered its way in between the street's half-timber houses. The exhibitions change frequently, so pick up a brochure from a tourist office to see what artist's works the museum will be showing when you visit. The language of the exhibition materials typically corresponds to the nationality of the artists. ✉ *St. Alban-Rheinweg 60, Grossbasel* ☎ *061/2728183* ⊕ *www.mgkbasel.ch* 🎫 *10 SF, includes admission to Kunstmuseum* ⊙ *Tues.–Sun. 11–5.*

★ ☾ ㉕ Museum Tinguely. Stay alert and be ready to get involved—the fascinating mechanized artworks of 20th-century master Jean Tinguely invite close inspection and interaction. As you circle the installations, some a story high, you may wonder: how do they work? what do they mean? and where did he find this stuff? Born in Fribourg, Tinguely is best known for his whimsical *métamécaniques* (mechanical sculptures), which transform machinery, appliances, and items straight from the taxidermy shop into ironic and often macabre statements. For instance, *Le Ballet des Pauvres,* from 1961, suspends a hinged leg with a moth-eaten sock, a horse tail and fox pelt, a cafeteria tray, and a blood-soaked nightgown, all of which dangle and dance on command. The Barca, a wing projecting over the Rhine, has a splendid river view of Basel. Many of the museum's "sculptures" play on timers, typically every 5–15 minutes, and it pays to wait and see them in action. Schedules are listed on each work's nameplate, and information sheets are available in English. ✉ *Paul Sacher-Anlager 1, Kleinbasel* ☎ *061/6819320* ⊕ *www.tinguely.ch* 🎫 *7 SF* ⊙ *Tues.–Sun. 11–7.*

⑤ Naturhistorisches Museum (Natural History Museum). Under the same monumental roof as the Museum der Kulturen Basel, this museum outlines the earth's biological history from prehistoric to modern times, including some impressive examples of mammals, reptiles, and invertebrates. There's also a focus on local fossil finds and indigenous minerals from the Alps and Jura regions. Most descriptive materials are in German only. ⊠ *Augustinerg. 2, Grossbasel* ☎ *061/2665500* ⊕ *www.unibas.ch/ museum/nmb* ✉ *7SF, includes admission to Museum der Kulturen Basel* ☉ *Tues.–Sun. 10–5.*

⑲ Peterskirche (St. Peter's Church). Evidence of Basel's late-Gothic heyday, the 13th-century St. Peter's Church sits across from **Petersplatz**, a lovely park next to the **Universität** (University). In the rose-lighted chapel are some interesting 14th-century frescoes. Call for information about services. ⊠ *Across Peters-Graben from Peterspl., Grossbasel* ☎*061/2618724.*

⑳ Pharmazie-Historisches Museum (Museum of Pharmaceutical History). Although pharmaceuticals as the topic of an entire museum may seem like too much of a necessary thing, this collection showcases Basel's roots in the industry that dominates the banks of the Rhine today. There are original and re-created pharmacy counters and all kinds of beakers, flacons, and ceramic measures. The old remedies on display now seem like candidates for a witches' brew: insects, adders, even poisonous plants. The museum is housed in Zum Vorderen Sessel, a home once frequented by Erasmus. You can request an English-language information sheet. ⊠ *Totengässlein 3, Grossbasel* ☎ *061/2649111* ⊕ *www. pharmaziemuseum.ch* ✉ *5 SF* ☉ *Tues.–Fri. 10–6, Sat. 10–5.*

⑮ Puppenhaus Museum (Doll House Museum). Bordering on the Barfüsserplatz, this museum has several floors filled with 18th- and 19th-century toys (including a cast of 2,000 Teddy bears) and classic miniature furnishings, displayed in highly detailed settings and landscapes. ⊠ *Steinenvorstadt 1, Grossbasel* ☎ *061/2259595* ⊕ *www. puppenhausmuseum.ch* ✉ *7 SF* ☉ *Fri.–Wed. 11–5, Thurs. 11–8.*

★ ㉒ Rathaus (Town Hall). This bright red late-Gothic edifice, built to honor the city's entry into the Swiss Confederation in 1501, towers over the Marktplatz. Only the middle portion actually dates from the 16th century; pseudo-Gothic work was added in 1900. A massive clock with figures of the Madonna, the emperor Henry II, and his wife, Kunegunde, adorns the center of the facade; all around it is a series of colorful frescoes, painted in 1608. Step into the courtyard, where the frescoes continue. ⊠ *Marktpl., Grossbasel.*

need a break? Choose a few jewel-like pastries and order loose-leaf-brewed tea in the carved-wood, clubby upstairs tearoom of the **Café Schiesser** (⊠ Marktpl. 19, Grossbasel ☎ 061/2616077), steeping since 1870.

Rheinsprung. A row of 15th- and 16th-century houses and a handful of ink makers' shops line this steep little alley in Grossbasel. Number 11 housed Basel's university when it was founded in 1460. ⊠ *Grossbasel, parallel to and south of Rhine, between Eiseng. and Stapfelbg.*

⑧ St. Alban-Tor (St. Alban's Gate). This original medieval city gate is set amid a lovely garden near remnants of the town's ramparts. Parts of the gate date from the 13th century. ⊠ *St. Alban-Berg, St. Alban.*

⑱ Spalentor (Spalen Gate). Like the St. Alban-Tor, the Spalentor served as one of Basel's medieval city gates. More imposing than graceful, the 14th-century structure has a toothy wooden portcullis; also note Basel's coat of arms atop the gate. ⊠ *Spalenvorstadt, Grossbasel.*

Statue of Helvetia. What would the woman pictured on most Swiss coins do if freed from the confines of currency? With spear and shield set aside (and with a packed suitcase in hand) this humanistic interpretation shows her seemingly contemplating the possibilities from a perch not far from the border of her homeland and the wide world beyond. ⊠ *Klein-basel, northeastern bank of Rhine, near Mittlere Rheinbrücke, Kleinbasel.*

⑭ Zoologischer Garten (Zoological Garden). Referred to by Baslers as *Zolli*, and famed for its armored rhinoceroses as well as its gorillas, pygmy hippopotamuses, and Javanese monkeys, this is no ordinary zoo. It's very child-friendly, and the enormous restaurant-pavilion in the center serves kid-size meals. ⊠ *Binningerstr. 40, Grossbasel* ☎ *061/2953535* ⊕ *www. zoobasel.ch* ✍ *14 SF* ⊗ *May–Aug., daily 8–6:30; Mar., Apr., Sept., and Oct., daily 8–6; Nov.–Feb., daily 8–5:30.*

off the beaten path

LANGENBRUCK & ENVIRONS – In the German-speaking countryside south of Basel, known as the Baselbiet, you'll find a handful of stately little villages with sturdy old guesthouses and a range—from medieval to Roman—of historic sites to explore. Take the winding forest road (A12) west of the freeway between Liestal and Oensingen, watching for Balsthal, Holderbank, Oberer Hauenstein, and Langenbruck; the industrial stretch just south of Liestal is less attractive. **Landgasthof Bären** (☎ 062/3901414 ⊕ www.baeren-langenbruck.ch) in Langenbruck offers superb regional cooking, inexpensive prix-fixe menus, and locally brewed beer.

VITRA DESIGN MUSEUM – Ten kilometers (6 mi) across the border in the German town of Weil am Rhein, this museum is a startling white geometric jumble designed by American architect Frank Gehry as part of an avant-garde building complex associated with the Vitra furniture manufacturer. The Gehry section generally hosts traveling architectural exhibits. The permanent collection, including the soaring Wall of Chairs (just what it sounds like), is displayed in the nearby Vitra Fire Station, accessible only on the guided tour. To get here by car, take A5/E35 north from Basel toward Karlsruhe; turn right just after German customs onto Route 532, parallel to the parking lot, and turn left after exiting at Weil am Rhein. The museum is 1½ km (about 1 mi) ahead on the right. Or from the Deutscher Bahnhof in Basel (also known as the Badischer Bahnhof), take Bus 55 toward Kandern to the Vitra stop. Bring your passport and call ahead to arrange for an English-speaking tour guide. ⊠ *Charles-Eames-Str. 1, Weil am Rhein, Germany* ☎ 49/76217023200 ⊕ *www.design-museum.de* ✍ *€5.50* ⊗ *Tues.–Sun. 11–6.*

Colonia Augusta Raurica (Augst)

Founded in 44–43 BC, Augst is the oldest Roman settlement on the Rhine. The site is reachable by car from Basel in 10 minutes or, from mid-April to mid-October, via a leisurely boat trip up the river. To view the restoration areas scattered around the almost suburban neighborhood, be prepared to do some walking.

a good tour

A scenic 1 hour, 50 minute boat ride will take you to Kaiseraugst, known for its thermal spas. From there walk uphill, following the signs to the ruins of **Augusta Raurica,** a 2,000-year-old Roman settlement that has been almost entirely rebuilt. Stop in for a map and a peek at the excavated treasures in the **Römermuseum.** Boats (Basler Personenschiffahrts-Gesellschaft ☏061/6399500 ⊕www.bpg.ch) to Augst depart from the Shifflände three times a day in high season. For a round-trip fare of 42 SF, you'll cruise slowly up the Rhine, passing the Old Town and the cathedral.

TIMING Augst merits at least a half day, slightly more if you go by boat. Drinks and cold snacks are available on all cruises, hot meals on some. The last boat returning to Basel each day leaves Augst around 5 PM.

Sights to See

★ **Augusta Raurica.** The remains of this 2,000-year-old Roman settlement have been extensively rebuilt (one suspects the Swiss might have done the same with Rome's Colosseum if they had gotten their hands on it), with substantial portions of the ancient town walls and gates, streets, water pipes, and heating systems all in evidence. The 1st-century BC theater is being restored to reflect its various incarnations in the 1st century BC and the 2nd and 4th centuries AD. An open-air festival to celebrate completion is planned for spring 2007.

Römermuseum (Roman Museum). Roman daily life is vividly depicted in this rebuilt ocher-hue home. Everything from the thermal baths to the ancient board games in the sitting rooms has been completely recreated. The museum also exhibits a treasure trove of Roman-era coins and silver unearthed in 1962. The objects, dating mostly from the 4th century, are believed to have been buried by the Romans in 350 to protect them from the ravages of the Alemanni, the German tribes who drove the Romans out of Switzerland. Trilingual (English/French/German) brochures are available. ⊠ *Giebenacherstr. 17, Augst* ☏ *061/8162222* ⊕ *www.augusta-raurica.ch* ⊠ *5 SF* ⊗ *Mar.–Oct., Mon. 1–5, Tues.–Sun. 10–5; Nov.–Feb., daily 10–noon and 1:30–5.*

WHERE TO EAT

Of course Basel can't help but show the sophistication of generations of cosmopolitan influence, so the city boasts a wide variety of innovative eateries, many of them world-class (and priced accordingly). In fact, dining in Basel tends to be a pricey venture, whether your sausage is stuffed with lobster and truffles or merely pork scraps. To keep expenses down, stick to beer-hall fare or look out for lunch specials (*Tagesmenu*).

WHAT IT COSTS In Swiss francs				
$$$$	$$$	$$	$	¢
MAIN COURSE over 60	40–60	20–40	15–20	under 15

Prices are per person for a main course at dinner.

★ $$$$ ✗ **Bruderholz.** Chef Patrick Zimmermann continues in the vein of the late master chef Hans Stucki at what is still one of Basel's best spots (regulars still often call it by its old name, Stucki). Classics include frog's legs with black truffles and chestnut honey duck with Sicilian blood oranges. The service at this restaurant, in the leafy residential neighborhood of Bruderholz, is formal and the seating competitive: reserve as far ahead as possible. ✉ *Bruderholzallee 42, Bruderholz* ☎ *061/3618222* ✍ *Reservations essential* ▤ *AE, DC, MC, V* ⊘ *Closed Sun. and Mon.*

$$–$$$$ ✗ **Teufelhof.** Monica and Dominique Thommy have transformed a grand
Fodor'sChoice old mansion into a cultural center boasting two restaurants, a trendy bar,
★ and even medieval ruins in the basement. The formal Bel Étage showcases Michael Baader's masterly culinary inventions, including reindeer fillets in rose hip sauce and St. Pierre fillet with tarragon risotto and lobster sauce. Taste wines by the glass then buy the bottle in the house wineshop. The casual, high-tech *Weinstube* serves 10 dishes that change daily, plus a three-course menu. ✉ *Leonhardsgraben 49/Heuberg 30, Grossbasel* ☎ *061/2611010* ▤ *AE, MC, V* ⊘ *Closed Sun. and Mon. No lunch Sat.*

$–$$$$ ✗ **Schlüsselzunft.** This historic guildhall holds an elegant little restaurant with a ceramic stove, as well as an inexpensive courtyard brasserie and café called the Schlüsselhöfli. The restaurant, which draws a business-lunch crowd, serves well-bred seasonal cuisine such as *Bâloise,* meaning liver with onions, and a Basel-style salmon dish. The brasserie serves a cheaper menu that changes daily. ✉ *Freie Str. 25, Grossbasel* ☎ *061/2612046* ✍ *Reservations essential* ▤ *AE, MC, V* ⊘ *Closed Sun.*

$$$ ✗ **Chez Donati.** Restaurateurs Peter Wyss and Romano Villa serve up a selection of Italian standards at this much-loved establishment, which is famous for its antipasti. Other specialties include osso buco and braised beef. The traditional, gilt-framed Venetian paintings are supplemented with modern art, but you can still get a view of the Rhine from your white-draped table. ✉ *St. Johanns-Vorstadt 48, Grossbasel* ☎ *061/3220919* ▤ *No credit cards* ⊘ *Closed Sun. and Mon.*

$$–$$$ ✗ **St. Alban-Eck.** This bistro, a five-minute walk behind the Kunstmuseum, is a well-known landmark in the Old Town. In a half-timber historic home, it's a real *petit coin sympa* (friendly little place), with plank wainscoting in natural wood, framed historic prints and net curtains. The cuisine gracefully mixes Swiss and French favorites: sole, salmon, grilled entrecôte, and beef medallions in duck-liver sauce with market vegetables. ✉ *St. Alban-Vorstadt 60, St. Alban* ☎ *061/2710320* ▤ *AE, DC, MC, V* ⊘ *Closed Sun. No lunch Sat.*

$$–$$$ ✗ **Zum Goldenen Sternen.** This *Gasthof's* building, dating from 1506, was moved from the town center to its current Rhine-side site, but it preserves its atmosphere through its restored antique beams, stenciled ceilings, and unvarnished planks. The food is classic French, only slightly updated. Game and fish are strong suits; one favorite is the *Fisch Har-*

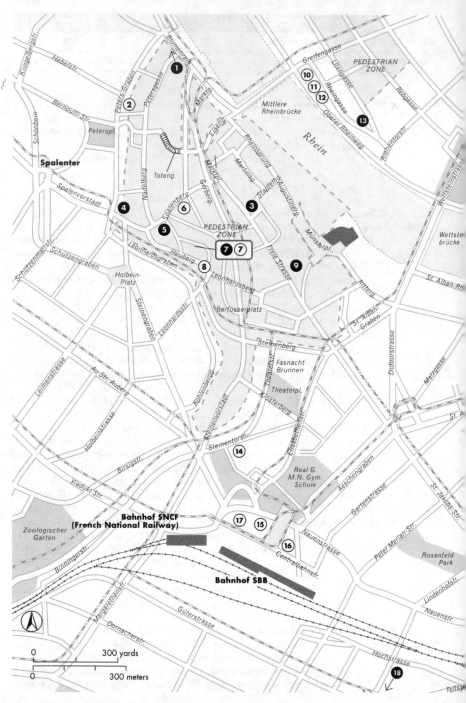

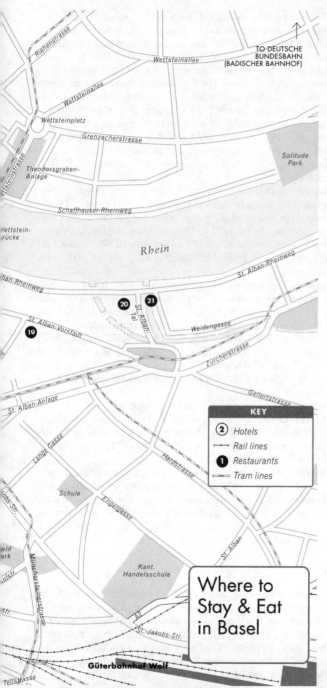

KEY

② Hotels
⊢—⊣ Rail lines
❶ Restaurants
⚊ Tram lines

Where to Stay & Eat in Basel

monie, a sampling of six kinds of fish with saffron sauce. There's also a seven-course tasting menu that changes monthly. The management does its best to discourage smoking and the use of cell phones. ⊠ *St. Alban-Rheinweg 70, St. Alban* ☎ *061/2721666* ▤ *AE, DC, MC, V.*

★ **$–$$** ✕ **Brauerei Fischerstube.** If you're serious about sampling the local color, stop in here for a cold one. The Fischerstube brews its own lagers and ales in the deep, frothing copper tanks at the end of the room. The house label, Ueli Bier, named for a Fasnacht clown, comes in a 5-liter tower served at your table or a 15-liter keg you can take home. Pretzels hang on racks on the sanded wooden tables, and the menu includes such local dishes as rump steak and grilled *Würstli* (sausages). There's a beer garden out back. ⊠ *Rheing. 45, Kleinbasel* ☎ *061/6926635* ▤ *MC, V.*

$–$$ ✕ **Löwenzorn.** This is a classic, comfortable gathering place serving typical Swiss food. The menu features everything from liver and kidney dishes to vegetarian offerings. Regulars come for a beer, a full plate, and some laughs with the friendly staff. With stained-glass lamps, ceramic stoves, and nice woodwork, it's a nice mix of bistro and beer hall. ⊠ *Gemsberg 2, Grossbasel* ☎ *061/2614213* ▤ *AE, DC, MC, V* ☉ *Closed Sun.*

★ **$–$$** ✕ **Restaurant/Café Papiermühle.** With the splashing of the paper mill's waterwheel in the background, this is a restful spot for lunch or an afternoon snack (it's only open until 6 PM). The hand-scrawled chalkboard and printed menus aren't translated, but most often include two set meals, brunch favorites (quiches and *Birchermüsli,* the original, creamy, fruity version of muesli), salads, soups, and pasta dishes. Hand signals, however, are all you'll need to point out one of the homemade cakes. ⊠ *St. Alban-Tal 35, St. Alban* ☎ *061/2724848* ▤ *No credit cards* ☉ *Closed Mon. No dinner.*

¢–$$ ✕ **Zur Harmonie.** University students pack this *Jugendstil* (art nouveau) marvel, with its parquet floors and etched mirrors. Choose from a selection of delicious French and Swiss favorites, such as mussels, Wiener schnitzel, or the popular bowl of salad and sausage. ⊠ *Petersgraben 71, Grossbasel* ☎ *061/2720220* ▤ *AE, DC, MC, V.*

¢–$ ✕ **Café Pfalz.** This bookish little self-service café, down a narrow street near the cathedral, dishes out veggie plates, sausages, and quiche in a trim beechwood-and-black contemporary setting. The impressive salad bar usually holds 25 different ingredients. There is also a juice bar and at least one hot daily special. ⊠ *Münsterberg 11, Grossbasel* ☎ *061/2726511* ▤ *No credit cards* ☉ *Closed weekends.*

WHERE TO STAY

With its industry, its banking, and its busy convention center offering a different trade fair most months, Basel is a city that prides itself on being a business center. The drawback, however, is that hotel prices tend to be steep, bargains in short supply, and amenities—minibars, data ports, fax machines—more important than atmosphere in the all-out competition for expense-account travelers. When there's a trade fair in town, every bed for miles can be filled, so book well ahead.

WHAT IT COSTS In Swiss francs					
	$$$$	$$$	$$	$	¢
DOUBLE ROOM	over 350	250–350	175–250	100–175	under 100

Prices are for two people in a standard double room in high season, including breakfast, tax, and service charge.

★ $$$–$$$$ **Euler.** An archetypal old-world hotel, this landmark attracts a loyal business clientele that mingles over a *Cüpli* (glass of champagne) in the famous leather-and-red-velvet bar. Duvets billow over the bed frames in some of the cushier rooms and suites; standard rooms are furnished classically with reproduction antique furnishings. All have triple-glazed windows to cut out tram-traffic noise, unavoidable because of its city center location. ✉ *Centralbahnpl. 14, Grossbasel, CH-4002* ☎ *061/2758000* 🖷 *061/2758050* 🌐 *www.hoteleuler.ch* *55 rooms, 9 suites* *2 restaurants, some in-room data ports, minibars, bar, babysitting, concierge, meeting rooms, parking (fee), no-smoking rooms; no a/c in some rooms* 💳 *AE, DC, MC, V.*

★ $$$–$$$$ **Teufelhof.** This bastion of style and cuisine has an Art Hotel whose nine rooms are works of art in their own right: each is redecorated by the owner, Dominique Thommy, every three years. By contrast, the serenely simple rooms of the adjoining Galery Hotel function collectively as a canvas for one particular artist to show off the work from one of his periods. There's a food-and-wine shop situated in the cellar. An in-house theater puts on various shows in German from mid-September to early May. In-room TVs are available upon request. The hotel is fitted with wireless computer connections. ✉ *Leonhardsgraben 49/Heuberg 30, Grossbasel, CH-4051* ☎ *061/2611010* 🖷 *061/2611004* 🌐 *www.teufelhof.ch* *29 rooms, 4 suites* *2 restaurants, café, bar, wineshop, theater, parking (fee); no a/c, no room TVs* 💳 *AE, MC, V* 🍴 *BP.*

★ $$$–$$$$ **Victoria.** Once you enter through the revolving doors into the marble-floor reception area with its Greek statue and high-tech lighting, you will understand this hotel's claim to combine old-fashioned elegance with modern comfort. The rooms are tastefully decorated with useful modular furniture accented by carefully chosen antique reproductions. The bathrooms are black and white and evoke the art deco aesthetic. The restaurant and café are very popular with the locals and have a luxurious atmosphere. ✉ *Centralbahnpl. 3-4, Grossbasel, CH-4002* ☎ *061/2707070* 🖷 *061/2707077* 🌐 *www.victoria.balehotels.ch* *100 rooms, 9 suites* *Restaurant, café, in-room safes, minibars, exercise equipment, bar, business services, meeting rooms, parking (fee), no-smoking rooms* 💳 *AE, DC, MC, V.*

$$–$$$$ **Basel.** This all-modern hotel has become part of the Old Town neighborhood, its bars and restaurants filling with locals after work. The wood-panel rooms are accented with contemporary leather furniture and chrome; polished marble adds luster to the baths. The clientele during the week is almost exclusively business executives, which means there's plenty of room on the weekends. The hotel is fitted with wireless computer connections. ✉ *Münzg. 12, Grossbasel, CH-4001* ☎ *061/2646800* 🖷 *061/2646811* 🌐 *www.hotel-basel.ch* *69 rooms, 3 suites* *2 restaurants,*

café, in-room data ports, some in-room faxes, in-room safes, minibars, bars, meeting rooms, no-smoking floors ☰ AE, DC, MC, V ❮O❯ BP.

$$–$$$ ▣ **Krafft.** Smack on the waterfront sits this elegant mansion with a mo-
Fodor'sChoice saic-tile entrance hall, elaborate moldings, glittering chandeliers, and a
★ sinuous atrium stairwell. The service more than makes up for the oc-
casional signs of wear and tear. Many of the rooms have a mix-and-match feel to them. There's a traditional dining room with river views for break-fast and dinner, but the downstairs Zem Schnooggeloch (Mosquito's Den) is where everyone gathers for wine and cheese. The waterfront terrace café is justifiably popular. ✉ Rheing. 12, Kleinbasel, CH-4058 ☎ 061/ 6909130 ✍ 061/6909131 ⊕ www.hotelkrafft.ch ✍ 50 rooms, 45 with bath ⟋ Restaurant, Stübli; no a/c ☰ AE, DC, MC, V ❮O❯ CP.

$$–$$$ ▣ **Merian am Rhein.** This hotel has a modern, airy look accented with touches of gray wood and russet leather. The best rooms overlook the river. The Café Spitz has been a meeting place since the early 13th cen-tury, but you wouldn't guess it to look at it; now it's done in light wood, linens, and halogen lamps. Fish dominate the decor as well as the menu. ✉ Rheing. 2, Kleinbasel, CH-4005 ☎ 061/6851111 ✍ 061/6851101 ⊕ www.merian-hotel.ch ✍ 65 rooms ⟋ Restaurant, café, minibars, in-room VCRs, meeting rooms, parking (fee), no-smoking floor; no a/c ☰ AE, DC, MC, V ❮O❯ CP.

★ **$$–$$$** ▣ **Radisson SAS.** This business hotel is one of the largest in the city, but you'd never think so when you see it from the street. It's built in a fig-ure-eight pattern around two courtyards, ensuring that most of the gen-erously sized rooms have garden views. Although the lobby seems cold with its white walls and gray marble, the staff offers a warm welcome. The hotel is fitted with wireless Internet connections. ✉ Steinentorstr. 25, Grossbasel, CH-4001 ☎ 061/2272727 ✍ 061/2272828 ⊕ www. basel.radissonsas.com ✍ 197 rooms, 8 suites ⟋ Restaurant, café, room service, in-room data ports, in-room safes, minibars, cable TV, pool, ex-ercise equipment, massage, sauna, steam room, bar, Internet, meeting rooms, parking (fee), no-smoking floors ☰ AE, DC, MC, V.

$$ ▣ **Bad Schauenburg.** About 10 km (6 mi) southeast of Basel, this charm-ing country inn has suites decorated in Biedermeier-era antiques and a restaurant serving cuisine de marché (market-fresh food). Take the main road toward Liestal, then follow the signs after the turnoff in Frenk-endorf. ✉ Schauenburgerstr. 76, Liestal CH-4410 ☎ 061/9062727 ✍ 061/9062700 ⊕ www.badschauenburg.ch ✍ 31 rooms, 3 suites ⟋ Restaurant, Internet, meeting rooms; no a/c ☰ AE, DC, MC, V ◷ Closed mid-Dec.–mid-Jan. ❮O❯ BP.

★ **$$** ▣ **Central.** If you hadn't just picked up your key from the reception desk of a four-star hotel, you might have reservations about making your way down an alleyway near the train station to get to your room. But this hotel is under the same management as the nearby Euler, which ensures that you'll receive the same level of service. Rooms can be on the small side but are tasteful and cheerful—dashes of vivid color include tangerine bedspreads. Rooms with high-speed Internet connections are available. ✉ Kücheng. 7, Grossbasel, CH-4002 ☎ 061/2758000 ✍ 061/2758050 ⊕ www.hoteleuler.ch ✍ 23 rooms ⟋ Some in-room data ports, bar, park-ing (fee); no a/c ☰ AE, DC, MC, V.

$$ ⊞ **Rochat.** Location is this modest but roomy property's main asset; it's across from the university. The main building, a brownstone dating from 1898, has a dormlike feel, while the whitewashed annex, with its twisting hallways, comes across as a scaled-down inn. The restaurant does not serve alcohol. ⊠ *Petersgraben 23, Grossbasel, CH-4051* ☎ *061/2618140* 🖶 *061/2616492* ⊕ *www.hotelrochat.ch* ⇌ *50 rooms* ⚒ *Restaurant, café, minibars, meeting rooms, no-smoking rooms; no a/c* ⊟ *AE, DC, MC, V* ⏐⊙⏐ *BP.*

★ $–$$ ⊞ **Hotel Brasserie Au Violon.** The former residents here—priests and prisoners—never had it so good. Housed in a 12th-century building that served as a cloister and then a prison, the hotel now captivates its clientele with subdued elegance, a peaceful location, and a terrific restaurant. There are some reminders of the building's austere past—rooms overlooking the courtyard still conform to cell-block arrangements, with uniformly tight square footage. Rooms facing the town offer more space. The brasserie, with its mirrored bar, deco fixtures, and iron-leg tables, serves French classics. ⊠ *Im Lohnhof 4, Grossbasel, CH-4051* ☎ *061/2698711* 🖶 *061/2698712* ⊕ *www.au-violon.com* ⇌ *18 rooms, 2 suites* ⚒ *Restaurant; no a/c, no TV in some rooms* ⊟ *AE, DC, MC, V* ⊙ *Closed between Christmas and New Year.*

★ $ ⊞ **Hecht am Rhein.** Situated between two more expensive hotels, this budget lodging offers faded comfort and a friendly staff. The rooms here seem bigger than in the neighboring establishments and are simply furnished with aged leather chairs, wood-backed beds, and an astonishing selection of art prints. Each floor has a large seating area and clean, bright, and inviting showers. There is a welcoming breakfast room on the top floor. The popular terrace restaurant serves pizza in the summer. ⊠ *Rheing. 8, Kleinbasel, CH-4058* ☎ *061/6912220* 🖶 *061/6810788* ⊕ *www. huettenmoser.com* ⇌ *30 rooms* ⚒ *Restaurant; no a/c, no room TVs* ⊟ *AE, DC, MC, V* ⏐⊙⏐ *BP.*

NIGHTLIFE & THE ARTS

For a complete listing of events, pick up a copy of *Basel Live,* a booklet published every two weeks. It's written partially in English. *Events in Basel,* another listings publication, comes out every six months and is fully bilingual (German-English). Both are available at the tourist office and usually at hotel desks. If you'd like to play it by ear, the Steinenvorstadt is crowded with cinemas, bars, and young people, and on the Kleinbasel side, there are late-night bars along the Oberer Rheinweg.

Nightlife

Bars & Lounges

The extremely popular **Bar des Arts** (⊠ Barfüsserpl. 6, Grossbasel ☎ 061/2735737), a bistro/pub/lounge, pulls in an interesting mix of patrons. It began as an arty experiment, but the crimson interior of **Bar Rouge** (⊠ Level 31 Messeturm, Am Messepl., Kleinbasel ☎ 061/3613031) has caught on. The bar is on the top floor of the trade-fair tower. The landmark **Brauner Mutz** (⊠ Barfüsserpl. 10, Grossbasel ☎ 061/2613369) is a big beer hall with long wooden tables and a stein in every fist.

Campari Bar (⊠ Steinenberg 7, Grossbasel ☎ 061/2728383), behind the Kunsthalle and Tinguely Fountain, pulls in an artsy crowd with its pop-art interior and tree-canopied terrace. Inside the Hotel Euler, the **Euler Bar** (⊠ Centralbahnpl. 14, Grossbasel ☎ 061/2758000) draws a conservative crowd after work. **Zum Sperber** (⊠ Münzg. 12, Grossbasel ☎ 061/2646800) fills tables and bar stools with well-heeled workers at happy hour; there's live music some evenings.

Dancing & Nightclubs

Atlantis (⊠ Klosterberg 13, Grossbasel ☎ 061/2289698) hosts a regular roster of live blues, rock and alternative bands in a loftlike setting. The futuristic **Mad Max** (⊠ Steinentorstr. 35, Grossbasel ☎ 061/2814113) has two floors catering to the thirtysomething crowd, one playing rock and and the other playing disco. At **Plaza Dancing Club** (⊠ Am Messepl., Kleinbasel ☎ 061/6923206) the DJ spins pop hits.

Queen's Disco Bar (⊠ Blumenrain 10, Grossbasel ☎ 061/2613050) is an upscale discotheque. A traditional cabaret, **Singerhaus** (⊠ Marktpl., Grossbasel ☎ 061/2616466) opens at 7, and dancing starts at 9.

The Arts

Advance bookings for many live performances can be made inside Bider & Tanner at **au Concert** (⊠ Aeschenvorstadt 24, Grossbasel ☎ 061/2722229). You can also purchase tickets at **Musik Hug** (⊠ Freie Str. 70, Grossbasel ☎ 061/2723395).

Film

Movies in Basel are usually shown in the original language with subtitles. Most theaters are along Steinenvorstadt in the Old Town, and the titles and times are prominently posted. In summer there are open-air cinemas located in various locations, such as on the Münsterplatz.

Music

The **Musik-Akademie der Stadt Basel** (⊠ Leonhardsgraben 4–6, Grossbasel ☎ 061/2645757) is an important music academy drawing top-drawer international performers. The **Stadtcasino** (⊠ Steinenberg 14, Grossbasel ☎ 061/2263600) hosts the Basel Symphony Orchestra, the Basel Chamber Orchestra, and a wide range of visiting performers.

Theater

The **Musical Theater** (⊠ Feldbergstr. 53, Kleinbasel ☎ 061/6998899) is the venue for touring companies. **Theater Basel** (⊠ Theaterstr. 7, Grossbasel ☎ 061/2951133) hosts opera, operetta, and dance performances, as well as drama (usually in German). Book in advance Monday to Saturday 10 to 6:45. The box office opens one hour before the performance.

SPORTS & THE OUTDOORS

Golf

Golf & Country Club Basel (⊠ Hagenthal-le-Bas, France ☎ 033/389685091) is one of the most beautiful golf courses in Europe, with stunning views of the Black Forest. A half hour from Basel, the course is just across the French border. It's open to nonmembers on weekdays.

MAD ABOUT SOCCER

Founded in 1893, Fussball Club Basel is one thing that can encourage the city's normally reserved residents to wave their arms, stomp their feet, and scream at the top of their lungs. Although the soccer team enjoyed many successful seasons in the 1960s and 1970s, its luck then seemed to run out. This didn't squash the support of its loyal fans, however. With most of the city backing the team, and whole families turning out to watch the matches, tickets are hard to come by. Surprising really, when you realize that their home stadium, St. Jakob-Park, is one of Switzerland's largest arenas. But when there's a game against their rivals from Zürich, the 30,000 seats are filled. Such devotion has helped FC Basel to become, once again, one of the most successful clubs in Switzerland. In recent years the team has have topped the internal league more than once. All eyes are on the future now as Switzerland is set to cohost the 2008 European Soccer Championships with Austria.

Squash

Sportcenter Paradies (⊠ Bettenstr. 73 ☎ 061/4859580) has eight squash courts. You can rent equipment on the premises.

SHOPPING

The major downtown shopping district stretches along **Freie Strasse** and **Gerbergasse,** where you can find many one-of-a-kind boutiques. More reasonably priced shops along **Steinenvorstadt** cater to a younger crowd.

Department Stores

EPA (⊠ Gerberg. 4, Grossbasel ☎ 061/2699250) carries a wide selection of clothing and household goods, as well as groceries in the basement. **Globus** (⊠ Marktpl. 2, Grossbasel ☎ 061/2684545) is an upscale department store, with gourmet edibles and sleek clothes. Whether you're in need of socks, toothpaste, or chocolate on the cheap, head to **Manor** (⊠ Greifeng. 22, Grossbasel ☎ 061/6854699). In the main train station, the supermarket **Migros** (⊠ Centralbahnpl., Grossbasel ☎ 061/2799745) stays open until 10 PM.

Specialty Stores

Antique Books

Among many fine competitors, **Erasmushaus** (⊠ Bäumleing. 18, Grossbasel ☎ 061/2289933) has one of the city's largest collections of fine antique manuscripts, books, and autographs, mostly in German but including some multilingual art publications. If they can not help you in the search for a particular tome, they will be happy to supply the names of the other specialist shops in the Basel area.

Calligraphy

Abraxas (⊠ Rheinsprung 6, Grossbasel ☎ 061/2616070) is a great source for fine writing instruments and paraphernalia, from thick paper and delicate fountain pens to luxurious sealing waxes and reproductions of antique silver seals. **Scriptorium am Rheinsprung** (⊠ Rheinsprung 2, Grossbasel ☎ 061/2613900) mixes its own ink and carries calligraphy pens.

Coins

Münzen & Medaillen (⊠ Malzg. 25, Grossbasel ☎ 061/2727544) is a good place to find coins and medals dating from antiquity to the mid-19th century.

Crafts & Gifts

Though primarily specializing in home furnishings, **Atelier Baumgartner** (⊠ Spalenberg 8, Grossbasel ☎ 061/2610843) also stocks Swiss and European handicrafts, including music boxes and nutcrackers from the Erzgebirge region of Germany. **Heimatwerk** (⊠ Schneiderg. 2, Grossbasel ☎ 061/2619178) sells Swiss crafts from traditional ceramics to Basel-made embroidered silk ribbons. Highly specialized handiwork comes from **Johann Wanner** (⊠ Spalenberg 14, Grossbasel ☎ 061/2614826), which sells Christmas goods year-round, including handblown, hand-painted, and hand-molded ornaments, tin Victorian miniatures, Advent cards and calendars, and Christmas cards. **Zem Baselstab** (⊠ Schnabelg. 8, Grossbasel ☎ 061/2611016) has Fasnacht figurines and other Basel paraphernalia.

Food Specialties

Bachmann & Co. (⊠ Gerberg. 51, Grossbasel ☎ 061/2613583 ⊠ Blumenrain 1, Grossbasel ☎ 061/2614152 ⊠ Centralbahnpl. 7, Grossbasel ☎ 061/2712627) carries a Basel specialty called *Leckerli*, a chewy cookie made of almonds, honey, dried fruit, and kirsch. **Glausi's** (⊠ Spalenberg 12, Grossbasel ☎ 061/2618008) ages its own cheeses, which are sold alongside myriad fresh Swiss specialties. The famous **Läckerli-Huus** (⊠ Gerberg. 57, Grossbasel ☎ 061/2642323) sells a variety of sweets, including wonderful Leckerli. A large selection of gift canisters and a shipping service make getting gifts home a cinch. **Schiesser** (⊠ Marktpl. 19, Grossbasel ☎ 061/2616077), a convivial tearoom that opened in 1870, sells carefully crafted (and costly) confections in its downstairs shop.

Linens

Caraco (⊠ Gerberg. 77, Falknerstr. entrance, Grossbasel ☎ 061/2613577) sells handmade Swiss lace and embroidered goods. **Langenthal** (⊠ Gerberg. 26, Grossbasel ☎ 061/2610900) offers mostly Swiss products: tea towels, tablecloths, and folk-style aprons. **Sturzenegger** (⊠ Theaterstr. 4, Grossbasel ☎ 061/2616867) specializes in household items, including lace from St. Gallen.

Lingerie

Beldona (⊠ Freie Str. 103, Grossbasel ☎ 061/2731170) stocks Swiss cotton lingerie. **Fogal** (⊠ Freie Str. 44, Grossbasel ☎ 061/2617461 ⊠ Freie Str. 4, Grossbasel ☎ 061/2611220) sells its famous Swiss hosiery at two locations; both branches set out trays of clearance goods. **Sturzenegger**

(⊠ Theaterstr. 4, Grossbasel ☎ 061/2616867) carries an extensive line of undergarments with labels such as Hanro.

Men's Clothes
K. Aeschbacher (⊠ Schnabelg. 4, Grossbasel ☎ 061/2615058) carries unique Swiss silk ties, scarves, robes, and pajamas. For the smoking-jacket set, **Renz** (⊠ Freie Str. 2a, Grossbasel ☎ 061/2612991) has a small but impeccable selection of fine Swiss-cotton pajamas and Scottish cashmeres.

Shoes
Kropart (⊠ Schneiderg. 16, Grossbasel ☎ 061/2615133) specializes in trendy, comfort-oriented styles. **Müki** (⊠ Münsterberg 14, Grossbasel ☎ 061/2712436) focuses on functional yet stylish European-made kids' shoes, from patent-leather loafers to brightly colored fleece house slippers. **Rive Gauche** (⊠ Schneiderg. 1, Grossbasel ☎ 061/2611080) carries high-end designer shoes. This is the place to satisfy that Prada and Mui Mui craving.

Toys
Bercher & Sternlicht (⊠ Spalenberg 45, Grossbasel ☎ 061/2612550) has miniature trains and accessories. **Spielegge** (⊠ Rümelinspl. 7, Grossbasel ☎ 061/2614488) places an emphasis on wood, with chisel-carved puppets and whimsical watercolor puzzles of fairy-tale scenes. **Spielhuus** (⊠ Eiseng. 8, Grossbasel ☎ 061/2649898) is a good source for board games and reasonably priced children's toys, as well as fanciful Fasnacht costumes.

Women's Clothes
Le mouton à cinq pattes (⊠ Eiseng. 6, Grossbasel ☎ 061/2620007) sounds the siren call of a bargain; you'll find mostly cut-rate French and Italian styles. **Trois Pommes** (⊠ Freie Str. 74, Grossbasel ☎ 061/2729255) dominates the high end of fashion, with Jil Sander, Prada, Gucci and Dolce & Gabbana.

BASEL A TO Z

To research prices, get advice from other travelers, and book travel arrangements, visit www.fodors.com.

AIR TRAVEL
CARRIERS There are connecting flights from Zürich into EuroAirport on Swiss.
🚩 **Airlines & Contacts Swiss** ☎ 061/3253525 for reservations, 0848/852000 within Switzerland.

AIRPORTS & TRANSFERS
Basel uses EuroAirport (just across the border in France), which is shared by Mulhouse in France and Freiburg in Germany. Direct flights link Basel to most major European cities. The nearest intercontinental airport is Unique Zürich Airport, which is approximately 80 km (50 mi) southeast of Basel.
🚩 **Airport Information EuroAirport** ☎ 061/3252511. **Unique Zürich Airport** ☎ 0900/300313.

AIRPORT
TRANSFERS
Regular bus service runs between EuroAirport and the SBB train station in the center of Basel. The trip takes about 20 minutes and costs 3.60 SF per person.

One-way taxi fare from the airport to the Basel center is approximately 40 SF; it takes about 15 minutes in light traffic and up to 30 minutes at rush hours (around 7.30 AM to 8.30 AM, noon to 2 PM, and 5 PM to 7 PM). There are normally cabs at the taxi stand, but if you need to call one from the airport, make sure you leave the building on the Swiss side.
Taxis & Shuttles 33er Taxi ☎ 061/6333333. **Mini Cab** ☎ 061/2711111. **Taxi-Zentrale** ☎ 061/2712222.

CAR TRAVEL
The German Autobahn A5 enters Basel from the north and leads directly to the Rhine and the center of the city. From France, the auto route A35 (E9) peters out at the frontier, and secondary urban roads lead to the center. The A2 Autobahn leads off to the rest of Switzerland. Since most of the city's sights are within walking distance of downtown, it's advisable to park your car for the duration of your visit.

EMERGENCIES
For medical emergencies (including late-night pharmacy referrals) or to contact the police, refer to the phone numbers listed below.
Hospital (Kantonsspital) ☎ 061/2652525. **Medical Emergencies** ☎ 061/2611515. **Police** ☎ 117.

ENGLISH-LANGUAGE MEDIA
Bider & Tanner has a good range of fiction and nonfiction, plus travel-focused publications. Jäggi shelves plenty of best-sellers.
Bookstores Bider & Tanner ✉ Aeschenvorstadt 2, at Bankverein, Grossbasel ☎ 061/2069999. **Jäggi** ✉ Freie Str. 32, Grossbasel ☎ 061/2642626.

TOURS
Basel Tourismus organizes a daily two-hour walking tour of the city. This starts from the tourist information office in the Stadtcasino and caters to German, French, and English speakers. Tours take place from May to mid-October, Monday through Saturday at 2:30. From mid-October to April the walking tours are held every Saturday at 2:30. The cost is 15 SF. On Sunday afternoon the tour goes to the Roman ruins at Augusta Raurica.

TRAIN TRAVEL
There are two main rail stations in Basel. The Schweizerische Bundesbahnen connects to destinations in Switzerland as well as in France. The station is in Grossbasel. The Deutsche Bundesbahn, locally known as the Badischer Bahnhof, runs to Germany. The station is across the river in Kleinbasel.
Train Information Deutsche Bundesbahn ✉ Schwarzwalderstr. and Riehenstr., Kleinbasel ☎ 061/6901215. **Schweizerische Bundesbahnen** ✉ Centralbahnstr., Grossbasel ☎ 0900/300300.

TRAM TRAVEL

Most trams run every 6–7 minutes all day, every 12–15 minutes in the evening. Tickets must be bought at the automatic machines at every stop (which give change). Stops are marked with green-and-white signs; generally the trams run from 5.30 or 6 in the morning until midnight or shortly thereafter. As long as you travel within the central Zone 10, you pay 2.80 SF per ticket. If you are making a short trip—four stops or fewer—you pay 1.80 SF. *Mehrfahrtenkarten* (multijourney cards) allow you 12 trips for the price of 10 and can be purchased from the ticket office at Barfüsserplatz. *Tageskarten* (day cards) allow unlimited travel all day within the central zone and cost 8 SF. Guests at hotels in Basel receive a complimentary Basel Mobility Ticket for free use of all public transportation for the duration of their stay. Holders of the Swiss Pass travel free on all Basel public transport systems.

TRANSPORTATION AROUND BASEL

The best way to see Basel is on foot or by tram, as the landmarks, museums, and even the zoo, radiate from the Old Town center on the Rhine, and the network of rails covers the territory thoroughly. Taxis are costly, less efficient, and less available than the ubiquitous tram. Parking in the city center is competitive and in some areas nonexistent. If you've driven in by car, you'll save time and hassle by heading straight for an all-day garage, such as the Parkhaus Elisabethen, on Heuwaage near the SBB train station. Expect to pay around 25 SF per day.

TRAVEL AGENCIES

🚩 **Local Agent Referrals Reisebüro Müller** ✉ Steinenvorstadt 33, Grossbasel ☎ 061/2059797.

VISITOR INFORMATION

The main tourist information desk in Basel is in the Stadtcasino at Barfüsserplatz and is open weekdays 8.30–6.30, Saturday 10–5, Sunday, and holidays 10–4. The Basel tourism branch at the SBB train station can also help you with hotel reservations and museum information. The BaselCard provides admission to the city's museums and gives discounts and special offers at restaurants, galleries, and selected stores. It can be purchased for 20 SF, 27 SF, or 35 SF (for one, two, or three days, respectively) at Basel Tourismus and at most hotels.

🚩 **Tourist Information Basel Tourismus** (Basel Tourism) ✉ Stadt-Casino, Steinenberg 14, Grossbasel ☎ 061/2686868 🖷 061/2686870 ⊕ www.baseltourismus.ch. **Basel Tourismus** ✉ Bahnhof, SBB, Grossbasel ☎ 061/2686870.

FRIBOURG, NEUCHÂTEL & THE JURA

7

Updated by
Sue Birrer

SHOULDERED BY THE MORE PROMINENT CANTONS of Bern and Vaud, the cantons of Fribourg, Neuchâtel, and Jura are easily overlooked by hurried visitors. If they do stop, it is usually for a quick dip into Fribourg and Gruyères. That leaves the rest of this largely untouched area to the Swiss, who enjoy its relatively unspoiled nature and relaxed approach to life.

Although the strict cantonal borders are a messy reflection of historic power struggles, the regional boundaries are unmistakable, even to an outsider. Fribourg starts in the pre-Alpine foothills above Charmey and rolls down across green hills, tidy farms, and ancient towns until it reaches the silty shores of the Murten, Neuchâtel, and Biel lakes. The region of Neuchâtel begins in these silt-rich fields (which grow everything from lettuce to tobacco), sweeps across Lac Neuchâtel to its chateaux- and vineyard-lined western shore, and rises up to the Jura Mountains. The Jura is a deceptive region: its smoky, forested slopes, sheltering the "arc" of the Jurassian watchmaking industry, suddenly flatten out onto open, sunny plateaus, gentle pastures, and low-roof farmhouses. Its serpentine Doubs River and imposing falls cascade after the dam-created Lac des Brenets.

The Röstigraben (or Hash-Brown Trench, so called because Swiss Germans eat lots of *Rösti*) is the tongue-in-cheek name for the linguistic border where French meets German. It runs through Fribourg and butts up against the northern borders of the Jura and Neuchâtel. In some towns you can walk into a *boulangerie* (bread bakery) selling dark *Vollkornbrot* (whole-grain bread) or find a family named Neuenschwand who hasn't spoken German for generations.

Exploring Fribourg, Neuchâtel & the Jura

These three regions are roughly organized like a hand. At the wrist are the Alpine foothills of Fribourg; these curve gently down to the palm of flatter Neuchâtel, with the long ellipse of Lac Neuchâtel. The Jura's rugged fingers form valleys in the Jura Mountains and finally rest on the plateaus. The formal cantonal borders defy the Swiss penchant for neatness since they're based on medieval landholdings. For instance, the present-day cantonal borders of Fribourg still surround odd bits belonging to other cantons, such as the town of Avenches, which technically belongs to Vaud.

About the Restaurants

Both Fribourg and Neuchâtel have a plethora of top-quality, French-influenced, *gastronomique* (ultragourmet) restaurants. They offer far cheaper lunch menus (three or more courses) or at least an *assiette du jour* (daily special) for less than 20 SF. No one here lays down strict dress codes. Ever sensible, the Swiss expect common sense from their customers: the fancier the restaurant, the fancier the attire, but you won't be thrown out for not wearing a tie. Restaurants open about 6 in the evening, though diners tend to arrive closer to 7:30, and kitchens wind down between 9.30 and 10. Lunch is usually served from 11:30 to 2, but you can often get simple fare even after that. Try a *crêperie* for a quick, cheap meal that still has local flavor. The closer you are to France, the more of these you'll find.

WHAT IT COSTS In Swiss francs				
	$$$$	$$$	$$	$	¢
MAIN COURSE	over 60	40–60	25–40	15–25	under 15

Prices are per person for a main course at dinner.

About the Hotels

As they become more tourist-oriented, Fribourg, Neuchâtel, and Jura are developing a better hotel infrastructure. Fribourg is the best equipped, though there's still only a handful of choices in the Old Town. In Neuchâtel most lodgings are along the lake. Not all towns in the Jura have decent hotels; you may prefer to make excursions from Neuchâtel, La Chaux-de-Fonds, or Basel. Don't expect air-conditioning either; assume hotels don't have it unless it's specified. Many hotels offer more than one meal plan, so even if BP (breakfast plan) is specified in a review, it doesn't hurt to ask if another plan is available.

WHAT IT COSTS In Swiss francs				
	$$$$	$$$	$$	$	¢
DOUBLE ROOM	over 350	250–350	175–250	100–175	under 100

Prices are for two people in a standard double room in high season, including tax and service.

Timing

Throughout the year you'll encounter lighter tourist traffic here than in any other region. Summer is a lovely time in the Jura, when forest glades become ripe with the smells of the woods. Fribourg is also pleasant in summer, but crowds tend to pick up, especially in Gruyères. Spring and fall are beautiful times to visit anywhere in this region. January is great for winter sports. You can't be sure of snow in December, and in February, some canton or other (not to mention the Germans, English, Dutch, and Italians) will invariably have school vacations, so slopes get pretty crowded. When the snow lasts, March is also ideal.

FRIBOURG

With its landscape of green hills against the craggy peaks of the pre-Alps, Fribourg is one of Switzerland's most rural cantons. Its famous Fribourgeois cows—the Holsteins (black and white, the colors of the cantonal coat of arms)—provide the canton with its main income, although light industry is replacing the cows. Fondue was invented here, as was Gruyère cheese and Switzerland's famous *crème-double* (double cream).

Though the major sights themselves don't require too much time, they are scattered throughout the region so it takes time to get to them. You can easily explore much of this area by train, but renting a car will save you some time and allow you to go at your own pace (though many places are connected by two-lane roads often used by tractors).

Numbers in the text correspond to numbers in the margin and on the Fribourg, Neuchâtel, and the Jura map.

7

If you have 1 or 2 days

If you're coming from the east (Bern, Basel, or Zürich), start with the Old Town and lakefront promenade of ⊠ **Neuchâtel ⓫** ⌐. Go on to the medieval lakeside town of **Murten ⓵**, and continue to ⊠ **Fribourg ⓵**. Make a detour to **Gruyères ⓵** on your way to Lausanne or Geneva. If you're coming from the south (Geneva or Lausanne), reverse the order.

If you have 3 or more days

More time allows you to leisurely crawl over ancient ramparts, wander through a medieval town, and visit a 17th-century château. Visit ⊠ **Fribourg ⓵** ⌐, cut south to the castle at **Gruyères ⓵**, and from there circle northwest through the ancient towns of **Romont ⓵**, **Payerne ⓼**, **Avenches ⓽**, and **Murten ⓵** on your way to ⊠ **Neuchâtel ⓫**. From Neuchâtel you can either head south along the Route du Vignoble (Vineyard Road) to the château town of **Grandson ⓵** or travel northwest through watchmaking country to **La Chaux-de-Fonds ⓵**. Finish by enjoying the natural beauty of the Jura, perhaps stopping at **Saignelégier ⓵** to go horseback riding or at **St-Ursanne ⓵** to canoe down the Doubs River.

Fribourg

★ ⌐ ⓵   *34 km (21 mi) southwest of Bern.*

Between the rich pasturelands of the Swiss plateau and the Alpine foothills, the Sarine River (called the Saane by German speakers) twists in an S-curve, its sandstone cliffs joined by webs of arching bridges. In one of the curves of the river is the medieval city of Fribourg. The city grew in overlapping layers; it's an astonishing place of hills and cobblestones, ramparts and Gothic fountains, ancient passageways and worn wooden stairs, red-orange rooftops and sudden views. Only on foot can you discover its secret charm as one of the finer ensembles of medieval architecture in Europe.

Fribourg is a stronghold of Catholicism; it remained staunchly Catholic even during the Reformation. The evidence is everywhere, from the numerous chapels and religious orders to the brown-robed novitiates walking the sidewalks. Fribourg University, founded in 1889, remains the only Catholic university in Switzerland. It is also the only bilingual institution of its kind and reflects the region's peculiar linguistic agility. Two-thirds of the people of Canton Fribourg are native French speakers, one-third are native German speakers, and many switch easily between the two. In the Basse-Ville neighborhood, old-timers still speak a unique mixture of the two languages called Boltz. The city is officially bilingual, although French predominates.

At its very core, and a good place to start a walk, is the **Basse-Ville** (Lower City), tucked into a crook of the river. Here you'll find the 11th- through 16th-century homes of the original village as well as a lively café and cellar-theater scene. The oldest bridge in this city of bridges is the **Pont de Berne** (Bern Bridge), to the north of the Basse-Ville. Once the only access to the territory of Bern, it's made entirely of wood.

As the town expanded from the Basse-Ville, it crossed the river over the Pont du Milieu (Middle Bridge) to a narrow bank, the Planche-Inférieure, which has a row of tightly packed houses. As the town prospered, it spread to the more stately 16th- and 17th-century **Planche-Supérieure,** a large, sloping, open triangular *place* (square) that was once the busy livestock market. It's now lined with several upscale restaurants and cafés. From here you can walk up to the **Chapelle de Lorette** (Loreto Chapel), once a favored pilgrimage site, for the best view of Fribourg. When the Pont St-Jean was built in the 17th century, making the northern bank of the river readily accessible, the merchant houses and walled cloisters of the **Neuve-Ville** (New Town) popped up.

From the steep, cobbled rue Grand-Fontaine (best avoided at night unless you like red-light districts), you can spy narrow passageways and hidden courtyards, or you can take the funicular up and walk down the route des Alpes to the **Hôtel de Ville,** or Rathaus (Town Hall). This is the seat of the cantonal parliament, built on the foundations of the château of Berthold IV of Zähringen, who founded the town of Fribourg in 1157. The symmetrical stairways were added in the 17th century, as were the clockworks in the 16th-century clock tower. The place de Tilleul (Linden Square) buzzes with a busy local market every Wednesday and Saturday morning.

From the place de Tilleul, the shop-lined rue de Lausanne and rue des Alpes climb upward, their tightly spaced 18th-century buildings hiding terraced gardens of surprising size. The 19th- and 20th-century section of the city begins at the top of rue de Lausanne; nearby are the main buildings of the university. The 21st century has arrived in the form of the Fribourg Centre shopping mall, close to the station.

A block away from the Hôtel de Ville, the Gothic **Cathédrale St-Nicolas** (St. Nicholas Cathedral) rears up from the surrounding gray 18th-century buildings. Its massive tower was completed in the 15th century, two centuries after construction of the cathedral was begun in 1283. Above the main portal, a beautifully restored tympanum of the Last Judgment shows the blessed being gently herded left toward Peter, who holds the key to the heavenly gates; those not so fortunate head right, led by pig-face demons, into the jaws and cauldrons of hell. Inside you can see the famous 18th-century organ as well as the rare, restored 1657 organ. The exceptional stained-glass windows, dating from 1895 through 1936, are executed in a Pre-Raphaelite and art nouveau style. In the **Chapelle du St-Sépulcre** (Chapel of the Holy Sepulcher) a group of 13 polished-wood

Bicycling

Bicycling is popular here, and itineraries are varied. You can struggle up Alpine passes, bounce over mountain-bike trails, or coast along the flatlands around the lakes. Each region has miles of bicycle routes, and route maps can be picked up in most tourist offices or train stations. Swiss Federal Railways (CFF/SBB) offers reasonably priced rentals at many train stations throughout the three cantons. Bicycles must be reserved at least one day in advance; in summer you should call at least three days in advance. In addition, tourist offices in Fribourg run a unique program for the Broye region called Bike Broye. They've charted 20 different biking itineraries (a vineyard or abbey tour, for example), each of which can be paired with an overnight package. Contact the Avenches tourist office at least three weeks in advance, and for July, book at least two months in advance.

7

Hiking & Walking

Fribourg is ideal hiking and walking country for every level of difficulty, with its rugged pre-Alps and flat lake lands. Many major ski lifts run in summer, shuttling hikers instead of skiers. For the agile, Moléson has the kid-friendly Via Ferrata, a marked climbing trail. If city wandering is more your style, you might like strolling around Neuchâtel, which has one of the country's largest pedestrian zones. Hiking in the Jura offers open terrain, cool gorges, and thick forest. All trails are marked with yellow signs, but don't rely on the signs after October. When the Swiss decide the season is finished, they cover the signs in black garbage bags, lay them down, and hide them, to protect the signs, if not the lost tourists, over the winter. Instead get hiking maps from local tourist offices.

History

No matter what aspect of history interests you, you should find something to please you here: from prehistoric menhirs and the lifestyle of stilt-house people at Laténium, near Neuchâtel, to clambering over a Roman theater at Avenches (formerly Aventicum) to imagining the Battle of Murten from the city's ramparts. Perhaps you'd prefer Grandson's castle, with Charles the Bold's ridiculously bejeweled hat and life-size, fully armored replicas of jousting knights. If you love Gothic churches and religious art, you can have your fill, especially in Fribourg and Neuchâtel. There's stained glass at Romont, watchmaking at La Chaux-de-Fonds, and the sheer romantic thrill of medieval towns like St-Ursanne and Gruyères.

Regional Cuisine

The cuisines of these three regions all use robust, seasonal food: perch from the lakes, game and mushrooms from the forested highlands, and, of course, the dairy products of Fribourg and Gruyères. In the lake towns, menus are thick with *perche* (perch), *sandre* (a large cousin of the perch), *bondelle* (a pearly fleshed trout found exclusively in Lac Neuchâtel), or *silure* (catfish). Mushrooms are another strong suit, from the delicate *Schwämli* (*chanterelles* in French) to the robust *Steinpilz* (*bolets* in French), fat, fleshy mushrooms with a meaty texture and taste. These are particularly wonderful when sautéed and served with slices of dark bread or with local rabbit or venison, along with a glass of red Neuchâtel pinot noir.

The traditional autumn Fribourg feast, called Bénichon (Kilbi in Swiss German), embodies the region's love of fundamental food. This harvest feast fetes not only the return of the cattle from the high pastures to the plains but also the season's final yield: chimney-smoked ham, served hot with *moutarde de Bénichon* (sweet mustard); mutton stew with plump raisins and potato puree; and tart *poires-à-Botzi* (pears poached in liquor and lightly caramelized). The main feast takes place during the second week of September, but restaurants across the region serve versions of Bénichon all fall.

Winter Sports
Both the steeper pre-Alps and the gentler slopes of the Jura are littered with ski resorts. The downhill pistes are shorter but also less crowded and more family-friendly than those in the Alps. Provided there's enough snow (these mountains are not as high), you can downhill ski, snowboard, toboggan, or cross-country ski on marked trails till you drop. If you're not fond of lift lines, rent some touring skis and check the Avalanche Report (☎ 187), or book a guide through any ski school. Another way to get off the beaten trail is to ask at a sport or ski shop about itineraries and rentals of lightweight, plastic *raquettes de neige* (snowshoes).

---

figures dating from 1433 portrays the entombment of Christ. If you can handle the 365 steps, climb up the tower for a panoramic view. (During services, you won't be allowed in.) ⊠ *rue St-Nicolas* 🎫 *Free, tower 3.50 SF* ⊘ *Mon.–Sat. 7:30–7, Sun. 8.30 AM–9.30 PM; tower Mar.–Nov., Mon., Wed., Fri., and Sat. 10–noon and 2–5, Thurs. 10–noon, Sun. 2–5.*

From the cathedral slip through the rue des Épouses to the Grand-rue, lined with 18th-century patrician homes. At the end of this street is the **Pont de Zaehringen** (Zähringen Bridge), with views over the Pont de Berne, the Pont de Gottéron, and the wooden remains of the ancient towers that once guarded the entrance to the city. You're now in the area where Duke Berthold IV first established his residence and founded the city in 1157.

need a break? The terrace of **La Belvédère** (⊠ 36 Grand-rue ☎ 026/3234407) has a view up the river to the Planche-Supérieure. Inside it's a *café littéraire* by day and a lively bar and meeting spot at night. The friendly staff serves a selection of teas, coffees, and homemade syrups as well as alcohol, and you can get Asian snacks from the excellent Thai restaurant upstairs.

The 13th-century **Église des Cordeliers** (Church of the Franciscan Friars), north of the cathedral, is attached to a Franciscan friary. The lightness of its white walls and the rose-, gray-, and alabaster-color ceiling contrast with the Gothic darkness of the cathedral. A 16th-century polyptych by the anonymous Nelkenmeister, or Maîtres à l'Oeillet (who signed their works only with red and white carnations), hangs over the high altar. A carved wood triptych, believed to be Alsatian, and a 15th-century retable of the temptation of St. Anthony by the Fribourg artist Hans Fries, adorn the side walls. At the entrance to the cloister leading to the friary is a 13th-century five-panel fresco depicting the birth of

DAIRY DELIGHTS

Many regions of Switzerland are known for fondue, but Fribourg is the source of fondue fribourgeoise, the combination of the canton's two greatest cheeses—Gruyère and Vacherin—into a creamy moitié-moitié (half-and-half) blend. The Vacherin can be melted alone for an even creamier fondue, and potatoes can be dipped instead of bread. From the Jura comes the Vacherin Mont d'Or—wood-ringed cheese so creamy you can spoon it out—and the Tête de Moine (monk's head) cheese, which is stuck on a metal post and shaved off in nutty-flavored ruffles.

Those familiar cows that relieve the saturation of green in the Fribourg countryside yield more than cheese, however. An additional debt of gratitude is owed them for producing crème-double, a Gruyères specialty that rivals Devonshire cream. A rich, extra-thick, high-fat cream that—without whipping—almost supports a standing spoon, it is served in tiny carved-wood baquets (vats), to be spooned over a bowl of berries.

the Virgin Mary. ⊠ *6 rue de Morat* ☎ *026/3471160* 💷 *Free* ☉ *Mon.–Sat. 9–6, Sun. noon–6.*

Near the Église des Cordeliers, the **Musée d'Art et d'Histoire de Fribourg** (Fribourg Museum of Art and History) is housed in the Renaissance Ratzé mansion and, incongruously, an old slaughterhouse connected by an underground passage. The mansion displays 11th- to 18th-century art and a Fribourg archaeology collection. The 19th-century slaughterhouse, a stark stone structure modernized with steel-and-glass blocks, provides the setting for a provocative mix of sacred sculptures and the kinetic, scrap-iron whimsies of native son Jean Tinguely (1925–91). The attic gallery displays 19th- and 20th-century paintings from Delacroix, Courbet, and Ferdinand Hodler. With the expansion of the museum, a new section houses sculpture and paintings from around 1500, including several works by Hans Fries. Take a breather in the quiet sculpture garden overlooking the river. Limited descriptive material in English is available upon request, and guided tours in English can be booked in advance. ⊠ *12 rue de Morat* ☎ *026/3055140* ⊕ *www.fr.ch/mahf* 💷 *6 SF* ☉ *Tues.–Wed. and Fri.–Sun. 11–6, Thurs. 11–8.*

☙ Once the city's tram terminal, the **Espace Jean Tinguely–Niki de Saint Phalle** now houses a few whirring, tapping, spinning metal sculptures by Jean Tinguely and a wall full of the voluptuous, colorful work of his then-wife, Niki de Saint Phalle. Her works are titled in English, while his need no explanation. Kids (16 and under free) are often fascinated by Tinguely's work. Something is happening somewhere all the time: skis are walking, a potted plant is turning, a toy rabbit is being hit on the head. ⊠ *2 rue de Morat* ☎ *026/3055140* 💷 *6 SF* ☉ *Wed. and Fri.–Sun. 11–6, Thurs. 11–8.*

Deep in the catacombs beneath a 12th-century patrician home, the **Musée Suisse de la Machine à Coudre** (Swiss Sewing Machine Museum) displays an example of almost every sewing machine ever built (more

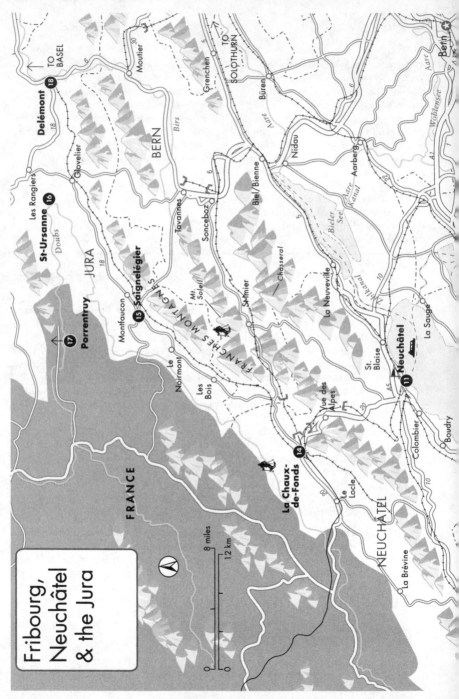

Fribourg, Neuchâtel
& the Jura

FRANCE

BERN

JURA

NEUCHÂTEL

FRANCHES MONTAGNES

TO BASEL
18 Delémont
Les Rangiers **16**
St-Ursanne
Porrentruy **17**
Montfaucon
15 Saignelégier
Le Noirmont
Les Bois
La Chaux-de-Fonds
Le Locle
La Brévine
Moutier
Grenchen
TO SOLOTHURN
Büren
Nidau
Glovelier
Tavannes
Soncebaz
Biel/Bienne
Chasseral
Mt. Soleil
St-Imier
La Neuveville
La Sauge
Vue des Alpes
St. Blaise
11 Neuchâtel
Colombier
Boudry
14
Birs
Doubs
Aare
Aare
Aare
Aare Kanal
Aarberg
Bieler See
Zihlkanal
Wohlensee
Bern

0
8 miles
0
12 km

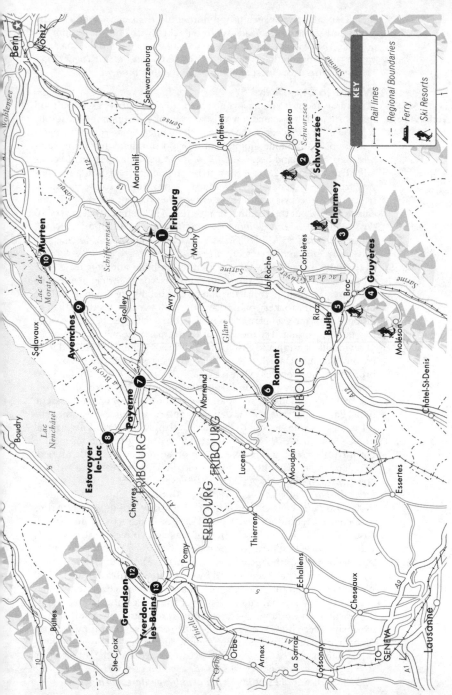

than 250), along with such useful household firsts as vacuum cleaners and washing machines. A side room is packed with curiosities from by-gone days, such as chestnut-hulling boots. Owner Edouard Wassmer will charm you with anecdotes and history. ⊠ *58 Grand-rue* ☎ *026/4752433* ⊕ *www.museewassmer.com* ⊑ *Free* ☉ *By appointment only.*

Where to Stay & Eat

$$-$$$
Fodor'sChoice
★
✕ **Des Trois Tours.** If you have a penchant for innovative, excellent food that is superbly presented, try this restaurant gastronomique just out-side town. You can eat in the sunny, plant-filled brasserie; in the more discreet ocher-and-blue dining room; or on the shady terrace in sum-mer. Fast beforehand because a *menu du marché* (market menu) costs 100 SF to 125 SF, and you'll want to relish it all. Perhaps you'll eat your way from the lasagna of crepes and wild mushrooms to the mosaic of fruits and sorbets via a mouthwatering series of mains and a groaning cheese trolley, but then again, perhaps not. The menu changes every 10 days. ⊠ *15 rte. de Bourguillon, Bourguillon* ☎ *026/3223069* ⚏ *Reservations essential* ⊟ *AE, DC, MC, V* ☉ *Closed Sun. and Mon. plus late July–early Aug. and late Dec.–early Jan.*

$$
✕ **La Grotta.** In the Basse-Ville, a friendly husband-and-wife team have created a rustic Piemonte (Piedmont) grotto from a former stable. The walls are part rock, part plaster; the ceiling beams are original; and the blue-and-white crockery on dark-wood tables completes the Italian il-lusion. The menu is simple and seasonal: truffles in September, *cabri* (suck-ling goat) in spring. Try the Piemonte: antipasti; homemade *agnolotti* (a ravioli-like pasta); and osso buco, rabbit, or guinea fowl served with creamy polenta. Daniel, one of the owners, will help you choose ap-propriate wines from his extensive cellar. ⊠ *5 rue d'Or* ☎ *026/3228100* ⊟ *MC, V* ☉ *Closed July and Aug. and Sun. and Mon. No lunch.*

$$
✕ **L'Epée.** It's a good idea to make reservations at this popular brasserie in the Basse-Ville. The food is delicious and reasonably priced, the staff is friendly, and the view up to the cathedral and the Neuve-Ville is a real draw—from inside or on the terrace, by day or night. Options include black truffle ravioli in sage cream, an oh-so-tender rack of lamb with basil, and meringues with *vin cuit* (cooked wine) ice cream and Gruyère cream. ⊠ *39 Planche-Supérieure* ☎ *026/3223407* ⊟ *MC, V* ☉ *Closed late July–late Aug. and Sun. No dinner Mon.*

¢
✕ **Xpresso Café.** On the fourth floor of the new Fribourg Centre, this café cum crêperie does waffles and crepes—both savory and sweet. Also choose from a wide selection of teas and coffees. ⊠ *10 av. de la Gare* ☎ *026/3417808* ⊟ *No credit cards* ☉ *Closed Sun. No dinner Sat.*

$$-$$$
✕▥ **Auberge de Zaehringen.** The oldest private house in Fribourg, now a lovely auberge, has been owned by only three families during its 700 years. The restaurant ($$-$$$) offers gracious service, elegant dishes such as roasted pigeon, and a view over the Basse-Ville. (Reservations are essential on weekends.) The warmly lit brasserie ($-$$) offers less-expensive specialties, such as wild mushrooms served on puff pastry with thyme sauce. Two luxurious guest rooms are outfitted with an-tiques and marble baths. There's free cab service from the train station if you phone in advance. ⊠ *13 rue de Zaehringen, CH-1700* ☎ *026/ 3224236* 🖷 *026/3226908* ⊕ *www.auberge-de-zaehringen.ch* ⏎ 2

suites ⚿ *2 restaurants, in-room safes, minibars, cable TV, bar, business services, meeting rooms, some pets allowed* ▭ *MC, V* ⊘ *Closed Sun. and Mon.* ‖⃝‖ *BP.*

★ **$$** ✕▦ **Au Sauvage.** The Sauvage began in the 1600s as a cloister, became an inn during the cattle-market days in the 18th and 19th centuries, and is now a sophisticated auberge with a striking blend of minimalism and medieval details. In the guest rooms, thick, whitewashed stone walls hide TVs, while sleek bathrooms include elegant vanities. The small dining room ($$–$$$; closed Sunday, Monday, and July), under the original vaulted ceiling, serves French-influenced cuisine, such as beef fillet with Gorgonzola and fish in a delicate ginger-lime sauce. One room (and bathroom) is wheelchair accessible. You can park free in the square: the staff will keep changing the blue card. ⊠ *12 Planche-Supérieure, CH-1700* ☏ *026/3473060* 🖷 *026/3473061* ⊕ *www.hotel-sauvage.ch* ⤶ *17 rooms* ⚿ *Restaurant, in-room safes, minibars, cable TV, bar, Internet, some pets allowed (fee), no-smoking floors* ▭ *AE, DC, MC, V* ‖⃝‖ *BP.*

$$ ▦ **Hôtel de la Rose.** In a typical 17th-century sandstone house, this hotel is within walking distance of museums, churches, the cathedral, and the Old Town. The hotel has a familial, friendly atmosphere. Rooms are done in off-white and brown; some are dark. Ask for a room that's been renovated with noise-proof windows. ⊠ *1 rue de Morat, CH-1702* ☏ *026/3510101* 🖷 *026/3510100* ⊕ *www.hotelrose.com* ⤶ *40 rooms* ⚿ *Restaurant, coffee shop, in-room safes, minibars, cable TV with movies, bar, laundry service, business services, meeting room, some pets allowed (fee), no-smoking rooms* ▭ *AE, DC, MC, V* ‖⃝‖ *BP.*

$$ ▦ **Hôtel Duc Berthold.** Berthold IV is said to have lived in this ancient building in the 12th century. The rooms have a comfortable, old-fashioned air, thanks to delicate florals and reproduction antique furniture. Triple-glaze windows keep out traffic noise. The hotel has air-conditioning. ⊠ *5 rue des Bouchers, CH-1700* ☏ *026/3508100* 🖷 *026/3508181* ⊕ *www.hotelducberthold.ch* ⤶ *36 rooms* ⚿ *2 restaurants, coffee shop, in-room safes, minibars, cable TV with movies, exercise equipment, sauna, bar, business services, meeting room, some free parking, some pets allowed* ▭ *AE, DC, MC, V* ⊘ *Closed late Dec.–early Jan.* ‖⃝‖ *BP.*

$$ ▦ **NH Hotel.** Conveniently located near the train station and next to a park with a spouting Tinguely fountain, this modern, multistory box offers stunning views of the pre-Alps and town. The spacious rooms are comfortable, with blue-and-gold decor. ⊠ *14 Grand-pl., CH-1700* ☏ *026/3519191* 🖷 *026/3519192* ⊕ *www.nh-hotels.com* ⤶ *121 rooms, 1 suite* ⚿ *Restaurant, in-room data ports, in-room safes, minibars, cable TV with movies, bar, laundry service, business services, convention center, free parking, some pets allowed (fee), no-smoking floors* ▭ *AE, DC, MC, V* ‖⃝‖ *BP.*

¢ ▦ **Ibis.** Near the northern *autoroute* (expressway) exit, this modern budget hotel (opened May 2004) appeals to those traveling by car. At the edge of town, it is close to the casino and the convention center (Le Forum). Rooms are simple, appointed in turquoise and ocher; triple-glaze windows keep out most of the noise from the main road. Some rooms have pull-out beds for children under 12 to sleep for free. Two rooms are accessible and fully equipped for people in wheelchairs. The hotel has air-conditioning. ✉ *21 rte. du Lac, CH-1763 Granges-Paccot* ☎ *026/ 4697900* 🖷 *026/4697910* ⊕ *www.accorhotels.com* 🛏 *82 rooms* ♨ *Snack bar, bar, laundry service, Internet, some pets allowed (fee), no-smoking floors* ▤ *AE, DC, MC, V.*

Nightlife

BARS   To get a feel for Fribourg's nightlife, try one of the cellar bars scattered throughout the Old Town. The bar at the **Hôtel de la Rose** (✉ 1 rue de Morat ☎ 026/3510101) serves pizza. The cellar bar of the **Hôtel Duc Berthold** (✉ 5 rue des Bouchers ☎ 026/3508181) has red leather seats and, surprisingly, a view of the river. Both bars stay open until 2 AM on Friday and Saturday. An 18th-century inn, seemingly in the middle of nowhere, has been turned into **Planet Edelweiss** (✉ Mariahilf, near Düdingen ☎ 026/4920505), a lively *restaurant de nuit* and disco. Its diverse crowd (ranging from bankers to farmers) doesn't get going until after 10, and the bar stays open until 2 Sunday–Wednesday, 3 on Thursday, and 4 on Friday and Saturday. The 12-minute taxi ride from town runs around 30 SF.

CASINO   Near the northern autoroute exit, the**Casino de Fribourg** (✉ 11 rte. du Lac, Granges-Paccot ☎ 026/4677000) opened in 2003. In addition to roulette, blackjack, stud poker, and 100 poker machines, the casino has a restaurant, banquet room for 200, and regular shows.

Schwarzsee

★ ☾ ➋   *26 km (16 mi) southeast of Fribourg.*

Known as Lac Noir (Black Lake) in French, Schwarzsee is an exceptionally pretty, dark lake (hence the name) and family resort, set at the end of a valley amid several 6,560-foot peaks. It is well worth visiting at any time of year. In November or December, the lake often freezes before the first snows, becoming a paradise for ice-skaters and parents pulling children on sleds. When snow comes, the resort fills with skiers and snowboarders, and there's a sled run for the younger ones. Bundle up well to visit the **Eis-Palaeste** (Ice Palaces), a few kilometers from Schwarzsee on your way back to Fribourg. When the snow melts, the hikers arrive. Stroll around the lake (but not on a sunny Sunday afternoon unless you like crowds), or climb to one of the ridgelines for stunning views. You can also cheat and take the chairlift to the Berghaus Riggisalp.

Skiing

A favorite with families, **Schwarzsee** has pistes of easy to medium difficulty and good ski and snowboard schools. The ski area has six lifts, which go up to 5,740 feet, for runs with spectacular views. There's also a small cross-country trail. Parking lots fill up on weekends, so arrive early or take the regional bus, which leaves from the Fribourg train station.

Where to Eat

¢–$ ✕ **Berghaus Gurli.** Enjoy a simple but good Swiss meal at this mountain chalet, complete with traditional Swiss charm and stunning views from its panoramic terrace. Listen to the jangling of cowbells as you enjoy a creamy cheese fondue or a Gurli cold platter: slivers of dried beef, bacon, salami, and sausage with cheese and crusty brown bread. You can hike up from Zollhaus or include it on your (much longer) ridgeline walk from the Schwyberg. You can also cheat and drive up the back way. Turn right at the upper (southern) end of Plaffeien (about halfway back to Fribourg), and follow the signs. ⊠ *Gurli* ☎ *026/4191913* 🚫 *No credit cards* 🕙 *Closed Nov.–Apr.*

Charmey

🥾 ❸ *30 km (18 mi) south of Fribourg.*

If you're traveling from Fribourg to Gruyères along the east side of the lake, a left turn at a fork brings you to this family-oriented resort in a bowl surrounded by forested peaks. At 2,953 feet, Charmey is known for skiing, but it is also a good base for hiking and climbing in summer. Teens enjoy **Charmey Aventures,** an adventure park not for the faint of heart. (Children must be at least 8 and accompanied by an adult until 14.) Even older teens are terrified by the black run. Admission includes the gondola ride. ⊠ *Mid-station of gondola* ☎ *026/9271990* ⊕ *www. charmeyaventures.ch* 🎟 *35 SF* 🕙 *May, June, Sept., and Oct., weekends 10–6:30; July and Aug., daily 10–6:30.*

off the beaten path

LA VALSAINTE – On the road to Charmey, after you've passed Crésuz, turn left on a narrow, winding road for a drive in this peaceful and green valley with few villages. The valley runs up along a stream, past the austere and impressive Chartreux Monastery (founded by followers of St. Bruno at the end of the 13th century).

Skiing

The Charmey ski area is located between Vounetz, at 5,337 feet, and the village itself. Slopes are of medium difficulty at best, and the resort's charms lie in its family-friendly atmosphere. Charmey has seven lifts including a gondola, 35 km (22 mi) of downhill runs, and 20 km (12½ mi) of cross-country trails.

Where to Eat

★ $$ ✕ **Pinte des Mossettes.** Overlooking a steep valley at the end of a winding road, this restaurant offers some of the most intriguing menus in Switzerland. Owner-chef Judith Baumann bases her dishes on wild herbs and locally grown ingredients. The menu changes monthly and includes surprising combinations, such as wild greens with bean mousse, dandelion soup, and Andalusian ham with Xeres vinaigrette. ⊠ *Road to La Valsainte, Cerniat* ☎☎ *026/9272097* 🍴 *Reservations essential* 🚫 *No credit cards* 🕙 *Closed Nov.–mid-Mar. and Mon. and Tues.*

en route

On the way from Fribourg or Charmey to Gruyères, chocoholics should consider stopping at the tantalizing **Nestlé chocolaterie** (chocolate factory), in the otherwise unassuming town of Broc. Founded by Alexandre Cailler in 1889 and bought by Nestlé in 1929, it offers a 40-minute tour and video, followed by a chocolate tasting. Look for chocolate-brown signs marking the way. Reservations are essential. ⊠ *Broc* ☎ *026/9215151* 🎟 *Free* 🕙 *May–Oct., weekdays 9–11 and 1:30–4.*

CloseUp

LA DÉSALPE

WHEN THE ALPINE GRASS thins out in the fall, the cows of Haute Gruyères are led down to the village stables—in style, with huge bells around their necks and flowers and pine branches attached to their horns. Not to be outdone by their beasts, the cowherds wear their Sunday best: a dark blue jacket with embroidered edelweiss motifs and puffy short sleeves that optically double the width of the wearer's shoulders. With their black-trimmed straw caps, fancy pipes, and bushy beards, the men are the real stars of the day. The women, in red-checked aprons and flat straw hats, stay in the background.

To avoid two weeks of continual congestion on the roads, the foothill villages of Charmey (last Saturday in September) and Albeuve (first Saturday in October) have the herds descend together, making a folk festival of it. Decorated cows, heifers, sheep, goats, and even pigs are paraded through the streets from 9 AM until about 3 PM. The partying goes on all day, with flag throwing, marching bands, alpenhorn playing, and stalls selling Bénichon specialities. (Originally a benediction of the church, Bénichon has become a harvest celebration.)

Watch for the poyas adorning the front walls of Gruyères farmhouses. These are naive-style paintings of cows filing up to the high pastures in spring. They advertise which breed the farmer owns and symbolize hope for a productive summer. (Before the 1820s, cheese was only made up on the Alps, where the cows had the lushest grass; so farmers had four months a year to make their living.)

Gruyères

❹ *35 km (21 mi) south of Fribourg.*

Fodor'sChoice ★

Rising above the plain on a rocky crag and set against a backdrop of Alpine foothills, the castle village of Gruyères seduces from afar. This perfect specimen of a medieval stronghold comes complete with a cobbled main street, stone fountains, and well-preserved houses whose occupants try to outdo each other with picturesque facades and geranium displays in summer. The town was once the capital of the Alpine estates of the Burgundian counts of Gruyères, and its traditional crest bears a stylized crane (*grue*). Gruyères is car-free, so you'll have to park in one of three lots outside town and either walk up or catch the tourist train; arrive early to beat the crowds.

Gruyères is known for its blue-and-white or dark-red-and-white pottery decorated with the grue, as well as for creamy, nutty cheeses (Vacherin and Gruyère, spelled without the town's *s*), and the 48%-butterfat crème-double, which is served with a bowl of berries or crumbly, sweet meringues.

Between 1080 and 1554, 19 counts held political power over this region, and they built and expanded the **château** here from the 11th century onwards. Little is known about them except for the last, Michael I, or Michel. A lover of luxury and a big spender, he expanded the estates and then fled his creditors in 1555, leaving vast holdings to Fribourg and Bern. In 1848 a wealthy Geneva family bought the old castle. As patrons of the arts, family members hosted the artist Corot; some of his panels grace the castle's drawing room. A tour will take you to the 13th-century dungeon and the living quarters, decorated in 16th- and 17th-century styles with tapestries, frescoes, and grand fireplaces. The Salle des Chevaliers (Knights' Room) has an impressive fresco cycle depicting local legends. Modern fantasy art by Woodroffe adorns the tower. ☎ 026/9212102 ⊕ www.chateau-gruyeres.ch 🎫 6.50 SF ⊙ Apr.–Oct., daily 9–6; Nov.–Mar., daily 10–4:30.

Most people will get enough of an idea about the enormously talented but equally tormented H.R. Giger from sitting in the Giger Bar, opposite the **Giger Museum.** Here you can admire ceiling buttresses that look like elongated backbones with ribs, and his ingenious trademark chairs: more spines and ribs, with pelvises for headrests. Giger won an Academy Award for his set design of the horror film Alien; he's not likely to win any prizes for his cheerful, healthy outlook on life (or women). That said, a few of his sculpture/furniture pieces are very good. Just avoid looking at the walls if you want to enjoy lunch afterwards. ⊠ Château St. Germain ☎ 026/9212200 ⊕ www.hrgigermuseum.com 🎫 10 SF ⊙ Apr.–Oct., weekdays 10–6, weekends 10–6:30; Nov.–Mar., Tues.–Fri. 11–5, weekends 10–6:30.

Before going up to town, you can visit the very touristy **Maison du Gruyère,** a demonstration fromagerie (cheese dairy) where the famous cheese is produced with fully modernized equipment. Demonstrations are given three or four times a day in season. ☎ 026/9218400 ⊕ www.lamaisondugruyere.ch 🎫 5 SF ⊙ Apr.–Sept., daily 9–11 and 1–3; Oct.–May, daily 2–3.

> **off the beaten path**
>
> **FROMAGERIE D'ALPAGE –** For a more authentic, historical perspective than the Maison du Gruyère provides, visit the Magnin family's cheese-making operation up on the Alp, in nearby Moléson-sur-Gruyères. Watch the true Gruyère cheese, called Gruyère d'alpage, being made in a cauldron over an open fire in the low-roofed chalet. An exhibit explains the development of cheese making since the 17th century, and a 15-minute video, subtitled in English, describes the process. A small restaurant serves traditional local dishes. ⊠ Moléson-sur-Gruyères ☎ 026/9211044 🎫 3 SF ⊙ Daily 9:30–6; demonstrations mid-May–late Sept., daily at 9:45 and 2:45.

Skiing

At 3,609 feet, **Moléson,** Gruyères's "house mountain," offers skiing up to 6,568 feet and wraparound views of the pre-Alps and on to Lac Léman (Lake Geneva). The area has three cable cars, four lifts, 20 km (12 mi) of downhill ski runs, and 8 km (5 mi) of cross-country trails.

Where to Stay & Eat

¢–$$ ✗ **Auberge de la Halle à Pied Cheval.** The unfussy interior of this medieval house, with its massive raftered ceiling and smooth stone floor, feels like a 16th-century burgher's home. Choose the front rooms for people-watching or the back terrace for admiring the town ramparts while you savor traditional Gruyères dishes, such as fondue with potatoes. ⊠ *Main street* ☏ *026/9212178* ▤ *AE, DC, MC, V.*

★ $$ ✗▣ **De Ville.** This welcoming hotel has large, airy rooms, tastefully renovated in 2000, that mix bright Tuscan colors with traditional pine furniture. Back rooms overlook the valley, front rooms the village. The restaurant ($–$$) serves steaming fondue, raclette, and other Swiss dishes. ⊠ *Main street, CH-1663* ☏ *026/9212424* 🖷 *026/9213628* 📞 *8 rooms* ⚭ *Restaurant, cable TV; no smoking* ▤ *AE, DC, MC, V* ⏐◉ *BP.*

$$ ✗▣ **Hostellerie St-Georges.** The management of this well-situated hotel changed in 2004, and it has since lost its conference room and upgraded its restaurant to gastronomique status. Spacious, cheerful rooms have traditional wood decor and white, edelweiss-embroidered bed linen, and their mountain views are breathtaking. A massive fireplace anchors the evening dining area; during lunch, enjoy the stunning views from the large, light-filled winter garden. ⊠ *Main street, CH-1663* ☏ *026/9218300* 🖷 *026/9218339* ⊕ *www.st-georges-gruyeres.ch* 📞 *14 rooms* ⚭ *Restaurant, in-room safes, cable TV* ▤ *AE, DC, MC, V* ⊘ *Closed late Dec.–early Jan.* ⏐◉ *BP.*

★ $–$$ ▣ **Hostellerie des Chevaliers.** This traditional, family-friendly hotel is also well-equipped for business conferences. Standing outside the main gates of Gruyères, it has the same views overlooking the valley and the castle as in-town lodgings, without the noise. Room decor mixes regional antiques, handsome woodwork, and ceramic stoves with contrasting color schemes. Though the hotel no longer has a restaurant, breakfast is served in the dining room, and additional meal plans are offered using the restaurant of the Hostellerie St-Georges. ⊠ *CH-1663* ☏ *026/9211933* 🖷 *026/9212552* ⊕ *www.gruyeres-hotels.ch* 📞 *34 rooms* ⚭ *Dining room, cable TV, Internet, meeting rooms, some pets allowed (fee), no-smoking rooms* ▤ *AE, DC, MC, V* ⊘ *Closed Jan. and Feb.* ⏐◉ *BP.*

$ ▣ **Fleur de Lys.** From its vaulted, stenciled reception area to its pine-and-beam restaurant, this is a welcoming little hotel. Plain rooms contain '50s-style wooden furniture, and a large rear terrace and garden have a wonderful view of the mountains and castle. ⊠ *CH-1663* ☏ *026/9218282* 🖷 *026/9213605* ⊕ *www.hotelfleurdelys.ch* 📞 *10 rooms* ⚭ *Restaurant, café, cable TV, bar, Internet, some pets allowed* ▤ *AE, DC, MC, V* ⊘ *Closed Feb.* ⏐◉ *BP.*

Sports & the Outdoors

In addition to skiing, Moléson is known for hiking and climbing in summer. Stuck with whining teenagers? Send them up the **Via Ferrata** (⊠ Moléson-sur-Gruyères ☏ 026/9272013 ⊕ www.mountainguide. ch), an assured climbing trail up the face of the mountain. It's challenging but idiotproof, provided you don't try it in a thunderstorm. You can rent equipment on the spot; children must be over 4 feet 7 inches tall. Moléson village also has a kids' play area with a bobsled run and go-carts, open mid-June–September, weather permitting.

Bulle

⑤ *5 km (3 mi) northwest of Gruyères, 31 km (19 mi) southwest of Fribourg.*

A small town of fewer than 10,000 people, Bulle condenses the attractions of a larger town: a castle (not open to the public), three-storied patrician houses lining the cobblestone main street, and a scenic backdrop so perfect you might think it has been painted. You can learn about Gruyères traditions at the **Musée Gruérien**, which contains displays of folk costumes, handicrafts, and farm tools—it even has a full reproduction of a flagstone farmhouse kitchen and dining room. ✉ *pl. du Cabalet* ☎ *026/9127260* ⊕ *www.bullech/culture* ✉ *5 SF* ⊗ *Tues.–Sat. 10–noon and 2–5, Sun. 2–5.*

Romont

⑥ *15 km (9 mi) northwest of Bulle, 49 km (30 mi) southwest of Fribourg.*

The best way to approach this 13th-century town of two broad streets is to leave the highway and drive up to its castle terrace. The fortress's 13th-century ramparts surround the town, forming a belvedere from which you can see the Alps—from Mont Blanc to the Berner Oberland. You'll also find a 12th-century Cistercian convent, the 17th-century Capuchin monastery, and the lovely 13th-century Collégiale, one of the purest examples of a Gothic church in Switzerland, with period (and modern) windows, sculptures, choir stalls, a screen, and an altarpiece.

Inside the castle, the **Musée du Vitrail** (Stained-Glass Museum) shimmers with crisscrossing shafts of colored light from its glass panels, both ancient and contemporary. A slide presentation traces the development of the craft, and a workshop area demonstrates current techniques. The museum is expanding further into the castle so that it can accommodate a donated collection of reverse painting on glass. Work should be finished by June 2006. ✉ *Château* ☎ *026/6521095* ⊕ *www.romont. ch* ✉ *7 SF* ⊗ *Apr.–Oct., Tues.–Sun. 10–1 and 2–6; Nov.–Mar., Thurs.–Sun. 10–1 and 2–5.*

Payerne

⑦ *15 km (9 mi) north of Romont, 18 km (11 mi) west of Fribourg.*

The meandering streets in this market town are filled with pastel-painted 18th-century buildings, now shops and restaurants. Above them stands a magnificent 11th-century *église abbatiale* (abbey church), one of the finest examples of Romanesque art in Switzerland. You can visit its restored austere abbey, including a grand barrel-vaulted sanctuary and primitive capital carvings on the pillars. The church hosts painting exhibitions (except in winter) and organ concerts (donations welcome) the first Saturday of the month at 6:15. ☎ *026/6626704* ✉ *12 SF, 3 SF if no exhibition* ⊗ *May–Sept., Tues.–Sun. 10–noon and 2–6; Oct.–Apr., Tues.–Sun. 10–noon and 2–5.*

Estavayer-le-Lac

❽ *7 km (4 mi) northwest of Payerne, 51 km (32 mi) southwest of Neuchâtel.*

Modest Estavayer-le-Lac, on the shore of Lac Neuchâtel, can still be navigated using a map drawn in 1599. It has retained much of its medieval architecture, from the arcades of the town center to the gracious, multitowered medieval **Château de Chenaux**, which now houses city government offices.

For something completely different, visit the quirky **Musée de Grenouilles** (Frog Museum). Here are displays of 108 embalmed frogs posed like people in scenes of daily life from the 19th century up through the mid-1900s. Other exhibits include an authentic 17th-century kitchen, various military and household artifacts dredged from Lac Neuchâtel, and more than 200 Swiss railroad lanterns, some up to 100 years old. ⊠ *rue des Musées* ☎ *026/6632448* 🖼 *4 SF* ⏱ *Mar., June, Sept., and Oct., Tues.–Sun. 10–noon and 2–5; July and Aug., daily 10–noon and 2–5; Nov.–Feb., weekends 2–5.*

Where to Stay

$ 🏨 **Hotel du Lac.** Although this blocky, semimodern hotel is short on old-world charm, it's the only lodging in town with a lakeside location. The harbor and grassy park are completely relaxing; you can watch the swans nesting from the terrace in spring. Rooms are unpretentious and in need of renovation. ⊠ *1 pl. du Pont, CH-1410* ☎ *026/6635220* 🖨 *026/6635343* 📞 *24 rooms* ⚙ *Restaurant, café, cable TV, Internet, meeting room, some pets allowed* 🟰 *AE, DC, MC, V* ⧖ *BP.*

Avenches

❾ *5 km (3 mi) northeast of Estavayer-le-Lac, 13 km (8 mi) northwest of Fribourg.*

Avenches (technically in Canton Vaud) is the old capital of the Helvetians, which, as Aventicum, grew into an important city that reached its peak in the 2nd century AD. In its prime, the Roman stronghold was surrounded by some 6 km (4 mi) of 6-foot-high stone walls. The Alemanni destroyed it in the 3rd century. The town's **château** was built at the end of the 13th century by the bishops of Lausanne. It has a Renaissance-style facade and portal.

You can still see the remains of a Roman forum, a bathhouse, and an amphitheater—today the **Musée et Théâtre Romains** (Roman Museum and Theater)—where bloodthirsty spectators once watched the games. Now opera lovers gather here for an annual July evening spectacle; contact the tourist office well in advance for tickets. The collection of Roman antiquities at the museum is noteworthy, including an excellent copy of a gold bust of Marcus Aurelius, unearthed at Avenches in the 1920s, the original of which is in Lausanne. (Just east of town, there's a small Roman theater; farther up the hill are parts of the Roman wall.) ☎ *026/6751727* 🌐 *www.avenches.ch* 🖼 *2 SF* ⏱ *Apr.–Sept., Tues.–Sun. 10–noon and 1–5; Oct.–Mar., Tues.–Sun. 2–5.*

Murten

⑩ *6 km (4 mi) northeast of Avenches, 17 km (11 mi) north of Fribourg.*

Fodor's Choice
★

The ancient town of Murten, known in French as Morat, is a popular resort on the Murtensee/Lac de Morat (Lake Murten). The bilingual town has a boat-lined waterfront, Windsurfer rentals, a lakeside public pool complex, grassy picnic areas, and a promenade as well as a superbly preserved medieval center. Leave your car in the parking area in front of the 13th-century gates and stroll the fountain-studded cobblestone streets. Climb up the worn wooden steps to the town ramparts for a view of the lake over a chaos of red roofs and stone chimneys.

The town's most memorable moment came on June 22, 1476, when the Swiss Confederates—already a fearsomely efficient military machine—attacked with surprising ferocity and won a significant victory over the Burgundians, who were threatening Fribourg under the leadership of Duke Charles the Bold. Begun as a siege 12 days earlier, the battle cost the Swiss 410 men, the Burgundians 12,000. The defeat at Murten prevented the establishment of a large Lothringian kingdom and left Switzerland's autonomy unchallenged for decades. Legend has it that a Swiss runner, carrying a linden branch, ran from Murten to Fribourg to carry the news of victory. He expired by the town hall, and a linden tree grew from the branch he carried. Today, to commemorate his dramatic sacrifice, some 15,000 runners participate annually on the first Sunday in October in a 17-km (11-mi) race up the steep hill from Murten to Fribourg. As for the linden tree, it flourished in Fribourg for some 500 years, until 1983, when it was ingloriously felled by a drunk driver. It has been replaced with a steel sculpture.

The **Musée Historique** (Historical Museum) is in the town's old mill, complete with two water-powered mill wheels. On view are prehistoric finds from the lake area, military items, and trophies from the Burgundian Wars. ⊠ *Lausannestr., southern end of historic center* ☎ *026/6703100* ⊕ *www. museummurten.ch* 🖾 *6 SF* ☉ *Apr.–Oct., Tues.–Sun. 11–5.*

Where to Stay & Eat

$–$$$ ✕ **Ringmauer.** Whether in the simpler brasserie or the dining section, this rustic restaurant in the city wall offers good value for the money. Try the confit *de canard* (duck leg in a garlic and parsley sauce) or the regional pan-fried perch fillets. You can enjoy the terrace in summer and take your predinner drinks by the fire in winter. (There are even some hotel rooms, which should be renovated by 2005.) ⊠ *Deutsche Kirchg. 2* ☎ *026/ 6701101* ⊟ *MC, V* ☉ *Closed Sun. and Mon.*

★ **$$$$** ✕⊡ **Le Vieux Manoir au Lac.** A manicured park spreads around this stately, turreted mansion just 1 km (½ mi) south of Murten on Lac de Morat. The decor is an eclectic mix of parquet and Persian rugs, wing chairs, Biedermeier, and country prints; rooms blend chintz, gingham, and toile de Jouy. The restaurant's ($$$) seasonal sampling menus have a French-Continental bent. Options might include roast lamb with mustard sauce or a lasagna of asparagus with truffle butter. At this writing, the hotel had not finalized the times of year it would close for holidays.

✉ *rue de Lausanne, CH-3280 Meyriez* ☎ *026/6786161* 🖷 *026/6786162* ⊕ *www.vieuxmanoir.ch* ⌨ *30 rooms* ♿ *Restaurant, in-room safes, minibars, cable TV, bicycles, business services, meeting rooms, free parking, some pets allowed (fee)* ▤ *AE, DC, MC, V* ⍾ *BP.*

★ **$$–$$$** ╳🖾 **Weisses Kreuz.** Owned by the same family since 1921, this hotel has two buildings: one with lake views and the other wing across the street with Old Town views. The latter has rooms extraordinarily furnished with complete antique bedroom sets—Biedermeier, art nouveau, Louis XVI, Empire. Simpler rooms, in pine or high-tech style, cost less. The lovely formal dining room ($$–$$$), open May to September, specializes in fish: whitefish with chanterelles and cucumbers, timbale of three lake fish, pike braised in dill. ✉ *Rathausg. 3, CH-3280* ☎ *026/ 6702641* 🖷 *026/6702866* ⊕ *www.weisses-kreuz.ch* ⌨ *27 rooms* ♿ *Restaurant, cable TV, business services, convention center* ▤ *AE, DC, MC, V* ⊘ *Closed Dec. and Jan.* ⍾ *BP.*

$$ ╳🖾 **Schiff am See.** The Schiff nabbed an ideal setting; its sheltered terrace gives onto a shady park and the waterfront promenade. Inside you'll find an eclectic collection of heavy wood furniture and antiques. The ambitious French restaurant, Lord Nelson ($–$$$; closed Wednesday and Thursday), has lake views and wraps around the garden. Specialties may include risotto with porcini mushrooms or local fish. A pizzeria and terrace are open on fine days. The Schiff is a "velo-hotel"; bicycles are welcome, and the staff can help you rent one in town. ✉ *53 Ryf, CH-3280* ☎ *026/6702701* 🖷 *026/6703531* ⊕ *www.hotel-schiff.ch* ⌨ *15 rooms* ♿ *Restaurant, pizzeria, minibars, cable TV, lake, bar, meeting room, some pets allowed (fee)* ▤ *AE, DC, MC, V* ⍾ *BP.*

(**en route**) The **Papiliorama and Nocturama,** formerly in Neuchâtel, are now just north of Kerzers, a small detour en route from Murten to Neuchâtel. Literally crawling with life, these two separate domes contain completely different tropical biospheres. The Papiliorama pulses with humid tropical plants, lily ponds, more than 1,000 living butterflies, dwarf caimans, tortoises, birds, fish, and gigantic tropical insects—the latter, fortunately, in cages. The Nocturama is filled with bats, opossums, raccoons, skunks, and other nocturnal creatures. Outdoor areas include a children's zoo and a Swiss butterfly garden; a new Jungle Trek dome, with birds and lizards to ogle, is planned for 2005. ✉ *Kerzers* ☎ *031/7560460* ⊕ *www.papiliorama.ch* ▦ *13 SF* ⊘ *Apr.–Sept., daily 9–6; Oct.–Mar., daily 10–5.*

LAC NEUCHÂTEL

The region of Neuchâtel belonged to Prussia from 1707 to 1857, with a brief interruption caused by Napoléon and a period of dual loyalty to Prussia and the Swiss Confederation between 1815 and 1857. Yet its French heritage remains untouched by Germanic language, diet, or culture. Some boast that the inhabitants speak "the best French in Switzerland," which is partly why so many summer language courses are taught here.

Neuchâtel

★ ▶ ⑪ *28 km (17 mi) northwest of Murten, 48 km (30 mi) northwest of Fribourg.*

At the foot of the Jura Mountains, flanked by vineyards, and facing southeast, the city of Neuchâtel enjoys panoramic views of Lac Neuchâtel and the range of the middle Alps, including the majestic mass of Mont Blanc and the Bernese Oberland. Lac Neuchâtel, at 38 km (24 mi) long and 8 km (5 mi) wide, is the largest located entirely within Switzerland. (The much larger lakes of Geneva and Constance are shared with France and Germany, respectively.) A prosperous city, Neuchâtel has a reputation for precision work, beginning with watchmaking in the early 18th century. Broad avenues in the lower part of town bordering the lake are lined with neo-Romanesque yellow-sandstone buildings, which inspired author Alexandre Dumas to call Neuchâtel "a city with the appearance of an immense *joujou* [toy] dressed in butter." The cathedral and the 12th-century castle, which today houses the cantonal government, sit gracefully above the city's bustling old marketplace. You can stroll (or cycle or rollerblade) along the lakeside promenade as far as Hauterive, the next village to the north. Neuchâtel's biggest annual festival is the winemakers' three-day celebration of the grape harvest, the *fête des vendanges*. It's celebrated the last weekend of September with parades and fanfare throughout the city.

The extent of French influence in Neuchâtel is revealed in its monuments and architecture, most notably at the **Église Collégiale** (Collegiate Church). The handsome Romanesque and Burgundian Gothic structure dates from the 12th century, with a colorful tile roof. The church contains a strikingly realistic and well-preserved grouping of life-size painted figures called *le cénotaphe,* or monument, to the counts of Neuchâtel. Dating from the 14th and 15th centuries, this is considered one of Europe's finest examples of medieval art. Anyone not wanting to climb steep streets can reach the church from the Promenade Noire off the place des Halles by an inconspicuous elevator—*ascenseur publique.* ⊠ *12 rue de la Collégiale* ☎ *032/8896000* ☞ *Free* ⊙ *Weekdays 8–noon and 1:30–5.*

The **Tour des Prisons** (Prison Tower), which adjoins the Collegiate Church, has panoramic views from its turret. On your way up, stop in one of the original wooden prison cells. ⊠ *rue Jeanne de Hochberg* ☎ *No phone* ☞ *1 SF* ⊙ *Apr.–Sept., daily 8–6.*

The architecture of the **Old Town** demonstrates a full range of French styles. Along rue des Moulins are two perfect specimens of the Louis XIII period, and—at its opposite end—a fine Louis XIV house anchors the place des Halles (market square), also notable for its turreted 16th-century **Maison des Halles.** The Hôtel de Ville (⊠ rue de l'Hôtel de Ville) opened in 1790 east of the Old Town. It was designed by Pierre-Adrien Paris, Louis XVI's architect. There are also several fine patrician houses, such as the magnificent **Hôtel DuPeyrou** (⊠ 1 av. DuPeyrou), home of the friend, protector, and publisher of Jean-Jacques Rousseau, who studied botany in the nearby Val-de-Travers. Most of the Old Town is a pedestrians-only zone, though public buses do run through it.

Behind the Hôtel DuPeyrou, the new **Galeries de l'Histoire** house models of Neuchâtel from the year 1000 to 2000. ✉ *7 av. DuPeyrou* ☎ *032/7177920* ⊕ *www.mahn.ch* 💲 *Free* ⊙ *Tues.–Sun. 1–5.*

★ Thanks to a remarkably unprovincial curator, the **Musée d'Art et d'Histoire** (Museum of Art and History) displays a striking collection of paintings gathered under broad themes—nature, civilization—and mounted in a radical, evocative way. Fifteenth-century allegories, early impressionism, and contemporary abstractions pack the walls from floor to ceiling: interacting, conflicting, demanding comparison. You may climb a platform (itself plastered with paintings) to view the higher works. This aggressive series of displays is framed by the architectural decorations of Neuchâtel resident Clement Heaton, whose murals and stained glass make the building itself a work of art.

This novel museum also has the honor of hosting three of this watchmaking capital's most exceptional guests: the **automates Jaquet-Droz**, three astounding little androids, created between 1768 and 1774, which once toured the courts of Europe like young mechanical Mozarts. Pierre Jaquet-Droz and his son Henri-Louis created them, and they are moving manifestations of the stellar degree to which watchmaking had evolved by the 18th century. Le Dessinateur (the Draughtsman) is an automated dandy in satin knee pants who draws graphite images of a dog, the god Eros in a chariot pulled by a butterfly, and a profile of Louis XV. La Musicienne (the Musician) is a young woman playing the organ. She moves and breathes subtly with the music and actually strikes the keys that produce the organ notes. L'Écrivain (the Writer) dips a real feather in real ink and writes 40 different letters. Like a primitive computer, he can be programmed to write any message simply by changing a steel disk. The automatons come alive only on the first Sunday of the month, at 2, 3, or 4 (or by appointment), but the audiovisual show recreates the thrill. ✉ *quai Léopold-Robert* ☎ *032/7177925* ⊕ *www.mahn. ch* 💲 *7 SF, free Wed.* ⊙ *Tues.–Sun. 10–6.*

Named after the Swiss writer and artist Friedrich Dürrenmatt, the **Centre Dürrenmatt,** perched high above Neuchâtel, houses an exhibition area devoted to modern literature and visual arts. Architect Mario Botta designed a curving, skylit underground space connected to Dürrenmatt's former home (now a private library and offices). Many of Dürrenmatt's paintings are disturbing, reflecting a bleak world view that tends to be softened by the humor, albeit acerbic, in his writing. Letters and excerpts of his books are also on display, and each artwork is accompanied by a quote. Fifty-minute group tours with an American guide can be booked in advance. ✉ *74 chemin du Pertuis-du-Sault* ☎ *032/202060* ⊕ *www. cdn.ch* 💲 *8 SF* ⊙ *Wed.–Sun. 11–5.*

★ ☾ Opened on the lakeshore in 2001, **Laténium,** an interactive archaeological museum, displays artifacts discovered in and around the lake and explains (in French and German) how they were recovered. The lifestyles of the *la Tène* Celts and Bronze Age lake dwellers are skillfully depicted. A sculpted menhir from Bevaix, a village southwest of Neuchâtel, resembles a man. Inside the museum you can see the remains of a 60-foot-long Gallo-Roman barge; outside in the park, its reconstruction is moored near a full-scale wooden Bronze Age house on stilts. There is a pamphlet in English, and guided tours in English can be booked in advance. ⊠ *2068 Hauterive* ☎ *032/8896917* ⊕ *www.latenium.ch* 🖃 *9 SF* ⊙ *Tues.–Sun. 10–5.*

Where to Stay & Eat

$$–$$$ ✗ **Au Boccalino.** Just north of Neuchâtel, this restaurant gastronomique has a tiny winter-garden brasserie and a main dining room discreetly decorated in pale gray and muted blue. Despite its proximity to the lake, there's neither terrace nor view, and charming owner-chef Claude Frôté wants it that way. Customers should come for his innovative regional food (an evening menu will cost between 120 SF and 150 SF—without cheese and dessert) and, above all, his wine. He keeps 25,000 bottles in stock, and connoisseurs can reserve a predinner *apéro* in the cellar (for up to 12 people). Try traditional tripe, pork tongue, foie gras of duck with passion fruit, or veal poached with vanilla and mint. ⊠ *11 av. Bachelin, St-Blaise* ☎ *032/7533680* ⌲ *Reservations essential* ☰ *AE, DC, MC, V* ⊙ *Closed Sun. and Mon.; mid-July–mid-Aug.; and late Dec.–early Jan.*

$–$$$ ✗ **Du Banneret.** The chef often emerges to greet diners in the brasserie portion of this popular restaurant, housed in a late-Renaissance building at the foot of the rue du Château. Dishes are mostly regional fare, such as homemade pasta with fresh wild mushrooms and lake trout. In the upstairs dining room, the food takes a strong Italian twist. ⊠ *1 rue Fleury* ☎ *032/7252861* ☰ *AE, DC, MC, V* ⊙ *Closed Sun. and Mon.*

$–$$$ ✗ **Le Cardinal Brasserie.** Stop and have a perfect café crème (coffee with cream) or a light meal along with the Neuchâteloise at one of the most authentic cafés in the Old Town. The interior has some striking art nouveau elements; the molded ceiling, etched windows, and blue-and-green decorative tile all date from 1905. Fish is the specialty, and large platters of *fruits de mer* (shellfish) in season are a delicious treat. ⊠ *9 rue du Seyon* ☎ *032/7251286* ☰ *AE, MC, V.*

¢ ✗ **Bach & Buck.** Simply furnished and seating 70, this crêperie opposite the Jardin Anglais is an ideal spot to grab a cheap but tasty meal. The 130 types of crepes include savory, vegetarian, sweet, and with liqueurs. The Provençale (tomatoes, cheese, herbes de Provence, plus your choice of other ingredients) is a lunchtime favorite. ⊠ *22 av. du 1er-Mars* ☎ *032/7256353* ☰ No credit cards ⊙ *No lunch Sun. July–Aug.*

$$ ✗▥ **Auberge de l'Aubier.** A 15-minute drive west of Neuchâtel, this small ecoretreat comes complete with organic farm, solar panels on the barn, and washing machines that use rainwater. Rooms are different but are all simply decorated and color-coordinated in shades designed to soothe the soul. Many have balconies or bay windows with lake views. An annex with 10 smaller, cheaper rooms (incongruously called "bungalows") has been added. The restaurant ($–$$$; closed Monday) emphasizes fresh, local ingredients, turning out such dishes as red-pepper terrine and homegrown pork. ⊠ *CH-2205 Montézillon* ☎ *032/7322211* 🖶 *032/7322200* ⊕ *www.aubier.ch* ⌁ *25 rooms* ⌂ *Restaurant, bicycles, hiking, cross-country skiing, shop, meeting rooms; no smoking* ☰ *AE, DC, MC, V* ⊙ *Closed early Jan.* ¶⊙ *BP.*

$-$$ ✕▥ **La Maison du Prussien.** In the gorge of Vauseyon, 10 minutes from Neuchâtel, this restored 18th-century brewery nestles alongside a roaring woodland stream. Polished beams, yellow sandstone highlights, and lush views are undeniably atmospheric. Every room is different, and three have fireplaces. The winter-garden restaurant ($$$) offers innovative seasonal cuisine, such as duck breast sautéed with saffron and coulis of blackberry; you can have a simpler lunch on the terrace overlooking the stream. Take the tunnels under Neuchâtel toward La Chaux-de-Fonds, exit toward Pontarlier-Vauseyon, and watch for the hotel's signs. ⊠ *Gor du Vauseyon, CH-2000* ☎ *032/7305454* 🖳 *032/7302143* ⊕ *www.hotel-prussien.ch* ⌨ *6 rooms, 4 suites* ♿ *Restaurant, café, minibars, in-room DVD, bar, meeting room, some pets allowed (fee)* ▤ *AE, DC, MC, V* ⊘ *Closed July, late Dec.–early Jan.*

$ ✕▥ **Du Marché.** Opening directly onto the place des Halles, this is a delightful place for a hearty plat du jour or a carafe of local wine. Inside, pass through the lively bar-café to the steamy, old-wood brasserie for a bowl of tripe in Neuchâtel wine or salt pork with lentils. Upstairs, a pretty little dining room (¢–$$$) serves more sophisticated fare. Plain, functional rooms with tidy tile bathrooms down the hall are good value. Double-glaze windows keep out the noise. ⊠ *4 pl. des Halles, CH-2000* ☎ *032/7232330* 🖳 *032/7232333* ⊕ *www.hoteldumarche.com* ⌨ *10 rooms* ♿ *Restaurant, café, cable TV* ▤ *AE, DC, MC, V* ⊙⏐ *BP.*

★ $$$$ ▥ **Beau-Rivage.** This thoroughly elegant restored 19th-century hotel sits gracefully on the lakeshore; on a clear day there's a splendid view of the Alps. The warmly lit interior, with high ceilings and wild-cherry wood, exudes calm. Two-thirds of the spacious rooms have lake views. The sophisticated dining room, done in pale green, offers a fine selection of wines, after-dinner cigars, and brandies. The hotel has air-conditioning. ⊠ *1 esplanade du Mont Blanc, CH-2001* ☎ *032/7231515* 🖳 *032/7231616* ⊕ *www.beau-rivage-hotel.ch* ⌨ *65 rooms* ♿ *Restaurant, in-room data ports, in-room safes, minibars, cable TV, bar, babysitting, business services, convention center, some free parking, some pets allowed (some for fee)* ▤ *AE, DC, MC, V.*

$$ ▥ **Alpes et Lac.** This modest 19th-century hotel across from the train station overlooks tile rooftops, the sparkling lake, and the white-capped Alps. Although the building was modernized, it preserves the original parquet floors and stone steps. Along the pale yellow corridors, fresh flowers hide in niches. The gold-and-red-checked bedspreads in the guest rooms echo the colors found throughout this sunny hotel. A lovely park surrounds the terrace. ⊠ *2 pl. de la Gare, CH-2002* ☎ *032/7231919* 🖳 *032/7231920* ⊕ *www.alpesetlac.ch* ⌨ *30 rooms* ♿ *Restaurant, in-room safes, minibars, cable TV, Internet, meeting rooms, some free parking, some pets allowed* ▤ *AE, DC, MC, V* ⊙⏐ *BP.*

★ $-$$ ▥ **Le Café-Hôtel de L'Aubier.** In the pedestrian zone at the foot of the château, this delightful hotel offers light, modern, spacious rooms whose warm color schemes are inspired by the spice they are named after. Cheaper rooms have their own sink but share a bathroom. The central location sometimes makes it noisy on weekends. The café (closed Monday breakfast and Sunday) and terrace offer inexpensive but good fare: breakfasts, salads, and desserts (try the chocolate tart), with a selection of teas and coffees. ✉ *1 rue du Château, CH-2000* ☎ *032/7101858* 📠 *032/ 7101859* ⊕ *www.aubier.ch* ⇆ *9 rooms, 3 with bath* ♿ *Café, some pets allowed, no-smoking floors; no TV in some rooms* ☰ *MC, V.*

Sports & the Outdoors

GOLF There's an 18-hole golf course at **Voëns sur St-Blaise** (☎ 032/7535550) open to anyone with proof of membership in another club.

SWIMMING There are **public beaches** at many villages and resorts on the lake. A **municipal complex** (✉ Nid du Crô, 30 rte. des Falaises ☎ 032/7226222) has outdoor and indoor pools.

Nightlife

Neuchâtel has an ever-changing selection of restaurants de nuit and *bars musicaux,* establishments that pulse with disco music until the wee hours of the morning and sometimes serve food—along the lines of steak *frites* (steak and fries)—to keep you going. **Café Trio** (✉ 3 rue des Moulins ☎ 032/7242224) is open until 2 on Friday and Saturday. **Casino de la Rotonde** (✉ 14 Faubourg du Lac ☎ 032/7244848) houses the Discothèque le Jocker, open 10–4, and the **Sunset Bar,** open 5–2.

en route To the west of Neuchâtel lie some of Switzerland's best vineyards, their grapes producing chiefly white and rosé wines that are light and slightly sparkling. The wines are bottled before the second fermentation, so they have a rather high carbonic acid content. **Château Boudry** offers wine tasting by appointment and houses the **Musée Cantonale de la vigne et du vin** (Cantonal Museum of Vines and Wines). ✉ *Tour de Pierre* ☎ *032/8421098* 🎫 *Museum 5 SF* ⊙ *Museum Wed.–Sun. 2–6.*

Grandson

⑫ *29 km (18 mi) southwest of Neuchâtel.*

This lakeside village in Canton Vaud has a long history. It is said that in 1066 a member of the Grandson family accompanied William of Normandy (better known as the Conqueror) to England, where he founded the English barony of Grandison. Otto I of Grandson took part in the Crusades. When the Burgundian Wars broke out in the late 15th century, the **Château de Grandson** (Grandson Castle), built in the 11th century and much rebuilt during the 13th and 15th centuries, was in the hands of Charles the Bold of Burgundy. In 1475 the Swiss won it by siege, but early the next year their garrison was surprised by Charles, and 418 of their men were captured and hanged from the apple trees in the castle orchard. A few days later the Swiss returned to Grandson and, after crushing the Burgundians, retaliated by stringing their prisoners from the same apple trees. After being used for three centuries as a residence by the Bernese bailiffs, the castle was bought in 1875 by the de Blonay family, who restored it to its current impressive state, with high, massive walls and five cone turrets. Inside, you can see reproductions of Charles the Bold's Burgundian war tent and two jousting knights astride their horses—in full armor. There are also *oubliettes* (dungeon pits for prisoners held *in perpetua*), torture chambers, and a model of the Battle of Grandson, complete with 20-minute slide show (in English if you get in quickly enough to push the right button). Cassette-guided tours of the town are available at the castle reception desk. The dungeons now house an extensive vintage car museum, with motorbikes and even a Penny Farthing bicycle. ☎ 024/4452926 ⊕ *www.grandson.ch* 🎫 *12 SF* ⊙ *Apr.–Oct., daily 8.30–6; Nov.–Mar., Mon.–Sat. 8:30–11 and 2–5, Sun. 8.30–5.*

Yverdon-les-Bains

⑬ *6 km (4 mi) southwest of Grandson, 36 km (22 mi) southwest of Neuchâtel.*

This pastel-color lakefront town at the southernmost tip of Lac Neuchâtel has been appreciated for its thermal waters and sandy, willow-lined shoreline since the Romans first invaded and set up thermal baths here. In the 18th century its fame spread across Europe. Today the **Thermal Center** is completely up-to-date, with medicinal and recreational pools. Swim caps are mandatory. ✉ *22 av. des Bains* ☎ *024/4230232* 🎫 *16 SF* ⊙ *Mon.–Sat. 8 AM–9:30 PM, Sun. 9–5.30.*

In the center of the Old Town sits the turreted, mid-13th-century **Château de Yverdon-les-Bains.** Most of the castle is now a museum, with exhibits on locally found prehistoric and Roman artifacts, Egyptian art, natural history, and of course, local history. A special room is dedicated to the famous Swiss educator Johann Heinrich Pestalozzi (1746–1827), who spent 20 years here. His influential ideas on education led to school reforms at home and in Germany and England. ☎ *024/4259310* 🎫 *8 SF* ⊙ *June–Sept., Tues.–Sun. 10–noon and 2–5; Oct.–May, Tues.–Sun. 2–5.*

In front of Yverdon's Hôtel de Ville—notable for its Louis XV facade—stands a bronze monument of Pestalozzi, grouped with two children. The charming, bustling town center is closed to traffic. Along the waterfront you'll find parks, promenades, a shady campground, and a 5-km (3-mi) stretch of little beaches.

en route   Reaching north from Neuchâtel into the Jura Mountains, Highway 20 climbs 13 km (8 mi) from Neuchâtel to the **Vue des Alpes,** a parking area on a high ridge that, on a clear day, affords spectacular views of the Alps, including the Eiger, Mönch, Jungfrau, and Mont Blanc.

THE JURA

Straddling the French frontier from Geneva to Basel is a range of low-riding mountains (few peaks exceed 4,920 feet), which fall steeply down to the mysterious River Doubs, Lac des Brenets, and Doubs Falls to the north and to Lac Neuchâtel and the Lac de Bienne to the south. The secret of this region, known as the Jura, is the sunny plateau atop the mountains, especially in the Montagnes Neuchâteloise and the

Franches-Montagnes. These lush pastures and gentle woods have excellent hiking, biking, horseback riding, and cross-country-skiing opportunities—perfectly organized yet unspoiled. (Be warned, though, that it can get chilly in winter: La Brévine, between Le Locle and Les Verrières, is known as the Swiss Siberia.) Watchmaking concentrates around Le Locle and La Chaux-de-Fonds, and horse breeding and tourism flourish in the Franches-Montagnes. Jura is the youngest Swiss canton. In 2004, it celebrated the 25th anniversary of its independence.

La Chaux-de-Fonds

⑭ *22 km (14 mi) north of Neuchâtel.*

Actually part of Canton Neuchâtel, La Chaux-de-Fonds (called "Tschaux" by locals) sits high on the Jura plateau. In the early 18th century, watchmaking was introduced as a cottage industry to create income for an area otherwise completely dependent on farming. Over the years the town became the watchmaking capital of Switzerland. Destroyed by fire at the end of the 18th century, the city was rebuilt on a grid plan around the central, broad, tree-lined avenue Léopold-Robert. It is a city of incongruities: pastel-painted town houses and stone villas, working-class cafés and cultural institutions.

Famed architect Charles-Édouard Jeanneret, otherwise known as Le Corbusier, was born here. His birthplace can be seen, although not toured, along with the École d'Art, where he taught, and several villas he worked on between 1906 and 1917. Only one of his buildings is open to the public: the **Villa Turque,** north of the main avenue. It has a glowing terra-cotta-brick facade, rounded wings, and curved edges. A 20-minute video about Le Corbusier is available in English. The tourist office has a brochure outlining a walk that passes by his buildings. ⊠ *147 rue du Doubs* ☎ *032/9123123* ☜ *Free* ☉ *1st and 3rd Sat. of month 10–4 or by appointment; call weekdays 9–11 and 2–5.*

The **Musée des Beaux-Arts** (Museum of Fine Arts), a striking neoclassical structure, was designed by Le Corbusier's teacher, L'Éplattenier. It contains works by Swiss artists Léopold Robert and Ferdinand Hodler as well as three of Le Corbusier's works: a furniture set, an oil painting (*Femme au Peignoir*), and a tapestry (*Les Musiciennes*). The museum also usually has a temporary exhibit. ⊠ *33 rue des Musées* ☎ *032/9130444* ☜ *8 SF, Sun. 10–noon free* ☉ *Tues.–Sun. 10–5.*

★ The **Musée International d'Horlogerie** (International Timepiece Museum) displays a fascinating collection of clocks and watches that traces the development of timekeeping and the expansion of watchmaking as an art form. You can see audiovisual presentations on the history and science of the craft, observe current repairs on pieces from the collection in an open work area, and browse the gift shop, which sells replicas as well as the latest timepieces by stellar local watchmaking firms (Corum, Girard-Perregaux, Ebel, and so on). Some explanatory material is in English, and group tours in English can be arranged. ⊠ *29 rue des Musées* ☎ *032/9676861* ⊕ *www.mih.ch* ☜ *10 SF* ☉ *Tues.–Sun. 10–5.*

Where to Stay & Eat

★ **$-$$** ✕ **Auberge de Mont-Cornu.** Just southeast of town, this converted farm-house has an idyllic setting. Friendly staff serve everything from simple sandwiches to traditional regional dishes; the fondue with cream is renowned. Rooms are wood-paneled and chock-full of authentic extras: a grandfather clock, a gramophone with record, and a huge glazed-tile oven. In summer sit outside in the flower-filled garden and take in the view of wooded hills and the sound of distant cowbells. The restaurant is open only by advance reservation in December, mostly for groups. ✉ *116 Mont-Cornu* ☎ *032/9687600* ⚠ *Reservations essential* ▭ *AE, MC, V* ⊘ *Closed Mon. and Tues. and Dec.–Feb.*

$$$ ✕▥ **Grand Hôtel les Endroits.** Set in a tranquil green suburb above town, this modern, family-run hotel offers just about everything. Rooms are spacious and light, with discrete pastels and warm wood set off by touches of black. Many have balconies or open onto a grassy area. Eat in the no-smoking restaurant ($–$$$), in the brasserie (¢–$$), or on the large terrace. Enjoy a Jacuzzi after a day of skiing or a strenuous bike ride. ✉ *94–96 bd. des Endroits, CH-2300* ☎ *032/9250250* 🖨 *032/9250350* ⊕ *www.hotel-les-endroits.ch* ⤴ *42 rooms, 4 suites* ⚹ *Restaurant, café, in-room safes, minibars, cable TV with movies, sauna, bicycles, Ping-Pong, recreation room, playground, Internet, business services, convention center, some pets allowed (fee), no-smoking rooms* ▭ *AE, DC, MC, V* ⦿ *BP.*

$$ ▥ **Fleur-de-Lys.** This low-key hotel offers comfortable rooms in muted mauves and aquas and a few extra perks, such as the fresh fruit and snacks waiting for you on top of the minibar. The windows were replaced in 2004 to keep out the noise of the main thoroughfare and the annual two-week music festival. A number of meal plans are available (in the Italian restaurant), as are weekend package deals. ✉ *13 av. Léopold-Robert, CH-2300* ☎ *032/9133731* 🖨 *032/9135851* ⊕ *www.fleur-de-lys.ch* ⤴ *33 rooms* ⚹ *Restaurant, in-room safes, minibars, cable TV, bar, Internet, convention center* ▭ *AE, DC, MC, V* ⦿ *BP.*

Skiing

La Chaux-de-Fonds is very close to cross-country ski areas and some modest downhill runs as well. The **Tête-de-Ran,** beyond Vue des Alpes, tops 4,592 feet and provides panoramic views toward the Bernese Alps. Together, Vue des Alpes, Tête-de-Ran, La Corbatière, and Le Locle count 31 lifts, 27 km (16 mi) of downhill runs, and 400 km (nearly 250 mi) of cross-country trails.

Saignelégier

⑮ *26 km (16 mi) northeast of La Chaux-de-Fonds, 36 km (22 mi) south-west of Delémont.*

A small, fairly modern town, Saignelégier is known mostly for its lush surroundings, horseback riding, and cross-country skiing. The Marché-Concours National de Chevaux (National Horse Fair), held since 1897, takes place on the second Sunday in August and draws crowds from throughout Switzerland and France, as does the Fête des Montgolfières (Hot-Air Balloon Festival) the second weekend of October.

Where to Stay & Eat

$$$–$$$$ ✕ **Hôtel-Restaurant Georges Wenger.** One of Switzerland's top gourmet
Fodor'sChoice restaurants is just 6 km (4 mi) from Saignelégier. Chef Georges Wenger
★ creates elegant, savory dishes with both a regional and seasonal bent
and has a flair for unusual combinations, such as langoustines with a
subtle, gingery almond-milk and rhubarb sauce. An excellent selection
of cheeses and a fine wine cellar round out the experience. If you feel
you can't tear yourself away, you can spend the night; upstairs are a hand-
ful of luxurious, individually decorated rooms. ⊠ *2 rue de la Gare, Le
Noirmont* ☎ *032/9576633* 🖷 *032/9576634* ⊕ *www.georgeswenger.
grandestables.ch* ⊟ *AE, DC, MC, V* ⊘ *Closed late July–early Aug., late
Dec.–late Jan., and Mon. and Tues.*

¢–$ ▦ **Café Du Soleil.** For the bohemian at heart, the Soleil is a great gather-
ing place. Artists, writers, musicians, and passersby come for the artwork,
live music (classical or jazz), and fresh vegetarian food. Rooms are spar-
tan but clean; all have writing desks. It's just across from the town's eques-
trian center. The restaurant is closed on Monday. Some cheaper rooms
share bathrooms. ⊠ *CH-2350* ☎ *032/9511688* 🖷 *032/9512295* ⊕ *www.
cafe-du-soleil.ch* ⊠ *23 rooms, 21 with bath, 1 dormitory* ⚄ *Restaurant,
café, minibars; no TV in some rooms* ⊟ *MC, V* ⦿⦿ *BP.*

Sports & the Outdoors

This is terrific horseback-riding country. Many individual farms offer
riding packages that include accommodations and are geared for fam-
ilies. For information, contact the tourist office. You can also rent horses
at the **Manège de Saignelégier** (☎ 032/9511755).

St-Ursanne

⑯ *27 km (17 mi) northeast of Saignelégier, 22 km (14 mi) west of Delémont.*

This lovely, quiet medieval town in a valley carved by the River Doubs
is best known to outdoors enthusiasts—fishermen, bicyclists, canoeists,
and, believe it or not, bat watchers. The 12th-century church, la Collé-
giale, is a mixture of Romanesque and early Gothic architecture; the large
cloisters are Gothic. The old stone bridge over the River Doubs, with
its statue of St. John of Nepomuk, the patron saint of bridges, best catches
the romantic spirit of St-Ursanne.

Porrentruy

⑰ *13.5 km (8 mi) northwest of St-Ursanne, 28 km (17 mi) northwest of
Delémont.*

A small detour toward the French border brings you to the center of
the Ajoie region and to this city that was once the seat of the bishop-
princes of Basel and that today has an excellently preserved medieval
town center. The impressive Château de Porrentruy towers over the Old
Town and is now used for cantonal offices. The 13th-century Tour Ré-
fouse (Refuge Tower), next to the castle, provides a beautiful view and
is always open to the public. The Porte de France, a remnant of the walls
of the city, and the old stone houses alongside it dramatically reflect a
medieval character.

Delémont

⑱ *81 km (50 mi) northeast of Neuchâtel.*

Set in a wide, picturesque valley, this is the administrative seat of Canton Jura. Though it's on the French-German language divide, the official language is French. In the 11th century Delémont was annexed by the bishop-princes of Basel, who often used it as a summer residence; it remained an annex until the 18th century. The town center is still atmospheric, with cobblestone streets and splashing 17th-century fountains.

All kinds of artifacts illuminate the region's history in the **Musée Jurassien d'Art et d'Histoire** (Museum of Art and History of the Jura). A fascinating collection of archaeological finds includes Roman terra-cotta and bronze pieces; there are also ancient religious objects, mementos from the Napoleonic era, and 18th-century furnishings. ⊠ *12 pl. de la Gare* ☎ *032/4228077* ⊕ *www.jura.ch/musees/arthist.htm* ☞ *6 SF* ⊙ *Tues.–Sun. 2–5.*

A mile northeast of town is the pilgrimage church **Chapelle du Vorbourg**, perched on a wooded outcropping. The door is usually open; masses are held Sunday and holidays at 9:30 AM.

⌐ off the
⌐ beaten
⌐ path

MOUTIER – Just 11 km (6½ mi) south of Delémont, this medieval town produces the creamy, piquant Vacherin Mont d'Or and Tête de Moine cheeses, the only reminder of the town's once-renowned monastery of Bellelay.

Where to Stay & Eat

$ ✕⌹ **Hotel du Midi.** This unassuming, charming restaurant-hotel faces the train station and houses three restaurants (¢–$$$ between them; closed Wednesday and dinner Tuesday), ranging from gastronomique to brasserie. Fare is as simple as spaghetti Bolognese or as sophisticated as pigeon stuffed with cabbage and olives. The large rooms are tucked under the roof on the third floor and yield views toward the town or the station. Some were redecorated with pale wood and cheerful fabrics in 2002. ⊠ *10 pl. de la Gare, CH-2800* ☎ *032/4221777* ⌂ *032/4231989* ☞ *7 rooms* ♨ *2 restaurants, café, cable TV* ⊟ *DC, MC, V* ⑽ *BP.*

FRIBOURG, NEUCHÂTEL & THE JURA A TO Z

To research prices, get advice from other travelers, and book travel arrangements, visit www.fodors.com.

AIR TRAVEL

Frequent flights from the United States and the United Kingdom arrive on Swiss and other international carriers, either at Geneva's Cointrin or Unique Zürich airports.

AIRPORTS

Fribourg lies between Geneva's Cointrin Airport (138 km [86 mi] to the southwest) and Unique Zürich Airport (180 km [112 mi] to the northeast). Train connections to both are good. The Bern-Belp Airport is a small international airport 34 km (21 mi) northeast of Fribourg, near Bern.

🔁 **Airport Information** Bern-Belp Airport ☎ 031/9602111. **Cointrin Airport** ☎ 022/7177111, 0900/571500 for arrivals and departures. **Unique Zürich Airport** ☎ 0900/300313.

BOAT & FERRY TRAVEL

There are boat trips on the lakes of Neuchâtel, Murten (Morat), and Biel (Bienne), as well as on the Aare River and the Broye Canal, a natural wildlife sanctuary. Schedules vary seasonally but in summer are frequent and include evening trips. Contact Navigation Lacs de Neuchâtel et Morat for more information.

🔁 **Boat & Ferry Information** Navigation Lacs de Neuchâtel et Morat ☎ 032/7299600.

BUS TRAVEL

Postbus connections, except in the principal urban areas, can be few and far between; plan excursions carefully using the bus schedules available at the train station.

CAR TRAVEL

An important and scenic trans-Swiss artery, the A12 expressway, cuts from Bern to Lausanne, passing directly above Fribourg. A parallel route to the northwest extends the A1 between Zürich and Bern, connecting Bern to Murten, Payerne, and Lausanne. The expressway between Neuchâtel and Yverdon is still mostly under construction, but the one connecting Neuchâtel and La Chaux-de-Fonds is now complete. From Basel, the slow but scenic highway 18 meanders through the Jura by way of Delémont.

The charms of this varied region can be seen best by car, and there are scenic secondary highways throughout. Keep in mind that some towns, like Gruyères, are car-free or have pedestrians-only centers; in these cases, parking lots are easy to find.

EMERGENCIES

In case of any emergency, dial ☎ 117. For an ambulance and/or doctor, dial ☎ 144.

🔁 **Emergency Contacts** Fribourg police ☎ 117 or 026/3051818. **Neuchâtel police** ☎ 117 or 032/7222222.

🔁 **Medical Contacts** Dental referrals ☎ 026/3223343 in Fribourg, 032/7222222 in Neuchâtel. **Medical referrals** ☎ 144.

TOURS

Fribourg, Neuchâtel, and Murten tourist offices organize guided city walking tours for groups in English. Tourist offices will also organize package deals with hotels and sights or transportation.

TRAIN TRAVEL

The main train route connecting Basel, Zürich, and Geneva passes through the Fribourg station between Bern and Lausanne. Trains generally arrive twice an hour.

Secondary connections are thin, but they allow visits to most towns. To visit Gruyères, you must take a bus out of Broc.

𝄜 Train Information Fribourg station ✉ av. de la Gare ☎ 0900/300300 [1.19 SF per min].

VISITOR INFORMATION

The regional office for Canton Fribourg is based in Fribourg. The regional office for Canton Neuchâtel (as well as its city tourist office) is based in Neuchâtel. The Jura's regional office is found in Saignelégier.

𝄜 Local Tourist Offices Avenches ✉ 3 pl. de l'Église, CH-1580 ☎ 026/6769922 ⊕ www.avenches.ch. **Charmey** ✉ CH-1637 ☎ 026/9275580 ⊕ www.charmey.ch. **Estavayer-le-Lac** ✉ pl. du Midi, CH-1470 ☎ 026/6631237 ⊕ www.estavayer-le-lac.ch. **Fribourg** ✉ 1 av. de la Gare, CH-1700 ☎ 026/3501111 🖶 026/3501112 ⊕ www.fribourgtourism.ch. **Gruyères** ✉ CH-1663 ☎ 026/9211030 ⊕ www.gruyeres.ch. **La Chaux-de-Fonds** ✉ 1 Espacité, CH-2302 ☎ 032/9196895 ⊕ www.chaux-de-fonds.ch. **Moléson-sur-Gruyères** ✉ Moléson-Village CH-1663 ☎ 026/9218500 ⊕ www.moleson.ch. **Murten** ✉ 6 Franz-Kirchg., CH-3280 ☎ 026/6705112 ⊕ www.murten.ch. **Porrentruy** ✉ 5 Grand-rue, CH-2900 ☎ 032/4665959 ⊕ www.porrentruy.ch. **St-Ursanne** ✉ CH-2882 ☎ 032/4613716 ⊕ www.jura.ch/st-ursanne. **Schwarzsee** ✉ CH-1716 ☎ 026/4121313 ⊕ www.schwarzsee.ch. **Yverdon-les-Bains** ✉ 1 pl. de la Gare, CH-1400 ☎ 024/4236101 ⊕ www.yverdon-les-bains.ch/tourisme.

𝄜 Regional Tourist Offices Fribourg ✉ 1107 rue de la Glâne, CH-1700 ☎ 026/4025644 🖶 026/4023119 ⊕ www.pays-de-fribourg.ch. **Neuchâtel** ✉ Hôtel des Postes, CH-2001 ☎ 032/8896890 🖶 032/8896291 ⊕ www.neuchateltourisme.ch. **Saignelégier** ✉ pl. du 23-Juin, CH-2350 ☎ 032/9521952 🖶 032/9521955 ⊕ www.juratourisme.ch.

BERN

WITH A SIDE TRIP TO THE EMMENTAL

8

BROWSE THE BRUNNEN
Bern's allegorical fountains ⇨*p.249*

GRIN AND BEAR IT
feeding bears at the Bärengraben ⇨*p.251*

WITNESS FEATS OF KLEE
at the Zentrum Paul Klee ⇨*p.254*

FOLLOW THE POLS
to lunch at Della Casa ⇨*p.258*

MEANDER THE MARKETS
on cobblestone plazas ⇨*p.266*

OGLE THE ALPS
from the Bundeshaus portico ⇨*p.251*

SAY "CHEESE!"
in the dairy capital of Emmental ⇨*p.267*

Updated by
Kay
Winzenried

BERN IS THE SWISS CAPITAL, yes, but you won't find much cosmopolitan nonsense here. The annual fair celebrates the humble onion, the mascot is a common bear, and the seven members of the coalition government, each of whom serves a year as president, have to find their own places to live when in Bern. In fact, there's not even an official presidential residence, and the leader of the Swiss Confederation is likely to take the tram to work.

Bern wasn't always so self-effacing. It earned its pivotal position through a history of power and influence that dates from the 12th century, when Berchtold V, duke of Zähringen, established a fortress on this gooseneck in the River Aare. He chose Bern not only for its impregnable location but also for its proximity to the great kingdom of Burgundy, which spread across France and much of present-day French-speaking Switzerland.

By the 14th century Bern had grown into a strong urban republic. When the last Zähringens died, the people of Bern defeated their would-be replacements and, shedding the Holy Roman Empire, became the eighth canton to join the rapidly growing Swiss Confederation. It was an unlikely union: aristocratic, urban Bern allied with the strongly democratic farming communities of central Switzerland. But it provided the Bernese with enough security against the Habsburg Holy Roman Empire to continue westward expansion.

Despite a devastating fire that laid waste to the city in 1405, by the late 15th century the Bernese had become a power of European stature—a stature enhanced exponentially by three decisive victories over the duke of Burgundy in 1476 and 1477. Aided by the other cantons and prompted by Louis XI, king of France and bitter enemy of the Burgundians, the Bernese crushed Charles the Bold and drove him out of his Swiss lands. Not only did the Bernese expand their territories all the way west to Geneva, but they also acquired immense wealth—great treasures of gold, silver, and precious textiles—and assumed the leading role in Switzerland and Swiss affairs.

Bern stayed on top. Through the 17th and 18th centuries, the city's considerable prosperity was built not so much on commerce as on the export of troops and military know-how. The city and her territories functioned essentially as a patrician state, ruled by an aristocracy that saw its raison d'être in politics, foreign policy, the acquisition of additional lands, and the forging of alliances. At the same time, her landed gentry continued to grow fat on the fruits of the city's rich agricultural lands. Napoléon seized the lands briefly from 1798 until his defeat in 1815, but by the 1830s the Bernese were back in charge, and when the Swiss Confederation took its contemporary, democratic form in 1848, Bern was a natural choice for its capital.

Today Bern is the country's geographic, educational, and political hub. But it was the perfectly preserved arcades, fountains, and stone buildings of Bern's Old Town that caused UNESCO to award Bern World Cultural Heritage status, putting the city on a par with Rome and Florence.

8

If you have
1 or 2
days

You can take in the highlights of Bern in a single day, but two days will allow you a more leisurely pace, with time for shopping and a museum or two. Starting at the *Hauptbahnhof* (main train station), move eastward through the arcades and plazas. Check your watch as you pass the Zytglogge, on the Kramgasse, and if you're there just before the hour, pause to watch the animated performance on the clock tower's east side. A walk to the site of Bern's founding at the Nydeggkirche will take you past several of the city's famous fountains. Here you can cross over the bridge to feed the indolent bears at the Bärengraben and climb uphill to the Rosengarten for one of the best views of the city, or double back to the Münster, for panoramic city views, and the Bundeshaus, both must-sees.

If you have
3 to 5
days

If you're staying a few more days, start by exploring Bern as described above. Assuming your visit coincides with a market day, plan to spend several hours perusing one of these classic Bern experiences, and allow additional time for a museum. The Bernisches Historisches Museum and new Zentrum Paul Klee are both good options. To take in some of Switzerland's beautiful scenery, escape for an overnight to the Emmental, where you can sample some Emmentaler and see how the traditional holey Swiss cheese is made. Burgdorf's castle town and museums are reason enough for the excursion.

EXPLORING BERN

Because Bern stands on a high, narrow peninsula formed by a gooseneck in the Aare, its streets seem to follow the river's flow. The original town began by what is now the Nydegg bridge and expanded westward. The *Zeitglockenturm* (or *Zytglogge*, in local dialect), a clock tower constructed in 1191, marks the city's first western gate. Another entrance to the growing city was finished in 1256; it's located where the Käfigturm now stands.

The active, commercial City Center, around the train station and tram hub, transitions into the Old Town once you cross the Bärenplatz or pass through the Käfigturm. Marzili and Matte, formerly working-class neighborhoods, lie together along the deeply carved riverbed of the Aare. All these areas are easily explored on foot, but in Marzili and Matte you may want to take your cue from the locals: walk down, ride up. To get to the cluster of museums in Kirchenfeld, on the opposite side of the river, you can walk or hop on a tram.

Numbers in the text correspond to numbers in the margin and on the Bern map.

Old Town & City Center

With its cobblestone streets and solid stone buildings, the Altstadt (Old Town), at the historical heart of the city, retains a distinctly medieval appeal. After a fire destroyed its predominately wooden structures, the city was rebuilt in sandstone, with arcades stretching for some 6 km (4mi) away from the banks of the Aare. The 800-year-old area east of the Zytglogge contains beautiful old buildings as well as souvenir shops and many of the city's more upscale stores. Arcaded walkways extend beyond these ancient walls toward the Hauptbahnhof in the newer City Center. Although the facades and stone streets look similar, the commercial district concentrated between the main railroad station and the Zytglogge contains department stores and chain boutiques mixed with restaurants and upper-level office suites.

a good walk ▶

Start your tour at the southernmost end of the Hauptbahnhof, at the foot of the escalator leading to the Loeb department store. Here you'll find remnants of the **Christoffelturm ❶ ▶**, including a medieval city gate and parts of a moat.

Take the escalator from the Christoffelunterführung (underpass) up to street level. Before you is Spitalgasse. Following the trams, head down this wide street and walk *outside* the arcades to see some of the city's stunning architecture and an array of flags.

In the middle of Spitalgasse you'll come across the Pfeiferbrunnen (Bagpiper Fountain). Continue to the first intersection, Bärenplatz. Here, trams pass through the **Käfigturm ❷**, once a prison tower. Continue down the street (now called Marktgasse) to admire the Anna Seilerbrunnen, an allegory on moderation, and the Schützenbrunnen (Musketeer Fountain), a tribute to a troop commander from 1543.

At the end of Marktgasse, turn left on the Kornhausplatz to view the imposing 18th-century **Kornhaus ❸**, now the site of two restaurants and the Forum für Media und Gestaltung. On the Kornhausplatz, the Kindlifresserbrunnen is worth a second look: an ogre is munching on a meal of small children.

From the Kornhaus continue past the Stadttheater, site of theatrical and dance productions, and cross the street. Take the Kornhausbrücke over the river, stopping in the middle of the bridge. On a cloudy day you'll have a view of the Berner Altstadt and possibly the Gurten, Bern's local hill, behind it. If the air is clear, the sky in the distance will look like the backdrop for an opera, filled with the majestic gray-and-white peaks of the Alps.

Return from the Kornhausbrücke to the intersection where the trams turn. On your left, dominating town center, is the mighty **Zytglogge ❹**. Head under the clock to its far side and turn around to view the mechanical figures, which entertain hourly.

From the Zytglogge continue down Kramgasse, a lovely old street with many guild houses, some fine 18th-century residences, more arcades, and, of course, more fountains: first the Zähringerbrunnen (Zähringer Fountain), a monument to Bern's founder, Berchtold V; then the powerful depiction of Samson in the Simsonbrunnen. In the arcades at the right is No. 49, the **Einsteinhaus ❺**, once the apartment and workplace of Albert Einstein.

8

Arcades & Fountains
Like a giant cloister, Bern is crisscrossed by *Lauben* (arcades) that shelter stores of every kind and quality. Stout 15th-century pillars support the low vaulted roofs, which extend to the edge of the pavement below. At the base of many arcades, nearly horizontal cellar doors lead down into interesting underground eateries and businesses. Throughout Bern, brilliantly colored and skillfully carved *Brunnen* (fountains) provide relief from the sturdy severity of these medieval structures. Most fountains are the work of Hans Gieng, who created them between 1539 and 1549.

Markets
In the Middle Ages, Bern was a great marketing center, and markets are still an integral part of daily life. Of the seasonal markets, the most elaborate is the Zwibelemärit (Onion Market), which dates from the 1405 fire, when, in gratitude for assistance given by Fribourg, Bern granted farmers the unrestricted right to sell their onions in the city's market square. All over downtown, stalls display an unimaginable array of items made from onions—everything from wreaths to alarm clocks. Pot after pot of colorful draping flowers are sold to fill window boxes in spring Geranienmarkt (Geranium Market), and by December the air fills with the scent of evergreens and holiday excitement during the Weihnachtsmarkt (Christmas Market).

Bern shoppers also stock their wicker baskets and wheeled carts during weekly and monthly markets. Displayed with Swiss precision, fruits and vegetables sit scrubbed and color-coordinated on wooden tables. Old-fashioned pan scales wait to tabulate the weight of a handful of apricots or a bunch carrots. It's courtesy to ask for assistance, not to serve yourself. Aproned women and men in smocks stand at attention behind cases of cheese—towers of stacked wheels, bricks, logs, and tiny rounds—waiting for directions and moving around each other in a synchronized waltz. Hesitate and they will move on to the next customer pressing in behind you. Mobile cooling trailers serve butchers and fishmongers, each with an array of offerings that look like they must have been snared at dawn. A tangle of shoppers and carts spill out from coffee bars, where a respite before tackling the next item or a chat with a friend is required. Note there are no strolling "to go" cups in the crowd. Market shopping demands your full attention.

From Kramgasse turn left at Kreuzgasse, a tiny, alleylike street. From here you can see the Rathaus, the Bernese town hall. In the square before it stands the Vennerbrunnen (Ensign Fountain), with the figure of a Bernese standard-bearer.

At Kreuzgasse, the main street running through the Altstadt becomes Gerechtigkeitsgasse. Beyond the Gerechtigkeitsbrunnen (Justice Fountain) are some lovely 18th-century houses. At No. 7 is the Gasthaus zum Goldenen Adler. Built between 1764 and 1766, it has an ornate coat of arms by locksmith Samuel Rüetschi.

A left turn at the bottom of Gerechtigkeitsgasse will take you steeply down Nydeggstalden through one of the oldest parts of the city; the **Nydeggkirche** ❻ is on your right. At the bottom of the hill, stop to visit the Läuferbrunnen (Messenger Fountain) before taking the Untertorbrücke, or Lower Gate Bridge, across the Aare.

From the Untertorbrücke it's a short, steep climb to the east end of the high Nydeggbrücke. Across the street you're likely to find several of the city's mascots begging for carrots in the **Bärengraben** ❼.

Behind the Bärengraben is the Altes Tramdepot (Old Tram Depot), which served as the terminal for the city's trams from 1890 to 1901. The building now houses a restaurant and brewery as well as a tourist information center with a multimedia history of Bern.

Bern's carefully tended **Rosengarten** ❽ sits above the city across Grosser Muristalden. It is an additional hike past another fountain up the cobblestone Alter Aargauerstalden to a footpath that veers off to the left just before the first house. At the top you'll enjoy an exceptional view of the Altstadt. A refreshment kiosk within the gardens provides a break before you backtrack to the Nydeggbrücke.

Back in the Altstadt, make the first left at Junkerngasse, notable for its fine old houses. The facade of No. 22 is painted with silhouettes that depict an old-time street scene. After peeping into the courtyard of No. 47, the Erlacherhof, seat of the municipal government, step out into the street to view the gorgeous, unrestored, painted facade at No. 51.

At the end of Junkerngasse you come to the pride of the city: the magnificent, Gothic **Münster** ❾. To your left, on the south side of the cathedral, is the Münsterplatform. From here you can see the terraces of the patrician houses overlooking the Matte neighborhood. At the front of the platform you have a view of the Kirchenfeldbrücke. Walk around the park to the small gate leading to the Münsterplatz and the entrance to the cathedral.

After visiting the Münster, pass by the Mosesbrunnen and head up Münstergasse. Take a moment to check out No. 62, the Mayhaus—the huge, enclosed 1895 balcony connecting two 16th-century houses is held up by a muscled figure whose facial expression is worth a second look. At the end of Münstergasse, turn left to the Casinoplatz (a restaurant and concert locale); then cross the street that extends to the Kirchenfeldbrücke. A walkway skirts the terrace behind the Hotel Bellevue Palace and leads to the portico of the **Bundeshaus** ❿. Midway you'll come to a lookout where you can study a diagram of the Alps' principal peaks. Below are the tile rooftops of the Marzili, a chic, bohemian neighborhood along the banks of the Aare. To your right, the bright red Marzilibahn, a cable railway, transports pedestrians down (and more often up) the short, steep hill. At the end of the semicircular gallery of the capitol building, turn right, exiting to Bundesplatz to admire the parliament house and the fountain plaza from the front. To return to where the walk began, turn left at Schauplatzgasse, which leads to the train station escalators at the Loeb entrance.

You'll probably want to plan separate outings to visit the **Kunstmuseum** ⑪ and the **Zentrum Paul Klee** ⑫, in Schöngrün. To get to the fine arts museum from the Hauptbahnhof, take Genfergasse north to the end. A half-block detour on Aarbergergassewill take you to the 11th fountain, Ryfflibrunnen (Crossbowman Fountain). To get to the Klee center from the station, take the Number 12 bus.

TIMING You can tour the town center in a single day, with brief stops at the Bärengraben, Münster, and Bundeshaus. Try to stop by the Zytglogge a few minutes before the hour to see its mechanical figures go through their paces. If you'll be in Bern longer, a half day will allow a visit to the Kunstmuseum, Rosengarten, or Zentrum Paul Klee with time to indulge your whims in the arcade shops.

What to See

★ ☺ ❼ **Bärengraben** (Bear Pits). Since the late 1400s, this has been home to the city's mascots: fat brown bears that clown and beg for carrots tossed by tourists and loyal townsfolk. According to legend, Berchtold V announced that he would name the city for the first animal he killed. It was a bear; in those days the woods were full of them. The German plural for bears is *Bären,* and you'll see their images everywhere in Bern, from the coat of arms to chocolate to umbrellas. ⊠ *East end of Nydeggbrücke, Bärengraben* ☎ *No phone* ☒ *Free* ☉ *June–Sept., daily 9–5:30; Oct.–May, daily 9–4.*

❿ **Bundeshaus** (Houses of Parliament). This hulking, domed building is the
Fodor'sChoice beating heart of the Swiss Confederation and meeting place of the 46-
★ member Council of States and 200-member National Council, patterned after the U.S. Senate and House of Representatives. In front is a plaza with fountain jets representing each canton; views from the rear portico encompass the Altstadt rooftops, countryside, and the Alps. Free guided tours include entry to the parliamentary chambers, where there's a spectacular mural of Lac Léman, considered the cradle of the confederation. Security is tight; a passport or photo ID is required for entrance. No tours are given during session and on official holidays. When parliament is in session, you can sit in the gallery and listen to discussions in Swiss German, Italian, and French. ⊠ *Bundespl., City Center* ☎ *031/3228522* ⊕ *www.parlament.ch* ☒ *Free* ☉ *Tours Mon.–Sat. at 9, 10, 11, 2, 3, and 4.*

▶ ❶ **Christoffelturm** (Christoffel Tower). Remnants of the city's third gate, built between 1344 and 1366, were uncovered in the train station during construction of a pedestrian passageway in the 1970s. The archaeological site, oddly juxtaposed with the modern train station, includes the massive stone foundation of the tower as well as parts of a moat built in 1488.

❺ **Einsteinhaus** (Einstein's House). For a bit of intellectual history, you can visit the apartment and workplace of Albert Einstein. It was during his stay from 1903 to 1905 that, at the age of 26, he published his *Special Theory of Relativity.* ⊠ *Kramg. 49, Altstadt* ☎ *031/3120091* ⊕ *www. einstein-bern.ch* ☒ *3 SF* ☉ *Feb.–Nov., Tues.–Fri. 10–5, Sat. 10–4.*

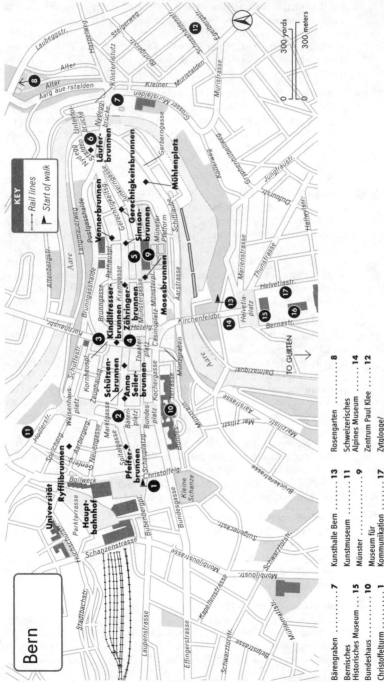

Bern

KEY
→ Rail lines
▲ Start of walk

② Käfigturm (Prison Tower). In 1641, work began on this tower located at the site of what had been a city entrance in the 13th and 14th centuries. The Käfigturm served as a prison from 1643 until 1897. ⊠ *Marktg. 67, City Center.*

③ Kornhaus (Granary). The imposing 18th-century Kornhaus has a magnificent cellar, now a popular Bernese restaurant. The upper stories house the **Forum für Media und Gestaltung** (Forum for Media and Design), which hosts exhibitions and events devoted to design, architecture, contemporary media, video, photography, and applied art. ⊠ *Kornhauspl. 18, Altstadt* ☎ *031/3129110* ⊕ *www.kornhausforum. ch* 🖭 *Varies with exhibition or event* ☉ *Tues.–Fri. 10–7, weekends 10–5.*

★ **⑪ Kunstmuseum** (Art Museum). Though the world's largest collection of works by Paul Klee—more than 2,000 examples by this native son—will be moved to a new center in mid-2005, there will be plenty left to see. From another Bern native, the symbolist Ferdinand Hodler, there are striking allegories (some enormous), landscapes, and portraits. Works by Swiss artists Stauffer, Anker, and Böcklin are also shown. But the Kunstmuseum's concentration isn't entirely Swiss; its holdings span artists ranging from Fra Angelico to Cézanne, Rouault, and Picasso. ⊠ *Hodlerstr. 8–12, City Center* ☎ *031/3280944* ⊕ *www. kunstmuseumbern.ch* 🖭 *7 SF* ☉ *Tues. 10–9, Wed.–Sun. 10–5.*

⑨ Münster (Cathedral). Started in 1421 by master mason Matthäus Ensinger,
Fodor'sChoice Bern's famous cathedral was planned on lines so spacious that half the
★ population could worship in it at one time. The smaller church on the site was kept intact and functioning during construction. Only later was it demolished and removed piece by piece through the main portal of the enlarged cathedral, whose construction went on for centuries. Even the Reformation, the impact of which converted it from a Catholic to a Protestant church, didn't halt the work. Daniel Heinz directed construction for 25 years (from 1573 to 1598), completing the nave and the tower. The finishing touch, the tip of the 328-foot steeple (the highest in Switzerland), was added only in 1893. Today you can ascend a dizzying 344-step spiral staircase to enjoy a panoramic view of Bern.

At the entrance to the church, the **main portal** contains a magnificent representation of the Last Judgment (1490), completed immediately before the Reformation. It's composed of 234 carved figures: ivory-skinned angels with gilt hair fill heaven on the left; green demons with gaping red maws fill hell on the right.

Inside the church, although the elaborately carved pews and choir stalls are worth your attention, note the **stained glass,** especially the 15th-century windows of the choir, dealing as much with local heraldry as with Christian iconography. A shop in the entry has information and church-related souvenirs, including pieces of stone taken from the church walls during renovations. The Münster frequently hosts concerts, its 5,404-pipe organ boosted by grand acoustics. ⊠ *Münsterpl. 1, Altstadt* ☎ *031/3120462* 🖭 *Steeple 3 SF* ☉ *Easter–Oct., Tues.–Sat. 10–5, Sun. 11:30–5; Nov.–Easter, Tues.–Fri. 10–noon and 2–4, Sat. 10–noon and 2–5, Sun. 11:30–2.*

⑥ Nydeggkirche (Nydegg Church). Built in 1341–46, the church stands on the ruins of Berchtold V's first fortress (destroyed about 1260–70), the site of Bern's founding. Although the church was completely renovated in the 1950s, there's still a wooden pulpit from 1566. ⊠ *Nydegg, Altstadt* ⊙ *Mon.–Sat. 10–noon and 2–5:30, Sun. 10–noon.*

⑧ Rosengarten (Rose Garden). You'll find a riot of color from April to October in this splendidly arranged and well-maintained garden. A popular place for a Sunday stroll, it offers not only 27 types of rhododendrons, 200 kinds of roses, and 200 varieties of irises, but also a splendid view of the bridges, red roofs, and major buildings of downtown Bern. ⊠ *Alter Aargauerstalden/Laubeggstr.* ☎ *No phone* ⊠ *Free* ⊙ *Daily sunrise–sunset.*

⑫ Zentrum Paul Klee (Paul Klee Center). Designed by Renzo Piano, this three-part center showcases the collection of the 20th-century Swiss expressionist Paul Klee. Exhibit space, an activity center, and a music performance hall are embedded into the hilly landscape of Schöngrün, on the east side of the city. Nearly 4,000 works of the Klee Foundation are on deposit here, including paintings, drawings, and personal notes. Expansive facilities include a sculpture garden, Internet café, gift shop, and café. It opens June 2005. ⊠ *Monument im Fructland 3, Schöngrün* ☎ *031/3590101* ⊕ *www.zpk.org* ⊠ *14 SF* ⊙ *Tues., Wed., and Fri.–Sun. 10–7, Thurs. 10–9.*

④ Zytglogge/Zeitglockenturm (Clock Tower). The mighty tower, built in 1191
Fodor'sChoice as the western gate to the then-smaller city, dominates the town center
★ with its high copper spire and a massive astronomical clock and calendar, built on its east side in 1530. From the 15th to the 19th centuries, all clocks were set according to this one. Today, tourists gather five minutes before the hour to watch the clock's mechanical figures perform. Tours of the clock tower in English are offered daily through Bern Tourismus. ⊠ *Kramg. at Hotelg., Altstadt* ⊠ *Tour 9 SF* ⊙ *Tours May, June, Sept., and Oct., daily at 11:30; July and Aug., daily at 11:30 and 4:30.*

Museum District

a good walk

Most of Bern's museums are clustered in a quadrant at the end of Kirchenfeldbrücke, in a tranquil tree-filled neighborhood also home to embassies and consulates. From the Casinoplatz cross the panoramic Kirchenfeldbrücke to Helvetiaplatz. On your left, just after the bridge, is the contemporary **Kunsthalle Bern** ⑬ ⌐. If you cross the street and pass the building on the corner you'll reach the **Schweizerisches Alpines Museum** ⑭. Across the square, behind the massive fountain of Mother Helvetica, is the castlelike **Bernisches Historisches Museum** ⑮. From the history museum turn left and follow Bernastrasse to the **Naturhistorisches Museum** ⑯. And finally, to reach the **Museum für Kommunikation** ⑰ you'll need to go around the block. (You can follow Bernastrasse to Hallwylstrasse and take the flight of steps on the left to eventually reach Helvetiastrasse.)

TIMING You can explore a couple of these museums in half a day. In clear weather, an afternoon at the Gurten takes you above the city for spectacular views of the mountains and countryside.

BERN'S ARTISTIC SON

T'S IRONIC that expressionist painter Paul Klee (1879–1940), one of Switzerland's most prolific and talented artists, wasn't a Swiss citizen during his life. Though he was born near Bern and spent most of his life in the country, his nationality was determined by the lineage of his father, who was German.

From a musical family, Klee awoke to the arts early, doodling and sketching in his schoolbooks. At age 19 he left for Germany—first to study and later to teach—but he couldn't support himself with his art, so he returned to Bern (1902–04) to live with his parents. An accomplished violinist, he played the violin with the Bern Symphony until he earned enough money to return to Munich and marry pianist Lily Strumpf. But art, especially drawing, was his passion.

A trip to Tunisia in 1914 introduced color to his work. "Color has taken possession of me," he said, and color and wit became his signatures. In the 1920s his recognition grew, with exhibitions in Paris and New York, but when the Nazis rose to power in 1933, Klee was labeled a degenerate, much of his work was confiscated, and his academic position was terminated. Once again he returned to his parents in Switzerland. The apartment he later took in Elfenau, not far from his childhood playground, became his studio for the rest of his life.

Two years after his return Klee began to show symptoms of severe fatigue. Misdiagnosed as the measles, he actually suffered from scleroderma. Yet Klee continued to paint, and some term this period his most expressive. In 1939 he applied for Swiss citizenship and sought a more agreeable climate in the Ticino. He died there in 1940, but his body is buried in Bern's Schlosshalde cemetery, near where he once lived and where the Zentrum Paul Klee stands today. A month after his death he became a citizen.

What to See

★ ⑮ **Bernisches Historisches Museum** (Historical Museum of Bern). Much of this enormous, enlightening collection is booty from victories over Burgundy, including magnificent tapestries "acquired" in 1476–77, when the Bernese pushed Charles the Bold back into France. There are armor and arms, lavish church treasures (including 15th- and 16th-century stained-glass windows), and the original Last Judgment sculptures from the cathedral's portal. Don't miss the novel three-way portrait of Calvin, Zwingli, and Luther. Among the important exhibitions about the outside world is an exceptional Islamic collection. ⊠ Helvetiapl. 5, Kirchenfeld ☎ 031/3507711 ☎ 5 SF, can be higher during special exhibitions ⊙ Tues. and Thurs.–Sun. 10–5, Wed. 10–8.

off the beaten path

GURTEN – Bern's very own hill offers a panoramic view of the city and surrounding countryside in good weather. Take the three-minute trip to the hilltop on the bright red funicular, then head left to the hill's east end, where there's a diagram labeling more than 200 peaks of the distant mountains. At the west end you can climb the Gurtenturm's 122 steps for a 360-degree view of the area. From early April to late October, children can ride on model trains pulled by steam and electric engines. Nature lovers can bypass the funicular and walk up (a real workout) or down (hard on the knees) through pleasant woods and countryside. A choice of restaurants, from self-service to linen tablecloths, serve up exceptional vistas. ⊠ *Wabern, tram stop Gurtenbahn* ☎ *031/9703333* ⊕ *www.gurtenpark.ch* 🎫 *Funicular 9 SF round-trip, 5 SF one-way* ⊙ *Funicular Mon.–Sat. 7:10 AM–11:40 PM, Sun. 7:40 AM–10:10 PM.*

▶ ⑬ **Kunsthalle Bern** (Bern Art Gallery). Not to be confused with the traditional Kunstmuseum, this groundbreaking contemporary art venue has no permanent collection but displays temporary exhibitions of living artists, usually before anyone's heard of them. Built in 1918 in heroic classical style to boost local artists—Kirchner, Klee, Hodler—it grew to attract the young Kandinsky, Miró, Sol LeWitt, Richard Long, Cy Twombly—and a parade of newcomers of strong potential. ⊠ *Helvetiapl. 1, Kirchenfeld* ☎ *031/3500040* ⊕ *www.kunsthallebern.ch* 🎫 *8 SF* ⊙ *Tues. 10–7, Wed.–Sun. 10–5.*

⑰ **Museum für Kommunikation** (Museum of Communication). This is Switzerland's only museum dedicated exclusively to communication—starting with bonfire signals and working its way through time to the transmission of complex digital information. There's an interactive museum; documents, art, and artifacts related to the history of mail and telecommunications; and the world's largest public display of postage stamps. ⊠ *Helvetiastr. 16, Kirchenfeld* ☎ *031/3575555* ⊕ *www.mfk.ch* 🎫 *9 SF* ⊙ *Tues.–Sun. 10–5.*

★ ☕ ⑯ **Naturhistorisches Museum** (Museum of Natural History). In this slick and spacious museum, considered one of Europe's finest, you'll find evocative wildlife dioramas, a splendid collection of Alpine minerals, and exhibits on master builders ranging from moles to ants. The museum's quirkiest trophy: the stuffed body of Barry, a St. Bernard that saved more than 40 people in the Alps in the 1800s. ⊠ *Bernastr. 15, Kirchenfeld* ☎ *031/3507111* ⊕ *www.nmbe.ch* 🎫 *7 SF* ⊙ *Mon. 2–5, Tues., Thurs., and Fri. 9–5, Wed. 9–6, weekends 10–5.*

⑭ **Schweizerisches Alpines Museum** (Swiss Alpine Museum). This museum, known for its topographical maps and reliefs, also covers the history of mountain climbing and life in the mountains. There are fine old photos, as well as a magnificent Hodler mural of the tragic conquest of the Matterhorn. ⊠ *Helvetiapl. 4, Kirchenfeld* ☎ *031/3510434* ⊕ *www. alpinesmuseum.ch* 🎫 *7 SF* ⊙ *Mon. 2–5, Tues.–Sun. 10–5; hrs may be extended for special exhibits.*

WHERE TO EAT

Dining in Bern is usually a down-to-earth affair, with Italian home cooking running a close second to the standard local fare: German-style meat and potatoes. The most widespread specialty is the famous *Bernerplatte*, a meaty version of Alsatian *choucroûte*—great slabs of salt pork, beef tongue, smoky bacon, pork ribs, and mild, pink pork sausages cooked down in broth and heaped on a broad platter over juniper-scented sauerkraut, green beans, and boiled potatoes. Another classic is the Berner version of *Ratsherrtopf* (veal shank cooked in white wine, butter, and sage), traditionally enjoyed by the town councillors.

WHAT IT COSTS In Swiss francs				
$$$$	**$$$**	**$$**	**$**	**¢**
MAIN COURSE over 60	40–60	25–40	15–25	under 15

Prices are per person for a main course at dinner.

$$$–$$$$ ✕ **Meridiano.** Young superstar chef Fredy Boss presides over this contemporary space with complex Mediterranean cooking that is as vibrant as the setting. Not a typical hotel dining room, the Meridiano is styled in gold and black with red accents and plate chargers that add a rainbow burst of color. Amazing views of the lighted Altstadt silhouetted by the Alps make it a romantic spot. ⊠ *Hotel Allegro, Kornhausstr. 3, Kornhausbrücke* 🕾 *031/3395500* ⌚ *Reservations essential* 🖃 *AE, DC, MC, V.*

$$$–$$$$ ✕ **Schultheissenstube.** The intimate, rustic dining room, with a clublike **Fodor'sChoice** bar and an adjoining, even more rustic all-wood *Stübli* (tavern-café),
★ looks less like a gastronomic haven than a country pub, but this is formal dining at its best. The cooking is sophisticated, international, and imaginative, and seafood and game preparations are noteworthy. Consider poached and grilled lobster served on potato-crabmeat *galettes* (pancakes) or roasted saddle of reindeer seasoned with cumin-sherry sauce. Jackets are required in the dining room. ⊠ *Hotel Schweizerhof Bern, Bahnhofpl. 11, City Center* 🕾 *031/3268080* ⌚ *Reservations essential* 🖃 *AE, DC, MC, V* ⊘ *Closed Sun.*

$$–$$$$ ✕ **Jack's Brasserie.** This dining room with high ceilings, wainscoting, and roomy banquettes is airy, bustling, and cosmopolitan. Enjoy a drink at a bare-top table by day, or settle in at mealtime for smartly served Swiss standards and French bistro classics: veal liver in an herb sauce with *Rösti* (fried shredded potatoes) or lamb knuckle sautéed in a merlot reduction served with polenta. The Sunday brunch buffet, one of the few in town, draws a crowd. ⊠ *Hotel Schweizerhof Bern, Bahnhofpl. 11, City Center* 🕾 *031/3268080* 🖃 *AE, DC, MC, V.*

★ **$$–$$$** ✕ **Kornhauskeller.** Entering the Kornhauskeller is like entering a cathedral, except that the stunning vaulted ceilings and frescoes are all underground. At various times a granary, a post office, and a beer hall, this historic building is now a classy gathering spot with an emphasis on Mediterranean cuisine. In the gallery overlooking the restaurant you'll find a bar (65 varieties of whiskey), casual seating, and a humidor. ⊠ *Kornhauspl. 18, Altstadt* 🕾 *031/3277272* ⌚ *Reservations essential* 🖃 *AE, DC, MC, V.*

★ **$$–$$$** ✕ **Zimmermania.** This deceptively simple bistro, hidden away on an alleylike street near the Rathaus, has been in business for more than 150 years and is a local favorite for authentic French-bourgeois cooking. In a city that celebrates the onion, this is a good place to try the soup. Veal kidneys in mustard sauce and the ever-popular *Kalbsleber* (calves' liver) are sure bets. For a special vintage, ask for the separate French wine list.

Lunch specials around 20 SF are a good deal. ⊠ *Brunng. 19, Altstadt* ☎ *031/3111542* ☐ *AE, MC, V* ⊘ *Closed Sun. and Mon.*

$$–$$$ ✕ **Zum Zähringer.** For a different view of Bern, take the 183 steps or the funky little outdoor elevator (1 SF) from the cathedral terrace down to this restaurant in the Matte neighborhood. Here the emphasis is on fresh, local ingredients, and the menu changes according to the season and the whims of the chef. You might find delicate pumpkin ravioli, a meaty veal shank with a subtle wine sauce, or an original vegetarian dish. One constant: the daily fish special is always a hit. ⊠ *Badg. 1, Matte* ☎ *031/ 3113270* ☐ *MC, V* ⊘ *Closed Sun.*

$–$$$ ✕ **Harmonie.** Sporting slightly scuffed blond wood, this mainstay of Swiss cuisine has a separate menu for cheese dishes, as the tinge in the air confirms. Fondue—classic, *moite-moite* (half Gruyère, half Vacherin), and bobbing with morels or truffles—arrives at the table accompanied by endless baskets of crusty bread. *Käseschnitte* (open-face sandwiches with melted cheese) and velvety *Chäshörnli* (macaroni and cheese) use generous amounts of the nation's notable export. For the lactose averse, there are rich preparations of veal, liver, and beef served with traditional sauces and a helping of crispy brown Rösti or *Spätzli* (dumplings). ⊠ *Hotelg. 3, Altstadt* ☎ *031/31311141* ☐ *AE, DC, MC, V* ⊘ *Closed weekends.*

$–$$$
Fodor'sChoice
★ ✕ **Lorenzini.** It must be good: chicly clad professionals and members of the Swiss parliament meet here for traditional, homemade Italian pastas and desserts. Signature dishes include escalope of veal with ham, sage and saffron risotto, and osso buco. The restaurant, on the second floor, serves warm food as late as 11:45, while the street level has two bars: a cocktail bar facing Hotelgasse and a coffee bar facing Theaterplatz. In the latter you can listen to music and order sandwiches (made fresh three times a day). ⊠ *Theaterpl. 5/Hotelg. 8, Altstadt* ☎ *031/3117850* ☐ *AE, DC, MC, V* ⊘ *Closed Sun.*

¢–$$$ ✕ **Markthalle.** Think of a cuisine and it's likely to be represented at this converted open-air market turned global food court. Stand-up bars and full-service restaurants have been fashioned out of produce stalls. Choices change with tenants: soup, bratwurst, sushi, pizza, seafood, and upscale Continental. Intermingled among the eateries are a flower boutique, tea salon, and lifestyle shops. It's frantic at lunch and hosts a late-dining crowd. ⊠ *Bubenbergpl. 9, City Center* ☐ *MC, V.*

$$
Fodor'sChoice
★ ✕ **Della Casa.** Affectionately nicknamed "Delli," this favorite has been serving generous platters of local specialties—such as schnitzel, oxtail stew with fried macaroni, and calves' liver with herbs—for more than a century. The waitresses are "wonderfully prickly dragons," according to one Swiss food magazine, but no one seems to mind. The yellowed downstairs Stübli and the wood-paneled upstairs rooms are unofficial parliament headquarters; they buzz during lunch. The patio menu is limited. ⊠ *Schauplatzg. 16, City Center* ☎ *031/3112142* ☐ *AE, DC, MC, V* ⊘ *Closed Sun. No dinner Sat.*

$–$$ ✕ **Altes Tramdepot.** Three varieties of house beer and one specialty beer—all brewed on-site in a microbrewery—are offered each month in this uncomplicated restaurant located in the high-ceilinged, barnlike building that once housed the city's trams. Traditional dishes of Switzerland,

Munich, and Vienna include everything from black bread topped with a warm garlic pesto to venison (during hunting season). There's a nice view of the Aare and Altstadt and in warm months the pleasant outdoor garden can seat a throng. ⊠ *Grosser Muristalden 6, Bärengraben* ☎ *031/3681415* ☱ *AE, DC, MC, V.*

$–$$ ✕ **Gartenrestaurant Marzilibrücke.** On the west side of the Aare, this small, relaxed restaurant has white benches and scuffed wood tables. The varied menu could include pumpkin soup or a whole squid with chili and saffron sauce. Your best bet, though, is the *gebratene Maispoularde,* an Indian dish combining tender chicken, a lentil paste, mango chutney, and a tasty sauce. On Sunday, brunch is served from 10 to 2, and in the summer you can eat out in the garden. ⊠ *Gasstr. 8, Marzili* ☎ *031/3112780* ☱ *AE, MC, V.*

$–$$ ✕ **Kornhaus Café.** Decorated in a modern style with cool shades of white and gray, this trendy café serves light meals, homemade pastries, and 14 kinds of coffee from early in the morning to late at night. Toward evening it becomes a popular bar, and from mid-March to mid-October you can sit outside at tables along the Kornhausplatz. ⊠ *Kornhauspl. 18, Altstadt* ☎ *031/3277270* ☱ *AE, DC, MC, V.*

¢–$$ ✕ **Verdi.** Framed pieces of opera memorabilia, chandeliers, and velvet drapes grace this restaurant, but amazingly, it isn't the least bit kitschy. Chef Giovanni D'Ambrogio even cooks specialties from the eponymous composer's hometown region of Emilia-Romagna. Try his spaghetti Scarpara, with an excellent, garlicky tomato sauce, or the sliced steak on a bed of arugula with Parmesan. ⊠ *Gerechtigkeitsg. 5, Altstadt* ☎ *031/3126368* ⌲ *Reservations essential* ☱ *AE, DC, MC, V.*

¢–$ ✕ **Tibits.** You'll find quick, healthy eating on an upper level of the glass box surrounding the train station. It's a sister restaurant to Zürich's wildly popular vegetarian pacesetter Hitl, and you'll have to vie for a table in this town, too. Choose from an assortment of just-squeezed juices (carrot-orange or fennel-apple-lemon), multiflavor coffees, and organic wines. Signature soups (pumpkin, lentil, or green pea with peppermint) come with wedges of hearty bread, as does the bountiful salad buffet sold by the gram. Take-out service lets you dine on the train or in the park. ⊠ *Bahnhofpl. 10, City Center* ☎ *031/3129111* ☱ *AE, DC, MC, V.*

WHERE TO STAY

As a frequent host to conventioneers, tourists, and visiting members of parliament, Bern is well equipped with hotels in all price ranges. Rooms are harder to find in March, June, September, and December, when parliament is in session, so book well ahead.

WHAT IT COSTS In Swiss francs				
	$$$$	**$$$**	**$$**	**$**	**¢**
DOUBLE ROOM	over 350	250–350	175–250	100–175	under 100

Prices are for two people in a standard double room in high season, including tax and service.

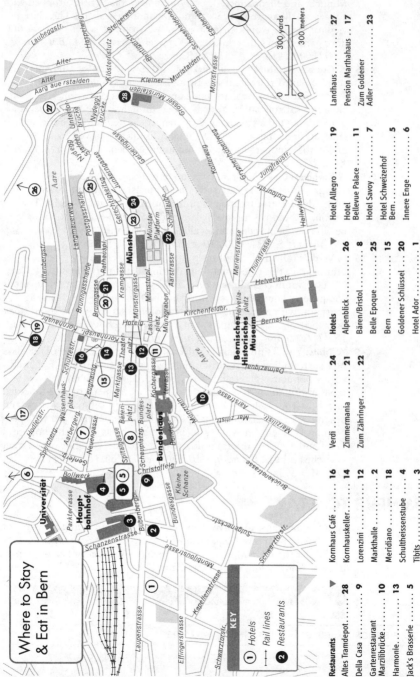

Where to Stay & Eat in Bern

KEY

1 Hotels
—+— Rail lines
2 Restaurants

Restaurants

Altes Tramdepot	28
Della Casa	9
Gartenrestaurant Marzilibrücke	10
Harmonie	13
Jack's Brasserie	5
Kornhaus Café	16
Kornhauskeller	14
Lorenzini	12
Markthalle	2
Meridiano	18
Schultheissenstube	4
Tibits	3
Verdi	24
Zimmermania	21
Zum Zähringer	22

Hotels

Alpenblick	26
Bären/Bristol	8
Belle Epoque	25
Bern	15
Goldener Schlüssel	20
Hotel Ador	1
Hotel Allegro	19
Hotel Bellevue Palace	11
Hotel Savoy	7
Hotel Schweizerhof Bern	5
Innere Enge	6
Landhaus	27
Pension Marthahaus	17
Zum Goldener Adler	23

300 yards
300 meters
0
0

$$$$ 🏨 **Hotel Bellevue Palace.** Bern's grande dame is both stately and mod-
Fodor'sChoice ern. Politicos and corporate execs have cocktail parties in reception areas
★ that are true to the hotel's original character, but intricate moldings,
cherub-filled frescos, crystal chandeliers, and art nouveau stained glass
give way to cosmopolitan refinement and techno-smarts in guest rooms
of warm yellow and abstract florals. Reclaimed space under the eaves
has a contemporary style, with platform beds, whimsical carpets, and
chrome lighting. The elegant Bellevue Grill, with a terrace, keeps pace
with gastronomic trends while holding on to old-line service standards.
Rooms in back and outdoor diners both get stunning views of the
Bernese Alps. ⊠ *Kocherg. 3–5, Altstadt, CH-3001* ☎ *031/3204545*
🖶 *031/3114743* ⊕ *www.bellevue-palace.ch* ⇆ *130 rooms ⚴ Restaurant, in-room data ports, in-room safes, minibars, cable TV with movies,
bar, concierge, business services, parking (fee), no-smoking rooms* ⊟ *AE,
DC, MC, V* ⑩ *BP.*

$$$$ 🏨 **Hotel Schweizerhof Bern.** This landmark across from the Hauptbahnhof is decidedly nonpalatial: the lobby is deluxe but on a relatively
intimate scale, and the broad corridors are lined with antiques and ob-
jets d'art. Square lines and subdued patterns lend an Edwardian feel,
and original artwork adds an individual touch. Street-side rooms are
solidly soundproof. Little extras abound, such as the next day's weather
report on your pillow beside the requisite truffle. ⊠ *Bahnhofpl. 11, City
Center, CH-3001* ☎ *031/3268080* 🖶 *031/3268090* ⊕ *www.schweizerhof-
bern.ch* ⇆ *72 rooms, 12 suites ⚴ 2 restaurants, in-room data ports,
in-room safes, minibars, cable TV with movies, bar, concierge, business
services, parking (fee), no-smoking floors* ⊟ *AE, DC, MC, V* ⑩ *BP.*

★ **$$$** 🏨 **Belle Epoque.** This hotel has so many authentic *Jugendstil* (art nou-
veau) antiques that it could almost pass for a museum. Romantics find
it an irresistible hideaway, especially on weekends when rates are re-
duced. Each room has its own color palette, using subtle wallpapers
and white-on-white spreads as backdrops for jewel-tone splashes in head-
boards and draperies. The hotel bar is one of the most beautiful in the
city. Quieter rooms on the *Innenhof* (inner side) avoid the clatter of
vehicles on cobblestone. ⊠ *Gerechtigkeitsg. 18, Altstadt, CH-3011*
☎ *031/3114336* 🖶 *031/3113936* ⊕ *www.belle-epoque.ch* ⇆ *15
rooms, 2 suites ⚴ Restaurant, café, minibars, cable TV, bar, no-smok-
ing floor; no a/c* ⊟ *AE, DC, MC, V.*

$$$ 🏨 **Innere Enge.** Eighteenth-century origins and art nouveau updates are
discreetly discernible in this quiet hotel located in a pleasant area out-
side the City Center. Rooms, named for jazz musicians, are spacious,
light, and airy, with generous windows facing the Bernese Alps. Memorabilia of greats like Lionel Hampton and John Lewis have been incorporated into the decor. The parklike setting and nearby walking
trails offer a welcome change from the cityscape. From January to June
and September to December, don't miss the hot jazz acts playing in Marians Jazzroom. From the Hauptbahnhof, take Bus 21 (marked BREM-
GARTEN) to Innere Enge. ⊠ *Engestr. 54, Innere Enge, CH-3012* ☎ *031/
3096111* 🖶 *031/3096112* ⊕ *www.zghotels.ch* ⇆ *11 rooms, 15 suites
⚴ Restaurant, café, in-room data ports, minibars, cable TV, bar, nightclub, free parking; no a/c in some rooms* ⊟ *AE, DC, MC, V.*

$$–$$$ ▦ **Bären/Bristol.** These dependable, business-class Best Western properties orbit the city's hub of shopping, banking, and government. (Standing reservations from parliament officials and financial clients can make it difficult to secure a room.) Their fresh, modern rooms are decorated in blues and yellows. The hotels are connected on one level and share some amenities, including bicycles you can use free of charge. ⊠ *Bären: Schauplatzg. 4, City Center, CH-3011* ☎ *031/3113367, 800/780–7234 in U.S.* 🖷 *031/3116983* ⬐ *57 rooms* ⊕ *www. baerenbern.ch* ⊠ *Bristol: Schauplatzg. 10, City Center, CH-3011* ☎ *031/3110101, 800/780–7234 in U.S.* 🖷 *031/3119479* ⊕ *www. bristolbern.ch* ⬐ *92 rooms* ⚲ *Snack bar, in-room data ports, in-room safes, cable TV, sauna, bicycles, bar, laundry facilities, no-smoking rooms* ⊟ *AE, DC, MC, V* ⑩ *BP.*

$$–$$$ ▦ **Hotel Allegro.** In a town renowned for its antiquity, the Allegro caters to guests who prefer everything modern, from state-of-the-art technical facilities to decorative art. Connected to the Kursaal, a conference and entertainment center with casino, the Allegro is just across the Kornhausbrücke from the Altstadt. Rooms come in a range of styles: "Panorama" (with a view of the Alps) and "Comfort" rooms both have parquet floors, light wood, and TVs with built-in Internet. Splurge on a penthouse room with eye-popping views, leather furniture, designer toiletries, and a towel warmer. Piazza, the outdoor café by the entry pond, is a relaxing spot to linger over an espresso and the *Herald Tribune.* ⊠ *Kornhausstr. 3, Kornhausbrücke, CH-3000* ☎ *031/ 3395500* 🖷 *031/3395510* ⊕ *www.allegro-hotel.ch* ⬐ *161 rooms, 2 suites* ⚲ *2 restaurants, café, in-room data ports, in-room safes, minibars, cable TV with movies, gym, hot tub, sauna, 2 bars, casino, concert hall, dance club, business services, parking (fee), no-smoking rooms* ⊟ *AE, DC, MC, V* ⑩ *BP.*

$$ ▦ **Hotel Ador.** Convenient and efficient, this boxy hotel near the train station and tram stops makes a good base to the west of City Center. The stone lobby sparkles. Hallways to guest lodgings transition to matte-painted concrete. Modular furniture, color-block carpets, and baths with chrome fixtures add a modern touch. Vending machines on each level replace in-room minibars, and the small lobby restaurant serves tasty Swiss cuisine with vegetarian options. ⊠ *Laupenstr. 15, city west, CH-3001* ☎ *031/3880111* 🖷 *031/3880101* ⊕ *www.hotel-ador.ch* ⬐ *52 rooms* ⚲ *Restaurant, in-room data ports, in-room safes, cable TV, parking (fee), no-smoking rooms; no a/c* ⊟ *AE, DC, MC, V* ⑩ *BP.*

$$ ▦ **Hotel Savoy.** A duo with long-standing hotelier-family histories runs this neat hotel, which is a straight shot from the Hauptbahnhof escalator. Tailored rooms in warm yellows are stocked with all the essentials. Although the hotel has no full-service restaurant, the café, which offers light meals and cocktails, is a lively gathering spot in a neighborhood overflowing with shopping and dining choices. Jazz fans will be pleased by discounted admission to Marians Jazzroom, in the Innere Enge, a sister property. ⊠ *Neueng. 26, City Center, CH-3011* ☎ *031/3114405* 🖷 *031/3121978* ⊕ *www.zghotels.ch* ⬐ *56 rooms* ⚲ *Café, in-room data ports, in-room safes, minibars, cable TV, bar; no a/c in some rooms* ⊟ *AE, DC, MC, V.*

$-$$ ☒ **Bern.** City flags flutter above the entrance of this energetic establishment popular with businesspeople. Small but tidy rooms feature a white-on-white color scheme with a compact work space. Quieter quarters can be found away from the street, which is animated with daytime traffic and evening entertainment. Guests appreciate the 10% discount offered at the hotel's restaurants. ☒ *Zeughausg. 9, Altstadt, CH-3011* ☎ *031/3292222* 🖷 *031/3292299* 📞 *97 rooms, 1 suite* ♿ *2 restaurants, in-room data ports, in-room safes, minibars, cable TV, bar; no a/c* ⊟ *AE, DC, MC, V* ⦿ *BP.*

$-$$ ☒ **Zum Goldener Adler.** Built in a magnificent patrician town house, this guesthouse has been lodging travelers since 1489, though the current structure dates from 1764. One family has run it for 100-odd years. Despite the striking exterior with its coat of arms, the rooms are modest, with standard platform beds, white duvets, and small baths. Still, the ambience is comfortable and welcoming. ☒ *Gerechtigkeitsg. 7, Altstadt, CH-3011* ☎ *031/3111725* 🖷 *031/3113761* ⦿ *www.goldener-adler-bern.ch* 📞 *40 rooms* ♿ *Restaurant, cable TV; no a/c* ⊟ *AE, DC, MC, V* ⦿ *BP.*

$ ☒ **Alpenblick.** This family-operated hotel in a quiet residential neighborhood minutes from downtown (Tram 9 to Breitenrainplatz) faces the parklike grounds of the Kaserne, once an army barracks. Rooms are in two adjoining buildings connected by a glassed-in entry hall. All rooms have modern tile bathrooms and functional furniture; the rooms in the newer addition are slightly larger. The restaurant serves traditional Swiss dishes cooked by the owner; you can eat on the terrace when the weather is warm. ☒ *Kasernenstr. 29, Breitenrain, CH-3013* ☎ *031/3356666* 🖷 *031/3356655* ⦿ *www.alpenblick-bern.ch* 📞 *48 rooms* ♿ *Restaurant, in-room data ports, cable TV, parking (fee); no a/c* ⊟ *AE, DC, MC, V* ⦿ *BP.*

$ ☒ **Goldener Schlüssel.** This little hotel sits midway between the Rathaus and the Zytglogge. The friendly proprietors receive guests at an alcove at the end of the entry hallway, and floral duvets perk up the rather spartan guest rooms, some with shared baths. The good, inexpensive restaurant serves rib-sticking dishes such as bratwurst with Rösti. ☒ *Rathausg. 72, Altstadt, CH-3011* ☎ *031/3110216* 🖷 *031/3115688* ⦿ *www. goldener-schluessel.ch* 📞 *29 rooms, 21 with bath* ♿ *Restaurant, Stübli, cable TV; no a/c* ⊟ *AE, MC, V* ⦿ *BP.*

$ ☒ **Landhaus.** Just across the river from the Altstadt, this simple, clean, and bright hotel/hostel has natural wood floors and soothing pastel walls. Rooms range from a dorm-style cubicle to a double room with shower. Cook for yourself in the community kitchen or dine at the hotel's trendy restaurant, which has live jazz. A computer with Internet access is available for use by guests for a fee. ☒ *Altenbergstr. 4/6, Altenberg, CH-3013* ☎ *031/3314166* 🖷 *031/3326904* ⦿ *www.landhausbern.ch* 📞 *6 rooms, 2 dormitories* ♿ *Restaurant, kitchens, cable TV, bicycles, bar, laundry facilities, Internet; no a/c* ⊟ *AE, DC, MC, V* ⦿ *BP.*

¢-$ ☒ **Pension Marthahaus.** This cheery pension stands at the end of a quiet cul-de-sac in a residential neighborhood, equidistant from the Hauptbahnhof and the heart of Altstadt. The comfortable rooms are bright and sunny; most have shared baths but in-room sinks. Dormitory accommodations are available, and there is a community kitchen and coin laundry. Community rooms offer cable TV and Internet access. From the Hauptbahnhof, take Bus 20 across the Lorrainebrücke to the first stop, Gewerbeschule. ⊠ *Wyttenbachstr. 22a, Lorraine, CH-3013* ☎ *031/ 3324135* 🖨 *031/3333386* ⊕ *www.marthahaus.ch* ↩ *40 rooms, 6 with bath* ⚲ *Kitchen, bicycles, laundry facilities, Internet, parking (fee), no-smoking floors; no a/c, no room TVs* 🖃 *MC, V* ⍾ *BP.*

NIGHTLIFE & THE ARTS

What's On, published every month, lists special events, concerts, entertainment, museum exhibits, and a variety of useful telephone numbers. Portions of the text are in English. The booklet is free from Bern Tourismus.

Nightlife

Bars

Adriano's (⊠ Theaterpl. 2, Altstadt ☎ 031/3188831) is a tiny coffee bar where you can get fresh croissants early in the morning and a variety of sandwiches, wine, and beer until late at night. The plush leather and upholstered chairs at the café **Du Théâtre** (⊠ Hotelg. 10/Theaterpl. 7, Altstadt ☎ 031/3123031) attracts a smart young professional crowd for a mellow glass of wine after work. For history, head for **Klötzlikeller** (⊠ Gerechtigkeitsg. 62, Altstadt ☎ 031/3117456), said to be the oldest wine bar in Bern.

Among Bern's top hotel bars, the **Arcady** (⊠ Hotel Schweizerhof) has a mellow piano bar. At the **Bar Toulouse Lautrec** (⊠ Belle Epoque), you can enjoy a drink surrounded by art nouveau treasures. Political deal makers and well-heeled travelers gather at the **Bellevue Bar** (⊠ Hotel Bellevue Palace).

Casino

The **Allegro Grand Casino** (⊠ Kornhausstr. 3, Kornhausbrücke ☎ 031/ 3305500), in the Kursaal above the Hotel Allegro, has slot machines and gaming tables.

Dancing

Quality Dance in InSide (⊠ Kornhausstr. 3, Altstadt ☎ 031/3395148), in the Kursaal, has dancing on Friday and Saturday nights, with a *thé dansant* (tea dance) on Sunday afternoons from 3:30 to 7. For Latin music, salsa dancing, and tropical drinks head to **Shakira** (⊠ National Hotel, Hirschengraben 24, City Center ☎ 031/3811988). For late-night partying (to 3:30), **Toni's the Club** (⊠ Aarbergerg. 35, City Center ☎ 090/ 0575150) has two dance floors with music ranging from disco to hip-hop to trance.

Jazz Club

Marians Jazzroom (⊠ Engestr. 54, Innere Enge ☎ 031/3096111 ⊕ www. mariansjazzroom.ch), an intimate club in the cellar of the Innere Enge hotel, hosts top live acts from September to May. There are shows from Tuesday to Saturday at 7:30 and 10, plus a "late-night groove" starting at 11:45.

The Arts

Music

The **Bern Symphony Orchestra** (Ticket office ✉ Herreng. 25, Altstadt ☎ 031/3114242) is the city's most notable musical institution. Concerts take place at the **Casino** (✉ Casinopl., Altstadt) or the **Münster**. A five-day **International Jazz Festival** takes place in early May. Tickets go on sale in February at **Der Bund TicketCorner** (✉ Bubenbergerpl. 8 ☎ 084/8800800 ⊕ www.ticketcorner.com).

Opera & Ballet

Bern's resident opera company and contemporary dance troupe perform at the **Stadttheater** (✉ Kornhauspl. 20, Altstadt ☎ 031/3295151); tickets are sold next door at No. 18, weekdays 10 to 6:30, Saturday 10 to 4, and Sunday 10 to 12:30.

Theater

Although you can see traditional and modern plays at the **Stadttheater**, Bern also has a range of little theaters, mostly found in cellars in the Altstadt.

The **Berner Puppen Theater** (✉ Gerechtigkeitsg. 31, Altstadt ☎ 031/3119585) produces funny, action-packed puppet shows—enjoyable even if you don't speak the language. **Kleintheater** (✉ Kramg. 6, Altstadt) has a modern repertoire; buy tickets at **Müller & Schade** (✉ Kramg. 50, Altstadt ☎ 031/3202626). Avant-garde plays, satires, and burlesques (in Swiss German), pantomime, modern dance, and productions of the English-language amateur theater group UPSTAGE are performed at **Theater am Käfigturm** (✉ Spitalg. 4, City Center ☎ 031/3116100).

SPORTS & THE OUTDOORS

Bicycling

There are about 300 km (185 mi) of marked trails around Bern. Bikes can be rented at the Hauptbahnhof. There's also the tourism office's *Bern Rollt* program; you can borrow a bike with a 20 SF deposit and ID from late April to late October.

Golf

The **Golf and Country Club Blumisberg** (✉ 18 km [11 mi] west of town ☎ 026/4963438) has 18 holes and a clubhouse with a restaurant, bar, showers, and swimming pool. The club admits visitors weekdays, provided they're members of any golf club with handicaps. Only local members and their guests are admitted on weekends.

Swimming

Join the throngs of people on the lawn and in the pools at **Aarebad Marzili** (✉ Marzilistr. 29, Marzili ☎ 031/3110046). Sections of the river are roped off for swimming, but the cold, swift-running water should be entered with caution.

Bern's numerous public swimming areas have multiple pools for swimmers of all ages and abilities. Outdoor pools (open from May to October) are generally free. Indoor pools *(Hallenbäder)* have an entrance fee.

Hallenbad Hirschengraben (⊠ Maulbeerstr. 14, City Center ☎ 031/3813656) is closest to downtown.

A unique bathing experience for adult swimmers of all abilities is offered at **Solbad Schönbühl** (⊠ Mattenweg 30 Schönbühl ☎ 031/8593434), in a nearby Bern suburb. The heated indoor and outdoor baths, open year-round, have mineral-rich waters, underwater massage nozzles, and bubbling jets. Bathing suits, swim caps, and towels can be rented with a deposit. Admission is 23 SF.

SHOPPING

Store hours in Bern vary from most store hours throughout the rest of Switzerland. Stores in downtown Bern open between 8 and 9 in the morning; some Altstadt stores open later. Closing times are more consistent: 6:30 on Monday through Wednesday and Friday, 9 on Thursday, and 4 on Saturday. On Sunday all stores except the Hauptbahnhof stores are closed; some stores are closed Monday morning as well.

Department Stores

In **Globus** (⊠ Spitalg. 17–21, City Center ☎ 031/3118811) you'll find a wide variety of designer labels. Head downstairs to the food hall for imported and gourmet edibles. **Loeb** (⊠ Spitalg. 47–51, City Center ☎ 031/3207111) is a general department store worth visiting for its imaginative and often outrageous display windows.

Markets

The elaborate annual **Zwibelemärit** opens at 4 AM on the fourth Monday in November. All around downtown, you can find things oniony. Beginning in mid-May and with a later start time, the **Geranienmarkt** sells the classic blooms along the Bundesplatz. During December's **Weihnachtsmarkt,** garlands and trees plus handicrafts are on sale in the plazas at Waisenhaus and Münster.

During **Tuesday and Saturday markets,** Waisenhausplatz fills with awning-covered stalls selling clothing, music, art, toys, and household goods. It's an adventure to wander through the maze to find unusual herbs, a cheese grater, or a hand-carved rocking horse. Closer to the parliament building on Bundesplatz and Bärenplatz, shoppers stock their wicker baskets and wheeled carts with fresh produce and flowers, stopping for meat, poultry, and cheese along Münstergasse.

If it's an antique hand mirror or a cherry armoire you are looking for, a ramble through the fabulous **Matte flea market,** in Bern's bohemian district along the river, is filled with discoveries the third Saturday of the month from May to October.

Shopping Streets

East of the Zytglogge, along **Kramgasse** and **Gerechtigkeitsgasse** and, farther to the north, **Postgasse,** you'll find quirkier, bohemian spots and excellent antiques stores. Don't overlook the cellar shops, accessible from the street outside the arcades. Countless shops are concentrated in arcades and passageways between the Hauptbahnhof and the Zytglogge; **Spitalgasse** and **Marktgasse** are considered the main drags. **Junkerngasse** has numerous art galleries and avant-garde fashion boutiques. Münstergasse is another artsy shopping area.

Specialty Stores

Antiques
The best antiques shops line Gerechtigkeitsgasse and Postgasse; their wares range from cluttery *brocante* (collectibles) to good antiques from all over Europe. The **Puppenklinik** (⊠ Gerechtigkeitsg. 36, Altstadt ☎ 031/3120771) is just this side of a museum, packed with lovely—if slightly eerie—old dolls and toys.

Books
Stauffacher (⊠ Neueng. 25–37, City Center ☎ 084/4880040), a bookstore with three floors and two wings, is easy to get lost in. On the third floor in the west wing you'll find the English Bookshop. Readings in both German and English are held regularly in the Café Littéraire, on the second floor.

Chocolate
Abegglen (⊠ Spitalg. 36, City Center ☎ 031/3112111) has great chocolate-covered almonds. Don't leave **Beeler** (⊠ Spitalg. 29, City Center ☎ 031/3112808) without trying its champagne chocolates. **Eichenberger** (⊠ Bahnhofpl. 5, City Center ☎ 031/3113325) is known for its hazelnut *Lebkuchen* (a flat spice cake). Pop into the tearoom in the back for a rich hot chocolate or a luscious dessert. **Tschirren** (⊠ Kramg. 73, Altstadt ☎ 031/3111717) has been making sweets for more than 80 years. The mandarin chocolates and florentines are divine.

Gifts & Souvenirs
Heimatwerk Bern (⊠ Kramg. 61, Altstadt ☎ 031/3113000) offers a broad, high-quality range of Swiss-made handicrafts, textiles, and ceramics. **Langenthal** (⊠ Marktg. 15, City Center ☎ 031/3118786) is where you'll find fine embroidery and linens.

SIDE TRIP TO THE EMMENTAL

The city of Bern anchors a large and lovely region tourists often overlook: the Berner Mittelland, the rural lowlands of the enormous Canton Bern. These mist-covered, velvety green foothills lap the base of the Bernese Alps. Fodor'sChoice The Mittelland's most famous region is the **Emmental,** the valley of the ★ River Emme, where Switzerland's trademark cheese (Emmentaler, the one with the holes) is made. In the 19th century, Swiss clergyman Jeremias Gotthelf was so inspired by the virtues of family life and Christian beliefs in this breathtaking valley that he turned to writing novels and short stories about the Emmentalers. His efforts revealed a prodigious literary talent, making him one of Switzerland's most famous writers. Much of the Emmental has remained the same since Gotthelf's time.

The gentle hills of Emmental are dotted with some of Switzerland's most beautiful farmhouses—plump, broad boxes topped with deep-curving roofs that slope nearly to the ground. On a typical farmstead, the enormous *Bauernhaus* (main building) shelters the living quarters of the farmer and his family. At the back of the house, built into the central plan, is the cowshed; grains and feed are stored upstairs, under the deep roof. Next door, in a separate house, lives the older generation. When a farmer retires, he passes the entire farm on to his youngest son and moves into the *Stöckli*, a kind of guesthouse, conceding the home to the inheriting family. A third building, the *Spycher*, is used for storing the harvest and, in olden days, the family's savings. If the farm caught fire, this building would be saved before the main house.

To get a true feel for the Emmental, make its castle town, Burgdorf, your base. Stay overnight to enjoy a leisurely visit to the upper and lower parts of the city and its museums before driving to the demonstration dairy in Affoltern. Outside the city, the steady grade of the hillside roads, narrow and twisting, requires extra time, as does stopping at lookouts to photograph the stunning views, which seem to pop out at every switchback. Following the river, you'll drive into the heart of the valley through a sequence of villages marked by covered bridges, town squares, and museums that highlight regional folklore and crafts, especially ceramics.

Numbers in the text correspond to numbers in the margin and on the Emmental map.

Burgdorf

❶ *30 km (19 mi) northeast of Bern via the A1 and Hwy. 23.*

Burgdorf's sizable Gothic castle, built in the early 13th century by the Zähringens, the family responsible for founding the cities of Bern, Fribourg, Murten, and Burgdorf, dominates the *Oberstadt* (upper city). Its square turrets and boxy main tower painted with the Bernese flag are markers on the horizon for miles, especially at night when illuminated. The *Unterstadt* (lower city), where tradespeople had their workrooms and storehouses, remains an active commercial area extending from the base of the massive stone outcropping along the Emme to the train station.

A pedestrian-only zone, the upper town holds a weekend open-air market, its arcades filled with smart shops, galleries, and restaurants. The *Stadtkirche* (church) and *Rathaus* (city hall) anchor one of the broad plazas. Follow the Schloss/Museum signs through town to stone steps that climb up to the castle fortress. Enormous wooden doors mark the entry to the castle ramparts, where you can stroll the restored fortifications and take in stunning views of green hillsides and farmsteads backed by icy white Alpine peaks.

The **schloss** (castle) was turned into a museum more than 100 years ago. The **Schlossmuseum Burgdorf** (Burgdorf Castle Museum) and the smaller **Helvetisches Goldmuseum** (Swiss Gold Museum) occupy separate spaces within the tower confines. A walk through the Knights' Hall and the various rooms, towers, and battlements introduces you

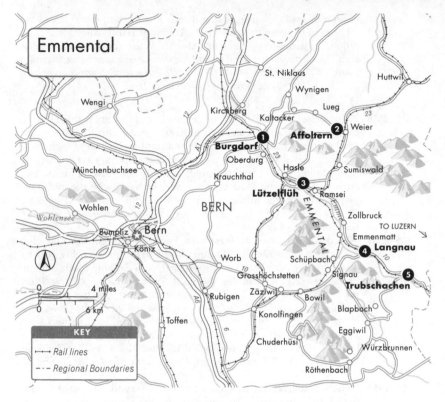

Emmental

St. Niklaus
Wynigen
Huttwil
Wengi
Kirchberg
Lueg
Weier
Kaltacker
Affoltern ❷
Burgdorf ❶
Oberdurg
Hasle
Sumiswald
Münchenbuchsee
Krauchthal
Lützelflüh ❸
Ramsei
Wohlen
BERN
Zollbruck
Wohlensee
TO LUZERN
Bumpliz ⊗ Bern
Emmenmatt
Köniz
❹ **Langnau**
Worb
Schüpbach
Grosshöchstetten
Signau
❺
Rubigen
Zäziwil
Trubschachen
Bowil
Blapbach
Toffen
Konolfingen
Eggiwil
Chuderhüsi
Würzbrunnen
Röthenbach

0   4 miles
0   6 km

KEY
⊢—⊦ *Rail lines*
- - - *Regional Boundaries*

to the history and culture of Burgdorf and the Emmental. There are additional exhibits of regional ceramics and period furniture. To learn about the discovery of gold and precious-metal mining in Switzerland, follow the exhibits in the Goldmuseum. ☎ *034/4230214* ⊕ *www. schloss-burgdorf.ch, www.helvetisches-goldmuseum.ch* 🎫 *Fortifications free, museums 5 SF* ☉ *Apr.–Oct., Mon.–Sat. 2–5, Sun. 11–5; Nov.–Mar., Sun. 11–5.*

In the lower village, the **Kornhaus**, a former granary, now houses the Swiss Center for Folk Culture. An extensive collection of costumes from all over the country, many still worn at regional celebrations, shows the intricate details and embroidery of dresses, suits, and headgear that reflect people's place of origin. Phonographs, musical instruments, and a room for yodelers have permanent space. The museum hosts special exhibits and concerts. ✉ *Kornhausg. 16* ☎ *034/4231010* ⊕ *www. kornhaus-burgdorf.ch* 🎫 *10 SF* ☉ *Mid-Mar.–Oct., Tues.–Fri. 10–12:30 and 1:30–5, weekends 10–5; Nov.–mid-Mar., Tues.–Fri. 1:30–5, weekends 10–5.*

A contemporary box amid historical structures, the **Museum Franz Gertsch** showcases the work of its eponymous artist. His paintings and graphics occupy huge canvases; using color and woodblocks, he creates his version of reality in painstaking detail. The modern museum is a collaboration between the artist and local industrialist Willy Michel. Additional galleries have changing exhibits. A café and video lounge runs an artist documentary by day and music videos for evening entertainment. ⊠ *Platanenstr. 3* ☎ *034/4214020* ⊕ *www.museum-franzgertsch. ch* ⌨ *10 SF* ⊘ *Tues.–Fri. 11–7, weekends 10–5.*

Where to Stay & Eat

★ **$$$–$$$$** ✕ **Emmenhof.** Part of the fun of getting out of the city is the discovery of great restaurants in the most unlikely places. This fine-dining spot on the town's main drag attracts restaurant guide–toting enthusiasts and well-heeled locals. Cool colors and contemporary art brighten the main dining room. Sophisticated, light dishes such as almond-encrusted crayfish in a Madras curry sauce contrast with the traditional Swiss dishes in the adjacent Stübli. ⊠ *Kirchbergstr. 70, Unterstadt* ☎ *034/4222275* ⊟ *AE, DC, MC, V* ⊘ *Closed Mon. and Tues. and mid-July–mid-Aug.*

$$$–$$$$ ✕ **Restaurant Brauerei Schützenhaus.** Formerly a target-shooting clubhouse (notice the flip-out windows in the bar), this microbrewery has several dining options: a lively sports bar, casual dining room, and umbrella-covered picnic tables outdoors. Start with a large *Bretzel* (soft pretzel) and a draft. The *Bierbrauerbrett,* a large platter of smoked and air-dried cold cuts plus cheese, is best shared by the table, especially with refills of crusty farmer's bread. Multicourse meals and blue-plate specials are largely from the regional cookbook. After eating, take a stroll on the path along the riverbank for a look at the wooden covered bridge. ⊠ *Wynigenstr. 13, Unterstadt* ☎ *034/4288200* ⊟ *AE, DC, MC, V.*

$$$–$$$$ ⊡ **Hotel Stadthaus.** Set amid cobblestone streets and covered arcades on the hilltop dominated by the castle towers, this inn promises a very quiet stay. Traffic is restricted, although guests can drive up to the entrance. Built in the mid-1700s as the gathering place for the city council, the hotel has smartly furnished rooms with antiques on loan from the Schlossmuseum. Two restaurants give you a choice between elegant French and brasserie-style dining. ⊠ *Kirchbühlstr. 2, Oberstadt, CH-3402* ☎ *034/4288000* ⊟ *034/4288008* ⊕ *www.stadthaus.ch* ⇌ *16 rooms, 1 suite* ♿ *2 restaurants, cable TV, bar, parking (fee); no a/c* ⊟ *AE, DC, MC, V* ⫶⨀⫶ *BP.*

$$ ⊡ **Hotel Berchtold.** Old and new combine in the restoration and expansion of one of the town's vintage buildings, near the train station. The lobby hums around the clock with clusters of coffee drinkers from the connecting *confiserie* (specialty bakery) and patrons of the bar and restaurant. Clean lines, whimsical lighting, and graphics by local artists fill the public areas and guest rooms. Blond modular furniture, black accents, and white-on-white bedding give a business-casual feeling. Top-floor rooms have access to a rooftop terrace. ⊠ *Bahnhofstr. 90, Unterstadt, CH-3401* ☎ *034/4288428* ⊟ *034/4288484* ⊕ *www. hotel-berchtold.ch* ⇌ *36 rooms* ♿ *Restaurant, in-room data ports, in-room safes, minibars, cable TV, bar, shops, parking (fee), no-smoking rooms* ⊟ *AE, DC, MC, V* ⫶⨀⫶ *BP.*

en route

For a **back-roads drive to Affoltern,** take the main road out of Burgdorf toward Wynigen. Cross the Emme River, and in less than a kilometer (½ mi), turn right on a small road signed LUEG, KALTACKER, AFFOLTERN. This narrow road winds uphill through stands of evergreens, past sprawling farmhouses and cultivated fields. At the crossroads hamlet of Hüb, continue straight; then turn right when the road ends near Gütisberg. Up on this sunny shelf you get bird's-eye views back to the castle town and out to the Bernese Alps.

Consider a stop at the wayside inn **Landgasthof zum Hirschen** (✉ Kaltacker ☎ 034/4223216). You might not expect English to be spoken at this remote eatery, but hostess and chef welcome guests with a cordial exchange and multilingual menus filled with traditional Emmentaler dishes and international creations from their travels. Walk off your meal with a stop for the panoramic views from **Lueg,** about 3 km (2 mi) farther. Here is a war monument and a map that indicates the distant peaks.

Affoltern

★ ☾ ❷ *11 km (7 mi) east of Burgdorf.*

Affoltern, a small traditional village, has some strong examples of Emmental architecture. The main attraction is the **Schaukäserei Affoltern** (demonstration dairy), which allows you to see Swiss cheese in the making. In four different buildings, techniques from previous periods are shown. Watch from a glassed-in balcony as more than 1,000 gallons of milk are stirred in copper cauldrons, the curd is separated from the whey in great sieves, and the heavy solids are eased into molds to be brine-soaked and then stored. Try to be here between 9 and 11 or between 2 and 4, when the most active stages of cheese making take place. You can try the cheese at the source at the factory's simple restaurant, where the menu covers cheese dishes—fondue, Käseschnitte—as well as local cold meats. There's also a crafts boutique, bakery, and children's play area. ☎ *034/4351611* 🎫 *Free* ◷ *Daily 8:30–6:30.*

Where to Eat

$–$$$ ✕ **Sonne.** If the dining hall atmosphere of the Schaukäserei doesn't suit, this nearby archetypal restaurant with guest quarters will. Set on a sunny hill with more of those picture-perfect views of countryside and mountains, the restaurant serves rich, hearty cooking based on ingredients straight off the farm. There are satiny soups, unusually well-executed veal dishes, and freshwater fish. Leave room for the meringue, fluffed to enormous proportions with farm-fresh Emmental egg whites. ☎ *034/4358000* 🍴 *MC, V* ◷ *Closed Wed. and Thurs.*

Lützelflüh

❸ *9 km southeast of Burgdorf.*

This little town is perhaps best known for the beloved author Jeremias Gotthelf. The **Gotthelf-Stube,** a museum honoring the writer-laureate, contains photographs, handwritten manuscripts, and rare editions of his books, carefully tended by local volunteers. To get here, park near the church and walk uphill on Rainsgergliweg. Continue past the driveway of the parsonage and community house, behind which stands the Spycher that was converted into the museum. ☎ 034/4601611 ⌨ 4 SF ⊙ Apr.–Oct., Mon.–Sat. 2–5, Sun. 10:30–11:30 and 2–5.

Langnau

❹ 11 km southeast of Lützelflüh.

This graceful old market town serves as capital of the region and clearinghouse for its cheese. Here you'll find the **Regional Museum Chüechli-hus,** named for the tarts served in the first-floor coffeehouse. Traditional crafts, tools, and furniture, as well as military paraphernalia, are on display in this enormous chalet. Although it's closed from November through March, private tours can be arranged for groups of six or more during these months; call ahead to reserve. ⊠ Bärenpl. 2a ☎ 034/4021819 ⌨ 4 SF ⊙ Apr.–Oct., Tues.–Sun. 1:30–6.

Trubschachen

❺ 6 km southeast of Langnau.

This center for the region's folk-style ceramics sits in the shadow of the 3,920-foot Blapbach ridge. Here the **Heimatmuseum Hasenlehn,** arranged among the three traditional buildings of a farm, displays crafts and household antiques in the Spycher and Stöckli. To watch local craftspeople at work, visit the **Schautöpferei** (demonstration pottery studio), where you'll also find a shop full of local ceramics and a cozy upstairs café. ⊠ Hafenlehnmattstr. 1 ☎ 034/4956038 museum, 034/4956029 studio ⌨ Museum 5 SF, studio free ⊙ Museum Apr.–Nov., Sun. 2–4 or by appointment; studio weekdays 8–noon and 1:30–6.

en route On your way out of the Emmental, make a **scenic loop along the Emme** past nine restored bridges to another spectacular lookout point. From Schüpbach follow the river to Eggiwil, and continue to Röthenbach. Stop to stretch your legs at the country church in Würzbrunnen, which has been featured in films made about Jeremias Gotthelf and his stories. From here a road zigzags up to the summit of Chuderhüsi (3,650 feet), where there's a basic restaurant but an excellent view of the Alps. A pleasant 10-minute walk through the woods will bring you to a tower with a 360-degree view of the Emmental. From Chuderhüsi follow signs to Bowill and on to Highway 10, direction Zäziwil. You can stop in the next village, Grosshöchstetten, at the excellent restaurant **Landgasthof Sternen** (☎ 031/7102424) or continue on Highway 10 through Worb to A6 and either back to Bern or toward Thun and the Berner Oberland.

BERN A TO Z

To *research prices, get advice from other travelers, and book travel arrangements, visit www.fodors.com.*

AIR TRAVEL

CARRIERS Swiss, Switzerland's international and domestic airline, flies directly from Bern-Belp to Basel, Lugano, and Paris. A number of discount airlines, such as InterSky and AirAlps, have initiated service from here, too.

🚹 Airlines & Contacts **AirAlps** ☎ 031/9602127 ⊕ www.airalps.at. **InterSky** ☎ 055/7448800 ⊕ www.intersky.biz. **Swiss** ☎ 031/9602121 ⊕ www.swiss.com.

AIRPORTS & TRANSFERS

Bern's small airport, located 9 km (6 mi) south of the city in Belp, has connecting flights to most major European cities. A shuttle bus runs regularly between the Bern train station and the Belp airport. The fare each way is 15 SF; the ride takes 20 minutes. A taxi from the airport to the Hauptbahnhof costs about 40 SF.

🚹 Airport Information **Belp Airport** ⊠ Belp ☎ 031/9602111.

BUS TRAVEL WITHIN BERN

Bus and tram service is excellent, with fares ranging from 1.50 SF to 2.40 SF. Buy individual tickets from the dispenser at the tram or bus stop: find the name of the stop closest to your destination on the map, and then check the fare on the list of stops. An unlimited-travel Visitor's Card—7 SF for 24 hours, 11 SF for 48 hours, and 15 SF for 72 hours—is available at the tourist office in the Hauptbahnhof or at the public transportation ticket office on Bankgässchen (from the train station follow signs for Bus 13). A Swiss Pass includes free travel in Bern.

CAR TRAVEL

Bern is connected conveniently by expressway to Basel and Zürich via A1, to the Berner Oberland via A6, and to Lac Léman and thus Lausanne, Geneva, and the Valais via A12. Bern's many pedestrian zones make parking in city garages a virtual necessity. There are electric signs on all the incoming thoroughfares giving up-to-the-minute counts on space availability.

EMBASSIES

🚹 Embassies **Canada** ⊠ Kirchenfeldstr. 88, Kirchenfeld ☎ 031/3573200. **United Kingdom** ⊠ Thunstr. 50, Kirchenfeld ☎ 031/3597700. **United States** ⊠ Jubiläumsstr. 95, Kirchenfeld ☎ 031/3577234.

EMERGENCIES

🚹 **Ambulance** ☎ 144. **Police** ☎ 117. **Emergency Medical, Dental, and Pharmacy Referrals** ☎ 0900/576747.

🚹 Hospitals **Inselspital (Hospital)** ⊠ Freiburgstr. 18 ☎ 031/6322111. **Inselspital Frauenklinik (Women's Hospital)** ⊠ Schanzeneckstr. 1 ☎ 031/3001111.

TAXIS

Direct traffic routes are almost nonexistent in Bern, and taxis are a cumbersome and expensive alternative to walking or taking a bus or tram. To go from the Hauptbahnhof to the Bärengraben will cost approximately 18 SF by taxi. There's a cab stand at the train station's side entrance, or call to order one.

🚹 Taxi Companies **Barem Taxi** ☎ 031/3711111. **Kull Taxi** ☎ 031/3205020.

TOURS

Walking and bus tours with English commentary covering Bern's principal sights are offered daily June through September and on Saturday the rest of the year. Buy tickets at Bern Tourismus in the Hauptbahnhof; the bus tour costs 29 SF, the walking tour 15 SF.

To arrange for a private guide or to schedule excursions outside the city, contact Bern Tourismus.

TRAIN TRAVEL

Bern is a major link between Geneva, Zürich, and Basel. Intercity trains, which make the fewest stops, leave almost every hour from the Hauptbahnhof. Bern is the only European capital to have three high-speed trains: the ICE from Berlin takes 9 hours; the TGV from Paris takes 4½ hours, and the Pendolino from Milan takes 3–4 hours.

🚹 Train Information **Hauptbahnhof** ☎ 0900/300300.

VISITOR INFORMATION

Bern Tourismus provides free brochures and information and organizes a variety of tours. A branch at the Altes Tramdepot, next to the Bear Pits, offers a free multimedia show titled *Bern Past and Present*. Discounts at shops and restaurants are available with the purchase of a Bern Card.

Burgdorfer Tourismus and Pro Emmental are extremely helpful, providing information about local attractions and maps and routes for hikes in the region. Both offices are open daily. The Emmental office closes over lunch.

🚹 Tourist Information **Bern Tourismus** ✉ Bahnhofpl., at main train station, City Center, CH-3001 ☎ 031/3281212 🖷 031/3121233 ⊕ www.bernetourism.ch. **Burgdorfer Tourismus** ✉ Bahnhofstr. 44, CH-3401 Burgdorf ☎ 034/4236905 🖷 034/4236901 ⊕ www.burgdorf-tourismus.ch. **Pro Emmental** ✉ Schlossstr. 3, CH-3550 Langnau ☎ 034/4024252 🖷 034/4025667 ⊕ www.emmental.ch.

BERNER OBERLAND
GSTAAD, INTERLAKEN, WENGEN

GET YOUR JUST DESSERTS
in the meringue capital of Meiringer ⇨*p.307*

SLAY A DRAGON
in the caves of St. Beatus-Höhlen ⇨*p.283*

IMPERSONATE JAMES BOND
at the glamorous resort of Mürren ⇨*p.290*

HEAD INTO THE CLOUDS
at the world's highest train station ⇨*p.292*

GET THE BLUES
at a craggy, steel-colored glacier ⇨*p.295*

HAVE A COW
or any number of carved-wood creatures ⇨*p.298*

Updated by
Katrin Gygax

THERE ARE TIMES WHEN THE REALITY of Switzerland puts postcard idealization to shame, surpassing tinted-indigo skies and advertising-image peaks with its own astonishing vividness. Those times happen often in the Berner Oberland, for this rugged region concentrates some of the best of rural Switzerland: awesome mountain panoramas, massive glaciers, crystalline lakes, gorges and waterfalls, chic ski resorts, dense pine forests, and charming gingerbread chalets.

After contemplating the Staubbach Falls in 1779, the great German writer Johann Wolfgang von Goethe was moved to write one of his most celebrated poems, "Gesang der Geister über den Wassern" ("Song of the Spirits over the Waters"). Rousseau spread word of the region's astounding natural phenomena to Paris society. Then the Romantics began to beat a path to this awe-inspiring area. Lord Byron came to investigate; it's said he conceived his *Manfred* in barren, windswept Wengernalp. Shelley followed, then William Thackeray, John Ruskin, the composer Johannes Brahms, and Mark Twain; the master landscape painter J. M. W. Turner recorded the views; and Queen Victoria herself came, beginning a flood of tourism that changed the Berner Oberland's—and Switzerland's—profile forever.

Before the onslaught of visitors inspired the locals to switch from farming to inn-keeping, agriculture was the prime industry—and is still much in evidence today. As if hired as props to style a photo opportunity, brown and white cows dot the hillsides. The houses of the Berner Oberland are classics, the definitive Swiss chalets, with broad, low, deep-eaved roofs covering scalloped and carved gables. Facades are painted with the family dedication on wood weathered to dark sienna. From early spring through autumn, window boxes spill torrents of well-tended geraniums and petunias, and adjacent woodpiles are stacked with mosaiclike precision.

The region is arranged tidily enough for even a brief visit. Its main resort city, Interlaken, lies in green lowlands between the gleaming twin pools of the Brienzersee and the Thunersee, which are linked by the River Aare. Behind them to the south loom craggy, forested foothills with excellent views, and behind those foothills stand some of Europe's noblest peaks, most notably the snowy crowns of the Eiger (13,022 feet), the Mönch (13,445 feet), and the fiercely beautiful Jungfrau (13,638 feet). Because nature laid it out so conveniently, the region has become far and away the most popular for tourism, with its excursion and transportation systems carrying enormous numbers of visitors to its myriad viewpoints, overlooks, and wonders. The railroad to the Jungfraujoch transports masses of tour groups to its high-altitude attractions, and on a peak-season day its station can resemble the Sistine Chapel in August or the Chicago Board of Trade. But the tourist industry can handle the onslaught, offering such an efficient network of boats, trains, and funiculars, such a variety of activities and attractions, and such a wide range of accommodations, from posh city hotels to rustic mountain lodges, that every visitor can find the most suitable way to take in the marvels of the Bernese Alps.

Ten days in the Berner Oberland give you the luxury of exploring each of the valleys and lakes of this varied region, but you can experience it *en passage* as well, depending on your travel pace.

Numbers in the text correspond to numbers in the margin and on the Berner Oberland map.

9

If you have 3 days Base yourself in bustling ⬚ **Interlaken ❶** ↳ or the quieter ⬚ **Bönigen ❷**, one day taking a boat trip across the Thunersee to ⬚ **Thun ⑫**, the next day a driving tour around the Brienzersee to ⬚ **Brienz ❾** and the Freilichtmuseum Ballenberg. The third day (or best-weather day) head up the Lauterbrunnen Valley and take the famous rail trip from ⬚ **Wengen ❻** to the **Jungfraujoch ❺**, returning via ⬚ **Grindelwald ❼**.

If you have 5 days Follow the tours above, and while in the Lauterbrunnen Valley, take the cable cars or cogwheel rail up to ⬚ **Mürren ❹** and the Schilthorn. On Day 5, drive up to ⬚ **Kandersteg ⑬** to hike to the Oeschinensee, or wind through the forest by car or on the Golden Pass Panoramic Express train to visit famous ⬚ **Gstaad ⑭**.

If you have 10 days Expand your five-day itinerary to take in the lesser sights as you cruise around the varied region. Visit the Trümmelbach Falls in the Lauterbrunnen Valley; see the castles at Hilterfingen and Oberhofen on the Thunersee; explore the St. Beatus caves just above the Thunersee near Interlaken; and take another high-altitude excursion out of Interlaken to Harder Kulm, Heimwehfluh, or Schynige Platte. Go to Meiringen and visit the Reichenbach Falls. Or spend an overnight in Gstaad, and take the cable car to the Diablerets glacier.

Exploring Berner Oberland

The central, urban-Victorian resort of Interlaken makes a good base for excursions for visitors who want to experience the entire Jungfrau region, which includes the craggy, bluff-lined Lauterbrunnen Valley and the opposing resorts that perch high above it: Mürren and Wengen. Busy Grindelwald, famous for its variety of sporting possibilities, and isolated Kandersteg, ideal for hiking and cross-country skiing, are both easily accessible from Interlaken. Each lies at the dead end of different gorge roads that climb into the heights. Spreading east and west of Interlaken are the Brienzersee and Thunersee, both broad, crystalline lakes, surrounded by forests, castles, and waterfront resorts, including Brienz, Thun, and Spiez. From Spiez, you can head southwest through the forest gorge of the Simmental to the Saanenland and glamorous Gstaad. Connections by rail or car keep most highlights within easy reach.

About the Restaurants

Most restaurants are at the high-end hotels, especially in the smaller mountain villages. If you're on a tight budget or tired of three-course meals, grab a quick bite at the counter of a cheese and butcher shop. These places offer delicious local specialties and sandwiches. Get there early though, as some are closed at lunch hour.

WHAT IT COSTS In Swiss francs				
$$$$	$$$	$$	$	¢
MAIN COURSE over 60	40–60	25–40	15–25	under 15

Prices are per person for a main course at dinner.

About the Hotels

Outside of the larger towns, such as Interlaken and Thun, which have more modern architecture, Berner Oberland tradition mandates charming chalet-style exteriors replete with steeply sloped roofs, scalloped-wood balconies, and cascades of brilliant geraniums. A few landmarks have preserved interiors that reflect their lovely facades. Although a vast majority of the hotels are still family-owned and -run, big businesses are creeping in, scooping up properties that private families can no longer carry, and creating competition that forces even more family-run places to go under, a sad scenario that is actively being fought in some communities.

Small towns may not have street addresses; in those cases, hotels large and small are clearly signposted. Prices below are average for the Berner Oberland; note that such car-free resorts as Wengen, Mürren, and Gstaad run well above this curve, especially during ski season. Half board, or *demipension* (breakfast and one hot meal) is often the thrust of regional hotels. Remember that many properties post rates on a per-person basis.

Some two dozen hotels in the Interlaken/Jungfrau area have cooked up a distinctive special offer: during the winter season, guests celebrating a birthday during their stay will be given free accommodations and a complimentary ski pass as long as there is an accompanying paying adult. Contact the Interlaken tourist bureau for further details.

WHAT IT COSTS In Swiss francs				
$$$$	$$$	$$	$	¢
DOUBLE ROOM over 350	250–350	175–250	100–175	under 100

Prices are for two people in a standard double room in high season, including tax and service.

Timing

In high summer, the Berner Oberland is the most popular tourist area in Switzerland and can feel overrun. June or September to early October—when the weather still holds but the crowds thin—can be delightful. Ski season begins in mid-December and runs through Easter vacation. May and November are low season, with November being the lowest of the low. Some towns all but roll up their sidewalks; many hotels and cable cars shut down for maintenance, and, depending on snow conditions, some excursions may be closed into June or may shut down

9

Cruises Steamers ply the lakes of Brienz and Thun, trailing leisurely across crystal waters past rolling panoramas of forested hills and craggy, snowcapped peaks. With buslike schedules, they allow passengers to step off at any port for a visit; just choose the best boat to catch next.

Dining Meals in the Berner Oberland tend to be down-to-earth. You might start with a hearty soup, a slawlike salad, or a platter of thinly sliced, air-dried beef or mountain cheese. Desserts are sizable. Fried or broiled *Egli* (perch) and *Felchen* (whitefish) are usually local and freshly caught from the nearest lake. Waterfront resorts such as Spiez, Brienz, and Iseltwald specialize in fish. Meat dishes represent Bernese and Zürich cuisines: *Ratsherrentopf* is a mixed grill, *Geschnetzeltes Kalbsfleisch* is veal in cream sauce. *Rösti* (hash brown potatoes) is served plain or with any number of accompaniments, such as fried eggs, ham, or wild mushrooms. *Älplermagronen* (baked macaroni and cheese) is made with potatoes and onions and sometimes bacon, and is served mainly in rural areas. Colorful mixed salads include freshly shredded celery root, beet, carrot, and cabbage as well as tomato and cucumber. Fondue and raclette (a dish of melted cheese served over boiled potatoes with pickles) are winter-evening staples.

The valley town of Meiringen claims to have invented meringue. Whether true or not, the region consumes enough to corner the culinary market. Enormous, crisp, ivory meringue puffs come with or without vanilla ice cream but are always served under mounds of whipped cream.

Hiking Partly because of its spectacular ski-transport network woven throughout the region, the Berner Oberland offers a wealth of highly developed walking and hiking options. The scenery is magnificent and the options varied, from rough trails toward glaciers to smooth postbus roads. From May through October you'll be unlikely to find yourself alone for long on any given trail; you'll even find company on a snowy trail since nearly a third of the region's visitors come for winter hiking. A wide variety of topographical maps and suggested itineraries, along with information about overnight huts and *Berghotels* (mountain inns), are available at tourist offices in each town. In summer, some farmers offer their barns for *Schlaf im Stroh* (sleeping in the hay). Local tourist bureaus will provide information.

Skiing As one of Switzerland's winter-sports capitals, the Berner Oberland provides a dazzling variety of choices to skiers. Each resort offers its own style of transit and its own peculiar terrain, from nursery slopes to the deadly narrow pistes of the Schilthorn. The lift lines are a fair bit more tolerable here, although the region as a whole is not as snow-sure as is, for example, the Engadine.

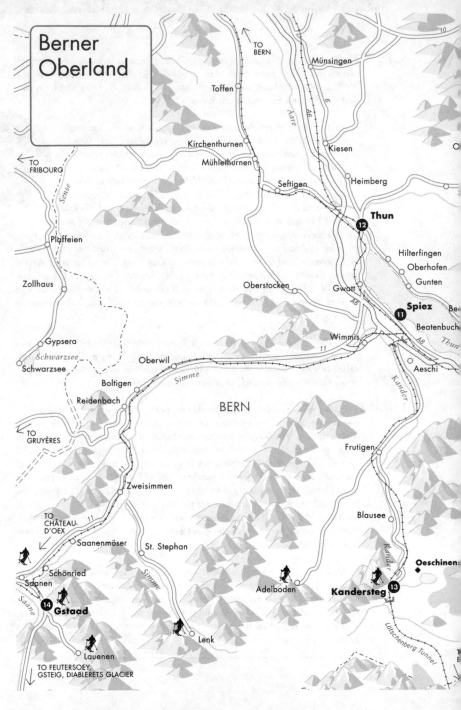

Berner Oberland

TO BERN

Münsingen

Toffen

Kiesen

Kirchenthurnen

Mühlethurnen

TO FRIBOURG

Sense

Seftigen

Heimberg

Thun **12**

Pfaffeien

Hilterfingen

Oberhofen

Zollhaus

Oberstocken

Gwatt

Gunten

Spiez **11**

Be

Beatenbuch

Gypsera

Schwarzsee

Wimmis

Thu

Schwarzsee

Oberwil

Simme

Aeschi

Boltigen

BERN

Kander

Reidenbach

TO GRUYÈRES

Frutigen

Zweisimmen

Blausee

TO CHÂTEAU-D'OEX

Saanenmöser

St. Stephan

Kander

Oeschinen

Schönried

Simme

Adelboden

Kandersteg **13**

Saanen

Saane

Gstaad **14**

Lenk

Lauenen

TO FEUTERSOEY, GSTEIG, DIABLERETS GLACIER

Lötschenberg Tunnel

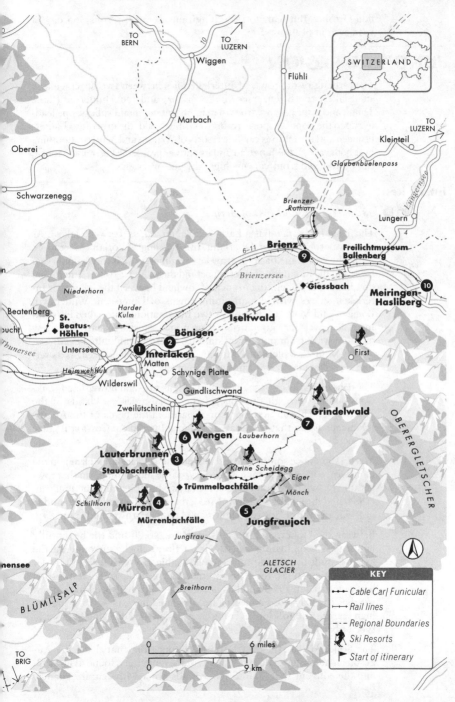

SWITZERLAND

TO
BERN

TO
LUZERN

Wiggen

Flühli

TO
LUZERN

Marbach

Kleinteil

Oberei

Glaubenbüelenpass

Lüngernsee

Schwarzenegg

Brienzer-
Rothorn

Lungern

6–11   **Brienz**

Freilichtmuseum
Ballenberg

9

Niederhorn

Brienzersee

♦ **Giessbach**

Beatenberg

*Harder
Kulm*

8

10

**Meiringen-
Hasliberg**

St.
Beatus-
Höhlen

Iseltwald

ucht

Thunersee

Unterseen

Bönigen

First

Heimwehfluh

1 **Interlaken**

Matten

Wilderswil

Schynige Platte

Gundlischwand

Grindelwald

7

Zweilütschinen

**O
B
E
R
E
R
G
L
E
T
S
C
H
E
R**

6 **Wengen**

Lauberhorn

Lauterbrunnen

3

Kleine Scheidegg

Staubbachfälle

Eiger

♦ **Trümmelbachfälle**

Mönch

Schilthorn

Mürren **4**

5

Mürrenbachfälle

Jungfraujoch

Jungfrau

nensee

ALETSCH
GLACIER

Breithorn

BLÜMLISALP

TO
BRIG

KEY
●━● *Cable Car/ Funicular*
┼━┼ *Rail lines*
─·─ *Regional Boundaries*
🎿 *Ski Resorts*
▶ *Start of itinerary*

0 ————— 6 miles

0 ————— 9 km

mid-October. But fear not: the Jungfraujoch rail trip runs 365 days a year, even in pea-soup fog.

JUNGFRAU REGION

The thriving resort town of Interlaken lies between two spectacularly sited lakes, the Brienzersee (Lake Brienz) and the Thunersee (Lake Thun), and is the gateway to two magnificent mountain valleys, one leading up to the popular sports resort of Grindelwald, the other into Lauterbrunnen and the famous car-free resorts of Wengen and Mürren. Looming over both valleys, the Jungfrau and its partner peaks, the Eiger and Mönch, can be admired from various high-altitude overviews.

Interlaken

▶ ❶ *58 km (36 mi) southeast of Bern.*

The name *Interlaken* has a Latin source: *interlacus* (between lakes). As a gateway to the Berner Oberland, this bustling Victorian resort town is the obvious home base for travelers planning to visit the region's two lakes and the mountains towering behind them. At 1,870 feet, Interlaken dominates the Bödeli, the branch of lowland between the lakes that Interlaken shares with the adjoining towns of Unterseen, Wilderswil, Bönigen, and Matten. The town's two train stations, Interlaken East and Interlaken West, are good orientation points; most sights are just a few minutes' walk from one of the stations. There are unlimited excursion options, and it's a pleasant, if urban, place to stay put as well, as its setting is spectacular and its ambience genteel.

The **Höheweg** is the city's main promenade, its tree- and flower-lined walkways cutting through the edge of the broad green parklands of the Höhematte. This 35-acre park once pastured the herds of the Augustinian monastery that dominated medieval Interlaken. Cows still graze in fenced-off areas.

Mark Twain once sojourned at the **Grand Hotel Victoria-Jungfrau**, on the Höheweg, conceived to take in the view of the snowy Jungfrau that towers above town. The hotel originated as two humbler inns, the Jungfrau (1864) and the Chalet Victoria (1865); these were merged and expanded in 1895, and the facade redesigned and landmark tower added in 1899.

Between the Höheweg and the River Aare, you'll find the beautifully landscaped grounds, complete with a floral clock, surrounding the **Kursaal**. Built in 1859 in a dramatic combination of Oberland-chalet and Victorian styles, the Kursaal (meaning a public room at a resort) was renovated in 1968 and has become once again a social focal point for the city. Plays and concerts are presented here, mostly during the high season, and folklore evenings are held in the adjoining *Spycher* (a type of barn).

The **Schlosskirche** (Castle Church) was once the chapel for the Augustinian monastery. All that remains of the monastery, founded in 1133, and the convent that shared its grounds are a 14th-century chancel and a wing of the cloister. The rest of the convent was incorporated into a private castle in 1745. ☒ *At the end of Höhematte, south of Hotel du Nord.*

☯ Surrounding a geodesic sphere a bit like the one at Epcot, **Mystery Park** is devoted to natural and supernatural events. Designed by extraterrestrial theorist Erich von Däniken, the theme park has seven pavilions that explore topics such as the Nazca lines of Peru, the pyramids of Egypt, and the possibility of a space station on Mars. The park is near the Interlaken East train station. ☒ *Hauptstr. 43* ☎ *033/8275757* ⊕ *www. mysterypark.ch* ☒ *48 SF* ☉ *Daily 10–6.*

On the north side of the River Aare is the tiny town of **Unterseen,** with its picturesque Old Town and Marktplatz (Marketplace). Founded in 1279 on land rented from the Augustinians, Unterseen retains some of the region's oldest buildings, including the 17th-century **Stadthaus** (city hall) and the 14th-century **church,** its steeple dating from 1471. The **Schloss Unterseen** (Unterseen Castle), built in 1656 for the reigning Bernese nobleman, stands at the opposite end of the square from these structures, near a medieval arched gateway. You can get here via a 10-minute bus ride from Interlaken's center, or even by walking; it's near the Interlaken West train station.

Fronting on the Unterseen Marktplatz is the **Touristik-Museum der Jungfrau Region,** which traces the history of tourism in the area over the last 200 years. Exhibits include models of early transportation and primitive mountain-climbing and skiing equipment. ☒ *Obereg. 28* ☎ *033/8229839* ☒ *5 SF* ☉ *May–mid-Oct., Tues.–Sun. 2–5.*

┌─────────┐
│ off the │
│ beaten │
│ path   │
└─────────┘

ST. BEATUS-HÖHLEN – The legend of the St. Beatus caves goes back to the 6th century, when the missionary St. Beatus arrived on the Thunersee to find the local population terrorized by a dragon who lived in the lake and surrounding grottoes. Exorcised by Beatus, the fleeing dragon fell to his death on the rocks plunging down to the lake. The caves then became the hermit's home; today you can see the stalagmites, stalactites, and pools inside. There's even a replica of Ponzo, the dragon, for children to explore, and a Ponzo-decorated steamship plies the Thunersee. You can reach the caves by taking Bus 21 from the Interlaken West train station or by crossing by boat to Sundlaunen. ☒ *Opposite Interlaken on east coast near Sundlaunen* ☎ *033/8411643* ⊕ *www.beatushoehlen.ch* ☒ *17 SF* ☉ *Apr.–mid-Oct., daily 10:30–5.*

HARDER KULM – Take the 12-minute funicular ride up Harder Kulm (4,297 feet); from there, hike uphill to views south over the city, the lakes, and the whole panorama of snowy peaks. A turreted, Gothic, chalet-style restaurant offers sumptuous meals on a sunny terrace with views of the surrounding mountains. The funicular runs every 20 to 30 minutes. ✦ *Funicular station north of River Aare near Interlaken East, across Beaurivagebrücke* ☎ *033/8287339* ☒ *Funicular round-trip: 22 SF* ☉ *Funicular: May–Oct., daily 9–6.*

HEIMWEHFLUH – An old-fashioned, red funicular railway leads to the top of this 2,194-foot mountain, where you will get views over both lakes and an elevated peek at the Jungfrau, the Eiger, and the Mönch. A restaurant and playground have been built at the top, complete with a 985-foot bobsled run, and there's a show of model trains every 30 minutes. The funicular station is a five-minute walk from the Interlaken West station down the Rugenparkstrasse, with a departure every 15 minutes. If you hike to the top, the train show costs just 6 SF. ☎ 033/8223453 ☜ 16 SF, includes model train show ⊙ Late Apr.–Oct., daily 10–5:30.

SCHYNIGE PLATTE – For the most splendid overview in the region, make the ambitious trip to this 6,445-foot peak for a picnic, a wander down any of numerous footpaths, or a visit to the Alpine Botanical Garden, where more than 520 varieties of mountain flowers grow. A cogwheel train dating from 1893 takes you on the round-trip journey, though you may opt to walk either up or (more comfortably) down. Make sure to specify when you buy your ticket. Trains run from approximately 7:45 to 6. To get here, take six-minute ride on Bernese Oberland Railway from Interlaken East to Wilderswil. ☒ Wilderswil ☎ 033/8287233 ☜ One-way 33 SF; round-trip 58 SF ⊙ Late May or early June–late Oct., daily, depending on snow conditions.

Where to Stay & Eat

★ $$–$$$ ✕ **Alpenblick.** Just 2 km (1 mi) south of Interlaken, this carved-wood-and-shingle 17th-century landmark attracts both locals and travelers with its two restaurants. One serves old-style Swiss cuisine (Rösti with wild mushrooms); the other showcases chef Richard Stöckli's renowned international fare, such as marinated lake fish tartare, duck-liver pâté with onion confit, or pigeon with rhubarb confit and rosemary-bacon potatoes. ☒ Oberstr. 8, Wilderswil ☎ 033/8283550 ▤ AE, DC, MC, V.

★ $$–$$$ ✕ **Im Gade.** This welcoming hybrid of carved-wood coziness and sleek formality fills up with appreciative locals who recognize fresh, fine cooking and alert service. Details count here: even that dab of smoky sauerkraut in your crisp mixed salad is made on the premises. Choose seasonal specialties such as bärlauch (wild garlic) ravioli, veal with morel sauce, or trout with horseradish mousse. The curried carrot soup makes a tasty starter. ☒ Hotel du Nord, Höheweg 70 ☎ 033/8275050 ▤ AE, DC, MC, V ⊙ Closed mid-Nov.–mid-Dec.

$$–$$$ ✕ **Krebs.** A sunny, front-porch serving area overlooks the street, but head for the more formal dining room, glassed-in yet still opening onto the main promenade. A classic old-world resort spot, serving upscale Swiss cuisine (such as veal medallions) and homey daily plates (look for the fish dishes) with starched-collar style, this place has been in Interlaken— and the Krebs family—since 1875. ☒ Bahnhofstr. 4 ☎ 033/8227161 ▤ AE, DC, MC, V ⊙ Closed Nov.–Apr.

$–$$$ ✕ **Schuh.** With a luxurious shady terrace spilling into the Höhematte in summer and mellow piano enhancing the old-fashioned elegance inside, this sweet shop and café-restaurant serves everything from tea to rich, hot Swiss meals. Leave room for the chocolate specialties and pastries, like the glossy strawberry tarts, which you'll also find in the adjoining shop. ⊠ *Höheweg 56* ☎ *033/8229441* ▤ *AE, DC, MC, V.*

★ $–$$ ✕ **Laterne.** You'll find this unpretentious local favorite, with a sports-bar ambience, a bit off the tourist track, east of the center near the A8 ring road (a 10-minute walk from Interlaken West). The rustic, woodsy setting is a perfect backdrop for the hearty meat dinners and Swiss specialties: seven kinds of Rösti served in iron skillets and eight kinds of cheese fondue. To top it all off, the prices are reasonable. There's live Swiss folk music every other Friday. ⊠ *Obere Bönigstr. 18* ☎ *033/8221141* ▤ *AE, DC, MC, V.*

★ $–$$ ✕ **Stellambiente.** For something nicely out of the ordinary, try this restaurant in the Stella Hotel. The modern, flavorful cuisine includes several vegetarian options, with locally grown ingredients and an extraordinary variety of salads. Order the "surprise" menu and you'll be treated to six inventive courses served on beautiful, individually selected pieces of china. An attractive terrace, complete with fountain, turns summer dining into a garden idyll. ⊠ *Waldeggstr. 10* ☎ *033/8228871* ▤ *AE, DC, MC, V.*

$–$$ ✕ **Zum Bären.** Just across the river, this jolly establishment in Unterseen has been a restaurant since 1674. The latest incarnation has been run by the same family for more than 150 years. Standard Swiss dishes, such as breaded veal or pork scallops, are perfectly prepared and served; the Rösti, crisp on the outside and tender within, is a real treat. Piped-in Swiss-German country music and the occasional yodel from the kitchen round out the experience. ⊠ *Seestr. 2, Unterseen* ☎ *033/8227526* ▤ *AE, MC, V.*

★ $$$$ ▦ **Grand Hotel Victoria-Jungfrau.** Grand says it all. Mark Twain may have slept in this 1865 landmark, but its restoration has taken it firmly into the 21st century, with glitzy postmodern touches such as the burled-wood entryway. There are plenty of facilities, including indoor master golf. The rooms are gorgeous, with styles shifting from marble columns to fresh gingham and waxed wood floors. Nearly all take in the obligatory view. A terrific new casual restaurant, La Pastateca, joins the flashy formal dining room, La Terrasse. ⊠ *Höheweg 41, CH-3800* ☎ *033/8282828* 🖶 *033/8282880* ⊕ *www.victoria-jungfrau.ch* 🛏 *188 rooms, 28 suites* ⚴ *3 restaurants, in-room safes, 7 tennis courts, pool, hair salon, spa, billiards, 2 bars, meeting rooms* ▤ *AE, DC, MC, V.*

★ $$$–$$$$ ▦ **Beau Rivage.** This Interlaken old-timer is steeped in luxury. Set well back from the road and surrounded by gardens, it maintains an unruffled calm. Rich in brocades, muted tones, and patterned carpets, the rooms have views of either the mountains or the quiet Aare. Delicate market-fresh cuisine is served in the highly regarded, hearth-warmed restaurant. Try the tomato mousse and salmon terrine followed by the entrecôte with pepper sauce on the enchanting summer terrace. The location, close to the Interlaken East train station, is perfect. ⊠ *Höheweg 211, CH-3800* ☎ *033/8267007* 🖶 *033/8267008* ⊕ *www.lindnerhotels.ch* 🛏 *98 rooms, 3 suites* ⚴ *2 restaurants, in-room data ports, in-room safes, minibars, pool, health club, bicycles, 2 bars; no a/c* ▤ *AE, DC, MC, V* ⊘ *Closed mid-Nov.–mid-Dec.*

$$$-$$$$ ⊞ **Metropole.** As Berner Oberland's only skyscraper, this 18-story concrete high-rise gobbles up the scenery and ruins everyone's view but its own—which is spectacular. The rooms have dark furniture, floral drapes, and enormous closets. In the rooftop restaurant you can feast your eyes on more staggering vistas while having a light lunch or snack. ⊠ *Höheweg 37, CH-3800* ☎ *033/8286666* 🖷 *033/8286633* ⊕ *www.metropole-interlaken.ch* 📞 *97 rooms* ⌂ *2 restaurants, minibars, pool, massage, sauna; no a/c* ⊟ *AE, DC, MC, V.*

$$-$$$$ ⊞ **Interlaken.** A former guesthouse run by the local monastery, the oldest hostelry in town (Felix Mendelssohn and Lord Byron slept here) may date back to the 14th century, but its comfortable rooms are quite up-to-date, with sleek furnishings and pastel accents. A multicultural air is added by the elaborate Japanese garden, Italian bistro, and excellent Cantonese restaurant. It's a short walk to the Interlaken East train station, making excursions a snap. ⊠ *Höheweg 74, CH-3800* ☎ *033/8266868* 🖷 *033/8266869* ⊕ *www.interlakenhotel.ch* 📞 *60 rooms* ⌂ *2 restaurants, in-room safes, minibars, sauna, bar, no-smoking rooms* ⊟ *AE, DC, MC, V* ⏐⊘⏐ *BP.*

$$-$$$ ⊞ **Du Lac.** The riverboat docks behind this dependable hotel, with its lovely location across from a wide, woodsy bank of the Aare. Despite hourly trains at the nearby Interlaken East station until 11:30 PM, nights are comparatively quiet, especially on the riverside, as the hotel is just outside downtown. Managed by the same family for more than 100 years, the carefully maintained Du Lac has high-ceiling rooms, with touches of French classical and Queen Anne styles. ⊠ *Höheweg 225, CH-3800* ☎ *033/8222922* 🖷 *033/8222915* ⊕ *www.bestwestern.ch/dulacinterlaken* 📞 *40 rooms* ⌂ *Restaurant, Stübli, bar, babysitting, free parking, no-smoking rooms; no a/c* ⊟ *AE, DC, MC, V* ⊘ *Closed Jan. and Feb.* ⏐⊘⏐ *BP.*

$-$$$ ⊞ **Royal–St. Georges.** If you are a fan of Victoriana, this impeccably restored grand hotel is a dream come true, with original moldings, built-in furnishings, and fantastical art nouveau bath fixtures. In the lobby, you pass beautifully carved columns on your way to the staircase that sweeps you upstairs. The wellness facilities, recently renovated, are a great retreat after a long day of sightseeing. ⊠ *Höheweg 139, CH-3800* ☎ *033/8227575* 🖷 *033/8233075* ⊕ *www.royal-stgeorges.ch* 📞 *89 rooms, 6 suites* ⌂ *Restaurant, hot tub, sauna, steam room, bar; no a/c* ⊟ *AE, DC, MC, V* ⊘ *Closed Nov.–Jan.*

★ $-$$$ ⊞ **Stella.** This small, family-run gem defies its outdated '60s exterior and residential neighborhood setting. Inside you'll find marvelous, friendly service; innovative, cozy rooms; and special, personal touches such as rose petals strewn across your duvet in welcome. This is a small hotel that truly does try harder—and does so successfully. Its personal touch carries over to the restaurant, the Stellambiente. ⊠ *Waldeggstr. 10, CH-3800* ☎ *033/8228871* 🖷 *033/8226671* ⊕ *www.stella-hotel.ch* 📞 *30 rooms* ⌂ *Restaurant, in-room safes, minibars, pool; no a/c* ⊟ *AE, DC, MC, V* ⏐⊘⏐ *BP.*

$$ ⊞ **Chalet Oberland.** With rustic decor and a city-crossroads position, this downtown lodge occupies both sides of the street and keeps expanding. The newest rooms (in the building pierced by a life-size statue of a cow) are chic, with warm wood tones and funkily designed bathrooms.

The rooms in the older wing have a heavy-on-the-browns decor. Folklore performances are held on Tuesday. ⊠ *Postg. 1, CH-3800* 🕾 *033/ 8278787* 🖷 *033/8278770* ⊕ *www.chalet-oberland.ch* ⇋ *137 rooms, 23 suites* ⚿ *2 restaurants, pizzeria, in-room safes, minibars, bar; no a/c* 🖹 *AE, DC, MC, V* ⦿*BP.*

$-$$ ▦ **Splendid.** Location is key here: you can't get more central to shopping and nightlife. It's a modest, family-run Victorian dwelling with some woodsy rooms and the occasional spindle bed enlivening the decor. The back rooms overlook a quiet street; the corner bays are prettiest. The proprietor is a hunter, so game in season is fresh and local. ⊠ *Höheweg 33, CH-3800* 🕾 *033/8227612* 🖷 *033/8227679* ⊕ *www.splendid.ch* ⇋ *35 rooms* ⚿ *Restaurant, in-room safes, minibars, pub; no a/c* 🖹 *AE, MC, V* ⊘ *Closed late Oct.–Christmas* ⦿*BP.*

$-$$ ▦ **Toscana.** Well situated in the pedestrian zone, this standard lodging emphasizes amenities such as elevators, indoor parking, angled mountain views. Rooms are spacious, if bland, but the restaurant stands out with good Tuscan cooking, prepared by the Italian owners. ⊠ *Jungfraustr. 19, CH-3800* 🕾 *033/8233033* 🖷 *033/8233551* ⇋ *20 rooms* ⚿ *Restaurant, café, in-room safes, minibars, cable TV, free parking; no a/c* 🖹 *AE, MC, V* ⊘ *Closed Jan. and Feb.* ⦿*BP.*

★ $ ▦ **Alphorn.** Comfortably old-fashioned, this lovely family-run Victorian bed-and-breakfast sits on a quiet side street between Interlaken West and the Heimwehfluh. Some rooms have tapestry wallpaper, waxed parquet floors, and original plaster moldings; florals and other patterns abound. Service is warm and welcoming. ⊠ *Rugenaustr. 8, CH-3800* 🕾 *033/ 8223051* 🖷 *033/8233069* ⊕*www.hotel-alphorn.ch* ⇋ *10 rooms* ⚿ *Bar; no a/c* 🖹 *AE, DC, MC, V* ⦿*BP.*

★ ¢ ▦ **Balmer's.** This popular youth hostel gives families and young travelers bare-bones rooms at rock-bottom prices. Kitchen access, washers and dryers, videos, two fireplaces, a convenience store, and self-service suppers add to the lively, collegiate party atmosphere. The English-speaking staff can help find the cheapest deals for all outdoor activities. Rooms, all with sinks, are available with one to five beds; you can also go for an even cheaper bed in the massive group tent pitched at the edge of town roughly from June through September. Checkout is at 10 AM; there are no lockers or day storage. ⊠ *Hauptstr. 23–25, CH-3800* 🕾 *033/8221961* 🖷 *033/8233261* ⊕ *www.balmers.com* ⇋ *50 rooms* ⚿ *Bar, library, laundry facilities; no a/c* 🖹 *AE, MC, V.*

¢ ▦ **Happy Inn Lodge.** Smack in the middle of town, this low-budget dorm-style hotel is clean, safe, and friendly. Rooms have bunk beds, doubles, or twins. Brasserie 17 downstairs is an incredibly popular nightspot— but since it closes at 12:30 AM you'll still get some sleep. ⊠ *Rosenstr. 17, CH-3800* 🕾 *033/8223225* 🖷 *033/8223268* ⊕ *www.happy-inn. com* ⇋ *16 rooms* ⚿ *Bar; no a/c* 🖹 *AE, MC, V.*

Nightlife & the Arts

BARS At the Happy Inn Lodge, you'll always find a lively, mixed crowd at **Brasserie 17** (⊠ Rosenstr. 17 🕾 033/8223225). **Buddy's Pub** (⊠ Höheweg 33 🕾 033/8227612), at Hotel Splendid, is a popular spot where locals and visitors actually mingle. **Jones' Blues Bar** (⊠ Bahnhofstr. 22 🕾 033/ 8234863) buzzes with canned blues and clever drinks.

CASINO   The **Casino Kursaal** (☎ 033/8276140) has American and French roulette, as well as 120 slot machines; it's open from noon until 2:30 AM daily. Las Vegas it's not, but there's a congenial atmosphere.

DANCING   In the Hotel Metropole, the dance club **Black & White** (✉ Höheweg 37 ☎ 033/8236633) attracts an upscale crowd. **High-Life** (✉ Rugenparkstr. 2 ☎ 033/8221550), near Interlaken West, brings back easygoing oldies. In Hotel Central Continental, **Hollywood** (✉ Bahnofstr. 43 ☎ 033/ 8231033) draws a painfully young crowd. **Johnny's Club** (✉ Höheweg 92 ☎ 033/8223821), in the Hotel Carlton, has been the definitive after-hours club for years. Don't get here too early, as the place comes alive at midnight.

FOLKLORE   Folklore shows—yodeling and all—are presented at the Kursaal in the **Folklore-Spycher** (✉ Off Höheweg ☎ 033/8276100). Admission is 16 SF, or 40 SF to 60 SF if you also want to sample typical dishes. Priority seating is given to diners. Meals begin at 7:30, shows at 9. At the restaurant at **Harder Kulm** (☎ 033/8225171), reached by funicular, on Friday only from June through September you can hear typical *Ländler* (traditional dance) music. If you're brave you can try a few steps yourself.

THEATER   For a real introduction to the local experience, don't miss the **Tell-**
Fodor'sChoice   **freilichtspiele,** an outdoor pageant presented in Interlaken every sum-
★   mer by a cast of Swiss amateurs. Wrapped in a rented blanket—which you'll need, since evenings can be chilly, even from June to September—and seated in a 2,200-seat sheltered amphitheater that opens onto illuminated woods and a permanent village set, you'll see 250 players in splendid costumes acting out the epic tale of Swiss hero Wilhelm Tell. The text is Schiller's famous play, performed in German with the guttural singsong of a Schwyzerdütsch accent—but don't worry; with galloping horses, flower-decked cows, bonfires, parades, and, of course, the famous apple-shooting climax, the operatic story tells itself. Tickets range from 22 SF to 38 SF and are available through the **Tellbüro** (✉ Bahnhofstr. 5A ☎ 033/8223722 ⊕ www.tellspiele.ch). Travel agents and hotel concierges can also secure tickets.

Sports & the Outdoors

HORSEBACK   The area between Lake Thun and Lake Brienz offers a number of scenic
RIDING   marked bridle paths through woods, over fields, and beside streams. Guided rides and classes are available from **E. Voegeli** (✉ Scheidg. 66, Unterseen ☎ 033/8227416 or 079/2188258 ⊕ www.reitschulevoegeli.ch).

MOUNTAIN   Contact **Alpin Center Interlaken** (✉ Wilderswil ☎ 033/8235523 ⊕ www.
CLIMBING   alpincenter.ch) to join tours led by accredited mountain guides.

SAILING   Lake Thun offers the area's best sailing. From April through October, Interlaken's **Von Allmen Sailing School** (☎ 033/8225693) offers courses and boat rental.

TENNIS   The **Victoria-Jungfrau Spa Tennis Center** (✉ Höheweg 41 ☎ 033/ 8282855) has three outdoor and four indoor courts; rental equipment is available.

Bönigen

➋ *2 km (1 mi) east of Interlaken.*

With Interlaken so close, Bönigen never got a fair chance to develop into a resort town. All the better if you want to be near the action but not in the middle of it. This quiet, charming lakeside village is a leisurely half-hour stroll or a five-minute car or bus ride from Interlaken. Somehow Bönigen escaped major fires in its 750-year history, so there remains a group of *beschnitzte Häuser,* original wooden houses dating from the 16th to the 18th centuries. The homes are covered with elaborate carvings—curling along posts and window frames, dripping off balconies and underscoring the eaves. Arrowed signs lead you past 18 of the nicest. Many of the sightseeing boats on the Brienzersee start or stop here.

Where to Stay & Eat

★ **$$–$$$$** ✕▥ **Seiler au Lac.** With heavy competition down the road in Interlaken, this charming lakefront hotel, in the same family for more than 100 years, makes up for its less prestigious address with expansive views of the lake and mountains and a genuinely friendly ambience. Rooms reflect the owners' novel tastes, with decorative tiles in the bathroom, triangular mirrors, or draperies swagging the headboards. In addition to the popular pizzeria, there's an upscale restaurant ($$–$$$$) specializing in lakefish dishes; the Rösti with tomato, bacon, and mozzarella is another excellent choice. ⊠ *Am Quai 3, CH-3806* ☎ *033/8289090* 📠 *033/ 8223001* ⊕ *www.seileraulac.ch* ↙ *45 rooms* ⚷ *Restaurant, pizzeria, bar, no-smoking rooms; no a/c* 🝙 *AE, DC, MC, V* ⊗ *Closed late Oct.–Christmas and mid-Jan.–late Feb.* ⦿| *BP.*

$ ▥ **Hotel Oberländerhof.** Comfortably worn at the edges, this century-old family-run hotel is worth a second look. Ignore the need for fresh paint and the worn red linoleum. Instead, notice the carved gargoyles making faces from the woodwork, the angels looking down from the plaster ceilings, the red-velvet curtains, and the central atrium, all recalling a more glamorous past. Rooms are clean and up to par. The service is friendly, and the café is filled with locals. ⊠ *Am Quai 1, CH-3806* ☎ *033/ 8221725* 📠 *033/8232866* ⊕ *www.oberlaenderhof.ch* ↙ *18 rooms* ⚷ *Café; no a/c* 🝙 *MC, V* ⦿| *BP.*

Lauterbrunnen

★ **➌** *10 km (6 mi) south of Interlaken.*

Below Interlaken the mountains part as you enter the bluff-lined Lauterbrunnen Valley. Around the village of Lauterbrunnen, grassy meadows often lie in shadow, as 1,508-foot rocky shoulders rise on either side. This tidy town of weathered chalets serves as a starting point for the region's two most spectacular excursions: to the Schilthorn and to the Jungfraujoch. Super-efficient parking and a rail terminal allow long- and short-term parking for visitors heading for Wengen, Mürren, the Jungfraujoch, or the Schilthorn. Consider choosing this valley as a home base for day trips by train, funicular, or cable, thereby saving considerably on hotel rates. But don't ignore its own wealth of hiking options through awe-inspiring scenery.

Magnificent waterfalls adorn the length of the Lauterbrunnen Valley, the most famous being the 984-foot **Staubbachfälle** (Staubbach Falls), which are illuminated at night and visible from town. Just beyond the Staubbachfälle are the spectacular **Trümmelbachfälle** (Trümmelbach Falls), a series of 10 glacier waterfalls hidden deep inside rock walls at the base of the Jungfrau, which you can access by underground funicular. Approach the departure point via a pretty, creek-side walkway and brace yourself for some steep stair climbing. Be sure to bring along a light jacket—the spray can be more than refreshing in the cool Alpine air. ⊠ *Follow signs from town* 🕾 *033/8553232* ⊕ *www.truemmelbach. ch* 🎫 *10 SF* ☉ *Apr.–June and Sept.–Nov., daily 9–5; July and Aug., daily 8:30–6.*

Where to Stay & Eat

$–$$ ✕🎫 **Silberhorn.** Though across from the train station and next to the cogwheel train to Mürren, this family-owned hotel, set in a lovely garden, is surprisingly quiet. Knotty *Arvenholz* (pine) panels the spic-and-span rooms. On clear days you may want to chill out in one of the wicker chairs on the sunny porch. The dependable restaurant ($–$$$) offers satisfying meals of Rösti and meat fondues. ⊠ *CH-3822* 🕾 *33/8562210* 🖷 *033/8554213* ⊕ *www.silberhorn.com* 🛏 *30 rooms* ⚐ *Restaurant, sauna, bar, free parking; no a/c* ⊟ *AE, DC, MC, V* ↾⚬↿ *BP.*

¢–$ 🎫 **Staubbach.** At the far end of town sits what is perhaps the best deal in the valley. Young owners have turned this local landmark into a clean, straightforward hotel. Although the emphasis is on keeping the prices low, there's no skimping on personal warmth and charm. The views of the Staubbach Falls are astounding. ⊠ *CH-3822* 🕾 *033/8555454* 🖷 *033/8555484* ⊕ *www.staubbach.ch* 🛏 *31 rooms* ⚐ *Laundry facilities; no a/c* ⊟ *MC, V* ☉ *Closed Nov.–mid-Dec.* ↾⚬↿ *BP.*

Shopping

A good source of Lauterbrunnen's handmade lace is **Handwärch Lädeli** (⊠ Near old schoolhouse 🕾 033/8553551).

Mürren

➍ 7 km (4 mi) southwest of Lauterbrunnen, 16 km (10 mi) south of In-
Fodor's Choice terlaken, plus a 5-min cable car ride from Stechelberg.
★

This lofty sports mecca (elevation 5,413 feet) offers extraordinarily peaceful mountain nights and an unrivaled panorama of the Jungfrau, Mönch, and Eiger. Skiers may want to settle here for daredevil year-round skiing at the top; hikers can combine bluff-top trails with staggering views. This is a car-free resort, so no parking lots spoil the scenery.

Mürren is the second stop along the popular cable car ride up the south side of the **Schilthorn** (9,742 feet), famed for its role in the James Bond thriller *On Her Majesty's Secret Service.* The peak of this icy Goliath is accessed by a four-stage cable-lift ride past bare-rock cliffs and stunning slopes. At each level, you step off the cable car, walk across the station, and wait briefly for the next cable car. At the top is a revolving restaurant, Piz Gloria. The cable car station is in the town of Stechelberg, near the spectacular Mürrenbachfälle (Mürrenbach Falls). ⊠ *Stechelberg*

HOW NOW, BROWN COW?

T'S DIFFICULT TO GROW *more than grass on the steep slopes of the Alps, so much of the area has traditionally been used to graze sheep, goats, and, of course, cattle, who supply fresh milk to the cheese and chocolate industries that makes up such an important part of the country's agricultural economy. The Brown Swiss cow, said to be the oldest breed in the world, has been a reliable producer of dairy products for centuries. Browns are highly prized in the region, as they adapt to all kinds of weather, have strong feet and legs, and produce more milk (which also happens to be higher in protein than that from other cows). Their robust nature has made them increasingly popular throughout the world, resulting in a current global population of about 7 million.*

The seasonal movement of livestock from lowland pastures to Alpine meadows is a tradition that goes back to ancient times. In spring, herders in regional costume spruce up their animals with flowers and embroidered bell collars and move them up to the grazing areas in a ceremony known as the Alpaufzug (Alpine ascent). In fall they come down the same way in the Alpabfahrt (Alpine descent). All cows are fitted with bells to help make them easier to find if they wander away from the rest of the herd, and the collective clang can echo through an entire valley. If you're driving along during one of the ceremonies, be prepared to pull over for a half hour or more while the cows lumber on past, taking up the entire road.

☎ *033/8562141* ⊕ *www.schilthorn.ch* ✉ *Round-trip cable car Stechelberg–Schilthorn 94 SF; 71 SF 7:25–8:55 or after 3:25 in May and mid-Oct.–mid-Nov.* ☉ *Departures daily year-round, twice hourly 6:25 AM–4:25 PM; last departure from the top 6:03 PM in summer, 5:03 PM in winter.*

A more affordable way to Mürren is the **funicular** whose station sits across the street from Lauterbrunnen's train station. You then connect to the cogwheel rail from Grütschalp, which runs along the cliff and affords some magnificent views. The whole trip takes about 30 minutes and drops you at the Mürren rail station, at the opposite end of town from the cable car stop. Trains depart every 15 to 20 minutes. As you ascend, point your binoculars at the gleaming dome on the Jungfraujoch across the valley: you can almost hear the winds howling off the Aletsch Glacier. ✉ *Lauterbrunnen* ☎ *0900/300300* ⊕ *www.sbb.ch* ✉ *18 SF.*

Skiing

Mürren provides access to the **Schilthorn,** where you'll find a 9-mi run that drops all the way through Mürren to Lauterbrunnen. At 5,413 feet, the resort has one funicular railway, two cable cars, seven lifts, and 65 km (40 mi) of downhill runs. A one-day pass covering the Schilthorn region costs 56 SF; a seven-day pass costs 265 SF.

Where to Stay

$$ 🏨 **Bellevue-Crystal.** Distinguished by its yellow-brick-and-shutter facade, this older landmark, with welcoming owners, presents itself as a traditional ski lodge with full modern comforts. Each room has a tiny balcony with fine views, and the decor is fresh pine and gingham. ⊠ *CH-3825* 🕿 *033/8551401* 📠 *033/8551490* ⊕ *www.muerren.ch/bellevue* 🛏 *17 rooms* ♨ *Restaurant, café, sauna, no-smoking rooms; no a/c* ▤ *MC, V* ⊙ *Closed Easter–early June* ⍓ *BP.*

$–$$ 🏨 **Alpenblick.** This simple, comfortable pension has balconies with astonishing views. Friendly owners (and their good home cooking) round out the experience. The modern facility is just beyond the center of town, near the train station. ⊠ *CH-3825* 🕿 *033/8551327* 📠 *033/8551391* ⊕ *www.muerren.ch/alpenblick* 🛏 *14 rooms* ♨ *Restaurant, café; no a/c* ▤ *AE, MC, V* ⊙ *Closed mid-Apr.–June and Nov.–mid-Dec.* ⍓ *BP.*

Jungfraujoch

❺
Fodor'sChoice
★

½-day cog railway excursion out of Interlaken, Lauterbrunnen, or Grindelwald.

The granddaddy of all high-altitude excursions, the famous journey to the Jungfraujoch, site of the highest railroad station in the world, is one of the most popular destinations in Switzerland. From the station at Lauterbrunnen you take the green cogwheel Wengernalp Railway nearly straight up the wooded mountainside, and watch as the valley and the village shrink below. From the hilltop resort of **Wengen** the train climbs up steep grassy slopes past the timberline to **Kleine Scheidegg**, a tiny, isolated resort settlement surrounded by vertiginous scenery. Here you change to the **Jungfraubahn,** another train, which tunnels straight into the rock of the Eiger, stopping briefly for views out enormous picture windows blasted through its stony face.

The **Jungfraujoch terminus** stands at an elevation of 11,400 feet; you may feel a bit light-headed from the altitude. Follow signs to the Top of Europe restaurant, a gleaming white glass-and-steel pavilion. The expanse of rock and ice you see from here is simply blinding.

If you're not sated with the staggering views from the Jungfraujoch terminus, you can reach yet another height by riding a high-tech 90-second elevator up 364 feet to the **Sphinx Terrace**: to the south crawls the vast Aletsch Glacier, to the northeast stand the Mönch and the Eiger, and to the southwest—almost close enough to touch—towers the tip of the Jungfrau herself. Note: even in low season you may have to wait in line for the elevator.

More than views are offered to the hordes that mount the Jungfraujoch daily. You can sign up for a beginner's ski lesson or a dogsled ride, or tour the chill blue depths of the **Ice Palace,** a novelty reminiscent of a wax museum, full of incongruous and slightly soggy ice sculptures. Admission to the attraction is included in the price of the excursion.

A few things to keep in mind for the Jungfraujoch trip: take sunglasses, warm clothes, and sturdy shoes; even the interior halls can be cold and slippery at the top. Some sensitive individuals may experience fatigue or headaches while at the top from the high altitude, which usually disappears on the train ride down. Return trains, especially toward the end of the day, can be standing-room only. To save money, take a guided tour with English commentary (called Jungfrau Tour, as opposed to *Jungfrau individuel*), which costs less. Tours leave once a day from Interlaken West, with stops at Interlaken East, Wilderswil, Lauterbrunnen, and Wengen before climbing to Kleine Scheidegg; the return trip is via Grindelwald. You can get to Lauterbrunnen or Grindelwald on your own steam, but you'll have to return the way you came and miss the full round-trip tour. ☎ *033/8287233* ⌨ *Round-trip Interlaken West–Lauterbrunnen–Wengen–Jungfraujoch (back via Grindelwald) 174 SF; departure from Interlaken East 169 SF* ☾ *June–Sept., daily 6:27* AM *(first train up)–5:10* PM *(last train down).*

Wengen

❻ *½-hr cog railway ride from Lauterbrunnen.*

Fodor's Choice
★
A south-facing hilltop resort perched on a sunny plateau over the Lauterbrunnen Valley, Wengen has magnificent panoramas down the valley. It rivals Mürren for its quiet setting, chic atmosphere, and challenging skiing, which connects with the trail network at Grindelwald; loyalists prefer Wengen for its memorable sunsets. In summer it's a wonderful place to hike. You can aim for centrally located upscale hotels, near shopping and nightlife options, or head downhill to pleasant, more isolated lodgings, all artfully skewed toward the view. Half board is just short of obligatory, as only a few restaurants are not attached to a hotel. It's a car-free town; most hotels have porters that meet the trains.

Skiing

Just over the ridge from Grindelwald, **Wengen** (4,265 feet–11,316 feet) nestles on a sheltered plateau high above the Lauterbrunnen Valley; from there, a complex lift system connects to Grindelwald, Kleine Scheidegg, and Männlichen. Wengen has six funicular railways, one cable car, 31 lifts, and 250 km (155 mi) of downhill runs. The Lauberhorn run is tough; it's used for the World Cup Ski Races in January. One-day lift tickets for Kleine Scheidegg–Männlichen cost 56 SF. A two-day pass costs 104 SF. Lift passes for the Jungfrau–Top-Ski-Region are available only for two or more days. A two-day ticket costs 120 SF; a three-day ticket, 165 SF; and a seven-day, 318 SF. For lessons, contact the **Swiss Ski & Snowboard School** (☎ 033/8552022).

Where to Stay & Eat

$$–$$$$ ✕⌨ **Regina.** It's all about atmosphere in this genteel Victorian hotel. Between the loyal clientele and the gracious owners, a genuinely familiar mood is palpable. Most large rooms have balconies and are done in mauve and rose; rooms under the eaves have loft beds. Paintings and rustic antiques (such as a huge wooden sled) are scattered throughout. The emphasis is on half board, and it's a treat; the dining room, which serves exceptionally creative seasonal fare, shares the chef with the hotel's popular restaurant, Chez Meyer's ($$–$$$$). Try the chestnut soup, the zucchini flowers filled with mushrooms, or the pheasant. ✉ *CH-3823* ☎ *033/8565858* 🖷 *033/8565850* ⊕ *www.wengen.com/hotel/regina* ⤳ *90 rooms ⚭ 2 restaurants, gym, hair salon, sauna, steam room, bar; no a/c* ▤ *AE, DC, MC, V* ⊘ *Closed Nov.* ¶◎ *BP.*

$$$–$$$$ 🏨 **Park Hotel Beausite.** Grandly situated on the hill above Wengen, this hotel encourages pampering in its new leisure area, which includes a lovely indoor pool. Relax with a massage followed by a steam bath or sauna. Rooms are spacious, some with elegant brass beds, others in a more traditional, rustic style. For a leisurely look at the view, sink into one of the couches in the front lounge off the lobby. Near the cable car station, the hotel is a 10-minute walk from the village. ✉ *CH-3823* ☎ *033/8565161* 🖷 *033/8553010* ⊕ *www.beausite-park-hotel.ch* ⤳ *46 rooms, 7 apartments ⚭ Restaurant, in-room data ports, in-room safes, minibars, indoor pool, massage, sauna, piano bar; no a/c* ▤ *AE, DC, MC, V* ¶◎ *BP.*

★ **$$–$$$$** 🏨 **Alpenrose.** Wengen's first lodging, this welcoming inn has been run by the same family for more than a century. The decor is homey, with knotty pine, painted wood, and skirted lamp shades. Rooms with south-facing balconies are slightly more expensive and well worth it. It's downhill and away from the center, with an emphasis on good half-board meals. The restaurant is for guests only. ✉ *CH-3823* ☎ *033/8553216* 🖷 *033/8551518* ⊕ *www.alpenrose.ch* ⤳ *50 rooms ⚭ Dining room; no a/c* ▤ *AE, DC, MC, V* ⊘ *Closed Easter–mid-May and early Oct.–Christmas* ¶◎ *BP.*

$$–$$$ 🏨 **Silberhorn.** Its 19th-century origins evident only in the roofline, this modern lodge just across from the cogwheel train station has a young staff and a lively ambience. Bright, generously sized rooms are full of pine and chintz, some with delicate floral and striped wallpaper. Heated floors in the bathrooms are a nice touch. ✉ *CH-3823* ☎ *033/8565131* 🖷 *033/8565132* ⊕ *www.silberhorn.ch* ⤳ *64 rooms ⚭ Restaurant, in-room safes, minibars, sauna, bar, dance club; no a/c* ▤ *AE, DC, MC, V* ¶◎ *BP.*

$–$$ 🏨 **Eden/Eddy's Hostel.** A shingled Victorian jewel box joins forces with an unpretentious crash pad—the Eden Hotel provides marvelous southern views, comfortable rooms with or without bathrooms, and pretty gardens, while Eddy's Hostel has a no-frills dorm rooms and a shower down the hall. The terrific proprietress will help organize hikes. There are plenty of occasions to mix with other guests at barbecues, over drinks, or at one of many summertime live music events. ✉ *CH-3823* ☎ *033/8551634* 🖷 *033/8553950* ⤳ *18 rooms, 6 with bath, 6 dorms ⚭ Restaurant, café; no a/c* ▤ *AE, DC, MC, V* ⊘ *Closed Nov.–mid-Dec.* ¶◎ *BP.*

★ **$–$$** 🏨 **Schweizerheim.** It's worth the hike to this family-run pension nestled well below the beaten path for the flawless full-valley views, the pristine gardens, and the terrace picnic tables balancing precariously over the Lauterbrunnen Valley. The rooms are a dated mix of wood paneling, Formica, linoleum, and carpet, but the experience is welcoming and fun—and the owner is a Swiss hand-organ celebrity. The restaurant serves guests only. ⊠ *CH-3823* ☎ *033/8551112* ⊞ *033/8552327* ⤴ *24 rooms* ⟁ *Dining room, bar; no a/c* ⊟ *MC, V* ⦿ *BP.*

$–$$ ⊞ **Zum Bären.** This chalet-style lodging just below the center of town is straightforward and bright, with good views and low rates. Rooms are done in blues, yellows, and pale wood; the watercolors are painted by the owner's mother. For extra-cheap sleeps (about 35 SF, including breakfast), you can stay in one of the two camp-style dorm rooms, each filled with 10 beds. ⊠ *CH-3823* ☎ *033/8551419* ⊞ *033/8551525* ⊕ *www.baeren-wengen.ch* ⤴ *14 rooms* ⟁ *Restaurant, café; no a/c* ⊟ *AE, DC, MC, V* ⊘ *Closed mid-Oct.–mid-Dec. and for 2 wks after Easter* ⦿ *BP.*

Nightlife & the Arts

DANCING Hit **Tiffany** (⊠ Hotel Silberhorn ☎ 033/8565131) for a good mix of locals and tourists.

Sports & the Outdoors

ICE SKATING Wengen has a **Natureisbahn** (outdoor ice rink) and a partially sheltered indoor rink. For hours of operation contact the **tourist office** (☎ 033/8551414).

Grindelwald

❼ *27 km (17 mi) southeast of Interlaken.*

Strung along a mountain roadway with two convenient train stations, Grindelwald (3,445 feet) is the most accessible of the region's mountaintop resorts. It makes an excellent base for skiing and hiking, shopping and dining—if you don't mind a little traffic.

★ From Grindelwald you can drive, take a postbus, or hike up to the **Obergletscher,** a craggy, steel-blue glacier. You can approach its base along wooded trails, where there's an instrument to measure the glacier's daily movement. For an equally fascinating experience, travel down into ★ the valley to Grund, below Grindelwald, and visit the **Gletscherschlucht** (Glacier Gorge). There you can walk along a trail through tunnels and over bridges about 1 km (½ mi) into the gorge itself. Although you can't see the glacier itself while walking along the edges of the spectacular gorge it sculpted, you'll get a powerful sense of its slow-motion, inexorable force. ⌦ *5 SF* ⊘ *Late May–mid-Oct.*

Also out of Grindelwald, you can take the **Firstbahn,** a 30-minute gondola ride to the lovely views and pistes of the **First** ski area (7,095 feet). A garden flourishes within easy walking distance (it's even wheelchair accessible). Here, you can see gentians, edelweiss, anemones, and Alpine asters.

Skiing

An ideal base for the Jungfrau ski area, **Grindelwald** provides access to the varied trails of Grindelwald First and Kleine Scheidegg–Männlichen. Grindelwald has eight funicular railways, three cable cars, 22 lifts, and 165 km (103 mi) of downhill runs. Some long runs go right down to the village; there are special areas for snowboarders and beginning skiers. One-day lift tickets for Kleine Scheidegg–Männlichen and First each cost 56 SF. A two-day pass costs 104 SF.

Where to Stay & Eat

$–$$ ✕ **Memory.** A no-fuss, family-style chalet restaurant, this welcoming place is known for its cheese and potato dishes, which extend beyond seven kinds of Rösti to include gratins with meat and potato-garlic soup. ⊠ *Eiger Hotel* ☎ *033/8543131* ⊟ *AE, DC, MC, V.*

★ **$–$$** ✕ **Onkel Tom's Hütte.** This tiny pizza parlor, set in a rustic A-frame cabin on the main drag, is as cozy as they come. Rough wooden floors accommodate ski boots, and eight wooden tables share space with a huge iron cookstove, where the young owner produces fresh pizzas in three sizes (the smallest of which is more than enough). There are also generous salads, freshly baked desserts, and a surprisingly large international wine list. Its popularity outstrips its size, so enjoy the delicious smells while you wait. ⊠ *Across from Firstbahn* ☎ *033/8535239* ⊟ *MC, V* ⊙ *Closed Mon. and Nov. and June.*

★ **$$$$** ✕🏠 **Schweizerhof.** Behind a dark-wood, Victorian-chalet facade dating from 1892, this big, comfortable hotel attracts a loyal clientele. Wing chairs and bookcases in the lobby lounge and dining rooms are inviting on rainy days. Rooms are decorated in carved pine and have tile baths. Service is attentive, unhurried, flexible, and extremely friendly. The restaurant ($–$$$) serves nouvelle Swiss cuisine—try lamb fillets with marinated lentils and rosemary-cream sauce, or something from their vegetarian selections. Breakfasts are generous and are offered until 11:30 AM (a rarity in these parts). ⊠ *CH-3818* ☎ *033/8532202* 🖷 *033/ 8532004* ⊕ *www.hotel-schweizerhof.com* ⬦ *41 rooms, 9 suites* ♨ *Restaurant, Stübli, in-room safes, minibars, pool, health club, hair salon, bowling; no a/c* ⊟ *AE, DC, MC, V* ⊙ *Closed Easter–late May and Oct.–late Dec.* ⍾⍾ *BP.*

★ **$$$–$$$$** ✕🏠 **Belvedere.** As you wind your way into Grindelwald, this large, pink structure, precariously perched above the road, comes into view. Interiors are tastefully designed: the Salon Louis Philippe, for instance, has period furniture and wood-inlay games tables. There are drop-dead views of the Eiger and surrounding peaks from almost every room. The staff and management radiate genuine warmth and absolute professionalism; the owner takes groups of guests skiing, hiking, and golfing weekly. At the restaurant ($–$$$), the fresh, creative menu includes vegetarian wild mushroom crepes or the classic tournedos with goose liver topping. Ask about the special rates for Fodor's users when making reservations. ⊠ *CH-3818* ☎ *033/8545454* 🖷 *033/8535323* ⊕ *www. belvedere-grindelwald.ch* ⬦ *55 rooms* ♨ *Restaurant, Stübli, pool, gym, hot tub, sauna, piano bar, recreation room; no a/c* ⊟ *AE, DC, MC, V* ⊙ *Closed late Oct.–mid-Dec.* ⍾⍾ *BP.*

★ **$–$$$** ✕🏠 **Fiescherblick.** This is the place to eat in Grindelwald, whether as a hotel guest or day-tripper: the same outstanding chef oversees the serious cuisine in the intimate restaurant and the more casual bistro ($–$$$). The seasonal menu might include *bärlauch* (wild garlic leaf) sausage, crepes with guinea fowl, or fish and shellfish pot-au-feu with fresh mushrooms and fennel ravioli. As for rooms, try to nab one of the "superior" ones, which are bright and spacious, if more expensive. Standard rooms tend to be on the unexciting functional-brown-decor side. ⊠ *CH-3818* ☎ *033/8545353* 🖷 *033/8545350* ⊕ *www.fiescherblick. ch* ⤴ *25 rooms* ⚭ *2 restaurants, in-room safes, minibars; no a/c, no TV in some rooms* 🖃 *AE, DC, MC, V* ☉ *Closed Easter–mid-May and mid-Oct.–mid-Dec.* †⊙⨏ *BP.*

$$$$ 🎴 **Grand Hotel Regina.** The turreted exterior dates from the turn of the last century, but this pricey hotel's interior is an elegant blend of old and new. Touches from the past, such as antiques and elaborate chairs from the owners' collection, grace the rooms and the reception area; a luxurious atmosphere runs throughout, with parquet floors and white-leather furnishings. The views are flawless, the location central, and the tennis courts may be some of the most spectacularly sited in the world. ⊠ *CH-3818* ☎ *033/8548600, 800/745–8883 in the U.S.* 🖷 *033/ 8548688* ⊕ *www.grandregina.ch* ⤴ *91 rooms, 9 suites* ⚭ *Restaurant, in-room safes, 2 tennis courts, pool, hair salon, massage, sauna, nightclub; no a/c* 🖃 *AE, DC, MC, V.*

$$–$$$ 🎴 **Gletschergarten.** In the same family for three generations, this atmospheric pension radiates welcome, from heirloom furniture and paintings (by the grandfather) to tea roses cut from the owner's garden. There's heraldry in the leaded-glass windows, a ceramic stove with built-in seat warmer, and a cozy lounge paneled in wood taken from an old Grindelwald farmhouse. All rooms have balconies, some with glacier views, others overlooking the emerald-green hills. Ask for a corner room, as the angle views are especially pleasing. ⊠ *CH-3818* ☎ *033/ 8531721* 🖷 *033/8532957* ⊕ *www.hotel-gletschergarten.ch* ⤴ *26 rooms* ⚭ *Restaurant, sauna, steam room, billiards, Ping-Pong, bar, laundry facilities; no a/c* 🖃 *AE, DC, MC, V* †⊙⨏ *BP.*

$ 🎴 **Gletscherschlucht.** Just below Grindelwald, at the entrance to the glacier gorge in Talgrund, is this neat-as-a-pin chalet-style hotel. Large, bright rooms welcome with cozy furnishings and shiny, tile baths; there's also a playroom for kids. ⊠ *CH-3818* ☎ *033/8536050* 🖷 *033/8536051* ⊕ *www.gletscherschlucht.ch* ⤴ *5 rooms* ⚭ *Restaurant, sauna; no a/c* 🖃 *V* †⊙⨏ *BP.*

$ 🎴 **Wetterhorn.** Overlooking the magnificent ice-blue upper glacier—as well as the sprawling parking lot where hikers leave their cars—this modest inn offers generous lunches outdoors, with full glacier views, and good regional dining inside its comfortable restaurant. The adjoining Gletscherstübli attracts locals as well as the hordes of tourists and hikers who come to marvel at its namesake. Up the creaky old stairs are simple, tidy, aged-pine rooms—some have glacier views—with sink and shared bath. A dormitory with 30 beds is also available. ⊠ *CH-3818* ☎ *033/8531218* 🖷 *033/8535818* ⤴ *9 rooms, 1 dormitory* ⚭ *Restaurant, café, Stübli; no a/c* 🖃 *AE, DC, MC, V* †⊙⨏ *BP.*

¢ 🎴 **Mountain Hostel.** This welcoming hostel sits at the foot of the Eiger in Grund, 2 km (1½ mi) from Grindelwald. The beds, offered with or without linens, are set up in bunk-bed rooms for two to six people. Showers and toilets are down the hall. The owners take groups out on hikes, and there are outdoor barbecues in summer. It's just a couple of minutes on foot from the Grund train station. ⊠ *CH-3818* ☎ *033/8543838*

⌂ 033/8543839 ⊕ *www.mountainhostel.ch* ↩ *20 rooms* ⌂ *Restaurant; no a/c* ☰ *MC, V* ☯ *Closed Nov.*

Nightlife & the Arts

DANCING **Challi** (✉ Hotel Kreuz ☎ 033/8545492) has a DJ who is happy to play requests. **Gepsi** (✉ Eiger Hotel ☎ 033/8532121) is open late; there's a fun crowd and weekly live music. A self-styled "ethno disco" (decorated with cows and alphorns), the **Plaza Club** (✉ Sunstar Hotel ☎ 033/8547777) plays music that is strictly modern (no yodeling here). **Regina** (✉ Grand Hotel Regina ☎ 033/8548600) offers live music nightly.

Sports & the Outdoors

HIKING Grindelwald is a hiker's paradise, both in summer and winter. Detailed maps of mountain trails are available at the tourist office.

MOUNTAIN **Grindelwald Sports** (☎ 033/8541280) offers daily and weekly courses to
CLIMBING mountain and glacier hikers.

SKATING The **Sportzentrum Grindelwald** (☎ 033/8541230) has indoor and natural rinks. You can rent skates at the indoor rink.

TENNIS Grindelwald has six **public courts** (☎ 033/8531912).

BRIENZERSEE

Reputedly the cleanest lake in Switzerland—which surely means one of the cleanest in the world—this magnificent bowl of crystal-clear water mirrors the mountain-scape and forests, cliffs, and waterfalls that surround it. You can cruise alongside Lake Brienz at high speed on the A8 freeway or crawl along its edge on secondary waterfront roads; or you can cut a wake across it on a steamer, exploring each stop on foot, before cruising to your next destination.

Iseltwald

❽ *9 km (6 mi) northeast of Interlaken.*

This isolated peninsula juts out into the lake, its small hotels, cafés, and rental chalets clustered at the water's edge. Every restaurant prides itself on its fish dishes, of course. From the village edge you may want to take off on foot; an idyllic forest walk of about 1½ hours brings you to the falls of the **Giessbach,** which tumbles in several stages down rocky cliffs to the lake. If you don't take the Brienzersee steamer, the most scenic route to Iseltwald from Interlaken is via the south-shore road; follow the black-and-white ISELTWALD signs. You can also take the A8 expressway, following the autoroute signs for Meiringen.

Brienz

★ **❾** *12 km (7 mi) northeast of Iseltwald, 21 km (13 mi) northeast of Interlaken.*

The romantic waterfront village of Brienz, world renowned as a woodcarving center, is a favorite stop for people traveling by boat as well as by car. Several artisan shops display the local wares, which range in quality from the ubiquitous, winningly simple figures of cows to finely modeled nativity figures and Hummel-like portraits of Wilhelm Tell. Brienz is also a showcase of traditional Oberland architecture, with some of its loveliest houses (at the west end of town, near the church) dating from the 17th century. Once an important stage stop, Brienz hosted Goethe and Byron at its 17th-century, landmark Hotel Weisses Kreuz; their names are proudly displayed on the gable.

Switzerland's last steam-driven cogwheel train runs from the center of Brienz, at the waterfront, up to the summit of **Brienzer-Rothorn,** 7,700 feet above the town. The ride takes one hour. Trains depart at least once an hour, but to avoid long waits at peak times, purchase your ticket for a particular train in advance on the day you will make the trip; they do not accept reservations. ☎ *033/9522222* ⊕ *www.brienz-rothorn-bahn. ch* 🚋 *72 SF round-trip* ☉ *June–Oct., daily; 1st train up Mon.–Sat. 8:15, Sun. 7:30; last train up 4:10, last train down 5:10.*

At Brienz you may want to try your hand at **wood carving.** During a two-hour lesson at the atelier of Paul Fuchs you can learn to carve the typical Brienzer cow. Make a reservation through the tourist office in Brienz or directly with Mr. Fuchs. You'll be placed in a class of a dozen or more. His workshop is in Hofstetten, between Brienz and Ballenberg. ⊠ *Scheidweg 19D, Hofstetten* ☎ *033/9511418* 🚋 *25 SF* ☉ *Apr.–Oct.*

off the beaten path

FREILICHTMUSEUM BALLENBERG – Just east of Brienz, a small road leads to this child-friendly outdoor park, where 80 characteristic Swiss houses from 18 cantons have been carefully reconstructed. Even the gardens and farm animals are true to type. Old handicrafts and trades like spinning, forging, and lace making are demonstrated using original tools. ☎ *033/9521030* ⊕ *www.ballenberg.ch* 🚋 *16 SF* ☉ *Mid-Apr.–Oct., daily 10–5.*

Where to Stay & Eat

★ $–$$$$ ✕ **Steinbock.** Whether you dine on the broad flower-lined terrace or inside this wonderful, carved-wooden chalet dating from 1787, you'll know you're at a proud local institution. Choose from no fewer than 11 interpretations of Lake Brienz whitefish and perch. The menu also has a range of veal classics. ⊠ *Hauptstr. 123* ☎ *033/9514055* 🗀 *AE, DC, MC, V* ☉ *Closed Tues. and Feb.*

$–$$ ✕ **Weisses Kreuz.** Generic modern improvements have erased some of the fine origins of this structure, built in 1688 and host to Goethe and Byron, but the idea of its antiquity and the hallowed names on the gable may be allure enough. The pine-lined restaurant offers omelets and *Käseschnitte* (cheese and bread baked in its own whey) as well as lake fish, steaks, and strudel. The sunny lake-view terrace café draws locals and tourists fresh off the boat. ⊠ *Hauptstr. 143* ☎ *033/9522020* 🗀 *AE, DC, MC, V.*

$$–$$$$ ✕🏨 **Grandhotel Giessbach.** The scenery is breathtaking from almost any vantage point in this belle epoque haven overlooking Giessbach Falls, across the lake from Brienz. The lobby has high, chandeliered

ceilings and period furnishings in golds, yellows, and soft pinks. Rooms are comfortable and spacious. The popular restaurant ($–$$$) sees a lot of day-trippers, so the menus are varied, ranging from tasty sandwiches and salads to more formal meals. ⊠ *am Brienzersee, CH-3855* ☎ *033/9522525* 🖷 *033/9522530* ⊕ *www.giessbach.ch* ⇗ *66 rooms, 4 suites ◊ 2 restaurants, tennis court, pool, hiking, bar, library, playground, meeting rooms; no a/c* ⊟ *AE, DC, MC, V* ⊙ *Closed late Oct.–late Apr.*

★ **$–$$** ⊡ **Lindenhof.** In a 1787 lodge high above the lakefront, families settle in for a week or two of evenings by the immense stone fireplace, in the panoramic winter garden, or on the spectacular terrace. The grounds are vast and beautifully manicured, the atmosphere familial and formal at once. At the popular restaurant, families with small children can dine together by the fire, apart from other guests. ⊠ *Lindenhofweg 15, CH-3855* ☎ *033/9522030* 🖷 *033/9522040* ⊕ *www.hotel-lindenhof.ch* ⇗ *40 rooms, 4 suites ◊ Restaurant, café, kitchenettes, pool, sauna, bar; no a/c* ⊟ *AE, MC, V* ⊙ *Closed Jan. and Feb.* ⟨○⟩ *BP.*

★ **$** ⊡ **Schönegg und Spycher.** Clinging to a steep, garden-covered hillside overlooking town, this snug pension is run by house-proud Christine Mathyer, who sees to it that all three small lodgings maintain their old-fashioned charm. There are flagstone floors, a fireplace lounge, and rooms with rustic painted furniture, flower-sprigged duvets, and chocolates on the pillow at night. Guests can relax in the sunny garden overlooking the lake, or easily walk up to the Lindenhof or down to the Steinbock for dinner. ⊠ *Talstr. 8, CH-3855* ☎ *033/9511113* 🖷 *033/9513813* ⇗ *16 rooms ◊ Ping-Pong, bar; no a/c* ⊟ *AE, MC, V* ⊙ *Closed Jan. and Feb.* ⟨○⟩ *BP.*

¢–$ ⊡ **Chalet Rothorn.** Family photos, various knickknacks, and a doll collection make this private bed-and-breakfast remarkably homey. Its perch above town gives it great lake views. Guest rooms are distributed between the family's home and a small house and a tiny chalet in the garden. One of the rooms in the garden chalet has its own balcony and makes a particularly nice getaway. ⊠ *Talstr. 17, CH-3855* ☎☎ *033/9512374* ⊕ *www.jobins.ch* ⇗ *6 rooms ◊ No a/c* ⊟ *No credit cards.*

Shopping

Brienz is the place for good selections of local wood carvings—everything from cows to plates to nativity figures. The wood carvings at **H. Huggler-Wyss** (⊠ Brunng. 17 ☎ 033/9521000) make it worth stopping by. Check out the wares and get a tour to boot at **Nordia Import** (⊠ Hauptstr. 111 ☎ 033/9511414).

Meiringen–Hasliberg

❿ *12 km (7 mi) east of Brienz, 35 km (22 mi) northeast of Interlaken.*

Set apart from the twin lakes and saddled between the roads to the Sustenpass and the Brünigpass, Meiringen is a resort town with 300 km (186 mi) of marked hiking trails and 60 km (37 mi) of ski slopes at the Hasliberg ski region. Its real claim to fame, though, is the **Reichenbachfälle** (Reichenbach Falls), where Sir Arthur Conan Doyle's fictional detective Sherlock Holmes and his archenemy, Professor Moriarty, plunged into the "cauldron of swirling water and seething foam in that bottomless abyss above Meiringen." In the center of town the **Sherlock Holmes Museum** has created an "authentic" replica of the fictional sleuth's front room at 221B Baker Street. ⊠ *Bahnhofstr. 26* ☎ *033/9714221* ⊕ *www. sherlockholmes.ch* ⊠ *4 SF* ⊙ *May–Oct., Tues.–Sun. 1:30–6; Nov.–Apr., Wed.–Sun. 4:30–6:00.*

Where to Stay

$–$$ ⊞ **Sporthotel Sherlock Holmes.** This hotel is ideal for families, hikers, and skiers. Though the building is modern and unspectacular, most rooms look out on Reichenbach Falls. Rooms are simple, but a meringue on your pillow adds a homey touch. The indoor pool, on the top floor, has a phenomenal view. ⊠ *Alpbachallee 3, CH-3860* ☎ *033/9729889* 🖷 *033/9729888* ⊕ *www.sherlock.ch* ⊅ *55 rooms* ☖ *Restaurant, pool, health club, billiards, Ping-Pong, bar; no a/c* ☰ *AE, DC, MC, V* ⊚ *BP.*

Sports & the Outdoors

HIKING   A private, 20-km (12½-mi) road to Grindelwald prohibits cars but provides a beautiful, seven-hour Alpine hike. To obtain maps of other local hiking trails, visit the tourist office.

THUNERSEE

If you like your mountains as a picturesque backdrop and prefer a relaxing waterfront sojourn, take a drive around the Thunersee (Lake Thun) or crisscross it on a leisurely cruise boat. More populous than Lake Brienz, its allures include the marina town of Spiez and the large market town of Thun, spread at the feet of the spectacular Schloss Zähringen (Zähringen Castle). There are other castles along the lake, and yet another high-altitude excursion above the waterfront to take in Alpine panoramas—a trip up the Niederhorn.

Spiez

⑪   *19 km (11¾ mi) west of Interlaken.*

Spiez is a summer lake resort with marinas for water-sports enthusiasts. Its enormous waterfront castle, **Schloss Spiez,** was home to the family Strättligen and, in the 13th century, its great troubadour, Heinrich. The structure spans four architectural epochs, starting with the 11th-century tower; its halls contain beautiful period furnishings, some from as long ago as Gothic times. The early Norman church on the grounds is more than 1,000 years old. ☎ *033/6541506* ⊠ *6 SF* ⊙ *Mid-Apr.–June and Sept.–mid-Oct., Mon. 2–5, Tues.–Sun. 10–5; July and Aug., Mon. 2–6, Tues.–Sun. 10–6.*

Where to Stay & Eat

$–$$ ✕⊞ **Seegarten Hotel Marina.** With a pizzeria in one wing and two dining rooms that stretch comfortably along the marina front, this is a pleasant, modern family restaurant ($–$$$). The lake fish specialties are excellent. Spiez Castle looms directly behind you, unfortunately out of sight. The rooms upstairs are spare and modern. ⊠ *Schachenstr. 3,*

CH-3700 ☏ *033/6556767* 🖶 *033/6556765* ⊕ *www.seegarten-marina. ch* ⬯ *42 rooms* ⚲ *Restaurant, café, pizzeria, minibars, bar; no a/c* ⊟ *AE, DC, MC, V* ⦿ *BP.*

$$–$$$$ ⛉ **Strandhotel Belvedere.** This graceful old mansion has beautiful lawns and gardens, and its manicured waterfront offers secluded swimming. Rooms are done in blue and rose, with homey touches such as canopy beds. Corner and lakeside rooms are worth the higher price. On the restaurant's excellent seasonal menu, look for pumpkin ravioli or succulent local chicken. Guests have free access to the city's heated outdoor pool. ⊠ *Schachenstr. 39, CH-3700* ☏ *033/6556666* 🖶 *033/6546633* ⊕ *www. belvedere-spiez.ch* ⬯ *33 rooms* ⚲ *Restaurant, in-room data ports, in-room safes, minibars, spa, beach; no a/c* ⊟ *AE, DC, MC, V* ⊗ *Closed Oct.–Mar.* ⦿ *BP.*

Thun

⑫ *10 km (6 mi) north of Spiez, 29 km (18 mi) northwest of Interlaken.*

Built on an island in the River Aare as it flows from Lake Thun, this picturesque market town is laced with rushing streams crossed by wooden bridges, and its streets are lined with arcades. On the Old Town's main shopping thoroughfare, pedestrians stroll along flowered terrace sidewalks built on the roofs of the stores' first floors and climb down stone stairs to visit the "sunken" street-level shops.

★ From the charming medieval Rathausplatz (Town Hall Square), a covered stairway leads up to the great **Schloss Thun** (Thun Castle), its broad donjon cornered by four stout turrets. Built in 1191 by Berchtold V, Duke of Zähringen, it houses the fine **Schlossmuseum Thun** (Thun Castle Museum) and provides magnificent views from its towers. The Knights' Hall has a grand fireplace, an intimidating assortment of medieval weapons, and tapestries, one from the tent of Charles the Bold. Other floors display local Steffisburg and Heimberg ceramics, 19th-century uniforms and arms, and Swiss household objects, including charming Victorian toys. ⊠ *Rathauspl.* ☏ *033/2232001* ⊕ *www.schlossthun.ch* 🎟 *7 SF* ⊗ *Apr.–Oct., daily 10–5; Nov.–Jan., Sun. 1–4; Feb. and Mar., daily 1–4.*

The **Vaporama Swiss Steam Engine Museum** has gotten under way in the lakeside neighborhood of Schadau. Among a comprehensive collection of stationary steam engines is the cruising star exhibit, the completely restored 1906 steamer *Blümlisalp*. Call ahead for hours. ⊠ *Seestr. 34/ 38* ☏ *033/2332324.*

Where to Stay & Eat

$$–$$$ ✕⛉ **Krone.** Positioned directly on the lovely Town Hall Square, this landmark has some fine river views. Although the exterior is classic, the airy interior is generally modern, except for the two lovely tower rooms— round, with bay windows and marble and gilt-edged decor—that are worth requesting. There are two eateries on the premises, one serving a broad range of Asian dishes and an upscale bistro ($-$$$) that whips up chic versions of regional dishes. ⊠ *Obere Hauptg. 2, CH-3600* ☏ *033/2278888* 🖶 *033/2278890* ⊕ *www.krone-thun.ch* ⬯ *27 rooms* ⚲ *2 restaurants, in-room safes, minibars; no a/c* ⊟ *AE, DC, MC, V.*

$ ⊞ **Zu Metzgern.** At the base of the castle hill, this shuttered and arcaded *Zunfthaus* (guildhall) overlooks the Town Hall Square. The grand old building has clean, comfortable rooms (bathrooms down the hall). There's atmospheric, traditional Swiss dining, too, whether in the wood-and-linen restaurant or on the intimate little terrace, tucked behind an ivy-covered trellis. ⊠ *Untere Hauptg. 2, CH-3600* ☎ *033/2222141* 🖷 *033/2222182* ⊕ *www.zumetzgern.ch* ⤳ *10 rooms* ⅃ *Restaurant, café; no a/c* ⊟ *MC, V.*

> **off the beaten path**

HILTERFINGEN AND OBERHOFEN – These two small towns, just a few miles southeast of Thun, are each dominated by a castle. Hilterfingen's castle, **Schloss Hünegg** (Hünegg Castle; ⊠ Staatsstr. 52 ☎ 033/2431982), was built in 1861 and furnished over the years with a bent toward Jugendstil and art nouveau. The stunning interiors have remained unchanged since 1900. Open from mid-May to mid-October, Monday through Saturday from 2 to 5 and on Sunday from 10 to noon and 2 to 5, admission is 10 SF. Oberhofen is topped with its own **Schloss Oberhofen** (Oberhofen Castle; ☎ 033/2431235), this one a hodgepodge of towers and spires on the waterfront. Begun during the 12th century, it was repeatedly altered over a span of 700 years. Inside, a historical museum has a display of the lifestyles of Bernese nobility. Open from mid-May through mid-October, Monday from 2 to 5 and Tuesday to Sunday from 11 to 5, admission is 9 SF.

NIEDERHORN – About eight miles east of Oberhofen, the town of Beatenbucht has a shore terminal that sends funiculars to Beatenberg daily in high season. From there you can either walk up a trail or catch a chairlift to the Niederhorn (6,294 feet), from which an astonishing panorama unfolds: Lake Thun and Lake Brienz, the Jungfrau, and even, on a fine day, Mont Blanc.

Shopping

A good spot for traditional pottery in Thun is **Töpferhaus** (⊠ Obere Hauptg. 3 ☎ 033/2227065). Just outside Thun in Heimberg, the **Museum Hänn** (⊠ Bahnhofstr. 4 ☎ 033/4381242) demonstrates and displays its traditional ceramic work, as it has since 1731.

KANDER VALLEY

Easily reached by car or the Lötschberg rail line from Interlaken via Spiez, the spectacular Kander Valley leads up from Lake Thun toward Kandersteg, an isolated resort strewn across a wide plateau. From Kandersteg, you can make a hiker's pilgrimage to the silty blue Oeschinensee.

Kandersteg

⑬ *45 km (28 mi) southwest of Interlaken.*

At 3,858 feet, Kandersteg stands alone, a quiet resort spread across a surprisingly broad, level—and thus walkable—plateau. Lofty bluffs, waterfalls, and peaks—including the **Blümlisalp**, at 12,018 feet, and the **Doldenhorn**, at 11,949 feet—surround the plateau, and at the end of its 4-km (2½-mi) stretch, the valley road ends abruptly.

Exploration above Kandersteg must be accomplished by cable car or on foot, unless (depending on Swiss army training schedules and weather) you find the tiny paved road into the magnificent **Gastern Valley** open. Carved into raw rock, portions of the road are so narrow that cars must pass one at a time. The local tourist office knows whether the road is passable.

Don't miss the **Oeschinensee,** an isolated, austere bowl of glacial silt at 5,176 feet. From Kandersteg you can walk there in about 1½ hours, or you can take the chairlift to the Oeschinen station, with a downhill walk of approximately 30 minutes through mountain-ringed meadows. You also may choose to hike back down to Kandersteg from the Oeschinensee, but be prepared for the steep slopes. Less ambitious hikers can circle back to the chairlift at the end of a relatively level walk.

Although it's a dead-end valley for cars confining themselves to Berner Oberland, Kandersteg is the source of one of Switzerland's more novel modes of transit: the rail-ferry tunnel through the **Lötschenberg.** After driving your car onto a low-slung railcar, you will be swept along piggyback through a dark and airless tunnel to Goppenstein, at the east end of the Valais region. Travel time is 15 minutes; the cost is 25 SF.

Where to Stay & Eat

$$–$$$
Fodor'sChoice
★
✕⊡ **Ruedihus.** This painstakingly restored 1759 chalet is set in a meadow beyond the center of the village. Rooms with bulging leaded-glass windows, authentically low ceilings and doors (watch your head), and aged woodwork hold antique beds with bleached homespun linens. These oldfashioned charms are counterbalanced by modern baths. Upstairs, the Biedermeier restaurant ($–$$) offers excellent meat specialties, but eat downstairs at least once: the Käse- und Wystuben serves nothing but Swiss products—local wines, greens, and sausages, and a variety of rich fondues. ✉ CH-3718 ☎ 033/6758182 ⊟ 033/6758185 ⊕ www. doldenhorn-ruedihus.ch ⌑ 9 rooms ♨ 2 restaurants, café; no a/c ⊟ AE, DC, MC, V ⊗ BP.

★ **$$–$$$**
⊡ **Waldhotel Doldenhorn.** On a forested hillside far from the road, this secluded retreat offers several options: large rooms with balconies and mountain views, smaller rooms opening onto the woods, or a separate budget chalet. All rooms gracefully combine modern and rustic styles. A cross-country ski trail starts at the hotel's door. ✉ CH-3718 ☎ 033/ 6758181 ⊟ 033/6758185 ⊕ www.doldenhorn-ruedihus.ch ⌑ 33 rooms, 1 apartment ♨ Restaurant, Stübli, some kitchenettes; no a/c ⊟ AE, DC, MC, V ⊗ BP.

$
⊡ **Edelweiss.** Built in 1903, this inn has sleek, impeccable rooms and an old-fashioned atmosphere, complete with low ceilings and burnished wood. There's a comfortable checkered-cloth Stübli serving only drinks. The pretty garden makes you forget you're on the main road, five minutes from the train station. ✉ CH-3718 ☎ 033/6751194 ⌑ 8 rooms ♨ Stübli; no a/c ⊟ No credit cards.

off the
beaten
path

BLAUSEE – The much-vaunted Blausee, or Blue Lake, is a natural pool above Frutigen. It is privately owned and so meticulously developed, with restaurant, shop, and boat rides, that you may think the lake itself is artificial. The summer admission price includes a boat ride, a visit to the trout nursery, and use of the picnic grounds. In winter the facilities are closed, but you're free to roam the area. ✉ *4 km (2½ mi) north of Kandersteg* ☏ *033/6723333* ⊕ *www. blausee.ch* 🎫 *5 SF* ⊙ *May–early Oct., daily 9 AM–10 PM.*

SIMMENTAL & GSTAAD

Separate in spirit and terrain from the rest of the Berner Oberland, this craggy forest gorge follows the Lower Simme into the Saanenland, a region as closely allied with French-speaking Vaud as it is with its Germanic brothers. Here the world-famous resort of Gstaad has linked up with a handful of neighboring village resorts to create the almost limitless outdoor opportunities of the Gstaad "Super-Ski" region. From Gstaad, it's an easy day trip into the contrasting culture of Lake Geneva and the waterfront towns of Montreux and Lausanne.

From Interlaken, take A8 toward Spiez, then cut west on A11 toward Gstaad. The forest gorges of the Simmental Valley lead you through Zweisimmen to the Saanenland and Gstaad.

Gstaad

⑭ *49 km (30 mi) southwest of Spiez, 67 km (42 mi) southwest of Interlaken, 68 km (43 mi) northwest of Montreux.*

The four fingerlike valleys of the Saanenland find their palm at Gstaad, the Berner Oberland's most glamorous resort. Linking the Berner Oberland with the French-speaking territory of the Pays-d'Enhaut of canton Vaud, Gstaad-Saanenland blends the two regions' natural beauty and their cultures as well, upholding Pays-d'Enhaut folk-art traditions such as *papier découpage* (paper silhouette cutouts) as well as decidedly Germanic ones (cowbells, wood carvings, and alphorns).

However, in Gstaad neither culture wins the upper hand. During high season, the folksy *Gemütlichkeit* (homeyness) of the region gives way to jet-set international style. Although weathered-wood chalets are the norm (even the two tiny supermarkets are encased in chalet-style structures), the main street is lined with designer boutiques. Prince Rainier of Monaco, Roger Moore, and Elizabeth Taylor have all owned chalets in Gstaad, as well as the late Yehudi Menuhin, who founded his annual summer music festival here. (The Menuhin festival takes place from mid-July through early September, and hotels fill quickly then—as they do for the Swiss Open tennis tournament, held every July.)

Gstaad is a see-and-be-seen spot, with equal attention given to its plentiful skiing and and its glamorous gatherings—après-ski, après-concert, après-match. The Christmas–New Year's season brings a stampede of glittering socialites to rounds of elite soirees. But you can escape the social scene. There are several unpretentious inns, hotels, and vacation apartments, and dozens of farmhouses that rent rooms, either in Gstaad itself, or in one of the nearby Saanenland hamlets (Gsteig, Feutersoey, Lauenen, Turbach, Schönried, Saanenmöser, Saanen). What paradoxically defies and maintains Gstaad's socialite status is its setting: richly forested slopes, scenic year-round trails, working dairy farms, and, for the most part, stubbornly authentic chalet architecture keep it firmly anchored in tradition. The center of Gstaad is reserved for pedestrians. You can leave your car at the parking facilities at either end of the main street.

The oldest building in the region, the **Saanen Church** was built between the 10th and 11th centuries. Just off Saanen's main street, the church is open daily for visits unless a service is being held. This Romanesque structure was renovated in the 20th century to reveal portions of medieval frescoes on the interior walls. On Saanen's main street next to and behind the Heimatwerk (handcrafts shop), the tiny **Museum der Landschaft Saanen** (Saanenland Museum) traces the history of the area through tools, transport, costumes, furniture, and decorative pieces. ☎ *033/7447989* ⊕ *www.museum-saanen.ch* ☉ *Mid-May–mid-Oct., Tues.–Sun. 2–6; mid-Dec.–Easter, Tues.–Sun. 2–5* 🖼 *6 SF.*

Skiing

Gstaad-Saanenland does not hesitate to call itself a "Super-Ski" region, and the claim is not far from the truth. With the building of the one-track railroad from Montreux at the beginning of the 19th century, Gstaad-Saanenland became increasingly popular, both for its ideal location at the confluence of several valleys and for the sunny mildness of its slopes, which, starting at 3,608 feet and soaring to 7,217 feet, stay relatively toasty compared with those of other resorts (except for the Diablerets Glacier).

Skiing in Gstaad-Saanenland is, in terms of numbers, the equivalent of Zermatt: 66 lifts can transport more than 50,000 skiers per hour to its network of 250 km (155 mi) of marked runs. In fact, these lifts are spread across an immense territory, 20 km (12 mi) as the crow flies, from Zweisimmen and St-Stefan in the east to Château-d'Oex in the west, and 20 km (12 mi) to the Diablerets Glacier in the south.

Gstaad's expansive area means that most of its lifts are not reachable on foot, and since parking is in short supply, public transport, either by the train or the postauto, is the best option. The flip side is that, except in very high seasons (Christmas and February) and in certain places, such as the lift for the Diablerets, waits for lifts are tolerable. A one-day ticket costs between 28 SF and 53 SF, depending on the sector; a six-day pass costs 263 SF. The **Gstaad Ski School** (☎ 033/7441865) gives lessons in downhill, snowboarding, and cross-country skiing (there are more than 50 km [30 mi] of well-groomed cross-country trails).

Where to Stay & Eat

$$$–$$$$ ✕ **Chesery.** This lively late-night dining scene, complete with piano bar, manages to combine the height of upscale chic with summits of culinary excellence. Chef Robert Speth marries exotic flavors, such as gin-

A MEIRINGER BY ANY OTHER NAME

According to local legend, meringues were invented in 1720 in the Bernese Oberland town of Meiringen by a Swiss confectioner named Gasparini. The popularity of the fluffy deserts was so great that they soon spread to neighboring France, where Marie Antoinette apparently was so taken with them that she was said to actually make them herself regularly at the Trianon. From the palaces of France the dish spread to the rest of the world, and it is the French angle that led to the name change: from the original meiringer to the more common meringue. Melt-in-your-mouth meringues are still a local specialty in Meiringen, where they are sold in dozens of pastry shops. To make them yourself, whip two parts egg whites together with one part sugar until the mass is light and fluffy. Bake for 3 hours at low heat, then let cool. Serve with a generous dollop of fresh whipped cream. Afterward, you might want to make an appointment with your personal trainer.

ger or mango, with market-fresh local ingredients. Watch for stuffed quail with truffle sauce or veal kidneys in mustard sauce. And do try the Brie stuffed with truffles along with your entrée or paired with a salad as a light meal. Book ahead in high season. An elegant little casino in the cellar adds that James Bond touch. ✉ *Lauenenstr.* ☎ *033/7442451* ▤ *AE, DC, MC, V* ☉ *Closed Mon. and Tues.*

★ **$$$$** ✕▨ **Olden.** At the eastern end of the main thoroughfare, this charming Victorian-style inn has an elaborately painted facade and intricately carved woodwork in every interior niche. Rooms are folksy and atmospheric, but have such modern details as lighted closets. The places to see and be seen are the hotel's bar and restaurant ($$$–$$$$). Offerings at the elegant establishment might include a succulent pigeon or fillet of sole with cherry tomatoes. A more economic way of scoping the Gstaad scene is to sip a coffee on the Olden's sidewalk terrace. ✉ *CH-3780* ☎ *033/7443444* 🖷 *033/7446164* ⊕ *www.hotelolden.com* ⟲ *17 rooms* ♦ *2 restaurants, café, bar; no a/c* ▤ *AE, DC, MC, V* ☉ *Closed mid-Apr.–mid-May and Oct.–mid-Nov.* ⦿ *BP.*

$$$$ ✕▨ **Palace.** This family-run landmark is the town's focal point dur-
Fodor'sChoice ing high season. An indoor-outdoor swimming pool (with a glass floor
★ placed on top for dancing on winter nights), a chauffeured Rolls-Royce, tennis weeks in summer, and an elaborate health club are but a few of many compelling amenities. The kitchen serves four lavish restaurants ($$$$), with renowned guest chefs conducting weeks of special cuisines from around the world. Rooms and suites have rustic touches but are undeniably opulent. ✉ *CH-3780* ☎ *033/7485000, 800/745–8883 in the U.S.* 🖷 *033/7485001* ⊕ *www.palace.ch* ⟲ *68 rooms, 6 suites, 1 apartment* ♦ *4 restaurants, 4 tennis courts, indoor-outdoor pool, health club, squash, ice-skating, lobby lounge, piano bar, nightclub; no a/c* ▤ *AE, DC, MC, V* ☉ *Closed late Mar.–mid-June and mid-Sept.–mid-Dec.* ⦿ *BP.*

$$$–$$$$ ✕⊡ **Le Grand Chalet.** On a hill just a 10-minute walk from the center of Gstaad, Le Grand Chalet commands a spectacular view of the surrounding mountains and village below. The spacious, comfortable rooms exude an informal elegance, with pale wood and fresh white curtains throughout. An open central fireplace separates the cozy lounge from La Bagatelle ($$–$$$$), the hotel's popular restaurant favored for its nouvelle Swiss cuisine. Try the pepper steak, baby chicken with tarragon, game in season, and marvelous local cheeses. Easy walking trails depart from the hotel's doorstep. ⊠ *Neueretstr., CH-3780* ☎ *033/7487676* 🖷 *033/7487677* ⊕ *www.grandchalet.ch* ⇆ *20 rooms, 4 suites* ⚭ *Restaurant, in-room safes, minibars, pool, gym, sauna, bar; no a/c* ⊟ *AE, DC, MC, V* ⊙ *Closed mid-Oct.–mid-Dec. and Apr.–early June* ⦿l *BP.*

★ **$$–$$$**   ✕⊡ **Posthotel Rössli.** This comfortable inn, the oldest in town, combines down-home knotty-pine decor with soigné style. Despite the mountain-cabin look, the clientele is young and chic, and the café, a local-landmark watering hole, draws crowds. The restaurant ($–$$$), full of linens and candlelight, serves good Swiss fare at reasonable prices. ⊠ *CH-3780* ☎ *033/7484242* 🖷 *033/7484243* ⊕ *www.posthotelroessli.ch* ⇆ *18 rooms* ⚭ *Restaurant, café, minibars; no a/c* ⊟ *AE, DC, MC, V* ⦿l *BP.*

★ **$$$$**   ⊡ **Grand Hotel Park.** This bustling, modern chalet-style hotel offers some of the best health facilities in the Saanenland, including an antistress program, aerobics and gymnastic classes, and an indoor saltwater pool. Treatment weeks offer an irresistible mix of glamour and virtue. Large, cheerful rooms feature flowered wallpaper, waxed wooden furniture, and wardrobes painted with Swiss folk-art scenes. ⊠ *CH-3780* ☎ *033/7489800* 🖷 *033/7489808* ⊕ *www.grandhotelpark.ch* ⇆ *88 rooms, 11 suites* ⚭ *3 restaurants, in-room safes, minibars, tennis court, 2 pools (1 indoors), hair salon, sauna, steam room, 2 bars* ⊟ *AE, DC, MC, V* ⊙ *Closed late Sept.–mid-Dec. and Apr.–early June* ⦿l *BP.*

$$$$ ⊡ **Grandhotel Bellevue.** Dating from 1914, this thoughtfully renovated property with its own park blends old-world charm with cutting-edge health and fitness facilities. The crisp and airy rooms, done in beige, gray and orange, are stuffed with entertainment and business tools, including notebook computers. Along with the gourmet standards, the restaurants offer lighter fare for the health conscious. ⊠ *Hauptstr., CH-3780* ☎ *033/7480000* 🖷 *033/7480001* ⊕ *www.bellevue-gstaad.ch* ⇆ *32 rooms* ⚭ *2 restaurants, in-room data ports, in-room fax, in-room safes, minibars, cable TV with movies, indoor pool, gym, sauna, 2 bars, wine bar* ⊟ *AE, DC, MC, V.*

$$–$$$$ ⊡ **Bernerhof.** Centrally located between the main street and the train station, this large, modern chalet-style inn is simple, solid, and surprisingly cozy, with tile baths, lots of natural pine, and a balcony for every room. There are good play facilities for children and the hotel is only half a block from the ice-skating rink. ⊠ *CH-3780* ☎ *033/7488844* 🖷 *033/7488840* ⊕ *www.bernerhof-gstaad.ch* ⇆ *34 rooms, 12 suites* ⚭ *3 restaurants, in-room safes, minibars, indoor pool, massage, sauna; no a/c* ⊟ *AE, DC, MC, V* ⦿l *BP.*

Nightlife & the Arts

BARS **Pinte** (☎ 033/7443444), in the Hotel Olden, is where people gather after a day on the slopes. Belly up to the beautiful wooden bar or huddle around the stone fireplace.

CONCERTS The **Menuhin Festival Gstaad** (✉ Postfach 65, CH-3780 ☎ 033/7488338 ☐ 033/7488339 ⊕ www.menuhinfestival.com) hosts a series of world-class concerts from mid-July to early September. **Les Sommets Musicaux de Gstaad** (✉ 36 rue de Montchoisy, case postale 1207, CH-1211 Geneva ☎ 022/7386675 ☐ 022/7368505 ⊕ www.sommets-musicaux. com) presents two weeks of classical music from late February to early March. Information for the festivals is available several months in advance, direct or from the Gstaad tourist bureau.

DANCING **Club 95** (☎ 033/7484422), in the Sporthotel Victoria, is popular with a younger crowd. **GreenGo** (☎ 033/7485000), a disco in the Palace Hotel, is open only in winter. There are two crowded bars, but the focal point is the massive dance floor fitted over the hotel's pool.

Sports & the Outdoors

GOLF **Gstaad-Saanenland** (☎ 033/7484030) has 18 holes in an idyllic setting just above Saanenmöser, on Route 11 past Schönried.

HORSEBACK In Gstaad, the **Reitzentrum Gstaad** (☎ 033/7442460) offers lessons for
RIDING beginners and guided outings for experienced riders.

MOUNTAIN Great treks and climbs are a stone's throw from Gstaad. **Alpinzentrum**
CLIMBING **Gstaad** (☎ 033/7484161) can supply you with mountain guides and snow-sports teachers. **Beats Adventure** (☎ 033/7441521) aims its tough sports excursions at very fit people. **Experience Gstaad** (☎ 033/7448800) is the place to go for guides for off-trail skiing, ice climbing, and snowshoe trekking.

TENNIS **Tennis Center Gstaad** (☎ 033/7441090) has three indoor and five outdoor courts. Rental equipment and lessons are available.

BERNER OBERLAND A TO Z

To research prices, get advice from other travelers, and book travel arrangements, visit www.fodors.com.

AIRPORTS

Belp Airport in Bern brings you within an hour via train of Interlaken, the hub of the Berner Oberland. Near Basel, EuroAirport (across the border in France) is 2¼ hours by train. The Unique Zürich Airport is 2½ hours away. Geneva's Cointrin is less than three hours away.

🛈 Airport Information **Belp** ☎ 031/9602111. **Cointrin** ☎ 022/7177111. **EuroAirport** ☎ 061/3252511. **Unique Zürich Airport** ☎ 0900/300313.

BOAT & FERRY TRAVEL

Round-trip boat cruises around Lake Thun and Lake Brienz provide an ever-changing view of the craggy foothills and peaks. The round-trip from Interlaken to Thun takes about four hours; the trip to Spiez takes about two hours and includes stopovers for visits to the castles of Oberhofen, Spiez, and Thun. A round-trip from Interlaken to Brienz takes around 2½ hours, to Iseltwald about 1¼ hours. These boats are public transportation as well as pleasure cruisers; just disembark whenever you feel like it and check timetables when you want to catch another. Tickets are flexible and coordinate neatly with surface transit: you can cruise across to Thun and then take a train home for variety. Buy tickets and catch boats for Lake Thun at Interlaken West station. For Lake Brienz, go to Interlaken East. The official boat company for both lakes is Schiffsbetrieb BLS Thuner- und Brienzersee.

🚢 Boat & Ferry Information Schiffsbetrieb BLS Thuner- und Brienzersee ☎ 033/3345211.

BUS TRAVEL

Postbuses (called postautos or postcars) travel into much of the area not served by trains, including most smaller mountain towns. In addition, a number of private motor-coach tours cover points of interest. Schedules are available from tourist offices and post offices.

CAR RENTAL

🚗 Major Agencies Avis ✉ Waldeggstr. 34a, Interlaken ☎ 033/8221939. **Hertz** ✉ Harderstr. 25, Interlaken ☎ 033/8226172.

CAR TRAVEL

Swift and scenic roads link both Bern and Zürich to Interlaken. From Bern, the autoroute A6 leads to Spiez, then A8 continues as the highway to Interlaken. From Zürich, the planned autoroute link with Luzern (Lucerne) is incomplete; travel by Highway E41 south, then pick up the autoroutes A4 and A14 in the direction of Luzern. South of Luzern, pick up the A4 again in the direction of Interlaken. From Geneva, the autoroute leads through Lausanne and Fribourg to Bern, where you catch A6 south, toward Thun. A long, winding, scenic alternative: continue on the autoroute from Lausanne to Montreux, then to Aigle; then, head northeast up the mountain on A11 from Aigle through Château-d'Oex to Gstaad and the Simmental.

Driving in the Berner Oberland allows you the freedom to find your own views and to park at the very edges of civilization before taking off on foot or by train. If you are confining yourself to the lakefronts, valleys, and lower resorts, a car is an asset. But several lovely resorts are beyond the reach of traffic, and train, funicular, and cable car excursions take you to places ordinary tires can't tread; sooner or later, you'll leave the car behind and resort to public transportation. Remember that Wengen, Mürren, and Gstaad are all car-free.

EMERGENCIES

🚑 Dental referrals ☎ 111. **Medical emergencies** ☎ 144. **Pharmacist referrals** ☎ 111. **Police** ☎ 117.

TOURS

Auto AG Interlaken offers guided coach tours and escorted excursions within the Berner Oberland. There are bus tours to Mürren and the Schilthorn (including trips on the cable car), to Grindelwald and Trümmelbach Falls, to Kandersteg and the Blausee, and to Ballenberg. Guests are picked up at either the Interlaken West or East train stations or at the Metropole or Interlaken hotels. Some tours are available with English commentary. The tourist office is the best source of information.

If you're traveling without either a Swiss Pass or a Regional Pass, remember that guided tours to the Jungfraujoch or to the Schilthorn, arranged through the railway and cable companies themselves, cost less than independent round-trip tickets.

For a nostalgic tour of the streets of greater Interlaken by horse-drawn carriage, line up by the Interlaken West train station.

🚅 Fees & Schedules **Auto AG Grindelwald** ☎ 033/8281717 for reservations. **Horsedrawn carriage** ✉ Charles Wyss Kutschenbetrieb ☎ 033/8222403.

TRAIN TRAVEL

Trains from Bern to Interlaken run once an hour between 6 AM and 11 PM, some requiring a change at Spiez. From Zürich, a direct line leads through Bern to Interlaken and takes about 2½ hours, departing hourly; a more scenic trip over the Golden Pass route via Luzern takes about two hours. From Basel trains run twice an hour via Olten (approximately a 2½-hour trip). Trains run hourly from Geneva (a 2¾-hour ride). Trains stop at the Interlaken West station first. Next stop is Interlaken East. West is the more central, but check with your hotel if you've booked in advance: some of the town's fine hotels are clustered nearer the East station, and all Brienzersee boat excursions leave from the docks nearby. For train information in Interlaken, ask at Interlaken West.

The Berner Oberland is riddled with federal and private railways, funiculars, cogwheel trains, and cable lifts designed with the sole purpose of getting you closer to its spectacular views. A Swiss Pass lets you travel free on federal trains and lake steamers, and gives reductions on many private excursions. If you're concentrating only on the Berner Oberland, consider a 15-day Regional Pass, which offers 450 km (279 mi) of free rail, bus, and boat travel for any five days of your visit, with half fare for the remaining 10 days, as well as discounts on some of the most spectacular (and pricey) private excursions into the heights. The price is 316 SF (first class) and 265 SF (second class). A seven-day pass allows you three days of travel for 263 SF (first class) and 220 SF (second class). These regional passes also grant a 50% discount for travel to Luzern, Zermatt, and Brig. With a Family Card (20 SF), children who are under 16 and accompanied by at least one parent travel free. Discount passes pay for themselves only if you're a high-energy traveler; before you buy, compare the price à la carte for the itinerary you have in mind.

🚅 Train Information **Swiss Rail** ☎ 0900/300300 ⊕ www.sbb.ch.

TRAVEL AGENCIES

🚅 Local Agent Referrals **Jungfrau Tours** ✉ Strandbadstr. 3, Interlaken ☎ 033/8283232. **Kuoni** ✉ Höheweg 12, Interlaken ☎ 033/8283636. **Vaglio** ✉ Höheweg 72, Interlaken ☎ 033/8270722.

VISITOR INFORMATION
Berner Oberland Tourismus dispenses tourist information for the entire region. It's not oriented toward walk-ins, so write or call ahead. The Interlaken Tourist Office, at the foot of the Hotel Metropole, provides information on Interlaken and the Jungfrau region. Arrange your excursions here.

ℹ Local Tourist Offices **Brienz** ✉ CH-3855 ☎ 033/9528080 ⊕ www.alpenregion.ch. **Grindelwald** ✉ CH-3818 ☎ 033/8541230 ⊕ www.grindelwald.ch. **Gstaad** ✉ CH-3780 ☎ 033/7488181 ⊕ www.gstaad.ch. **Kandersteg** ✉ CH-3718 ☎ 033/6758080 ⊕ www. kandersteg.ch. **Meiringen** ✉ Bahnhofstr. 22, CH-3860 ☎ 033/9725050. **Spiez** ✉ CH-3700 ☎ 033/6542020 ⊕ www.spiez.ch. **Thun** ✉ Bahnhof, CH-3600 ☎ 033/2222340 ⊕ www.thuntourismus.ch. **Wengen-Mürren-Lauterbrunnen** ✉ CH-3822, Lauterbrunnen ☎ 033/8568568 ⊕ www.wengen-muerren.ch.

ℹ Regional Tourist Offices **Berner Oberland Tourismus** ✉ Jungfraustr. 38, CH-3800 Interlaken ☎ 033/8230303 🖷 033/8230330 ⊕ www.berneroberland.ch. **Interlaken Tourist Office** ✉ Höheweg 37, CH-3800 ☎ 033/8265300 🖷 033/8265375 ⊕ www. interlaken.ch. **Meiringen-Hasliberg** ✉ Bahnhofstr. 22, CH-3860, Meiringen ☎ 033/9725050 🖷 033/9725015 ⊕ www.alpenregion.ch.

VALAIS
CRANS-MONTANA, VERBIER, LEUKERBAD, ZERMATT

Updated by
Kay
Winzenried

THIS IS THE BROAD UPPER VALLEY OF THE MIGHTY RHÔNE, a river born in the heights above Gletsch (Glacier), channeled into a broad westward stream between the Bernese and the Valaisan Alps, lost in the depths of Lac Léman (Lake Geneva), and then diverted into France, where it ultimately dissolves in the marshes of the Camargue. The region is still wild, remote, beautiful, and slightly unruly. Its *mazots* (typical little Valais barns balanced on stone disks and columns to keep mice out of winter food stores) are romantically tumbledown, its highest slopes peopled by nimble farmers who live at vertiginous angles. More than 500 km (310 mi) of mountains and glaciers span the Bietschhorn, Aletsch, and Jungfrau summits. In 2001 UNESCO named this area a World Heritage site, joining such other natural wonders as the Galapagos Islands, Yellowstone National Park, and the Serengeti desert.

The birthplace of Christianity in Switzerland, Valais was never reformed by Calvin or Zwingli, nor conquered by the ubiquitous Bernese—one reason, perhaps, that the west end of Valais seems the most intensely French of the regions of the Suisse Romande.

Its romance appeals to the Swiss. Longing for rustic atmosphere, they build nostalgic Valais-style huts in their modern city centers so they can eat raclette (melted cheese with potatoes and pickles) under mounted pitchforks, pewter pitchers, and grape pickers' baskets. For vacations, the Swiss come here to escape, to hike, and, above all, to ski. The renowned resorts of Zermatt, Saas-Fee, Crans-Montana, Verbier, and Leukerbad are all in the Valais, some within yodeling distance of villages barely touched by modern technology.

Exploring Valais

Valais is an L-shape valley with Martigny at its angle. Its long (eastern) leg, a wide, fertile riverbed flanked by bluffs, is the most characteristic and imposing. It's fed from the north and south by remote, narrow valleys that snake into the mountains and peter out in Alpine wilderness or lead to the region's most famous landmarks—including that Swiss superstar, the Matterhorn. Not all of Valais covers Alpine terrain, however. The western stretch—between Martigny and Sierre—comprises one of the two chief sources of wine in Switzerland (the other is in Vaud, along Lac Léman). Valaisan wines come from vineyards that stripe the hillsides flanking the Rhône.

The Val d'Entremont leads southward down an ancient route from Lac Léman to the Col du Grand St-Bernard (Great St. Bernard Pass), traversing the key Roman crossroads at Martigny. Up the Rhône Valley, past the isolated eagle's-nest village of Isérables, two magnificent castle-churches loom above the historic Old Town at Sion. From Sion, the Val d'Hérens winds up into the isolated wilderness past the stone Pyramides d'Euseigne (Pyramids of Euseigne) and the Brigadoon-like resorts of Évolène and, even more obscure, Les Haudères. The Val d'Anniviers, the valley winding south from Sierre, leads to tiny, isolated skiing and hiking resorts such as Grimentz. The most famous southbound valley, the Mattertal, leads from Visp to the stellar resort of Zermatt and its

10

Numbers in the text correspond to numbers in the margin and on the Valais map.

If you have 2 days

You'll feel unsated if you miss Switzerland's most photographed icon, the Matterhorn, so strike out on the most direct route to ⊞ **Zermatt** ❽ ➤. Allow a half day to get there and back, enjoying spectacular views from the train en route (you can't drive to Zermatt). If the weather is clear when you arrive, hustle to the end of the village to see the mountain. Then split your day of exploring between taking a lift or the train to higher elevations and strolling the narrow streets and shops, being sure to stop at one of the local restaurants for raclette.

If you have 5 days

To experience Valais, it's not necessary to explore every wild valley that ribs out from the Rhône; better to choose one region and spend a few days hiking, driving, or skiing. Enter from Lac Léman and visit the Gianadda museum in **Martigny** ❷ ➤. Spend the night and next day exploring the citadel and Old Town of ⊞ **Sion** ❺. Then make your selection: if you've never seen the Matterhorn, head directly for ⊞ **Zermatt** ❽, and spend three days shutter-snapping, riding cable cars for better views, and stuffing yourself with raclette. Other Alpine resort options—⊞ **Saas-Fee** ❾, ⊞ **Verbier** ❸, and ⊞ **Crans-Montana** ❻—are also magnificently sited. If you prefer wilderness and old-fashioned retreat, shun the famous spots, and make an excursion up the Val d'Hérémence, Val d'Hérens, or Val d'Anniviers.

If you have 10 days

You'll have time to visit the abbey and art treasures of **St-Maurice** ❶ ➤ and **Martigny** ❷ before heading up to the mountains and ⊞ **Verbier** ❸ for a couple of days of hiking or skiing. Set aside a full day for the monuments and museums of ⊞ **Sion** ❺, but leave time for backcountry walks or cross-country skiing in the Val d'Hérens, with stops to see the Grande Dixence dam and Pyramides d'Euseigne. Wine enthusiasts should add another half day to walk the vineyard trail between Sierre and Salgesch and visit the museums and tasting room. Then zip back to the heights. ⊞ **Crans-Montana** ❻, on the sunny shelf above Sierre, and the spa town of ⊞ **Leukerbad** ❼ provide contrasting options, as do the highly developed, Germanic ⊞ **Zermatt** ❽ and the understated ⊞ **Saas-Fee** ❾. Whichever you choose, staying three or four nights enables you to settle in and fully exploit the facilities. From these valleys, you can exit Valais via the **Simplon Pass** ⓫ or the **Furka Pass** ⓮. If you opt for the Furka route, take the aerial cable car from Fiesch for stunning views of the Bernese and Valaisan Alps and glaciers that make up the World Heritage site. Whenever time and road conditions permit, opt for the slow switchback crawl over the mountain passes rather than the more efficient tunnels.

mascot mountain, the Matterhorn. A fork off that same valley leads to spectacular Saas-Fee, another car-free resort in a magnificent glacier bowl. From Brig, back at the Rhône, a valley mounts southward to the Simplon Pass and Italy, and the river flows from the northeast and its glacier source, Gletsch, near the Furka Pass, which leads out of the region.

About the Restaurants

For Valaisans, the midday meal remains the mainstay. Locals gather at a bistro for a *plat chaud* (warm meal) that includes meat, vegetable or pasta, and salad for under 20 SF. Baskets of crusty *pain Valaisan* (bread made of wheat and cereal grains) freshly cut from thick loaves, never presliced, circulate around the table. The evening meal is lighter, perhaps comprising an *assiette* (platter) of cheese and cold cuts shared by the table, accompanied by another bread basket and fruit. For the time-pressed, sandwiches and quick meals can be picked up at a corner boulangerie or supermarket (Manor, Migros, or Coop), where food halls have buffets and inexpensive sit-down options. Dress and atmosphere are understated even at top-dollar restaurants, which eschew worn jeans but seldom require a jacket. Keep in mind that most eateries do not offer continuous service; lunch winds down around 2 and dinner does not begin before 6. Unless a host greets you or you have a reservation, it is fine to take a seat at an open table.

Multiple dining options can share the same entrance and kitchen. A brasserie or *Stübli* is the homey casual section just inside the doorway, with paper place mats, straightforward dishes, and lively conversation. The quieter *salle à manger* (dining room) has tables dressed in linen and a *carte* (menu) of multicourse meals and more complicated preparations. If cheese specialties are served, a *carnotzet,* a cozy space in the cellar or a corner away from main dining, is designated to confine the aroma and foster conviviality. Wine is a standard companion whether *vin ouvert* (open wine) poured from small pitchers or bottles selected from cellar holdings. The pace of eating is leisurely, and the server will not bring a check until you request it.

WHAT IT COSTS In Swiss francs					
	$$$$	$$$	$$	$	¢
MAIN COURSE	over 60	40–60	25–40	15–25	under 15

Prices are per person for a main course at dinner.

About the Hotels

The most appealing hotels in Valais seem to be old. That is, historic sites have maintained their fine Victorian ambience; postwar inns, their lodgelike feel. Most of those built after about 1960 popped up in generic, concrete-slab, balconied rows to accommodate the 1960s ski boom. They are solid enough but, for the most part, anonymous, depending on the personality and dedication of their owners.

Valais is home to some of Switzerland's most famous resorts, and prices vary widely between top-level Zermatt lodgings and simple, wayside auberges (inns) in humbler towns. The price categories below have been

Hiking As skiing is to winter, hiking is to summer in Valais, and the network of valleys that radiate north and south of the Rhône provides almost infinite possibilities. Sociable hikers can join the crowds on trails out of the big resorts—especially outside Saas-Fee and Zermatt, where the mountain peaks and glaciers are within tackling distance—but don't overlook wilder, more-isolated alternatives in the less-developed Val d'Hérens and Val d'Anniviers. Skilled trekkers opt for multiday hut-to-hut excursions into the higher elevations, skirting mountain peaks that fail to recognize official borders with France and Italy. Wine enthusiasts can explore the pathways connecting vineyards between Martigny and Visp, especially the well-defined trail between museums in Sierre and Salgesch. Good maps and suggested itineraries are available through the Valais regional tourist office in Sion.

10

Skiing With its plateaus and cavernous gorges, Valais has nurtured ski resorts for centuries. Zermatt and Saas-Fee, both rustic and car-free, contrast sharply with their high-tech peers to the west: Verbier and Crans-Montana are virtually purpose-built, with plenty of amenities but less charm. Smaller installations like Thyon, Nendaz, and Bettmeralp are tied to larger resorts, so you can enjoy the atmosphere of a tiny ski village with access to more runs. Snowboarders flock to the pipes and carved gullies of snow parks, but it is the extreme glide that attracts the fearless to off-slope descents. You can find all levels of difficulty and all kinds of snow—even in July—and it's not all downhill. Extensive cross-country tracks include a few boring ovals, but most are paths through the forests or to adjacent villages. Sledding and snowshoeing excursions are increasing in popularity. Family discount programs are available in most resorts.

A Wine & Cheese Party Though the French influence in the western portion of this region means a steady diet of cuisine bourgeoise, leading newcomers to think entrecôte with peppercorn sauce is a native dish, the elemental cuisine of Valais is much simpler. In a word: cheese.

The most popular way to enjoy this regional product is raclette, an exclusive invention of this mountain canton (though the French of Haute-Savoie embrace it as their own). Ideally, the fresh-cut face of a half wheel of Orsières (a mild cheese produced in the high pastures near Martigny) is melted before an open wood fire, the softened cheese scraped onto a plate and eaten with potatoes (always in their skins), pickled onions, and tiny gherkins. Nowadays, even mountain carnotzets with roaring fires depend on electric raclette heaters that grip the cheese in a vise before toasterlike elements. Fondue, of course, is omnipresent and is often made with a blend of the local Bagnes and Orsières. Its consumption is generally held to the cold months, although locals casually request raclette à discrétion (as much as you want) on a cool summer's eve.

The beverage of choice to accompany your raclette is a crisp, bubbly, fruity Fendant (a local white wine), but there are other regional favorites. Appellations and vintner names aren't as prominent in the Valais; it's the name of the grape that holds the spotlight. Winemakers welcome tasting guests most times of the year except harvest (late September through early October). A true Valaisan wouldn't enjoy a fine meal without a ruby red Dôle (pinot noir and gamay blend) swirled in a stemmed *ballon* (glass) or a sparkling white Fendant poured into a shot-size glass. On your way through the region follow custom and give a toast: *Santé.*

Cheese isn't the region's only culinary treasure, however. Valais rivals Graubünden in its production of *viande séchée* (air-dried beef), a block of meat marinated in herbs, pressed between planks until it takes on its signature bricklike form, and then dried in the open air. Shaved into thin, translucent slices, it can be as tender as a good prosciutto *crudo*—or as tough as leather. The flavor is concentrated, the flesh virtually fat-free.

---

equally applied, so the standards in a $$$-rated hotel in expensive Zermatt may be moderate compared with those in nonresort towns, and even the best hotels do not have air-conditioning. Often included in the price, *demipension* (half board)—also called Modified American Plan (MAP)—includes breakfast and a hot meal, either lunch or dinner; rates may be listed per person. There are sometimes enormous differences between high- and low-season prices, but, although some places offer low-season savings, others simply close their doors. If you're planning a vacation for fall or spring, remember that many resorts shut down altogether during the lulls in May and from November to mid-December and schedule their renovations and construction projects for these periods.

WHAT IT COSTS	In Swiss francs			
$$$$	**$$$**	**$$**	**$**	**¢**
DOUBLE ROOM over 350	250–350	175–250	100–175	under 100

Prices are for two people in a standard double room in high season, including tax and service.

Timing
Valais is at its sunny best in high summer and midwinter, with foggy dampness overwhelming the region in late autumn (its low season). Mid-December to Easter is peak ski season in the resorts. As Europeans vacation here for weeks at a time, book well ahead if you want to compete for lodging in August, at Easter time, and at Christmas and New Year's. And remember: May and November to mid-December are renovation and repair time, with many facilities closed.

VAL D'ENTREMONT

At Villeneuve the Rhône broadens deltalike into a flat valley that pours into Lac Léman, but head upriver (south), crossing from the canton of Vaud into Valais, and the valley and the river change character. The mountains—the Dents du Midi in the west and the Dents de Morcles to the east—begin to crowd in. The Rhône no longer flows placidly but gives a taste of the mountain torrent it will become as you approach its source. And at the Martigny elbow, the most ancient of Alpine routes leaves the Rhône and ascends due south to 8,098 feet at the Col du Grand St-Bernard before descending into Italy's Valle d'Aosta.

St-Maurice

▶ ❶ *46 km (28 mi) west of Sion, 56 km (35 mi) southeast of Lausanne.*

Pushed up against a stern, gray rock face, this village is quiet and peaceful, with patrician homes lining its Grand-rue. Once a customs station along the Roman route over the Col du Grand St-Bernard, in the 3rd century it witnessed the massacre of a band of Christian soldiers, the Theban Legion, and their chief, Maurice, who had refused to worship the Roman deities.

★ At the end of the 4th century the first bishop of the Valais built a sanctuary over Maurice's tomb, and in 515 the **Abbaye Saint-Maurice** (St. Maurice Abbey) was founded. Its treasury contains a stellar collection of religious offerings, with precious Romanesque and Gothic objects given in honor of the martyrs. Contemplate both sides of the stunning bronze doors with inscriptions honoring martyrs from around the world. Excavations near the baroque **église abbatiale** (abbey church) have revealed the foundations of the original building. ☎ *024/4860404* ✉ *Church free; guided tour 6 SF* ⊙ *Guided tours Apr.–June, Sept., and Oct., Tues.–Sat. at 10:30, 3, and 4:30, Sun. at 3 and 4:30; July and Aug., Tues.–Sat. at 10:30, 2, 3:15, and 4:30, Sun. at 2, 3:15, and 4:30; Nov.–Mar., Tues.–Sun. at 3.*

Where to Stay & Eat

★ $ ✕🏠 **Le St-Christophe.** Time your entry into the Valais to stop at this stone *relais* (inn), hewn of boulders from the gorge that separates Bex and St-Maurice. It's an unlikely location for a gourmet kitchen ($$–$$$), but the place has been operating successfully for decades. Two options await: the less-expensive, three-table anteroom turned bistro and the open dining room, where contemporary paintings soften the walls and enliven the atmosphere. Updated classics use ideas as refreshing as the art—puffy lardon-seasoned crispies on the salad, morel-filled ravioli with Parmesan cream sauce. Reserve one of the upper-level rooms, and you can stay put after dinner. ✉ *rte. St- Maurice (exit Bex direction Lavey) CH-1880* ☎ *024/4852977* 🖶 *024/ 4852445* 💤 *12 rooms* ⚒ *Restaurant, café, minibars, cable TV, free parking* ☰ *AE, DC, MC, V* ⊙ *Closed Sun. and Mon.* ⧖ *BP.*

Martigny

▶ ❷ *17 km (11 mi) south of St-Maurice, 23 km (14 mi) southwest of Sion.*

At the foot of the Col du Grand St-Bernard, Martigny has long been a commercial crossroads. Testimony to this past are the Gallo-Roman ruins discovered in 1976 by engineer Leonard Gianadda. When Gianadda's brother Pierre died in a plane crash, Leonard created a cultural center **Fodor**'s**Choice** in his memory. The **Fondation Pierre Gianadda** now rises in bold geometric ★ shapes around the ruins. Inside are three separate collections, and the foundation itself sponsors high-profile, themed art exhibits. Recent

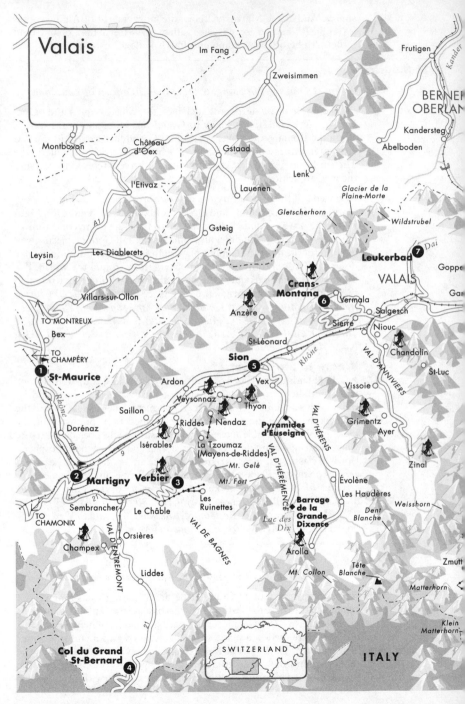

Valais

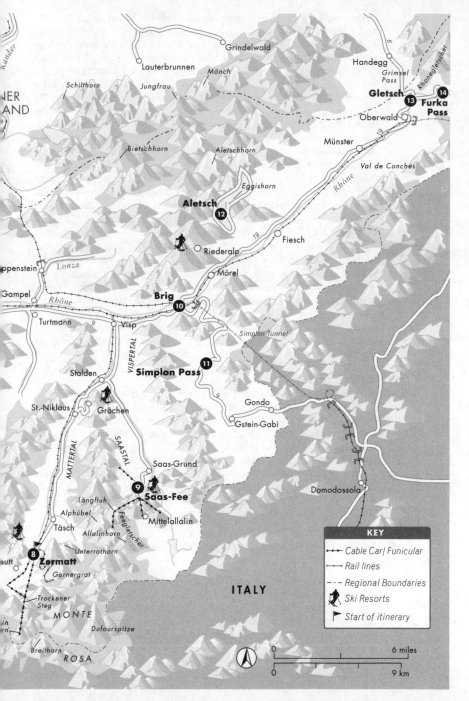

temporary exhibitions have spotlighted works by Albert Anker, Picasso, and Leonardo da Vinci, and its permanent holdings include works by Van Gogh, Cézanne, and Picasso. The **Musée Gallo-Romain** displays Gallo-Roman relics excavated from a 1st-century temple: striking bronzes, statuary, pottery, and coins. A marked path leads through the antique village, baths, drainage systems, and foundations to the fully restored 5,000-seat amphitheater, which dates from the 2nd century. In the gracefully landscaped garden surrounding the foundation, a wonderful **Parc de Sculpture** displays works by Rodin, Brancusi, Miró, Calder, Moore, Dubuffet, and Max Ernst. There's also a sizable **Musée de l'Automobile**, which contains some 50 antique cars, all in working order. They include an 1897 Benz, the Delauney-Belleville of Czar Nicholas II of Russia, and a handful of Swiss-made models. You may spot posters for concerts by international classical stars such as Cecilia Bartoli or Itzhak Perlman—the foundation doubles as a concert hall. ✉ *59 rue de Forum* ☎ *027/7223978* ⊕ *www.gianadda.ch* ✉ *15 SF* ◷ *June–Oct., daily 9–7; Nov.–May, daily 10–6.*

off the beaten path

SAILLON – Thirteen km (8 mi) northeast of Martigny on Route 9, the Saillon freeway exit leads to a narrow farm road, which winds through orchard groves and trellised vines to this hilltop town. Here you'll find plenty of cellars to begin identifying the distinctive, fruity wines of this part the valley. You'll also find the **Bains de Saillon** (☎ 027/7431170), a natural-spring aqua-center with indoor and outdoor pools, waterslides and play areas for children, and several therapeutic treatments to soothe away road weariness.

Where to Stay & Eat

$–$$ ✕▣ **Hôtel du Forum.** Martigny is something of a one-street town, but if it suits your itinerary to stop over, then this is a convenient choice. Though the pine-decorated rooms are comfortable, the real draw is the hotel's top-rated chef, who oversees both the more formal restaurant, Le Gourmet ($$$$), and a brasserie, l'Olivier ($$). The menu's temptations could include crayfish gazpacho and pigeon with an arabica-infused sauce. Take Bus 13 from the railway station to the Le Bourg stop. ✉ *74 av. de Grand-St-Bernard, CH-1920* ☎ *027/7221841* 🖷 *027/7227925* ➥ *29 rooms* ♧ *2 restaurants, cable TV* ▭ *AE, DC, MC, V* ⏏ *BP.*

Verbier

❸ *29 km (18 mi) east of Martigny (exit at Sembrancher), 58 km (36 mi) southwest of Sion.*

It's the skiing on sunny slopes that draws committed sports lovers to Verbier, a high-tech, state-of-the-art sports complex that links four valleys and multiple ski areas, including Thyon, Veysonnaz, Nendaz, and La Tzoumaz. Verbier has a huge aerial cableway, with two cabins accommodating 150, and 93 smaller transportation installations. There is plenty of vertical drop, as the extreme snowboard competitions can attest. Summer sports are equally serious: hang gliding and its variations compete with golf as the principal sports. Though it's perched on a sunny shelf high above the Val de Bagnes, with the 9,915-foot Mont Gelé towering behind and wraparound views, Verbier is too modern to be picturesque, but thanks to its compact layout and easygoing locals, the town has a friendlier feel than the traffic-snarled sprawl of Crans-Montana or hotel-packed Zermatt. Rail and cable car connections from Le Châble are an alternative to driving switchback roads to the resort. Once there, you can easily navigate the village on foot or shuttle bus, and all hotels are clearly signposted.

Skiing

At 4,921 feet, Verbier is the center of Switzerland's most famous transit network, **Televerbier**—which consists of 12 gondolas, five cable cars, 32 chairlifts, and 45 other ski lifts giving access to 410 km (253 mi) of marked pistes. From this resort an immense complex of resorts has developed—some more modest, others more exclusive—covering four valleys in an extended ski area whose extremities are 15 km (9 mi) or so apart as the crow flies and several dozen kilometers apart by way of winding mountain roads.

Les Ruinettes gives access to Verbier's entire upper ski area, which culminates at **Mont-Fort,** at 10,923 feet. This is reached by an aerial tram, *Le Jumbo,* equipped with a cab that accommodates 150. This entire sector is crisscrossed by a dense network of astonishingly varied pistes. There are several strategic passes, including **Les Attelas, Mont-Gelé, Col des Gentianes, Lac des Vaux,** and **Tortin.** One-day lift tickets cost 61 SF; six-day passes cost 314 SF. Automated ski passes streamline the lift check-in process, and family discounts are available.

If you're looking for a private instructor to fine-tune your ski or snowboard technique, stop in at the **Maison du Sport** (☎ 027/7753363).

Where to Stay & Eat

$$–$$$ ✕ **Le Millénium/El Toro Negro.** Bask in the sun on the terrace during lunch at this combination restaurant–grill house. The duck salad with berry vinaigrette and the perch fillet with matchstick potatoes are flawless. Head downstairs to the steak house for a menu heavy with meat and hearty side dishes. ✉ *pl. Centrale* ☎ *027/7719900* ▤ *AE, DC, MC, V.*

$–$$$ ✕ **La Grange.** To eat cheese or not to eat cheese will be the question here. In keeping with the traditional decor, you can sample regional specialties, such as fondue or dried beef, or you can go for more lofty epicurean choices from the open grill, such as mushroom *cassolette* (casserole) or liver pâté with plum sauce. The wine list includes an excellent selection of local vintages. ☎ *027/7716431* ▤ *AE, DC, MC, V* ☉ *Closed June.*

★ $$$$ ✕▥ **Chalet d'Adrien.** Named for the owner's grandfather, a baron, who discovered the village in the early 1900s, this luxury inn passes on the baron's aristocratic taste. Antiques and collectibles from old farmhouses and châteaux and a large number of suites contribute to the private ski mansion feel. Rooms, outfitted with hand-carved headboards, TV armories, safes, minibars, and couples baths, are named for wildflowers. South-facing rooms (many with balcony) look out on the French Alps backlit by the afternoon sun. To work out those après-ski kinks, visit the small spa or firelit lounge. The epicurean menu at Astrance ($$–$$$$) has imaginative dishes like lentils with foie gras or sole prepared with white endive and chervil butter. ⊠ *rte. des Creux, CH-1936* ☎ *027/ 7716200* 🖷 *027/7716224* ⊕ *www.chaletadrien.com* ↵ *10 rooms, 15 suites* ⚭ *2 restaurants, in-room data ports, in-room safes, minibars, cable TV, hot tub, sauna, spa, steam room, billiards, bar, video game room, free parking, no-smoking rooms* ⊟ *AE, DC, MC, V* ⊘ *Closed late Apr.–early July and late Sept.–early Dec.*

★ $$$$ ✕🖼 **Rosalp.** The rustic-chic pine decor of Pierroz ($$$$), the main restaurant here, sets a warm tone for one of Switzerland's great meals. Chef Roland Pierroz has earned an international following for such dishes as *rouget* (red mullet) with black truffles and crayfish bisque. For simpler, less pricey, but equally creative food, try La Pinte ($$–$$$). An outstanding cellar makes Rosalp the place to sample rare regional vintages. Reservations are essential. If you plan to stay overnight, ask for one of the newer rooms, which have marble baths. Upper rooms are smaller but quieter and have better views. ⊠ *rte. de Médran, CH-1936* ☎ *027/ 7716323* 🖷 *027/7711059* ⊕ *www.relaischateaux.ch/rosalp* ↵ *25 rooms, 5 apartments* ⚭ *2 restaurants, in-room data ports, in-room safes, minibars, cable TV, gym, hot tub, sauna, Turkish bath, bar* ⊟ *AE, DC, MC, V* ⊘ *Closed late Apr.–early July and late Sept.–early Dec.* ⏇*BP.*

$$$$ 🖼 **Hotel Montpelier.** This classy, chalet-style lodge sits apart from the town hub. Generously sized rooms with balconies are brightened with honey-colored wood and blue stenciled decorations. The half board is far from a hardship, as the cuisine is excellent; if you'd like a change of scenery, though, the owners will book you a table at their restaurant in the upper village. ⊠ *rue de la Piscine, CH-1936* ☎ *027/7716131* 🖷 *027/7714689* ⊕ *www.hotelmontpelier.ch* ↵ *46 rooms, 24 suites, 1 apartment* ⚭ *Restaurant, minibars, cable TV, indoor pool, sauna, steam room, mountain bikes, bar, free parking, parking (fee), no-smoking rooms* ⊟ *AE, DC, MC, V* ⊘ *Closed May and Nov.* ⏇*MAP.*

$$$$ 🖼 **Verbier Lodge.** In this village of modern and chalet architecture, log construction typical of the American West stands out. The lodge is on the way to the Médran lift, and the owners, competitive skiers and extreme-adventure guides, have created a convivial place for like-minded enthusiasts to gather, swapping stories at the attractive bar or in the hot tub. Rooms, some in duplex configurations, are up-to-date, though the emphasis is more on function than luxury. Brush up on your racing style, or book a heli-skiing package with your accommodations. ⊠ *chemin de Plénadzeuz, CH-1936* ☎ *027/7716666* 🖷 *027/7716656* ⊕ *www. verbierlodge.ch* ↵ *9 rooms, 4 suites* ⚭ *In-room safes, cable TV, gym, hot tub, sauna, Turkish bath, bar, free parking* ⊟*AE, DC, MC, V* ⏇*BP.*

$$$–$$$$ 🖼 **Hôtel Farinet.** With its central location, this hotel lures crowds year-round to its open-air patio. An Italian restaurant serves heaping plates of handmade pasta to tanned sports enthusiasts before they dive into the club downstairs. There's also a smoking lounge with a nice stock of Cuban cigars. The comfortable guest rooms mix contemporary and homey looks, with iron beds and mismatched dark furniture. Be sure to reserve a space for your car when you book your room. ⊠ *pl. Centrale, CH-1936* ☎ *027/7716626* 🖷 *027/7713855* ⊕ *www.hotelfarinet.*

ch 🛏 *18 rooms, 3 apartments* ⅋ *Restaurant, cable TV, bar, dance club, parking (fee)* ▤ *AE, MC, V* ⊘ *Closed May, Oct., and Nov.* ¶⊙¶ *BP.*

Nightlife & the Arts

DANCING The popular **Crok No Name** (✉ rte. des Creux ☎ 027/7716934) has live music or DJs nightly. The **Farm Club** (✉ Rhodania Hotel, rue de Verbier ☎ 027/7716121) is the place to be seen in Verbier. Apparently it's not fashionable to turn up before 1 AM. The club is closed Sunday. If you don't plan to hit the slopes early, you can party into the wee hours at **Marshal's** (✉ Hôtel Farinet, pl. Centrale ☎ 027/7713572). If you're looking for someplace unpretentious, head to **Scotch** (✉ rue de la Poste ☎ 027/7714394), where karaoke takes center stage on Wednesday and the dancing doesn't stop until 4 AM.

MUSIC For more than two weeks overlapping July and August the **Verbier Festival and Academy** (☎ 027/7718282 🖨 027/7717057 ⊕ www.verbierfestival.com) hosts an impressive classical music festival of performances and master classes. Musical director James Levine assembles celebrated guests such as Sarah Chang, Vadim Repin, and Yuri Temikanov to perform under a sprawling tent.

Sports & the Outdoors

Verbier offers a variety of summer and winter high-altitude sports, ranging from rock and ice climbing to rafting and snow tubing, all led by specialist outfitters.

BICYCLING Trails and routes (200 km [150 mi]) for the enthusiast range from difficult distance rides across the passes to simpler runs closer to town. The pros at **Jet Sports** (☎ 027/7712067) will help you plan your entire outing plus rent standard or high-performance bikes and helmets. **Medran Sports** (☎ 027/7716048), on the other side of the village, offers a choice of equipment and gear at competitive rates.

GOLF Keeping pace with the growing popularity of golf, Verbier has two 18-hole courses open to the public. **Les Esserts** (☎ 027/7715314) is adjacent to the upper settlement of Hameau. Closer to the main village, **Les Moulins** (☎ 027/7717693), a compact golf course, is a challenge at par 54.

HIKING & Sign up at **La Fantastique** (☎ 027/7714141) for hut-to-hut trekking
CLIMBING tours of the Mont Blanc region or technical rock climbing and rappelling sessions.

SPORTS CENTERS Verbier's **Centre Polysportif** (☎ 027/7716601) is a hub for the active, with indoor skating, swimming, curling, tennis, and squash, as well as whirlpools, saunas, and a solarium. There's even a backpackers' dorm and Internet café.

Col du Grand St-Bernard

★ ❹ *40 km (25 mi) south of Martigny, 69 km (43 mi) southwest of Sion.*

Breasting the formidable barrier of the Alps at 8,101 feet, this pass is the oldest and most famous of the great Alpine crossings, and the first to join Rome and Byzantium to the wilds of the north. Used for centuries before the birth of Christ, it has witnessed an endless stream of emperors, knights, and simple travelers—think of Umberto Eco's *The Name of the Rose,* with its two friars crossing on donkey back in howling winter winds. Napoléon took an army of 40,000 across it en route to Marengo, where he defeated the Austrians in 1800.

You'll have an easier time crossing today. If you simply want to get to Italy quickly, take the tunnel, which opens on the other side above the Valle d'Aosta. But by skipping the tiny winding road over the top, you'll miss the awe-inspiring, windswept moonscape at the summit and the hospice that honors its namesake. In 1038, the story goes, Bernard of Menthon, bishop of Aosta, came to clear the pass of brigands. When he reached the top, he found a pagan temple, which he covered with his chasuble. The shrine immediately crumbled to dust, and, by the same power, the brigands were defeated. Bernard established his hospice there.

The **hospice of St. Bernard** served international travelers throughout the Middle Ages. Kings and princes rewarded the hospice by showering estates upon the order. Nowadays its residents—Augustinian canons—train as mountain guides and ski instructors and accommodate youth groups. Behind the hospice, there's a kennel full of the landmark's enormous, furry namesakes: the famous St. Bernard dogs, who for centuries have helped the monks find travelers lost in the snow. They supposedly came to Switzerland with silk caravans from central Asia and were used by Romans as war dogs; nowadays they're kept more for sentimental than functional reasons. The most famous was Barry, who saved more than 40 people in the 19th century and today stands stuffed in Bern's Naturhistorisches Museum (Museum of Natural History). Souvenir stands sell plush versions of St. Bernards on either side of the pass. ☎ 027/7871236 ▨ *Kennel 6 SF* ☉ *June and Sept., daily 8:30–noon and 1–6; July and Aug., daily 8:30–6.*

SION & ENVIRONS

The Rhône Valley is most fertile just east of Martigny, its flatlands thick with orchards and vegetable gardens, its south-facing slopes quilted with vineyards. The region nurtures a virtual market basket of apples, pears, apricots, and delicate white asparagus, a specialty of early spring. The local blue-blood crop, however, is grapes: this is one of the primary wine-producing regions in the country, and the fruity Fendant and hearty red Dôle appear on lists throughout the area. Lesser known local varietals include Petite Arvine, Amigne, Cornalin, and Humagne. Once Valais wines were poured from hinged-lid tin or pewter pitchers called *channes*; reproductions are sold throughout the region. Also from the orchards come potent, intensely perfumed eaux-de-vie (or schnapps), especially *abricotine* (from apricots) and *williamine* (from pears).

This patch of Valais demonstrates the region's dramatic contrasts. Over the fertile farmlands looms the great medieval stronghold of Sion, its fortress towers protecting the gateway to the Alps. High up in the bluffs and valleys to the south are scores of isolated eagle's-nest towns, including Évolène and Isérables. The latter, set on a precarious slope that drops

3,280 feet into the lowlands, has narrow streets that weave between crooked old stone-shingle mazots. Since the arrival of the cable car, Isérables has prospered and modernized itself. Yet the inhabitants of this village still carry the curious nickname *Bedjuis*. Some say it's derived from "Bedouins" and that the people are descended from the Saracen hordes who, after the battle of Poitiers in 732, overran some of the high Alpine valleys.

Excursions to the sights and villages of these *haute vallées* (high valleys) can be accomplished in a day, with plenty of time to hike and explore before returning to the city. Keep in mind that narrow roads twist up and down steep grades and require additional time to navigate. Above the town of Vex, the road splits: to the west is the Val d' Hérémence, which terminates at the base of the Barrage de la Grande Dixence (Grande Dixence Dam); to the east is the Val d'Hérens, which begins near the Pyramides d'Euseigne and pushes toward the Dent Blanche. Expanses of wilderness are broken by clusters of chalets and small cultivated plots. Accommodations and services are modest and limited. The tourist office in Sion can assist with reservations for overnight stays or multiday hiking trips.

Sion

⑤ *158 km (98 mi) south of Bern.*

Rearing up in the otherwise deltalike flatlands of the western Valais, two otherworldly twin hills flank the ancient city of Sion. The two hills together are a powerful emblem of the city's 1,500-year history as a bishopric and a Christian stronghold. From the top of either hill are dramatic views of the surrounding flatlands and the mountains flanking the valley. The town itself can be comfortably explored on foot in an afternoon, unless you lose yourself in one of its museums or labyrinthine antiques shops. In summer a trolley called Le P'tit Sédunois shuttles between the train station, main plaza, and elevated sights.

Sion folk are fiercely proud and independent, as reflected in the fanatical support for their soccer team and their dogged attempts to host the Winter Olympics. (There was bitter disappointment when they lost the bid for the 2006 games to rivals across the border in Turin, Italy.) A shortage of high-quality hotels gives the impression that the town is not as hospitable to travelers as the tourist-oriented ski resorts, but don't be deterred; there are ample reasons to spend time here. As one example, the city walking tour includes a wine tasting.

★ Crowning Tourbillon, the higher of Sion's hills, the ruined **Tourbillon château** was built as a bishop's residence at the end of the 13th century and destroyed by fire in 1788. If you take the rugged walk uphill, try to time it for a visit to the tiny chapel with its ancient, layered frescoes. ◻ *Free* ⊙ *Mid-Mar.–mid-Nov., Tues.–Sun. 10–6; chapel Tues.–Sun. 11, 3, and 4.*

★ On Valère, Sion's lower hill, the **Église-Forteresse de Valère** (Church-Fortress of Valère) is a striking example of sacred and secular power combined—

reflective of the Church's heyday, when it often subjugated rather than served its parishioners. Built on Roman foundations, the massive stone walls enclose both the **château** and the 11th-century **Église Notre Dame de Valère** (Church of Our Lady of Valère). This structure stands in a relatively raw form, rare in Switzerland, where monuments are often restored to perfection. Over the engaging Romanesque carvings, 16th-century fresco fragments, and 17th-century stalls painted with scenes of the Passion, there hangs a rare **organ,** its cabinet painted with two fine medieval Christian scenes. Dating from the 14th century, it's the oldest playable organ in the world, and an annual organ festival celebrates its musical virtues.

The château complex also houses the **Musée Cantonal d'Histoire** (History Museum), which displays a wide array of medieval sacristy chests and religious artifacts. Expanded exhibits trace daily life and advances in the canton from these early centuries to present day, including soccer championships. Explanations are in three languages, including English. The museum is well worth the trek up uneven stone walkways and steep staircases. Guided tours are conducted at quarter past the hour. ☎ *027/6064710* ✉ *Church 3 SF; museum 6 SF; combination ticket 7 SF* ⊙ *Church June–Sept., Mon.–Sat. 10–6, Sun. 2–6; Oct.–May, Tues.–Sat. 10–5, Sun. 2–5; museum June–Sept., Tues.–Sun. 1–6; Oct.–May, Tues.–Sun. 1–5.*

The **Old Town,** down rue de Lausanne (take a left when leaving the tourist office on the place de la Planta), is a blend of shuttered 16th-century houses, modern shops, and a host of sights worth seeing.

The grand old **Maison Supersaxo** (House of Supersaxo), tucked into a passageway off rue Supersaxo, was built in 1505 by Georges Supersaxo, the local governor, to put his rivals to shame. This extravagantly decorated building includes a Gothic staircase and a grand hall, whose painted wood ceiling is a dazzling work of decorative art. ✉ *passage Supersaxo* ✉ *Free* ⊙ *Mon.–Sat. 8–noon and 2–6.*

The imposing **Hôtel de Ville** (Town Hall) has extraordinary historic roots: though it was built in the 1650s, it has transplanted stones in the entrance bearing Roman inscriptions, including a Christian symbol from the year AD 377. The 17th-century doors are richly carved wood, and the tower displays an astronomical clock. Upstairs, the **Salle du Conseil** (Council Hall) is also adorned with ornate woodwork. The only way to visit the Hôtel de Ville is by taking a guided walking tour of the town, which costs 8 SF and leaves from the Sion tourist office. Tours are held from mid-July to the end of August on Tuesday and Thursday mornings. ✉ *rue de Conthey and rue du Grand-Pont* ✉ *Free with walking tour.*

need a break?

It's a tight squeeze to get into Old Town's popular *vinotek* (wine store–tasting room) **La Verre à Pied** (✉ 29 rue du Grand-Pont ☎ 027/3211380), where 150 regional vintages are poured. For a few francs you can join winemakers and enthusiasts who swill and sip.

The **Musée Cantonal d'Archéologie** (Museum of Archaeology) displays a collection of excavated pieces, including fine Roman works found in Valais.

The narrow, cobbled rue des Châteaux, which leads up toward the twin fortifications, passes graceful old patrician houses, among them the museum. ⊠ *12 rue des Châteaux* ☎ *027/6064700* ⊡*4 SF* ☉ *June–Sept., Tues.–Sun. 1–6; Oct.–May, Tues.–Sun. 1–5.*

The cathedral, **Notre-Dame du Glarier** (Our Lady of Glarier), is dominated by its Romanesque tower, built in the Lombard, or Italian, style and dating from the 12th century. The rest of the church is late Gothic in style. ⊠ *rue de la Cathédrale.*

Just across from the cathedral, the **Tour des Sorciers** (Sorcerers' Tower) is the last remnant of the walls that once ringed the town. ⊠ *rue de la Tour* ⊡*3 SF* ☉ *June–Sept., Tues.–Sun. 1–6; Oct.–May, Tues.–Sun. 1–5.*

Where to Stay & Eat

$$–$$$ ✕ **La Croisette.** Don't be put off by the less-than-stylish front room, often filled with locals sipping a glass of Fendant. Once you're settled at a linen-topped table in back, the mood changes. The chef has a light and skillful touch with French dishes, such as chicken breast with mustard sauce and herb-grilled potatoes. ⊠ *21 rue de Rhône* ☎ *027/3224300* ⊟ *AE, DC, MC, V* ☉ *Closed late July–late Aug. No dinner Sun.*

$–$$ ✕ **Au Chevel Blanc.** Set on one of Old Town's cobblestone streets, this congenial bistro is bustling around noon, when locals take their midday meal accompanied by a glass of gamay or Walliser (beer). *Entrecôte avec frites* (steak and fries) and *moules à la mariniére* (mussels in white wine and parsley butter) hold top billing with such traditional dishes as *civet de chevreuil* with spaetzle (venison stew served with dumplings). ⊠ *23 rue du Grand-Pont* ☎ *027/3221867* ⊟ *AE, DC, MC, V* ☉ *Closed Sun. and Mon. and last 2 wks of Dec.*

$–$$ ✕ **L'Enclos de Valère.** If you've worked up an appetite climbing the Tourbillon, you may want to stop in this Old Town eatery on your way back down. Unfussy service, fine regional cuisine, and a rustic cottage setting make it a sentimental favorite. Seasonal items—mushrooms, asparagus, shellfish, and game—lend variety to the upscale menu. When it's not mealtime, drop in for a coffee or a channe of wine. ⊠ *18 rue des Châteaux* ☎ *027/3233230* ⌂ *Reservations essential* ⊟ *AE, DC, MC, V* ☉ *Closed Sun. and Mon. and Oct.–Apr.*

$$–$$$$ ⊞ **Hôtel des Vignes.** For a hotel with character, head a few km east of Sion to the village of Uvrier to find this sienna-color palazzo flanked by vineyards. The welcoming lobby has a central fireplace and a fountain; guest rooms are done in warm peach. ⊠ *9 rue du Pont, CH-1958 Uvrier* ☎ *027/2031671* ⊞ *027/2033727* ⊕ *www.hoteldesvignes.ch* ↫*33 rooms, 10 suites* ⌂ *Restaurant, tea shop, cable TV, driving range, 2 tennis courts, indoor pool, sauna, Turkish bath, bar, laundry service, helipad, free parking* ⊟ *AE, DC, MC, V* ☉ *Closed Jan.* ¹⊙¹ *BP.*

$$ ⊞ **Du Rhône.** The reception area of this cinder block property has a dated feel, with brown furniture and tired accents. The guest rooms are livelier, done in red, green, and blue with exhibition posters from the Fondation Pierre Gianadda. Operating under the Best Western flag, the lodging is located at the edge of Old Town and is handy to the castle walks. Consider it a comfortable, no-frills base. ⊠ *10 rue de Scex, CH-1950* ☎ *027/3228291* ⊞ *027/3231188* ⊕ *www.bestwestern.com* ↫*44* *rooms ♿ Restaurant, in-room data ports, in-room safes, minibars, cable TV, bar, parking (fee), no-smoking rooms* ▭ *AE, DC, MC, V* ⦿❘ *BP.*

Nightlife & the Arts

Sion attracts world-class musicians and scholars to its festivals celebrating the medieval organ in its church-fortress. The **Festival International de l'Orgue Ancien Valère** (International Festival of the Ancient Valère Organ; ☎ 027/3235767) takes place from July through late August.

Val d'Hérémence

16 km (10 mi) south of Sion.

Across Route 9 and past Vex, a right fork takes you up a narrow mountain road and into the Val d'Hérémence. Here you'll find the **Barrage de la Grande Dixence,** a gargantuan monolith of concrete built in the mid-1960s at the improbable altitude of 7,754 feet. Only the Swiss could have accomplished such a feat of Alpine engineering—an achievement that brings them millions of kilowatt-hours of electricity every year. You can walk the rim of the dam and view the pristine lake either by paying 7 SF for a cable car ride or by hiking to the top on the marked trail. Sturdy trekkers can take the ibex trail, a four-hour loop through the region's watershed.

Val d'Hérens

28 km (14 mi) southeast of Sion.

If you take the left (east) fork south of Vex, you'll drive up the Val d'Hérens, where the road transforms into a rural byway often edged in solid rock. As you wind farther into the valley's confines, passing an oncoming car can require precision gauging. Here are the **Pyramides d'Euseigne,** a group of bizarre geological formations: stone pillars formed by the debris of glacial moraines and protected by hard-rock caps from the erosion that carved away the material around them. The effect is that of enormous, freestanding stalagmites wearing hats. A car tunnel has been carved through the bases of three of them.

In a broad, fertile section of the valley sits **Évolène,** a town of ramshackle mazots and wooden houses edged with flower-filled window boxes that provide a picturesque setting for vacationers—mostly French—and mountaineers, who tackle nearby Mont-Collon and the Dent Blanche. If you're lucky, you'll see some of the older women villagers in the traditional dress of kerchiefs and flowered cottons they still favor. Travel farther into the valley to **Les Haudères,** little more than a scattering of chalets in a spectacular, isolated mountain valley. For those seeking a total retreat into the Alpine reaches, continue into the Val d'Arolla, where the road ends in the tiny resort village of **Arolla** (6,555 feet), home to mountain guides and skiers.

CONVERSION DE LA VALLÉE

Secured above the plateau north of Sierre and Leuk are the ski towns of Crans and Montana and the hot springs resort of Leukerbad, each with a different personality. Crans-Montana offers expansive skiing, pricey boutiques, and clubby restaurants. Though Leukerbad also has first-class hotels and ski runs (albeit fewer), it is the restorative pools and spas and authentic Alpine village that attract visitors here. Along this stretch of the Rhône, the switchback of language and culture begins. The Valais, as it is referred to by French speakers, is called Wallis by locals with Germanic ties. To the south the remote Val d'Anniviers offers a glimpse of a simpler life before high-speed lifts and Internet cafés.

Crans-Montana

6 *12 km (7 mi) northwest of Sierre, 19 km (11¾ mi) northeast of Sion.*

This well-known twin sports center rises above the valley on a steep, sheltered shelf at 4,904 feet. It commands a broad view across the Rhône Valley to the peaks of the Valaisan Alps, and its grassy and wooded plateau gets the benefit of Sierre's sunshine. Behind the towns, the **Rohrbachstein** (9,686 feet), the **Gletscherhorn** (9,653 feet), and the **Wildstrubel** (10,637 feet) combine to create a complex of challenging ski slopes. Every September, the 18-hole golf course is the site of the annual European Masters, a period the locals describe as "party week." The most direct route to Crans-Montana is from Sierre, just southeast, either by car, postbus, or funicular.

The resort towns themselves are highly developed and uncaptivating, lacking the regional color and grace of Zermatt. The streets are lined with designer boutiques and hotels. Car traffic is almost always heavy, so it's best to get around on foot or shuttle bus. As in other resorts, signs point the way to the hotels. The crowds are young, wealthy, and international, roving in cocoons of the fit, fun-loving, and fashionable.

Skiing

The pearl of the region is the **Plaine Morte,** a flat glacier 5 km–6 km (3 mi–3½ mi) long, which is perched like a pancake at an elevation of 9,840 feet and has snow year-round. A cross-country ski trail (watch out for your lungs at this altitude) of 10 km–12 km (6 mi–7½ mi) is open and maintained here seven months of the year. The ascent on the gondola from **Violettes Plaines-Morte,** virtually under assault by crowds during the high season and in good weather, will in itself justify your stay in Crans-Montana. Expert skiers may prefer the **Nationale Piste,** site of previous world championships. The incredibly steep-pitched **La Toula** is a challenge for pros. The eastern section of ski area connects to Aminona, where a park for snowboarders and a bobsled run drop from **Petit Bonvin,** at 7,874 feet. A one-day lift ticket costs 54 SF; a six-day pass costs 262 SF, permitting access to 160 km (100 mi) of runs and more than 30 ways to ride to the top.

Where to Stay & Eat

$$$$
Fodor'sChoice
★
✕ 🏨 **L'Hostellerie du Pas de l'Ours.** In a town known for blocklike towers, this petite auberge stands out. Plush and rich with amenities, the roomy suite-apartments have polished wood floors, stucco walls, balconies, fireplaces, and Jacuzzis. The restaurant ($$$–$$$$) draws a chic crowd, thanks to superb French cuisine such as almond-roasted lamb

with apricot reduction; book well in advance for a table. ⊠ *rue du Pas de l'Ours, CH-3963 Crans* ☎ *027/4859333* 📠 *027/4859334* ⊕ *www. relaischateaux.com/pasdelours* ⤳ *9 suites* ♦ *Restaurant, café, in-room data ports, in-room safes, minibars, cable TV, indoor-outdoor pool, sauna, steam room, bar, free parking* ⊟ *AE, DC, MC, V* ⊘ *Closed May and Nov.* ‖◯‖ *BP.*

$$$–$$$$ ✗▣ **Aïda-Castel.** This warm and welcoming complex has kept pace with the times. Its moderately isolated hillside, though quiet, requires a shuttle or uphill walk to activities. Public areas have carved or aged wood, stone, and stucco; the rooms, sturdy Alpine furniture, wrought iron, and stenciling. South-facing balconies fill with afternoon sun worshipers. The very popular public restaurant, La Hotte ($$$–$$$$), serves Italian fare, some prepared on the open grill, as well as raclette made at fireside—so good that reservations are essential. ⊠ *rue du Béthania, CH-3962 Montana* ☎*027/4854111* 📠*027/4817062* ⊕*www. aida-castel.ch* ⤳ *56 rooms, 4 suites* ♦ *3 restaurants, minibars, cable TV, pool, exercise equipment, massage, sauna, Turkish bath, bar, free parking* ⊟ *AE, DC, MC, V* ‖◯‖ *MAP.*

$$$$ ▣ **Alpina & Savoy.** The third generation of Mudry family oversees this rambling hotel on convenient middle ground between the two villages. Secluded in a hilltop park, it is buffered from the main thoroughfare by enormous evergreens. Shuttle service links in both directions, and the Crans-Cry-d'Err cable car is a five-minute walk uphill. Rooms, outfitted with familiar heavy furnishings and damask coverlets, undergo seasonal spruce-ups but remain homey, luring repeat guests. Activity areas, though a bit worn, are full of options, from games to workout equipment to a pool. An in-house spa is a plus, and the demipension meal plan means you won't have to vie for a reservation in town. ⊠ *rte. du Rawyl, CH-3963 Crans* ☎ *027/4850900* 📠 *027/4850999* ⊕ *www. alpina-savoy.ch* ⤳ *45 rooms, 5 suites* ♦ *Restaurant, Stübli, minibars, cable TV, indoor pool, exercise equipment, sauna, spa, steam room, billiards, Ping-Pong, piano bar, video game room, free parking* ⊟ *AE, DC, MC, V* ‖◯‖ *MAP.*

$$$$ ▣ **Grand Hôtel du Golf.** This grand, genteel, blue-blooded oasis offers urbane taste with few of life's nicks and scrapes. Built by English golfers in 1907, it feels like a country clubhouse—emerald and burgundy, a dash of the floral, spaniel prints, and the owner's pet scampering about. The hotel has been modernized outside and attentively tended within, with finely turned-out rooms done in pastels. In addition to a formal restaurant and homey café, the hotel has dining affiliations around town. Manicured grounds adjoin 9- and 18-hole golf courses, and an Asian-oriented spa adds pampering and beauty treatments. ⊠ *rte. du Rawyl, CH-3963 Crans* ☎ *027/4854242* 📠 *027/4854243* ⊕ *www.grand-hotel-du-golf. ch* ⤳ *76 rooms, 8 suites, 2 apartments* ♦ *Restaurant, café, cable TV, in-room VCRs, indoor pool, gym, hair salon, sauna, spa, Turkish bath, piano bar, concierge, Internet, business services, free parking* ⊟ *AE, DC, MC, V* ‖◯‖ *BP.*

$$$ ▣ **Mirabeau.** Done in pastels straight out of suburbia, this attractive midtown property keeps working at self-improvement, expanding activity areas and fluffing guest quarters. Views (of the street and other hotels) aren't spectacular, but the hotel *is* at the hub of the downtown dining and shopping scene, enabling you to park in the garage and leave your car until departure. After a day on the trails, pick up a game of pool in the lounge or steep tired muscles in the sauna. ⊠ *CH-3962 Montana* ☎ *027/4802151* 🖷 *027/4813912* ⊕ *www.hotelmirabeau.ch* ⤺ *40 rooms, 10 apartments* ৬ *Restaurant, in-room safes, minibars, cable TV, gym, hot tub, sauna, billiards, Ping-Pong, bar, parking (fee)* ⊟ *AE, DC, MC, V* ¶◯¶ *BP.*

$$ 🔲 **La Prairie.** Wally Cleaver might have stayed here on a school ski trip: there are rough-hewn fireplaces, indestructible furniture, and an active, rec-room atmosphere complete with Ping-Pong table, sports trophies, and a jukebox. Built in the 1930s, the updated dormlike rooms cover all the bases, and baths are modern. The hotel is away from the noisy center; a hotel shuttle runs frequently. ⊠ *rte. de la Prairie, CH-3962 Montana* ☎ *027/4854141* 🖷 *027/4854142* ⊕ *www.prairie.ch* ⤺ *30 rooms* ৬ *Restaurant, Stübli, in-room data ports, cable TV, pool, billiards, Ping-Pong, bar, parking (fee)* ⊟ *AE, DC, MC, V* ¶◯¶ *BP.*

$$ 🔲 **Le Mont-Paisible.** One of the hotel directors, an architect, lends his design expertise and eye for interiors to this lookout lodge, which takes in the sweep of Valaisan mountains. Slate floors, colorful stenciled furniture, and a raised-hearth fireplace set a sophisticated yet rustic mood. Paneled rooms with built-in furniture and a small sitting area are well thought out. The terrific location is away from the village hubbub but near the Violettes cable car station. ⊠ *chemin du Mont-Paisible, CH-3962 Montana* ☎ *027/4802161* 🖷 *027/4817792* ⊕ *www. montpaisible.ch* ⤺ *40 rooms* ৬ *Restaurant, Stübli, in-room data ports, in-room safes, cable TV, pool, sauna, bar, free parking* ⊟ *AE, DC, MC, V* ¶◯¶ *BP.*

Nightlife

BARS & DANCING If you've ever wondered what Salvador Dalí would have produced if he'd illustrated a vodka ad, then head for poster-filled **Absolut** (☎ 027/4816596), a Crans nightclub where martini-swilling and swaying don't get started until after 11 PM. The dance floor buzzes at **Barocke** (☎ 079/2211635), around the corner from Absolut, in Crans. If it's barhopping that interests you, **Punch** (☎ 027/4812083), in Crans's Plaza Restaurant, is a hot Cuban-theme venue. Up in Montana, the small but convivial **Amadeus** (☎ 027/4812985), beneath the Olympic Hotel, is a popular après-ski venue with the young crowd. **Le Tirbouchon** (☎ 027/4802608) is a chummy little Montana wine bar where you can catch up on regional vintages.

CASINO Roulette, blackjack, poker, and an abundance of slot machines are among the games you can play at the high-stakes **Casino Crans-Montana** (☎ 027/4859040), in Montana. You can also just stop in for a drink or dinner, as there is no pressure to play. The casino is open 3 PM–3 AM, but you'll need your passport for admission.

Sports & the Outdoors

BICYCLING The Tour de Suisse and other top-name bike competitions pass through the streets during racing season. Serious amateur mountain bikers can test the obstacle course set up in the parking lot of the Crans-Cry-d'Err cable car or the downhill practice run. Cycling enthusiasts find a full range of clothing and bike rentals at **Avalanche Pro Shop** (✉ Montana ☎ 027/4802424). **Montana Sports** (☎ 027/4812288) is a convenient shop, providing bikes for rent and information about the eight marked trails that radiate from the resort, as well as the lifts to use to gain altitude without pedaling.

BOATING **Lac Grenon and Lac Moubra,** two crystalline lakes near the connected villages, are filled with pedal boats and windsurfers on long summer days. Rentals are available at shoreside kiosks.

GOLF With three in-town courses (one 18-hole, two 9-hole), this is a golfer's destination. One of the 9-hole courses was designed by Jack Nicklaus; the full course, designed by and named for Severiano Ballesteros, is a challenge. A driving range and video simulator help even the best handicappers improve their strokes. For more information, contact **Golf Club Crans** (☎ 027/4859797), the organization that oversees all the golf courses in town.

SWIMMING If your hotel doesn't have a swimming pool or wellness center, trek over to **Club Hotel Valaisia** (✉ Montana ☎ 027/4812612). The lower-level complex, which is open to the public, has a large saltwater pool with jets and currents, hot tubs, and cold plunges. Reserve time for a sauna, steam, and massage.

TENNIS **Centre de Congrès & Sports** (✉ Crans ☎ 027/4811615) has five indoor and two outdoor tennis courts as well as squash courts. **Centre de Tennis** (✉ Montana ☎ 027/8415014) calls itself the largest tennis center in the Alps, with five indoor and six outdoor clay courts. Both offer private and group lessons.

en route Split between the towns of Sierre/Siders and Salquenen/Salgesch, the **Musée Valaisan de la Vigne et du Vin** (Valaisan Vine and Wine Museum) offers a two-part discovery of grape growing and wine making. To follow the process in order, start in Salgesch and conclude in Sierre. A walking path through the vineyards connects exhibits housed in a winemaker's home and merchant's villa, which also has a restaurant and tasting shop. ✉ *Château de Villa, 4 rue Ste-Catherine, Sierre* ☎ *027/4551986* ✉ *Zumofenhaus, Salgesch* ☎ *027/4564525* ⊕ *www.museevalaisanduvin.ch* ✄ *5 SF* ☉ *Villa daily 10:30–1 and 4:30–8:30; Zumofenhaus Mar.–Oct., Tues.–Sun. 2–5; Nov. and Dec., Fri.–Sun. 2–5.*

Val d'Anniviers

25 km (16 mi) south of Sierre.

If you drive east of Sierre and south of the Rhône, following signs for Vissoie, you enter a wild and craggy valley called Val d'Anniviers. The name is said to come from its curious and famous (among anthropologists, at least) nomads, known in Latin as *anni viatores* (year-round travelers). If you don't have time to follow the lengthy gorge to its end, climb the switchback road to the tiny village of **St-Luc** for a taste of rural life

A TRAIL OF TWO CULTURES

THE LINE BETWEEN FRENCH and German settlements in the Valais (also known as Wallis) is imperceptible. At a restaurant a server may speak French to one group of diners and German to the next. It's called "bi-lang." Locals drop in and out of languages at the drop of a chapeau (or hut), even if one language prevails as their native tongue.

On the wine trail that's called the sentier viticole at one end and the rebweg at the other, you cross that imaginary boundary somewhere between the Walliser Reb und Weinmuseum and the Musée Valaisan de la Vigne et du Vin, which comprise a museum dedicated to wine and wine growing. The two parts of this museum complement each other and the two cultures, as do the towns in which they are located: Salquenen and Sierre in French, Salgesch and Siders, respectively, in German. (You may choose to start at either end of the trail, though to follow the wine-growing and wine-making processes in order, you'll have to begin your journey in Salgesch/Salquenen.)

Germanic roots are visible in the converted farmhouse museum, the Zumofenhaus, in Salgesch. The multilevel, double-gabled structure has low rooms and is built of stucco and worn timbers in a style found in Bernese villages on the other side of the mountains. The size and comfort of the vineyard owner's home—including a basement press and cave and upper and lower family quarters—indicates that he was successful. Exhibits here focus on the agriculture of the vineyard, including the terroir (soil), cultivation techniques, and seasonal chores.

Outside the museum a well-marked trail (6–7 km [4 mi]) leads past current growers' homes into the vineyard. Here panels explain the grape varieties in the long rows of vines, which are shored up by trellises and stone walls. Traditional varietals pinot noir, Chasselas, and gamay, long the mainstays of Valaisan wine production, are being eased out by Humagne Rouge, Humagne Blanche, Petite Arvine, Amigne, Syrah, and lesser-known Malviosie, Cornalin, and Marsanne Blanche. Some of these grape varieties are nurtured in small isolated plots, and, ironically, much of the old rootstock came from the United States following a phylloxera epidemic.

The path dips downhill into a forested nature preserve along the Gorge Raspille, filled with boulders brought down from jagged ridgelines. Unusual pyramidlike formations emerge on a chalky wall, and a network of channels used to feed the hot vineyard floor fans out from the streambed. The agricultural zone becomes mixed with smaller villages as the trail nears its end.

The turreted entry and architecture of Château de Villa is decidedly French. It's an estate home of grand proportions with gardens and salons converted into a restaurant that serves typically Valaisan dishes. The actual wine museum is housed in the manor's outbuildings. At this end of the trail, the focus is on winemaking. Here you can see a collection of presses and exhibits on vinification processes and cellar storage.

The whole experience takes about three or four hours, two of which are spent on the walk. In that short period, you will have made the transition from German to French culture without knowing exactly where you crossed the invisible border. Since wine is the universal language, a tasting at L'Oenotheque (the wine store) is the perfect conclusion. Santé or Gesundheit, whichever toast you prefer.

and celestial viewing at the observatory. In summer you can continue down a narrow forest road to **Grimentz,** with the Weisshorn dominating the views. With a population of 370, this ancient 13th-century village has preserved its weathered-wood houses and mazots in its tiny center. **Zinal,** farther into the valley, is another isolated mountaineering center with well-preserved wood houses and mazots. A stopover in any one of these windswept mountain hideouts to walk, climb, ski, or relax by the fire is a reward.

Where to Stay & Eat

★ **$$** ✕⊞ **De Moiry.** This family-run country inn is draped in a profusion of geraniums in summertime and bundled in snowbanks in winter. Rooms are walled in pine and larch, with carved furniture and mounds of white linen on the beds. Hikers and skiers gather on the porch or near the stone hearth in the dining room ($–$$) for beer and hearty regional fare. Ask the owner, who's an experienced mountain guide and photographer, to show you some of his work; it will leave you breathless. ⊠ *CH-3961 Grimentz* ☎ *027/4751144* 🖷 *027/4752823* ⊕ *www.hoteldemoiry.ch* ⇔ *16 rooms* ⚹ *Restaurant, cable TV* 🖃 *AE, DC, MC, V* ⊺◎⊺ *BP.*

Leukerbad

❼ *21 km (13 mi) northeast of Sierre.*

At 4,628 feet, Leukerbad is Europe's highest spa village; travelers have been ascending to this Alpine retreat for centuries to take the curative waters and fill their lungs with cleansing mountain air. With 90 km (43 mi) of downhill and cross-country runs of varying difficulty, including some used for World Cup training and testing, Leukerbad is a pleasant alternative to the larger resorts, though it doesn't compete with the top names. However, Leukerbad has rejuvenating hot mineral pools, which are soothing for après-ski. The Torrent gondola whisks skiers to slopes; a one-day ski pass including a visit to one of the public spas is 62 SF; a six-day pass is 314 SF. Without the spa visit, ski passes cost 44 SF and 223 SF, respectively.

Summer brings hikers who love the combination of trekking and soaking. High-altitude crossings via the Gemmi Pass go back to 500 BC. The ancient connection between the Valais and the Berner Oberland can be traversed easily in a day.

Calcium sulphite hot springs flow beneath the village, filling stone troughs with warm vapor, keeping thoroughfares free of snow, and circulating to private tubs and public pools daily. In the late 1960s an arthritis and rheumatism treatment facility was established, but it has since been overshadowed by upscale wellness hotels and sports clinics. Don't forget to drink a glass of water from the tap, which is touted to have added health benefits.

The two largest bath facilities in Leukerbad are Burgerbad and Alpentherme. Both have pools, fountains, whirlpools, jets, and sprays of thermal waters at a temperature of 35°C (100°F). Towels and robes can be rented at the reception desk.

The multilevel **Burgerbad,** with both indoor and outdoor pools, resembles an aqua park and is often packed with families clad in multicolor swim gear. The facility also has exercise rooms, a sauna, solarium, and snack bar. ⊠ *Rathausstr.* ☎ *027/4722020* ⊕ *www.burgerbad.ch* 🖘 *22 SF* ⊘ *Sun.–Thurs. 8–8, Fri. and Sat. 8 AM–9 PM.*

★ Sporting expansive Palladian windows set in marble, the **Lindner Alpentherme** looks like a temple perched on the hill. It has facilities similar to the Bugerbad but in a more sophisticated setting. Annexes contain a beauty center, medical complex, and shopping arcade that includes a pharmacy specializing in natural remedies, *confiserie* (pastry shop), and juice bar. The unique spa treatment here is the *Bain Romano-Irlandais* (Roman-Irish bath), a two-hour succession of hot and cold soaks and vapor treatments. Massage, herbal wraps, scrubs, and medical consultations are also on the menu. Children under six aren't allowed at this spa. ⊠ *Dorfpl.* ☎ *027/4721010* 🖘 *36 SF* ⊘ *Mon.–Thurs. 8–7, Fri. and Sat. 8–8.*

Where to Stay & Eat

$$-$$$$ ✕🖾 **Lindner Alpenhof.** Two hotels, Maison Blanche and the Hotel de France, are merged under one banner. The more regal Maison Blanche, which hosts reception for both, has guest rooms and salons that take a contemporary approach, using wheat and sage to create a soothing mood. Across the plaza the de France imitates the village's Alpine roots with knotty woods and gingham checks. Alpentherme, the village's posh bath and spa complex, is under the same ownership, and an underground walkway permits you to tread to your appointment in robe and slippers. Packages include admission and treatments. Restaurant choices follow the ambience of each location: glitzy hotel dining room ($$$–$$$$) and convivial brasserie ($$–$$$). ⊠ *Dorfpl., CH-3954* ☎ *027/4721000* 🖶 *027/4721001* ⊕ *www.lindnerhotels.ch* 🖘 *123 rooms, 12 suites & 2 restaurants, in-room safes, minibars, cable TV, 2 tennis courts, indoor-outdoor pool, health club, spa, piano bar, parking (fee)* ⊟ *MC, V* ⦿¶ *MAP.*

★ **$-$$$** ✕🖾 **Waldhaus Grichting.** This is the prototypical *relais de campagne* (country inn): honey-color wood, cheerful rooms, and a vivacious proprietress. Set on a forested hillside convenient to both the Alpentherme and the Torrent station, this expanded chalet seems more like a private home than a hotel. The Stübli ($–$$) attracts locals for raclette and the daily special, and hotel guests are treated to a six-course meal in the dining room ($$–$$$), included in the price of the room. Pool and spa facilities are shared with a nearby sister hotel. ⊠ *On the Promenade, CH-3954* ☎ *027/4703232* 🖶 *027/4704525* ⊕ *www.grichting-hotels.ch* 🖘 *16 rooms & Restaurant, Stübli, cable TV, bar, parking (fee)* ⊟ *MC, V* ⦿¶ *MAP.*

ALPINE ZENTRUM

Immediately east of Sierre, you'll notice a sharp change: *vals* become *tals,* and the sounds you overhear at your next pit stop are no longer the mellifluous tones of the Suisse Romande but the lilting, guttural Swiss-

German dialect called Wallisertiitsch, a local form of Schwyzerdütsch. Welcome to Wallis (*vahl*-is), the Germanic end of Valais. This sharp demographic frontier can be traced back to the 6th century, when Alemannic tribes poured over the Grimsel Pass and penetrated as far as Sierre. Here the middle-class cuisine changes from steak frites to veal and *Rösti* (hash brown potatoes).

Zermatt

▶ **8**
Fodor'sChoice
★
29 km (18 mi) south of Visp, plus a 10-km (6-mi) train ride from Täsch.

Despite its fame—which stems from that mythic mountain, the Matterhorn, and from its excellent ski facilities—Zermatt is a resort with its feet on the ground. It protects its regional quirks along with its wildlife and its tumbledown mazots, which crowd between glass-and-concrete chalets like old tenements between skyscrapers. Streets twist past weathered-wood walls, flower boxes, and haphazard stone roofs until they break into open country that slopes, inevitably, uphill. Despite the crowds, you're never far from the wild roar of the silty river and the peace of a mountain path.

In the mid-19th century, Zermatt was virtually unheard of; the few visitors who came to town stayed at the vicarage. Along with the vicar, a chaplain named Joseph Seiler persuaded his little brother, Alexander, to start an inn. Opened in 1854 and named the Hotel Monte Rosa, it's still one of five Seiler hotels in Zermatt. In 1891, the cog railway between Visp and Zermatt took its first summer run and began disgorging tourists with profitable regularity—though it didn't plow through in wintertime until 1927. Today the town remains a car-free resort (there's a reason for those carriages). If you're traveling primarily by car, you can park it in the long-term lot in Täsch, where you catch the train into Zermatt.

Fodor'sChoice
★
Hordes of package-tour sightseers push shoulder to shoulder to get yet another shot of the **Matterhorn** (14,685 feet). Called one of the wonders of the Western world, the mountain deserves the title, though it has become an almost self-parodying icon, like the Eiffel Tower or the Empire State Building. Its peculiar snaggletooth form, free from competition from other peaks on all sides, rears up over the village, larger than life and genuinely awe-inspiring. As you leave the train station and weave through pedestrian crowds, aggressive electric taxi carts, and aromatic horse-drawn carriages along the main street, Bahnhofstrasse, you're assaulted on all sides by Matterhorn images—on postcards, sweatshirts, calendars, beer steins, and candy wrappers—though not by the original, which is obscured by resort buildings (except from the windows of pricier hotel rooms). But break past the shops and hotels onto the main road into the hills, and you'll reach a slightly elevated spot where you'll probably stop dead in your tracks. There it is at last, its twist of snowy rock blinding in the sun, weathered mazots scattered romantically at its base. Surely more pictures are taken from this spot than from anywhere else in Switzerland.

It was Edward Whymper's spectacular—and catastrophic—conquest of the Matterhorn, on July 14, 1865, that made Zermatt a household word. Whymper stayed at the Hotel Monte Rosa the nights before his departure and there named his party of seven for the historic climb: Michel Croz, a French guide; old Peter Taugwalder and his son, young Peter, local guides; Lord Francis Douglas, a 19-year-old Englishman; Douglas Hadow; the Reverend Charles Hudson; and Whymper himself. They climbed together, pairing "tourists," as Whymper called the Englishmen, with experienced locals. They camped at 11,000 feet and by 10 AM had reached the base of the mountain's famous hook. Wrote Whymper of the final moments:

The higher we rose the more intense became the excitement. The slope eased off, at length we could be detached, and Croz and I, dashing away, ran a neck-and-neck race, which ended in a dead heat. At 1:40 PM, the world was at our feet, and the Matterhorn was conquered!

Croz pulled off his shirt and tied it to a stick as a flag, one that was seen in Zermatt below. They stayed at the summit one hour, then prepared for the descent, tying themselves together in an order agreed on by all. Croz led, then Hadow, Hudson, Lord Douglas, the elder Taugwalder, then the younger, and Whymper, who lingered to sketch the summit and leave their names in a bottle.

I suggested to Hudson that we should attach a rope to the rocks on our arrival at the difficult bit, and hold it as we descended, as an additional protection. He approved the idea, but it was not definitely decided that it should be done.

They headed off, "one man moving at a time; when he was firmly planted the next advanced," Whymper recalled.

Croz . . . was in the act of turning around to go down a step or two himself; at this moment Mr. Hadow slipped, fell against him, and knocked him over. I heard one startled exclamation from Croz, then saw him and Mr. Hadow flying downward; in another moment Hudson was dragged from his steps, and Lord Douglas immediately after him. All this was the work of a moment. Immediately we heard Croz's exclamation, old Peter and I planted ourselves as firmly as the rocks would permit; the rope was taut between us, and the jerk came on us both as on one man. We held; but the rope broke midway between Taugwalder and Lord Francis Douglas. For a few seconds we saw our unfortunate companions sliding downward on their backs, and spreading out their hands, endeavoring to save themselves. They passed from our sight uninjured, disappeared one by one, and fell from precipice to precipice on to the Matterhorn glacier below, a distance of nearly 4,000 feet in height. From the moment the rope broke it was impossible to help them. So perished our comrades!

A "sharp-eyed lad" ran into the Hotel Monte Rosa to report an avalanche fallen from the Matterhorn summit; he had witnessed the deaths of the four mountaineers. The body of young Lord Douglas was never recovered, but the others lie in little cemeteries behind the park near the village church, surrounded by scores of other failed mountaineers, including an American whose tomb bears the simple epitaph I CHOSE TO CLIMB.

In summer the streets of Zermatt fill with sturdy, weathered climbers, state-of-the-art ropes and picks hanging at their hips. They continue to tackle the peaks, and climbers have mastered the Matterhorn literally thousands of times since Whymper's disastrous victory.

Zermatt lies in a hollow of meadows and trees ringed by mountains—among them the broad **Monte Rosa** and its tallest peak, the **Dufourspitze** (at 15,200 feet, the highest point in Switzerland)—of which visitors hear relatively little, so all-consuming is the cult of the Matterhorn.

It's quite simple to gain the broader perspective of high altitudes without risking life or limb. A train trip on the **Gornergrat–Monte Rose Bahn** functions as an excursion as well as ski transport. Part of its rail system was completed in 1898, and it's the highest open-air rail system in Europe (the tracks to the Jungfraujoch, though higher, bore through the face of the Eiger). It connects out of the main Zermatt train station and heads sharply left, at a right angle to the track that brings you into town. Its stop at the **Riffelberg,** at 8,469 feet, offers wide-open views of the Matterhorn. Farther on, from **Rotenboden,** at 9,246 feet, a short downhill walk leads to the **Riffelsee,** which obligingly provides photographers with a postcard-perfect reflection of the famous peak. At the end of the 9-km (5½-mi) line, the train stops at the summit station of **Gornergrat** (10,266 feet), and passengers pour onto the observation terraces to take in the majestic views of the Matterhorn, Monte Rosa, Gorner Glacier, and an expanse of scores of peaks and 24 other glaciers. Make sure to bring warm clothes, sunglasses, and sturdy shoes, especially if you plan to ski or hike down. ⊠ *Zermatt station* ☎ *027/ 9214711* 🖃 *67 SF round-trip, 34 SF one way* ☉ *Departures daily every 24 mins, 7–6.*

To get a real sense of the climber's risk and life in this high-altitude region, visit the **Alpine Museum** behind the ski and snowboard school. The personal accounts of local docents liven up the displays of antiquated equipment and clothing, a farmer's cottage interior, and stuffed and mounted animals. ☎ *027/9674100* 🖃 *8 SF* ☉ *June, Sept., and Oct., daily 10–noon and 4–6; July and Aug., daily 10–noon and 3–6; Nov.–May, Mon.–Sat. 4:30–6:30.*

Skiing

Zermatt's skiable terrain lives up to its reputation: the 70 lift installations are capable of moving well above 50,000 skiers per hour to reach its approximately 400 km (248 mi) of marked pistes—if you count those of Cervinia in Italy. Among the lifts are the cable car that carries skiers up to an elevation of 12,746 feet on the Klein Matterhorn, the small Gornergratbahn that creeps up to the Gornergrat, and a subway through an underground tunnel that gives more pleasure to ecologists than it does to sun-loving skiers.

This royal plateau has several less-than-perfect features, however, not least of which is the separation of the skiable territory into three sectors. **Sunegga-Blauherd-Rothorn** culminates at an elevation of 10,170 feet. **Gornergrat-Stockhorn** (11,155 feet) is the second. The third is the region dominated by the **Klein Matterhorn,** which goes to Italy; to go from this sector to the others, you must return to the bottom of the valley and lose considerable time crossing town to reach the lifts to the other elevations. The solution is to ski for a whole day in the same area, especially during high season. On the other hand, thanks to snowmaking machines and the eternal snows of the Klein Matterhorn, Zermatt is said to guarantee skiers 7,216 feet of vertical drop no matter what the snowfall—an impressive claim. Gravity Park, a snowboarding center on Theodul glacier below the Klein Matterhorn, has pipes, kickers, and rails to thrill. A one-day lift ticket costs 64 SF; a six-day pass costs 318 SF. Ask for the hands-free "Smart Card" or "Swatch Access Key" with computer chip gate activation and billing. A **ski and snowboard school** (✉ Skischulbüro, Bahnhofstr. ☎ 027/9662466) operates from mid-December until April and in July and August.

Where to Stay & Eat

Many Zermatt hotels, especially larger ones, decide on a year-by-year basis to close during low season, which lasts from "melt-down" (anywhere from late April to mid-June) until "preseason" (November through mid-December). If you plan to travel during the low season, be sure to call ahead. Summer can be more popular than the winter ski season, with rates and availability to match.

$–$$$ ✕ **Findlerhof.** Whether for long lunches between sessions on the slopes
Fodor'sChoice or for a panoramic break on an all-day hike, this mountain restaurant
★ is ideal. It's perched in tiny Findeln, between the Sunnegga and Blauherd ski areas; its Matterhorn views are astonishing. The food is decidedly fresh and creative. Franz and Heidi Schwery tend their own Alpine garden to provide lettuces for their salads and berries for vinaigrettes and hot desserts. The fluffy *Matterkuchen*, a bacon and leek quiche, will fortify you for the 30- to 40-minute walk down to the village. ✉ *Findeln* ☎ *027/9672588* ▭ *MC, V* ☻ *Closed May–mid-June and mid-Oct.–Nov.*

$–$$$ ✕ **Grill-Room Stockhorn.** The moment you step across the threshold into this low-slung, two-story restaurant decked with mountaineering memorabilia, tantalizing aromas of cheese melting and meat roasting on the open grill should sharpen your appetite. This is a great place to fortify yourself with regional dishes. The service and the clientele are equally lively. ✉ *Hotel Stockhorn, Riedstr. 11* ☎ *027/9671747* ▭ *AE, MC, V* ☻ *Closed mid-May–mid-June and Oct.*

★ **$–$$** ✕ **Zum See.** In a hamlet (little more than a cluster of mazots) of the same name, this restaurant turns out inventive meals that merit acclaim. Although it's in the middle of nowhere, it overflows until late afternoon with diners sunning on the terrace or packed into the 400-year-old log house. (The quickest way to get here is to walk or ski down from Furi.) Hosts Max and Greti Mennig masterfully prepare such daily specials as venison salad with wild mushrooms and handmade tortelloni with spinach ricotta filling. The selection of wines and brandies sets skiers aglow. ✉ *Zum See* ☎ *027/9672045* ⚞ *Reservations essential* ▭ *MC, V* ☻ *Closed mid-Apr.–June and Oct.–mid-Dec. No dinner.*

$–$$ ✕ **Whymperstube.** At this little restaurant in the Hotel Monte Rosa, plates of melted raclette and bubbling pots of fondue are delivered to tightly packed tables by an agile waitstaff. Imagine the climbers' stories that must have echoed within these walls. In the winter season, the place stays open until 1 AM. ✉ *Bahnhofstr. 80* ☎ *027/9672296* ▭ *AE, DC, MC, V.*

¢–$$ ✕ **Elsie's Bar.** This tiny log cabin of a ski haunt, directly across from the Zermatt church, draws an international crowd that selects from an extensive list of aged scotches and mixed cocktails. Light meals include cheese dishes, oysters, escargots, and would you believe spaghetti with caviar and crème fraîche? ✉ *Kirchepl. 16* ☎ *027/9672431* ▭ *AE, DC, MC, V* ☯ *Closed May and mid-Oct.–mid-Nov.*

$$$$ ✕▣ **Grand Hotel Schöegg.** From its position above the valley floor, this Relais & Chateaux affiliate captures some of the village's premiere views. The interiors cleave to elegance, with woods rubbed to a high sheen, ornately painted ceilings, and rich fabrics. The Restaurant Gourmetstübli ($$–$$$) is one of Zermatt's haute dining addresses; look for au courant dishes like rabbit ravioli with fig beurre blanc or lobster with soy butter, bok choy, and Chinese noodles. ✉ *Riedwg. 35, CH-3920* ☎ *027/9663434* 🖶 *027/9663435* ⊕ *www.relaischateaux.ch* ↩ *37 rooms, 2 suites ♨ 2 restaurants, in-room safes, minibars, cable TV, gym, hot tub, sauna, Turkish bath, 2 bars* ▭ *AE, DC, MC, V* ☯ *Closed late Apr.–late May, Oct., and Nov.* ⧖ *MAP.*

$$$$ ✕▣ **Julen.** The decor here happily shuns regional kitsch. Instead, rooms have a Bavarian style: century-old spruce-wood decor paired with primary-color carpets and silk curtains. Each suite is equipped with a green-tile stove. A three-floor wellness center includes an elaborate Roman bath where you can indulge in various therapies. The main restaurant ($$) offers international cuisine, and the welcoming Stübli ($–$$) serves unusual dishes prepared with lamb from local family-owned flocks. ✉ *Riedstr. 2, CH-3920* ☎ *027/9667600* 🖶 *027/9667676* ⊕ *www.zermatt.ch/julen* ↩ *27 rooms, 5 suites ♨ 2 restaurants, Stübli, minibars, cable TV, pool, gym, sauna, spa* ▭ *AE, DC, MC, V* ⧖ *MAP.*

★ $$$$ ✕▣ **Mont Cervin Hotel & Residences.** Part of the Seiler dynasty, this luxurious, urbane hotel isn't grandiose in either scale or attitude. Built in 1852, it's unusually low-slung for a grand hotel. Rooms are decorated with tasteful stripes and plaids in primary colors; many have Matterhorn views. The Residence, across the street, offers spacious apartments. The main restaurant ($$$) has a light, modern ambience with dishes to match, including grilled tuna with coconut milk and coriander. There's also a more casual dining option ($–$$). Reserve covered parking and transportation from Täsch. ✉ *Bahnhofstr. 31, CH-3920* ☎ *027/9668888* 🖶 *027/9688899* ⊕ *www.seilerhotels.ch* ↩ *87 rooms, 31 suites, 15 apartments ♨ 2 restaurants, in-room safes, minibars, cable TV, indoor pool, gym, hair salon, sauna, spa, piano bar, meeting rooms, no-smoking rooms* ▭ *AE, DC, MC, V* ☯ *Closed May–mid-June, Oct., and Nov.* ⧖ *MAP.*

$$$ ✕▣ **Pollux.** This modern, small-scale hotel is simple and tidy, with straightforward rooms trimmed in pine and leatherette. Though none of its windows looks onto the Matterhorn, its position directly on the main pedestrian shopping street puts you in the heart of resort activities. The restaurant ($$) is based on a village square, with garden furniture and a central fountain; an appealing, old-fashioned Stübli ($–$$) draws locals for its low-price lunches, snacks, and Valaisan cheese

dishes. Its popular T-Bar disco is always packed. ⊠ *Bahnhofstr. 28, CH-3920* ☎ *027/9664000* 🖷 *027/9664001* ⊕ *www.reconline.ch/pollux* ⇝ *33 rooms* ᗡ *Restaurant, Stübli, cable TV, sauna, bar, dance club, meeting rooms* ☰ *AE, DC, MC, V* ⦿ *BP.*

$$$$ ⊡ **Hotel Monte Rosa.** Alexander Seiler founded his first hotel in the core of this historic building, expanding it over the years to its current size. (This was the home base of Edward Whymper when he conquered the Matterhorn in 1865.) Behind its graceful, shuttered facade you'll find an ideal balance between modern convenience and history in the burnished pine, flagstone floors, original ceiling moldings, fireplaces, and Victorian dining hall. The beige room decor is impeccable; southern views go quickly and cost more. The bar is an après-ski must. The pool and health facilities are shared with Mont Cervin. ⊠ *CH-3920* ☎ *027/9660333* 🖷 *027/9660330* ⊕ *www.seilerhotels.ch* ⇝ *40 rooms, 7 suites* ᗡ *Restaurant, in-room safes, minibars, cable TV, bar, meeting room* ☰ *AE, DC, MC, V* ⊙ *Closed mid-Apr.–late June and late Oct.–mid-Dec.* ⦿ *MAP.*

★ **$$$$** ⊡ **Riffelalp Resort 2222.** This grand mountaintop hotel, at 7,288 feet, has a stunning location amid fields and Alpine forest. Its direct views of the Matterhorn are especially breathtaking in the orange glow of early morning. The expansive complex includes a wine cellar with tastings and a converted chapel for concerts. The sumptuous rooms have Jacuzzi tubs and Bose sound systems. Even transit is made memorable, as you can ride a private restored tram to and from the train station. ⊠ *CH-3920* ☎ *027/9660555* 🖷 *027/9660550* ⊕ *www.seilerhotels.ch* ⇝ *63 rooms, 2 suites, 2 apartments* ᗡ *3 restaurants, in-room data ports, in-room safes, cable TV, indoor pool, sauna, steam room, billiards, bowling, ski storage, piano bar, cinema, concierge, meeting room, helipad* ☰ *AE, DC, MC, V* ⊙ *Closed mid-Apr.–mid-June and mid-Oct.–mid-Dec.* ⦿ *MAP.*

$$$–$$$$ ⊡ **Apartmenthotel Zurbriggen.** Sleeping under the roof of Olympic medalist Pirmin Zurbriggen's six-unit apartment house may not make you a better skier, but the view will elicit dreams of starting gates and downhill races. Flexible configurations with fully stocked kitchenettes can sleep a couple or expand to include a pack of friends. Near the cable car to Klein Matterhorn, this ultramodern glass structure has plenty of tech-amenities: flat-screen TV, ISDN lines, CD players. ⊠ *Schulhmattstr. 68, CH-3920* ☎ *027/9663838* 🖷 *027/9663839* ⊕ *www.zurbriggen.ch* ⇝ *6 apartments* ᗡ *In-room data ports, in-room safes, kitchenettes, minibars, cable TV, indoor pool, hot tub, sauna, steam room, mountain bikes, Internet* ☰ *AE, DC, MC, V* ⦿ *BP.*

$$ ⊡ **Romantica.** Among the scores of anonymously modern hotels along the Zermatt plain, this modest structure offers an exceptional location directly above the town center, no more than a block up a narrow, mazot-lined lane. Its tidy, bright gardens, game trophies, and granite stove give it personality, and the plain rooms benefit from big windows and balconies. You can also stay in one of the two *Walliserstadel,* tiny (but charming), 200-year-old huts in the hotel's garden. Keep in mind that this is a *garni* hotel (no restaurant), so only breakfast is served. ⊠ *Churm 21, CH-3920* ☎ *027/9662650* 🖷 *027/9662655* ⇝ *13 rooms, 1 apartment, 2 cabins* ᗡ *Cable TV, bar* ☰ *AE, DC, MC, V* ⦿ *BP.*

$$ ▦ **Touring.** Reassuringly traditional architecture; snug, sunny rooms full of pine; and an elevated position apart from town with excellent Matterhorn views make this an appealing, informal alternative to the chic downtown scene. Hearty daily menus are served to pension guests in the cozy dining room (the same menu is available in the Stübli). ⊠ *Riedstr. 45, CH-3920* ☎ *027/9671177* 🖷 *027/9674601* ⊕ *www. touring.buz.ch* ⇥ *20 rooms* ⚭ *Restaurant, Stübli, cable TV, sauna, bar, playground, meeting room* ☰ *MC, V* ⦿❘ *MAP.*

$–$$ ▦ **Alpenhotel.** If steep resort prices don't suit your budget, stay downhill in the village of Täsch. Train connections to Zermatt are easy, though you'll have to compete with guests required to leave their cars in nearby lots. This Best Western standard has tidy rooms with blond modular furniture and tile showers, plus an on-premises bakery. ⊠ *CH-3929 Täsch* ☎ *027/9662644* 🖷 *027/9662645* ⊕ *www.bestwestern.ch* ⇥ *29 rooms* ⚭ *Restaurant, cable TV, gym, sauna, bar* ☰ *AE, DC, MC, V* ⦿❘ *BP.*

$ ▦ **Mischabel.** One of the least expensive hotels in this pricey resort town, the Mischabel provides comfort, atmosphere, and a central situation few places can match at twice the price. South-facing balconies frame a perfect Matterhorn view—the higher the better. Creaky, homey, and covered with *Arvenholz* (Alpine pine) aged to the color of toffee, some rooms have a private bath whereas others have sinks only and share the linoleum-lined showers on every floor. A generous daily menu, for guests only, caters to families and young skiers on the cheap. ⊠ *Hofmattstr. 20, CH-3920* ☎ *027/9671131* 🖷 *027/9676507* ⊕ *www.zermatt. ch/mischabel* ⇥ *28 rooms, 3 with bath* ⚭ *Dining room; no room TVs* ☰ *MC, V* ⦿❘ *BP.*

Nightlife

GramPi's Bar (☎ 027/9677788), located in what locals call the Bermuda Triangle because of the concentration of nightspots, is a lively, young-people's bar, where you can get into the mood for dancing downstairs with a Lady Matterhorn cocktail. For a double dose of folklore song and dance, an evening at the **Schwyzer Stübli** (☎ 027/9676767), in the Hotel Schweizerhof, is full of rowdy sing-alongs and accordion music. The **T-Bar** (☎ 027/9674000), below the Pollux hotel, plays more varied music than the generic disco-pop of the ski resorts. At **Vernissage** (☎ 027/9676636), you can see old and current films in the screening room, have a drink at the bar, or check out the art scene at the gallery.

Sports & the Outdoors

HIKING With 400 km (248 mi) of marked trails available, you'll have plenty of options for exploring the mountains on foot. Outfitted with scarred boots, rucksacks, and walking sticks, trekkers strike out in all directions for daylong excursions ranging from easy to exhausting. Maps and route guides are available at the tourist office. Be sure to pack rain gear and a warm jacket along with sunscreen, as the weather changes quickly. Multiday lift passes will ease the way up and leave some change in your pocket for an after-hike beer.

MOUNTAIN BIKING Mountain biking is severely limited by Zermatt authorities to prevent interference with hiking on trails. About 25 km (15 mi) have been set aside, however. A map is available at the tourist office. Bikes can be rented at **Slalomsport** (☎ 027/9662366).

MOUNTAIN
CLIMBING
The Matterhorn is one of the world's most awe-inspiring peaks, and many visitors get the urge to climb it. However, this climb must be taken seriously; you have to be in top physical condition and have climbing experience to attempt the summit. You also need to spend 7–10 days acclimatizing once in the area. Less-experienced climbers have plenty of alternatives, though, such as a one-day climb of the Riffelhorn (9,774 feet) or a half traverse of the Breithorn (13,661 feet). For those wanting a challenge without such extreme altitudes, try a guided trip across the rugged Gorner gorge. For detailed information, advice, instruction, and climbing guides, contact the **Zermatt Alpin Center** (✉ Bahnhofstr. 58 ☎ 027/9662460 ⊕ www.zermatt.ch/alpincenter).

Shopping

Zermatt may be Switzerland's souvenir capital, offering a broad variety of watches, knives, and logo clothing. Popular folk crafts and traditional products include large, grotesque masks of carved wood, and lidded channes in pewter or tin, molded in graduated sizes; they're sold everywhere, even in grocery stores.

You'll especially see stores offering state-of-the-art sports equipment and apparel, from collapsible grappling hooks for climbers to lightweight hiking boots in brilliant colors to walking sticks—pairs of lightweight, spiked ski poles for hikers to add a bit of upper-body workout to their climb. **Baynard** (✉ Bahnhofpl. 2 ☎ 027/9664950 ✉ Bahnhofstr. 35 ☎ 027/9664960) has sporting-goods shops scattered throughout the village, including these two main branches. **Glacier Sport** (✉ Bahnhofstr. 19 ☎ 027/9681300) specializes in ski and climbing equipment and accessories.

Saas-Fee

 36 km (22 mi) south of Visp.

At the end of the switchback road from Saas-Grund lies a parking garage where visitors must abandon their cars for the length of their stay in Saas-Fee. But even by the garage you'll be amazed, for the view on arriving at this lofty (5,871 feet) plateau is humbling. (In true Swiss-efficient fashion, you can drop off your bags curbside and call an electric shuttle that will arrive to fetch you in the time it takes to park your car.)

Saas-Fee is at the heart of a circle of mountains, 13 of which tower to more than 13,120 feet, among them the **Dom** (14,908 feet), the highest mountain entirely on Swiss soil. The town lies in a deep valley that leaves no doubt about its source: it seems to pour from the vast, intimidating **Fee Glacier,** which oozes like icy lava from the broad spread of peaks above. *Fee* can be translated as "fairy," and although Saas-Fee itself is a tourist-saturated resort, the landscape could illustrate a fairy tale.

★ Carved into the Allalinhorn at 11,482 feet, an **Eis Pavillon** (ice cave), considered the largest in the world, combines fascinating construction with a dash of kitsch. Twenty-six feet below the ice pack, the cavernous facility provides an impressive view of the surreal, frozen environment inside glacial formations. There are ice sculptures, exhibits on glaciology and crevasse rescue, and even a chapel-like room for meditation, concerts, and art shows. The ticket for the cable car and underground funicular is pricey, but if you are up on the mountain, spring for the entrance fee and have a look below the frozen surface of the earth. ⊠ *Mittelallalin* ☎ *027/9571414* 🖼 *8 SF* ☉ *Daily 8–4.*

Skiing

The first glacier to be used for skiing here was the **Längfluh** (9,414 feet), accessed by gondola, then cable car. The run is magnificent, sometimes physically demanding, and always varied. From the Längfluh you can take a lift to reach *the* ski area of Saas-Fee, the **Felskinn-Mittelallalin** sector (9,840–11,480 feet). Felskinn harbors its own surprise: in order to preserve the land and landscape, the Valaisans have constructed a subterranean funicular, the Métro Alpin, which climbs through the heart of the mountain to Mittelallalin, that is, halfway up the Allalinhorn (13,210 feet). Tourists debark in a rotating restaurant noted more for the austere grandeur of its natural surroundings than for the quality of its food. Felskinn-Mittelallalin's exceptional site, its high elevation, its runs (15 km [9 mi]), and its ample facilities (cable car, funicular, and five ski lifts) have made Saas-Fee the number one summer-skiing resort in Switzerland. It's also one of two official European snowboard centers sanctioned by the International Snowboard Federation. Lifts don't connect with other resorts in the valley—Saas Almagel, Saas Balen, or Saas Grund. However, good days of skiing can be found a bus ride away, and hiking trails open in winter and summer link all four valleys. A one-day lift ticket costs 60 SF; a six-day pass costs 299 SF. A savings program for parents who buy six-day passes permits free skiing for children under 16.

Where to Stay & Eat

$–$$ ✕ **Restaurant Skihütte.** During high season, you'll have to be quick in order to snag a table on the sun-filled deck of this charming spot. A great location at the bottom of the lift and good Walliser favorites hold you for another beer and a few more rays. ☎ *027/9589280* ▭ *AE, MC, V.*

$$$$ ✕🖼 **Beau-Site.** A proud family with unyielding standards tends this elegant hotel. Interiors of patinated wood, stacked stone, and leaded glass give the look of a respected manor house. Guest rooms have baths with modern fixtures; furnishings tastefully mix antiques with the more modern. The elegant main restaurant ($$–$$$) rates as one of the most romantic around. Intimate dining of a different type can be found at La Ferme ($–$$), a low-slung rustic restaurant with a central woodstove. ⊠ *CH-3906* ☎ *027/9581560* 🖷 *027/9581565* ⊕ *www.beausite.org* ⤴ *15 rooms, 3 suites, 16 apartments* ♨ *3 restaurants, café, in-room safes, minibars, cable TV, indoor pool, hot tub, massage, sauna, bar* ▭*DC, MC, V* ℹ◍ *MAP.*

★ **$$$$** ✕🖼 **Waldhotel Fletschhorn.** Once a customhouse, this quiet, sophisticated *Landgasthof* (country inn) is set apart from the resort at the end of a forested lane. Pine paneling, antiques, and serene views mellow the rooms' ultramodern fittings and contemporary art. The restaurant's ($$–$$$$) innovative French cuisine is based on local products; savor choices such as rabbit fillet with truffle puree and dim sum of veal and shrimp in an Asian beurre blanc. Reservations are essential. ☒ *CH-3906* ☎ *027/9572131* 🖷 *027/9572187* ⊕ *www.fletschhorn.ch* ⇗ *15 rooms* ⟁ *Restaurant, cable TV, hot tub, sauna* ⊟ *AE, DC, MC, V* ⊗ *Closed late Apr.–early June and mid-Oct.–early Dec.* ⦿⟊ *BP.*

$$$$ 🎫 **Dom Hotel.** Follow the snowboarders who flock to Popcorn, a wildly popular bar and gear boutique, to find a place where a traditional exterior belies a funky interior. Contemporary furnishings in vibrant colors and unusual shapes fill the lobby lounge. The amply sized rooms with modular furniture all have TV-stereo combinations loaded with Sony PlayStations. ☒ *CH-3906* ☎ *027/9575101* 🖷 *027/9572300* ⊕ *www. uniquedom.com* ⇗ *40 rooms* ⟁ *Restaurant, cable TV, sauna, 2 bars, Internet* ⊟ *AE, DC, MC, V* ⦿⟊ *BP.*

$$$$ 🎫 **Ferienart Resort & Spa.** Switzerland's first *minergie* (low-energy) hotel is loaded with amenities—whirlpools in the guest rooms, a mock-glacier pool with a waterfall, a "wellness zone" with every sort of thermal and medicinal bath, and even an art gallery. The generously sized rooms have modern birch furnishings and granite countertops in the bath. Although the hotel is in the center of town, it still has panoramic views on all sides. ☒ *CH-3906* ☎ *027/9581900* 🖷 *027/9581905* ⊕ *www.ferienart.ch* ⇗ *83 rooms, 5 suites, 4 apartments* ⟁ *4 restaurants, café, in-room data ports, in-room safes, minibars, cable TV, pro shop, pool, gym, hair salon, massage, sauna, piano bar, nightclub* ⊟ *AE, DC, MC, V* ⦿⟊ *MAP.*

$$$–$$$$ 🎫 **Allalin.** Families will especially appreciate the flexibility and up-to-date design of the suites and rooms here, all with kitchen equipment and balconies. In high season guests usually pay half board and eat one meal per day in the restaurant—no great punishment, as the kitchen is surprisingly sophisticated—although a breakfast-only arrangement can be made. Built in 1928, the hotel feels warm, bright, and natural. It's on the hill just east of the town center and a block from the main parking, and all doubles but one have a spectacular southern or southeastern view. ☒ *CH-3906* ☎ *027/9571815* 🖷 *027/9573115* ⊕ *www.allalin.ch* ⇗ *16 rooms, 11 suites* ⟁ *Restaurant, café, in-room safes, kitchenettes, cable TV, sauna, bar* ⊟ *AE, DC, MC, V* ⦿⟊ *MAP.*

Nightlife & the Arts

BARS & DANCING A popular dance zone, **Art Club** (☎ 027/9581900) is located at the Ferienart Walliserhof hotel. The **Metropol Hotel** (☎ 027/9571001) hosts late-night revelers with mixed music sets at **Crazy Night Disco** and distilled spirits at the **Whiskey Lounge.** The price of some shots from among their 300 labels will cost as much as a lift ticket. People often squeeze into **Nesti's** (☎ 027/9572112), a perennial après-ski favorite. Snowboarders and a younger crowd congregate for brews at **Popcorn** (☎ 027/9574006).

MUSIC Like other Alpine resorts, Saas-Fee is not without echoes of symphonies and chorus groups during its summer months. Two festivals, the **International Alpine Music Festival** and **Música Romântica** please audiences in June and August. Bookings and ticket information are available through the tourist office.

Sports & the Outdoors

MOUNTAIN
CLIMBING

The **Swiss Mountaineering School** (☎ 027/9574464) conducts daily guided forays year-round; you can rent season-appropriate equipment. Another popular activity is gorge crossing, which uses safety cables and pulleys to traverse the valley's deep divide.

SLEDDING

Your stay won't be complete without a few runs on the **Feeblitz** (☎ 027/9573111), the curved and looped track of the *rodelbobbahn* (bobsled) near the Alpin Express cable car station.

SPORTS CENTER

The **Bielen Recreation Center** (☎ 027/9572475) has a four-lane swimming pool, children's pool, whirlpools, steam baths, sauna, solarium, table tennis, billiards, badminton, and two indoor-tennis courts.

BRIG & THE ALPINE PASSES

This region is the Grand Central Station of the Alps. All mountain passes lead to or through Brig, as traffic and rail lines pour in from Italy, the Ticino, central Switzerland, and the Berner Oberland. It is also a transit link for Paris, Brussels, London, and Rome. The Simplon, Nufenen, Grimsel, and Furka passes provide exit options and stunning vistas dependent on destination. Northeast of this critical junction, the spectacular Aletsch Glacier, the largest in Europe, straddles the cantons of Valais and Bern. The Rhône River becomes increasingly wild and silty until it meets its source in Gletsch, at the end of the valley called Goms.

Brig

🔟 *209 km (129 mi) southeast of Bern.*

A rail and road junction joining four cantons, this small but vital town has for centuries been a center of trade with Italy. Often overlooked as merely a transit point, the town has a legacy that can be appreciated in a couple of hours: a restored core with cobblestone streets, shops, cafés, and the main attraction, the elegant merchant's castle.

The fantastical **Stockalperschloss,** a massive baroque castle, was built between 1658 and 1678 by Kaspar Jodok von Stockalper, a Swiss tycoon who made his fortune in Italian trade over the Simplon Pass. Topped with three gilt onion domes and containing a courtyard lined by elegant Italianate arcades, it was once Switzerland's largest private home and is now restored. Group tours in English are available upon request. To get here from the station walk up Bahnhofstrasse to Sebastienplatz; then turn left onto Alte Simplonstrasse. ⊠ *Alte Simplonstr. 28* ☎ *027/9216030* 💷 *7 SF* ☉ *May–Oct., Tues.–Sun., guided tours at 10, 11, 2, 3, and 4 plus June–Sept. at 5.*

Simplon Pass

⑪ *23 km (14 mi) southeast of Brig.*

Beginning just outside Brig, this historic road meanders through deep gorges and wide, barren, rock-strewn pastures to offer increasingly beautiful views back toward Brig. At the summit (6,593 feet), the **Hotel Bellevue Simplon-Kulm** shares the high meadow with the **Simplon Hospitz** (Simplon Hospice), built 150 years ago at Napoléon's request and now owned by the monks of St. Bernard. Just beyond stands the bell-towered **Alt Spital,** a lodging built in the 17th century.

From the summit you can still see parts of the old road used by traders and Napoléon, and it's easy to imagine the hardships travelers faced at these heights. Look north toward the Bernese Alps and a portion of the massive Aletsch Glacier. Beyond the pass, the road continues through Italy, and it's possible to cut across the Italian upthrust and reenter Switzerland in the Ticino, near Ascona.

off the
beaten
path

SIMPLON TUNNEL – If you'd rather ride than drive, you can take a train through this tunnel, which starts above the eastern outskirts of Brig and runs nearly 20 km (12 mi) before ending in Italian daylight. The first of the twin tunnels—the world's longest railway tunnels—was started in 1898 and took six years to complete.

Aletsch

Fodor's Choice
★

13 km (8 mi) north of Brig.

Ice-capped peaks with small mountain resorts staggered up their spines rim the Aletsch, a glacier that shares its name with the area surrounding it, paralleling the valley floor. A variety of ecological zones—from deep, frozen expanses in the center to forests emerging at the fringes—are part of a wilderness region that is now firmly in the hands of conservationists, protected as a UNESCO international nature site. In contrast to these extreme expanses, sunny south-facing slopes are active with skiers and hikers staying in the villages of Riederalp, Bettmeralp, and Fiescheralp.

Villa Cassel, a turn-of-the-20th-century mansion, is the headquarters for **Pro Natura Zentrum Aletsch,** an environmental education center. It offers guided tours, glacier walks, conservation camps, expeditions to spot marmots and eagles, self-directed walks, an Alpine garden, and even dorm and private rooms for overnight stays. Some information is available in English; prices vary according to the activity. The center is in a hamlet on the pass above the village of Ried (where you leave your car). ✉ *Riederalp* ☎ *027/9286220* ⊕ *www.pronatura.ch/aletsch* ☉ *June–Oct., daily 9–6.*

Skiing

The three resorts of **Riederalp, Bettmeralp,** and **Fiescheralp** are connected by trails, lifts, and shuttle buses. There are 33 lifts and 83 km (52 mi) of runs, a quarter of which are expert and peak at 9,415 feet. A one-day lift ticket for access to the whole Aletsch ski area costs 44 SF; a six-day pass costs 211 SF. All of the essentials are in place in these picture-book villages, but don't expect lots of amenities, varied dining choices, or glitzy nightlife. Riederalp is best known as the home of Art Furrer, who became famous in the United States as one of the pioneers of freestyle ski-

CloseUp

ALL ABOUT ALETSCH

EUROPE'S LONGEST GLACIER—24 km (15 mi)—was at its longest 150 years ago but now recedes 100–165 feet a year. Concern about the recession of the earth's ice formations has made preserving the Aletsch Glacier internationally significant. So UNESCO designated a 250-square-km (97-square-mi) area around the glacier, shared between the cantons of Valais (77%) and Bern (23%), as a protected site. Generations ago, the Swiss sensed the need to safeguard the area and began placing parts in conservationist hands.

The glacier's starting point, Concordia Platz, is the confluence of three ice masses that move down from the Bernese Alps. Here the ice has been measured as deep as 2,952 feet—over twice as tall as the Empire State Building. Another magnificent formation, the Mäjelensee is a lake with icebergs floating on top, carved into the glacier field with walls of ice and stone. As the glacier's ice recedes, nature reclaims the land, first with moss and small plants, then forest. Pro Natura, the conservation organization that oversees the region, describes the process as "forest emerging from ice." Though some of the area's pine and larch are 600–700 years old, extreme conditions keep them short. Animals thought to be extinct thrive here; chamois, marten, badgers, lizards, and birds have adapted to the elevation and temperature.

Cable cars ferry tourists to ridge tops above Ried and Fiesch, where 360-degree views of the sweep of ice are framed by extraordinary peaks. You can see the Bernese Alps, including the Sphinx station on the Jungfraujoch called the "Top of Europe"; the Valaisan Alps; and even into Italy and France. Hiking trails lead to the glacier's edge, and guides take trekkers across parts of the ice field. All around are places to admire nature's grandeur and be grateful for its protection.

ing. His ski school, the **Skischule Forum Alpin** (☎ 027/9284488 ⊕ www.artfurrer.ch) is still up and running.

Where to Stay

$$$ 🖫 **La Cabane.** This down-to-earth garni hotel is a good option for a stay in the middle of the region. The Mattig family will warmly welcome you to their small, chalet-style lodge with tidy rooms and sunny balconies. ⊠ CH-3992 Bettmeralp ☎ 027/9274227 🖷 027/9274440 ⊕ www.bettmeralp.ch/lacabane ⟿ 12 rooms ᗜ Cable TV, sauna, steam room, bar ⊟ AE, DC, MC, V ⊘ Closed Easter–early July and Nov.–mid-Dec. ⫶◎⫶ BP.

en route   If the day is clear, grab the chance for a spectacular ride to the top of one of the lofty peaks that shadows the roadway by taking the **Fiesch cable car** (☎ 027/9712700) up to Eggishorn (9,303 feet). The panoramic views of Alps and glaciers will leave you breathless. As the cable car rotates 360 degrees, you can tick off famous Bernese and Valaisan peaks. The Jungfrau, Eiger, Matterhorn, and Dom are clearly visible, as are peaks that lie across the border in Italy and France.

Gletsch

⑬ *48 km (30 mi) northeast of Brig.*

Summer travelers may want to go the distance of the remote Goms region to the tiny resort of Gletsch, named for its prime attraction: the glacier that gives birth to the Rhône. From this aerie crossroad, the views of ice fields and mountain peaks are magnificent, but accommodations are scarce. Make an exit by descending into the Bernese Oberland over the scenic Grimsel Pass (7,101 feet), or continue higher to the Furka Pass (7,975 feet) to the central and western parts of the country.

If you want to go the old-fashioned way, take the **Furka Cogwheel Steam Railway**. After more than 20 years in storage, the Realp/Gletsch steam engine once again pulls itself up to the Gletsch glacier cog by cog, passing through fantastic Alpine scenery, over bridges, and through tunnels as it crosses the Furka Pass. A one-way trip takes an hour and a half. Board at Realp or Gletsch; you can return via shuttle bus for a change of pace (included in the round-trip ticket). ☎ *084/8000144* ⊕ *www.furka-bergstrecke.ch/eng* ⊠ *154 SF round-trip* ⊙ *July and Aug., daily; Sept., Fri.–Sun., depending on weather; departures at 2 (10:10 in Realp).*

Furka Pass

⑭ *11 km (7 mi) east of Gletsch, 59 km (37 mi) northeast of Brig.*

Making the final ascent of Valais by way of the Furka Pass, travelers have a choice to drive the stunning alpine highway or take the train. Be aware that even in summer, adverse weather can close this thoroughfare. From Oberwald, the rail line cuts through the heights with a 15-km (9-mi) tunnel to Realp before leading down to central Switzerland. Passengers and cars are loaded at this base, offering an attractive alternative for reluctant and weary drivers and those trying to save time. Transit time once on board the train is approximately 15 minutes.

Whether from a lookout point or train window, the views are spectacular. Stark moonscapes are punctuated by the occasional Spielbergian military operations—white-clad soldiers melting out of camouflaged hangars carved deep into solid-rock walls. Should you choose to drive, the sleek, broad highway that snakes down toward Andermatt shows Swiss Alpine engineering at its best.

VALAIS A TO Z

To research prices, get advice from other travelers, and book travel arrangements, visit www.fodors.com.

AIR TRAVEL

You can choose between two airports when flying to Valais: Geneva Cointrin or Unique Zürich.

AIRPORTS

Geneva's Cointrin serves international flights and is nearest the west (French) end of Valais; it's about two hours away by train or car. Unique Zürich brings you closer to the east (German) side, but the Alps are in the way; you must connect by rail tunnel or drive over one of the passes.

🖪 **Airport Information Cointrin Airport** ☎ 022/7177111. **Unique Zürich Airport** ☎ 0900/300313.

CAR TRAVEL

Valais is something of a dead end by nature: a fine expressway (A9) carries you in from Lac Léman, but to exit—or enter—from the east end, you must park your car on a train and ride through the Furka Pass tunnel to go north or take the train through the tunnel under the Simplon Pass to go southeast. (The serpentine roads over these passes are open in summer; weather permitting; the Simplon road stays open all year.) You also may cut through from or to Kandersteg in the Berner Oberland by taking a car train to Goppenstein or Brig. A summer-only road twists over the Grimsel Pass as well, heading toward Meiringen and the Berner Oberland or, over the Brünig Pass, to Luzern.

If you want to see the tiny back roads—and there's much to be seen off the beaten path—you'll need a car. The A9/9 expressway from Lausanne turns into a well-maintained highway at Sierre that continues on to Brig. Distances in the north and south valleys can be deceptive: apparently short jogs are full of painfully slow switchbacks and distractingly beautiful views. Both Zermatt and Saas-Fee are car-free resorts, though you can drive all the way to a parking lot at the edge of Saas-Fee's main street. Zermatt must be approached by rail from Täsch, the end of the line for cars (there's a central, secure, long-term parking lot and garage).

EMERGENCIES

There are standardized telephone numbers throughout Switzerland for emergencies.

🖪 **Ambulance** ☎ 144. **Fire** ☎ 118. **Late-night Pharmacies** ☎ 111. **Police** ☎ 117. **Roadside Assistance** ☎ 140.

SPORTS & THE OUTDOORS

HIKING This is one of the hiking capitals of Switzerland, and it's impossible to overstate the value of setting off on a mountain path through the sweet-scented pine woods and into the wide-open country above the timberline. The trails are wild but well maintained here, and the regional tourist office publishes a thorough map with planned and timed walking tours. Ask for *Sentiers valaisans;* it's written in English, French, and German.

SKIING There are a dizzying number of fantastic ski opportunities in this region. The Valais tourist office puts out a helpful winter sports guide (available in English) that includes lift maps, special offers, and information on cross-country skiing, snowshoeing, and other sports.

TOURS

Guided coach tours of Valais, including lodging and dining packages, are offered by Valais Incoming. Sion's Air-Glaciers has several itineraries out of Sion for groups of four or six who want a bird's-eye view of Valais—from a helicopter. Prices start at 360 SF for 10 minutes.

◢ Tour Operators Air-Glaciers ☎ 027/3291415. **Valais Incoming** ✉ 6 rue du Pré-Fleuri, Sion ☎ 027/3273599.

TRAIN TRAVEL

There are straightforward rail connections to the region by way of Lausanne to the west and Brig/Brigue to the east. The two are connected by one clean rail sweep that runs the length of the valley. In winter a special extension of the high-speed train from France, TGV Neige, terminates in Brig. (Information is available through the SBB.) Routes into the tributary valleys are limited, although most resorts are served by cheap and reliable postbuses running directly from train stations. The Brig-Visp-Zermatt Railway, a private railway system, runs from Brig to Visp with connections to Zermatt. The SBB provides 24-hour information about all rail service.

◢ Train Information SBB Information ☎ 0900/300300 ⊕ www.rail.ch.

VISITOR INFORMATION

The main tourist office for Valais is in Sion, but there are also local offices in other Valaisan towns.

◢ Local Tourist Offices Bettmeralp ✉ CH-3992 ☎ 027/9286060 ⊕ www.bettmeralp. ch. **Brig** ✉ Train station, CH-3900 ☎ 027/9216030 ⊕ www.brig.ch. **Crans-Montana** ✉ CH-3963 ☎ 027/4850404 ⊕ www.crans-montana.ch. **Leukerbad** ✉ CH-3954 ☎ 027/4727171 ⊕ www.leukerbad.ch. **Martigny** ✉ 9 pl. Centrale, CH-1920 ☎ 027/7212220 ⊕ www.martignytourism.ch. **Riederalp** ✉ CH-3987 ☎ 027/9286050 ⊕ www.riederalp. ch. **Saas-Fee** ✉ CH-3906 ☎ 027/9581858 ⊕ www.saas-fee.ch. **St-Maurice** ✉ CH-1890 ☎ 024/4854040 ⊕ www.st-maurice.ch. **Sion** ✉ pl. de la Planta, CH-1950 ☎ 027/3277727 ⊕ www.siontourism.ch. **Verbier** ✉ CH-1936 ☎ 027/7753888 ⊕ www.verbier. ch. **Zermatt** ✉ CH-3920 ☎ 027/9678100 ⊕ www.zermatt.ch.

◢ Regional Tourist Office Valais Main Cantonal Tourist Office ✉ 6 rue Pré-Fleuri, CH-1951 Sion ☎ 027/3273570 📠 027/3273571 ⊕ www.valaistourism.ch.

VAUD

LAUSANNE, MONTREUX, LES ALPES VAUDOISES

11

Updated by
Kay
Winzenried

IN JUST ONE REGION, you can experience a complete cultural, gastronomic, and scenic sweep of Switzerland. Vaud (pronounced Voh) has a stunning Gothic cathedral (Lausanne) and one of Europe's most evocative châteaux (Chillon), palatial hotels and weathered-wood chalets, sophisticated culture and ancient folk traditions, snowy Alpine slopes and balmy lake resorts, simple fondue and the finesse of some of the world's great chefs. Everywhere there are the roadside vineyards with luxurious rows of vines and rich, black loam.

This is the region of Lac Léman (Lake Geneva), a grand body of water graced by Lausanne and Montreux. The lake's romance—Savoy Alps looming across the horizon, steamers fanning across its surface, palm trees rustling along its shores—made it a focal point of the budding 19th-century tourist industry and an inspiration to the arts. In a Henry James novella, the imprudent Daisy Miller made waves when she crossed its waters unchaperoned to visit Chillon; Byron's Bonivard languished in chains in the fortress's dungeons. From their homes outside Montreux, Stravinsky wrote *The Rite of Spring* and Strauss his transcendent *Four Last Songs*. There are resorts, of course—Leysin, Villars, Château-d'Oex—but none so famous as to upstage the region itself.

Throughout the canton, French is spoken, and the temperament the Vaudoise inherited from the Romans and Burgundians sets them apart from their Swiss-German fellow citizens. It's evident in their humor, their style, and—above all—their love of their own good wine.

Exploring Vaud

Lac Léman is a graceful swelling in the Rhône River, which passes through the northern hook of the Valais and channels between the French and Vaudoise alps before breaking into the open at Bouveret, west of Villeneuve. The lake is shared by three of Switzerland's great French cities, grandes dames of the Suisse Romande: Lausanne, Montreux, and Geneva. Though the lake's southern shore lies in France's Haute-Savoie, the green hillsides of the north portion and the cluster of nearby Alps that looms over its east end are all part of the canton of Vaud.

About the Restaurants

Because of its sunny, scenic position, the Lac Léman shore draws weekenders and car tourists who speed along the waterfront highway, careening through cobbled wine towns in search of the perfect lunch. As in all great wine regions, *dégustation* (wine tasting) and *haute gastronomie* (refined cuisine) go hand in hand, and in inns and auberges throughout La Côte and Lavaux (the two stretches of vineyard-lined shore) you'll dine beside ascoted oenophiles who lower their half lenses to study a label and order a multicourse feast to complement their extensive tastings.

To experience Vaud's best cuisine, look for *déjeuners d'affaires* (business lunches), plats du jour, and prix-fixe menus, which can offer considerable savings over à la carte dining.

WHAT IT COSTS In Swiss francs				
	$$$$	$$$	$$	$	¢
MAIN COURSE	over 60	40–60	25–40	15–25	under 15

Prices are per person for a main course at dinner.

About the Hotels

It's a pleasure unique to Vaud to wake up, part floor-length sheers, and look out over Lac Léman to Mont Blanc. A series of 19th-century grand hotels with banks of balconied lake-view rooms were created to offer this luxury to such grand-tourists as Strauss, Twain, Stravinsky, and Henry James. Yet there's no shortage of charming inns offering similar views on an intimate scale. Up another 3,936 feet you'll find the antithesis to an airy lakefront inn: the cozy, honey-gold Alpine chalet, with down quilts in starched white envelopes, balustrade balconies with potted geraniums, and also panoramic views.

The hotels of Lausanne and Montreux are long on luxury and grace, and low prices are not easy to find. Especially at peak periods—Christmas–New Year's and June–August—it's important to book ahead. Many hotels have been increasing in-room facilities; direct phone and fax lines, data ports, safes, and business centers are now the rule rather than the exception. Small auberges in the villages along the lake and the vineyards offer traditional dishes and simple comforts. Up in the Pays-d'Enhaut and the Alps southeast of the lake, there are comfortable mountain hotels in all price ranges—though rates are naturally higher in the resorts themselves. Charges are generally not as steep as those in the Alpine resorts of Graubünden or Valais. At the **cantonal tourist office Web site** (⊕ www.lake-geneva-region.ch), you can scan hotel facilities and rates, then click to reserve.

WHAT IT COSTS In Swiss francs				
	$$$$	$$$	$$	$	¢
DOUBLE ROOM	over 350	250–350	175–250	100–175	under 100

Prices are for two people in a standard double room in high season, including tax and service.

Timing

The lake sparkles and clouds lift from Mont Blanc from spring to fall; November tends to be drizzly gray, and then winter brightens things up above the plain (as they call the flatter terrain surrounding the lake). Crowds monopolize Montreux and Chillon year-round but overwhelm it in July (jazz festival time) and August (Europe-wide vacations). It's worth aiming for concert and dance season in Lausanne: from September through May. Prime ski time in the Alpes Vaudoises is from late December through Easter, and prices go up accordingly. Remember that at these latitudes summer daylight extends until 9 PM, allowing you to pack a lot into one day; the reverse is true in winter.

Numbers in the text correspond to numbers in the margin and on the Vaud and Lausanne maps.

If you have 3 days

If time is limited, fly into Geneva Cointrin and drive the shore highway through **Coppet** ❶ ⌐ to **Nyon** ❸ to visit the Roman museum and medieval castle. Overnight in one of the lake's smaller towns before taking a full day to immerse yourself in the sights, shops, and streetside cafés of the region's largest city, 🖾 **Lausanne** ❽–㉑. On the next day, set out for the winding Corniche de la Vaud, visiting a *vignoble* (vineyard) or two in **Lutry** ㉒, **Cully** ㉓, Épesses, or Chexbres. You'll end up at the lakefront town of **Montreux** ㉕, with its fabled **Château de Chillon** ㉖.

If you have 5 days

Spend two days savoring 🖾 **Lausanne** ❽–㉑ ⌐ and its Old Town, museums, and hyperactive waterfront. Lunch at one of the region's top restaurants will consume hours but is lighter on your wallet than dinner. On your third day, follow the Corniche route east as it winds through the vineyards of Lavaux. Stop for photos (pull-offs are strategically interspersed), walk a section of the wine trail, and definitely taste a glass of white wine. The harbor-front town of 🖾 **Vevey** ㉔ deserves a leisurely visit, especially its older section. A night's rest here or in 🖾 **Montreux** ㉕ will ready you to take in the glitzy, Riviera-like city's highlights before touring the **Château de Chillon** ㉖. Hop a late train from Montreux, or take the half-hour winding drive for a good night's sleep in the brisk mountain air of 🖾 **Villars-sur-Ollon** ㉘, where chalet architecture contrasts with contemporary museums and estate homes. Break in the new day with an Alpine walk before heading back down the steep canyon to the main roads that speed you west to **Nyon** ❸ for a last afternoon learning about the Roman influence.

If you have 10 days

Expand on the five-day itinerary by spending more time outside the cities in wine villages and mountain resorts. After launching your tour with a few days in 🖾 **Lausanne** ❽–㉑ ⌐, go west along the Route du Vignoble to **Morges** ❼, **Allaman** ❻, Aubonne, Rolle, and 🖾 **Nyon** ❸, which you can use as a base to explore this part of Vaud, including side trips to **Coppet** ❶ and **St-Cergue** ❹. (Lake steamers can serve as alternative transportation for town-hopping.) Backtrack east past Lausanne, and pick up the Corniche road for stops in **Cully** ㉓, Épesses, and St-Saphorin to taste local wines. If you arrive in 🖾 **Vevey** ㉔ on a Saturday, you may need a few extra hours to peruse the market, and if fatigue is creeping in, a spa appointment will remedy it. Next stop: the resort town of 🖾 **Montreux** ㉕ paired with a visit to the **Château de Chillon** ㉖. Leaving the lake behind, zigzag your way into the Alpes Vaudoises, which have been staring over your shoulder for days. Spend a couple of nights in 🖾 **Villars-sur-Ollon** ㉘ to hike, ski, or bask on a sunny balcony. Cross the Col des Mosses and the Gorges du Pissot into 🖾 **Château-d'Oex** ㉚ for another day or two of hiking and studying the folkloric chalets. In winter the passes are often closed. If snow is blocking your way, return to Montreux to board the Montreux–Oberland–Bernois Railroad (MOB), a spectacularly panoramic train ride.

11

LA CÔTE

Just northeast of Geneva, La Côte (the shore) of Lac Léman has been settled since Roman times, with its south-facing slopes cultivated for wine. It is thus peppered with ancient waterfront and hillside towns, castles, and Roman remnants. A car is a must if you want to wind through tiny wine villages, but do get out and walk—if only to hear the trickling of any number of Romanesque trough fountains. Be willing to traverse a few times from the slopes to the waterfront and back if you're determined to cover all the region's charms; sticking exclusively to either the diminutive Route du Vignoble or the shore road deprives you of some wonderful sights.

Coppet

► ❶ *9 km (6 mi) south of Nyon, 46 km (28 mi) southwest of Lausanne.*

Its pretty, arcaded main street, with occasional peeks through to the jettied waterfront, makes Coppet a pleasant stop for a stroll. But it's ★ the **Château de Coppet** that puts this lake village on the map. Enclosed within vast iron gates, the château has been kept in its original 18th-century form, with luxurious Louis XVI furnishings arranged in a convincingly lived-in manner; its grounds, which harbor grand old trees, hidden courtyards, and stone stairs, are equally evocative.

Built in the 1300s, the château was restored when purchased in 1784 by Jacques Necker, a Genevan banker who served as financial minister to France's Louis XVI. The turmoil of the French Revolution and Necker's opposition to Napoléon forced him into exile in this splendid structure, where his remarkable daughter, Madame de Staël, created the most intriguing salon in Europe. Her intellectual sparkle and concern for the fiery issues of the day attracted the giants of the early Romantic period: Lord Byron, the Swiss historian Jean-Charles Sismondi, the German writer August Wilhelm von Schlegel, and British historian Edward Gibbon. Part of the château is still occupied by family descendants, but you can see the interior on a guided tour. The language of the commentary is generally chosen according to the language of the tour participants. Tours in English are not always available. ✉ *3 chemin des Murs, uphill from waterfront hwy.* ☎ *022/7761028* ⊕ *www.swisscastles.ch* ☑ *10 SF* ☯ *Apr.–June, Sept., and Oct., daily 2–6; July and Aug., daily 10–noon and 2–6.*

Where to Stay & Eat

$$–$$$ ✕☐ **Hôtel du Lac.** First ranked as a *grand logis* in 1628 to distinguish it from a common roadhouse, this historic inn still feels like an exclusive men's club, catering to power-lunchers and well-heeled travelers. It fronts on the main road and is accessible by boat, with a sycamore-shaded terrace and rooms with exposed beams, niches, and antiques. Its inventive restaurant ($$–$$$) draws a regular clientele for its exquisite open-grill specialties, such as brochette St-Jacques (scallops or shrimp on a skewer) and chateaubriand with pinot noir sauce. Reservations for the restaurant are essential. ✉ *51 Grand-rue, CH-1296* ☎ *022/7761521* 🖷 *022/*

Canton-ese Cuisine

The marvelous culinary delights of the region range from the *cuisine marché* (cuisine based on fresh market produce) of top-drawer chefs to the simplest fare: *papet Vaudois* (a straightforward stew of leeks, potatoes, and cream served with superb local sausages), delicate *filets de perche* (local perch fillets, sautéed or fried), and even *malakoffs* (egg-and-Gruyère fritters), which hark back to the days when the soldiers of La Côte fought in the Crimean Wars. Fondue, the Swiss national dish, can be ordered in any season, but locals prefer chillier months or cooler climes before gathering around a *caquelon* (earthen pot) of bubbling cheese.

11

A generation of acolytes from the kitchen of renowned chef Fredy Girardet are now master performers in their own right, showcasing their culinary talents in villages scattered along the lake. Season after season, they fill their high-end dining rooms with scores of obsessed restaurant habitués and locals celebrating milestone events. Eating well does not mean you have to raise your credit card limit or book a table months in advance. There is hardly a village without a white-tablecloth dining area. It could be a nook of half a dozen tables or a carefully orchestrated salon, the space and the menu set apart. Your host has stocked the cellar with top-quality vintages from neighboring wineries as well as global selections, and the staff is aptly qualified to pair them with the *menu du jour*.

Be adventurous and stop when you see a sign or lace-curtained window you find inviting. There is probably an exceptional meal to be had—one that is in harmony with the character of the wines produced down the lane and appreciative of each head of sun-sweetened lettuce.

Châteaux

Home to magnificently restored Chillon, the most visited if not the best château in Switzerland, Vaud offers a variety of smaller draws as well, including Coppet, Nyon, Prangins, Rolle, Allaman, Aubonne, and Aigle. Most house museums and offer magnificent views. Their salons and gardens tell stories of a grand life often interrupted by hardship. As you travel main highways and back roads, you will see similar compounds appropriated by or constructed anew for rock stars and corporate chieftains seeking the same beauty and solitude of the vineyards, lake, and mountains.

Mountain & Water Sports

The Alpes Vaudoises are home to lovely, not overly developed high-altitude resorts—Villars, Les Diablerets, Leysin, Château-d'Oex—where you can experience all levels of skiing difficulty. Summer opens trails and high-altitude passes for hikers and mountain bikers. Well-marked paths in every direction give proof that the Swiss adore an outing, especially with the requisite rest stop at a *buvette* (snack bar) for a glass of wine or dish of ice cream. You can also take on a more unusual activity, such as strenuous river-gorge expeditions, breathtaking paragliding and hot-air ballooning, and even mountain surfing (zipping downhill on a skateboardlike scooter with handlebars).

On Lac Léman, sailing fever, which has always been embedded in the life of residents, reached a frenzied pitch when the America's Cup came to its shores. (Much of 2003 cup winner Alinghi's design and construction took place in a secure boatyard above Vevey.) Sailing schools and rentals—from pedal boats to yachts—are available at village marinas. Waterskiing and windsurfing alleys have been carved out of the shipping lanes plied by tourist steamers and commercial barges. But the best way to enjoy the lake is to take a plunge in the invigorating Alpine-fed water at any of the public beaches.

7765346 ⊕ *www.hoteldulac.ch* ⌁ *12 rooms, 4 suites, 3 apartments* ⬥ *Restaurant, some kitchens, minibars, cable TV, bar, some free parking, kennel* ▤ *AE, DC, MC, V.*

Céligny

❷ *6 km (4 mi) north of Coppet.*

With its lakefront, small port, lawns for sunbathing, and pier, this endearing village provides the best swimming opportunities for miles around. The enclave is wholly charming: rows of vineyards, a historic (but private) château and church, a village square adorned with flowers, a fountain, and its best-kept secret, the wonderfully *sympa* (friendly) Hôtel du Soleil. Céligny was home to Richard Burton during the last years of his life, and you can visit the village cemetery, the smaller one hugging the edge of the forest, to visit Burton's simple grave.

Where to Stay & Eat

★ $ ╳🖫 **Hôtel du Soleil.** Lured by the charm of Céligny and this 300-year-old building, California chef John Olcott and his German wife, Catrin, have established a wonderful auberge. Whether in the café up front or the quieter restaurant in back (both $–$$$; closed Monday dinner and Tuesday), the decor is a minimalist showcase for the chef's fetching presentations. The menu features such local standards as *Rösti* (hash browns) with grilled veal sausage as well as the chef's creative side (fish medallions with spinach and shrimp bisque). You'll need a reservation to snatch a table from the locals, especially on the terrace in summer. Up the stone staircase wait a handful of sweet guest rooms. ⊠ *10 rte. des Coudrées, CH-1298* ☎ *022/9609633* 🖷 *022/7760800* ⌁ *7 rooms* ⬥ *Restaurant, cable TV; no a/c* ▤ *AE, DC, MC, V* ⧆ *BP.*

Nyon

❸ *3 km (2 mi) north of Céligny, 27 km (17 mi) southwest of Lausanne.*

Lovely Nyon, with its waterfront drive, shops, museums, and a castle dominating its cliff-top Old Town, was founded by Julius Caesar around 45 BC as a camp for war veterans. The Romans called it Noviodunum and developed the entire region for miles around. Lovely views can be had from the château-museum's terrace and the town's waterfront promenade, where boats and swans bob in the waves.

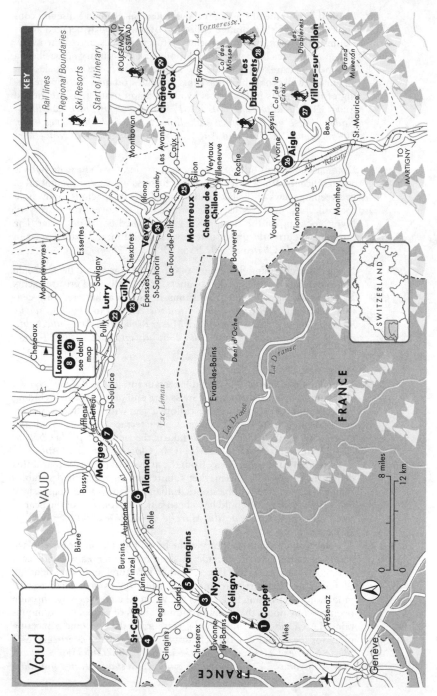

Vaud

KEY

↦ Rail lines
--- Regional Boundaries
🎿 Ski Resorts
▲ Start of itinerary

SWITZERLAND

TO ROUGEMONT, GSTAAD

29 Château-d'Oex

Montbovon

Les Avants
Chamby
Blonay
Les Pléiades

Col des Mosses

28 Les Diablerets

Leysin Col de la Croix

27 Villars-sur-Ollon

L'Etivaz

Glion
Caux

25 Montreux
Veytaux Villeneuve
Château de Chillon
Roche

Yvorne **26** Aigle

Bex
St-Maurice

TO MARTIGNY

Monthey

Vouvry
Vionnaz

Le Bouveret

Evian-les-Bains

Dent d'Oche

La Dranse

FRANCE

8 miles
12 km

Chexbres
La-Tour-de-Peilz

24 Vevey
St-Saphorin
Épesses

23 Cully
22 Lutry
Pully

Savigny
Esserts
Chexbres

Montpreveyres

Cheseaux

▲ **Lausanne 8 – 21** see detail map

St-Sulpice
Vufflens-le-Château
Chigny

7 Morges

6 Allaman
Aubonne
Rolle

Bière
Bussy

Bursins
Vinzel
Luins

4 St-Cergue
Begnins
Gingins

5 Prangins

3 Nyon
Gland
Chéserex
Divonne-les-Bains

2 Céligny
1 Coppet
Mies

Vésenaz

Genève

FRANCE

Lac Léman

★ Flanked by a statue of Caesar, the **Musée Romain** (Roman Museum) contains an attractively mounted collection of sumptuously detailed architectural stonework, fresco fragments, statuary, mosaics, and earthenware. The museum was built atop foundations of a 1st century AD basilica; a pristine miniature model inside and an excellent trompe l'oeil palace on an outside wall evoke the remarkable original structure. A complete listing of the exhibits in English is available upon request, as are guided tours. ⊠ *rue Maupertuis* ☎ *022/3617591* ⊕ *www.nyon.ch* ☒ *6 SF includes Musée du Léman* ⊘ *Apr.–June, Sept., and Oct., Tues.–Sun. 10–noon and 2–6; July and Aug., daily 10–noon and 2–6; Nov.–Mar., Tues.–Sun. 2–6.*

Dominating Nyon's hilltop over the waterfront, the **Château de Nyon** is a magnificent 12th-century multispire fortress with a terrace that takes in sweeping views of the lake and Mont Blanc. Its spacious rooms hold the collection of the **Musée Historique,** which covers the history of Nyon, focusing on the city's role as a renowned porcelain center. The museum is currently under extensive renovation and will reopen in 2005. ⊠ *pl. du Château* ☎ *022/3638361.*

Nestled in a charming floral park that parallels the water, the **Musée du Léman** exhibits models of lake steamers, crew shells, and private yachts as well as sizable lake-water aquariums, housed in a shuttered 18th-century hospital. ⊠ *8 quai Louis-Bonnard* ☎ *022/3610949* ⊕ *www. museeduleman.ch* ☒ *6 SF includes Musée Romain* ⊘ *Apr.–June, Sept., and Oct., Tues.–Sun. 10–noon and 2–6; July and Aug., daily 10–noon and 2–6; Nov.–Mar., Tues.–Sun. 2–6.*

Where to Stay & Eat

$–$$ ✕ **Auberge du Château.** This reliable restaurant, just steps from Nyon's château, serves straightforward Swiss fare and plats du jour, including veal five different ways (such as scalloped veal with lime and fresh ginger) and game in autumn. In summer, a big terrace lets diners study the château; in winter, broad windows take in the view. ⊠ *8 pl. du Château* ☎ *022/3616312* ⊟ *AE, DC, MC, V* ⊘ *Closed Wed. Oct.–Apr.*

$–$$ ✕ **Restaurant du Marché.** Away from the activity of the castle plaza, this delightful eatery near the market square has umbrella-shaded tables that spill out onto the cobblestones. Italian influences accent pasta, lake fish, and produce that could have been plucked from one of the nearby open-air stalls. ⊠ *3 rue du Marché* ☎ *022/3623500* ⊟ *MC, V* ⊘ *Closed Sun.*

$$$–$$$$ ▦ **Hôtel Real.** This contemporary white box stands out on the lower plaza across from the lake promenade. A sleek reception area with adjacent bar and seating has stone floors, leather furniture, and novel lighting. Bleached wooden furniture and crisp white linens give guest accommodations a refreshing feel, especially when lake breezes blow through open balcony doors that frame stunning views of sailboats and mountains. Le Grand Café, the hotel's restaurant, has become a meeting place for locals and day-trippers drawn to the active waterfront. ⊠ *1 pl. de Savoie, CH-1260* ☎ *022/3658585* ▤ *022/3658586* ⊕ *www. hotelrealnyon.ch* ☞ *29 rooms, 1 suite* ⊘ *Restaurant, in-room data* *ports, minibars, cable TV, in-room VCRs, bar, some free parking* ☰ *AE, DC, MC, V* ⦿ *BP.*

$–$$ 🏨 **Hôtel Ambassador.** Terra-cotta stucco and peaked dormers set off this petite hotel on Nyon's main thoroughfare. Request one of the "under the roof" rooms; these have hand-hewn dark wooden beams, floral bedding, and compact modern baths. The quiet garden terrace with its view of the castle (which is illuminated at night) is an exquisite spot for a glass of wine or a light meal. ✉ *26 rue St-Jean, CH-1260* ☎ *022/9944848* 🖨 *022/9944860* ⊕ *www.hotel-ambassador-nyon.ch* ⮎ *20 rooms* ⚅ *Restaurant, minibars, cable TV, bar; no a/c* ☰ *AE, DC, MC, V* ⦿ *BP.*

| en route | On your way from Nyon to St-Cergue, detour west to see two interesting sights. Absorb the exceptional color and design of the glass collection at the **Neumann Foundation.** The glowing glassworks include art nouveau pieces designed by L'Ecole de Nancy founders Auguste and Antonin Daum and Emile Gallé, and American artist Louis Comfort Tiffany. ✉ *6 km (4 mi) northwest of Nyon, Gingins* ☎ *022/3693653* ⊕ *www.fondation-neumann.ch* 🎫 *8 SF* ⊙ *Tues.–Fri. 2–5, weekends 10:30–5.* |

If you stay on the narrow back road to Chéserex, you'll come to the 12th-century **Abbaye de Bonmont,** a monastery with a stark white chapel and red-tile bell tower. You can glimpse evidence of the turbulence of the Reformation and Bernese invasion in the structural adjustments that converted the space into troop quarters, a granary, bakery, and warehouses. Concerts are especially dramatic in the acoustically strong chapel. The abbaye borders on the stately country lodging, the Château de Bonmont. ✉ *8 km (5 mi) northwest of Nyon, Chéserex* ☎ *022/3692368* 🎫 *5 SF* ⊙ *Apr.–June, Sept., and Oct., Sat.–Mon. 1–5; July and Aug., daily 1–5.*

St-Cergue

❹ *11 km (7 mi) northwest of Nyon.*

This petite time-capsule resort in the verdant Jura Range flourishes in both summer and winter—the first hint in Vaud of bigger Alpine sprawls to come—with good ski facilities for children, modest skiing for adults, mushing (dogsled races), and fine cross-country trails. It's also the birthplace of snowshoeing. In late September and the first week of October, look out for the annual *Fête Désalpe,* the ritual parade of cows coming down from the mountains. It lasts all of a Saturday morning, as hundreds of cows file through the streets in amazing floral headgear. If you prefer not to drive the switchback road, take the bright-red coaches of the private mountain railway **Nyon–St-Cergue–La Cure** (☎ 022/9942840). Note the contrast between the old rolling stock, museum pieces in themselves, and the modern passenger cars.

Prangins

⑤ *3 km (2 mi) northeast of Nyon.*

You'll see the elegant hillside chateau that's home to the national museum before you reach this little commune, where the pace of life moves gently between the boulangerie, post office, and café. The 18th-century
★ **Château de Prangins** is the Suisse Romande branch of the **Musée National Suisse** (Swiss National Museum). Its four floors detail (in four languages, including English) Swiss life and history in the 18th and 19th centuries. So, one exhibit might describe the country's history of international exports. Surrounded by parks and gardens (the estate once stretched all the way to Rolle), the museum is also a major venue for cultural events and regional celebrations. A café with terrace is open for lunch and refreshments. ☎ *022/9948890* ⊕ *www.musee-suisse.com* ✉ *7 SF* ◷ *Tues.–Sun. 10–5.*

> **need a break?**
>
> After strolling the galleries and gardens of the National Museum, head to **Rapp Chocolatier** (✉ 6 rue des Alpes ☎ 022/3617914), a petite chocolate shop in the heart of town. Here handmade confections are stacked in perfect pyramids, and a school and demonstration kitchen are adjacent, so if your timing is right you'll see artisans shaping molten cocoa and plying their forms with heavenly fillings. The family also has a *confiserie* (sweet shop) on the place Bel-Air in Nyon.

Where to Stay & Eat

$$$–$$$$ ✕▥ **La Barcarolle.** Hidden in a parklike setting off the lake road, this mustard-color complex is a modern *relais* (inn) amid historic châteaux and country homes. The hotel's name and musical theme reflect its owner's fondness for great classical composers. Guest rooms with lawn and lake views contain painted furniture and floral furnishings in red and gold. Spacious baths have granite countertops, separate tub and shower, and towel warmers. The bright breakfast room and fine dining area ($$–$$$$) spill onto a wide terrace. French cuisine dominates the menu, which ranges from regional fish specialties to guinea fowl in a honey-ginger sauce. ✉ *rte. de Promenthoux, CH-1197* ☎ *022/3657878* 🖷 *022/3657800* ⊕ *www.labarcarolle.ch* ⇆ *36 rooms, 3 suites* ⚘ *Restaurant, in-room data ports, minibars, cable TV, pool, lake, marina, bar, free parking, no-smoking floor* ▤ *AE, MC, V* ⦿ *BP.*

> **en route**
>
> Twelve km (7 mi) northeast of Nyon, the lakefront village of **Rolle** merits a detour for a look at its dramatic 13th-century **château,** built at the water's edge by a Savoyard prince. While in town, you can visit the Moinat Antiques and Decoration shop for a sample of what it takes to furnish a grand country home.

Route du Vignoble

36 km (22 mi) between Nyon and Lausanne.

Parallel to the waterfront highway, threading through the steep-sloping vineyards between Nyon and Lausanne, the Route du Vignoble (Vineyard Road) unfolds a rolling green landscape high above the lake, punctuated by noble manors and vineyards. **Luins,** home of the flinty, fruity white wine of the same name, is a typical pretty village. Just up the road, the village of **Vinzel** develops its own white wines on sunny slopes and sells them from the *vin-celliers* (wine cellars) that inspired its name. It is also the best source for a very local specialty, the malakoff. These rich, steamy cheese-and-egg beignets have always been a favorite of the Vaudois, but after the Crimean Wars they were renamed after a beloved officer who led his army of Vaud-born mercenaries to victory in the siege of Sebastopol. The route continues through **Bursins,** home of an 11th-century Romanesque church, and goes all the way to Morges. The road is clearly signposted throughout.

need a break?

While driving the Route du Vignoble, stop at a roadside eatery, such as **Au Coeur de la Côte** (⊠ Vinzel ☎ 021/8241141). There, as at the **Auberge Communale** (⊠ Luins ☎ 021/8241159), you can sample the local wine and munch a few rich, Gruyère-based malakoffs.

Allaman

❻ *17 km (10 mi) northeast of Nyon, 20 km (12 mi) west of Lausanne.*

This village is little more than a cluster of stone and stucco houses and red-tile-roof barns; the streets are so narrow that two cars can barely pass. The main draw is the stately 16th-century **Château d'Allaman,** built in the 12th century by the barons of Vaud, then reconstructed by the Bernois after a 1530 fire. It has been converted to a stunning antiques mall, its narrow halls lined with beeswaxed armoires and ancestral portraits, all for sale at lofty prices through private entrepreneurs who rent space within. The château's vaulted crypt offers wine dégustations for potential buyers. For more antiques, collectibles, and art at slightly better prices, head to the annex next door, known as **La Grange,** the château's erstwhile stables and barn. ⊠ *Between Aubonne and Allaman, signposted* ☎ *021/8073805* ▨ *Free* ☺ *Wed.–Sun. 2–6.*

Morges

❼ *9 km (6 mi) northeast of Allaman, 8 km (5 mi) west of Lausanne.*

On the waterfront just west of the urban sprawl of Lausanne, Morges is a pleasant lake town favored by sailors and devotees of its **Fête de la Tulipe** (Tulip Festival), held annually from mid-April to mid-May. The town's castle, built by the duke of Savoy around 1286 as a defense against the bishop-princes of Lausanne, now houses the **Musée du Château,** which combines three collections: weapons, military uniforms, and 10,000 miniature lead soldiers. In the Salle Général Henri Guisan, you'll find memorabilia of this World War II general, much honored for keeping both sides happy enough to leave Switzerland safely alone. ☎ *021/8048556* ▨ *7 SF* ☺ *Feb.–June and Sept.–mid-Dec., weekdays 10–noon and 1:30–5, weekends 1:30–5; July and Aug., Tues.–Sun. 10–5.*

In the heart of town, a 15th-century courtyard-centered mansion, once home to renowned engraver Alexis Forel, displays the holdings

CloseUp

WILD ABOUT WINE

A

S ONE OF THE MAIN wine-producing regions in Switzerland, Vaud is best savored when sampling the local vintages.

If you're only tangentially interested, check the blackboard listings in any café for local names of vins ouvert (open wines), sold by the deciliter: the fruity whites of Épesses and St-Saphorin of Lavaux (between Lausanne and Montreux); the flinty Luins, Vinzel, and other La Côte variations (between Lausanne and Geneva); or the flowery Yvorne and Aigle, the best-known names from Le Chablais (between Villeneuve and Bex). You'll be tasting the previous season's harvest (local vintages are not aged).

If time allows, drive down narrow, fountain-studded stone streets in tiny wine villages, where inns and vignobles (vineyards) offer tastings. Keep an eye peeled for hand-painted signs announcing CAVEAU OUVERT or DÉGUSTATION; this indicates that a cellar owner or cooperative is pouring wine. (Do designate a driver; laws are strict.)

Local vintners welcome visitors year-round, except during harvest, which is usually in October. Some vineyards have sophisticated tasting rooms; at others, a family member gathers guests around a tasting barrel within the working cellar. You may share a barrel top or slot at the bar with locals, as these are communal gathering spots. If there is a particular winemaker you want to visit, phone ahead for an appointment. Most cellars charge for tasting, and if you occupy the winemaker's time beyond a casual pour, it is appropriate to buy a bottle unless you find the label not to your liking.

In July and August you can head for a Saturday market in Vevey, where, for the price of a commemorative glass, winemakers and tasters move from booth to booth. To boost your knowledge of wine cultivation, processing, and labeling, go to the Château d'Aigle's Musée de la Vigne et du Vin.

Interconnected hiking trails (signposted in several languages, including English, and full of informative tidbits) span the length of the shore from Ouchy to Chillon, traversing vineyards and traffic arteries from the lakefront to hillside villages. Walking the entire 32-km (19-mi) parcours viticole (wine route) takes about 8½ hours, but you can also break it into smaller segments, allowing time for wine tastings and meals at local restaurants. Tourist offices can provide a copy of the specialized map that identifies the route and cellars open for tastings. (If you're doing a portion of the trail, you can easily catch a train back to your starting point, as there are hourly stops in every village along the lakefront.) Speaking of trains, if the distance and grade of the trails seem too much, you can take the bright yellow coaches of the Train des Vignes (vineyard train) through the rows of pinot noir, gamay, and chasselas vines. The train starts from Vevey's station, near the waterfront, and ends more than 2,000 feet above sea level in the village of Puidoux-Chexbres; its timetable is part of the regular CFF schedule.

of the **Musée Alexis Forel.** Although most of Forel's exceptional engravings are in the Musée Jenisch, in Vevey, here you can experience his home surroundings. Thick-beamed salons filled with high-back chairs, stern portraits, and delicate china remain as they were in the 1920s, when musicians and writers such as Stravinsky, Paderewski, and Rolland gathered for lively discussions and private concerts. An attic room has a selection of 18th-century puppets and porcelain dolls. ⊠ *54 Grand-rue* 🕾 *021/8012647* 🕾 *5 SF* ☉ *Apr.–early Dec., Tues.–Sun. 2–5:30.*

The oar-powered warships of the Greeks, Romans, and Phoenicians once crossed the waters of Lac Léman. Now you can follow in their wake on ☾ **La Liberté,** a reconstruction of a 17th-century galley. This brainchild of historian Jean-Pierre Hirt is part public works project, part historical re-creation. Unemployed workers helped handcraft the 183-foot vessel. You can visit the shipyard to see exhibits of the ship being carved and fitted. Christened in 2001, the ship sails the lake four times a day; the two-hour tour costs 44 SF. ⊠ *45 rue de Lausanne* 🕾 *021/8035031* 🕾 *Shipyard 5 SF* ☉ *Daily 10–6.*

---

off the beaten path

VUFFLENS-LE-CHÂTEAU – This village, 2 km (1 mi) northwest of Morges, is known for its namesake château, a 15th-century Savoyard palace with a massive donjon and four lesser towers, all trimmed in fine Piedmont-style brickwork. It's privately owned, but the grounds are open to the public.

Where to Stay & Eat

$$$$ ✕🔠 **L'Ermitage des Ravets.** A multicourse gastronomic treat awaits at the restaurant ($$$$; closed Sunday and Monday) of this 17th-century farmhouse, set beneath old, draping trees and edged by overflowing garden beds. Chef Bernard Ravet serves the classics with creative twists, such as medallions of Breton lobster flavored with olive oil and tarragon, baked with wild mushrooms, and served with a sorrel consommé. Reservations are essential. Chic rooms trimmed in dark green and burgundy are furnished with polished antiques and *canard* (duck) accessories to create a country setting that begs you to stay for more than just one superb meal. ⊠ *26 rte. du Village, CH-1134 Vufflens-le-Château* 🕾 *021/ 8046868* 🖶 *021/8022240* ⊕ *www.ravet.ch* ↝ *6 rooms, 3 suites* ♺ *Restaurant, in-room data ports, in-room safes, minibars, cable TV, bar, free parking* ▤ *AE, MC, V* ☉ *Closed late Dec. and Aug.* ⑩ *BP.*

$$–$$$ ✕🔠 **Hotel Fleur du Lac.** As the draperies are pulled back from south-facing windows, sun-splashed Mont Blanc comes into direct view. This lakefront oasis, just outside town on the main route to Lausanne, is surrounded by abundant seasonal plantings and stately old trees. Rooms are filled with a mix of antique and modern furniture. The terrace and dining room ($$–$$$) are the big draws. Fresh perch, a regional favorite, tastes even better when served lakeside. Book well in advance, as their guest return rate is unusually high. ⊠ *70 rue de Lausanne, CH-1110* 🕾 *021/8815811* 🖶 *021/8115888* ⊕ *www.fleur-du-lac.ch* ↝ *31 rooms, 7 suites* ♺ *Restaurant, cable TV, bar, free parking; no a/c* ▤ *AE, DC, MC, V.*

en route

Five km (3 mi) east of Morges, turn right toward the ancient waterfront village of St-Sulpice to visit the severe but lovely **Église de St-Sulpice** (Church of St. Sulpice). One of the best-preserved 12th-century Romanesque churches in Switzerland, it was built by monks from Cluny Abbey in Burgundy. Painted decoration softens the spare purity of its lines, and three original apses remain, although the nave has disappeared. The short bell tower is built of small stone blocks likely brought from the ruined Roman township at nearby Vidy. At one time the home of 40 monks, the adjoining priory was converted into a private residence in the 16th century. Today the church is a well-known venue for classical music concerts.

LAUSANNE

"Lausanne is a block of picturesque houses, spilling over two or three gorges, which spread from the same central knot, and are crowned by a cathedral like a tiara. . . . On the esplanade of the church . . . I saw the lake over the roofs, the mountains over the lake, clouds over the mountains, and stars over the clouds. It was like a staircase where my thoughts climbed step by step and broadened at each new height." Such was Victor Hugo's impression of this grand and graceful tiered city. Voltaire, Rousseau, Byron, and Cocteau all waxed equally passionate about Lausanne—and not only for its visual beauty. It has been a cultural center for centuries, the world drawn first to its magnificent Gothic cathedral and the powers it represented, then to its university, and during the 18th and 19th centuries to its vibrant intellectual and social life. Today the Swiss consider Lausanne a most desirable city in which to live.

Lausanne's importance today stems from its several disparate roles in national and world affairs. Politically, it is the site of the Tribunal Fédéral, the highest court of appeals in Switzerland. Commercially, although it is by no means in the same league as Zürich or Bern, it figures as the headquarters for many multinational organizations, corporations, and sports federations. On a major international rail route and at a vital national junction 66 km (41 mi) northeast of Geneva, Lausanne serves as a trade center for most of the surrounding agricultural regions and the expanding industrial towns of Vaud. This prosperity spills over into the arts; there's a surprising concentration of dance companies—including that of Maurice Béjart—as well as several theaters, jazz cellars, and a pair of excellent orchestras. Thousands of students come for the top-notch universities, private academies, and technology centers. Lausanne is also the world's Olympic capital; the International Olympic Committee has been based here since 1915 (its founder, Baron Pierre de Coubertin, is buried nearby at Montoie Cemetery).

The balance of old and new has not always been kept. The first 20 years after World War II saw an immense building boom, with old buildings and whole neighborhoods pulled down to make way for shining contemporary office and apartment buildings—an architectural exuberance that has given Lausanne a rather lopsided air.

Exploring Lausanne

Rising in tiers from the lakeside at Ouchy (1,181 feet) to more than 2,000 feet, the city covers three hills, which are separated by gorges that once channeled rivers. The rivers have been built over, and huge bridges span the gaps across the hilltops. On one hill in particular, modern skyscrapers contrast brutally with the beautiful proportions of the cathedral rising majestically from its crest. Atmospheric alleys and narrow streets have mostly been demolished, yet the Old Town clustered around the cathedral has been painstakingly restored.

Below the Old Town spreads the commercial city center, and in the bottom of the hollow between avenue Jules Gonin and rue de Genève is the Flon, a neighborhood with plenty of nightspots. Still farther south, along the lake, is the separate township of Ouchy, an animated resort area dominated by the Château d'Ouchy, with a tower dating from the Middle Ages.

a good tour

Lausanne has plenty of buses and a Métro (subway), the latter being the easiest and fastest way to traverse large stretches of this hilly town. To see the concentrated sights of the Old Town, however, it's best to go on foot. Wear comfortable shoes, as the city's steep inclines and multiple layers add considerable strain to getting around.

Begin in the commercial hub of the city, the **place St-François** ❽ ☞ (nicknamed Sainfe by the Lausannois), where you'll see the former Franciscan Église St-François. Behind the church, take a near hairpin turn right onto the fashionable main shopping street, the ancient **rue de Bourg** ❾. At the top of rue de Bourg, rue Caroline leads you left and left again over the Pont Bessières, where you can see the city's peculiar design spanning gorges and covered rivers.

Crossing the bridge and bearing right brings you up into the Old Town. On your left, the imposing palace of the Old Bishopric now houses the **Musée Historique de Lausanne** ❿. Adjacent is the **Musée de Design et d'Arts Appliqués Contemporains** ⓫ known as the Mudac to locals. Straight ahead, at the top of rue St-Étienne, towers the tremendous **Cathédrale de Notre-Dame** ⓬, which is on par with some of Europe's finest churches.

With the cathedral on your left, walk up the narrow passage of rue Cité-Derrière to the place du Château and its eponymous monument, the **Château St-Maire** ⓭. As you face the château, turn left and walk down the rue Cité-Devant. On your right is the Ancienne-Académie, the first Protestant theology school in Europe and now a secondary school. Farther on, as you pass the cathedral again, on your left, veer right toward a flight of wooden steps that leads down to the dramatic Escaliers du Marché, a wood-roof medieval staircase. At the bottom of the 150 covered steps, you'll run into the place de la Palud and the **Hôtel de Ville** ⓮, the seat of the municipal and communal councils. Turning right, just up rue Madeleine, you will come upon the place de la Riponne and the imposing **Palais de Rumine** ⓯, which houses a pack of museums covering subjects from archaeology to zoology.

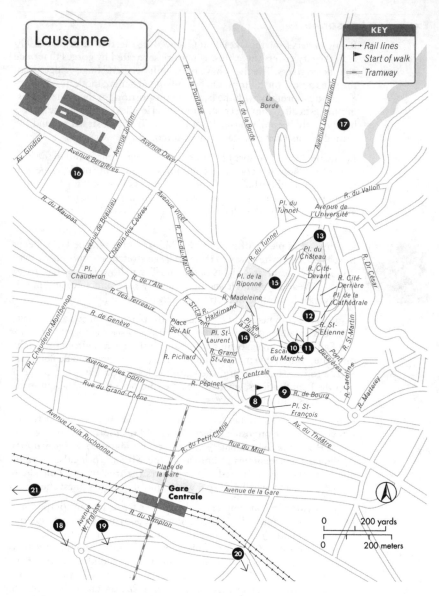

Lausanne

0   200 yards

0   200 meters

Cathédrale de
Notre-Dame **12**

Château St-Maire **13**

Collection
de l'Art Brut **16**

Débarcadère **18**

Fondation
de l'Hermitage **17**

Hôtel de Ville **14**

Musée de Design
et d'Arts Appliqués
Contemporains **11**

Musée de l'Elysée **20**

Musée Historique
de Lausanne **10**

Musée Olympique **19**

Musée Romain de
Lausanne-Vidy **21**

Palais de Rumine **15**

Place St-François **8**

Rue de Bourg **9**

Some of Lausanne's other worthwhile sights take a bit of extra effort to reach. You can fit one of them in at the end of your walking tour or save them for a separate adventure. A long hike up avenue Vinet, northwest of the Old Town, will take you to the **Collection de l'Art Brut** ⓰, an unusual museum of fringe art across from the Beaulieu convention center. To view the works of more classical, well-known painters, visit the **Fondation de l'Hermitage** ⓱, a 15-minute bus ride from the Old Town. Take Bus 3 from the Gare Centrale (central train station) or Bus 16 from place St-François. South of the Old Town, Ouchy's **Débarcadère** ⓲ has typical quayside attractions—vendors and people strolling on a promenade. It can be easily reached by the steep funicular Métro; there are stations across from the Gare Centrale and under the rue du Grand-Chêne in the Flon. (There's also a large underground parking garage, a boon in this space-pressed city.) Just east of Ouchy, on a hillside overlooking the lake, the dramatic **Musée Olympique** ⓳ tells about the history and sports of the Olympic Games. It's less than half a mile from the Débarcadère along the quai de Belgique, which turns into the quai d'Ouchy. Uphill and connected by garden pathways, the **Musée de l'Elysée** ⓴ is a photography museum housed in a restored 18th-century *campagne* (country manor home). West of Ouchy at Vidy is the **Musée Romain de Lausanne–Vidy** ㉑, where you can see a reconstructed private Roman home. Like the Musée Olympique, this is easy to get to on foot; it's just under a mile from the Débarcadère.

TIMING You can tour the Old Town in a couple of hours following the above route (do not reverse the order unless you're keen to walk up the Escaliers du Marché). But that's without stopping: if you have time, plan a full day to include visits to at least a few of the museums and the cathedral, not to mention some shops off the place du Palud. Or spend your afternoon in Ouchy and its nearby museums. Getting to Ouchy by car or Métro takes less than 10 minutes, and walking down the avenue d'Ouchy from the Gare Centrale to the Débarcadère takes about 15 minutes. Remember that most museums are closed on Monday.

What to See

⓬ **Cathédrale de Notre-Dame** (Cathedral of Our Lady). A Burgundian
FodorśChoice Gothic architectural treasure, this cathedral, also called the Cathédrale
★ de Lausanne, is Switzerland's largest church—and probably its finest. Begun in the 12th century by Italian, Flemish, and French architects, it was completed in 1275. Pope Gregory X came expressly to perform the historic consecration ceremony—of double importance, as it also served as a coronation service for Rudolf of Habsburg as the new Holy Roman Emperor. Rudolf brought his wife, eight children, seven cardinals, five archbishops, 17 bishops, four dukes, 15 counts, and a multitude of lesser lords to watch in the church's exquisitely proportioned nave.

Viollet-le-Duc, a renowned restorer who worked on the cathedrals of Chartres and Notre-Dame-de-Paris, brought portions of the building to Victorian Gothic perfection in the 19th century. His repairs are visible as paler stone contrasting with the weathered local sandstone; his self-portrait appears in the face of King David, harp and scroll in hand, to the right of the main portal. Streamlined to the extreme, without radiating chapels or the excesses of later Gothic trim, the cathedral wasn't always so spare; in fact, there was brilliant painting. Zealous Reformers plastered over the florid colors, but in so doing they unwittingly preserved them, and now you can see portions of these splendid shades restored in the right transept. The dark and delicate choir contains the 14th-century tomb of the crusader Otto I of Grandson and exceptionally fine 13th-century choir stalls, unusual for their age alone, not to mention their beauty. The church's masterpiece, the 13th-century painted portal, is considered one of Europe's most magnificent. Constant repairs and renovations often shroud parts of the structure in scaffolding.

Protestant services (the cathedral was reformed in the 16th century) exclude nonworshipping visitors on Sunday at 10 AM and 8 PM. You may want to come instead for the evening concerts given on an almost-weekly basis in spring and autumn; call ahead for a precise schedule. Guided tours are given July to mid-September. ⊠ *pl. de la Cathédrale, Old Town* ☎ *021/3167161* ⊙ *Apr.–Oct., weekdays 7–7, weekends 8–7; Nov.–Mar., weekdays 7–5:30, weekends 8–5:30.*

⑬ Château St-Maire. The fortresslike elements of this 15th-century stone cylinder certainly came into play. The castle was built for the bishops of Lausanne; during the 16th century, the citizens wearied of ecclesiastical power and allied themselves with Bern and Fribourg against the bishops protected within. Before long, however, Bern itself marched on Lausanne, put a bailiff in this bishops' castle, and stripped the city fathers of their power. The Bernese imposed Protestantism on the Lausannois, and their Catholic churches and cathedral were ransacked to fill the coffers of Bern. Today the Château St-Maire is the seat of the cantonal government. ⊠ *pl. du Château, Old Town.*

★ ⑯ Collection de l'Art Brut. This singular museum focuses on the genre of fringe or "psychopathological" art, dubbed *l'art brut* (raw art) in the 1940s by French artist Jean Dubuffet. His own collection forms the base of this ensemble of raw material from untrained minds—prisoners, schizophrenics, or the merely obsessed. Strangely enough, the collection is housed in the Château de Beaulieu, a former mansion of Madame de Staël, she of the sophisticated salons. The exhibits range from intricate yarn and textile pieces to a wall full of whimsical seashell masks. One of the most affecting works is a panel of rough carvings made by an asylum patient in solitary confinement; it was shaped with a broken spoon and a chamberpot handle. You can get here by walking up avenue Vinet or by taking Bus 2 from place St-Laurent in the direction of Le Désert. ⊠ *11 av. des Bergières, Beaulieu* ☎ *021/6475435* ⊕ *www.artbrut.ch* ⊠ *6 SF* ⊙ *July and Aug., daily 11–1 and 2–6; Sept.–June, Tues.–Sun. 11–1 and 2–6.*

☝ ⑱ Débarcadère (Wharf). In fine weather, the waterfront buzzes day and night—strollers, diners, concertgoers, in-line skaters, artisans selling their wares—while the white steamers that land here add to the traffic. It's as if sedate Lausanne lifts her skirts a bit at the shoreline. ⊠ *pl. du Port, Ouchy.*

⑰ Fondation de l'Hermitage. A 15-minute bus ride from the Old Town takes you to this beautifully set 19th-century country home. The estate is now an impressive art gallery with a fine permanent collection of Vaudois artists and headline-grabbing, yet seriously presented, blockbuster shows. Exhibits have included the works of Picasso, Giacometti, and the American impressionists. Details of the elegant villa have been preserved, including intricate moldings, carved fireplaces, and multipatterned parquet floors. Allow time for a walk on the grounds and a coffee or light meal at **L'esquisse,** the café backdropped by the outlying orangerie. Call ahead to check the museum's hours, since it shuts down during transition periods between exhibits and for private events. To get here, take Bus 3 from Gare Centrale to the Motte stop or Bus 16 from place St-François to Hermitage. ⊠ *2 rte. du Signal, Sauvabelin* ☎ *021/3125013* ⊕ *www.fondation-hermitage.ch* 🖾 *15 SF* ☉ *Tues., Wed., and Fri.–Sun. 10–6, Thurs. 10–9.*

⓮ Hôtel de Ville (Town Hall). Constructed between the 15th and 17th centuries, this is the seat of municipal and communal councils. A painted, medieval **Fontaine de la Justice** (Justice Fountain) draws strollers to lounge on its heavy rim. Across the street, you can watch the modern **animated clock,** donated to the city by local merchants; moving figures appear every hour on the hour. A street market is held in the square every Wednesday and Saturday morning. ⊠ *2 pl. de la Palud, city center* ☎ *021/ 3152223* 🖾 *Free.*

★ ⓫ Musée de Design et d'Arts Appliqués Contemporains (Museum of Contemporary Design and Applied Arts). A museum of contemporary design seems amiss in this ancient quarter of the city; yet it demonstrates the passion for art in everyday life. Temporary and permanent installations feature glassworks, textiles, and graphics. Creative and performing arts merge in multimedia shows. ⊠ *6 pl. de la Cathédrale, Old Town* ☎ *021/3152530* ⊕ *www.mudac.ch* 🖾 *6 SF* ☉ *Tues.–Sun. 11–6.*

⓴ Musée de l'Elysée. Stark white walls and parquet floors form an inviting backdrop for the changing array of contemporary photography assembled by this museum in an 18th-century country manor. Recent shows have included "Finding Face: The Death of the Portrait" and Robert Walker's "Color is Power." Wander the rooms, cellar, and attic spaces to view multiple exhibitions—some interactive and designed especially for children. The park surrounding the estate is a quiet place to find a shaded bench and critique the current show. ⊠ *18 ave. de l'Elysée, Ouchy* ☎ *021/3169911* ⊕ *www.elysee.ch* 🖾 *8 SF* ☉ *Daily 11–6.*

⓾ Musée Historique de Lausanne (Lausanne Historical Museum). The Ancien-Évêché (Old Bishopric) holds a wealth of both temporary and permanent historical exhibits about the city. Don't miss the 250-square-foot scale model of 17th-century Lausanne, with its commentary illuminating the neighborhoods' histories. Also look for the re-created 19th-century shop windows. ⊠ *4 pl. de la Cathédrale, Old Town* ☎ *021/ 3121368* 🖾 *4 SF* ☉ *Tues., Wed., and Fri.–Sun. 11–6, Thurs. 11–8.*

☾ ⓳ Musée Olympique (Olympic Museum). With high-tech presentation and
Fodor'sChoice touching mementos, this complex pays tribute to the athletic tradition
★ in ancient Greece, to the development of the modern Games, to the evolution of the individual sports, to Paralympic competitions, and to the

athletes themselves. There are art objects—an Etruscan torch from the 6th century BC, Rodin's *American Athlete*—as well as archival films and videos, interactive displays, photographs, coins and stamps, and medals from various eras throughout Olympic history. A museum shop, a lovely café overlooking the lake and sculpture park, and occasional Sunday-afternoon classical concerts complete this ambitious, world-class endeavor. Brochures and guided tours are available in English. ⊠ *1 quai d'Ouchy, Ouchy* ☎ *021/6216511* ⊕ *www.museum.olympic.org* 🕾 *14 SF* ⊙ *May–Sept., daily 9–6; Oct.–Apr., Tues.–Sun. 9–6.*

㉑ **Musée Romain de Lausanne–Vidy** (Lausanne-Vidy Roman Museum). Two Roman communities, Lousonna and Vidy, flourished near the lakefront from 15 BC into the 4th century; excavations of their ruins have brought these ancient settlements to light. A reconstructed private home serves as the museum's headquarters, where displays include a small treasure trove of coins, votive figures, mosaics, and objects from daily life—carved combs, toga pins, jewelry. On request you can get guided tours in English of the museum and the vast archaeological sites. The museum is west of Ouchy, just off the Lausanne-Maladière exit from E25/A1. Bus 1 stops at Maladière. ⊠ *24 chemin du Bois-de-Vaux, Vidy* ☎ *021/6251084* 🕾 *4 SF* ⊙ *Tues., Wed., and Fri.–Sun. 11–6, Thurs. 11–8.*

🚸 ⑮ **Palais de Rumine.** Built at the turn of the last century, this enormous neo-Renaissance structure houses several museums, all with a local spin. The **Musée Cantonal de Géologie** (Cantonal Geology Museum; ☎ 021/6924470 🕾 4 SF ⊙ Tues.–Thurs. 11–6, Fri.–Sun. 11–5) has an excellent fossil collection, including a mammoth skeleton. Besides its collection of regional fauna, the **Musée Cantonal de Zoologie** (Cantonal Zoology Museum; ☎ 021/3163460 🕾 4 SF ⊙ Tues.–Thurs. 11–6, Fri.–Sun. 11–5) has a rare collection of comparative anatomy. The top exhibit at the **Musée Cantonal d'Archéologie et d'Histoire** (Cantonal Archaeology and History Museum; ☎ 021/3163430 🕾 4 SF ⊙ Tues.–Thurs. 11–6, Fri.–Sun. 11–5) is the gold bust of Marcus Aurelius discovered at nearby Avenches in 1939. The **Musée Cantonal des Beaux-Arts** (Cantonal Museum of Fine Arts; ☎ 021/3163445 🕾 6 SF ⊙ Tues.–Wed. 11–6, Thurs. 11–8, Fri.–Sun. 11–5) has an enlightening collection of Swiss art, not only by the Germanic Hodler and Anker but also by Vaud artists—especially Bocion, whose local landscapes are well worth study during a visit to this region. Each museum has some descriptions or an abbreviated guide in English. There are no combination entrance tickets, but all museums offer free admission the first Sunday of each month. ⊠ *6 pl. de la Riponne, city center.*

▶ ⑧ **Place St-François** (St. Francis Square). The brick-paved square is dominated by the massive post office and the former Franciscan **Église St-François** (Church of St. Francis), built during the 13th and 14th centuries. From 1783 to 1793, Gibbon lived in a house on the site of the post office and there finished his work on *The Decline and Fall of the Roman Empire*. In those days, the square, now reserved for pedestrians, was a popular riding circuit. ⊠ *St-François.*

need a break?

Le Saint François (⊠ 5 pl. St-François ☎ 021/3202751), a see-and-be-seen gathering spot opposite the church, serves decadent pastries and inventive light meals in a sleek blond-wood setting or outside on the plaza. Just behind the restaurant is an epicurean boutique chockfull of gourmet items, including private-label products from regional gastronomic star Philippe Rochat.

❾ Rue de Bourg. Once a separate village isolated on a natural ridge, this is now Lausanne's fashionable main shopping street. Narrow and cobblestoned, it's lined with platinum-card stores such as Hermès and Louis Vuitton plus home-furnishings emporiums and jewelry salons. Boutiques have been built into the centuries-old buildings, though some have added fittingly modern facades. Tony stores notwithstanding, the street has its down-to-earth moments; on weekends a fresh-produce market makes things even more crowded. ⊠ *St-François.*

Where to Stay & Eat

$$$$ ✕ **Restaurant de l'Hôtel de Ville–Philippe Rochat.** Secure in his position as
Fodor'sChoice heir to the legendary chef Fredy Girardet, Philippe Rochat reigns as culi-
★ nary don of the region. It's a quick drive west from Lausanne to his understated manse. Service and presentation are spectacular, and the food is absolutely stellar. For these finely orchestrated prix-fixe menus, the ingredients are key—lamb raised in the Pyrenees, cardoons (an artichokelike vegetable) grown in the village. Pace yourself, reserving time and room for selections from the immense cheese cart or celestial desserts. Make reservations as far ahead as possible—lunch may be your only option. ⊠ *1 rue d'Yverdon, Crissier, 7 km (4 mi) west of Lausanne* ☎ *021/6340505* ⌂ *Reservations essential* ⊟ *AE, MC, V* ⊙ *Closed Sun. and Mon. and late July–mid-Aug.*

$–$$$$ ✕ **Louis, Villa, et Dépendances.** This multilevel, multivenue industrial restoration has brought new daytime action to late-night-oriented Flon. Brainchild of international restaurateur Louis Godio, the building houses a fast-paced bistro and vinothéque (wine bar) on the first floor ($–$$), with seating that expands onto outdoor decking. Upstairs, L'Atelier Gourmand ($$–$$$$) is an elegant epicurean salon complete with exhaustive wine cellar and cheese cave. Preparations range from updated bistro dishes on the ground floor to dazzling tasting menus on the second. A cigar-cognac lounge and nightclub complete the complex. ⊠ *pl. de l'Europe, Flon* ☎ *021/2130300* ⊟ *AE, MC, V* ⊙ *No lunch Sat. Atelier closed Sun. and Mon.*

★ **$$–$$$** ✕ **Café Beau-Rivage.** As if turning its back on the aristocratic Beau-Rivage Palace, which shelters it, this young, lively brasserie-café faces the lake and the Ouchy waterfront scene. Its flashy brass-and-Biedermeier dining area and bar fill with smart Lausannois and internationals enjoying trendy cuisine du marché. Despite the brasserie atmosphere, there are no paper place mats: linen, silver, and monogrammed damask set the tone. In summer the pillared terrazzo terrace (protected from embarcadero traffic by rose gardens) is the place to be seen. ⊠ *pl. du Général-Guisan, Ouchy* ☎ *021/6133330* ⌂ *Reservations essential* ⊟ *AE, DC, MC, V.*

$$-$$$ ✕ **Café Restaurant du Théâtre.** Locals come here for smoky, oven-fired in-dividual-size pizza, but the home-style pasta and risotto are also robust and flavorful. The stucco-walled dining room is tight and toasty in win-ter; in summer there is nothing more delightful than sitting under the gar-den's sprawling trees and umbrellas. Entrances connect to a theater complex, making it a natural for pre- and post-performance dining. ⊠ *12 av. du Théâtre, city center* ☎ *021/3515115* ☰ *AE, MC, V* ☉ *Closed Sun.*

$-$$$ ✕ **À la Pomme de Pin.** Behind the cathedral, this winsome *pinte* (wine pub)—one of Lausanne's oldest—produces an eclectic menu ranging from French to Italian to Swiss (rabbit and Rösti, anyone?) along with rea-sonable plats du jour, served both in the casual café and the adjoining linen-decked restaurant. ⊠ *11–13 rue Cité-Derrière, Old Town* ☎ *021/ 3234656* ☰ *AE, MC, V* ☉ *Closed Sun. No lunch Sat.*

★ **$-$$** ✕ **Bleu Lézard.** A cross section of Lausanne urbanites—hip artists, yup-pies, shoppers, university students—fights for tables at this stylish restau-rant. Dishes such as salmon ravioli, *moules et frites* (mussels and fries), and duck confit Provençal are available at remarkably low prices. A tongue-in-cheek decor of found-object art and easygoing waiters dressed in whatever they found near the bed that morning add to the laid-back ambience. Mixed drinks and live music draw a nocturnal clientele down-stairs. ⊠ *10 rue Enning, city center* ☎ *021/3123830* ☰ *AE, MC, V.*

$-$$ ✕ **Café du Grütli.** Tucked in between the place de la Palud and the covered stairs to the cathedral, this is a typical old-style Suisse Romande restaurant, with a bentwood-and-net-curtain café on the ground floor and a simple, more formal dining room upstairs. There are several fondues as well as brasserie classics—boiled beef vinaigrette, rabbit in mustard sauce, prof-iteroles, and tarte tatin. Have one of several open Vaud wines or a *café pomme* (coffee with a side shot of apple eau-de-vie). ⊠ *4 rue de la Mercerie, city center* ☎ *021/3129493* ☰ *DC, MC, V* ☉ *Closed Sun. No dinner Sat.*

★ **$-$$** ✕ **Café Romand.** All the customers seem to know each other at this vast, smoky dining institution, where shared wooden tables and clattering china create the perfect ambience for fondue feasts, mussels, *choucroûte* (sauerkraut), or a sausage plate. Prominent members of Lausanne's arts community swarm here after rehearsals and concerts as service contin-ues until 10 PM, late by Swiss standards. ⊠ *2 pl. St-François, St-François* ☎ *021/3126375* ☰ *MC, V* ☉ *Closed Sun.*

¢-$ ✕ **Manora.** If you're fed up with heavy Vaud cheese dishes and local sausage, this cheery self-service chain offers startlingly inexpensive op-tions. Stir-fries sizzle in huge woks under silent no-smoke hoods; there are also iced pitchers of fresh-squeezed fruit juices, four sizes of salad, a fruit bar, a pasta station, and a dessert buffet. No one dish costs more than 20 SF, and the no-smoking dining room is a lifesaver in this city of chain-smokers. ⊠ *17 pl. St-François, St-François* ☎ *021/3209293* ⌯ *Reservations not accepted* ☰ *No credit cards.*

$$$$ ⌂ **Alpha Palmiers.** Behind this historic facade you'll find a courtyard hotel of modern proportions. Filled with light from the atrium, the stream-lined rooms have ample work space and a safe large enough to store a laptop. A bamboo garden and palm trees add freshness to the active re-ception-restaurant areas. Though the hotel is close to the train station, the walk uphill is a bit of a challenge with luggage. ⊠ *34 rue du Petit-*

Chêne, CH-1003 ☎ *021/5555599* 🖷 *021/5555998* ⊕ *www.fhotels.ch* 🛏 *210 rooms* ⚭ *2 restaurants, in-room data ports, in-room safes, minibars, cable TV, gym, hair salon, sauna, Turkish bath, bar, laundry service, parking (fee), no-smoking rooms* ⊟ *AE, DC, MC, V.*

★ **$$$$** ⊡ **Beau-Rivage Palace.** Of the scores of luxury hotels in Switzerland, this gleaming grande dame stands apart, its neoclassical structure seamlessly restored to period opulence, its vast waterfront grounds manicured like a country estate. Every inch of marble, crystal, and polished mahogany sparkles like new. Rooms have many modern touches—remote light controls, towel heaters, wireless connections. The hotel has a pair of first-class restaurants: the romantic La Rotonde (jacket required) and the Café Beau-Rivage (see above). ⊠ *17–19 pl. du Port, Ouchy, CH-1006* ☎ *021/6133333* 🖷 *021/6133334* ⊕ *www.beau-rivage-palace.ch* 🛏 *155 rooms, 20 suites* ⚭ *2 restaurants, in-room data ports, in-room safes, minibars, cable TV with movies, 2 tennis courts, indoor-outdoor pool, gym, sauna, spa, Turkish bath, 2 bars, babysitting, laundry service, concierge, parking (fee), no-smoking rooms* ⊟ *AE, DC, MC, V.*

$$$$ ⊡ **Hôtel de la Paix.** Anchored hillside in the center of town, this upscale turn-of-the-20th-century hotel has some of the city's best views and is near corporate addresses, shopping, and nightlife. No wonder so many business types are repeat visitors. The fresh-market bistro buzzes with multilingual conversations, while Jacky's, the piano bar, is a Lausanne institution. Cheery rooms are decked out in creamy tones accented with blond wood and tailored furnishings. ⊠ *5 av. Benjamin-Constant, St-François, CH-1003* ☎ *021/3107171* 🖷 *021/3107172* ⊕ *www. hoteldelapaix.net* 🛏 *109 rooms, 6 suites* ⚭ *Restaurant, café, in-room data ports, in-room safes, minibars, cable TV with movies, piano bar, laundry service, concierge, business services, parking (fee), no-smoking rooms* ⊟ *AE, DC, MC, V* ⦿ *BP.*

★ **$$$$** ⊡ **Lausanne Palace & Spa.** This Edwardian landmark, distinctly urban in setting and style, stands on a hill high over the lake, with layers of city scenery draped behind. It faces a city street, so to take advantage of its views you need a back room. Rooms have Empire reproduction decor with period details such as inlaid wood and dramatic art deco baths. The sleek, calming Aveda spa offers a wide array of treatments and classes. You are likely to spot International Olympic Committee officials exiting the meeting areas; the city's influential professionals dine at the polished Brasserie du Grand Chêne. ⊠ *7–9 rue du Grand-Chêne, city center, CH-1002* ☎ *021/3313131* 🖷 *021/3232571* ⊕ *www.lausanne-palace.ch* 🛏 *121 rooms, 31 suites* ⚭ *3 restaurants, in-room data ports, in-room safes, minibars, cable TV with movies, indoor pool, health club, spa, 2 bars, nightclub, shops, babysitting, concierge, laundry service, business services, parking (fee), no-smoking rooms* ⊟ *AE, DC, MC, V.*

★ **$$$–$$$$** ⊡ **Hôtel Angleterre & Résidence.** Within four graceful 18th- and 19th-century villas and a historic hotel near the waterfront, this small complex has been modernized without ruffling its gentility or disturbing its graceful stone arches, marble floors, or discreet gardens. The hotel, where Lord Byron penned *The Prisoner of Chillon*, anchors the compound. A private courtyard with glass pavilion receives guests and dispenses them to quarters furnished in styles ranging from contemporary historical to garden-party floral. A meal taken on the terrace of L'Accademia, the quay-facing Italian bistro, provides a glimpse of lakefront lifestyle. It's the best of both worlds: small-hotel attentiveness plus access to the facilities of the grand Beau-Rivage Palace next door. ⊠ *11 pl. du Port, Ouchy, CH-1006* ☎ *021/6133434* 🖷 *021/6133435* ⊕ *www.angleterre-residence.ch* 🖘 *62 rooms, 12 suites* ♨ *2 restaurants, in-room data ports, in-room safes, minibars, cable TV with movies, pool, bar, laundry service, parking (fee), no-smoking rooms* ⊟ *AE, DC, MC, V.*

$$$–$$$$ ⊡ **Meliá Carlton.** A quiet tree-lined street in one of Lausanne's nicest neighborhoods masks this lodging's close proximity to the train station. Rococo-style architecture is emphasized by embossed wallpapers, textured upholstery, and sweeping draperies in guest rooms and dining areas. Relax with a glass of wine and plate of tapas in the Mediterranean-influenced Nash Bar, knowing you are minutes from the Métro and the lakefront promenade. ⊠ *4 av. de Cour, CH-1007* ☎ *021/6130707* 🖷 *021/6130710* ⊕ *www.solmelia.com* 🖘 *35 rooms, 9 suites* ♨ *Restaurant, in-room data ports, in-room safes, minibars, cable TV, bar, free parking* ⊟ *AE, DC, MC, V.*

$$–$$$$ ⊡ **Mövenpick.** A five-minute drive from the city center, this link in the well-known business-hotel chain is across the street from the busy marina but nicer than other hotels along this stretch of lake. Rooms are spacious for a European hotel and are outfitted with wireless technology and sand-color furnishings. Guests can use the underground parking, at a premium in this part of town. Try a couple of scoops from the ice-cream bar; the Mövenpick brand is synonymous with flavor and high quality. ⊠ *4 av. de Rhodanie, Ouchy, CH-1006* ☎ *021/6127612* 🖷 *021/6127611* ⊕ *www.movenpick-hotels.com* 🖘 *258 rooms, 7 suites* ♨ *3 restaurants, in-room data ports, cable TV, gym, bar, parking (fee), no-smoking rooms* ⊟ *AE, MC, V.*

$$$ ⊡ **City.** It's hard to believe this onetime steam-heated dinosaur has been transformed into such a thoroughly modern hotel. Curved chrome planes and an escalator flanked by a waterfall give the lobby a space-age feel, and rooms have fresh duvets, some kitchenettes, and pink-tile baths. Slick and soundproof, the City is a stalwart in a tight-knit trio of family-owned hotels, including Alpha Palmiers (above) and Agora. ⊠ *5 rue Caroline, city center, CH-1003* ☎ *021/3202141* 🖷 *021/3202149* ⊕ *www.fhotels.ch* 🖘 *50 rooms* ♨ *In-room data ports, some kitchenettes, minibars, cable TV with movies, bar, no-smoking rooms* ⊟ *AE, DC, MC, V.*

$$–$$$ ⊡ **Hostellerie les Chevreuils.** Retreat to the nearby countryside (20 minutes from city center) for an inn with character. Rooms are lived-in and unfussy, with dark-wood furniture, upholstered reading chairs, and foamy white duvets. Happily, gourmet dining was not left in town. Café Mijoté offers uncomplicated elegant dishes and professional but not overly formal service. To get here take E62 to route 1, 8 km (5 mi) northeast of Lausanne past Èpalinges. ⊠ *CH-1000 Vers-chez-les-Blanc* ☎ *021/7842021* 🖷 *021/7841545* ⊕ *www.chevreuils.ch* 🖘 *30 rooms* ♨ *Restaurant, café, cable TV, bar; no a/c* ⊟ *AE, DC, MC, V* �ⵔⵉ *BP.*

$$ ⊡ **Hôtel Regina.** Owners at this friendly lodging spent more than a decade in the United States, so the language barrier is nonexistent.

Guest rooms are neatly squared away with color-coordinated carpets and upholstery, most with shower-baths. Some have panoramic views of the cathedral, while others look out onto red-tile rooflines. Rooms on the top floor are modern multilevel spaces with bleached-plank ceilings and cherrywood furniture. The hotel is well situated in a pedestrian zone with parking access. ⊠ *18 rue Grand-St-Jean, city center, CH-1003* ☎ *021/3202441* 🖷 *021/3202529* ⊕ *www.hotel-regina.ch* ⇆ *36 rooms* ♿ *In-room data ports, in-room safes, minibars, cable TV, laundry service, Internet, free parking, no-smoking floors; no a/c* ⊟ *MC, V* ⦿| *BP.*

¢ 🏠 **Lausanne Guest House.** This tidy 19th-century town house not far from the train station is run by a brother-and-sister team. Rooms are spread over five floors—some private with baths, others dorm-style with shared showers and toilets. You can prepare meals in the community kitchen or on the outdoor grill, or get caught up at the Internet corner with multiple terminals. The guest house is ecologically conscious, using solar heating and a special ventilation system, which makes smoking off-limits. ⊠ *4 Epinettes, CH-1007* ☎ *021/6018000* 🖷 *021/6018001* ⊕ *www. lausanne-guesthouse.ch* ⇆ *25 rooms, 6 with bath* ♿ *Picnic area, BBQs, bicycles, laundry facilities, Internet, parking (fee); no a/c, no room phones, no room TVs, no smoking* ⊟ *AE, DC, MC, V.*

Nightlife & the Arts

Nightlife

BARS Pints and pitchers of international beers, giant-screen sports broadcasts, dueling pianos, and waiters in kilts make the **King Size Pub** (⊠ 16 Port Franc, Flon ☎ 021/6190650) a larger-than-life, rowdy English-style watering hole. It's part of a cinema complex. One of the city's chicest and liveliest gathering spots is **Le Bar** (⊠ Beau-Rivage Palace, Ouchy ☎ 021/6133330). There's a sophisticated armchair-filled lounge and a tiny wine bar inside the hotel's lower lobby entrance, where you can sip local or imported vintages. The Lausanne Palace serves the after-hours crowd in the stately **Le Bar du Palace** (⊠ City center ☎ 021/3313131); the hotel's stylish, pared-down **LP Bar** is just a corridor away. Tapas and exotic cocktails make the bilevel restaurant-lounge **Minuit Soleil** (⊠ 23 rue Central, city center ☎ 021/3235364) a popular evening stop. The mood is coastal Mediterranean with DJ selections to match.

DANCING Since most nighttime activity is centered on the Flon and place St-François areas, it's easy to sample several hot spots. If you pass a crowded club where the music is to your taste, duck in. It may be one of the happening locations too new or ephemeral to list here. Latin and tropical music fill **Atelier Volant** (⊠ 12 rue des Côtes-de-Montbenon, Flon ☎ 021/3235280). Inside the **D! Club** (⊠ 4 rue du Grand-Pont, city center ☎ 021/3213847), there's a mix of film, fashion, and music. Special-effect lighting and video screens lend tech appeal at **Loft Electroclub** (⊠ 1 pl. de Bel-Air, Flon ☎ 021/3116400), whose multiple floors and bars come to life Wednesday through Saturday. Clubbers come from as far away as Zürich and Basel for trance concerts and live performances at **MAD** (⊠ 23 rue de Genève, Flon ☎ 021/3116400). On Sunday night the club hosts a gay crowd.

JAZZ CLUBS In a city with its own jazz music school, look for a range of styles at the clubs that fill quickly with diehard fans. **Le Chorus** (✉ 3 av. Mon Repos, city center ☎ 021/3232233) has a renowned jazz cellar and also serves food and drinks. For acoustic jazz, drop in at **Pianissimo Onze** (✉ Foyer du Théâtr'Onze, 11 rue des Deux-Marchés, city center ☎ 021/3120043).

The Arts

Lausanne is one of Switzerland's arts capitals. Event seasons generally run from September to May, though summer brings outdoor concerts and more casual events. For ticket outlets contact Lausanne's tourist office, whose calendar of monthly events and bimonthly *Reg'art* (in French) give information on upcoming activities. Check out the daily newspaper *24 Heures* for listings as well. Tickets for many performances can be purchased through the **Billetel toll line** (☎ 090/155390).

The **Opéra de Lausanne** (✉ 12 av. du Théâtre, city center ☎ 021/3101600) stages classics in its eponymous hall. The riveting experiments of the **Maurice Béjart** ballet company take the stage at the **Salle Métropole** (✉ 1 pl. Bel-Air, city center ☎ 021/3111122), which is also home to the **Orchestre de Chambre de Lausanne**. The **Théâtre de Beaulieu** (✉ 10 av. des Bergières Beaulieu ☎ 021/6432111), right across from the Collection de l'Art Brut, hosts full-scale musical performances like those of the **Orchestre de la Suisse Romande**, which Lausanne shares with Geneva. **Théâtre Kléber-Méleau** (✉ 9 chemin de l'Usine-à-Gaz, Lausanne-Malley ☎ 021/6258400) offers a variety of French-language theater, old and new. **Théâtre-Municipal Lausanne** (✉ 12 av. du Théâtre, city center ☎ 021/3126433), an underground fortification in the heart of Lausanne, is one of the city's key performance venues for concerts, plays, and dance. **Théâtre Vidy-Lausanne** (✉ 5 av. Émile-Jacques-Dalcroze, Vidy ☎ 021/6194545) presents classical and contemporary theater in French.

Sports & the Outdoors

Bicycling

Gare CFF de Lausanne (train station; ✉ 1 pl. de la Gare, Baggage Service, city center ☎ 051/2242162) rents bikes. You must make a reservation at least one day in advance; in summer three days is recommended. For a lakefront ride, check out a set of wheels at **Blade & Bike Rental** (✉ 6 pl. de la Navigation, Ouchy ☎ 079/4139969).

Sailing

Ecole de Voile d'Ouchy (✉ Port d'Ouchy, Ouchy ☎ 021/6355887) is open for classes and rentals from March through September. The **Surf Shop** (✉ la plage, Préverenges ☎ 021/8021616) rents windsurfing gear and gives lessons.

Skating

The city hills may seem formidable, but there are miles of paths good for rollerblading along the waterfront. Another option is **La Fiévre Skate Park** (✉ 36 av. Sévelin, outside city center ☎ 021/6263793). You can rent in-line skates at **Blade & Bike Rental** (✉ 6 pl. de la Navigation, Ouchy ☎ 079/4139969).

Open-air ice-skating rinks in the Lausanne area operate from October to March. **Patinoire de Montchoisi** (✉ 30 av. du Servan, outside city center ☎ 021/6161062) has 35,000 square feet of ice surface. **Patinoire de la Pontaise** (✉ 11 rte. Plaines-du-Loup, outside city center ☎ 021/6468163) attracts urban crowds. Rental skates are available at both rinks.

Swimming

Bellerive (✉ 23 av. de Rhodanie, Ouchy ☎ 021/6178131) has access to the lake and three pools, one Olympic-size, plus generous lawns and a self-service restaurant. The indoor pool at **Mon-Repos** (✉ 4 av. du Tribunal-Fédéral, city center ☎ 021/3234566) stays open from late August through June. The pool at **Piscine de Montchoisi** (✉ 30 av. du Servan, outside city center ☎ 021/6161062) makes artificial waves; it's open from May through August.

Shopping

The main shopping circle centers on **place St-François, rue St-François, rue de Bourg**, and **rue du Grand-Pont**. Less-expensive shopping is along **rue St-Laurent** and **rue de l'Ale**.

Books

For magazines, travel guides and other books, and music, **FNAC** (✉ 6 rue Genève, Flon ☎ 021/2138585) is *the* superstore.

Department Stores

Bon Génie (✉ 10 pl. St-François, St-François ☎ 021/3204811) has clusters of designer areas on several levels. **Globus** (✉ rue Centrale at rue du Pont, city center ☎ 021/3429090) is a large upscale department store with a splendid basement food hall. Value-priced **Manor** (✉ 7 rue St-Laurent, city center ☎ 021/3213699) stocks a full range of merchandise, including logo items and souvenirs. It has nice food service, too.

Markets

There are fruit and vegetable markets in Lausanne along **rue de l'Ale, rue de Bourg**, and **place de la Riponne** every Wednesday and Saturday morning. **Place de la Palud** adds a flea market to its Wednesday and Saturday produce markets and is the site of a handicrafts market the first Friday of the month from March through December.

Watches

Most watch shops are in the St-François neighborhood. **Bucherer** (✉ 1 rue de Bourg ☎ 021/3206354) sells Rolex and Piaget. **Greumser** (✉ 10 rue de Bourg ☎ 021/3124826) specializes in Baume & Mercier. **Junod** (✉ 8 pl. St-François ☎ 021/3122745) carries Blancpain. **Roman Mayer** (✉ 12 bis pl. St-François ☎ 021/3122316) carries Audemars Piguet, Ebel, and Omega.

LAVAUX VIGNOBLES & RIVIERA

To the east of Lausanne stretches the Lavaux, a remarkably beautiful region of vineyards that rise up the hillsides all the way from Pully, on the outskirts of Lausanne, to Montreux—a distance of 24 km (15 mi).

Brown-roof stone villages in the Savoy style, old defense towers, and small baronial castles stud the green-and-black landscape. The vineyards, enclosed within low stone walls, slope so steeply that all the work has to be done by hand. Insecticides, fungicides, and manure are carried in baskets, and containers are strapped to workers' backs. In early October pickers harvest the fruit, carrying the loads to the nearest road and driving them by tractor to the nearest press. Some Lavaux vintages are excellent and in great demand, but unfortunately, as with so much of Switzerland's wine, the yield is small, and the product is rarely exported. Throughout the year, especially on weekends, winegrowers' cellars and some of the private châteaux-vignobles open for tastings (and, of course, sales).

Fodor's Choice ★ The scenic **Corniche de la Vaud** stretches some 17 km (10 mi) through Lavaux, threading above the waterfront from Lausanne to Vevey, between the autoroute and the lakeside Route 9. This is Switzerland at its most Franco-European, reminiscent in its small-scale way of the Riviera or the hill towns of Alsace. You'll career around hairpin turns on narrow cobbled streets, with the Savoy Alps glowing across the sparkling lake and the Dents du Midi looming ahead. Stop to gaze at roadside overlooks or wander down a side lane into the fields of Riex, Épesses, Rivaz, or the Dézaley, the sources of some of Switzerland's loveliest white wines and typically magical little Vaudois villages.

Lutry

22 *5 km (3 mi) southeast of Lausanne*

From its origins as a simple fishing village, this medieval town on the skirt hem of Lausanne expanded in the 11th century with the installation of the Benedictine monks from Savigny-en-Lyonnais. The religious order is credited with taming the wild hillsides, terracing them, and expanding the cultivation of wine grapes—a tradition that thrives today. Celebrated at the end of September, the Fête des Vendanges (harvest festival) is but one of the lively events that brings families and tourists to the plaza for food, wine, and entertainment.

In the sweep of the Reformation, the monastic order was closed and the church converted from its modest configuration to a more elaborate center of worship. The Église de Lutry is worth a stop for its stained-glass windows and 16th-century Flemish paintings, which cover the nave and choir. Lutry eschews becoming an urban annex, its character preserved in narrow streets that follow the contour of the land dropping from estate vineyards to the waterfront, twisting in and out of rugged walls once protective fortifications. Follow your instincts exploring back alleys and crooked passageways. You're likely to discover a jewelry studio or tearoom hidden in a nook or bend. For a history lesson, pause to read the multilanguage panels. The beach and park, at opposite ends of the waterfront, call for a blanket and picnic, but if relaxing is not on your schedule, take in the shoreline aboard one of the steamers that pulls up to the dock, or head uphill for a view from a vineyard aerie.

Where to Stay & Eat

$–$$ ✕ **Café de la Poste.** There are a number of dishes served at this narrow eatery, with entrances on the main street and the promenade, but the most ordered is *filets de perche* (perch fillets). Served with a garden salad, frites or *pommes vapeur* (steamed potatoes), and savory tartar sauce, it's a weekly routine for many families and couples. Without a reservation in summer, you will have to wait for a table outside; two small dining rooms connected by an open kitchen have difficulty containing the faithful in any season. ✉ *48 Grand-rue* ☎ *021/7911872* 🖬 *MC, V* ⊘ *Closed Sun. and Mon.*

$–$$ 🏨 **Hôtel Restaurant du Rivage.** The only choice on the waterfront, this calm, unpretentious lodging is in the village's pedestrian zone. Neat, unfussy rooms are sparkling; many open to views of the active harbor set against the Savoy Alps. The dining room, which serves typical Swiss cuisine, has a grand fireplace, but you will want to take your meals on the terrace when the weather warms. ✉ *1 pl. de l'Hôtel de Ville, CH-1095* ☎ *021/7967272* 🖨 *021/7967200* ⊕ *www.hotelrivagelutry.ch* ➴ *33 rooms, 3 suites* ⚅ *Restaurant, café, minibars, cable TV with movies, parking (fee)* 🖬 *AE, MC, V* ⦿ *BP.*

Cully

㉓ *4 km (2.5 mi) southeast of Lutry, 9.5 km (6 mi) southeast of Lausanne.*

The cluster of businesses, homes, barns, and cellars in Cully epitomizes the Lavaux lifestyle. Although it's not as picturesque as some lakeside or hill towns, as you pass through this narrow crossroads you can get a glimpse of what a vintner's life is really like, full of hard work and good eating. From the waterfront where the whistle of lake steamers marks the time of day, the community moves upward through a narrow clutch of shops and cafés until it reaches vineyard terraces banked against the rail line and highway. The *caveau* (cellar operated by local winegrowers), just off the main street on the walkway to the boat landing, opens for tastings on Thursday, Friday, and Saturday evenings. On summer weekends a miniature train connecting Cully and Lutry travels along grape-growers' paths through the heart of these appellations. In March the commune swells with jazz enthusiasts who come for a weeklong festival that some find more authentic than the world-famous one in Montreux.

Where to Stay & Eat

$$$–$$$$ ✕🏨 **Auberge du Raisin.** Fashionably dressed families, romantic couples, and international business teams gather here to celebrate birthdays, weddings, and deal closings. In the center of the animated dining room ($$$$), rotisserie hooks and spits twirl in a raised-hearth grill, as the chef seasons, times, and dispatches meats to the servers (side dishes are synchronized in the kitchen). In the auberge's guest rooms, puffy spreads cover the draped four-posters, and the brightly painted armoires and chests are a change from the usual fruitwoods; some of the large baths have skylights. Reservations are essential for the restaurant. ✉ *1 pl. de l'Hôtel de Ville, CH-1096* ☎ *021/7992131* 🖨 *021/7992501* ⊕ *www.relaischateaux.ch* ➴ *7 rooms, 3 suites* ⚅ *Restaurant* 🖬 *AE, MC, V* ⦿ *BP.*

---

en route For a more modern take on sampling the appellations, stop in the hamlet of Rivaz. Here **Bacchus** (☎ 021/9461113), a petite wine bar that's closed Monday–Tuesday and January and February, is carved out of a stone building on the steeply graded main street. Parking, halfway between the lake and church, is in a modern underground garage camouflaged by the vineyards.

Vevey

㉔ *9.5 km (6 mi) east of Cully, 19 km (12 mi) east of Lausanne.*

This soigné waterfront town was the setting for Anita Brookner's evocative 1985 novel *Hotel du Lac,* about a woman retreating to a lake resort to write; her heroine was attracted to the site, in part, because of its slightly stuffy 19th-century ways. In the 1870s Henry James captured this mood of prim grace while writing (and setting) *Daisy Miller* in the Hôtel des Trois Couronnes. Indeed, despite its virtual twinning with glamorous Montreux, Vevey retains its air of isolation and old-world gentility. Loyal visitors have been returning for generations to gaze at the Dent d'Oche (7,288 feet), across the water in France, and make sedate steamer excursions into Montreux and Lausanne. Today there are some who come just to see the bronze statue of Charlie Chaplin, in a rose garden on the lakefront quai, and to take the funicular or mountain train up to Mont Pèlerin. Vevey is also a great walking town, with more character in its shuttered Old Town; better museums, landmarks, and shops; and more native activity in its wine market than cosmopolitan Montreux can muster.

Among the notables who have been drawn to Vevey are Graham Greene, Victor Hugo, Jean-Jacques Rousseau (who set much of his *Julie, ou la Nouvelle Héloïse* here), Fyodor Dostoyevsky, Gustave Courbet, Oskar Kokoschka, Charlie and Oona Chaplin (buried in the cemetery at Corsier), and Swiss native Édouard Jeanneret, known as Le Corbusier. By following an excellent brochure/map published by the tourist office, you can travel "On the Trail of Hemingway"—and to the homes and haunts of some 40 other luminaries.

★ Le Corbusier's **Villa le Lac,** a single-story white house built directly on the Vevey waterfront, was constructed for his parents in 1923. It remains unaltered, with his original furnishings and details preserved within. Shingled in corrugated sheet metal, with a white-metal railed balcony looking over the water and a "birdhouse" chimney in molded concrete, it is typically sculptural and, in a modest way, visionary. ✉ *Western outskirts, just west of marina, Corseaux* ☎ *021/9235371* ✇ *Free* ☉ *Self-guided tours Apr.–Oct., Wed. 1:30–5.*

The Nestlé Foundation, a dynamic force in the region, sponsors an
↺ unconventional museum, the **Alimentarium.** A sculpture of an apple at the entrance of the 19th-century lakefront mansion symbolizes the museum's purpose: the celebration and study of food. In a stainless-steel kitchen chefs demonstrate their skills, and displays on food preparation cover everything from the campfire to futuristic equipment. Other

sections focus on merchants, supermarkets, food presentation, and marketing; you can also stroll through herb and vegetable gardens. The exhibits have material in English; some are interactive. ✉ *quai Perdonnet* ☎ *021/9244111* ⊕ *www.alimentarium.ch* ☞ *10 SF* ⊗ *Tues.–Sun. 10–6.*

The **Musée Jenisch** owes its considerable inventory of the works of the expressionist Oskar Kokoschka to his retirement on Vevey's shores. If it's strictly the Kokoschkas you want to see, you may need to plan ahead. His works are not always on display, but advance arrangements can be made to view the holdings in the archives. The museum's partner wing, the **Cabinet Cantonal des Estampes** (Cantonal Print Collection) contains a rich assortment of engravings, including some by Dürer and Rembrandt. ✉ *2 av. de la Gare* ☎ *021/9212950* ⊕ *www.museejenisch.ch* ☞ *12 SF* ⊗ *Daily 11–5:30.*

The **Musée Historique du Vieux Vevey** (Historical Museum of Old Vevey) occupies a grand 16th-century manor house, briefly home to Charlotte de Lengefeld, wife of Friedrich von Schiller. It retains some original furnishings as well as collections of arms, art, keys, and wine-making paraphernalia. The first floor serves as headquarters for the Brotherhood of Winegrowers, the organization that stages the mammoth Fêtes des Vignerons (Winegrowers' Festival). The festival is held roughly every 25 years; you can get a taste of the most recent celebration (1999) from the costumes, photographs, and memorabilia on display. ✉ *2 rue du Château* ☎ *021/9210722* ⊕ *www.vevey.ch/museehistorique* ☞ *6 SF* ⊗ *Tues.–Sat. 10:30–noon and 2–5:30, Sun. 11–5.*

The **Musée Suisse de l'Appareil Photographique** (Swiss Camera Museum) displays an impressive collection of cameras, photographic equipment, and mounted work. It also hosts *Images*, a biennial multimedia show held in the fall of even-numbered years. ✉ *99 Grande-pl.* ☎ *021/ 9252140* ⊕ *www.cameramuseum.ch* ☞ *6 SF* ⊗ *Mar.–Oct., Tues.–Sun. 11–5:30; Nov.–Feb., Tues.–Sun. 2–5:30.*

need a break? Pause for a glass of a local or imported vintage at the storefront wine bar **Les Dix Vins** (✉ 24 rue des Deux-Marchés ☎ 021/9223033), on a side street between market plazas. The owner's friendly enthusiasm adds to the pleasure of time spent toasting, chatting, or people-watching. If sweets are more your mood, pick a luscious pastry from the case at **Poyet** (✉ 8 rue du Théâtre ☎ 021/9213737), on the pedestrian walkway near the tourist office.

Just east of town, the **Musée Suisse du Jeu** (Game and Toy Museum) fills a 13th-century castle. Games of strategy and chance, ranging from dice to video games, are represented in displays spanning centuries. Its excellent gift shop is stocked with Legos, puzzles, and board games. Tours and notes are available in English. ✉ *1½ km (1 mi) east of Vevey on rte. 9, La Tour-de-Peilz* ☎ *021/9444050* ⊕ *www.museedujeu.com* ☞ *6 SF* ⊗ *Mar.–Oct., Tues.–Sun. 11–5:30; Nov.–Feb., Tues.–Sun. 2–5.*

off the beaten path

BLONAY–CHAMBY RAILROAD – From Vevey and Montreux, a number of railways climb into the heights, which in late spring are carpeted with an extravagance of wild narcissi. If you like model railroads, you will especially enjoy a trip on the Blonay–Chamby Railroad, whose real steam-driven trains alternate with electric trains. You can depart from either end (parking is more plentiful in Blonay); trains make a stop at a small museum of railroad history in between. The trip takes about 20 minutes each way, not including a browse in the museum. ✐ *Case Postale 366, CH-1001 Lausanne* ☎ *021/9432121* ⊕ *www.blonay-chamby.ch* ✉ *Round-trip ticket 14 SF* ⊙ *May–Oct., weekends 9:55–6:35.*

Where to Stay & Eat

$$$$ ✕ **À la Montagne.** This elegant, intimate restaurant is set in a restored home in the wine village of Chardonne. Perched on a sunny shelf high above the Nestlé corporate complex, it offers a view of the lake (from part of the dining room) that is worthy of a champagne toast. Traditional French preparations like beef medallions and rack of lamb are straightforward, smartly garnished, and paired with fresh herbs and vegetables. A well-composed wine list of Swiss and international selections offers breadth to match. Those who like a stroll before and after dinner can take the mostly flat five-minute walk to the funicular, an easy way to access these upper reaches. ✉ *21 rue du Village, Chardonne* ☎ *021/9212930* ▭ *AE, DC, MC, V* ⊙ *Closed July.*

¢–$$ ✕ **Le Mazot.** Offerings at this tiny pinte are limited. Regulars favor the tender steak—entrecôte of beef or *cheval* (horse)—accompanied by an overflowing plate of fries or a half-moon of crispy Rösti. After years of overseeing bubbling pots of fondue, the other popular draw, handpainted murals and mirrors set in dark frames have a smoky patina. The narrow room is crowded with scarred booths and bare tables, which can be moved together in long chains. It's a casual neighborhood place where local wines are poured from pewter pitchers and the people at the next table eavesdrop. ✉ *7 rue du Conseil* ☎ *021/9217822* ▭ *MC, V* ⊙ *Closed Wed. No lunch Sun.*

★ $$$$ ✕▦ **Le Mirador.** On a ledge above Vevey, this combination spa resort and elite conference center is set among the meadows and modest villages of Mont-Pèlerin. Breathtaking panoramic views of lake, Alps, and vineyards can be had from elegant guest rooms trimmed in marble, parquet, and brocade. The luxurious Givenchy spa has a broad treatment menu, from jet-lag relief to cosmetic pampering. La Trianon ($$$–$$$$), the fine-dining restaurant, ranks as one of the best haute tables and wine cellars in this gastronomic region. Not to fear, the calorie-conscious are accommodated in all dining venues. ✉ *5 chemin du Mirador, CH-1801 Mont-Pèlerin* ☎ *021/9251111* 📠 *021/9251112* ⊕ *www.mirador.ch* ↩ *74 rooms, 19 suites* ♨ *3 restaurants, in-room data ports, in-room safes, minibars, cable TV with movies and video games, 3 tennis courts, indoor-outdoor pool, health club, hair salon, spa, bar, concierge, business services, helipad, free parking, no-smoking rooms* ▭ *AE, DC, MC, V.*

FOND OF FONDUE

THOUGH FONDUE IS DE RIGUEUR in any Alpine setting, Vaud is a fanatical stronghold. In the Pays-d'Enhaut (Highlands), cattle head uphill in summer, and production of local cheeses—the firm, fragrant Gruyère and L'Etivaz—soars. They are sold at various stages: young and mild, ripe and savory, or aged to a heady tang. Take a guided hike from Chateaux-d'Oex to the highland pastures to see all aspects of cheese making and then share a bubbly pot of perfection.

Fondue is simply cheese melted together with white wine, garlic, and a dash of kirsch. Aficionados debate the perfect blend of cheeses and whether to include mushrooms, tomatoes, and even chunks of potatoes. Most restaurants serve a blend of Gruyère, Emmental, and Appenzeller; others have their own recipe. The especially popular moite-moite (half and half) is half Gruyère and half bold l'Etivaz or creamy Vacherin.

Diners dip chunks of bread on long forks into the bubbling mixture. Many restaurants serve fondue in an adjoining carnotzet or Stübli (French and German versions of a cozy pub)—both to re-create a rustic Alpine experience and to spare fellow diners the fierce aromas of cheese, garlic, and the fuel that keeps the fondue melted. It's a dish best suited to winter.

Appropriate accompaniments are a fruity white wine or plain black tea—never red wine, beer, or cola—and the traditional coup du milieu (shot in the middle), a reviving midmeal shot of kirsch. The salty cheese will make you yearn for water; go light and never with ice. Custom dictates that if you lose your bread in the caquelon, women must kiss the host or nearest man, while men buy another round.

★ **$$$$** ⌂ **Hôtel des Trois Couronnes.** Honeycombed by dramatic atrium stairwells that look down on marble columns and gleaming floors inlaid with golden coronets, this regal landmark was Henry James's home base when he wrote (and set here) the novella *Daisy Miller*. A vast lakefront terrace with pool overlooks the pollards, the promenade, and the steamers plying the lake. Burgundy and gold swags and coverlets contrast boldly with neutral striped wallpaper in generously sized guest rooms. The spa, called Puressens (Pure Senses), offers a full range of restorative services that are a relaxing extension to time spent in the lower-level pool. ⊠ *49 rue d'Italie, CH-1800* ☎ *021/9233200* ⎙ *021/9233399* ⊕ *www.hoteldestroiscouronnes.com* ⌕ *55 rooms* ⚫ *Restaurant, café, in-room data ports, minibars, cable TV, indoor pool, health club, hair salon, spa, bar, business services, free parking* ⊟ *AE, DC, MC, V.*

$$$–$$$$ ⌂ **Hôtel du Lac.** Anita Brookner set her novel *Hotel du Lac* in this lesser sister of the Trois Couronnes: its readers may be disappointed to find the hotel lacking the discretion, refinement, and even the stuffiness she so precisely described. Instead, there are plenty of reminders that this is a link in the Best Western chain. Though some rooms are done in prim florals or chic burled wood, others retain decor of another era. Its location is the hotel's main attraction, as a sheltered terrace restaurant, garden, and pool are all just across the street from the waterfront. ⊠ *1 rue d'Italie, CH-1800* ☎ *021/9211041* 🖷 *021/9217508* ⊕ *www. bestwestern.com* ⇝ *56 rooms* ⚐ *Restaurant, café, in-room data ports, in-room safes, minibars, cable TV with movies, pool, bar, concierge, business services, parking (fee), no-smoking rooms; no a/c in some rooms* ⊟ *AE, DC, MC, V* ⊗ *Closed Dec. and Jan.* ⦿*❘ BP.*

$$$–$$$$ 🏨 **Hotel Pavillon.** Offering the best of old and new, this hotel contains 1920s frescoes of a winegrowers' festival on the ceiling of La Brasserie, the old-fashioned restaurant, as well as a modern annex of guest rooms wired with up-to-the-minute technology. Colors are strong—plaid spreads and geometric-print draperies in bold orange and red, cherry-wood furniture, and carpets dominated by dark green or blue. Adjacent to the train station, the outdoor café and coffee bar are convenient rendezvous points. The hotel is a congenial family-run place, and you will likely see the different generations checking on details and greeting guests. ⊠ *pl. de la Gare, CH-1800* ☎ *021/9250404* 🖷 *021/9250400* ⊕ *www.pavillon.ch* ⇝ *85 rooms, 3 suites, 2 apartments* ⚐ *3 restaurants, snack bar, in-room data ports, in-room safes, minibars, cable TV with movies, gym, sauna, steam room, bar, laundry facilities, concierge, parking (fee), no-smoking rooms* ⊟ *AE, DC, MC, V* ⦿*❘ BP.*

$$–$$$ 🏨 **Hostellerie Bon Rivage.** This hotel blends right in with the estates facing the lake on the main road between Vevey and Montreux. Its breezy rooms with blond modular furniture overlook a small marina and the turrets of the village castle. The building was once home to the Order of St. Joseph; the nuns still maintain a small chapel on the main floor. Request a lakefront room not only for the superb view, but to avoid street noise. Keep an eye out for l'Olivier's chef harvesting herbs and vegetables for Provençal-inspired dishes from the walled garden below. ⊠ *18 rue de St-Maurice, CH-1814 La Tour-de-Peilz* ☎ *021/9770707* 🖷 *021/ 9770799* ⇝ *50 rooms* ⚐ *Restaurant, in-room data ports, cable TV, bar, free parking, some pets allowed, no-smoking rooms; no a/c* ⊟ *AE, MC, V* ⦿*❘ BP.*

$ 🏨 **Des Négociants.** Handy to the market and near the lake, this comfortable and lively lodging is in the Old Town. Rooms have bright colors and modular blond-wood furniture, and bathrooms have showers only. The arcaded restaurant and terrace have a vivacious hum at mealtimes, courtesy of the guests who gather for Alsatian specialties and homemade desserts. ⊠ *27 rue du Conseil, CH-1800* ☎ *021/9227011* 🖷 *021/ 9213424* ⊕ *www.hotelnegociants.ch* ⇝ *23 rooms* ⚐ *Restaurant, in-room data ports, cable TV, free parking; no a/c* ⊟ *AE, DC, MC, V* ⦿*❘ BP.*

Nightlife

Despite its quiet, small-town appearance, Vevey has gathering spots where the music is loud and revelers dance until dawn. For dance, concerts, and jam sessions, head over to the multivenue complex **Les Temps Modernes** (⊠ 6 rue des Deux Gares ☎ 021/9222721). **National** (⊠ 9 rue du Torrent ☎ 021/9237625), just off the place du Marché, combines music and late food. At **Neury's Club** (⊠ 30 av. General Guisan ☎ 021/ 9212196), people warble karaoke Monday through Wednesday before full-throttle clubbing takes over for the weekend.

Sports & the Outdoors

As you drive along the highway you will see sunbathers lounging on rocks jutting out into the lake and swimmers playing on the stony beaches. It's difficult to tell if they are on private property or have public access. There *are* swimming areas open to everyone that include a mix of facilities—toilets, showers, changing cabins, and snack bars—but lifeguards are only at the pools, so be careful. Slippery rocks, drop-offs, and water traffic on the lake require special attention. **Jardin Doret** (⊠ Off pl. du Marché ☎ 021/6178131) provides access to the lake, a generous lawn with play area, and a snack bar. The indoor pool at **Piscine les Mousquetaires** (⊠ 13 pl. des Anciens-Fossés, La Tour-de-Peilz ☎021/9770307) is open most of the year; there's also a beach at the port. The **Vevey/ Corseaux Plage** (⊠ 19 av. de Lavaux, Corseaux ☎ 021/9212368), west of Nestlé headquarters, has both lake swimming and two large pools (indoor and outdoor).

Shopping

Boutiques and galleries in the Old Town east of place du Marché deserve attentive shopping. **L'Air du Temps** (⊠ 26 rue des Deux-Marchés ☎ 021/9222303) carries gifts for the home plus wine accessories. Next door is the town's best cheese shop, **La Grenette** (⊠ 27 rue des Deux-Marchés ☎ 021/9212345). **Saint-Antoine** (⊠ 1 ave. Général-Guisan), a modern, multilevel complex diagonally across from the train station, clusters large and small retailers within its glass panels. An extra bonus: its underground parking is a smart alternative to the cramped, restricted parking in the Old Town.

Vevey is a marketing center for regional wines, and the local white is sold in summer at its waterfront **Saturday market** (⊠ Grande-pl.), alongside fresh produce; you buy your own glass and taste *à volonté* (at will).

Montreux

4 km (2 mi) southeast of Vevey, 21 km (13 mi) southeast of Lausanne.

Montreux could be called the Cannes of Lac Léman—though it might raise an eyebrow at the slur. Spilling down steep hillsides into a sunny south-facing bay, its waterfront thick with magnolias, cypresses, and palm trees, the historic resort earns its reputation as the capital—if not the pearl—of the Swiss Riviera. Unlike the French Riviera, it has managed, despite overwhelming crowds of conventioneers, to keep up appearances. Its Edwardian-French deportment has survived considerable development, and though there are plenty of harsh modern high-rises with parking-garage aesthetics, its mansarded landmarks still unfurl yellow awnings to shield millionaires from the sun.

The site where Stravinsky composed *Petrouchka* and *Le Sacre du Printemps* and where Vladimir Nabokov resided in splendor, Montreuxand its suburbs have attracted artists and literati for 200 years: Byron, Shelley, Tolstoy, Hans Christian Andersen, and Flaubert were drawn to its lush shoreline. When its casino opened in 1883, tourism began in earnest. Even rock star Freddie Mercury came under the resort's spell; a statue of the late Queen singer stands on the quay. But the resort is best known for its annual jazz festival, which lately has strayed from its original focus to include rock, R&B, Latin, and hip-hop. Each July, Montreux's usually composed promenade explodes in a street festival of food tents, vendor kiosks, and open band shells, which complement standing-room-only concert hall venues.

Above the train station, a complex of 17th-century homes once belonging to the town's successful winemakers is now the **Musée du Vieux-Montreux** (Museum of Old Montreux). This historical museum traces regional development from the time when Roman coins were used as tender, focusing on agricultural life and the shift to tourism. Profiles of famous residents and visitors who lived and worked in the area are highlighted. The museum's cellar restaurant is a good place to sample typical cuisine. ✉ *40 rue de la Gare* ☏ *021/9631353* ⊕ *www.museemontreux. ch* 🖅 *6 SF* ☉ *Apr.–Nov, daily 10–noon and 2–5.*

Montreux's cultural center, the **Maison Visinand,** is housed in a restored mansion in the Old Town. Its calendar of events mixes exhibitions and performances with classes and studios for painting, photography, and dance. ✉ *32 rue du Pont* ☏ *021/9630726* ⊕ *www.centreculturelmontreux.ch* 🖅 *Free* ☉ *Wed.–Sun. 3–6.*

need a break?
The lunch-and-tearoom set (ladies with poodles, Brits in tweeds, fashion plates in Gucci) regularly descends on **Zurcher** (✉ 45 av. du Casino ☏ 021/9635963), the irresistible confiserie on Montreux's main drag. A green salad, the *potage du jour* (soup of the day), and a chocolate-striated torte make a great quick meal. The café is closed on Monday.

Fodor'sChoice
★
Certainly the greatest attraction at Montreux and one of Switzerland's must-sees is the **Château de Chillon,** the awe-inspiring 12th-century castle that rears out of the water at Veytaux, down the road from and within sight of Montreux. Chillon was built on Roman foundations under the direction of Duke Peter of Savoy with the help of military architects from Plantagenet England. For a long period it served as a state prison, and one of its shackled guests was François Bonivard, who supported the Reformation and enraged the Savoyards. He spent six years in this prison, chained most of the time to a pillar in the dungeon, before being released by the Bernese in 1536.

While living near Montreux, Lord Byron visited Chillon and was so transported by its atmosphere and by Bonivard's grim sojourn that he was inspired to write his famous poem "The Prisoner of Chillon." He charts the prisoner's despair and brief moments of hope, culminating in the realization on release that "these heavy walls to me had grown/A hermitage—and all my own!/ . . .So much a long communion tends/To make us what we are:—even I/Regain'd my freedom with a sigh." Like a true tourist, Byron carved his name on a pillar in Bonivard's still-damp and chilly dungeon; his graffito is now protected under a plaque.

In high season visitors to Chillon must now file placidly from restored chamber to restored turret, often waiting at doorways for entire busloads of fellow tourists to pass. Yet the restoration is so evocative and so convincing, with its tapestries, carved fireplaces, period ceramics and pewter, and elaborate wooden ceilings, that even the jaded castle hound may become as carried away as Byron was. While you're waiting your turn, you can gaze out the narrow windows over the sparkling, lapping water and remember Mark Twain, who thought Bonivard didn't have it half bad. ✉ *Veytaux, less than 3 km (2 mi) south of Montreux* ☎ *021/9668910* ⊕ *www.chillon.ch* 🎫 *9 SF* 🕙 *Mar. and Oct., daily 9:30–5; Apr.–Sept., daily 9–6; Nov.–Feb., daily 10–4.*

LES AVANTS – The Montreux–Oberland–Bernois (MOB) railroad leads to the resort village of Les Avants (3,181 feet) and then on to Château-d'Oex, Gstaad, and the Simmental. Noël Coward bought his dream home in Les Avants, at No. 8 route de Sonloup. Ernest Hemingway wrote to his family and friends of the village's fields of daffodils—and, more in character, of its bobsled track.

Where to Stay & Eat

$$$$ ✕ **Le Pont de Brent.** Tucked on a hillside next to its namesake bridge in
Fodor'sChoice the suburb of Brent, this small but elegant establishment ties with
★ Philippe Rochat's restaurant for the honor of best table in Switzerland. Who would guess that the pale stone exterior of this unassuming building screens showstopping cuisine? Norman chef Gérard Rabaey performs alchemy with local ingredients to turn out dishes almost too pretty to eat, such as ravioli of rabbit with chanterelles and baby fava beans as well as fillet of wild turbot with a citron-thyme sauce. All is warm here, from the ocher walls to the welcome and service. ✉ *rte. de Brent, 7 km (4½ mi) northwest of Montreux, Brent* ☎ *021/9645230* 🍴 *Reservations essential* ▤ *MC, V* 🕙 *Closed Sun. and Mon., last 2 wks of July, late Dec.–early Jan.*

$$–$$$ ✕ **La Vielle Ferme.** Follow the winding road into the village of Chailly. Past the fountain and across the street, you'll see the stone facade of a 14th-century farmhouse restored to rustic elegance and said to be the oldest in the region. Dining rooms that were once stalls and family quarters have stucco and wooden beams. The owner's philosophy—*A BON MANGER, BON BOIRE* (good food and good drink)—is carved above the raised fireplace that doubles as a grill. The cuisine is true to the heritage of the homestead: lamb chops prepared with herbs, chicken simmered in honey and lemon. If it's a fondue or raclette you prefer, a separate carnotzet serves these cheese specialties. ✉ *rue de Bourg, Chailly-sur-Montreux* ☎ *021/9646465* ▤ *AE, MC, V* 🕙 *Closed Mon. and Tues.*

$–$$ ✕ **Du Pont.** In the Old Town, high on the hill over Montreux's waterfront, this bustling, old restaurant-café takes its food and its customers seriously. You can relax in the smoky café (where jeans aren't out of place) or enjoy full service and pink linens in the lovely dining room upstairs. Suit your whim: the menu and the prices are exactly the same, including a cheap daily special—whether you order upstairs or down. ✉ *12 rue du Pont* ☎ *021/9632249* ▤ *AE, DC, MC, V.*

★ **$$$–$$$$** ✕▣ **L'Ermitage.** Freestanding on its own waterfront-garden grounds, this genteel, intimate retreat offers top-drawer haute gastronomie and a few luxurious rooms upstairs. The guest rooms are lightened with fresh flowers, lacquered cane furniture, and lake views; many rooms have balconies.

Chef Étienne Krebs's exceptional menu may include cannelloni of rabbit stuffed with foie gras or pan-sautéed lake fish with a tomato, chanterelle, and basil jus. A bit less formal than the dining room ($$$$; closed late December to late January and Sunday and Monday September to May), a terrace is open daily in summer for alfresco dining. ⊠ *75 rue du Lac, CH-1815 Clarens* ☎ *021/9644411* 🖶 *021/9647002* ⊕ *www.ermitage-montreux.com* ⇆ *4 rooms, 3 suites* ♨ *Restaurant, in-room data ports, minibars, cable TV, free parking* ▤ *AE, DC, MC, V* ☉ *Closed late Dec.–late Jan.* ⑩ *BP.*

$$$$ 🏨 **Grand Hôtel Suisse Majestic.** It's not unusual to mistake the similar belle epoch architecture and repeating yellow awnings for the Palace down the street. Half the size and less ritzy, the Majestic has a gracious ambience of its own plus the convenience of being across the street from the train station and in the heart of shopping and dining. Rooms have crown molding and fireplaces; lake views are definitely worth the extra charge. At the lively terrace restaurant, you can dine perched above the hubbub; the station-side café is great for people watching. ⊠ *43 ave. des Alpes, CH-1820* ☎ *021/9663333* 🖶 *021/9663300* ⊕ *www.suisse-majestic.ch* ⇆ *139 rooms* ♨ *Restaurant, café, minibars, cable TV with movies, bar, business services, parking (fee)* ▤ *AE, DC, MC, V.*

$$$$
Fodor'sChoice
★

🏨 **Le Montreux Palace.** Silver mansards and yellow awnings flag this vast institution as a landmark, though its aristocratic interiors are now filled with cell-phone-chatting travelers. This colossal belle epoque folly of stained glass, frescoes, and flamboyant molded stucco opened in 1906 and counts Vladimir Nabokov among its notable residents (a bronze of the author stands in the lakeside gardens). Updated facilities do not compromise the allure of this grand hotel. You can be cyber-connected from any corner or secluded in a massage suite at the Amrita wellness center. Guest rooms have fruitwood furniture, bold accessories, and Jacuzzis trimmed in granite and marble. For an American cocktail or sandwich, Harry's Bar sates your appetite. ⊠ *100 Grand-rue, CH-1820* ☎ *021/9621212* 🖶 *021/9621717* ⊕ *www.montreux-palace.com* ⇆ *185 rooms, 50 suites* ♨ *4 restaurants, in-room data ports, in-room safes, cable TV with movies, tennis court, 2 pools, health club, hair salon, spa, 2 bars, nightclub, concierge, convention center, parking (fee), no-smoking rooms* ▤ *AE, DC, MC, V.*

$$$–$$$$ 🏨 **Royal Plaza.** Neighbor to Auditorium Stravinski at the quiet end of town, this contemporary complex is a stylish complement to the lakefront. An advantageous layout affords three-quarters of the guest rooms irresistible views of Lac Léman and the Savoy Alps. Soft color palettes and Asian accents adorn the rooms, which have generous sitting and work areas. A small spa with workout area takes care of your wellness needs. The Sunset Bar is a choice spot for late-afternoon drinks; the fine-dining restaurant, La Croisette, features such seafood specialties as baked sea bass marinated in lemongrass and ginger, and scallop brochette with green salsa and fennel. ⊠ *97 Grand-rue, CH-1820* ☎ *021/9625050* 🖶 *021/9625151* ⊕ *www.royalplaza.ch* ⇆ *123 rooms, 24 suites* ♨ *3 restaurants, in-room data ports, in-room safes, minibars, cable TV with movies, indoor pool, gym, sauna, spa, steam room, 2 bars, laundry service, concierge, parking (fee), no-smoking floors* ▤ *AE, DC, MC, V.*

$–$$ ⌂ **Masson.** If you're traveling by car or enjoy being away from the downtown resort scene, look up this demure little inn on a hillside in Veytaux, between Chillon and Montreux. Since it was built in 1829, it has had only four owners, and the current family takes pride in its genteel period decor and the personalized attention that attracts repeat guests season after season. You'll find floral prints, brass beds, pristine linens, buffed parquet, and expansive lake views from the numerous balconies. The breakfast buffet is generous, with homemade breads and jams. ⌂ *5 rue Bonivard, CH-1820 Veytaux* ☎ *021/9660044* 🖷 *021/9660036* ⊕ *www.hotelmasson.ch* ⤴ *33 rooms* ⚷ *Restaurant, in-room safes, minibars, cable TV, hot tub, sauna, free parking; no a/c* ▤ *AE, MC, V* ☾ *Closed Oct.–Apr.* ⦿⦸ *BP.*

Nightlife & the Arts

Montreux's famous festivals and arts events are listed in a seasonal booklet published by the tourist office; tickets are sold from its booth at the waterfront. The renowned **Montreux Jazz Festival** takes place every July in the ultramodern **Auditorium Stravinski** (⌂ 95 Grand-rue) and other lakeside venues. For tickets to these popular events, it's easiest to monitor the schedule (not released until late April or May) on the Web site (⊕ www.montreuxjazz.com). Popular events sell out in hours so be ready to purchase online. The **Ticket Corner** also sells tickets at (☎ 900/800800). In summer Montreux offers a variety of free outdoor concerts from its bandstand on the waterfront near the landing stage.

BARS The swank **Harry's New York Bar** (⌂ 100 Grand-rue ☎ 021/9621212), at the Montreux Palace, has a pianist after 5. Adjacent to a popular Italian restaurant (La Rouvenaz), the eclectic **Il Baretto** (⌂ 1 rue du Marché ☎ 021/9621212) is the smallest bar in town. An urbane, designer-clad crowd flocks to the **Mayfair Café** (⌂ 52 Grand-rue ☎ 021/9667979) to take in the afternoon sun and make plans for the evening.

CASINO The **Casino Barrière** (⌂ 9 rue du Théâtre ☎ 021/9628383) has dancing, slot machines, table games, and multiple dining venues. Revised gambling regulations have upped the betting limits, making it a major gaming center. Be sure to bring your passport, as no other ID will get you in. Table games don't begin until 4 PM. The casino is open from 11 AM to 3 AM, Friday and Saturday to 4.

DANCING A DJ spins at the **Copy Cat** (⌂ 100 Grand-rue ☎ 021/9633444), the Montreux Palace's hot spot for dancing. Funk, techno, and Latin sounds lure the young set at **Ned** (⌂ 19 rue du Marché ☎ 021/9612540), where weekend partying goes until 3 AM. The sound takes a salsa turn at the **Tropical Bar** (⌂ 5 rue d'Auberge ☎ 021/9638888).

Sports & the Outdoors

BOATING Pedal boats are popular along Montreux-Vevey's waterfront. Rentals are available by the convention center and at the quai du Casino. **Ecole de Voile de Montreux** (⌂ Clarens ☎ 021/4691338) is the local sailing club. Montreux offers its hotel guests free and supervised use of its waterfront facilities for windsurfing and waterskiing; in the afternoon a fee is charged at the **Ski-Nautique Club** (⌂ Clubhouse du Casino ☎ 021/9634456).

SWIMMING **La Maladaire** (⊠ Clarens ☎ 021/9645703) has an Olympic-size indoor pool. The **Casino Barrière** (⊠ 9 rue du Théâtre ☎ 021/9628383) has a pool on an outdoor terrace with a bar.

en route

Several family entertainment complexes lie in the border village of Le Bouveret, on the lake's southern shore. The admission charges are similar to those in American amusement parks, but the facilities are not on a grand scale. At the indoor water park **Aqua Parc,** Captain Kid's Land and Jungle Land are filled with pirate-themed flumes, chutes, and slides. Paradise Land mimics a Caribbean getaway for adults, complete with a swim-up bar. ⊠ *Le Bouveret* ☎ *024/ 4820000* ⊕ *www.aquaparc.ch* 🎟 *43 SF* ⊙ *July and Aug., daily 10–10; Sept.–June, Sun.–Thurs. 10–7:30, Fri. and Sat. 10–10.*

The miniature railway circuit laid out in green **Swiss Vapeur Parc** is great for younger kids. Here you can straddle the tiny models and cruise around a reduced-scale landscape. ⊠ *Le Bouveret* ☎ *024/ 4814410* ⊕ *www.swissvapeur.ch* 🎟 *13 SF* ⊙ *Mid-Mar.–mid-May and late Sept.–Oct., weekdays 1:30–6, weekends 10–6; mid-May–mid-Sept., daily 10–6.*

LES ALPES VAUDOISES

At the eastern tip of Lac Léman, the Alps on the French and Swiss sides close in on the Rhône, and the lakefront highways begin a gradual, ear-popping ascent as the scenery looms larger and the mountains rise around you. The high-altitude Alpine resorts of Villars, Leysin, and Les Diablerets each have their charms for winter-sports fans and summer hikers; a visit to any one of the three would suffice for a mountain retreat. On the other hand, the Pays-d'Enhaut, over the Col des Mosses, is a rustic, lower-altitude region surrounded by rocky ridges and velvet hillsides sprinkled with ancient carved-wood chalets; either Château-d'Oex or Rougemont would serve well as home base for a sojourn in this gentle resort area. You can make a beeline from one to another, but rail connections are limited and driving often torturous; you'd do well to choose one dreamy spot and stay put—by the fireplace, on the balcony—for as many days as your itinerary allows.

The resorts of the Alpes Vaudoises, although anything but household words to most ski buffs, offer the bonus of a transportation linkup and lift-ticket package with the sprawling Gstaad "Super-Ski" region. This skiing mecca takes in the entire Saanen Valley from Zweisimmen to Château-d'Oex and even dovetails with the parallel valley resorts of Adelboden and Lenk, justifying a visit for skiers who want to cover a lot of territory during their stay.

Aigle

❷❻ *17 km (10 mi) south of Montreux, 38 km (24 mi) southeast of Lausanne.*

On a smooth plain flanked by the sloping vineyards of the region of Le Chablais, Aigle is a scenic wine center. Its spired and turreted **Château**

de Savoie, originally built in the 13th century, was almost completely destroyed—and then rebuilt—by the 15th-century Bernese.

At the **Château d'Aigle,** both the novice and wine aficionado can get a close-up look at wine-making history and promotion. First peruse display casks, bottles, presses, and winemakers' tools within the wood-beamed chambers of the **Musée de la Vigne et du Vin** (Museum of Viticulture and Wine), in the chateau. Some living quarters are reproduced, and there's even a collection of costumes worn over the centuries at the local Fête des Vignerons. The separate **Musée de l'Étiquette** (Museum of Wine Labels), in a timbered attic in an adjacent warehouse called the Maison de la Dîme, chronicles the history of prestigious vintages through a collection of labels representing more than 50 countries and dating back 200 years. You need go no farther for a tasting: the Pinte du Paradis wine bar is just downstairs, overlooking the vineyards. ☎ 024/4662130 ⊕ www.chateauaigle.ch ≋ 9 SF ☉ Apr.–June, Sept. and Oct., Tues.–Sun. 10–12:30 and 2–6; July and Aug., daily 10–6; Nov.–Mar., tours by appointment.

Lance Armstrong devotees and other cycling enthusiasts will find the **Centre Mondial du Cyclisme** (World Cycling Center) a fascinating stop. Headquarters of the UCI, cycling's international sports federation, the contemporary silver-tone facility has an exhibition hall, athlete training facility, and indoor velodrome—all state-of-the-art and used by world-class competitors. The track is open to the public in the off-season, and guided tours can be arranged. Both require advance booking. ⊠ chemin de la Mêlée ☎ 024/4685885 ⊕ www.cmc-aigle.ch ≋ Free ☉ Weekdays 8–6.

Shopping

Chasselas grapes are cultivated on the steep shale and sandstone terraces by Aigle and Yvorne; these local wines flare with exuberance. Generations of the Badoux family have tended the land around Aigle held by *murailles* (stone walls), producing a signature wine identified by the lizard on the label. **La Boutique du Lézard** (⊠ 18 av. du Chamossaire ☎ 024/ 4688888), a lovely wineshop, is just the place to scout a local find. Browse the shelves for select vintages, etched decanters, and corkscrews.

Villars-sur-Ollon

㉗ *15 km (9 mi) southeast of Aigle, 53 km (33 mi) southeast of Lausanne.*

At 4,264 feet, this welcoming ski center spreads comfortably along a sunny terrace, the craggy peaks of Les Diablerets (10,528 feet) behind it and before it a sweeping view over the Rhône Valley all the way to Mont Blanc. Balanced along its ridge and open to the vast space below, the busy little downtown—sports shops, cafés, resort hotels—tapers off quickly into open country. Though it's thriving with new construction, Villars retains a sense of coziness and tradition, and some of its family-owned hotels have preserved the feel of mountain lodges that's rare these days in Switzerland. What Villars lacks in glitz, it amply compensates for with unpretentious good cheer. A network of lifts connecting with Les Diablerets makes this a good choice for skiers or hikers who want to experience Suisse Romande relatively unspoiled. The boarding schools headquartered in the area keep the town animated with teen adrenaline, backing sports such as snowboarding, mountain biking, in-line skating, and rock climbing.

Skiing

Villars nicely balances sophistication and Alpine isolation, thanks to a compact village, 36 lifts, and 100 km (67 mi) of downhill runs. The main ski area above the village can be reached easily either by cable car to **Roc d'Orsay** (6,560 feet) or by cog railway from the center to **Bretaye** (5,925 feet); either site allows access to the lifts that fan out over a sunny bowl riddled with intermediate runs and off-trail challenges. From Bretaye, you can also take lifts up to **Grand Chamossaire** (6,954 feet) for gentle, open runs. Trails from Chaux Ronde are easy enough for beginners, but the more advanced can find jumps and trees enough to keep them more than alert. Just beyond Villars, the linking resort of **Gryon**, with runs that pitch off **Les Chaux**, presents a few more options and a change of scenery, again with trails for all levels of skill. For serious skiers, the link to **Les Diablerets Glacier** provides stepped-up challenges in vertical territory that is used for training professionals. One-day lift tickets cost 54 SF. If you are going to ski for six days, purchase the region's all-inclusive pass for 263 SF, which provides access to Glacier 3000 at Les Diablerets, Leysin, and Mosses. There are also 44 km (27 mi) of cross-country trails plus sledding and snowshoeing.

Where to Stay & Eat

★ ¢–$$ ✕ **Le Refuge de Frience.** Detour off the scenic route from Villars to Gryon at Barboleuse to get to this 18th-century Heidi-esque chalet in the highland pastures. It combines the grist of Alpine legend with good, honest food. Three cheery rooms glowing with log fires under low, beamed ceilings give way to unfettered views of the mountains. You won't see many tourists here; it's a word-of-mouth place that packs in locals and weekend expats in the know. They go for the fondue and raclette, river trout, and plates of fresh regional mushrooms—and wine spouting from an old *fontaine*, a wrought-iron contraption rarely seen in restaurants. ⊠ *4½ km (3 mi) from Villars, Alpe des Chaux* ☎ *024/4981426* 🖃 *MC, V* ☉ *Closed Tues., Apr.–May, and mid-Nov.–mid-Dec.*

$$$$ 🏨 **Grand Hôtel du Park.** You can't sleep any closer to the slopes than this upscale lodge at the base of the mountain, which has been run by the same family for generations. Its park setting is enjoyable in all seasons, and the honey-colored wood interior says ski chalet. Themed culinary weeks feature round-the-world cuisine, a delightful change from regional dishes. ⊠ *rue Centrale, CH-1884* ☎ *024/4962828* 🖶 *024/4953363* ⊕ *www.parcvillars.ch* ➴ *60 rooms* ♨ *4 restaurants, minibars, cable TV, bar, free parking; no a/c* 🖃 *AE, DC, MC, V* ☉ *Closed Nov.* ⦿ *BP.*

$$$–$$$$ 🏨 **Le Bristol.** This resort hotel, one of the poshest in town, rose from the ashes of an older landmark. Despite the Colorado-condo exterior with balconies that jut from every room, it is furnished with a light, bright, and convincingly regional touch. Interiors are mostly white with mauve accents and carved blond pine, and picture windows are angled to take

in the views. There are good fitness facilities and a choice of attractive restaurants, including one on a terrace above the valley. ✉ *rue Centrale, CH-1884* ☎ *024/4963636* 🖷 *024/4963637* ⊕ *www.bristol-villars.ch* 🔊 *87 rooms, 23 suites ⚐ 2 restaurants, minibars, cable TV, indoor pool, gym, hot tub, massage, sauna, steam room, bar, free parking; no a/c* 🖃 *AE, DC, MC, V* �’❶ *BP.*

$–$$ 🖃 **Écureuil.** Although there's a restaurant downstairs and a carnotzet for fondue, nearly every room in this warm family-run inn has a kitchenette, so you can make yourself at home mountain cabin–style. Opened in 1947 and now run by the son of the founder, the hotel has lots of homey touches: books and magazines, swing sets, and a piano parlor. An older stone-base chalet on the grounds offers bigger rooms; both buildings stand across the street from the Bristol and therefore don't have direct access to those Villars views. ✉ *rue Centrale, CH-1884* ☎ *024/4963737* 🖷 *024/4963722* ⊕ *www.hotel-ecureuil.ch* 🔊 *27 rooms ⚐ Restaurant, Stübli, in-room data ports, in-room safes, some kitchenettes, cable TV, Ping-Pong, Internet, free parking; no a/c* 🖃 *MC, V* ❶❶ *BP.*

$–$$ 🖃 **La Renardière.** This group of three classic chalets, set back from the resort center and surrounded by tall firs, appears beset with a '50's identity crisis, but behind rustic walls modern attributes have kept pace with the times. It's still got its golden pine, plaid curtains, and log bar. The lounges and sitting areas have fireplaces; the rooms are simple, done in pine and chenille. In the traditional restaurant, linens, crystal, and fresh flowers soften the rustic edges, and there's an agreeable terrace café that serves good lunches under the evergreens. ✉ *rte. des Liyeux, CH-1884* ☎ *024/4952592* 🖷 *024/4953915* 🔊 *20 rooms, 5 suites ⚐ Restaurant, café, cable TV, bar; no a/c* 🖃 *AE, DC, MC, V* ❶❶ *BP.*

Sports & the Outdoors

GOLF Precipitously sited, the **Golf Club Villars** (✉ rue Centrale ☎ 024/4954214), open from June to October, has 18 holes and an upscale restaurant.

HIKING There are 300 km (186 mi) of hiking trails in the region. Most only require a map (pick one up at the tourist office) and a good pair of hiking shoes. If you would like to tackle more difficult routes or add mountaineering to your outing, **Villars Experience** (✉ rue Centrale ☎ 024/4954138 ⊕ www.villars-experience.ch) has guides and equipment.

SPORTS CENTERS The **Centre des Sports** (✉ chemin de la Gare ☎ 024/4951221 ✉ rte. du Col de la Croix ☎ 024/4953030) has two locations. One has an indoor skating rink (skates available for rent) and an indoor pool, whereas the other offers an extensive range of activities—from badminton to wall climbing—as well as an outdoor pool.

Les Diablerets

②⑧ *19 km (12 mi) northeast of Aigle, 59 km (37 mi) southeast of Lausanne.*

This small resort (3,806 feet) lies at the base of the 10,525-foot peak of the same name—which sheds the dramatic namesake 9,840-foot glacier. The village was named after a folklore tale of devils who played skittles among the desolate glacier peaks. A compact handful of hotels, shops, and steep-roof chalets are strung along a winding road. The valley brightens only when sun finds its way over crags and crests, which may be why skiing is guaranteed year-round and the Swiss team trains here in summer. To get here from Villars during those warm months, car travelers can cut along spectacular heights on a tiny 13%-grade road over the Col de la Croix (5,832 feet). Train travelers have to descend to Bex and backtrack to Aigle.

Fodor'sChoice
★
The ride on **Glacier 3000**, an aerial cableway strung from its station at Col du Pillon 7 km (4 mi) outside the resort village to a shelf at Scex-Rouge, is a thrill and well worth the steep fare. Vistas of Alpine peaks, vast meadows, and clusters of sloping-roof farmhouses extend to Lac Léman and the Jura mountains. The 20-minute ascent is done in two segments, ending at the metallic, jewel box–shaped restaurant designed by world-famous architect Mario Botta. In warm weather, skiers share the glacial zone with snowcat (motorized vehicle) and dogsled tours. ☎ *024/4923377* ⊕ *www.glacier3000.ch* ✉ *54 SF* ◎ *Mid-June–July, daily 8:20–4:50; Aug.–Oct., daily 9–4:50; Nov.–May, daily 9–4:30.*

Skiing

The connection of Les Diablerets' ski facilities with those of Villars adds considerably to ski options—including summer skiing on the glacier itself. The lift to **Meilleret** (6,394 feet), the peak that lies directly above the village of **Les Diablerets** (3,806 feet) serves as the aerial linchpin with Villars. A cable car from another station in the village lifts skiers to **Isenau**, which has intermediate and expert runs cascading from the peak of **Floriettaz** (6,956 feet). But it is the glacier—and the dramatic peak-top pistes at **Quille du Diable** and **Scex-Rouge** that many come to ski. Take a bus to Col du Pillon, where a series of gondolas ascend along the sheer wall to mountaintop ski stations. From Scex-Rouge, a popular run carries you around the top of the **Oldenhorn** and down to **Oldenegg**, a wide-open intermediate run through a sheltered valley. For an additional adrenaline rush, there's one gravity-defying expert slope, directly under the gondola, from **Pierre-Pointes** back to the valley.

Before purchasing your tickets, study ski maps carefully and assess your stamina and skill level. Lift rates are often priced in combinations. A one-day pass for Les Diablerets/Villars is 46 SF; Isenau is 39 SF. Adding Glacier 3000 takes the cost up to 54 SF, but you will have 74 lifts and 200 km (137 mi) of runs from which to choose. (Reduced family prices are available.)

Cross-country skiers can explore 42 km (26 mi) of trails, some tracking through woods and meadows.

Where to Stay & Eat

$ ✕☲ **Auberge de la Poste.** The Pichard family, keepers of this weathered centuries-old inn, hold dear the inn's heritage of lodging stagecoach passengers and Alpine enthusiasts. The rustic chalet has carved eaves with hand-painted designs, creaky floors, and old, rippled, handblown-glass windows. The simplicity of this relais has attracted celebrities from Stravinsky to David Bowie. The restaurant (¢–$$) has heavy wood furniture and serves hearty fare, including fondue and platters of air-dried meats and cheese with crusty bread. ✉ *rue de la Gare, CH-1865* ☎ *024/*

4923124 🏠 *024/4921268* 🗨 *12 rooms* ♨ *Restaurant, cable TV, free parking; no a/c* ☰ *MC, V* ☯ *Closed Nov.* ⑩ *BP.*

$$$ ▥ **Hôtel des Diablerets.** Carved wooden eaves and ornate balconies frame this chalet-style hotel. It practically breathes Alpine ambience, from the heavy, carved blond-wood furniture to the starched white mile-high duvets. The café and brasserie are true to type, serving traditional Alpine dishes. The hotel is just minutes from the lifts—and it has outstanding, inspiring views. ⊠ *chemin du Vernex, CH-1865* 🕾 *024/4920909* 🏠 *024/4922391* ⊕ *www.hoteldesdiablerets.ch* 🗨 *54 rooms, 5 suites* ♨ *Restaurant, café, minibars, cable TV, indoor pool, sauna, steam room, bar, parking (fee); no a/c* ☰ *AE, DC, MC, V* ☯ *Closed late Apr.–June, Oct., and Nov.* ⑩ *BP.*

Sports & the Outdoors

You can satisfy your taste for adventure with activities ranging from leisurely to extreme. **Centre ParAdventure** (⊠ rue de la Gare 🕾 024/4922382) can take you hang gliding, canyoning, sledding, dirt biking, and zorbing (rolling down the mountainside in a huge plastic ball). **Mountain Evasion** (⊠ Parc des Sports 🕾 024/4921232 ⊕ www.mountain-evasion.ch) organizes luge, snowshoeing, canyoning, rock climbing, and dirt-biking excursions, among others. Both have English-speaking guides.

For a real tobogganing experience, try the 7-km (4.5-mi) run from **Vioz-Mazots,** accessible from the Meilleret lift, at night. You can rent sleds at any of the village sports stores; the ticket to the top costs 10 SF. Alternatively, you can book an all-inclusive excursion (transportation, equipment, and hot cider aprés sled run) with Mountain Evasion or Center ParAdventure. Evening outings start with a delicious fondue dinner followed by a torchlit race to the bottom.

en route From the switchback highway A11, a small mountain road leads up to **Leysin,** a family resort with easy skiing and a spectacular, sunny plateau looking directly onto the Dents du Midi. The crowd, many of whom spill out of nearby boarding schools, is young and athletic. Snowboarding hot shots and mountain bikers swarm the trails—home to qualifying training runs and championship competition. The best views are from Kukulos, a revolving restaurant in the glass tower on Berneuse, a peak 6,720 feet above the village.

PAYS-D'ENHAUT

Separated from the high-altitude Alpine resorts by the modest Col des Mosses (4,740 feet), the Pays-d'Enhaut (Highlands) offers an entirely different culture from that of its Vaud cousins. Here the architecture begins to resemble that of the Berner Oberland, which it borders. Deep-eaved wooden chalets replace the Edwardian structures of the lake lands, and the atmosphere takes on a mountain-farm air. The Pays-d'Enhaut once belonged to Gruyères, then was seized by Bern; when Vaud was declared a canton, the Pays-d'Enhaut went with it. A stone's throw up the valley, you cross the Sarine/Saanen and the so-called Rösti Border, where the culture and language switch to Bernese German.

This is still Gruyère cheese country. A style known as L'Etivaz is made from milk drawn exclusively from cows grazed on pastures at elevations between 3,280 feet and 7,216 feet. The sweet, late-blooming flowers they eat impart a flavor that lowland cheeses can't approach. Visitors passing through the eponymous village after crossing the Col des Mosses can stop at the Caves à Fromages (a cheese-makers' cooperative), where a worker in rubber boots will be happy to sell you brick-size chunks of both young and old cheeses at prices well below those at resort groceries.

The highlands are also the source of one of Switzerland's most familiar decorative arts: *papier découpé*, delicate, symmetrical paper cutouts. They are cut in black, often with simple imagery of cattle and farmers, and fixed on white paper for contrast. The real thing is a refined craft and is priced accordingly, but attractive prints reproducing the look are on sale at reduced prices throughout the region.

Château-d'Oex

㉙ *33 km (20 mi) northeast of Aigle, 64 km (40 mi) east of Lausanne.*

At the crossroads between the Col des Mosses highway to Aigle and the Valais and the route to the Berner Oberland lies Château-d'Oex (pronounced *day*), a popular sports resort that connects with the greater Gstaad ski region. Its perhaps even greater claim to fame these days is ballooning, with periodic hot-air-balloon competitions that draw mobs of international enthusiasts and fill hotels throughout the region. In spring 1999 the Breitling *Orbiter 3* balloon launched from the valley floor for its record-breaking nonstop trip around the world. The town itself is a mix of Edwardian architecture with weathered-wood chalets, spreading over a green forest-top hillside above the highway. It heads the French end of the valley of the Sarine River—also known, in the Berner Oberland, as Saanenland.

★ In Château-d'Oex's small center, the **Musée Artisanal du Vieux Pays-d'Enhaut** (Artisan and Folklore Museum of the Old Highlands) gives you insight into life in these isolated parts. Complete interiors are evocatively reproduced: two kitchens, a farmer's home, a cheese-maker's house, and a carpenter's studio. Marvelous wood carving and ironwork, a variety of ceramics, plus displays of old papier découpé, furniture, and popular art round out the collection. ⊠ *Grand-rue* ☎ *026/9246520* 💰 *5 SF* ☉ *Tues.–Sun. 2–5.*

Le Chalet is a reproduction of a mountain cheese-maker's home, with afternoon demonstrations over an open fire. Visitors sit at café tables (and are sold drinks or cheese dishes) while they watch the hot labor of stirring milk in a vast copper vat. The restaurant and a shop selling regional crafts and dairy products is open throughout the day. ⊠ ☎ *026/9246677* 💰 *Free; a purchase or consumption is expected* ☉ *Tues.–Sun. 1:30–5.*

Skiing

Château-d'Oex has links to **La Braye,** a sunny shelf that sits above the village at 5,348 feet. One of the region's smaller ski areas, it has 30 km (18 mi) of expert and intermediate trails—enough to fill a day—but offers additional options because of its proximity to Rougemont and Gstaad. Runs are accessed from a gondola, two chairlifts, and six T-bars. A one-day lift ticket costs 37 SF; a six-day pass costs 180 SF. La Braye has an equipment test center where you can try out the latest snowboards and skis; you can also rent sleds at the summit and coast downhill on the 3.2-km (2-mi) sled run.

Where to Stay & Eat

$ ✕ **Hôtel Buffet de la Gare.** This easygoing and convenient train-station café draws a regular local crowd for light meals and a dependable plat du jour. Stick with *croûtes* (rich toasted-cheese sandwiches) and salads, and opt for the casual—and smoky—café rather than the more formal restaurant, though it's fun to watch the trains roll by the latter. ☎ *026/ 9247717* ☰ *MC, V.*

$$ ✕🍴 **Ermitage.** Hoteliers Fabio and Françoise Piazza spent nearly a decade converting this once-ordinary mountain hotel into a cozy inn. Timbered ceilings and stenciled detailing warm up the amply sized rooms, which are furnished with traditional, blond-wood armoires and fluffy cotton-encased duvets. The terrace is the perfect perch for watching balloon takeoffs—it overlooks the launch field. Bistro ($–$$) meals are drawn from Piazza's grandmother's recipes. An excellent five-course prix fixe meal (85 SF) has the faithful driving up from glitzy Gstaad to the main dining room ($$–$$$) for smoked guinea fowl and fillet of veal. ✉ *CH-1837* ☎ *026/9246003* 🖷 *026/9245076* ↵ *14 rooms, 4 suites* ⚑ *Restaurant, café, minibars, cable TV, playground, free parking; no a/c* ☰ *AE, DC, MC, V* ⟊*⟊ BP.*

★ $–$$ ✕🍴 **Bon Accueil.** In a beautifully proportioned 18th-century weathered-wood chalet on the outskirts of town, this is the quintessential French-Swiss country inn. Rooms mix aged pine planking, spindle furniture, and antiques, and under the old low-beam ceilings the floors creak agreeably. Up-to-date amenities, immaculate appointments, and fresh flowers—inside and out—keep standards well above rustic. The restaurant ($$–$$$; reservations essential) is even more civilized, and the menu ranges from duck breast with truffle potatoes to sea scallops with chive oil and young beans. Winter nights there's a firelit stone cellar bar with low-key jazz. ✉ *CH-1660* ☎ *026/9246320* 🖷 *026/9245126* ↵ *18 rooms* ⚑ *Restaurant, cable TV, sauna, bar, free parking; no a/c* ☰ *AE, DC, MC, V* ⊘ *Closed mid-Mar.–mid Apr. and mid-Oct.–mid-Dec.* ⟊*⟊ BP.*

Sports & the Outdoors

BALLOONING The annual hot-air ballooning festival gets off the ground in late January. On Friday night a *night glow* is held. Scramble to the top of the hill that has the church (look for the steeple) for a stunning view of brilliantly colored, backlit balloons choreographed to music. A lively village fair follows. If you'd like to get up in the air yourself, you can arrange for an accompanied flight year-round through **Sky Event** (✉ CH-1837 ☎ 026/ 9242520 ⊕ www.skyevent.ch).

BICYCLING This graceful region of rolling hills and steep climbs is great for mountain biking. It's convenient to rent a bike at the **MOB Train Station** (☎ 026/ 9246458). You can also rent bikes at the lift for trails leading down from **La Braye** (☎ 026/9246794).

HIKING   You can see traditional cheese making firsthand with a hike to high-altitude summer pastures and huts. An overnight excursion can be arranged through the Chateau-d'Oex tourist office.

Mike Horn (✉ CH-1660 ☎ 026/9246794 ⊕ www.telechateaudoex.ch), a South African explorer who circumnavigated the globe along the equator, has adopted Chateau-d'Oex as his home and leads unusual adventure excursions and scavenger hunts in summer and winter.

RIVER SPORTS   Several gorges near Château-d'Oex offer excellent rafting as well as two unusual white-water sports: hydrospeeding (running rapids lying on your stomach atop a rubber inflatable) and canyoning (hiking a river bottom). A popular destination is the **Gorges du Pissot,** a canyon wilderness accessed along a precarious cliff-side road between L'Etivaz and Château-d'Oex. Sports lovers in wet suits canyon under the white waters of the Torneresse River. **Rivières et Aventures** (⌂ Case Postale 68, CH-1660 ☎ 079/4347089) organizes hiking, rafting, and kayaking excursions to the Gorges du Pissot. You can also arrange supervised initiations into these sports through the tourist office.

SKATING   There's an outdoor rink at the **Parc des Sports** (☎ 026/9242450).

SNOWSHOEING   Secure a guide and rent snowshoes at **Haute Pression Sports** (☎ 026/9245653).

SWIMMING   In summer Château-d'Oex opens a heated 50-meter **open-air pool with restaurant** (☎ 026/9246234). Admission is 6 SF.

VAUD A TO Z

To research prices, get advice from other travelers, and book travel arrangements, visit www.fodors.com.

AIR TRAVEL
Geneva's Cointrin is the second-busiest international airport in Switzerland, servicing flights from European and international destinations on Swiss as well as other international carriers. From Cointrin, Swiss connects to secondary airports throughout the country. Low-cost carrier easyJet also serves a number of European destinations.

CARRIERS   🔁 Airlines & Contacts **easyJet** ☎ 084/8888222 ⊕ www.easyjet.com. **Swiss** ☎ 084/8852000 toll free within the country ⊕ www.swiss.com.

AIRPORTS
🔁 Airport Information **Cointrin** ✉ 55 km [34 mi] southwest of Lausanne ☎ 022/7177111.

BOAT & FERRY TRAVEL
Like all fair-size Swiss lakes, Lac Léman is crisscrossed with comfortable and reasonably swift steamers. They sometimes run more often than the trains that parallel their routes. With a Swiss Pass you travel free. For boat schedule and docking information contact Compagnie Générale de Navigation or pick up a timetable in any tourist office.
🔁 Boat & Ferry Information **Compagnie Générale de Navigation** ☎ 084/8811848 ⊕ www.cgn.ch.

BUS TRAVEL

A useful network of postbus routes covers the region for the resourceful traveler with plenty of time; some routes are covered only once or twice a day. Schedules are available from tourist offices and rail stations. In smaller towns you can also check with the post office. Lausanne has a good city bus network. The Vevey–Montreux city service is extremely convenient, as it's hard to find a parking place in these towns. If you have a Swiss Pass, you can travel free on city buses and funiculars in Montreux, Vevey, and Lausanne.

CAR TRAVEL

There are two major arteries leading to Lac Léman, one entering from the north via Bern and Fribourg (A12), the other arcing over the north shore of Lac Léman from Geneva to Lausanne (A1), then to Montreux and on south through the Alpes Vaudoises toward the Col du Grand St-Bernard (A9) in Canton Valais. They are swift and often scenic expressways, and the north-shore artery (A1 and A9) traces a route that has been followed since before Roman times. Secondary highways parallel the expressways, but this is one case where, as the larger road sits higher on the lakeside slopes, the views from the expressway are often better than those from the highway. Be sure, however, to detour for the Corniche road views between Lausanne and Montreux.

A web of secondary highways cuts north into the hills and then winds east of the southbound expressway into the Alpine resorts, giving the driver maximum flexibility.

EMERGENCIES

There are standardized telephone numbers throughout Switzerland for emergencies.

🚑 Ambulance ☎ 144. **Fire** ☎ 118. **Late-night pharmacies** ☎ 111. **Police** ☎ 117. **Roadside Assistance** ☎ 140.

TOURS

BUS TOURS The two drop-by branches of the Lausanne tourist office run a daily two-hour coach trip into the Old Town, including a visit to the cathedral and an extended city coach tour that takes in the Lavaux vineyards.

🚌 **Fees & Schedules Lausanne tourist office** ✉ Gare Centrale, 9 pl. de la Gare ✉ Ouchy Métro Station, 4 pl. de la Navigation.

WALKING TOURS Walking tours led by local historians in Lausanne, Vevey, and Montreux are increasingly popular. They are organized by the town's tourist office and are given daily between April and September. English-speaking guides are often available, but you should call in advance to check. Most local tourist offices offer daily general tours in summer to Gruyères, to Chamonix and Mont Blanc, to the Alps by coach, and to Les Avants and Château-d'Oex by the Montreux–Oberland–Bernois Railroad line's panoramic train. There is also a chocolate excursion to the Nestlé factory in Broc. To ensure a tour with English commentary, reserve in advance.

TRAIN TRAVEL

Lausanne lies on a major train route between Bern and Geneva, with express trains connecting from Basel and Zürich. From Geneva, trains take about 30 minutes and arrive in Lausanne up to four times an hour; from Bern, they take a little more than an hour and arrive twice an hour. TGVs (high-speed trains) run from Paris 10 times a day and take approximately four hours. The Cisalpino train has daily departures to Milan and to Venice. From June to September extra trains are scheduled. There is also a Euronuit (night sleeper) connection to Italian cities. The ICE, the German high-speed train, has departures to northern destinations with only one change in Basel or Bern. The SBB provides information on international trains.

Trains along the waterfront, connecting major lake towns, are frequent and swift (unless you board one of the hourly locals that service every village). There are also several private rail systems leading into small villages and rural regions, including the Montreux–Oberland–Bernois (MOB) Railroad, which climbs sharply behind Montreux and cuts straight over the pre-Alps toward Château-d'Oex and the Berner Oberland. There is also the Blonay–Chamby Railroad. The Swiss Pass is accepted on these private lines, but there may be an additional fee for panoramic excursions. Inquire at local tourist offices or train stations about a regional pass that combines rail, boat, bus, and cable car excursions on these private lines at a reduced fee. It can be used for unlimited travel for three out of seven days and discounts on the other four days.

Lausanne has a tiny but essential Métro that runs every seven minutes until 11:30 PM, connecting the waterfront at Ouchy to the train station and the place St-François. Tickets are less than 3 SF, and a day pass costs 7.20 SF.

🚆 Train Information **Blonay–Chamby Railroad** ☎ 021/9432121 ⊕ www.blonay-chamby.ch. **Montreux–Oberland–Bernois Railroad (MOB)** ☎ 021/9898181 ⊕ www.mob.ch. **SBB** ☎ 090/0300300 ⊕ www.rail.ch.

VISITOR INFORMATION
The Office du Tourisme du Canton de Vaud has general information on the region.

🚆 Local Tourist Offices **Aigle** ✉ CH-1860 ☎ 024/4663000 ⊕ www.aigle.ch. **Château-d'Oex** ✉ CH-1837 ☎ 026/9242525 ⊕ www.chateau-doex.ch. **Lausanne** ✉ 2 av. de Rhodanie, CH-1006 ☎ 021/6137373 ⊕ www.lausanne-tourisme.ch ✉ Gare Centrale, 9 pl. de la Gare ✉ Ouchy Métro Station, 4 pl. de la Navigation. **Les Diablerets** ✉ CH-1865 ☎ 024/4923358 ⊕ www.lesdiablerets.ch. **Lutry** ✉ quai Gustav-Doret, CH-1095 ☎ 021/7914765 ⊕ www.lutry.ch. **Montreux-Vevey** ✉ 5 rue du Théâtre, CH-1820 Montreux ☎ 084/8868484 ⊕ www.montreux.ch ✉ 1 pl. du Débarcadère, Montreux ✉ 29 Grand-pl., Vevey. **Morges** ✉ rue du Château, CH-1110 ☎ 021/8013233 ⊕ www.morges.ch. **Nyon** ✉ 7 av. Viollier, CH-1260 ☎ 022/3616261 ⊕ www.nyon.ch. **Villars** ✉ CH-1884 ☎ 024/4953232 ⊕ www.villars.ch.

🚆 Regional Tourist Office **Office du Tourisme du Canton de Vaud** ✉ 60 av. d'Ouchy, CH-1000 Lausanne ☎ 021/6132626 🖷 021/6132600 ⊕ www.lake-geneva-region.ch.

GENEVA

Updated by
Jennifer
McDermott

GENEVA WAS KNOWN FOR ENLIGHTENED TOLERANCE long before
Henry Dunant founded the International Red Cross here (1864) and
the League of Nations moved in (1919). Today the world's largest center for multilateral diplomacy, this postcard-perfect city of 185,000
gave refuge to religious reformers John Knox and Jean Calvin and sheltered the writers Voltaire, Victor Hugo, Alexandre Dumas, Honoré
de Balzac, and Stendhal. Lord Byron, Percy Bysshe and Mary Shelley,
Richard Wagner, and Franz Liszt all fled to Geneva when scandal erupted
at home.

There were limits to this tolerance, however. A staunchly Calvinist city
government forced the liberal philosopher (and Geneva native) Jean-
Jacques Rousseau into exile in 1762 and burned his books. Nonbeliev-
ers left Geneva in the mid-16th century as it absorbed ever-greater
waves of Protestant refugees. But as the English fled Bloody Mary,
Protestant Italians the wrath of the pope, Spaniards the Inquisition, and
Huguenots the oppressive French monarchy, Calvin's city flourished as
a multilingual stronghold of Protestant reform.

Geneva's history as a crossroads stretches back farther still. The Genevois
controlled the only bridge over the Rhône north of Lyon when Julius
Caesar breezed through in 58 BC; the early Burgundians and bishop-princes
who succeeded the Romans were careful to maintain this control. The
strategically placed (and wealthy) city-state fell to the French in 1798,
then made overtures to Bern as Napoléon's star waned. Geneva finally
joined the Swiss Confederation as a canton in 1815. Now corporate executives jet in and out on business ranging from financial services to humanitarian aid.

EXPLORING GENEVA

The Canton de Genève (Canton of Geneva) shares more than 96% of
its border, as well as its language, with France. It also commands
panoramic views of the French Alps and the French Jura from its well-
groomed position at the southwestern tip of *Lac Léman* (Lake Geneva).
The water bisects the city's center, then tapers off into the River Rhône
en route to Lyon and the Mediterranean, leaving museums, shops, and
parks to jostle for space on its south shore, the historic *Rive Gauche*
(Left Bank), whose busy shopping streets underline the hilltop Old
Town. To the west lies the Plaine de Plainpalais; Eaux-Vives stretches
along the quays to the east. The *quartier international* (International Area),
the train station, and sumptuous waterfront hotels dominate the north
shore, or *Rive Droite* (Right Bank). St-Gervais, just north of the Ponts
de l'Ile, was once a watchmaking quarter. Les Pâquis, an unruly mix of
artists, ethnic communities, and scrappy pleasure-seekers, sits right behind the palace hotels. The International Area, on the northern edge of
the city, is a short tram ride from downtown; the other neighborhoods
are easily toured on foot.

*Numbers in the text correspond to numbers in the margin and on the
Geneva map.*

12

If you have
2 days

Spend your first morning exploring the downtown waterfront, with its boats, swans, 15-foot-wide flowered clock face, and feathery Jet d'Eau. Then window-shop your way along the Rues-Basses and up into the Vieille Ville. Have lunch on place du Bourg-de-Four, and investigate the Espace St-Pierre, an umbrella term for the starkly beautiful Cathédrale St-Pierre, the cavelike archae-ological ruins underneath it, and the Musée International de la Ré-forme. Don't forget the contemplative Auditoire de Calvin; the Monument de la Réformation sums it all up. The next day head for the International Area. Spend the morning at the Palais des Na-tions and the Musée International de la Croix-Rouge et du Crois-sant-Rouge, have lunch at the Château de Penthes, spend the afternoon wandering the Jardin Botanique, and find yourself some *filets de perches* (perch fillets) for dinner.

If you have
4 days

Follow the two-day plan above. On your third morning, head back to the Vieille Ville and the Maison Tavel, Espace Rousseau, Musée Barbier-Mueller, and/or Musée Rath. Then take a break from museum fare, and spend the afternoon swimming, sailing, paddle-boating, or, in winter, riding the waves of Lac Léman on a Compagnie Générale de Navigation (CGN) paddle steamer. Follow this up with a concert, indoors or out. Start Day 4 with a morning walk through the Right Bank waterfront parks and the Musée d'Histoire des Sciences. Have lunch at La Perle du Lac (outdoors in summer). Then take the Mouettes Genevoises ferry across the lake to Port Noir, and climb the rampe de Cologny to the stel-lar Fondation Martin Bodmer. Watch the sun set over the city from the Auberge du Lion d'Or or the bottom of the hill, and then take in a film at Cinélac (July–Au-gust) or wander home along the quays.

If you have
6 days

Two additional days will allow you to complete the tour of Geneva's museums and explore outside the city center. Start Day 5 with the Musée d'Art et d'His-toire, have lunch in Carouge, and head back into town for a look at the watch-making treasures in the Patek Philippe Museum. On your last day, weather permitting, head for the ski slopes or rent a bicycle and ride out past Cologny; in about 15–20 minutes you'll be surrounded by vineyards and sweeping vistas.

The Waterfront

Geneva is centered on water. The city's quays line the downtown area, link the Right and Left Banks, and form a horseshoe-shape continuum of scrupulously tended parkland, historical sites, grand hotels, monu-ments, and breathtaking views.

a good walk

From Gare Cornavin, take Bus 1 to the Secheron stop, and walk through the gate labeled RESTAURANT LA PERLE DU LAC. The second paved path to your left after the parking lot leads to the Villa Bartholoni, home of the superb **Musée d'Histoire des Sciences** ❶ ▶.

Turn right as you exit the museum, and make your way down to the water. On a clear day, **Mont Blanc** floats above the hills on the far side of the lake like a sugar-dusted meringue. Keep the water to your left as you head past the Mouettes Genevoises landing dock, La Perle du Lac, and spectacular seasonal flower beds.

Continue straight along quai Wilson as the traffic curls down to meet you. The stately **Palais Wilson** ❷, on your right, housed the League of Nations from its creation after World War I until 1936. Follow the manicured lawns and ornate town houses around a sharp curve to the right. The Bains des Pâquis, hugely popular public baths with a protected space to swim and sunbathe, occupy most of the jetty extending to your left. The Noga Hilton, a bit farther along to your right, opens the Right Bank parade of grand hotels.

Keep walking past the Port des Mouettes and Hotel d'Angleterre. The slender statue of Sissi, Empress Elizabeth of Austria, on your left, was erected in 1998 to celebrate the centennial of her death; she was stabbed as she left the **Beau-Rivage** ❸ to board one of the paddle steamers docked alongside the quay. Make a brief detour out to the end of the jetty, now used by the CGN, for a close-up view of the boats and the city center. Then cross the street in front of the Beau-Rivage and angle left to the elaborate **Monument Brunswick** ❹.

Cross back to the quay at the far end of the block, turn right past the plaque marking the spot where Sissi was stabbed, and take the last staircase before the pont du Mont-Blanc down to the left. Head straight under the bridge. When you surface in front of the Hotel des Bergues, make two lefts onto the pedestrians-only pont des Bergues. The **Ile Rousseau** ❺, halfway across, harbors a statue of its philosophical namesake. The sober **Temple de la Fusterie** ❻, on the far side of the bridge, was the first church to be built in Geneva after the Reformation.

Turn left when you reach dry land, and follow the quay under the pont du Mont-Blanc a second time. Turn left at the top of the ramp, then right toward the statue commemorating the union of Geneva and the Swiss Confederation on September 12, 1814. Keep to the left of the statue, follow the path as it arcs to the right, and keep walking until the **Horloge Fleurie** ❼ comes into view on the left. Continue past the floral clock face and into the Jardin Anglais, toward its graceful 19th-century fountain. Rejoin the quay where it veers to the left by the bust of Gustave Ador.

Take the steps down and angle left toward *La Neptune* ❽, the only original boat of its kind still in service on Lac Léman. Sticking out of the water to the right of *La Neptune* are the Pierres du Niton, two glacial erratics deposited during the last Ice Age. Guillaume-Henri Dufour designated the larger one as the base reference point (1,222 feet above sea level) for all altitude measurements taken during the 19th-century land survey that produced the first map of Switzerland.

Return to the upper promenade by the next set of stairs, continue to your left past more flower beds, and veer back to the lower level where rue du 31-Décembre meets quai Gustave-Ador. Walk out along the stone jetty toward the **Jet d'Eau** ❾, Europe's tallest fountain, which

12

Festivals Nothing is too small, it seems, to be feted in Geneva. The Genevois enthusiastically support an almost constant stream of celebrations, including tomato, wine-harvest, jazz, and cinema-arts festivals. The three-day Fête de la Musique comprises more than 500 free open-air concerts to mark the summer solstice, while Escalade is the Vieille Ville's December celebration of 17th-century independence. The Fêtes de Genève, the city's 10-day August block party, begins and ends with meticulously choreographed fireworks; sandwiched in between are a loud (and flamboyantly raunchy) Lake Parade, air shows, outdoor discos, and food from around the world.

Food & Wine Geneva's many restaurants teem with innovative, experimental menus and chefs with lofty pedigrees, but its traditional cooking is simple, earthy, full of flavor, and solidly middle class. *Cardon* (cardoon, a locally grown vegetable related to the artichoke and available in winter) is baked with cream and Gruyère cheese. Lac Léman yields abundant fish—perch, trout, *féra* (related to salmon), and *omble* (char)—in summer. *La chasse* (wild game) turns up on menus between late September and mid-December. The culinary influence of Lyon, 150 km (94 mi) to the southwest, can be felt year-round in dishes such as *pieds de cochon* (pigs' feet), *longeole* (unsmoked pork sausage stuffed with cabbage and fennel), *petit salé* (salt pork), *fricasée de porc* (simmered pork), *abats* (organ meats), *andouillettes* (chitterling sausages), and *boudin noir* (rich, rosy-brown blood pudding, best eaten in cold weather). Potatoes (often served au gratin) are a favorite side dish. Pears in the form of a spiced compote, a delicate tart, or a light eau-de-vie have a well-established role come dessert.

Think local when choosing your wine. The Romans brought vines to Geneva, and today vintners working in the countryside around the city produce red, white, and sparkling wines that are finally beginning to attract serious notice. (Bartholie, a boutique sparkling wine, has been known to trump French champagnes in international competition.) Small, ancient Chasselas grapes lead the charge of whites; the round, generous taste of gamay dominates the reds. You'll also find excellent local bottles of chardonnay, pinot blanc, pinot gris, gewürztraminer, Aligoté, pinot noir, Gamaret, and cabernet sauvignon. The hilly area around Satigny, Dardagny, and Russin (known for its annual harvest festival) is by far the canton's most productive.

Museums Geneva is, and has long been, a meeting place for people and ideas. To visit its museums is to experience the span and contradictions of history and culture: you can visit a military museum up the hill from the Red Cross's examination of the horrors of war; weigh the extremes of ancient and contemporary ceramics; examine archaeological treasures from Egypt and the Far East; compare primitive art from well before the time of Christ with its contemporary incarnation; and see how human thought and creativity have expressed themselves on paper, in science, and inside the case of a tiny pocket watch. Top it all off with a visit to the Palais des Nations, the ultimate living (and working) museum of 20th-century history.

Shopping Calvin created watchmakers out of less-utilitarian jewelers and gold-smiths, but the urge to create beautiful baubles never died in Geneva. Teams of expert craftsmen still toil steadily behind chic shop walls, and Geneva watchmakers are rightfully known for unparalleled excellence. But great shopping is not confined to timepieces. Handmade chocolates are an art form here. Stores just off the beaten path can be extraordinarily vibrant, and the Vieille Ville has no shortage of antiques shops. Geneva is also a city of markets; chatty fruit and vegetable vendors, taciturn flea-market regulars, and craftspeople clustered in designated squares continue the legacy of the medieval trade fairs once held along the department-store-lined Rues-Basses.

---

gushes straight up from the lake. The spray, should you run through it, feels like the mother of all sprinklers; the lighthouse at the end of the jetty has a superb view of the Centre Ville.

Return to the quay and continue to the left past the city's main marina. Look back for a great view of the cathedral just before you reach the statue of La Bise (the North Wind). Then turn right when the asphalt ends, and cross the street opposite **Parc La Grange** ⑩.

Have a peek at the park and return to the quay, or wander through the rose garden on the left inside the gates, make your way into the neighboring Parc des Eaux-Vives, and return to the quay farther down the road. Regardless of which park exit you use, cross the street and continue to the right past parallel beds of roses and terrific Jura, lake, and city views. At Port Noir, where the formal quay ends, a simple nautical monument commemorates the June 1, 1814, arrival of Swiss troops sent to guarantee Geneva's safety in the period immediately following Napoléon's rule.

If you're feeling energetic and time permits, continue past Port Noir, cross the street at the traffic light, and follow the steep, leafy rampe de Cologny about 1 km (½ mi) up to the hilltop village of Cologny, where Byron's guest, Mary Shelley, wrote *Frankenstein*. Head straight through the small traffic circle to the parking lot of the Auberge du Lion d'Or for sweeping views of the city, lake, and Jura; turn right at the traffic circle if the sweeping vista of human thought at the **Fondation Martin Bodmer** ⑪ is more your style.

Retrace your steps or take the peaceful pedestrian chemin du Righi, just below the museum, back down the hill; then head left to Port Noir. If the sun is setting, stay awhile and watch the city lights flicker on. In July and August, settle in for an open-air film at Cinélac. When you're ready to head home, cross the street, and take Bus 2 (direction Bernex) to the Métropole stop, from which you can take the 8 (direction OMS) or walk across the pont du Mont-Blanc to the train station.

TIMING Discounting its final uphill loop through Cologny, this walk covers 5 km (3 mi) of largely flat, paved promenade—the perfect way to spend a leisurely day following the sun. Wear sunscreen and comfortable shoes, bring a book and binoculars if you have them, and give yourself at least a few hours to stroll and linger—there are always boats coming in, swans to feed, benches to rest on, and people to watch.

What to See

❸ Beau-Rivage. Jean-Jacques Mayer's descendants still own and operate the hotel he built in 1865. It has discreetly witnessed the birth of a nation (Czechoslovakia, in 1918), the death of an empress (Empress Elizabeth of Austria, in 1898), the sale of royal treasure (the Duchess of Windsor's jewels, in 1987), and the passage of crowned heads from around the world. Sotheby's commandeers its conference rooms for jewelry auctions twice a year. ⊠ *13 quai du Mont-Blanc, Les Pâquis* ☎ *022/7166666* ⊕ *www.beau-rivage.ch.*

⓫ Fondation Martin Bodmer (Martin Bodmer Foundation). The stated purpose of Martin Bodmer's enormous collection of original text in all Fodor'sChoice media—from cuneiform tablets and papyrus scrolls to a first edition of ★ *Ulysses*—is to illustrate the human mind's urge to create. Dramatic displays of bas-reliefs and dimly lit Egyptian books of the dead give way to handwritten Gospels according to Matthew and John; an exquisitely preserved Gutenberg Bible; Martin Luther's Manifesto; Dante's *Divine Comedy; The Canterbury Tales;* Shakespeare's complete works (published 1623); first editions of *Paradise Lost, Don Quixote, Oliver Twist,* and the *Communist Manifesto;* a handwritten score by Mozart; and galley text meticulously annotated by Proust. The inspirational setting, at the top of a hill overlooking Geneva, could not be better suited to its lofty subject. A comprehensive printed guide is available in English. ⊠ *19-21 route du Guignard, Cologny* ☎ *022/7074433* ⊕ *www. fondationbodmer.org* 🖾 *8 SF* ☉ *Tues.–Sun. 2–6.*

❼ Horloge Fleurie (Flower Clock). The city first planted this gigantic, and accurate, floral timepiece in 1955 to highlight Geneva's seminal role in the Swiss watchmaking industry. Some 6,500 plants are required each spring and fall to cover its 16-foot-wide surface. ⊠ *Corner quai du Général-Guisan and pont du Mont-Blanc, Centre Ville.*

❺ Ile Rousseau. Jean-Jacques Rousseau, the son of a Genevois watchmaker, is known to history as a liberal *French* philosopher and social reformer in part because Geneva's conservative government so thoroughly rejected his views. Though he praised the city in his writings on education and politics, he was forced into exile and his books were burned. His statue on this former city bastion, erected reluctantly in 1834 (56 years after his death), was surrounded by trees and effectively hidden from view. The 1862 construction of the pont du Mont-Blanc, from which the statue is hard to miss, gave Rousseau the last laugh. ⊠ *Off pont des Bergues, Centre Ville.*

⦿ ❾ Jet d'Eau (Fountain). The direct descendant of a 19th-century hydroelectric Fodor'sChoice safety valve, Europe's tallest fountain shoots 130 gallons of water 390 ★ feet into the air every second at 120 mph (wind conditions permitting). The water is aerated on the way up by a special nozzle, making it white. ⊠ *Off quai Gustave-Ador, Eaux-Vives.*

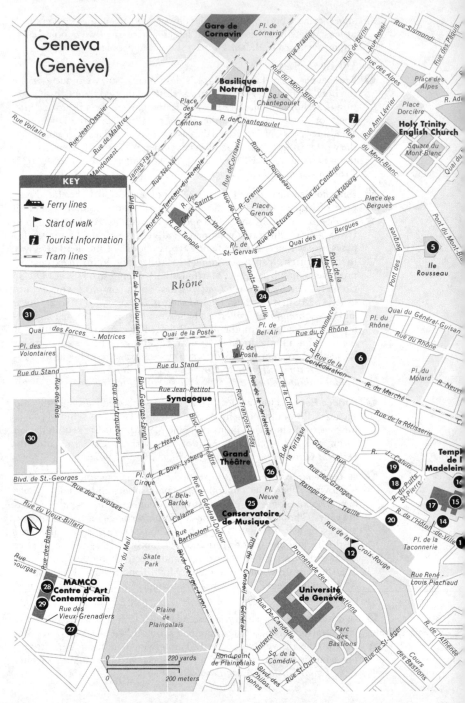

Geneva
(Genève)

Gare de
Cornavin

Pl. de
Cornavin

Basilique
Notre Dame

Sq. de
Chantepoulet

Place
des
22
Cantons

R. de Chantepoulet

Place des
Alpes

Place
Dorcière

Holy Trinity
English Church

Square du
Mont Blanc

Rue Voltaire

Rue Jean-Dassier

Rue de Malatrex

Mandement

James-Fazy

Rue Necker

Rue Terreaux-du-Temple

R. des
Corps Saints

R. du Temple

Pl. de la Coulouvrenière

R. Grenus

R. Varin

Place
Grenus

Rue de Coutance

Rue des Etuves

Pl. de
St. Gervais

Rue J.-J. Rousseau

Rue du Mont-Blanc

Rue du Cendrier

Rue Kléberg

Place des
Bergues

Rue Ami Lévrier

du Mont-Blanc

Quai du

R. Ad.

KEY

🚢 Ferry lines

🚩 Start of walk

ℹ️ Tourist Information

▬▬▬ Tram lines

Rhône

Quai des

Bergues

Pont du Mont-Bl.

Pont des Bergues

Ile
Rousseau

5

Pont de la
Machine

24

Pl. de
Bel-Air

Quai des Forces - Motrices

Quai de la Poste

Rue du Commerce

Rue du Rhône

Pl. du
Rhône

Quai du Général-Guisan

31

Pl. des
Volontaires

Rue du Stand

Pl. de
la Poste

Rue de la Confédération

Rue du Rhône

Pl. du
Molard

R. Neuve

30

Rue du Stand

Blvd.-Georges Favon

Rue de l'Arquebuse

Rue des Rois

Rue Jean-Petitot

Synagogue

Blvd. du Théâtre

R. Hesse

R. Bovy-Lysberg

Blvd. du Théâtre

Rue François-Diday

Rue de la Corraterie

R. de la Cité

R. du Marché

Rue de la Rôtisserie

6

Blvd. de St.-Georges

Pl. du
Cirque

Grand
Théâtre

26

Pl.
Neuve

25

Conservatoire
de Musique

R. de la Terrasse

Grand'-Rue

Rue des Granges

R. J.-Calvin

Temple
de l
Madelein

19

18

R. du Puits-
St.-Pierre

17

16

15

14

Rue de Vieux-Billard

Rue des Savoises

Pl. Béla-
Bartók

Calame

Rue
Bartholoni

Rampe de la Treille

20

R. de l'Hôtel-de-Ville

Pl. de la
Taconnerie

1

Rue des Bains

Av. du Mail

Skate
Park

Blvd.-Georges-Favon

Rue De-Candolle

Rue du Général-Dufour

Rue de la Croix-Rouge

12

Pl. de la
Taconnerie

Rue René-
Louis-Piachaud

Rue
ourgas

28

MAMCO
Centre d'Art
Contemporain

29

Rue des
Vieux-Grenadiers

27

Plaine
de
Plainpalais

Rond-point
de Plainpalais

Sq. de
la Comédie

Blvd.-des-
Philos-
ophes

Université

Rue St.-Ours

Université
de Genève

Promenade des Bastions

Parc
des
Bastions

Rue de St.-Léger

Cours des Bastions

R. de l'Athénée

0   220 yards

0   200 meters

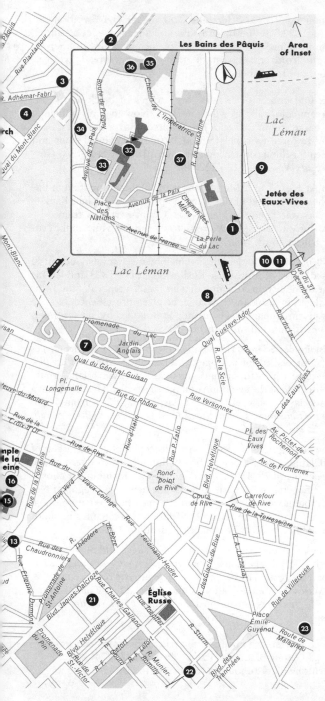

Les Bains des Pâquis

Area of Inset

Lac Léman

Jetée des Eaux-Vives

La Perle du Lac

Lac Léman

need a break? The ice-cream maestros at **Arlecchino** (⊠ 1 rue du 31-Décembre, Eaux-Vives ☎ 022/7367060), across the street from the Jet d'Eau, crank out more than 50 homemade flavors, including ginger-lime, tiramisu, *pannacotta* (cream custard), rhubarb, gingerbread, licorice, and three options for diabetics.

⑧ La Neptune. Old photos of Geneva show scores of black masts and graceful, cream-color sails crowding the lake. Now the only authentic traditional barge still in existence here is hired out for day sails. Built in 1904 and restored twice, in 1976 and 2005, she hauled stone and sand between far-flung construction sites until 1968. ⊠ *Off quai Gustave-Ador, Eaux-Vives* ☎ 022/7322944.

★ Mont Blanc. At 15,767 feet, Mont Blanc is the highest mountain in Europe and the crown jewel of the French Alps. Geneva's Right Bank—particularly its waterfront parkland—has a front-row view framed by a trio of less-lofty acolytes: Les Voirons, to the left; Le Môle, in the center; and Le Salève, to the right.

❹ Monument Brunswick. Charles d'Este-Guelph, the famously eccentric (and deposed) duke of Brunswick, died in Geneva in 1873 and left his vast fortune to the city on condition that his tomb, a replica of the 14th-century Scaligeri mausoleum in Verona, be given prominence. No one is sure why his sarcophagus faces inland. ⊠ *Bounded by rue des Alpes, quai du Mont-Blanc, and rue Adhémar-Fabri, Les Pâquis.*

★ ▶ ❶ Musée d'Histoire des Sciences (Museum of the History of Science). Age-old sundials, astrolabes, microscopes, gloŁbes, and barometers are displayed like jewels in walk-around glass cases in Switzerland's only museum to document the evolution of modern science. The collection's exquisite neoclassical home, the Villa Bartholoni, dates from 1828. ⊠ *128 rue de Lausanne, International Area* ☎ *022/4185060* ⊕ *mah. ville-ge.ch* ☒ *Free* ۩ *Wed.–Mon. 10–5.*

❷ Palais Wilson. Inaugurated in 1875 as the Hotel National, the largest of Geneva's palatial hotels, this dignified building leapt to international prominence on April 29, 1919, when Geneva was unanimously chosen by the peace negotiators in Paris to house the newborn League of Nations. Hotel rooms were converted to offices, and 700 international civil servants began work here in September 1920. It was renamed in honor of U.S. President Woodrow Wilson on his death in 1924.

By 1936, the faltering League had run out of space and moved to the custom-built Palais des Nations. Ten years later it was dismantled. The Palais Wilson was gutted by fire in 1987, meticulously restored in 1998, and now houses the United Nations Office of the High Commissioner for Human Rights. It is not open to the public. ⊠ *51 rue des Pâquis, Les Pâquis.*

need a break? The crowded and shaded open-air cafeteria at the **Bains des Pâquis** (⊠ 30 quai du Mont-Blanc, Les Pâquis ☎ 022/7322974) serves its hearty lunchtime plats du jour on (almost in) the water.

☝ ⑩ **Parc La Grange.** Two theaters, the Orangerie and the Théâtre de Verdure, stage performances here June through early September; new varieties of roses angle for prominence in a competition each June; and the remnants of a first-century Roman villa crown the hillside in this gracious, sun-dappled park, once the private grounds of an 18th-century villa overlooking the lake. William Favre's bequest of his family's domain to the city in 1917 stipulated that the park be made available to the public during the day and closed at night. It is still the only green space in Geneva to be locked when the sun goes down. ✉ *quai Gustave-Ador, Eaux-Vives.*

⑥ **Temple de la Fusterie.** Designed by Huguenot refugee Jean Vennes and completed in 1715, Geneva's first truly Calvinist church was built to accommodate the flood of immigrant French Protestants that followed the 1685 revocation of the Edict of Nantes. The plain, rectangular shape of the building disguised its religious purpose; the circular seating pattern allowed 750 people to hear every word the minister said. ✉ *pl. de la Fusterie, Centre Ville* ☎ *022/9097000* ⊕ *www.protestant. ch* 💬 *Free* ☉ *1st Sat. of month, 3–5.*

Old Town

Geneva's Old Town (Vieille Ville), a tight cluster of museums, boutiques, and sidewalk cafés capped by the cathedral, represents the city's core. The cantonal government's executive, legislative, and judicial branches operate within its walls; the Left Bank radiates out from its slopes.

a good walk

Begin at place Neuve, Geneva's musical hub. Walk straight through the gates of the Parc des Bastions. To the right is the Université de Genève, founded by Calvin as an academy in 1559. The enormous **Monument de la Réformation** ⑫ ▶ dominates the left side of the park. Relax on the terrace steps—made of Mont Blanc granite—to take it all in. Then climb the steps to the right of the Monument, ascend the ramp, cross rue de la Croix-Rouge, and follow rue René-Louis Piachaud straight into the Vieille Ville.

Turn left onto rue de St-Léger. When you reach the bottom of the tiered plateau and medieval marketplace known as **place du Bourg-de-Four** ⑬, climb the steps to your left and angle uphill on rue de l'Hôtel-de-Ville. Cut right into place de la Taconnerie. Christie's auction house, on the left, symbolically balances the small Gothic **Auditoire de Calvin** ⑭, Geneva's 16th-century training ground for Protestant missionaries, on the right where the road curves.

Circle around the back of the Romanesque-Gothic **Cathédrale St-Pierre** ⑮, and turn left into rue du Cloître. The **Musée International de la Réforme** ⑯, inaugurated in 2005, traces the history of Calvinism on the site where Geneva agreed, in 1536, to be reformed. Continue on to the cour St-Pierre, turn left, and enter the cathedral between the huge columns of its neoclassical facade. Climb the north tower for a bird's-eye view of the city; then exit the cathedral through the main doors, turn left, and take the stairs down to the **site archéologique** ⑰. Once you've resurfaced after an underground tour of the ruins, angle left toward rue du Soleil-Levant, and follow it to the **Maison Tavel** ⑱, Geneva's oldest house.

Wind your way to the attic and compare pre-1850 Geneva with what you just saw from the cathedral tower; then turn left as you leave the museum and head for rue Jean-Calvin. The site of his residence (No. 11) lies just across the street from the **Musée Barbier-Mueller** ⑲, home to ever-changing portions of a large private collection of primitive art. Turn left up rue de la Pélisserie by the plaque commemorating George Eliot's brief visit to Geneva, then left again onto the Grand-rue. Among the street's many boutiques, antiques stores, and art galleries you can also spot Argentinian writer Jorge Luis Borges's former residence (No. 28) and Ferdinand Hodler's painting studio (No. 33). The Espace Jean-Jacques Rousseau, a 25-minute audiovisual tour (in English) of the philosopher's life, occupies No. 40, where Rousseau was born. Follow the Grand-rue to the cannons by the city's 17th-century Arsenal. The sober facade of the **Hôtel de Ville** ⑳, across the street, conceals a stately inner courtyard and the offices of today's cantonal government.

Continue straight back to place du Bourg-de-Four, cross the square, dip right down rue Etienne-Dumont, and follow it to place Franz-Liszt, so named because the composer lived in the corner house on the right in 1835–36. Turn left onto promenade de St-Antoine, and descend the second set of steps marked *site archéologique* for a stroll through the Vieille Ville parking garage—it's built carefully around the massive remains of Geneva's medieval ramparts. Ride the elevator back up and cross the bridge on your right to the **Musée d'Art et d'Histoire** ㉑. When you've exhausted its many rooms of archaeological treasures and paintings, exit and turn right. To the left, off rue Charles-Galland, six gilt cupolas crown the 19th-century Église Russe, whose interior is decorated in neo-Byzantine style. Continue past the church, turn right onto rue François-Le-Fort, and left on rue Munier-Romilly. At the end of the block on the right is the **Collections Baur** ㉒, a superb private museum of Asian ceramics, jade, and lacquerware.

Walk straight from the museum back to rue Charles-Galland and turn right. Turn left on boulevard des Tranchées and head for the **Muséum d'Histoire Naturelle** ㉓, the modern black-and-white building on the far side of route de Malagnou. From here you can catch Bus 8 (direction OMS) for the Right Bank or follow rue Ferdinand-Hodler and boulevard Jaques-Dalcroze back toward the waterfront.

TIMING About an hour is required to complete this walk at a steady clip, but stretch it out over a day if you can, allowing time for detours into shops and side streets as well as the many exhibits you'll encounter. Most of the museums on this route are closed on Monday.

What to See

⑭ **Auditoire de Calvin** (Protestant Lecture Hall). John Knox, the Scots reformer, preached here from 1556 to 1559; Jean Calvin founded his academy here in 1559. Calvin also used this sober Gothic chapel to teach missionaries his doctrines of puritanical reform and encouraged Protestant refugees from around Europe to hold services in their native English, Italian, Spanish, German, and Dutch. The Auditoire is still used by the Church of Scotland, the Dutch Reformed Community, and the Waldensian Church of Italy; the Church of Scotland welcomes visitors to its Sunday-morning service at 11. ✉ *1 pl. de la Taconnerie, Vieille Ville* ☎ *022/9097000* ✆ *Free* ⊘ *Mon.–Sat. 10–noon and 2–5.*

★ ⑮ **Cathédrale St-Pierre** (St. Peter's Cathedral). Construction began in 1160 and lasted 150 years, by which time this towering Romanesque cathedral had acquired Gothic accents; a massive neoclassical facade was added in 1750. The austerity of the nave reflects its 1536 conversion from a Catholic cathedral to a Protestant church; Calvin's followers destroyed statuary and frescoes like those restored to the 15th-century, neo-Gothic **Chapel of the Maccabees,** to the right of the main entrance. The panoramic view from the **north tower** (to the left at the far end of the nave) is worth the climb. ✉ *cour St-Pierre, Vieille Ville* ☎ *022/3117575* ✆ *North tower 3 SF* ⊘ *June–Sept., Mon.–Sat. 9:30–6:30, Sun. noon–6:30; Oct.–May, Mon.–Sat. 10–5, Sun. noon–5.*

㉒ **Collections Baur** (Baur Collections). Spanning more than 10 centuries of Asian art, Alfred Baur's lovingly preserved collection of Far Eastern art is Switzerland's largest. Fine Chinese ceramics and jade, Japanese smoking paraphernalia, prints, netsuke, lacquerware, and elaborate sword fittings have filled this tranquil 19th-century town house since 1964. Temporary exhibits inhabit the basement; general texts in English introduce each room. ✉ *8 rue Munier-Romilly, Centre Ville* ☎ *022/3461729* ⊕ *www.collections-baur.ch* ✆ *5 SF* ⊘ *Tues.–Sun. 2–6.*

⑳ **Hôtel de Ville** (Town Hall). The cantonal government still inhabits this elegant vaulted compound—of which the oldest part, the Tour Baudet (Baudet Tower), dates from 1455—but the horses and sedan chairs that once clogged the cobbled ramp to the State Council Chamber on the third floor have disappeared. Sixteen countries signed the first Geneva Convention in the ground-floor **Alabama Hall** on August 22, 1864, making it the birthplace of the International Red Cross. On November 15, 1920, the League of Nations convened its first assembly in the hall, whose name refers to a ship at the center of a British-American dispute settled here in 1872. Whenever possible, the tourist office works a brief visit into its morning walking tour of the Vieille Ville. ✉ *2 rue de l'Hôtel-de-Ville, Vieille Ville* ☎ *022/9097030.*

⑱ **Maison Tavel** (Tavel House). Geneva's oldest house traces the development of urban life in the city from 1334 to the 19th century. The vaulted cellars and the ground-floor kitchens display medieval graffiti, local coins, 15th-century tiles, and a guillotine. Seventeenth-century ironwork, doors, and other fragments of long-demolished houses fill the first floor; a bourgeois home complete with 18th-century wallpaper is re-created on the second. The enormous Magnin Model, which depicts Geneva as it looked before the city's elaborate defense walls came down in 1850, is housed in the attic. Temporary exhibits rotate through the basement. Don't miss the little room full of photographs on the first floor. ✉ *6 rue du Puits-St-Pierre, Vieille Ville* ☎ *022/4183700* ⊕ *mah.ville-ge.ch* ✆ *Free* ⊘ *Tues.–Sun. 10–5.*

▶ ⑫ **Monument de la Réformation** (Wall of the Reformers). Conceived on a grand **Fodor'sChoice** scale—it measures 325 feet long, 30 feet high—and erected between 1909 ★ and 1917, this phalanx of enormous granite statues pays homage to the

16th-century religious movement spearheaded by Guillaume Farel, Jean Calvin, Théodore de Bèze, and John Knox. Solemn 15-foot likenesses of the four reformers are flanked by smaller statues of major Protestant figures, bas-reliefs, and inscriptions connected with the Reformation. Oliver Cromwell is surrounded by bas-reliefs of the Pilgrim fathers praying on the deck of the *Mayflower* and the 1689 presentation of the Bill of Rights to King William and Queen Mary by the English Houses of Parliament. The Reformation's—and Geneva's—motto, *Post Tenebras Lux* (After Darkness, Light), spreads over the whole. ⊠ *Parc des Bastions, Centre Ville.*

★ ⑲ **Musée Barbier-Mueller.** Josef Mueller began acquiring fine primitive art from Africa, Oceania, Southeast Asia, and the Americas in 1907. Today his family's vast, inspired collection of sculpture, masks, shields, textiles, and ornaments spans six continents and seven millennia. A small selection is on view at any given time, displayed like jewels in a warm, spotlit vault of scrubbed stone. Basement galleries focus consistently on pre-Columbian America, Africa, and Southeast Asia. ⊠ *10 rue Jean-Calvin, Vieille Ville* ☎ *022/3120270* ⊕ *www.barbier-mueller.ch* ⊠ *5 SF* ⊙ *Daily 11–5.*

㉑ **Musée d'Art et d'Histoire** (Museum of Art and History). The city's huge archaeology, fine arts, and applied arts collections moved from the overcrowded Musée Rath to this custom-built museum in 1910. Among the more noteworthy holdings are Switzerland's largest collection of Egyptian art and a roomful of intricate weapons from the early 1600s. The fine art collection includes the 15th-century *Miracle of the Fishes,* by Swiss painter Konrad Witz, in which Christ paces the waters of Lac Léman; an impressive array of Alpine landscapes; and a rich range of contemporary work. The front rooms are devoted to temporary exhibits. ⊠ *2 rue Charles-Galland, Vieille Ville* ☎ *022/4182600* ⊕ *mah.ville-ge.ch* ⊠ *Free* ⊙ *Tues.–Sun. 10–5.*

⑯ **Musée International de la Réforme** (International Museum of the Reformation). This engaging and meticulously conceived museum, slated to open in spring 2005, was lovingly installed in a 1723 building constructed on the site of the cloister where, on May 21, 1536, the Genevois voted to adopt Calvin's radical new religious doctrine. Using audiovisuals and historical artifacts, it traces the Protestant Reformation from its 16th-century roots through its influence on today's world. Printed and audio guides are available in English; underground passageways link the museum with the cathedral and the subterranean site archéologique. ⊠ *2 rue du Cloître, Vieille Ville* ⊕ *www.musee-reforme.ch* ⊠ *10 SF, 16 SF with cathedral towers and site archéologique* ⊙ *Tues.–Sun. 10–5.*

㉓ **Muséum d'Histoire Naturelle** (Museum of Natural History). Local school groups enthusiastically support this museum, so don't be surprised if it's overrun with kids. Large, evocative wildlife dioramas complete with sound effects are the biggest draw for young children; older visitors can study human evolution, precious stones, Swiss geology, exotic birds, coral reefs, or the history of the solar system. Gigantic crystals, a case full of polyhedrons, beehives, large quantities of fossils, and a multimedia display on plate tectonics round out the collection. Most labels are in French. ⊠ *1 rte. de Malagnou* ☎ *022/4186300* 🎫 *Free* 🕑 *Tues.–Sun. 9:30–5.*

★ ⓭ **Place du Bourg-de-Four.** Vestiges of the ancient roads that led south to Annecy and Lyon and east to Italy and the Chablais are still visible in this layered Vieille Ville square. Once a Roman cattle market, later flooded with Protestant refugees, it's still the quintessential Genevois crossroads. Shoppers, lawyers, workers, and students strike an easy balance between scruffy bohemia, genteel tradition, and slick gentrification as they meet for drinks around an 18th-century fountain. ⊠ *Intersection of rue Verdaine, rue des Chaudronniers, rue Étienne-Dumont, and rue de l'Hôtel-de-Ville, Vieille Ville.*

need a break? La Clémence (⊠ 20 pl. du Bourg-de-Four, Vieille Ville ☎ 022/3122498), an old and much-loved sidewalk café named for the largest of the cathedral bells, serves its breakfast *tartines* (baguettes with butter and jelly) in the middle of the busy square.

🕑 ⓱ **Site archéologique.** Archaeologists found multiple layers of history un-
Fodor'sChoice derneath the Cathédrale St-Pierre when its foundations began to falter
★ in 1976. Excavations have so far yielded remnants of two 4th-century Christian sanctuaries, mosaic floors from the late Roman Empire, portions of three early churches, and an 11th-century crypt. The first Romanesque cathedral on the site was built in 1000; today audio guides in English and careful lighting help you navigate the (reinforced) underground maze that remains. ⊠ *cour St-Pierre, Vieille Ville* ☎ *022/3117574* 🎫 *5 SF* 🕑 *Tues.–Sun. 11–5.*

Plainpalais

Reclaimed from the swamps that formed the confluence of the Rhône and Arve rivers as recently as the mid-19th century, the area centered on the diamond-shape Plaine de Plainpalais is now home to contemporary art galleries, traveling circuses, the Université de Genève, local and regional media, weekly flea markets, and remnants of a late-19th-century industrial past.

a good walk Begin by facing the mid-river tourist information booth on pont de la Machine. Follow either walkway around the building, and keep to the left of the Ile de la Cité. A plaque on the side of the **Tour de l'Ile** ㉔ ☛ notes the passage of Julius Caesar in 58 BC.

Heading onto the Left Bank, cross place de Bel-Air to the historic center of the banking district, rue de la Monnaie (literally, Small Change Street). Turn right at the fountain commemorating Geneva's Escalade victory, follow the tram lines to the left onto rue de la Corraterie, and continue past city walls that bore the brunt of the 1602 Savoyard attack. To your immediate right when you reach **place Neuve** ㉕ is the **Musée Rath** ㉖. The Grand Théâtre, to its right, is modeled on the Opéra Garnier in Paris. At the far end of the square is the Italianate Conservatoire de Musique, built—as is everything that follows—on reclaimed land.

CloseUp

SWORDS & SOUP

Geneva's Escalade is a celebration of victory and independence. In 1536 Geneva formally adopted the Protestant faith and rid itself of the Catholic bishop-princes who had ruled it since the 12th century. This set up a conflict with the Duke of Savoy, who controlled most of the region around Geneva and hoped to make the city his Catholic capital north of the Alps. Tensions rose, and on the night of December 11–12, 1602, the duke sent men to scale the city walls with ladders.

His plans went awry when the city's entire population turned out to fight. One resourceful housewife wielded a marmite (pot) of hot soup to devastating effect—an act commemorated each year with cauldrons made of chocolate. Geneva's 18 dead are honored with an elaborate parade, period outfits and weapons are worn in the Vieille Ville, and costumed children go door to door singing "Cé qu'è laîno," Geneva's victory song.

Follow rue Alexandre-Calame to the right of the Conservatoire, keeping the experimental Maison des Arts du Grütli (Grütli Arts Center) on your right. After crossing boulevard Georges-Favon at the traffic light to your right, you reach a fountain. Head left along the side of the park, cross both lanes of rue Harry-Marc, and continue straight under the plane trees, keeping the skateboard park and boccie pitches to your left. Farther to your left is the Plaine de Plainpalais, Geneva's all-purpose open space and fairgrounds, which hosts a constant stream of outdoor markets, fun fairs, circuses, and exhibitions.

Head south and a block west to rue des Vieux-Grenadiers, where the **Patek Philippe Museum** ㉗ offers a dazzling detour through the world of watchmaking and enameling. The combined entrance to the **Centre d'Art Contemporain** ㉘ and **Mamco (Musée d'Art Moderne et Contemporain)** ㉙, Geneva's mother lode of contemporary art, lies across the street at the end of the block.

Leave the world of modern art by the door through which you entered it and turn right onto rue des Bains. Head past the somewhat musty private Musée Jean Tua de l'Automobile, and keep going for three blocks. Keep the traffic circle to your right as you cross boulevard de Saint-Georges, and continue straight down rue des Rois to the peaceful **Cimetière de Plainpalais** ㉚, on your left.

Continue on rue des Rois, and turn left onto rue de la Coulouvrenière. The entrance to the imposing **Bâtiment des Forces Motrices** ㉛, a 19th-century hydroelectric plant turned opera house, lies to the right across place des Volontaires. Take a brief detour along the river to the left of the building, where the Barrage du Seujet, inaugurated in 1995, maintains the river water level, generates hydroelectricity, and lets fish and boats through separate sets of locks; then follow the quai back along the length of the opera house to the footbridge just before the road begins to climb.

Turn right when you get to the narrow mid-river park, and continue straight through the tunnel under the pont de la Coulouvrenière and into the passageway in the side of the rounded former market building known today as Les Halles de l'Ile. You'll emerge in an open-ended atrium flanked by art galleries and bookshops. Continue straight to place de l'Ile, and follow the quai on either side of the buildings back to pont de la Machine.

TIMING   Two hours more than suffices to complete this utterly flat stroll through Geneva's working downtown; an afternoon would allow you to investigate the museums, dawdle a little, and people-watch as you go. Late-afternoon sun gives the river a warm glow.

What to See

③①   **Bâtiment des Forces Motrices** (Hydroelectric Power Station). Two of the original 18 turbines remain in the vast L-shape lobby of Geneva's second opera house. The building's mid-river position and 19th-century industrial architecture present further reminders that it was built (in 1886 under the direction of the Genevois engineer Théodore Turrettini) to supply potable water, harness the river's energy for local industry, and keep the lake level steady. These days the 985-seat theater, built in 1997, hosts overflow from the Grand Théâtre—several operas, recitals, and the bulk of the ballet company's season—as well as traveling productions. It is not open during the day. ⊠ *2 pl. des Volontaires, Plainpalais* ☎ *022/3221220* ⊕ *www.bfm.ch.*

②⑧   **Centre d'Art Contemporain** (Center for Contemporary Art). Geneva's Kunsthalle (art institute) has been encouraging new work and organizing exhibits by cutting-edge contemporary artists since 1974. Shows have included work by Andy Warhol, Cindy Sherman, Nan Goldin, Pippilotti Rist, Thomas Scheibitz, and Shirana Shabhazi; parallel programs include multidisciplinary projects, performances, and lectures. ⊠ *10 rue des Vieux-Grenadiers, Plainpalais* ☎ *022/3291842* ⊕ *www.centre.ch* ☞ *3.50 SF* ☉ *Tues.–Sun. 11–6.*

③⓪   **Cimetière de Plainpalais** (Plainpalais Cemetery). Originally part of a 15th-century hospital complex built on dry ground outside the city to isolate victims of the plague, these verdant 7 acres bordering the city's tax offices hold the mortal remains of Jean Calvin, Simon Rath, Guillaume-Henri Dufour, William Favre, Ernest Ansermet (founder of the Orchestre de la Suisse Romande), Jorge Luis Borges, and the United Nations diplomat Sergio Vieira de Mello. The paucity of tombstones reflects a turbulent history of flooding and neglect, not lack of use; funeral monuments were introduced in the 19th century. ⊠ *10 rue des Rois, Plainpalais* ☎ *022/3292129* ☞ *Free* ☉ *Daily 8–noon and 1:30–5:30.*

②⑨   **Mamco (Musée d'Art Moderne et Contemporain)** (Museum of Modern and Contemporary Art). Concrete floors and fluorescent lighting set the tone for this gritty collection of stark, mind-stretching, post-1960 art housed in a former factory building. The industrial surroundings help juxtapose aesthetic approaches; temporary exhibits add current artists to the mix. ⊠ *10 rue des Vieux-Grenadiers, Plainpalais* ☎ *022/3206122* ⊕ *www. mamco.ch* ☞ *8 SF* ☉ *Tues.–Fri. noon–6, weekends 11–6.*

㉖ **Musée Rath.** Switzerland's original fine arts museum, inaugurated in 1826 and named for its late benefactor, Simon Rath, housed Geneva's growing collections of art and archaeology until they overflowed to the Musée d'Art et d'Histoire in 1910. Now the Rath hosts two annual temporary exhibitions ranging in focus from archaeology to contemporary art. Richard Wagner's impact on the visual arts is slated for examination in late 2005–early 2006. ⊠ *pl. Neuve, Centre Ville* ☎ *022/4183340* ⊕ *mah.ville-ge.ch* ⊡ *Varies by exhibit, up to 10 SF* ⊘ *Tues. and Thurs.–Sun. 10–5, Wed. noon–9.*

㉗ **Patek Philippe Museum.** This former watchmaking workshop owned by
Fodor'sChoice   Patek Philippe, one of Geneva's most venerable watchmaking compa-
★   nies, is now filled with meticulously restored workbenches, audiovisual displays, classical music, a horological library, and display upon softly lit glass display. Cases are filled with delicate gold watch cases, complicated watch innards, lifelike miniature portraits, and enameled objects ranging from fans, pens, pocket knives, snuffboxes, and telescopes to vanity pistols that shoot singing birds. You can take an exquisite 2½-hour guided tour of horology and enameling from the 16th century to the present. (The one on Friday at 2:15 is in English, as is all signage.) ⊠ *7 rue des Vieux-Grenadiers, Plainpalais* ☎ *022/8070910* ⊕ *www. patekmuseum.com* ⊡ *10 SF* ⊘ *Tues.–Fri. 2–5, Sat. 10–5.*

㉕ **Place Neuve.** Aristocratic town houses overlook Geneva's opera house, the Musée Rath, the Conservatoire de Musique, and the wrought-iron entrance to the Parc des Bastions. The equestrian statue at the center of the square honors Guillaume-Henri Dufour, the first general of Switzerland's federal army and the first person to map the country. A large bust of Henry Dunant, founder of the International Red Cross, marks the spot where public executions once took place. ⊠ *Intersection of blvd. du Théâtre, rue de la Corraterie, rue de la Croix-Rouge, and rue Bartholoni, Centre Ville.*

▶ ㉔ **Tour de l'Ile.** The lone surviving fragment of Bishop Aymon de Grandson's 13th-century fortified château served as a prison during the Reformation. It's not open to the public. ⊠ *ponts de l'Ile, Centre Ville.*

International Area

Geneva's humanitarian and diplomatic zone, of which the Palais des Nations forms the core, lies seven minutes north of the Gare Cornavin by tram. Modern structures housing UN agencies such as the WHO (World Health Organization), ILO (International Labour Organization), ITU (International Telecommunications Union), and UNHCR (United Nations High Commissioner for Refugees) are threaded between embassies, 19th-century villas full of nongovernmental organizations, and a handful of museums.

a good walk   Take Tram 13 (direction Nations) from the Gare Cornavin to the end of the line. Get off at place des Nations, by the Broken Chair monument to land-mine victims; have a look at the flags flying in front of the **Palais des Nations** ㉜ ▶, European headquarters of the United Nations; and walk west on avenue de la Paix. The domed palace set back from the road on your right is the **Musée Ariana** ③, home to the Musée Suisse de la Céramique et du Verre. The **Musée International de la Croix-Rouge et du Croissant-Rouge** ㉞, a fiercely moving museum that traces the history of humanitarian assistance, lies directly opposite the visitors' entrance to the Palais.

Avenue de la Paix becomes route de Pregny as it curves up and to the left past the headquarters of the Comité International de la Croix-Rouge (International Committee of the Red Cross). You'll pass the Pregny-Rigot campus of the International School of Geneva, on the right, and the American Mission to the UN, on the left, at the top of the hill. Turn right onto chemin de l'Impératrice. The arcadian grounds of the 19th-century Château de Penthes are open to the public; the building itself houses the **Musée des Suisses dans le Monde** ㉟, a permanent exhibit that traces the activities of Swiss people outside Switzerland. The **Musée Militaire Genevois** ㊱, set in one of the château's former stables, chronicles local military history.

Continue along chemin de l'Impératrice as it winds past panoramic Alpine views and down toward the **Jardin Botanique** ㊲, which spreads out on both sides of the road just after a small underpass. Enter by the main gate, on the right, and wander past pink flamingos, sweeping lawns, huge trees, and Alpine rock gardens to the exit gate at place Alfred-Thomas. Keep the headquarters of the World Trade Organization on your left as you cross avenue de la Paix and catch Bus 1 (direction Rive) back to the Gare Cornavin.

TIMING Make sure to devote a full day to this part of town—there's a lot of territory, both literal and figurative, to cover. Wear good walking shoes, check opening times in advance, and balance the museum shuffle with brisk strides in the fresh air.

What to See

㊲ **Jardin Botanique** (Botanical Garden). Geneva's 19th-century fascination with botany gave rise to 69 contemplative acres of winding paths and streams, mountain views and rock gardens, trees that predate 1700, exotic hothouses, beds of irises, rose gardens, an aviary, a deer park, a garden of scent and touch, a living catalog of economically useful and medicinal plants, and a formidable research institute. ⊠ *1 chemin de l'Impératrice, International Area* ☎ *022/4185100* ⊕ *www.ville-ge.ch/ cjb* ☜ *Free* ☉ *Apr.–Sept., daily 8–7:30; Oct.–Mar., daily 9:30–5.*

㉝ **Musée Ariana.** An architectural anachronism when it was built in 1884 and named for someone's mother, this serene Italianate structure ceded its parkland to the Palais des Nations and now houses the **Musée Suisse de la Céramique et du Verre** (Swiss Museum of Ceramics and Glass). Its enormous collection of stoneware, earthenware, porcelain, and glass covers 700 years of East-West exchange; contemporary work rotates through the basement. ⊠ *10 av. de la Paix, International Area* ☎ *022/ 4185450* ⊕ *mah.ville-ge.ch* ☜ *Free* ☉ *Wed.–Mon. 10–5.*

㉟ **Musée des Suisses dans le Monde** (Museum of Swiss Citizens in the World). In room after creaky room of the 19th-century Château de Penthes, models, paintings, documents, and other objects highlight the considerable achievements of Swiss people outside Switzerland since the 1200s. As you climb the stairs, Swiss Guards and military men give way to artists, bankers, explorers, doctors, writers, archaeologists, chocolatiers, and inventors. Many, like Louis Chevrolet, are surprisingly prominent. ⊠ *18 chemin de l'Impératrice, International Area* ☎ *022/ 7349021* ⊕*www.chateau-de-penthes.ch.* ☜*5 SF* ⊙*Jan.–Mar., Wed.–Sun. 10–noon and 2–5; Apr.–Dec., Tues.–Sun. 10–noon and 2–6.*

Have a generous plat du jour or a slice of homemade fruit tart on the summer terrace at **Les Cent Suisses** (⊠ 18 chemin de l'Impératrice, International Area ☎ 022/7344865), a lunch-only spot on the grounds of the Château de Penthes.

☾ ③④ **Musée International de la Croix-Rouge et du Croissant-Rouge** (International Red Cross and Red Crescent Museum). Powerful mute statues speak to the need for human kindness in the face of disaster, and balanced but often grim exhibits trace the history of the struggle to provide it in this carefully nonjudgmental museum buried in the hillside beneath the headquarters of the International Committee of the Red Cross.

Fodor's Choice ★

Audiovisuals show the postbattle horrors at Solferino that moved Henry Dunant to form the Red Cross. Endless aisles of file boxes hold 7 million records of World War I prisoners, and there's a replica of a 6½-foot by 6½-foot concrete cell in which Red Cross workers discovered 17 political prisoners. The **Mur du Temps** (Wall of Time), a simple time line punctuated by armed conflicts and natural disasters in which more than 10,000 people died, puts the overall story into sobering perspective. Good news, in the form of disaster-relief kits and snapshots used to reunite Rwandan families after the 1994 genocide, is also on display. Guided tours and museum literature are available in English. ⊠ *17 av. de la Paix, International Area* ☎ *022/7489525* ⊕ *www. micr.org* ☜ *10 SF* ⊙ *Wed.–Mon. 10–5.*

③⑥ **Musée Militaire Genevois** (Geneva Military Museum). Switzerland has not waged war outside its borders since 1292, but its military has not been idle. The weapons, uniforms, prints, and documents on display in this former stable tell the colorful story of *la Garde Genevoise* from 1814 to the present. ⊠*18 chemin de l'Impératrice, International Area* ☎ *022/ 7344875* ☜ *Free* ⊙ *Late Jan.–late Dec., Tues.–Sat. 2–5, Sun. 10–noon and 2–5.*

▶ ③② **Palais des Nations** (Palace of Nations). Built between 1929 and 1936 for the League of Nations, this monumental compound became the European branch of the United Nations in 1946. Today the Palais is the largest center for multilateral diplomacy in the world—it hosts some 9,000 conferences and 25,000 delegates each year—and the largest nexus for United Nations operational activities after New York.

You'll need to show your passport and join a tour to see the interior. Points of particular interest include the **Assembly Hall,** the largest of 34 conference rooms, where the UN General Assembly and scores of world leaders have met, and the ornate **Council Chamber,** home to the Conference on Disarmament, which glows with allegorical murals by Catalan artist José Maria Sert. Tours last about an hour and are available in English. There are no set starting times.

The Museum of the League of Nations and the United Nations Philatelic Museum are also quartered in the Palais (though access to the former is restricted and both are closed on weekends); admission is included in the general entrance fee. Temporary exhibitions and film screenings round out the options on any given day; the UN bookstore covers human rights, peacekeeping, and everything in between. ⊠ *14 av. de la Paix, International Area* ☎ *022/9174896* ⊕ *www.unog.ch* ⊠ *10 SF* ⊙ *Jan.–Mar. and Nov.–mid-Dec., weekdays 10–noon and 2–4; Apr.–June, Sept., and Oct., daily 10–noon and 2–4; July and Aug., daily 10–5.*

WHERE TO EAT

Genevois menus tend to follow the seasons, changing three or four times a year on average. Fast food consists of complex salads, fresh sandwiches, and warm quiche to go, and lunchtime plats du jour and bakeries with tearooms are delicious budget options. Many restaurants close on weekends, so be sure to call ahead.

WHAT IT COSTS In Swiss francs				
$$$$	**$$$**	**$$**	**$**	**¢**
MAIN COURSE over 60	40–60	25–40	15–25	under 15

Prices are per person for a main course at dinner.

$$$$ ✕ **Domaine de Châteauvieux.** Philippe Chevrier's expansive kitchen, in
Fodor'sChoice the heart of Geneva's wine country, has a glowing (and growing) rep-
★ utation for simple, elegant, unpretentious quality. Seasonal dishes highlight asparagus in spring, seafood in summer, game come October, and truffles in winter; the cellar houses top local vintages. Ancient beams, antique winepresses, weathered stone, and a summer terrace overlooking the vines complete the country setting. Mountain views are tremendous. Take a boat up the Rhône to Peney or drive 20 minutes from Geneva. ⊠ *Peney-Dessus, Satigny* ☎ *022/7531511* ⊕ *www.chateauvieux.ch* ⌦ *Reservations essential* ☐ *AE, DC, MC, V* ⊙ *Closed Sun. and Mon.*

★ **$$$–$$$$** ✕ **Le Lion d'Or.** Cologny is Geneva's Beverly Hills with a view, and this sleek, sophisticated dining room takes full advantage of its real estate. Picture windows and the lounge upstairs overlook the city, the lake, and the Jura. Local celebrity chefs Gilles Dupont and Tommy Byrne roast their line-caught sea bass to perfection, serve cardons au gratin with truffles, and grow their herbs in the garden below the terrace. The bistro next door shares the restaurant's kitchen, not its prices—grab a cab and come for lunch. ⊠ *5 pl. Pierre-Gautier, Cologny* ☎ *022/7364432* ⌦ *Reservations essential* ☐ *AE, DC, MC, V* ⊙ *Closed weekends.*

$$$ ✕ **La Perle du Lac.** The dining room stays open from February to December, but this chalet-style former guesthouse in the midst of Geneva's Right Bank waterfront park comes dramatically into its own in summer. The large flowered (and covered) terrace looks straight out over the lake at Mont Blanc; the Mouettes Genevoises water taxis dock di-

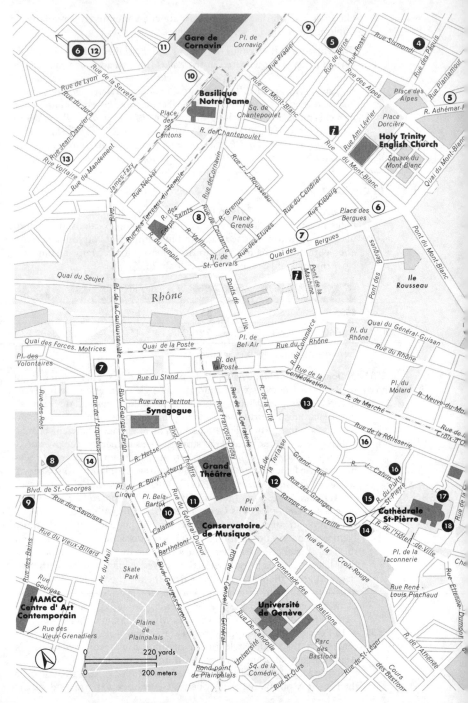

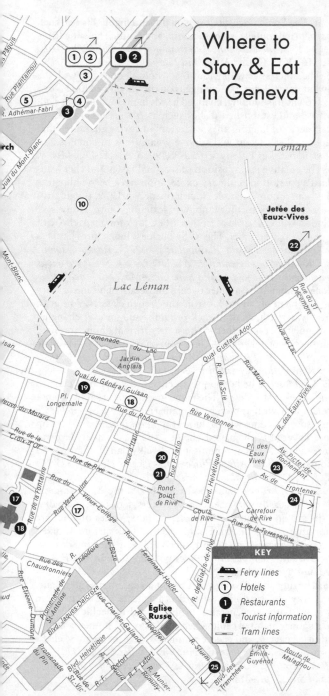

Where to Stay & Eat in Geneva

KEY

🛥 *Ferry lines*
① *Hotels*
❶ *Restaurants*
🛈 *Tourist information*
▬ *Tram lines*

rectly in front. The French-accented seasonal menu highlights fish such as *rouget barbet* (red mullet), sole, sea bass, and trout. The wine list is exhaustive. ⊠ *126 rue de Lausanne, International Area* ☎ *022/9091020* ⊟ *AE, DC, MC, V* ⊘ *Closed Mon. and Jan.*

$$$ ✕ **Le Cygne.** The timeless view of Mont Blanc doesn't quite jibe with the slick, somewhat dated decor, but change is on the way. The Hotel Noga Hilton, which owns the building, changed hands in mid-2004. That said, a loyal fan base and established dishes such as *filet de bœuf* (fillet of beef) and carpaccio of langoustines with Iranian caviar guarantee that chef Rodolphe Collet's menu will survive whatever is to come. ⊠ *19 quai du Mont-Blanc, Les Pâquis* ☎ *022/9089085* ⊟ *AE, DC, MC, V.*

$$–$$$$ ✕ **Le Béarn.** The creative juxtaposition of seasonal tastes and chef Jean-Paul Goddard's passion for culinary exploration have been hallmarks of this hushed gastronomic temple since it opened in 1979. (Goddard's wife, Denise, runs the peach-color Empire-style dining room.) House specialities include a winter soufflé of fresh truffles; look for gazpacho with lobster and avocado in summer. The 65 SF business lunch lures bankers at midday. ⊠ *4 quai de la Poste, Plainpalais* ☎ *022/3210028* ⊕ *www.lebearn.ch* ⚇ *Reservations essential* ⊟ *AE, DC, MC, V* ⊘ *Closed 6 wks July–Aug., weekends June–Sept., and Sun. Oct.–May. No lunch Sat.*

$$–$$$$ ✕ **Le Chat Botté.** Dominique Gauthier tweaks the details of his menu every few months, but he never strays far from the French classics. Foie gras, salt- and freshwater fish, roasted rack of lamb, and an ever-changing vegetarian menu are served either in the stately formal dining room or, from May through September, on the lakefront balcony-terrace. The wine cellar is exceptional. ⊠ *13 quai du Mont-Blanc, Les Pâquis* ☎ *022/7166920* ⚇ *Reservations essential* ⊟ *AE, DC, MC, V.*

$$–$$$ ✕ **Bistrot du Bœuf Rouge.** Belle epoque accents add a touch of class to
Fodor'sChoice the tongue-in-cheek bistro decor. The menu groans with rich Lyonnaise
★ classics. Boudin noir with apples, homemade rillettes, and *quenelles de brochet* (pike soufflé) come with light gratin *dauphinois* (baked cream and potatoes covered with melted cheese); the tender filet de bœuf barely requires a knife. Dessert options include silky flan au caramel and chestnut mousse. ⊠ *17 rue Alfred-Vincent, Les Pâquis* ☎ *022/7327537* ⊟ *AE, DC, MC, V* ⊘ *Closed weekends.*

★ $$–$$$ ✕ **Bistrot du Boucher.** Art nouveau woodwork, bright tile, and a stained-glass ceiling coexist easily with cheeky cow posters, figurines, and paintings. Aperitifs are on the house. The *côtes de bœuf* (sides of beef) are presented for approval prior to carving, and the steak tartare is mixed to your taste. Try the one-of-a-kind chocolate-pear tart for dessert. ⊠ *15 av. Pictet-de-Rochemont, Eaux-Vives* ☎ *022/7365636* ⊟ *AE, MC, V* ⊘ *Closed Sun. No lunch Sat.*

$$–$$$ ✕ **La Favola.** The tiny dining room at the top of a vertiginous spiral staircase in this quirky life-size dollhouse strikes a delicate balance between rustic and fussy, with lace curtains, embroidered tablecloths, rough beams, and a sponge-painted ceiling. Seasonal risottos, homemade pastas, paper-thin carpaccio, and classic tiramisu reflect the Ticinese chef's roots in Locarno. ⊠ *15 rue Jean-Calvin, Vieille Ville* ☎ *022/3117437* ⊕ *www.lafavola.com* ⊟ *No credit cards* ⊘ *Closed weekends Apr.–Aug., Sat. lunch and Sun. Sept.–Mar.*

★ **$$–$$$** ✕ **Le Vallon.** A rosy facade, snappy green awnings, and hanging grapevines set the scene at this century-old village restaurant. Seasonal dishes—from lobster cannelloni with green asparagus in a carrot-ginger emulsion to boudin blanc (white blood sausage) at Christmas and crème brulée—are served in two cozy dining rooms or outside amid the vines. ⊠ *182 rte. de Florissant, Conches* ☎ *022/3471104* ▬ *AE, DC, MC, V* ⊗ *Closed weekends.*

$$–$$$ ✕ **Roberto.** Roberto Carugati and his daughter, Marietta, have perfected an easy formality that lures lawyers, bankers, politicians, and fashionable Italians to their red-gold dining room. Parmesan cheese arrives in lieu of bread. The menu includes pasta in saffron sauce, buttery sole, and risotto served from shining copper and silver pots. Unusual and rare Italian wines help relax the somewhat stuffy atmosphere as the night wears on. ⊠ *10 rue Pierre-Fatio, Centre Ville* ☎ *022/3118033* ▬ *AE, MC, V* ⊗ *Closed Sun. No dinner Sat.*

★ **$–$$$** ✕ **Brasserie Lipp.** Green-and-white tiles, mustard-yellow ceilings, warm wood, and busy waiters in ankle-length aprons channel Paris, as Genevois intellectuals of all stripes linger over *choucroûte* (sauerkraut), veal blanquette, and heaping platters of seafood. The dining room expands to include a delightful summer terrace at the foot of the Vieille Ville. The kitchen stays open from noon to 12:30 AM (later than most). ⊠ *Confédération-Centre, 8 rue de la Confédération, Centre Ville* ☎ *022/3111011* ▬ *AE, DC, MC, V.*

$–$$$ ✕ **Café Lyrique.** Black-and-white floor tiles offset warm, yellow walls and high wedding-cake ceilings in this relaxed corner brasserie at the heart of Geneva's musical quarter. Images of Beethoven, Verdi, Strauss, and Liszt watch as pretheater diners tuck into elegant salads and carpaccios, homemade pastas, and *mignons de bœuf* or *magret de canard* (duck breast). Croissants are served from 7 AM, and the place Neuve setting and the dessert cart make for a terrific afternoon tea. ⊠ *12 blvd. du Théâtre, Centre Ville* ☎ *022/3280095* ▬ *AE, DC, MC, V* ⊗ *Closed weekends.*

$–$$$ ✕ **Les Armures.** Dark beams, wrought iron, medieval arms, and a robust Swiss menu that covers fondue, raclette, *Schübling* (sausage), and *Rösti* (hash browns) have lured local street sweepers, foreign heads of state, and everyone in between to this Vieille Ville institution. The kitchen serves until midnight (11:30 on Sunday), unusually late for Geneva. ⊠ *1 rue du Puits-St-Pierre, Vieille Ville* ☎ *022/3103442* ▬ *AE, DC, MC, V.*

$–$$$ ✕ **L'Hôtel-de-Ville.** The kitchen serves until 11:30 PM, the dining room transfers to the sidewalk in summer, and the location, at the political heart of the Vieille Ville, guarantees a loyal, smoky crowd of civil servants. The menu favors regional specialties, such as filets de perches, longeole, choucroûte, and game (in season). The Dégustation Genevois menu is a guided culinary tour with wine. ⊠ *39 Grand-rue, Vieille Ville* ☎ *022/3117030* ▬ *AE, DC, MC, V.*

$$ ✕ **Le Relais de l'Entrecôte.** It is rare to find a line of people waiting for **Fodor'sChoice** a table anywhere in Geneva, so the fact that it's commonplace out-★ side this bustling wood-panel Parisian import means the tender strips of grilled steak drenched in herb-based *sauce maison* (house sauce) are a true cut above. A crisp green salad sprinkled with walnuts, robust house wine, and thin, golden fries complete the only option on the menu;

don't worry, there's a second portion on the way. ✉ *49 rue du Rhône, Centre Ville* ☎ *022/3106004* ⚄ *Reservations not accepted* ▤ *MC, V* ⊘ *Closed July.*

$–$$ ✗ **Au Pied-de-Cochon.** Crowded, noisy, smoky, and gruff, this clattering white-tile bistro is anchored by its whitewashed beams and worn zinc bar. Simple regional dishes include andouillettes, choucroûte, boudin noir, longeole with lentils, filets de perches, and the namesake pigs' feet, served grilled, stuffed, or boned. ✉ *4 pl. du Bourg-de-Four, Vieille Ville* ☎ *022/3104797* ▤ *AE, DC, MC, V.*

$–$$ ✗ **Café du Grütli.** Black-clad artists, actors, and students from the nearby Université de Genève congregate in this sun-soaked, smoky restaurant on the ground floor of the Grütli arts center. The menu changes daily—lunch options include three plats du jour—but dishes are reliably generous and beautifully presented. Brunch is served from 10 AM to 3 PM on Sunday. ✉ *16 rue du Général-Dufour, Centre Ville* ☎ *022/3215158* ▤ *AE, DC, MC, V.*

★ **$–$$** ✗ **Café Léo.** Daniel Carugati's tiny, smoky, sunny corner bistro serves homemade ravioli and tortellini, veal *piccata* (breaded veal cutlets) in a raspberry-vinegar or mustard sauce, and a noteworthy *tarte au citron* (lemon tart). Trendy locals descend for lunch, then linger over coffee. ✉ *9 rond-point de Rive, Centre Ville* ☎ *022/3115307* ▤ *AE, MC, V* ⊘ *Closed Sun. No dinner Sat.*

$–$$ ✗ **Jeck's Place.** Even by Genevois standards, this unassuming little restaurant near the train station presents a staggering mix of cultures. Owner Jeck Tan, a native of Singapore and Swiss hotel-school graduate, greets his guests warmly in English and presents a menu written in Malay, Chinese, Thai, and French. The food—whether smooth, deep-fried bean curd with peanut sauce, chicken in green curry, fried *mee hoon* vermicelli, or roast duck *au diable*—keeps the international clientele coming back for more. ✉ *14 rue de Neuchâtel, Les Pâquis* ☎ *022/7313303* ▤ *AE, DC, MC, V* ⊘ *No lunch weekends.*

$–$$ ✗ **L'Echalotte.** Artists and journalists jostle for space on the polished wood banquettes. The handwritten seasonal menu stretches from vegetarian options to the namesake *onglet à l'échalotte* (steak in shallot butter). Buttery *crème de courge* (pumpkin soup), moussaka made with lamb, and a sinful chocolate terrine are served promptly with casual flair. ✉ *17 rue des Rois, Plainpalais* ☎ *022/3205999* ▤ *MC, V* ⊘ *Closed weekends.*

$–$$ ✗ **L'Opera Bouffe.** The ambience is casual-chic and friendly, with wine bottles stacked floor to ceiling, large framed mirrors, classical music in the background, and opera posters on the walls. The Syrian chef rolls out subtle updates of traditional bistro fare and overhauls the menu once a month. Be sure to leave room for a slice of warm tarte tatin with Gruyère cream. ✉ *5 av. de Frontenex, Eaux-Vives* ☎ *022/7366300* ▤ *AE, DC, MC, V* ⊘ *Closed Sun. and Mon. No lunch Sat.*

$–$$ ✗ **Ú Bobba.** The tomato-red and bright-yellow color scheme and the whimsical monthly menu reflect owner Sylvie Begert-Zanella's exuberant sense of fun. She named the restaurant after a Sardinian tuna factory and made up the character whose story is written on the walls. The staff is multinational, as are the influences behind the menu, and vegetarians will always find something, even when the rooftop summer terrace features grilled meats. ✉ *21 rue de la Corraterie, Centre Ville* ☎ *022/3105340* ▭ *AE, DC, MC, V* ⊙ *Closed Sun. and Mon. No lunch Sat.*

$ ✕ **Taverne de la Madeleine.** The city's temperance league owns and operates this big, plain, friendly canteen, so it serves no alcoholic beverages. The kitchen also closes early—3 PM from September to June, 4 PM in July and August—but produces wholesome plats du jour, choucroûte (in winter), filets de perches, homemade fruit tarts, and chocolate or citrus mousse. The sunny, elevated stone terrace looks across at the Temple de la Madeleine, a merry-go-round, and an outdoor crafts fair. ✉ *20 rue Toutes-Âmes, Vieille Ville* ☎ *022/3106070* ▭ *AE, DC, MC, V* ⊙ *Closed Sun. No dinner.*

★ ¢ ✕ **Le Thé.** The delicate red-clay teapots lining the walls are for sale. Scores of rare, scented, and little-known brews complement succulent rice-flour crepes stuffed with shrimp, dim sum, steamed bread, and wobbly cubes of tapioca cake. It is easy to miss this microscopic piece of China, lodged as it is behind a nondescript storefront near Mamco, but call ahead or drop by after 1:30 for lunch—the nine tiny tables fill up fast. ✉ *65 rue des Bains, Plainpalais* ☎ *079/4367718* ▭ *No credit cards* ⊙ *Closed Sun.*

12

WHERE TO STAY

Hotel rack rates in Geneva are comparable to those in most European capitals, but the huge number of conferences held here make weekend deals and group rates easy to secure. Book well in advance—large events can suddenly fill entire hotels—and remember that rates plummet most dramatically at luxury hotels on weekends.

WHAT IT COSTS In Swiss francs

	$$$$	$$$	$$	$	¢
DOUBLE ROOM	over 350	250–350	175–250	100–175	under 100

Prices are for two people in a standard double room in high season, including tax and service.

★ $$$$ 🏨 **Beau-Rivage.** There's water at the hushed, genteel heart of this grand old Victorian palace: the four-story atrium is centered on a murmuring fountain. Rooms have period furniture, original frescoes, triple phone lines, enormous safes, plush bathrobes, and a pervading sense of romance; front rooms overlook the harbor and Mont Blanc. The Mayer family's guest list since 1865 has included Richard Wagner, Jean Cocteau, Sarah Bernhardt, and Catherine Deneuve. ✉ *13 quai du Mont-Blanc, Les Pâquis, CH-1201* ☎ *022/7166666* 🖷 *022/7166060* 🌐 *www.beau-rivage.ch* *82 rooms, 11 suites* *2 restaurants, in-room safes, cable TV, piano bar, meeting rooms, parking (fee), no-smoking floors* ▭ *AE, DC, MC, V.*

$$$$ 🏨 **D'Angleterre.** Impeccable taste and a tangible passion for detail mark this stylish boutique hotel. Minibars are stocked with green tea and dried fruit, desks are equipped with office supplies, and afternoon tea can be served in your room. The Leopard Room bar has a working fireplace and live music Tuesday through Saturday; Windows, the quayside winter-garden restaurant, serves light meals with a view of Mont Blanc. ✉ *17 quai du Mont-Blanc, Les Pâquis, CH-1201* ☎ *022/9065555* 🖷 *022/ 9065556* ⊕ *www.dangleterrehotel.com* ➳ *39 rooms, 6 suites* ⚭ *Restaurant, minibars, cable TV, gym, sauna, bar, meeting rooms, parking (fee)* ▭ *AE, DC, MC, V.*

$$$$ 🖵 **Des Bergues.** Silk brocades, graceful statues, and unpretentious,
Fodor'sChoice friendly service give the first Four Seasons in Switzerland and the old-
★ est, least-self-conscious of Geneva's grand hotels an inner glow. The Louis-Philippe elegance, crystal chandeliers, and sumptuous marble bathrooms mesh seamlessly with modern conveniences like flat-screen TVs that turn toward you, high-speed wireless Internet access, 24-hour room service, and luxuriously thick mattresses. The bar serves afternoon tea and light fare throughout the day. ✉ *33 quai des Bergues, Centre Ville, CH-1201* ☎ *022/9087000* 🖷 *022/9087090* ⊕ *www.hoteldesbergues.com* ➳ *70 rooms, 24 suites* ⚭ *Restaurant, cable TV, gym, bar, Internet, business services, meeting rooms, parking (fee)* ▭ *AE, DC, MC, V.*

$$$$ 🖵 **Le Richemond.** Colette, Charlie Chaplin, and Marc Chagall have all signed the guest book. As of this writing, the hotel's new owners plan to close this opulent, slightly stuffy 1875 landmark during 2006 in order to update, expand, and draw out its essence. Whatever form that may take, it is certain that the Gentilhomme restaurant will remain Lebanese, individual balconies will still overlook the Monument Brunswick and the cathedral, and Rolls-Royces will continue to angle for space outside. ✉ *Jardin Brunswick, Les Pâquis, CH-1201* ☎ *022/7157000* 🖷 *022/7157001* ⊕ *www.roccofortehotels.com* ➳ *105 rooms, 20 suites* ⚭ *3 restaurants (1 seasonal), cable TV, gym, spa, bar, meeting rooms, parking (fee)* ▭ *AE, DC, MC, V.*

★ **$$$$**   🖵 **Les Armures.** Original 17th-century stonework, frescoes, painted beams, and tapestries adorn the lobby and some rooms in this low-key luxury hotel. Somber antiques mix easily with glowing glass-and-tile baths, fresh flowers, thick bathrobes, and wireless Internet access. Two very quiet rooms give onto a tiny inner courtyard; those overlooking rue du Perron have scenic cobblestone views. ✉ *1 rue du Puits-St-Pierre, Vieille Ville, CH-1204* ☎ *022/3109172* 🖷 *022/3109846* ⊕ *www.hotel-les-armures.ch* ➳ *28 rooms, 4 suites* ⚭ *Restaurant, cable TV, bar, Internet, business services, meeting room, parking (fee)* ▭ *AE, DC, MC, V* ❙⊘❙ *BP.*

$$$$ 🖵 **President Wilson.** Huge, fragrant flower arrangements punctuate the public areas of this expansive hotel (yes, named for Woodrow); 17th-century tapestries, colorful paintings, and Greco-Roman stonework balance green marble floors and sleek wood throughout. Many of the stylish, modern rooms take in sweeping views of the lake, Cologny, or the French Alps. The heated outdoor swimming pool is a rare treat. ✉ *47 quai Wilson, Les Pâquis, CH-1211* ☎ *022/9066666* 🖷 *022/9066667* ⊕ *www.hotelpwilson.com* ➳ *197 rooms, 33 suites* ⚭ *3 restaurants (1 seasonal), cable TV, pool, gym, hair salon, spa, lobby lounge, piano bar, shops, business services, meeting rooms, parking (fee), no-smoking floors* ▭ *AE, DC, MC, V.*

$$$$ 🖵 **Swissôtel Métropole.** Massive scrubbed-stone arches give this 1854 Left Bank palace a grand air, belied by the lopsided drink glasses in the Bistropole restaurant. Guest rooms come with espresso machines, and bathrooms in executive rooms and suites have TVs perched in a watertight alcove. High-voltage rue du Rhône shopping is literally just outside, but windows are triple-glazed to ensure silence. The wraparound view from the roof is much envied during Fêtes de Genève fireworks. ✉ *34 quai du Général-Guisan, Centre Ville, CH-1204* ☎ *022/3183200* 🖷 *022/3183300* ⊕ *www.swissotel-geneva.com* ⟳ *111 rooms, 16 suites* ⚭ *2 restaurants, cable TV, gym, piano bar, business services, meeting rooms, parking (fee)* ▤ *AE, DC, MC, V.*

★ **$$$$** 🏨 **Tiffany.** The designers of this intimate belle epoque jewel near the plaine de Plainpalais took their cue from the restored ceiling painting in the reception area, then got all the details right. Stained-glass lamps, ivy-clad wall sconces, period paintings, and curved wood accent the rose-and-green public areas. Rooms have blue-and-yellow stenciling, art nouveau bath tiles, fluffy bathrobes, and wireless Internet access, and suites have Jacuzzis. The brasserie's painted walls and ceiling are works of art. ✉ *1 rue des Marbriers, Plainpalais, CH-1204* ☎ *022/7081616* 🖷 *022/7081617* ⊕ *www.hotel-tiffany.ch* ⟳ *44 rooms, 2 suites* ⚭ *Restaurant, cable TV, bar, lounge, Internet, business services* ▤ *AE, DC, MC, V.*

$$$–$$$$ 🏨 **Ambassador.** Don't let the airport-lounge lobby fool you—each room in this central Right Bank hotel is fresh, colorful, and full of natural light. Many of the huge doubles would be called suites elsewhere, and bathrooms gleam with white tile. Ask for a (large) corner room if you're traveling with kids. The seventh floor delivers early morning sun and Vieille Ville views. ✉ *21 quai des Bergues, St-Gervais, CH-1211* ☎ *022/9080530* 🖷 *022/7389080* ⊕ *www.hotel-ambassador.ch* ⟳ *82 rooms* ⚭ *Restaurant, cable TV, meeting rooms, parking (fee)* ▤ *AE, DC, MC, V.*

$$$–$$$$ 🏨 **Cornavin.** The comic book character Tintin made this hotel famous with *L'Affaire Tournesol* (*The Calculus Affair*) in 1956. Now the nine-story clock pendulum in the lobby, the deft manipulation of frosted glass and natural light on the top three floors, the spectacular glassed-in breakfast hall, and enviable panoramic views compete for attention. The 14 large triples and six interconnecting doubles are great for families; double-glazed windows keep things quiet. ✉ *Gare de Cornavin, Centre Ville, CH-1201* ☎ *022/7161212* 🖷 *022/7161200* ⊕ *www.fhotels.ch* ⟳ *158 rooms, 4 suites* ⚭ *Cable TV, meeting rooms* ▤ *AE, DC, MC, V.*

$$–$$$ 🏨 **Domaine de Châteauvieux.** Delicate stenciling, marble sinks, and bright
Fodor'sChoice calico reflect a happy marriage of good taste and warm country spirit
★ at this former château complex surrounded by vineyards and sweeping hilltop views. The owners' cats roam the hallways, and the *chambre romantique* has a hot tub. Breakfast includes homemade bread and pastries, local honey, and jams made in-house from local fruit. The hotel is 20 minutes by car from Geneva's waterfront. ✉ *Peney-Dessus, CH-1242 Satigny* ☎ *022/7531511* 🖷 *022/7531924* ⊕ *www.chateauvieux.ch* ⟳ *12 rooms* ⚭ *Restaurant, cable TV, bar* ▤ *AE, DC, MC, V* ⟡ *BP.*

$$–$$$ 🏨 **International et Terminus.** The leafy outdoor terrace, soft yellow facade, and peach-paneled lobby with dark rose chairs impose civility on this modest hotel's central but chaotic location, just down the hill from the Gare Cornavin. Rooms have spanking-new tile bathrooms, sleek wood furniture, and restful rose, green, and raspberry color schemes. All win-

dows are impervious to noise. ⊠ *20 rue des Alpes, Les Pâquis, CH-1201*
☏ *022/9069777* 🖷 *022/9069778* ⊕ *www.international-terminus.ch*
↘*60 rooms ☖ Restaurant, fans, in-room safes, minibars, cable TV, parking (fee); no a/c* ☰ *AE, DC, MC, V* ♨ *BP.*

$$–$$$ ⊡ **Le Montbrillant.** Front rooms in this busy family-run hotel a stone's
throw from the back of the Gare Cornavin have a terrific view of the
TGV as it arrives from Paris. Double-glazed windows and ceiling fans
keep it quiet and cool. Studio apartments on the fifth floor have kitchenettes, dormer windows, and cathedral ceilings (also air-conditioning
and monthly rates). Nineteenth-century stone walls accent clean lines,
rosy wallpaper, and crisp blue-gray trim throughout. ⊠ *2 rue de Mont-*
brillant, Les Grottes, CH-1201 ☏ *022/7337784* 🖷 *022/7332511*
⊕ *www.montbrillant.ch* ↘ *58 rooms, 24 studios ☖ 2 restaurants,*
fans, in-room safes, some kitchenettes, minibars, cable TV, meeting
rooms, free parking, no-smoking floor; no a/c in some rooms ☰ *AE,*
DC, MC, V ♨ *BP.*

$ ⊡ **Bel'Espérance.** Rooftop views of the lake, bright yellow-and-blue
Fodor'sChoice rooms, tile baths, and a graceful Louis-Philippe–style breakfast salon
★ put this family-run former *foyer pour dames* (ladies' boarding house)
near place du Bourg-de-Four on a par with much pricier hotels. Communal kitchen space is available; the Salvation Army owns the building, so alcohol is not allowed. ⊠ *1 rue de la Vallée, Vieille Ville,*
CH-1204 ☏*022/8183737* 🖷*022/8183773* ⊕*www.hotel-bel-esperance.*
ch ↘ *36 rooms, 3 studios ☖ Cable TV, laundry facilities, Internet, no-*
smoking floor; no a/c ☰ *AE, MC, V* ♨ *BP.*

★ **$** ⊡ **Central.** Christine and Erik Gangsted have made flexibility and style
the focus of this low-cost hotel wedged into the top of a Left Bank shopping street. Warm Indonesian wood, intense pastel greens and blues,
sponge-painted terra-cotta, and exotic flowers reflect the family ties to
Bali. Sleeping configurations include budget rooms with a bunk bed
and shower, expansive apartments for four, and everything in between.
Whichever you choose, you're guaranteed a balcony, modem connection, voice mail, in-house videos, and breakfast in bed. ⊠ *2 rue de la*
Rôtisserie, Centre Ville, CH-1204 ☏ *022/8188100* 🖷 *022/8188101*
⊕ *www.hotelcentral.ch* ↘ *30 rooms, 1 suite, 2 apartments ☖ Some*
fans, in-room data ports, cable TV; no a/c in some rooms ☰ *AE, DC,*
MC, V ♨ *BP.*

$ ⊡ **Ibis.** Breakfast starts at 4 AM, the staff is on duty 24 hours a day, and
the train station is five minutes away, making this cheerful chain hotel
ideal for off-hours travelers. Smooth wood and apricot accents add
warmth to green pinstripes on awnings and walls. The bright, well-ap-
pointed rooms are spotless. ⊠ *10 rue Voltaire, St-Gervais, CH-1201*
☏*022/3382020* 🖷*022/3382030* ⊕*www.accorhotels.com* ↘*65 rooms*
☖ *Cable TV, bar, no-smoking floors* ☰ *AE, DC, MC, V.*

★ **¢–$** ⊡ **De la Cloche.** Christian Chabbey keeps friendly watch over his guests
in this first-floor apartment one block from the lake. The flocked wallpaper and creaky parquet floors suit the kindly spirit of the place. Three
of the eight plain, bright rooms have compact modular bathrooms (each
with a shower—the bathtub is down the hall), and breakfast is delivered to your door. Two rooms overlook a quiet inner courtyard; one of
the three facing rue de la Cloche has a balcony. ⊠ *6 rue de la Cloche,*

Les Pâquis, CH-1201 ☎ *022/7329481* 🖨 *022/7381612* ⊕ *www.geneva-hotel.ch/cloche* ⌷ *8 rooms, 3 with bath* ⚬ *Fans, cable TV; no a/c* ☰ *AE, DC, MC, V* ⍥ *BP.*

¢–$ 🖼 **St-Gervais.** Red tartan carpeting and creamy linen warm the garret-like rooms in this old Right Bank inn near the train station. Breakfast is served in the tiny, wood-panel café space on the ground floor. Most major bus lines stop right around the corner. ✉ *20 rue des Corps-Saints, St-Gervais, CH-1201* ☎☎ *022/7324572* ⊕ *www.stgervais-geneva.ch* ⌷ *26 rooms, 2 with bath* ⚬ *No a/c* ☰ *AE, DC, MC, V* ⍥ *BP.*

NIGHTLIFE & THE ARTS

Each week, **Genève Agenda** lists concerts, performances, temporary exhibits, restaurants, and clubs, in French and English. The bilingual monthly **Genève Le Guide** (⊕ www.le-guide.ch) profiles current films, dance events, theatrical performances, and restaurants outside the city center. Free copies of both are available from tourist information booths and hotels.

Nightlife

A successful night out in Geneva—whether exclusive, trendy, or pub-based—can hinge on understanding that you are not in a major metropolis. Though bars and clubs have lots of life, much of it English-speaking, it may not be possible to party till dawn.

Bars

Little-known wines from well-known places flow freely around communal tables until 8 PM on weekdays (5 PM on Saturday) at **Boulevard du Vin** (✉ 3 blvd. Georges-Favon, Plainpalais ☎ 022/3109190). **Flanagan's** (✉ 4 rue du Cheval-Blanc, Vieille Ville ☎ 022/3101314) has the worn, crowded, beer-stained feel of a sprawling Irish pub. The downstairs disco plays live music Thursday to Saturday. **La Clémence** (✉ 20 pl. du Bourg-de-Four, Vieille Ville ☎ 022/3122498) fills with university students and explodes into the street. **Mr. Pickwick's Pub** (✉ 80 rue de Lausanne, Les Pâquis ☎ 022/7316797) serves fish-and-chips, shows English football, and staves off homesickness in British expats. The Guinness is on tap and the accents robustly Irish at **Mulligan's** (✉ 14 rue Grenus, St-Gervais ☎ 022/7328576), on the Right Bank. The cocktail bar at the **Roi Ubu** (✉ 30 Grand-rue, Vieille Ville ☎ 022/3107398) draws a lively, young international crowd. Classic pub comfort and large-screen TVs draw sports enthusiasts to the **Spring Bros. Pub** (✉ 23 Grand-rue, Vieille Ville ☎ 022/3124008).

Dancing

Wine-red upholstery adds spice to the stylish bar at **B'Club—Le Baroque** (✉ 12 pl. de la Fusterie, Centre Ville ☎ 022/3110515 ⊕ www.lebaroque. com). Jet-setting sophisticates move downstairs to dance after 11 PM. Celebrity DJs and an upscale, black-tie crowd head to **Griffin's Club** (✉ 36 blvd. Helvétique, Eaux-Vives ☎ 022/7351218 ⊕ www.griffins-club. com). Live performances by up-and-coming artists of all musical stripes keep the bar hopping at **Le Chat Noir** (✉ 13 rue Vautier, Carouge ☎ 022/

GENEVA'S RIVAL CITY

For most of its history, convivial Carouge (from quadruvium, the Latin word for crossroads), to the south of Geneva, was a mere hamlet on the road to place Neuve. Things began to evolve in 1754, when the King of Sardinia (aka the Duke of Savoy) took control. The town grew so fast that the royal planners in Turin drew up five development plans between 1772 and 1783. To this day their harmonious architecture, plazas, and courtyard gardens give the town a Mediterranean

feel. Carouge failed to become a commercial rival to Geneva, but the artists and craftspeople established there, from fashion designers to glassblowers, give it a creative buzz. Rue St-Joseph and rue Ancienne are particularly vital, and the town is accessible by tram. Prior to its annexation by the canton in 1816, Carouge also developed a reputation as Geneva's pleasure dome. It still has one of the more dynamic nightspots around, Le Chat Noir.

3434998 ⊕ www.chatnoir.ch). Techno, reggae, disco, hits from the 1980s, salsa, and classic rock fill 10 throbbing dance floors until 6 AM at **Macumba** (✉ 403 rte. d'Annecy, St. Julien-en-Genevois, France ☎ 0033/450492350 ⊕ www.macumba.fr), just across the French border to the south. Local DJs spin a mix of past and present dance hits at **Shakers** (✉ 7 rue de la Boulangerie, Vieille Ville ☎ 022/3105598 ⊕ www. shakers.ch), a cubbyhole with stone walls and potent drinks.

The Arts

Geneva's legacy as a cultural crossroads has produced an unusually rich arts scene for a city of its size. Most of the performance spaces in town are roadhouses through which flow a steady stream of foreign as well as Swiss artists. Tickets remain on sale from theater box offices up to the day of performance. If you'd rather book ahead, the third-floor ticket booth at **Globus** (✉ 48 rue du Rhône, Centre Ville ☎ 022/3195583) handles concerts and theatrical performances throughout the Lac Léman region; note that it does not accept credit cards.

Film

Undubbed versions of English-language films are always screened somewhere in town. Check local newspaper listings for the initials *v.o.*, short for *version originale* (original version). The **CAC Voltaire** (✉ 16 rue du Général-Dufour, Centre Ville ☎ 022/3207878) hosts ongoing, undubbed classic film minifestivals in the basement of the Grütli Arts Center. The open-air lakeside theater at **Cinélac** (✉ Port-Noir, Cologny ☎ 022/3196111 ⊕ www.orangecinema.ch) screens a different film every night from July through August.

Music & Dance

Musical improvisation and contemporary jazz dominate the program at **AMR–Sud des Alpes** (✉ 10 rue des Alpes, Les Pâquis ☎ 022/7165630

⊕ www.amr-geneve.ch). The **Salle Théodore Turrettini,** constructed inside the mid-river **Bâtiment des Forces Motrices** (✉ 2 pl. des Volontaires, Plainpalais ☎ 022/3221220 ⊕ www.bfm.ch), a 19th-century pumping station, hosts an eclectic lineup of classical music, opera, jazz, theater, and ballet. Select recitals and chamber music concerts are open to the public at the **Conservatoire de Musique** (✉ pl. Neuve, Centre Ville ☎ 022/3196060 ⊕ www.cmusge.ch). The **Grand Théâtre** (✉ pl. Neuve, Centre Ville ☎ 022/4183130 ⊕ www.geneveopera.ch) stages eight full-scale operas, five ballets, and six recitals each season (September to June). The **Orchestre de la Suisse Romande** (☎ 022/8070017 ⊕ www.osr.ch) has made **Victoria Hall** (✉ 14 rue du Général-Dufour, Centre Ville ☎ 022/4183500) its Geneva home.

Theater

The creative, colorful French-language children's theater **Am Stram Gram** (✉ 56 rte. de Frontenex, Eaux-Vives ☎ 022/7357924 ⊕ www.regart. ch/amstramgram) draws inspiration from myth, folktales, lyric poetry, Shakespeare, and contemporary writing. Artistic Director Anne Bisang has brought international classics (translated into French), modern drama, and innovative staging to the venerable **Comédie de Genève** (✉ 6 blvd. des Philosophes, Plainpalais ☎ 022/3205001 ⊕ www.comedie.ch). The experimental **Théâtre du Grütli** (✉ 16 rue du Général-Dufour, Centre Ville ☎ 022/3289868 ⊕ www.grutli.ch) fills its spare, flexible space with contemporary Swiss and foreign plays, all in French.

SPORTS & THE OUTDOORS

Boating

Les Corsaires (✉ 33 quai Gustave-Ador, Eaux-Vives ☎ 022/7354300) rents paddle-, motor-, solar-powered, and sailboats for as little as a half hour.

Golf

Lush fairways, spectacular views, and unrestricted public access distinguish the 18-hole course at the **Domaine de Divonne** (✉ Divonne-les-Bains, France ☎ 0033/450403434), just over the border. You can also rent equipment.

Ice-Skating

The free outdoor **Patinoire de Noël** (✉ pl. du Rhône, Centre Ville ☎ 022/9097000), at the heart of the Left Bank shopping area, stays open daily until late evening from early December through March. Indoor skating is available Tuesday through Sunday from October to March at the **Patinoire des Vernets** (✉ 4–6 rue Hans-Wilsdorf ☎ 022/4184022). Both rinks rent skates.

Skiing

Geneva is surrounded by terrific downhill skiing, most of it in the French Alps. From early December until mid-April ski buses depart daily or on weekends from the **Gare Routière de Genève** (✉ pl. Dorcière, Les

Pâquis ☏ 022/7320230) for Chamonix, Les Contamines, Flaine, and Morzine-Avoriaz. Trips take 1½–2 hours, and the 50–70 SF fare includes a ski-lift pass.

Swimming

Lac Léman is certified clean and safe to swim in, and Geneva's beaches are crowded from the moment they open in April until closing time in October. The popular midharbor **Bains des Pâquis** (✉ 30 quai du Mont-Blanc, Les Pâquis ☏ 022/7322974) lures winter bathers with champagne fondue and an outdoor sauna. The concrete sunbathing area and nude beach are open all summer. Take Bus 2 to the end of the line for the green lawns, outdoor pool, lake access, and water slide at **Genève-Plage** (✉ Port Noir, Cologny ☏ 022/7362482). The **Piscine de Carouge** (✉ 53 rte. de Veyrier, Carouge ☏ 022/3432520) has an Olympic-size outdoor pool, volleyball courts, and a waterslide next to the River Arve. The indoor **Piscine de Varembé** (✉ 46 av. Giuseppe-Motta, International Area ☏ 022/7331214), near the UN, stays open year-round.

Tennis

The **Tennis Club de Genève** (✉ 41 rte. de Vessy, Vessy ☏ 022/7842566) has indoor and outdoor courts but does not rent equipment. You'll find tennis, badminton, and squash courts at the **Tennis Club du Bois Carré** (✉ 14 chemin des Bûcherons, Vessy ☏ 022/7843006) as well as equipment rentals. Both clubs are easy to reach by taxi and require same-day reservations—if a court is available, nonmembers may play.

SHOPPING

Official store open hours are Monday to Wednesday from 9 to 7, Thursday from 9 to 9, Friday from 9 to 7:30, and Saturday from 9 to 6. Smaller shops may open later Monday and/or close earlier Thursday.

Auctions

As a jewelry capital rivaled only by New York and an international center for Swiss watchmakers, Geneva regularly hosts high-profile auctions by the major houses. **Antiquorum** (✉ 2 rue du Mont-Blanc, Centre Ville ☏ 022/9092850) specializes in antique timepieces. **Christie's** (✉ 8 pl. de la Taconnerie, Vieille Ville ☏ 022/3191766) organizes sales of wine and jewelry twice a year. **Sotheby's** (✉ 13 quai du Mont-Blanc, Les Pâquis ☏ 022/9084800) puts lots of jewelry and watches on display in May and November before they are sold.

Department Stores

Bon Génie (✉ 34 rue du Marché, Centre Ville ☏ 022/8181111) sells expensive designer clothing and cosmetics on floor after hushed floor. **Globus** (✉ 48 rue du Rhône, Centre Ville ☏ 022/3195050) forms a physical link between the main Left Bank shopping streets. Service is good, and the home accessories, men's clothing, sport, and food sections are exceptional.

Markets

Les Halles de Rive (✉ 17 rue Pierre-Fatio/29 blvd. Helvétique, Centre Ville) sells fresh cheeses, meats, pasta, and fish all day Monday through Saturday. A vibrant seasonal fruit-and-vegetable market fills **boulevard Helvétique**, just outside, on Wednesday and Saturday mornings. Arts-and-crafts vendors crowd **place de la Fusterie** every Thursday. The **Plaine de Plainpalais** hosts a horde of flea market stalls on Wednesday and Saturday, and a fruit-and-vegetable market moves in on Tuesday and Friday mornings.

Shopping Streets

Geneva's two principal shopping arteries, known collectively as the **Rues-Basses** (Low Streets), run parallel along the Left Bank. **Rue du Rhône,** closest to the river, marks the epicenter of luxury shopping. One block in is the more popular thoroughfare known variously as **rue de la Confédération, rue du Marché, rue de la Croix-d'Or,** and **rue de Rive.** Galleries, antiques shops, home-furnishings emporia, and chic boutiques line the **Grand-rue** and streets radiating out from **place du Bourg-de-Four. Rue du Mont-Blanc,** on the Right Bank, is choked with souvenir stores.

Specialty Stores

Antiques

Antiquités Scientifiques (✉ 19 rue du Perron, Vieille Ville ☎ 022/3100706) buys, sells, and restores telescopes, barometers, microscopes, binoculars, typewriters, and clocks. Gorgeous art deco furniture and art objects from 1930s France are displayed at **Galerie la Ligne Droite** (✉ 28 rue de St-Léger, Vieille Ville ☎ 022/3108660). Head to **Librairie Ancienne** (✉ 20 Grand-rue, Vieille Ville ☎ 022/3102050) for leather-bound and gilt first editions (not in English). **Montparnasse** (✉ 40 Grand-rue, Vieille Ville ☎ 022/3116719) deals in unusual old books, prints, and maps. Well-polished English furniture fills the **Regency House** (✉ 3 rue de l'Hôtel-de-Ville, Vieille Ville ☎ 022/3103540). **Rue des Belles Filles** (✉ 8 rue Étienne-Dumont, Vieille Ville ☎ 022/3103131) is a treasure trove of vintage jewelry, crystal, china, and silver.

Books

French giant **FNAC** (✉ 16 rue de Rive, Centre Ville ☎ 022/8161220) holds readings and devotes its block-length first floor to current French (and a few English) titles. **Librairie Archigraphy** (✉ 1 pl. de l'Ile, Centre Ville ☎ 022/3116008) sells art, design, and architecture books in a setting worthy of its subjects. **Librairie Bernard Letu** (✉ 2 rue Jean-Calvin, Vieille Ville ☎ 022/3104757) carries an inspired range of multilingual art and photography titles. French-language books about Geneva, Switzerland, and the Haute Savoie crowd the front room at **Librairie Jullien** (✉ 32 pl. du Bourg-de-Four, Vieille Ville ☎ 022/3103670). **L'Oreille Cassée** (✉ 9 quai des Bergues, St-Gervais ☎ 022/7324080) serves devotees of hardcover *bandes dessinées* (Franco-Belgian comic books). **Off the Shelf** (✉ 15 blvd. Georges-Favon, Plainpalais ☎ 022/3111090) lures English-speaking browsers with a sunny space and a hand-picked selection. The commercial chain **Payot** (⊠ 5 rue de Chantepoulet, Les Pâquis ☎ 022/7318950 ⊠ 16 rue du Marché, Centre Ville ☎ 022/3197940) sells current titles in French, English, and German.

Chocolate

Silky, handmade white-chocolate truffles top the winter selection at **Arn** (⊠ 12 pl. du Bourg-de-Four, Vieille Ville ☎ 022/3104094). The original *pavés glacés,* creamy bite-size Genevois delicacies, were made by **Auer** (⊠ 4 rue de Rive, Centre Ville ☎ 022/3114286) and shaped like local cobblestones. **Du Rhône** (⊠ 3 rue de la Confédération, Centre Ville ☎ 022/3115614) has sold bittersweet hot chocolate since 1875. **Merkur** (⊠ 32 rue du Marché, Centre Ville ☎ 022/3102221 ⊠ Galerie marchande de Cornavin, Les Pâquis ☎ 022/7324182) stocks Swiss-theme gift boxes, individual bars, and huge champagne truffles. **Rohr** (⊠ 3 pl. du Molard, Centre Ville ☎ 022/3116303 ⊠ 4 rue d'Enfer, Centre Ville ☎ 022/3116876) models its smooth, rich signature truffles after old Geneva garbage cans. Don't let the shape fool you; it's the best chocolate in town.

Jewelry

Bucherer (⊠ 45 rue du Rhône, Centre Ville ☎ 022/3196266) sells luminous pearls and diamonds of all sizes. **Bulgari** (⊠ 30 rue du Rhône, Centre Ville ☎ 022/3177070) favors heavy gold necklaces and rings crusted with jewels. **Cartier** (⊠ 35 rue du Rhône, Centre Ville ☎ 022/8185454 ⊠ 90 rue du Rhône, Centre Ville ☎ 022/3102040) sets its rubies, emeralds, and diamonds in a variation on its trademark panther. **Chopard** (⊠ 8 rue de la Confédération, Centre Ville ☎ 022/3113728 ⊠ 27 rue du Rhône, Centre Ville ☎ 022/3107050) paves its watches and necklaces with diamonds. Interchangeable stones wrapped in curvaceous, coral-like gold settings distinguish work by Geneva veteran **Gilbert Albert** (⊠ 24 rue de la Corraterie, Centre Ville ☎ 022/3114833). **Ludwig Muller** (⊠ 2 rue de la Cité, Centre Ville ☎ 022/3102930) draws inspiration from commedia dell'arte and uses rare blue gold.

Watches

Bucherer (⊠ 45 rue du Rhône, Centre Ville ☎ 022/3196266) carries more prestigious, indestructible Rolex models than anyone else in town. **Franck Muller** (⊠ 1 rue de la Tour-de-l'Ile, Centre Ville ☎ 022/8180030) creates complicated modern timepieces. **Patek Philippe** (⊠ 1 pl. Longemalle, Centre Ville ☎ 022/7812448) is renovating its shop's usual quarters, the 1839 building at 41 rue du Rhône where Antoine Norbert de Patek invented the winding mechanism inside all watches. **Piaget** (⊠ 40 rue du Rhône, Centre Ville ☎ 022/8170200) wraps its ultraflat timepieces in white gold. **Vacheron Constantin** (⊠ 1 rue des Moulins, Centre Ville ☎ 022/3161740), the world's oldest manufacturer of watches, sold its first sober design in 1755.

Wine

La Cité des Vins (⊠ 3 bis rue de Coutance, St-Gervais ☎ 022/7322222) has a knowledgable staff and more than 1,000 labels from around the world. Hard-to-find Bordeaux and boutique champagnes are stored in backlit stone vaults at **Le Caveau de Bacchus** (⊠ 5 cours de Rive, Centre Ville ☎ 022/3124130).

GENEVA A TO Z

To research prices, get advice from other travelers, and book travel arrangements, visit www.fodors.com.

AIR TRAVEL

British Airways, easyJet, and Swiss fly direct between London and Cointrin, the second-largest international airport in Switzerland, 5 km (3 mi) northwest of downtown Geneva. Swiss and Continental operate direct service from New York. Swiss also schedules frequent connections to its hub in Zürich.

CARRIERS 🛪 **Airlines & Contacts British Airways** ☎ 0848/801010 ⊕ www.ba.com. **Continental** ☎ 022/4177280 ⊕ www.continental.com. **easyJet** ☎ 0848/888222 ⊕ www.easyjet.com. **Swiss** ☎ 0848/852000 ⊕ www.swiss.com.

AIRPORTS & TRANSFERS

🛪 **Airport Information Cointrin** ☎ 022/7177111 ⊕ www.gva.ch.

AIRPORT TRANSFERS The No. 10 bus runs regularly between the airport departure level and downtown Geneva. The ride lasts about 20 minutes and the fare is 2.60 SF. Taxis are plentiful but expensive. You'll pay at least 35 SF to reach the city center, plus 1.50 SF per bag. Limousine services provide buses, minivans, or Mercedes sedans; Privilège has a stretch Rolls-Royce. Most drivers speak English. Trains run about every 15 minutes between Cointrin and the Gare Cornavin, Geneva's main train station, from 6 AM to midnight; the six-minute trip costs 2.60 SF each way.
🛪 **Limousine Services Globe** ☎ 022/7310750 ⊕ www.globelimousines.ch. **Privilège** ☎ 022/7383366 ⊕ www.privilegelimousine.ch.

BIKE TRAVEL

Bike lanes, indicated by a yellow line and a yellow bicycle symbol on the pavement, are ubiquitous downtown. Yellow signs indicate routes elsewhere in the canton. Genèv'Roule rents out bicycles between May and October in Centre Ville and year-round in Les Grottes. They're free from May to October, but you'll have to pay a deposit of 50 SF and return the bike by 9:30 PM.
🛪 **Bike Rentals Genèv'Roule** ✉ 17 pl. Montbrillant, Les Grottes ☎ 022/7401343 ✉ Bains des Pâquis, Les Pâquis ✉ pl. du Rhône, Centre Ville ✉ Plaine de Plainpalais, Plainpalais ✉ Port Noir, Cologny.

BOAT & FERRY TRAVEL

The Compagnie Générale de Navigation sends its belle epoque steamers up and down the lake between Geneva and port towns in Switzerland, such as Nyon, Lausanne, Vevey, Montreux, and the Château de Chillon as well as Yvoire, Thonon, and Évian-les-Bains, in France. The fare is waived for holders of the Swiss Pass; those with a Swiss Boat Pass pay half price. The Mouettes Genevoises operate smaller-scale lake connections, including a shuttle service across Geneva's harbor.
🛪 **Boat & Ferry Information Compagnie Générale de Navigation** (CGN) ☎ 0848/811848 ⊕ www.cgn.ch. **Mouettes Genevoises** ✉ 8 quai du Mont-Blanc, Les Pâquis ☎ 022/7322944 ⊕ www.mouettesgenevoises.ch

BUS & TRAM TRAVEL

Gare Routière de Genève, Geneva's central bus station, just off rue du Mont-Blanc on the Right Bank, handles buses arriving from and departing for points across Europe. Local buses and trams operate every few minutes on all city routes from 5 AM to midnight. Buy a ticket from the vending machine at the stop before you board (instructions are given in English). For 2.60 SF you can use the system and transfer at will between buses, trams, airport-bound trains, and the Mouettes Genevoises harbor ferries for one hour. A *carte journalière* (daily pass), available for 8 SF from the vending machines and the Transports Publics Genevois (TPG) booths at the train station and cours de Rive, buys all-day unlimited city-center travel. Holders of the Swiss Pass travel free.

🚌 Bus & Tram Information **Gare Routière de Genève** ✉ pl. Dorcière, Les Pâquis ☎ 022/ 7320230 ⊕ www.coach-station.com. **Transports Publics Genevois (TPG)** ☎ 0900/ 022021 ⊕ www.tpg.ch.

CAR TRAVEL

Geneva's long border with France makes for easy access from the south. Grenoble (to the south), Lyon (to the southwest), and Chamonix (to the southeast) are all one to two hours away on the French A40 expressway (l'Autoroute Blanche). The French south shore of Lac Léman gives access to the Valais via Évian-les-Bains. The Swiss A1 expressway, along the north shore of the lake, connects Geneva to the rest of Switzerland by way of Lausanne.

CONSULATES

There's no lack of diplomatic activity in Geneva; most countries maintain at least a consular agent in the city.

🏛 Embassies **Australia** ✉ 2 chemin des Fins, International Area ☎ 022/7999100. **Canada** ✉ 5 av. de l'Ariana, International Area ☎ 022/9199200. **New Zealand** ✉ 2 chemin des Fins, International Area ☎ 022/9290350. **United Kingdom** ✉ 37–39 rue de Vermont, International Area ☎ 022/9182400. **United States** Consular Agent ✉ 7 rue Versonnex, Eaux-Vives ☎ 022/8405160.

EMERGENCIES

In case of an emergency, dial ☎ 117 for the police or ☎ 144 for an ambulance.

🏥 Doctors **Doctor Referral** ☎ 022/3222020.

🏥 Hospitals **Hôpital Cantonal de Genève** ✉ 24 rue Micheli-du-Crest, Plainpalais ☎ 022/ 3723311 ⊕ www.hcuge.ch.

🏥 24-hour Pharmacies **Pharmacies** *de garde* 24-hour pharmacy hotline ☎ 111.

TAXIS

Taxis are clean and drivers are polite, but be prepared to pay a 6.30 SF minimum charge plus 3.20 SF per km (about ½ mi) traveled. In the evening and on Sunday the rate climbs to 3.80 SF per km. Cabs won't stop if you hail them; go to a designated taxi stand (marked on the pavement in yellow) or call.

🚕 Taxis **Taxi-Phone** ☎ 022/3314133 ⊕ www.taxi-phone.ch.

TOURS

BOAT TOURS Swissboat and the Mouettes Genevoises jointly operate guided lake cruises past castles, famous homes, ports, and parkland along the lower end of the lake every day from April to October. Tours last anywhere from 40 minutes to two hours, and recorded commentary is in English. The boats leave from quai du Mont-Blanc opposite the Monument Brunswick and from the Eaux-Vives waterfront between the Jet d'Eau and the Jardin Anglais. The Mouettes Genevoises also operate two-hour, 45-minute natural-history tours of the Rhône. Live commentary is in English, and the boats depart from place de l'Ile.
🚹 Fees & Schedules **Mouettes Genevoises** ✉ 8 quai du Mont-Blanc, Les Pâquis ☎ 022/ 7322944 ⊕ www.mouettesgenevoises.ch. **Swissboat** ✉ 4 quai du Mont-Blanc, Les Pâquis ☎ 022/7324747 ⊕ www.swissboat.com.

BUS TOURS Key Tours conducts two-hour bus-and-minitrain tours of the International Area and the Vieille Ville, leaving from place Dorcière daily at 2 PM as well as at 10 AM May–October and 3:15 PM July and August. Each circuit costs 35 SF (39 SF May–October), and commentary is in English. Between May and October, if the weather is good, you can also opt to catch the minitrain (independent of the bus tour) at place du Rhône for a trip around the Vieille Ville. Between March and October, a second minitrain leaves from the quai du Mont-Blanc for a tour of the Right Bank parks, and a third departs the Jardin Anglais for a ride along the Left Bank quays. Each loop lasts 30–40 minutes; the cost is 7–8.90 SF. Afternoon bus tours of the Geneva countryside are also available May–October.
🚹 Fees & Schedules **Key Tours** ✉ 7 rue des Alpes, Les Pâquis ☎ 022/7314140 ⊕ www. keytours.ch.

WALKING TOURS English-speaking guides linked to Geneva's tourist office lead a two-hour walk through the Vieille Ville every Saturday at 10 AM. Additional circuits are added at 10 AM weekdays and at 6:30 PM on Tuesday and Thursday between mid-June and late September. The cost is 15 SF. Less regularly scheduled thematic tours cost 20 SF and trace the history of watchmaking, Henry Dunant's legacy, literary Geneva, or one of 12 other subjects. English-language audio guides to the Vieille Ville last 2½ hours and cost 10 SF plus a 50 SF deposit. The map, cassette, and player must be returned within four hours.
🚹 Fees & Schedules **Service des Guides** ✉ 18 rue du Mont-Blanc, Les Pâquis ☎ 022/ 9097030.

TRAIN TRAVEL
Express trains from most Swiss cities arrive at and depart from the Right Bank Gare Cornavin every hour. The French TGV provides a frequent link to Paris; the Cisalpino connects Geneva with Milan twice every morning.
🚹 Train Information **Gare Cornavin** ✉ pl. Cornavin ☎ 0900/300300 ⊕ www.cff.ch.

TRAVEL AGENCIES
🚹 Local Agent Referrals **American Express** ✉ 7 rue du Mont-Blanc, Centre Ville ☎ 022/ 7317600 ⊕ www.americanexpress.ch. **Carlson Wagonlit Travel** ✉ 5 rue du Nant, Eaux-Vives ☎ 022/7372230 ⊕ www.carlsonwagonlit.ch. **Kuoni Voyages** ✉ 8 rue de Chantepoulet ☎ 022/9086910 ⊕ www.kuoni.ch.

VISITOR INFORMATION

Genève Tourisme is headquartered halfway between the pont du Mont-Blanc and the Gare Cornavin. Additional information booths serve the airport, the city center, and, from June through September, the train station.

◪ Tourist Information Booths **Airport** ⊠ Cointrin Arrivals ☏ 022/7178083. **Mid-River** ⊠ pont de la Machine, Centre Ville ☏ 022/3119827. **Right Bank** ⊠ 18 rue du Mont-Blanc, Les Pâquis ☏ 022/9097000. **Train Station** ⊠ Gare Cornavin ☏ 022/9097050.

◪ Tourist Office **Genève Tourisme** ⌂ 18 rue du Mont-Blanc, Case Postale 1602, CH-1211 Genève 1 ☏ 022/9097000 🖷 022/9097011 ⊕ www.geneva-tourism.ch.

UNDERSTANDING
SWITZERLAND

THE GOOD, THE BAD & THE TIDY

U P IN THE HOARY, windswept heights and black fir forests of the Alps, an electric eye beams open a glistening all-glass door—and reveals the honey-gold glow of wood, the sheen of copper, the burnt-chocolate tones of ancient wooden rafters. Candles flicker; Sterno radiates blue-white flames under russet pots of bubbling fondue. The cheery *boomp-chick boomp-chick* of an accordion filters down from high-tech stereo speakers cleverly concealed behind oversize cowbells. Waitresses in starched black dirndls and waiters in spotless white ties scuttle briskly from kitchen to table, table to kitchen, while platters of gravy-laden veal, sizzling *Rösti* (hash brown potatoes), and rosy entrecôte simmer over steel trivets—preheated, electrically controlled—ready to be proudly, seamlessly served.

Coziness under strict control, anachronism versus state-of-the-art technology: strange bedfellows in a storybook land. Nowhere else in Europe can you find a combination as welcoming and as alien, as comfortable and as remote, as engaging and as disengaged as a glass cable car to the clouds. This is the paradox of the Swiss, whose primary national aesthetic pitches rustic Alpine homeyness against high-tech urban efficiency. Though they're proud, sober, self-contained, independent culturally and politically, disdainful of the shabby and the slipshod, painfully neat, rigorously prompt—the Swiss have a weakness for cuteness, and they indulge in incongruously coy diminutives: a German *Bierstube* (pub) becomes a *Stübli*, *Kuchen* (cake) becomes *Küchli*, *Wurst* becomes *Würstli*, and a *coupe* (glass) of champagne becomes a *Cüpli*.

It is lucky for travelers, this dichotomy of the folksy and the functional. It means your trains get you to your firelit lodge on time. It means the cable car that sweeps you to a mountaintop has been subjected to grueling inspections. It means the handwoven curtains are boiled and starched, and the high-thread-count bed linens are turned back with a chocolate at night. It means the scarlet geraniums that cascade from window boxes on every carved balcony are tended like prize orchids. It means the pipe smoke that builds up in the Stübli at night is aired out daily, as sparkling clean double-glazed windows are thrown open on every floor, every morning, to let sharp, cool mountain air course through hallways, bedrooms, and fresh-bleached baths.

Yet there is a stinginess that peeks around the apron of that rosy-cheeked efficiency. Liquor here is measured with scientific precision into glasses marked for one centiliter or two, and the local wines come in carafes reminiscent of laboratory beakers. Despite the fine linens and puffs of down that adorn each bed, double beds have separate mattresses with sheets tucked primly down the middle, sometimes so tightly you have to lift the mattress to loosen the barrier. And if you wash out your socks and hang them loosely on the shower rod in the morning, you may return at night and find them straightened, spaced, toes pointing the same direction, as orderly as little lead soldiers.

Nevertheless there is an earthiness about these people, as at ease with the soil as they are appalled by dirt. A banker in Zürich may rent a postage-stamp parcel of land in a crowded patchwork outside town, sowing tight rows of cabbages and strawberries, weeding bright borders of marigolds, and on Sunday he may visit his miniature estate, pull a chair out from the tidy toolshed, and simply sit and smoke, like Heidi's Alm-Uncle surveying his Alpine realm. An elderly woman may don knickers and loden hat and board a postbus to the mountains and climb steep, rocky trails at a brisk clip, cheeks glowing, eyes as icy bright as the glaciers above her.

There's a 21st-century counterpoint to this: the high-tech, jet-set glamour that splashes vivid colors across the slopes at St. Moritz, Gstaad, Zermatt, Verbier. Step out of a bulbous steel-and-glass cable car onto a concrete platform at 6,560 feet and see Switzerland transformed, its workers' blue overalls and good wool suits exchanged for ski suits. Wholesome, healthy faces disappear behind mirrored goggles and war-paint sunblock, and gaudy skis and poles bristle militarily, like the pikes and halberds in the Battle of Sempach.

The contradictions mount: while fur-clad socialites raise jeweled fingers to bid at Sotheby's on Geneva's quai du Mont-Blanc, the women of Appenzell stand beside the men on the Landsgemeindeplatz and raise their hands to vote locally—a right not won until 1991. While digital screens tick off beef futures in Zürich, the crude harmony of cowbells echoes in velvet mountain pastures. While a Mercedes roars down an expressway expertly blasted through solid rock, a horse-drawn plow peels back thin topsoil in an Alpine garden plot, impossibly steep, improbably high.

And on August 1, the Swiss national holiday, while spectacular displays of fireworks explode in sizzling colors over the cities and towns, the mountain folk build the bonfires that glow quietly, splendidly, on every hillside of every Alp, uniting Swiss citizens as they celebrate their proud independence, their cultural wealth, and above all their diversity. It's that diversity and those quirky contradictions that make Switzerland a tourist capital—the folksy, fiercely efficient innkeeper to the world.

— Nancy Coons

AFTER TWO CABLE CAR RIDES, we sit in a mountain restaurant thousands of feet above the resort village of Verbier. On the table in front of us are two cups of hot chocolate, and one tiny glass of bubbly white Fendant wine from Sion. Our legs are tired from a long day of skiing. We catch our breath before the evening run, while the slopes below empty themselves of skiers and fill up with evening light. Outside, Mont Blanc is an island of ice rising out of a sea of summits along the Franco-Swiss border. Peaks and passes stretch as far as the eye can see, an art director's Alpine fantasy in late light.

Verbier skiing is one reason I've returned to Switzerland in winter, faithfully, for the past 25 years. This is a giant of a ski area in a region of giant ski areas, perched high in the French-speaking southwest of Switzerland, draped over four mountain valleys, embracing six villages, a labyrinth of interconnected lifts (more than 100), interlaced slopes (too many to count)—a ski area you can't explore in a week or even exhaust in a season.

For passionate skiers every trip to Switzerland is a homecoming. All our skiing archetypes originate here. White sawtooth horizons point to the sky, picture-postcard chalet roofs poke up under great white hats of snow, necklaces of lifts and cable cars drape themselves over the white shoulders of fairy-tale mountains, and runs go on forever.

These are big mountains, with vertical drops twice the length of those of the Rockies. In the Alps you can often drop 4,000, 5,000, or 6,000 vertical feet in one run. Here runs are so long that halfway down you need a break—which you'll find at a little chalet restaurant in the middle of nowhere, where the views are as exhilarating as the schnapps that's so often the drink of choice.

These are pure white mountains, too, whiter than we're used to. In the Alps, the tree line is low, often only 6,000 feet above sea level, and many ski areas stretch upward from there. The skier's playing field is white on white; marked pistes are white rivers of groomed snow snaking down equally white but ungroomed flanks of Alpine peaks. There are more treeless bowls than you can hope to ski in several skiers' lifetimes.

When European skiers tell you that the western Alps are higher and more glaciated, more likely to have good snow in a dry year, and that the eastern Alps are lower in elevation but full of charm, with more intimate, more richly decorated villages, they are usually referring to the difference between the French Alps and Austria. In fact, they could just as well be talking about the mountains and ski resorts of southwest Switzerland versus those of eastern Switzerland, Graubünden, and the Engadine; for Switzerland, with its many cantons, is a microcosm that mirrors the diversity of skiing all across the greater Alps. You can test your credit card limits at the Palace Hotel in worldly St. Moritz, ride the cog railways of modest Kleine Scheidegg, or ponder the hearty existence of mountain farmers among the peaks of Valais—but always, the local mountain culture will be part of your ski experience.

As varied as the regions are the people who ski them. The ski pistes of Switzerland are the polyglot crossroads of Europe, where stylish Parisians in neon outfits rub elbows with Brits in navy blue, Munich businessmen in Bogner suits, and Swedish students with punk haircuts. And yet, when you're surrounded by mountains that will outlast fashions, lifetimes, and languages, such differences fade, and the mountains are all you can see.

We walk uphill through knee-deep powder toward the summit of the Allalinhorn—the friendliest of Canton Wallis's many 13,120-foot peaks. Early morning sunshine rakes the corniced ridges around us; the village of Saas-Fee still hides in shadow below. With climbing skins glued to the bottom of our skis, we've shuffled up the Feegletscher to earn a morning's bliss in deep untracked snow. This glacier highway is taking us above the domain of passes and ski lifts and groomed slopes, into a world of icy north walls, pure knife-edge ridges, undulating mile-long coverlets of fresh powder, summits of whipped meringue, and snow crystals sparkling at our feet. Munching cheese and chocolate as we climb, thinking that we must look like silhouettes in one of Herbert Matter's prewar Swiss travel posters, breathing deeply, climbing slowly, we daydream our way to the top. Our tracks, like zippers in the snow, stretch up to a vanishing point in the midnight-blue sky above.

* * *

IT'S A SOFT APRIL MORNING AT LES DIA-BLERETS, a ski area on the frontier between francophone Vaud and the German canton of Bern. It's already 11 AM and the frozen corn snow is only now softening up on the wide glacier beneath the dark, thumblike peak of the Oldenhorn. From the topmost lift we can see west toward Lake Geneva, south toward the giant peaks of the Valais, and northeast toward the dark brooding peaks of the Berner Oberland. An observation deck on the roof of the Alps reveals mountains filling space to its farthest corners, to the hazy horizon. On the deep valley flanks below Les Diablerets, winding west toward the Rhône Valley, the slopes are greening up with no respect for commonsense color—pastures of eye-dazzling kelly green under dark forests and crags. Only a few miles away, down the eastern German-speaking side of the mountains, the chic resort of Gstaad seems deserted; its jet-set winter guests have already hung up their skis and headed for the Mediterranean. The mountains are ours for a day.

At the top of the lift we break through the clouds. A sea of fog fills the Rhône Valley below us, a fluffy false plain, punctured only by snowy peaks, stretching to the horizon. Somewhere under these clouds is Lake Geneva, and far across, Les Dents du Midi ("The Teeth of Noon") rise out of the clouds like ice-sheathed knuckles. Villars-Gryon is a ski resort so small most American skiers have never heard of it, even though it's bigger than half the ski areas in Colorado. Alone, we ski along the edge of the piste, where the slope steepens and drops away in a succession of rocky ledges. Just over the border that separates the skier's world from the mountaineer's, we see a lone ibex, posing on a rock outcrop against the clouds, scimitar-shape horns swept back in wide twin arcs. We christie to a stop, stand in awe wishing we had cameras, and realize eventually that the ibex is not going to bolt. These are its Alps, its domain; we are the newcomers, birds of passage, intruders. It feels like a privilege to share the roof of Europe with this ibex, a privilege that our Swiss hosts have slowly earned over 700 years by farming basically unfarmable mountainsides, by making this land their domain. We push off, the cold snow squeaking under our skis. Behind our backs the ibex still stares off into the distance.

These images stay with me, indelible as the Alps themselves. Say the word *Switzerland* and I see the gentle slopes of the Plateau Rosa above Zermatt, perforated by the dotted lines of T-bars, peppered with tiny bright-color skiers, slopes lapping in white waves against the base of the Matterhorn. Near St. Moritz I see the blue-green crevasses of the Morteratsch Glacier, a frozen white-water rapid, spilling down from the ski area.

That Switzerland has some of the best skiing in the world goes without saying. In the end, though, it's not the skiing I remember, or the runs. It's the mountains I remember. And so will you.

— Lito Tejada-Flores

Winter Activities at the Resorts

Resort	Lift-Ticket Cost (SF) * (one day/six day)	Elevation (m/ft)	Number of Lifts	Lift Capacity (number of riders per hour in thousands)	Maintained Trails (km/mi)	Snowmaking
Arosa	49/219	1,800–2,650 m 5,900–8,700 ft	16	21.7	70/43	✗	
Crans-Montana	56/262	1,500–3,000 m 4,920–9,843 ft	30	38.6	160/100	✗	
Davos-Klosters	54/268	1,560–2,844 m 5,118–9,330 ft	54	46.0	320/199	✗	
Flims-Laax	59/324	1,160–3,292 m 3,808–10,798 ft	29	42.0	220/140	✗	
Gstaad-Saanenland	50/233	1,100–3,000 m 3,600–9,843 ft	66	53.0	250/160	✗	
La Vallée de Conches (cross-country)	n/a	1,300–1,450 m 4,265–4,757 ft	n/a	n/a	n/a	✗	
Le Val D'Anniviers	40/210	1,350–3,000 m 4,430–9,843 ft	45	25.0	250/155	✗	
Les Portes du Soleil (Champery and 14 linked Swiss and French areas)	48/219	1,000–2,500 m 3,280–8,200 ft	219	228.8	650/400	✗	
Verbier (including 6 linked areas of Quatre-Vallées)	56/282	820–3,330 m 2,690–10,925 ft	100	74.0	400/248	✗	
Saas-Fee	58/270	1,800–3,600 m 5,900–11,800 ft	26	26.4	100/50	✗	
St. Moritz (Upper Engadine)	53/274	1,950–3,300 m 6,396–10,824 ft	55	65.0	350/34	✗	
Grindelwald-Wengen (Jungfrau Region)	52/244	1,300–3,450 m 4,265–11,300 ft	45	40.0	213/132	✗	
Zermatt	62/306	1,260–3,820 m 4,132–12,530 ft	73	70.7	245/152	✗	

*varies according to extent of areas selected to ski in
ᵗdepending on type and quality of snow, as well as grooming of slopes

Average Annual Snowfall (cm/in)	Difficulty of Terrain: % Beg/Int/Exp	Cross-Country (km/mi of trails)	Glacier Skiing	Heli-Skiing	Para/Hang Gliding	Ice-Skating	Luge Runs	Skibob Runs	Ballooning	Accommodations (bed in hotels, chalets and apartments)
692/272	31/57/12	26/16			✗	✗	✗		✗	8,000
518/204	38/50/12	40/25	✗	✗	✗	✗	✗	✗	✗	40,000
491/193	29/50/21	75/46		✗	✗	✗	✗			24,250
440/173	50/30/20	60/37	✗	✗	✗	✗	✗		✗	10,800
627/247	40/40/20	127/75	✗	✗	✗	✗	✗	✗	✗	12,300
522/206	n/a	180/53				✗				20,000
348/137	30/40/30	82/51		✗	✗	✗	✗	✗		20,000
619/244	25/40/35	250/155		✗	✗	✗				93,000
491/193	32/42/26	42/33	✗	✗	✗	✗	✗	✗		25,000
357/141	25/25/50	54/34	✗			✗	✗			7,600
368/145	35/25/40	180/112	✗	✗	✗	✗	✗	✗	✗	36,500
389/153	30/50/20	17/10		✗	✗	✗	✗	✗		10,000
434/131	30/40/30	10/6	✗	✗	✗	✗				13,500

CHEESE: THE SWISS CURE

Grandfather sat himself down on a three-legged stool and blew up the fire with the bellows till it was red and glowing. As the pot began to sing, he put a large piece of cheese on a toasting fork and moved it to and fro in front of the fire until it became golden yellow all over. . . . Heidi took up the bowl of milk and drained it thirstily. . . . She ate her bread with the toasted cheese, soft as butter, which tasted delicious, and every now and then she took a drink. She looked as happy and contented as anyone could be.

—*Heidi,* by Johanna Spyri*

I T WAS SWISS CHEESE that put the apples in the cheeks of the hardy little mountain girl named Heidi, the heroine earth-child who inspired Victorians to leave dark city streets for clear Alpine air; to climb in high, flower-carpeted meadows; to rise early, work hard, and—first and foremost—eat cheese three times a day.

A creature of fiction but set by her creator in the very real verdant heights above Maienfeld, near the borders of Liechtenstein and Austria, Heidi grew strong, wise, and honest under her reclusive grandfather's bushy-browed gaze and his steady diet of goat's milk, black bread, and great slabs of cheese. She drank milk for breakfast, packed a fat chunk of cold cheese for lunch (with an occasional helping of cold meat), had fire-toasted cheese at supper, and drank more bowls of creamy milk, warm from the goat, before she climbed into the hayloft to sleep.

One wonders that she didn't waddle instead of climb. Despite the conspicuous absence of fruit and vegetables—even, say, a jar of canned cabbage from the pantry—Heidi flourished like the green bay tree. She even seduced her crippled friend Clara to leave dank, beshadowed Frankfurt and take an Alpine cure. The daily cheese and goat's milk worked a mountain miracle on Clara as well, and when her father came to take her home, she walked down the hillside to greet him.

It is the elements of freshness and purity in plain, wholesome cheese that captured the imagination of the Victorians—a true, untreated *cuisine du marché* carried from barn to table with all nature's goodness intact. Butterfat was a virtue; cholesterol, a concept unborn.

Cheese is still a way of life in Switzerland, eaten in dishes of such simplicity that they may seem uninspired to a palate grown used to trendy international cuisine. Raclette, the famous cheese specialty of canton Vaud, is nothing more than a great wheel of cheese cut in half, its exposed side held to an open fire and the softening semiliquid scraped onto a plate; this plain yellow puddle is enhanced only by a couple of crisp pickles and potatoes roasted in their jackets. Aelpler Magrone, found in variation throughout the mountain regions but particularly around Appenzell, makes America's macaroni and cheese (the national dish of the 1950s) seem sophisticated by comparison: The Swiss version simply tosses boiled macaroni and potatoes in melted butter and grated cheese, a few curls of butter-fried onions providing its sole textural contrast.

In German regions you'll find *Käseschnitte* (the French Swiss call it *croûte*), closest to Heidi's own toasted cheese: slabs of bread are topped with grated cheese and butter, then baked in a casserole until the whey and butterfat saturate the bread and the cheese turns golden brown. (Variations may combine wine, ham, mushrooms, or

*From translations by Helen B. Dole (New York: Grosset & Dunlap, 1927) and Eileen Hall (London: Penguin Books, 1956).

eggs.) *Chäschüchli* from the Valais region are ramekins of baked cheese, egg, and bread crumbs. *Käseknopfli* are chewy little fingers of noodle dough—*Spätzle* to Germans—served in a creamy mountain cheese sauce so pungently aromatic that you may rear back from the steamy plate. The flavor, though, is surprisingly sweet, fresh, and mild.

And of course fondue (from *fondre*—"to melt"), though it went in and out of vogue in America with the '60s ski rage, remains a winter fixture here: with its pungent crushed garlic and sting of kirsch stirred through the creamy molten mass, its flavors are relatively complex. Different regions press the subtlety further by demanding specific blends of the local cheese to create the only *true* fondue: proportions of aged Gruyère and milder Emmental vary, and in Fribourg, it's made with creamy Vacherin. (The convivial system of sharing fondue around a table dates back to the ancient peasant tradition of circling around a common pot for the family meal. It is rendered all the more convivial today by the tradition of downing a shot of 90-proof kirsch halfway through the pot: the *coup du milieu*.)

* * *

CHEESE IS AVAILABLE AROUND THE CLOCK, today as in Heidi's time. A good Swiss breakfast, especially in German cantons, won't be served without a fan of brown-skin slices of Gruyère, Emmental (the one with the holes that gave "Swiss cheese" its name), or Appenzeller. Cubed cheese may show up in your lunch salad (*Käsesalat*), along with nuts, potatoes, and greens. And after a French-style meal, there's always the cheese course: in addition to the usual array of aged hard cheeses, there's usually a token *tomme* (a creamy-white fresh cheese from cow, sheep, or goat's milk) and the mild but novel Tête de Moine from the Jura, shaved off in spiraling ruffles with a crank. The best L'Etivaz, an Alpine Gruyère-style cheese from

near Château-d'Oex, is aged three years and then scraped across a wooden plane: its grainy sheets, nutty as a good Reggiano Parmesan, are rolled into tight curls (*rebibes*), which are eaten by hand. In the Italian canton of Ticino, you may end a simple meal in a mountain grotto with a squeaky-fresh mold of goat cheese, called *formaggini*.

In Heidi's world, cold meat—yet another source of animal fats—seems to provide the only relief from her dairy diet. The meat she packed off to eat high in the goats' grazing meadows was probably air-dried beef, an Alpine delicacy that fills the role of Italy's *prosciutto crudo* as a first-course cold meat. Its texture—at best, tender and sliced paper thin; at worst, cut crudely and taking on the texture of bookbinding—reflects the simple process of its creation: it's dried outdoors in the mountain breeze. (A much rarer, though tastier, variation—and worth looking for—is Appenzeller *Mostbröckli*, which is marinated in cider before being dried in air.)

Had Heidi not lived alone on a mountaintop, her diet might have been richer still—indeed, it might have killed her. Today as in Heidi's day, hot meat dishes in Switzerland are served from large chafing dishes containing portions enough for two healthy farm boys. Often, two or more cutlets will be offered. When one heaping dinner plate has been cleared and the diner is ready to sigh in relief, the server reappears with a clean plate—and fills it completely again. The pan-Swiss dish called *Geschnetzeltes Kalbfleisch* or *émincé de veau* appears in nearly every middle-class dining room, its mounds of cut veal wallowing in rich, buttery cream. This rib-sticking mainstay inevitably comes with *Rösti*, an oil-crisped patty of hash browns often more than 8 inches in diameter.

And that's not all. Many of the simple stews and meaty *plats du jour* (daily specials) come swimming in a savory brown gravy, a distant cousin of *sauce borde-*

laise. Frequently—even usually—its basic flavor has been given a boost with the ubiquitous brown condiments that stock all but the most enlightened Swiss kitchens. They are made by the soup magnates Maggi and Knorr, and their primary ingredients are salt and monosodium glutamate (*Geschmackverstärker* or *exhausteur de goût*). If the gravy hasn't been boosted enough already, chances are you can season it to taste from the handy MSG shakers on your table, standing by in baskets made to fit with the salt, pepper, and toothpicks.

* * *

AT LEAST HEIDI'S DIET, though heavy in fats, was chemically pure. And when she climbed up to pasture the goats every day, she did carry hard black bread with her cheese. She coveted the aristocratic white rolls of Frankfurt and hoarded them during her urban sojourn—but only to smuggle them back to her friend Peter's grandmother, whose aged teeth couldn't handle a proper chunk of bread. Nowadays, though the countries that surround Switzerland still prize refined flour (Styrofoamlike baguettes in France are that country's weakest culinary link these days), it is coarse, crusty brown loaves that the Swiss offer with even their finest foods, especially in the German cantons. More generously leavened than in Heidi's day but chewy nonetheless, it is served simply fresh-sliced or, at breakfast buffets, as a whole loaf wrapped in a snowy linen napkin to be sawed at the last possible moment. In Heidi's time and until the turn of the 20th century, these whole-grain breads offered the only cereal roughage in a diet that was relentlessly high in animal fats. They were often, of course, heaped with cheese and sweet butter.

It was in reaction, in part, to Swiss cheese that Dr. R. Bircher-Benner, at a clinic in Zürich, developed the antidote that changed Swiss eating habits for good: Bircher-Müsli. A simple cereal blend of soaked raw oats, nuts, and whole apples (skins, pips, and all), it is eaten for breakfast or as a light supper—the latter, in fact, a throwback to the modest plate of evening gruel Swiss peasants once faced before tapping into the wealth of protein-rich cheese in their own backyard.

With one foot on the farm, the other in the factory, the cheese industry today reveals much about Switzerland's perpetually split personality, from its humble mountain huts that produce one cheese a day to its high-tech, high-volume, steel-and-tile factories. At L'Etivaz in canton Vaud, independent farmers graze their family's few cows on green Alpine slopes only during summer months, when the snow at elevations above 3,280 feet recedes enough for sweet grass to break through. In old copper pots over wood fires, each family stirs its own daily milk, gathers up the thick curd in broad cheesecloth, squeezes out excess whey with a wooden press, and molds the cheese into a round wheel to drain. Each cheese is stamped with the family brand and carried down to the village, where a modern cooperative *affineur* carefully supervises its aging until the farmer reclaims the finished product to sell or keep as he likes.

* * *

THE DIRECTNESS OF THE PROCESS is striking. A family Subaru, manure spattered on its fenders, backs up to the co-op door; a wiry, sunburned farmer opens the hatch and rolls out a pale, waxy new cheese wheel; a worker wades in rubber boots through the puddles of pungent whey, greets the farmer, takes a bacterial sample, and rolls the cheese onto a rack. It joins the ranks of similar cheeses, all bearing family brands, on long wooden shelves that stretch on and on like library stacks, each cheese to be washed and turned according to a schedule well tested over the centuries.

The great commercial cheese factories of Emmental and Gruyères still stir their cheeses in vast copper cauldrons, and their fires are still fueled by wood. The difference, of course, is in volume. At the *Schaukäserei* (demonstration factory) in Affoltern, outside Bern, 10,000 kilos (22,000 pounds) of milk a day (2,900,000 kilos a year) pour in from 59 suppliers throughout the Emmental valley. In pots as big as smelters, it is heated over fires fueled by a steady conveyor-belt flow of wood chips gleaned from Swiss lumber mills—250 tons a year. The storage racks—the stacks, as it were—could rival those of the Library of Congress.

It is Swiss science and industry in action. It may be disappointing to the romantic to learn that even the holes in Emmentaler cheese—the type Americans call "Swiss

cheese"—no longer swell naturally from the internal gases of fermentation but are carefully controlled by the addition of bacteria known to produce holes of a dependable size.

Yet a traveler, cruising Switzerland's emerald hills and villages far from industrial turf, can't help but notice the damp, fresh, earthy ephemera of the dairy that hangs in the air—a mild, musky tang that scents the cream, thickens the chocolate, and wafts through cool, muddy farmyards. That essence, mingled with crystalline mountain air, worked miracles in *Heidi*. It is the essence of Swiss cheese itself.

— Nancy Coons

BOOKS & MOVIES

Books

Wilhelm Tell, by Friedrich von Schiller, is the definitive stage version of the dramatic legend. "The Prisoner of Chillon," by Lord Byron, is an epic poem inspired by the sojourn of François Bonivard in the dungeon of Chillon. *A Tramp Abroad,* by Mark Twain, includes the author's personal impressions—and tall tales—derived from travels in Switzerland. *Arms and the Man,* by G. B. Shaw, was the source of Oscar Straus's Viennese operetta *The Chocolate Soldier;* both are about a Swiss mercenary with a sweet tooth.

Novels set at least partially in Switzerland include *Daisy Miller,* by Henry James (Lac Léman, Chillon); *Tender Is the Night,* by F. Scott Fitzgerald; *A Farewell to Arms,* by Ernest Hemingway; Thomas Mann's *The Magic Mountain* (Davos); Albert Cohen's *Belle du Seigneur* (Geneva); *Hotel du Lac,* by Anita Brookner (Vevey); Katharine Weber's *Objects in Mirror Are Closer Than They Appear* (Geneva); John le Carré's *The Night Manager* (Zürich); and Patricia Highsmith's *Small g: A Summer Idyll* (Zürich). A couple of fine contemporary Swiss authors, whose works reflect 20th-century Switzerland and are found in good English translations, are Max Frisch (*I'm Not Stiller*) and Friedrich Dürrenmatt (*End of the Game* and *The Visit*).

The best-known children's book set in Switzerland is, of course, *Heidi,* by Johanna Spyri (Maienfeld). Newbery Medal–winning *The Apple and the Arrow,* by Mary and Conrad Buff, tells the story of Wilhelm Tell from the point of view of his son. *Banner in the Sky,* by James Ramsey Ullman, is a powerful children's book about a boy's attempt to climb Switzerland's most challenging mountain.

La Place de la Concorde Suisse, by John McPhee, was developed from a series of *New Yorker* pieces the author wrote after traveling with members of the Swiss army. *Heidi's Alp,* by Christine Hardyment, a first-person account of a family traveling in a camper-van in search of the Europe of fairy tales, includes an adventure with a latter-day alm-uncle in a cabin above Maienfeld. *Terminal,* by Colin Forbes, is a murder-mystery tale with fantastic descriptions of Swiss cities.

There's no shortage of spellbinding mountain-climbing accounts. In *The Climb Up to Hell,* Jack Olsen details the dramatic 1957 Eiger expedition. Heinrich Harrer's *The White Spider: The Classic Account of the Ascent of the Eiger,* covering his successful 1938 ascent, was recently reprinted. *A Guide to Zermatt and the Matterhorn,* Edward Whymper's memoirs of his disastrous climb up the Matterhorn, is out of print, but it may be available in a library (excerpts appear in this guide's chapter on the Valais).

Movies

Heidi is undoubtedly the best-known film to be shot in Switzerland. Make sure you see the 1937 version directed by Allan Dulan, starring Shirley Temple. Swiss air must agree with James Bond; several films have Swiss scenes in them, including *Goldfinger* (1964) and *Goldeneye* (1995); *On Her Majesty's Secret Service* (1969) shows dazzling ski scenes of the Schilthorn in central Switzerland. You can also get glimpses of Swiss scenery in the 1994 version of *Frankenstein. Trois Couleurs Rouge (Three Colors Red),* the last in director Krzysztof Kieslowski's trilogy, and a big hit in Europe, is set in Geneva's Old Town, and Peter Greenaway's 1993 *Stairs* shows Geneva through the director's unique artistic vision. Gstaad and its Palace Hotel are featured in Peter Sellers's *Return of the Pink Panther. The Unbearable Lightness of Being* follows a couple fleeing from the 1968

Russian invasion of Czechoslovakia. The moving *Reise der Hoffnung (Journey of Hope)*, directed by Xavier Koller in 1990, centers on a Kurdish family fleeing Turkish persecution to seek sanctuary in Switzerland. In French director Claude Chabrol's *Rien Ne Va Plus* (*The Swindle*; 1997), Isabelle Huppert and Michel Serrault play a pair of con artists who attempt an out-of-their-league scam; a section was shot in Sils Maria, and a Swiss Army knife comes into play.

VOCABULARY

	English	French	French Pronunciation
Basics			
	Yes/no	Oui/non	wee/no
	Please	S'il vous plaît	seel voo **play**
	Thank you	Merci	mare-**see**
	You're welcome	De rien	deh ree-**enh**
	Excuse me	Pardon	pahr-**doan**
	Hello	Bonjour	bohn-**zhoor**
	Goodbye	Au revoir	o ruh-**vwahr**
Numbers			
	One	Un	un
	Two	Deux	deuh
	Three	Trois	twa
	Four	Quatre	**cat**-ruh
	Five	Cinq	sank
	Six	Six	seess
	Seven	Sept	set
	Eight	Huit	weat
	Nine	Neuf	nuf
	Ten	Dix	deess
Days			
	Today	Aujourd'hui	o-zhoor-**dwee**
	Tomorrow	Demain	deh-**menh**
	Yesterday	Hier	yair
	Morning	Matin	ma-**tenh**
	Afternoon	Après-midi	ah-pray-mee-**dee**
	Night	Nuit	nwee
	Monday	Lundi	**lahn**-dee
	Tuesday	Mardi	**mahr**-dee
	Wednesday	Mercredi	**mare**-kruh-dee
	Thursday	Jeudi	**juh**-dee
	Friday	Vendredi	**vawn**-dra-dee
	Saturday	Samedi	**sam**-dee
	Sunday	Dimanche	**dee**-mawnsh

*Prevalent Swiss-German dialect

German	German Pronunciation	Italian	Italian Pronunciation
Ja/nein	yah/nine	Sí/No	see/no
Bitte	**bit**-uh	Per favore	pear fa-**voh**-reh
Danke	**dahn**-kuh	Grazie	**grah**-tsee-ay
Bitte schön	**bit**-uh **shern**	Prego	**pray**-go
Entschuldigen Sie *Äxgüsi	ent-**shool**-de-gen-zee **ax**-scu-see	Scusi	**skoo**-zee
Guten Tag *Grüezi *Grüss Gott	**goot**-en **tahk** **grit**-zee groos got	Buon giorno	bwohn **jyohr**-noh
Auf Widersehen *Ufwiederluege *Tschüss (*familiar*)	Auf **vee-der**-zane oof-**vee-der**-lawgah choohs	Arrivederci	a-ree-vah-**dare**-chee

Eins	eints	Uno	**oo**-no
Zwei	tsvai	Due	**doo**-ay
Drei	dry	Tre	tray
Vier	fear	Quattro	**kwah**-troh
Fünf	fumph	Cinque	**cheen**-kway
Sechs	zex	Sei	say
Sieben	**zee**-ben	Sette	**set**-ay
Acht	ahkt	Otto	**oh**-to
Neun	noyn	Nove	**no**-vay
Zehn	tsane	Dieci	dee-**eh**-chee

Huete	**hoi**-tah	Oggi	**oh**-jee
Morgen	**more**-gehn	Domani	do-**mah**-nee
Gestern	geh-**shtairn**	Ieri	ee-veh-ree
Morgen	**more**-gehn	Mattina	ma-**tee**-na
Nachmittag	nahkt-**mit**-ahk	Pomeriggio	po-mer-**ee**-jo
Nacht	nahkt	Notte	Noh-teh
Montag	**mohn**-tahk	Lunedì	**loo**-neh-dee
Dienstag	**deens**-tahk	Martedì	**mahr**-teh-dee
Mittwoch	**mit**-vohk	Mercoledì	**mare**-co-leh-dee
Donnerstag	**doe**-ners-tahk	Giovedì	**jo**-veh-dee
Freitag	**fry**-tahk	Venerdì	**ven**-air-dee
Samstag	**zahm**-stahk	Sabato	**sah**-ba-toe
Sonntag	**zon**-tahk	La Domenica	lah doe-**men**-ee-ca

	English	French	French Pronunciation

Useful Phrases

English	French	French Pronunciation
Do you speak English?	Parlez-vous anglais?	par-lay-vooz awng-**gleh**
I don't speak French/German/Italian.	Je ne parle pas français.	juh nuh parl pah fraun-**seh**
I don't understand.	Je ne comprends pas.	juh nuh kohm-prawhn **pah**
I don't know.	Je ne sais pas.	juh nuh say **pah**
I am American/British.	Je suis américain/anglais	jhu sweez a-may-ree-**can**/awn-**glay**
I am sick.	Je suis malade.	juh swee ma-**lahd**
Please call a doctor.	Appelez un docteur s'il vous plâit.	a-pe-lay uhn dohk-**tore** seel voo **play**
Have you any rooms?	Est-ce que vous avez une chambre?	Ehskuh vooz ah-vay-oon **shahm**-br
How much does it cost?	C'est combien?	say comb-bee-**enh**
Do you accept . . . (credit card)	Est-ce que vous acceptez . . .	Ehskuh voo zahksehptay . . .
Too expensive	Trop cher	troh **shehr**
It's beautiful.	C'est très beau.	say tray boh
Help!	Au secours!	o say-**koor**
Stop!	Arrêtez!	a-ruh-**tay**

Getting Around

English	French	French Pronunciation
Where is . . .	C'est où . . .	say oo
The train station?	la gare?	la gahr
The post office?	la poste?	la pohst
The hospital?	l'hôpital?	lo-pee-**tahl**
Where are the rest rooms?	Où sont les toilettes?	oo sohn lay **twah**-let
Left	A gauche	a **gohsh**
Right	À droite	a **drwat**
Straight ahead	Tout droit	**too drwat**

Dining Out

English	French	French Pronunciation
Waiter/Waitress	Monsieur/Mademoiselle	muh-**syuh**/mad-mwa-**zel**
Please give me . . .	S'il vous plait, donnez-moi . . .	see voo **play** doh nay **mwah**

*Prevalent Swiss-German dialect

German	German Pronunciation	Italian	Italian Pronunciation
Sprechen Sie Englisch?	Shprek-hun zee eng-glish	Parla inglese?	par-la een glay-zay
Ich sprech kein Deutsch.	ihkh shprek-uh kine doych	Non parlo italiano.	non par-lo ee-tal-yah-no
Ich verstehe nicht.	ihkh fehr-stay-eh nikht	Non capisco.	non ka-peess-ko
Ich habe keine Ahnung.	ihkh hah-beh kine-eh ah-nung	Non lo so.	non lo so
Ich bin Amerikaner(in). Engländer(in).	ihkh bin a-mer-i kah-ner(in)/eng-glan-der(in)	Sono americano(a)/ Sono inglese.	so-no a-may-ree-kah-no(a)/so-no een-glay-zay
Ich bin krank.	ihkh bin krahnk	Sto male.	sto ma-lay
Bitte rufen einen Arzt.	bit-uh roof-en ine-en ahrtst	Chiami un dottore per favore.	kee-ah-mee oon doe-toe-ray pear fah-voh-reh
Haben sie ein Zimmer?	Ha-ben zee ine tsimmer	C'e una camera libera?	chay oo-nah cam-er-ah lee-ber-eh
Wieviel kostet das?	vee-feel cost-et dahs	Quanto costa?	kwahn-toe-coast-a
Nehmen Sie . . .	nay-men zee . . .	Posso pagare . . .	pohs-soh pah-gah-reh . . .
Es kostet zu viel.	es cost-et tsu feel	Troppo caro	troh-poh cah-roh
Das ist schön.	dahs is shern	É bello(a).	eh bell-oh
Hilfe!	hilf-uh	Aiuto!	a-yoo-toe
Halt!	hahlt	Alt!	ahlt
Wo ist . . .	vo ist	Dov'è . . .	doe-veh
Der Bahnhof? Die Post?	dare bahn-hof dee post	la stazione? l'ufficio postale?	la sta-tsee-oh-nay loo-fee-cho po-sta-lay
Das Krankenhaus? *Das Spital?	dahs krahnk-en-house dahs shpee-tahl	l'ospedale?	lo-spay-dah-lay
Wo ist die Toilette?	vo ist dee twah-let-uh	Dov'è il bagno?	doe-vay eelbahn-yo
Links	links	a sinistra	a see-neess-tra
Rechts	rechts	a destra	a-des-tra
geradeaus	geh-rod-uh ouse	Avanti dritto	a-vahn-tee dree-to
Herr Ober/ Fraülein	hehr oh-ber froy-line	Cameriere(a)	kah-meh-ryeh-reh(rah)
Bitte geben sie mir . . .	bit-uh gay behn zee-meer	Mi dia pear-fah-voh-reh . . .	mee dee-a

English	French	French Pronunciation
The menu	La carte	la cart
The bill/check	L'addition	la-dee-see-**ohn**
A fork	Une fourchette	ewn four-**shet**
A knife	Un couteau	uhn koo-**toe**
A spoon	Une cuillère	ewn kwee-**air**
A napkin	Une serviette	ewn sair-vee-**et**
Bread	Du pain	due penh
Butter	Du beurre	due bur
Milk	Du lait	due lay
Pepper	Du poivre	due **pwah**-vruh
Salt	Du sel	due sell
Sugar	Du sucre	due **sook**-ruh
Coffee	Un café	uhn kahfay
Tea	Un thé	uhn tay
Mineral water *carbonated/still*	De l'eau minéral *gazeuse/non gazeuse*	duh loh meenehrahl gahzuhz/noh(n) gahzuhz
Wine	Vin	venh
Cheers!	A votre santé!	ah vo-truh sahn-**tay**

*Prevalent Swiss-German dialect

German	German Pronunciation	Italian	Italian Pronunciation
Die speisekarte	dee **shpie**-zeh-car-tuh	Il menù	eel may-**noo**
Die Rechnung	dee **rekh**-nung	Il conto	eel **cone**-toe
Eine Gabel	**ine**-eh-**gah**-buhl	Una forchetta	oona for-**ket**-a
Ein messer	I-nuh-**mess**-ehr	Un coltello	oon kol-**tel**-o
Einen Löffel	I-nen **ler**-fuhl	Un cucchiaio	oon koo-kee-**ah-yo**
Die Serviette	dee zair-vee-**eh**-tuh	Il tovagliolo	eel toe-va-lee-**oh-lo**
Brot	broht	Il pane	eel **pa**-nay
Butter	**boo**-tehr	Il burro	eel **boo**-roh
Milch	meelch	Il latte	eel **lot**-ay
Pfeffer	**fef**-fehr	Il pepe	eel **pay**-pay
Salz	zahlts	Il sale	eel **sah**-lay
Zucker	**tsoo**-kher	Lo zucchero	loh **tsoo**-ker-o
eine Kaffee	**ine**-eh **kah**-feh	un caffè	oon kahf-**feh**
einen Tee	**ine**-en tay	un tè	oon teh
Mineral wasser	mi-neh-**raal**-**vahs**-sehr	L'acqua minerale	l'ah kwa mee-neh-**rah**-leh
mit gas/ohne gas	mit gahz/**oh**-nuh gahz	*gassata/naturale*	gahs-**sah**-tah/nah-too-**rah**-leh
Wein	vine	Il vino	eel **vee**-noh
Zum Wohl! *Proscht	zoom vole prosht	Salute!	sah-**loo**-teh

INDEX

sports and outdoor activities,
279, 288, 291–292, 293,
295–296, 298, 301, 306, 309
Thunersee, 301–303
timing the visit, 278, 282
transportation, 309–310, 311
travel agencies, 311
visitor information, 312
Bernisches Historisches
Museum, 254, 255
Beschnitzten Häuser, 289
Bethlehemhaus, 177
Biasca, 125
Bicycling, F35–F36
Bern, 265
Crans-Montana, 333–334
Davos, 90
Eastern Switzerland, 62
Fribourg, Neuchâtel, and the
Jura, 217
Geneva, 441
Graubünden, 81, 82, 85, 90,
94, 101, 108
Klosters, 85
Lausanne, 380
Liechtenstein, 62
Luzern and Central
Switzerland, 166, 169, 175,
176, 180
St. Moritz, 108
Valais, 325, 333–334, 344–345
Vaud, 395, 401
Verbier, 325
Zermatt, 344–345
Zürich, 30–31
Bierhalle Kropf ✕, F28, 21
Bierlialp ✕, 169
Bistrot du Boeœuf Rouge ✕,
F27, 428
Bistrot du Boucher ✕, 428
Black Madonna, 177–178
Blätzli (festival), F23
Blaues und Weisses Haus,
186, 189
Blausee, 305
Bleu Lézard ✕, 376
Blonay-Chamby Railroad, 386
Blues to Bop Festival, F21
Boat and ferry travel, F36
Berner Oberland, 309–310
Brissago Islands, 130
Eastern Switzerland, 65
Fribourg, Neuchâtel, and the
Jura, 243
Geneva, 441
Luzern and Central
Switzerland, 180
Ticino, 145
Vaud, 402

Boating and sailing
Berner Oberland, 288
Davos, 90
Eastern Switzerland, 52
Geneva, 437
Graubünden, 90, 111
Lausanne, 380
Luzern and Central
Switzerland, 166
Montreux, 393
Rorschach, 52
Sils, 111
Valais, 334
Vaud, 360, 380, 393
Bobsledding, 108, 331
Bodensee, 51
Bogn Engiadina Scuol, 92
Bon Accueil ✕☶, 401
Bönigen, 289
Books and movies, 456–457
Bourbaki-Panorama, 152,
156
Brasserie Lipp ✕, 429
Brauerei Fischerstube ✕, 202
Briefmarkenmuseum, 60
Brienz, 298–300
Brienzer-Rothorn, 299
Brienzersee, 298–301
Brig, 348
Brissago Islands, 130
British Classic Car Meeting,
F21
Broc, 225
Brunnen, F29
Bulle, 229
Bundesbriefmuseum, 177
Bundeshaus, F29, 250, 251
Bündner Kunstmuseum, 75
Burgdorf, 268–271
Bürgenstock, 171–172
Bürgenstock Hotels and Resort
☶, F26, 171–172
Burgerbad, 337
Bürglen, 175
Burg-Museum, 179
Bursins, 365
Bus travel, F37
Bern, 273
Berner Oberland, 310
Eastern Switzerland, 65
Fribourg, Neuchâtel, and the
Jura, 243
Geneva, 442
Graubünden, 111–112
Luzern and Central
Switzerland, 180
Ticino, 145
Vaud, 403
Business hours, F36–F37

C
Cable cars
Berner Oberland, 283, 284,
290–291
Eastern Switzerland, 53, 59
Fribourg, Neuchâtel, and the
Jura, 227
Les Diablerets, 398
Luzern and Central
Switzerland, 168, 172, 176
Ticino, 137–138
Valais, 350
Vaud, 398
Caduff's Wine Loft ✕, 21
Café Beau-Rivage ✕, 375
Café Léo ✕, 430
Café Romand ✕, 376
Cameras and photography,
F37
Camping, F51
Campione, 142–143
Canyoning, 399, 402
Car rental, F37–F38, 310
Car travel, F38–F40
Basel, 210
Bern and the Emmental, 273
Berner Oberland, 310
Eastern Switzerland, 65–66
Fribourg, Neuchâtel, and the
Jura, 243
Geneva, 442
Graubünden, 112
Luzern and Central
Switzerland, 181
Ticino, 145–146
Valais, 352
Vaud, 403
Zürich, 33
Carnevale, F23
Carriage rides, 101, 108, 111
Casa dei Canonici, 126
Casa Rusca, 126
Casinos
Arosa, 80
Bern, 264
Berner Oberland, 268, 288
Crans-Montana, 333
Fribourg, 224
Graubünden, 107
Interlaken, 288
Luzern, 164
Montreux, 393
Neuchâtel, 237
St. Moritz, 107
Ticino, 128, 141, 143
Vaud, 393
Castagnola Parks, 137
Castelgrande, 120–121

NOTES

NOTES

FODOR'S KEY TO THE GUIDES

America's guidebook leader publishes guides for every kind of traveler.
Check out our many series and find your perfect match.

FODOR'S GOLD GUIDES
America's favorite travel-guide series
offers the most detailed insider reviews
of hotels, restaurants, and attractions in
all price ranges, plus great background
information, smart tips, and useful maps.

COMPASS AMERICAN GUIDES
Stunning guides from top local writers
and photographers, with gorgeous
photos, literary excerpts, and colorful
anecdotes. A must-have for culture
mavens, history buffs, and new residents.

FODOR'S CITYPACKS
Concise city coverage in a guide plus a
foldout map. The right choice for urban
travelers who want everything under
one cover.

FODOR'S EXPLORING GUIDES
Hundreds of color photos bring your
destination to life. Lively stories lend
insight into the culture, history, and
people.

FODOR'S TRAVEL HISTORIC AMERICA
For travelers who want to experience
history firsthand, this series gives in-
depth coverage of historic sights, plus
nearby restaurants and hotels. Themes
include the Thirteen Colonies, the Old
West, and the Lewis and Clark Trail.

FODOR'S POCKET GUIDES
For travelers who need only the
essentials. The best of Fodor's in pocket-
size packages for just $9.95.

FODOR'S FLASHMAPS
Every resident's map guide, with dozens
of easy-to-follow maps of
public transit, restaurants, shopping,
museums, and more.

FODOR'S CITYGUIDES
Sourcebooks for living in the city:
thousands of in-the-know listings for
restaurants, shops, sports, nightlife,
and other city resources.

FODOR'S AROUND THE CITY WITH KIDS
Up to 68 great ideas for family days,
recommended by resident parents.
Perfect for exploring in your own
backyard or on the road.

FODOR'S HOW TO GUIDES
Get tips from the pros on planning the
perfect trip. Learn how to pack, fly
hassle-free, plan a honeymoon or cruise,
stay healthy on the road, and travel with
your baby.

FODOR'S LANGUAGES FOR TRAVELERS
Practice the local language before you
hit the road. Available in phrase books,
cassette sets, and CD sets.

KAREN BROWN'S GUIDES
Engaging guides—many with easy-to-
follow inn-to-inn itineraries—to the
most charming inns and B&Bs in the
U.S.A. and Europe.

SEE IT GUIDES
Illustrated guidebooks that include the
practical information travelers need,
in gorgeous full color. Thousands of
photos, hundreds of restaurant and
hotel reviews, prices, and ratings for
attractions all in one indispensable
package. Perfect for travelers who want
the best value packed in a fresh, easy-
to-use, colorful layout.

OTHER GREAT TITLES FROM FODOR'S
Baseball Vacations, The Complete
Guide to the National Parks, Family
Vacations, Golf Digest's Places to Play,
Great American Drives of the East,
Great American Drives of the West,
Great American Vacations, Healthy
Escapes, National Parks of the West,
Skiing USA.